OBSERVER'S HANDBOOK 2008

The Royal Astronomical Society of Canada is dedicated to the promotion of astronomy and its related sciences; this Handbook espouses the scientific method, and supports dissemination of discoveries and theories based on that well-tested method.

EDITOR
PATRICK KELLY

ONE-HUNDREDTH YEAR OF PUBLICATION

© THE ROYAL ASTRONOMICAL SOCIETY OF CANADA
136 DUPONT STREET, TORONTO ON M5R 1V2
2007

ISSN 0080-4193
ISBN 978-0-9738109-5-0

Mixed Sources
Product group from well-managed
forests and other controlled sources
www.fsc.org Cert no. SW-COC-1326
© 1996 Forest Stewardship Council
FSC

PRINTED IN CANADA
BY THISTLE PRINTING LIMITED

TABLE OF CONTENTS

Key to Marginal Chapter Symbols

Basic Data 1_2^3

Time

Optics and Observing

The Sky Month by Month

Eclipses and Transits

The Moon

The Sun

Planets and Satellites

Asteroids

Meteors, Comets, and Dust

Stars

Nebulae and Galaxies

E Expanded from previous edition
F Featured object updated this edition
N New section with this edition
R Revised significantly with this edition

LIST OF CONTRIBUTORS

JAY ANDERSON, Prairie Storm Prediction Centre, Winnipeg, Manitoba...................................
(Frequency of Nighttime Cloud Cover, Star-Party Weather, Weather for Eclipses)

RANDY ATTWOOD, Toronto, Ontario ....(Voyages in our Solar System)

ALAN H. BATTEN, Dominion Astrophysical Observatory, Victoria, British Columbia ....
(The Nearest Stars)

ROY BISHOP, Avonport, Nova Scotia...(Binoculars, Eclipse Patterns,
Electromagnetic Spectrum, Expired Stars, Filters, Interplanetary Dust
Mars oppositions diagram, Map of Moon, Maps of the Night Sky,
Midnight Twilight and Midnight Sun, Orbital Motion, Rainbows, Saturn ring diagram,
Some Astronomical and Physical Data, Telescope Exit Pupils,
Tides and the Earth–Moon System, Time and Time Scales)

LARRY D. BOGAN, Cambridge Station, Nova Scotia ..... (Configurations of Jupiter's Galilean
satellites, Configurations of Saturn's Brightest Satellites)

RANDALL BROOKS, Canada Science and Technology Museum, Ottawa, Ontario...................
(Astronomical Twilight and Sidereal Time)

PETER BROWN, University of Western Ontario, London, Ontario ....(Meteors)

IAN CAMERON, University of Manitoba, Winnipeg, Manitoba ....(Pluto finder chart)

MARGARET CAMPBELL-BROWN, University of Calgary, Calgary, Alberta...........(Meteors)

DAVID L. CRAWFORD, Kitt Peak National Observatory, Tucson, Arizona.....(Light Pollution)

TERENCE DICKINSON, Yarker, Ontario.. (The Planets for 2008)

DAVID W. DUNHAM, International Occultation Timing Association, Greenbelt, Maryland..........
(Occultations by the Moon, Planetary and Asteroidal Occultations)

ALAN DYER, Telus World of Science, Calgary, Alberta .... (Deep-Sky Challenge Objects,
Deep-Sky Observing Hints, The Finest NGC Objects, The Messier List)

JAMES EDGAR, Melville, Saskatchewan (Selected Observatories, Star Parties, and Planetaria)

LEO ENRIGHT, Sharbot Lake, Ontario....................................(David Levy's Deep-Sky Gems)

FRED ESPENAK, NASA/Goddard Space Flight Centre, Greenbelt, Maryland..... (Eclipses in 2008)

REV. ROBERT EVANS, Hazelbrook, New South Wales, Australia...(Amateur Supernova Hunting)

ROBERT F. GARRISON, University of Toronto, Richmond Hill, Ontario .... (The Brightest Stars)

PHILIP GEBHARDT, Pickering, Ontario .... (Radio Detection of Meteors)

PAUL GRAY, Fredericton, New Brunswick...(Dark Nebulae)

RAJIV GUPTA, University of British Columbia, Vancouver, British Columbia........................
(Polar Alignment, Times of Moonrise and Moonset, Times of Sunrise and Sunset, Twilight,
right-hand pages of The Sky Month by Month (librated lunar graphics))

ARNE A. HENDEN, American Association of Variable Star Observers, Cambridge, Maryland.
(Variable Stars)

WILLIAM HERBST, Wesleyan University, Middletown, Connecticut...................(Galactic Nebulae)

RICHARD K. HERD, Geological Survey of Canada, Ottawa, Ontario...... (Meteorite Identification)

ALAN HILDEBRAND, University of Calgary, Calgary, Alberta................................(Fireballs)

JASON HINES, University of New Brunswick, Fredericton, New Brunswick...........................
(Meteorite Impact Craters of North America)

PETER JEDICKE, Fanshawe College, London, Ontario .... (Star Clusters)

LEE JOHNSON, Vancouver, British Columbia (Magnification and Contrast in Deep-Sky Observing)

TOOMAS KARMO University of Toronto, Richmond Hill, Ontario .... (The Brightest Stars)

DAVID LANE, Saint Mary's University, Halifax, Nova Scotia...
(finder charts for Neptune, Uranus, and Vesta, left-hand pages of The Sky Month by Month
(tables), nebular filter transmission chart)

DAVID H. LEVY, Vail, Arizona .... (David Levy's Deep-Sky Gems, Observing Comets)

ALISTER LING, Edmonton, Alberta .... (Deep-Sky Challenge Objects)

BARRY F. MADORE, Caltech, Pasadena, California .... (Galaxies: Brightest and Nearest,
Galaxies with Proper Names)

PAUL MARKOV, Toronto, Ontario...(The Observing Logbook)

BRIAN G. MARSDEN, Smithsonian Astrophysical Observatory, Cambridge, Maryland............
(Asteroidal osculating elements and ephemerides, Comets in 2008)

BRIAN D. MASON, U.S. Naval Observatory, Washington, D.C. ....(Double and Multiple Stars)

ANTHONY MOFFAT, Université de Montréal, Montréal, Québec....................... (Star Clusters)

PHILIP D. NICHOLSON, Cornell University, Ithaca, New York ...(Natural Satellites of the Planets)

JOHN R. PERCY, University of Toronto, Mississauga, Ontario..
(Teaching and the *Observer's Handbook,* Variable Stars)

DOUGLAS PITCAIRN, Dartmouth, Nova Scotia .... (Limiting Magnitudes)

ALLAN RAHILL, Canadian Meteorological Centre, Dorval, Québec...
(Weather Resources on the Internet)

EBERHARD RIEDEL, München, Germany.................................... (Occultations by the Moon)

WILLIAM ROBERTS, Vancouver, British Columbia ....
(Magnification and Contrast in Deep-Sky Observing)

JOHN SPRAY, University of New Brunswick, Fredericton, New Brunswick.............................
(Meteorite Impact Craters of North America)

JAMES STAMM, International Occultation Timing Association, Tucson, Arizona....................
(Planetary and Asteroidal Occultations)

KEN TAPPING, Dominion Radio Astrophysical Observatory, Penticton, British Columbia........
(Radio Sources, Solar Activity)

ELIZABETH O. WAAGEN, American Association of Variable Star Observers, Cambridge, Maryland ....
(Variable Stars)

ALAN WHITMAN, Penticton, British Columbia...
(Southern-Hemisphere Splendours, left-hand pages of The Sky Month by Month (text))

THE *OBSERVER'S HANDBOOK*

The *Observer's Handbook* is one of Canada's oldest scientific publications. Created by C.A. Chant, Professor of Astronomy at the University of Toronto, it first appeared over a century ago as *The Canadian Astronomical Handbook for 1907,* a small (13 × 17 cm), 108-page publication. A second edition covered the year 1908, but for the following two years most of the information that would have appeared was published instead in installments in the *Journal of the RASC.* The Council of the Society decided to return to a separate publication for 1911 with a new name—the *Observer's Handbook*—and it has been published annually ever since.

Each year some 12000 copies of the Handbook are distributed to many countries throughout the world, to amateur and professional astronomers, to educators at school and university levels, and to many observatories, planetaria, and libraries. The Handbook is the main source of income for the Royal Astronomical Society of Canada. Since the first edition in 1907, the various editors, assistant editors, editorial assistants (see p. 9), and contributors (see pp. 4–5) have voluntarily contributed their time and expertise to produce this unique book.

EDITORS OF THE *OBSERVER'S HANDBOOK*

		Position	Editions	RASC President
C.A. Chant	(1865–1956)	Editor	1907–1957	1903–1907
Frank Hogg	(1904–1951)	Assistant Editor	1939–1951	1940–1942
Ruth Northcott	(1913–1969)	Assistant Editor	1952–1957	1962–1964
		Editor	1958–1970	
John Percy	(1941–	Editor	1971–1981	1978–1980
Roy Bishop	(1939–	Editor	1982–2000	1984–1986
Rajiv Gupta	(1958–	Editor	2001–2006	2002–2004
Patrick Kelly	(1958–	Editor	2007–	

The *Observer's Handbook* is intended to be "a companion which the observer would wish always to have in his pocket or on the table before him."

C.A. Chant, Toronto, 1906

"We believe that the *Observer's Handbook* is a truly significant contribution that Canadian astronomy in general and our Society in particular has been making to the dissemination of astronomical knowledge for half a century. I trust that it will still occupy the same position of respect after the first hundred years."

Ruth Northcott, Ottawa, 1964

"The more one knows, the more one can benefit from the Handbook. It inspires all who leaf through its pages to learn and question what the tables, graphs and data mean, perhaps to speculate on the mysteries of the Universe, and above all, to get out and look beyond our world. You have in your hands a key to the Universe—a key which will fit many doors. Please use it well and treasure it."

Peter Broughton, Toronto, 1992
Author of *Looking Up, A History of the RASC*

"The *Observer's Handbook* is the single most useful publication for the observational astronomer. Its combination of authoritative data, informative diagrams, and concise text is unique. Anyone interested in astronomy, beginner or expert, amateur or professional, student or teacher, will find the *Observer's Handbook* indispensable. Its international reputation for quality is a credit both to its many contributors and to Canadian astronomy."

Roy Bishop, Halifax, 2000

HOW TO USE THIS HANDBOOK

This Handbook is a concise, high-density compilation of information that is of interest to observers. By reading the following points, you will allow yourself to reap maximum benefit from it.

(1) The Handbook is composed of various *sections*. Related sections are grouped into chapters, as listed in the CONTENTS. Chapter titles are given in large dark-grey boxes and section titles against light background shades, both of which extend to the edge of the page. The section title and chapter title are given in headers at the top of the pages. In addition, staggered marginal symbols (see p. iii for a key) mark the edges of the pages in each chapter. These various identifiers are meant to facilitate the quick location of desired material.

(2) References to other sections are given in SMALL CAPITAL TYPE, and this type is generally reserved for this purpose. Internet email addresses and Web sites are also given in a distinctive font.

(3) The INDEX at the back contains a listing of keywords.

(4) Alternate blocks of rows are shaded in most tables, in order to make the location of entries easier. Every table has a shaded header with the titles of the various columns given in bold type. Detailed explanation of the meaning of the columns is usually given in accompanying text.

(5) SI symbols and abbreviations are used throughout. See pp. 33 and 36 in the section SOME ASTRONOMICAL AND PHYSICAL DATA for the most common abbreviations. The letter "m" is used to denote both minutes of right ascension and metres; the meaning will be clear from the context. Minutes of time are usually abbreviated "min".

(6) The time scale Universal Time is generally used. Times of day are usually given in the 24-hour clock, using numerals separated by colons. The section TIME AND TIME SCALES on pp. 42–48 explains the various time scales used in astronomy.

(7) The section TERMINOLOGY AND SYMBOLS on p. 20 lists Greek letters (and other symbols) and defines some basic terms.

(8) The section TEACHING AND THE *OBSERVER'S HANDBOOK* on pp. 17–19 gives an overview of the contents of this Handbook.

(9) The Web site of the Handbook is www.rasc.ca/handbook. Resources related to the Handbook, including a page of links to all Web sites cited in the Handbook, are given at this site, and any updates and corrections will also be posted there.

Cover photos

The image on the front cover depicts the galaxy NGC 7331 and its neighbours. It was taken by Toronto astrophotographers Paul Mortfield, Dietmar Kupke, and Stefano Cancelli using a 20-inch f/8.4 Ritchey-Chretien telescope and SBIG ST10XME CCD camera. The image is a composite of three hours of total exposure, and was processed using CCDStack and Adobe Photoshop. At a distance of 46 million light-years the galaxy is well placed for observing on autumn evenings in the constellation Pegasus. You can find it listed as the third item of THE FINEST NGC OBJECTS section on p. 290 of this Handbook.

The back cover shows the front of the Handbook as it appeared in the first year of each of the six editors: Chant (1907), Northcott (1958), Percy (1971), Bishop (1982), Gupta (2001), and Kelly (2007). The background image is a section of the Hubble Deep Field, which many would argue is the most important astronomical image taken during the Handbook's existence.

EDITOR'S COMMENTS

Welcome to the 100th edition of the Handbook! One of the "tools" that comes with the position of editor is a complete, bound collection of every edition. As you can imagine, flipping through these older issues one can see just how much has changed in the field of astronomy since 1907. For those who want a more detailed history of the Handbook, former editor Roy Bishop has prepared a paper on the topic, which will appear in an upcoming issue of the *Journal*.

At 324 pages, this is the thickest edition to date. You may have already looked at the table of contents and noticed part of that is due to new sections. Two have been contributed by Roy Bishop. One is THE ELECTROMAGNETIC SPECTRUM (p. 37), and looks at the medium by which we know the universe; the other is RAINBOWS, HALOS, SUNDOGS, PILLARS, CORONAE, GLORIES, AND HEILIGENSCHIEN (p. 185) and is a wonderful explanation of various atmospheric phenomena that astronomers are expected to know "because they are in the sky." While some could argue that the topic is "atmospheric" and not strictly astronomical, one could make the same claim about aurorae and meteors! Jay Anderson has produced a listing of star-party weather, for those who like to observe while travelling. The last new section is by David Levy and Leo Enright and is a wonderful list of objects for those who enjoy the challenge of tracking down new jewels of the night sky.

In addition to new sections, there are several sections of the Handbook that have been expanded with new material this year. James Edgar has added a page to the SELECTED OBSERVATORIES, STAR PARTIES, AND PLANETARIA (p. 12) and the title has been changed to reflect the extra content. Allan Rahill has provided additional material for the WEATHER RESOURCES ON THE INTERNET section (p. 78), and Rajiv Gupta has expanded the POLAR ALIGNMENT section (p. 83) to include alignment charts for the southern hemisphere.

Of course there are many sections that are revised totally each year. These may be as simple as an updated table of data, such as the ephemeris for the Sun, or may require a complete rewrite of the material, such as that needed for the weather predictions along the path of totality of a solar eclipse. Sometimes a section that one would think of as totally static does get revised. For example, in this edition the ASTRONOMICAL TWILIGHT AND SIDEREAL TIME section (p. 52) has been revised so that it can now be used in both northern and southern hemispheres.

Another type of change, highlighted in the table of contents, is of sections that contain a "feature object." There is often a lot to be learned by reading about these case studies, and they are usually updated every year or two. Unless one is aware of that change, one might expect these sections to be the same from year to year.

Lastly, in many cases, the changes are subtle, values are changed in one table in a larger body of text, URLs are updated, or small revisions are made to the data. These changes do not often leap off the page, but it is that sort of dedication from the authors of each section that has contributed so much to the success of the Handbook.

Another new feature, suggested by a reader, found on the lower-right corners of THE SKY MONTH BY MONTH section is a black corner tab so that readers can quickly find that section. You can even cut off the corner tabs of each month as time passes to make finding the current month easier (at least for those who don't cringe at the thought of using scissors on a Handbook).

There are two changes in authorship with this edition, Damien Lemay is stepping down from the FIREBALLS section; and Richard Grieve and James Whitehead are stepping down from the METEORITE IMPACT CRATERS OF NORTH AMERICA section. I thank them for their contributions to the Handbook.

The editorial team will have to consider two things between now and the next edition. You may have noticed that Pluto's status has not changed in this edition. While no longer an official "planet," both the 2008 edition of the *Astronomical Phenomena* and *Astronomical Almanac* did "business as usual" and that is also the case for the 2009 *Astronomical Phenomena*. The other issue is the listing of natural satellites—while the

Handbook has traditionally listed all satellites, at the current discovery rate of small satellites some sort of cut-off may be needed. I would welcome comments from readers.

While the 100th edition will hopefully be well received, you can look forward to several new and expanded sections already being planned for the 101st edition.

chalmey Huv.

Patrick Kelly
handbookeditor@rasc.ca
Falmouth, Nova Scotia
2007 Sep. 6

When Ruth Northcott wrote her hopes in 1964 that the *Observer's Handbook* would command the same respect in the second century of its existence as in the first, little could she imagine the Handbook as it exists today. It has evolved into a larger, more interesting, and much more useful book; one that is well placed for a continued existence in its second century.

Each summer for the past seven years I have looked forward eagerly to the Handbook production team collaborations in making it the best it can be—error free, grammatically correct, and eminently useful.

It pleases me greatly that we have been able to accomplish this goal, each of us in our scattered places; we wouldn't be able to do what we do without the Internet. This 100th, greatly expanded Handbook is a pleasure to have, to cherish, and to use. The impressive list of volunteer contributors makes it all the more valuable. Enjoy!

James Edgar
Melville, Saskatchewan
2007 Aug. 14

My personal collection of RASC *Observer's Handbooks* covers a deceptively small section of one bookshelf, yet now stretches across a quarter century. Each compact volume is indispensable during its year at the front of the row, and continues to be a frequent historical resource thereafter. A compendium of thousands of astronomical facts, this almanac is of equal value to the active observer and the theoretician.

It is a testament to the Handbook's staying power that just six people have served as Editor during its 100 years of publication. The list of contributors is a veritable who's who of the Society, ably supported by a sprinkling of well-known astronomers from around the globe, each expert in their field.

Over the past four years that I have served a small role on the production team, it has been a source of both pride and pleasure to work with dedicated volunteers like Pat Kelly and Rajiv Gupta, James Edgar and Betty Robinson. These amateurs exhibit the best kind of professionalism in their dedication to the monumental task of maximizing content while minimizing errors and maintaining our flagship publication's respected place in the international astronomy community.

Bruce McCurdy
Edmonton, Alberta
2007 Sep. 8

THE *OBSERVER'S* HANDBOOK

EDITOR
Patrick Kelly

EDITOR'S ASSISTANT AND PROOFREADER
James Edgar

COPY EDITOR
Betty Robinson

PROOFREADER
Bruce McCurdy

In addition to the 48 contributors listed on pp. 4 & 5, several other individuals and organizations played a role in the production of this Handbook.

Some of the data contained herein comes from the publications *Astronomical Phenomena for the Year 2008* and *The Astronomical Almanac 2008*, both prepared jointly by the U.S. Naval Observatory's Nautical Almanac Office and Her Majesty's Nautical Almanac Office.

Corrections or suggestions for improvement that were incorporated in this edition were provided by Jeff Baldwin, Roy Bishop, Anne Cowley, Ted Dunphy, Donna Giesler, Anton Jopko, Ken Kingdon, John Pazmino, and Alan Whitman.

THE ROYAL ASTRONOMICAL SOCIETY OF CANADA

The beginnings of the Royal Astronomical Society of Canada go back to the mid-1800s. Then, in 1890, the Society was incorporated within the province of Ontario, received its Royal Charter from King Edward VII in 1903, and was federally incorporated in 1968. The National Office of the Society (containing the business office and library) is located at 136 Dupont St, Toronto ON M5R 1V2; telephone: (416) 924-7973 or (888) 924-7272 from within Canada; email: nationaloffice@rasc.ca; Web site: www.rasc.ca.

The RASC has more than 4500 members, who are from many countries and all walks of life. Members receive the *Observer's Handbook* (published in September for the next calendar year) and electronic access to the bimonthly *Journal of the RASC,* which contains review articles, research papers on historical and contemporary topics, education notes, general notes of astronomical interest, book reviews, news items concerning the Society and its Centres, informal articles, and letters. (A print version of the *Journal of the RASC* is available at an extra cost.) Also included in membership is *SkyNews,* Canada's popular bimonthly astronomy magazine.

Membership fees are $55 per year, with a reduced rate for persons under 21 years of age. Life membership is $2100. (For members outside of Canada, these figures are to be read as U.S. dollars, to cover higher mailing costs.) An applicant may affiliate with one of the Centres of the Society across Canada or join the Society directly as an unattached member (some Centres levy a surcharge above the regular membership fee).

The Society currently has 28 Centres located throughout Canada, in every province and in most major Canadian cities. Most Centres hold monthly meetings at which prospective members are welcome. Details on each Centre's activities as well as contact information for the Centre are available at its Web site; for links to the Centres' Web sites, visit www.rasc.ca.

REPORTING OF ASTRONOMICAL DISCOVERIES

To report a possible significant discovery (e.g. a new comet, nova, or supernova), a message should be sent to the International Astronomical Union's Central Bureau for Astronomical Telegrams. Send electronic mail to cbat@cfa.harvard.edu. Messages are monitored at all times. If this preferred method of communication is unavailable, a telephone call may be made to (617) 495-7244 or -7440 or -7444, but telephone calls are discouraged and these numbers will not be answered at all times. Also, a follow-up letter should be sent to the Central Bureau at 60 Garden St, Cambridge MA 02138, USA. Inexperienced observers should have their observation checked before contacting the Central Bureau.

For any new object, specify the date and time of observation, RA and Dec (with equinox), magnitude, and some physical description. For photographic and CCD discoveries, confirmation with a second image is highly desirable. In the case of a new comet, the rate of motion in RA and Dec should also be indicated.

Reports may instead be filled out at www.cfa.harvard.edu/iau/cbat.html. Recent IAU circulars and subscription information are also available at this URL.

RECOMMENDED READING AND ATLASES

Astronomy, a nontechnical monthly magazine for amateur astronomers (Canada and U.S.: (800) 533-6644; www.astronomy.com).

The Backyard Astronomer's Guide (2nd. ed.), by Terence Dickinson and Alan Dyer. Firefly Books (Canada: (800) 387-6192, United States: (800) 387-5085), 2002. The best guide to equipment and techniques for amateur astronomers, by two experienced observers.

Catalogue of the Astronomical Society of the Pacific ((415) 337-1100; www.astrosociety.org), an excellent source of astronomical educational resources such as books, slides, videos, globes, posters, software, teachers' classroom activity guides, and more.

Catalogue of Sky Publishing Corporation, a good source of books, atlases, globes, slide sets, software, and posters ((866) 644-1377; www.shopatsky.com).

Exploring the Night Sky, by Terence Dickinson. Firefly Books (see above), 1987. A guide to stargazing, recommended for children.

A Field Guide to the Stars and Planets, by Jay M. Pasachoff. Houghton Mifflin Company, New York, 2000. In the Petersen Field Guides series, this classic work (currently in its 4th edition) is packed with star maps and accessible information.

Nightwatch (3rd ed.), by Terence Dickinson. Firefly Books (see above), 1998. An excellent introductory observing guide.

Sky & Telescope, a monthly magazine widely read by both amateur and professional astronomers ((866) 644-1377; www.skyandtelescope.com).

SkyNews, the Canadian magazine of astronomy and stargazing, published bimonthly ((866) 759-0005; www.skynewsmagazine.com).

Starlight Nights, by Leslie Peltier (1900–1980), 1965. Sky Publishing Corporation. Anyone who enjoys the night sky should read this book.

Atlas of the Moon, by Antonín Rükl. Sky Publishing Corporation, 2004. A first-rate lunar atlas for amateur astronomers.

Bright Star Atlas 2000.0, by Wil Tirion. Introductory atlas containing 9000 stars to magnitude 6.5 and 600 clusters, nebulae, and galaxies on 10 charts.

Millennium Star Atlas, by Roger Sinnott and Michael Perryman. A comprehensive atlas based on data from the *HIPPARCOS* satellite. Three volumes, each covering 8 hours in RA. Contains more than 1 000 000 stars to magnitude 11 and more than 10 000 clusters, nebulae, and galaxies on 1548 charts.

Sky Atlas 2000.0 (2nd ed.), by Wil Tirion and Roger Sinnott, 1998. Large format and well done. Contains 81 000 stars to magnitude 8.5 and 2700 clusters, nebulae, and galaxies on 26 charts; laminated version available.

Uranometria 2000.0 Deep Sky Atlas, by Wil Tirion, Barry Rappaport, and Will Remaklus. A second edition of the popular atlas, with stellar data from the *HIPPARCOS* satellite. Contains more than 280 000 stars to magnitude 9.75 and 30 000 clusters, nebulae, and galaxies on 220 double-page charts.

Computer-based Planetarium Programs: Several are available, for example, *ECU (Earth Centered Universe), MegaStar, RedShift 5, Starry Night, TheSky,* and *Voyager 4,* For more information, see the catalogues listed above or do an Internet search at, for example, www.google.com.

Many of these items are available from Sky Publishing, A New Track Media Company, 90 Sherman Street, Cambridge MA 02140, USA; (866) 644-1377, www.skyandtelescope.com.

SELECTED OBSERVATORIES, STAR PARTIES, AND PLANETARIA
BY JAMES EDGAR

Some observatories and selected *star parties* with URL, latitude and longitude to nearest minute, and elevation in metres and feet are given below, ordered by longitude from east to west.

Location	Lat.	Long.	Alt. (m/ft.)
Anglo-Australian Observatory — Siding Spring, Australia www.aao.gov.au	31°17'S	149°04'E	1164/3819
Mount Stromlo Observatory — Canberra, Australia www.mso.anu.edu.au/home.php	35°19'S	149°00'E	767/2516
Perth Observatory — Bickley, Australia www.wa.gov.au/perthobs	32°00'S	116°08'E	380/1247
Effelsberg Radio Telescope — Effelsberg, Germany www.mpifr-bonn.mpg.de/div/effelsberg	50°31'N	6°53'E	343/1125
Greenwich Observatory — Greenwich, England www.rog.nmm.ac.uk	51°29'N	0°00'	31/102
Lovell Radio Telescope — Jodrell Bank, England www.jodrellbank.manchester.ac.uk	53°14'N	2°18'W	89/292
Armagh Observatory — Armagh, Northern Ireland www.arm.ac.uk/home.html	54°21'N	6°39'W	43/144
"Leviathan" Great Telescope — Birr, Ireland www.birrcastle.com/index.asp	53°05'N	7°54'W	59/194
Isaac Newton Telescope — La Palma, Canary Islands www.ast.cam.ac.uk/~dwe/SRF/camc.html	28°45'N	17°53'W	2327/7634
Butterpot Star Party — Butter Pot Prov. Park, Newfoundland www.sji.ca/rasc/star-party-2007.html	47°23'N	53°04'E	164/538
Nova East — Smileys Provincial Park, Nova Scotia halifax.rasc.ca/ne/home.html	45°01'N	63°58'W	150/492
St. Croix Observatory — Windsor, Nova Scotia halifax.rasc.ca/sco.html	44°57'N	64°02'W	65/213
Arecibo Observatory — Arecibo, Puerto Rico www.naic.edu/index.htm	18°21'N	66°45'W	307/1007
Paranal Observatory (ESO) — Cerro Paranal, Chile www.eso.org/paranal/site/paranal.html	24° 40'S	70°25'W	2635/8645
Las Campanas Observatory — Cerro Las Campanas, Chile www.lco.cl	29°00'S	70°42'W	2282/7486
Gemini South Observatory — Cerro Pachon, Chile www.gemini.edu	30°14'S	70°44'W	2722/8930
La Silla Observatory (ESO) — Cerro La Silla, Chile www.ls.eso.org/index.html	29°15'S	70°44'W	2400/7980
Cerro Tololo Inter-American Observatory — Cerro Tololo, Chile www.ctio.noao.edu	30°10'S	70°49'W	2200/7220
Mont Mégantic Observatory — Mont Mégantic, Québec www.astro.umontreal.ca/omm	45°27'N	71°09'W	1114/3654
Stellafane — Springfield, Vermont www.stellafane.com	48°16'N	72°31'W	387/1270
Van Vleck Observatory — Middletown, Connecticut www.astro.wesleyan.edu	41°33'N	72°40'W	65/213
CAFTA — St-Timothée, Québec membres.lycos.fr/cdadfs/cafta.html	45°18'N	74°03'W	38/125

Location	Lat.	Long.	Alt. (m/ft.)
Helen Sawyer Hogg Observatory — Ottawa, Ontario www.sciencetech.technomuses.ca	45°24′N	75°53′W	58/190
SMARTScope — Ottawa, Ontario ottawa.rasc.ca/smartscope/smartscope.html	45°21′N	75°53′W	58/190
Algonquin Adventure — Algonquin Park, Ontario toronto.rasc.ca/content/Algonquin2007.shtml	45°57′N	78°31′W	404/1325
David Dunlap Observatory — Toronto, Ontario www.astro.utoronto.ca/DDO	43°52′N	79°25′W	244/800
Green Bank Telescope — Green Bank, West Virginia www.gb.nrao.edu/gbt	38°26′N	79°50′W	803/2634
Hamilton Centre Observatory — Waterdown, Ontario www.hamiltonrasc.ca/observatory.htm	43°23′N	79°55′W	104/341
Allegheny Observatory — Pittsburgh, Pennsylvania www.pitt.edu/~aobsvtry	40°29′N	80°01′W	380/1247
Carr Astronomical Observatory — Collingwood, Ontario toronto.rasc.ca/content/CAO.shtml	44°30′N	80°23′W	176/577
Starfest — Mount Forest, Ontario www.nyaa-starfest.com	44°04′N	80°50′W	400/1312
Winter Star Party — Camp Wesumkee, Florida www.scas.org/wsp.htm	24°39′N	81°19′W	1/4
Sudbury Neutrino Observatory — Creighton, Ontario www.sno.phy.queensu.ca/sno	46°46′N	81°20′W	−2073/−6800
Manitoulin Star Party — Gordon's Park, Ontario www.gordonspark.com/astronomy.html	45°40′N	81°58′W	235/771
Hallam Observatory — Comber, Ontario www.rascwindsor.com/pages/history.php	42°14′N	82°31′W	181/594
Astrofest — Kankakee, Illinois chicagoastro.org/af/index.html	41°09′N	87°51′W	194/636
Yerkes Observatory — Williams Bay, Wisconsin astro.uchicago.edu/yerkes	42°34′N	88°33′W	334/1050
Texas Star Party — Fort Davis, Texas www.texasstarparty.org	30°36′N	103°57′W	1500/4921
McDonald Observatory — Fort Davis, Texas www.as.utexas.edu/mcdonald/mcdonald.html	30°40′N	104°01′W	2075/6808
Kalium Observatory — Regina, Saskatchewan telescope.ras.sk.ca	50°26′N	104°37′W	577/1894
Apache Point Observatory — Sunspot, New Mexico www.apo.nmsu.edu	32°47′N	105°49′W	2788/9147
Sleaford Observatory — Saskatoon, Saskatchewan www.usask.ca/psychology/sarty/rasc/sleaford.html	52°06′N	105°57′W	526/1728
Very Large Array — Socorro, New Mexico www.vla.nrao.edu	34°05′N	107°37′W	2123/6965
Saskatchewan Summer Star Party — Cypress Hills Park, Sask. www.usask.ca/psychology/sarty/rasc/starparty.html	49°39′N	109°31′W	1272/4174
Steward Observatory — Tucson, Arizona james.as.arizona.edu/~psmith/61inch	32°25′N	110°44′W	2510/8230
Fred Lawrence Whipple Observatory — Amado, Arizona cfa-www.harvard.edu/facilities/flwo	31°41′N	110°53′W	2554/8379
Kitt Peak National Observatory — Tucson, Arizona www.noao.edu/kpno	31°57′N	111°36′W	2120/7049
Lowell Observatory — Flagstaff, Arizona www.lowell.edu	35°12′N	111°40′W	2175/7250

U.S. Naval Observatory—Flagstaff, Arizona www.nofs.navy.mil	35°11'N 111°44'W	2262/7421
TELUS World of Science—Edmonton, Alberta www.odyssium.com/observatory.html	53°34'N 113°34'W	677/2221
Wilson Coulee Observatory—Okotoks, Alberta calgary.rasc.ca/tourrequest.htm	50°46'N 114°02'W	1127/3697
Alberta Star Party—Caroline, Alberta calgary.rasc.ca/asp.htm	52°08'N 114°43'W	1072/3517
Riverside Telescope Makers Conference—Camp Oakes, Calif. www.rtmcastronomyexpo.org	34°14'N 116°45'W	2316/7600
Palomar Observatory—San Diego, California www.astro.caltech.edu/palomar	33°21'N 116°52'W	1706/5597
Mt. Wilson Observatory—Pasadena, California www.mtwilson.edu	34°13'N 118°03'W	1740/5700
Dominion Radio Astrophysical Observatory—Penticton, B.C. www.drao-ofr.hia-iha.nrc-cnrc.gc.ca	49°19'N 119°37'W	545/1788
Mount Kobau Star Party—Osoyoos, British Columbia www.mksp.ca	49°07'N 119°44'W	1860/6102
Oregon Star Party—Ochoco National Forest, Oregon www.oregonstarparty.org	44°18'N 120°08'W	1499/4918
Fall Star Quest—Loon Lake, British Columbia www.merrittastronomical.com	49°53'N 120°30'W	1159/3802
Table Mountain Star Party—Ellensburg, Washington www.tmspa.com	47°35'N 120°35'W	1937/6357
Goldendale Observatory—Goldendale, Washington www.perr.com/gosp.html	45°51'N 120°47'W	640/2100
Pine Mountain Observatory—Pine Mountain, Oregon pmo-sun.uoregon.edu	43°47'N 120°57'W	1905/6250
Lick Observatory—San Jose, California mthamilton.ucolick.org	37°21'N 121°38'W	1290/4232
Prince George Centre Observatory—Prince George, B.C. www.vts.bc.ca/pgrasc/tour.html	53°45'N 122°51'W	691/2296
Gordon Southam Observatory—Vancouver, B.C. www.hrmacmillanspacecentre.com/observatory.htm	49°16'N 123°09'W	6/21
Dominion Astrophysical Observatory—Victoria, B.C. www.hia-iha.nrc-cnrc.gc.ca/dao/index_e.html	48°31'N 123°25'W	238/780
RASCALS Star Party—Malahat, British Columbia victoria.rasc.ca/events/StarParty	48°33'N 123°34'W	345/1132
James Clerk Maxwell Telescope—Mauna Kea, Hawaii www.jach.hawaii.edu/JCMT	19°49'N 155°28'W	4092/13 426
Canada-France-Hawaii Telescope—Mauna Kea, Hawaii www.cfht.hawaii.edu	19°49'N 155°28'W	4204/13 793
Gemini North—Mauna Kea, Hawaii www.gemini.edu/public	19°49'N 155°28'W	4213/13 824

A selection of North American planetaria with URL, phone number, and related information, ordered alphabetically by city, is given below.

Planetarium	Notes
Lodestar Astronomy Center—Albuquerque www.unm.edu/~cygnus (505) 841-5955	Part of University of New Mexico outreach; Infinity Express multimedia program; astronomy store; astrophoto contests
Fiske Planetarium—Boulder fiske.colorado.edu (303) 492-5001	Evening shows and weekend matinees; observatory available following shows for stargazing; school groups welcome

TELUS World of Science—Calgary
www.calgaryscience.ca
(403) 268-8300

Join "Seymour Sky" at the Planetarium dome; several programs, multimedia shows, and kits available for kids of all ages

Adler Planetarium—Chicago
www.adlerplanetarium.org/home.shtml
(312) 922-7827

Historic, first in Western Hemisphere; large collection of historic instruments; Doane Observatory on-site

Christa McAuliffe Planetarium—Concord
www.starhop.com/home.htm
(603) 271-7827

Dedicated to first "Teacher In Space" who tragically died in shuttle *Challenger* disaster 1986 Jan. 28

TELUS World of Science—Edmonton
www.telusworldofscience.com/edmonton
(780) 451-3344

Observatory; IMAX theatre; exhibit galleries; science camps and courses, planetarium shows, computer lab; robotics lab, gift shop

Burke Baker Planetarium—Houston
www.hmns.org/see_do/planetarium.asp
(713) 639-4632

One of the Challenger Centres; dome is used for training astronauts to identify star fields; SkyScan digital stars; theatre seats 232

Samuel Oschin Planetarium—Los Angeles
www.griffithobservatory.org/bsoplanet.html
(213) 473-0800

Newly renovated with state-of-the-art technology; 300-seat theatre; Zeiss Mark IX star projector; and Digistar 3-laser system

ASTROLab du Mont Mégantic—Mont Mégantic
www.astrolab-parc-national-mont-megantic.org
(819) 888-2941

Cosmic Rhythms multimedia show; dark skies; astronomy evenings; on-site lodging; open house for teachers; school programs

Planétarium de Montréal—Montréal
www.planetarium.montreal.qc.ca
(514) 872-4530

Programs for all ages and groups; activity sheets; classroom kits; advanced workshop for teachers and educators

Mystic Seaport Planetarium—Mystic
www.mysticseaport.org
(850) 572-5315

Celestial navigation workshops; 30-foot dome; specialized group programs; history of navigation exhibit; GPS workshop

Hayden Planetarium—New York
www.amnh.org/rose
(212) 769-5100

At American Museum of Natural History; programs, courses, and lectures; Zeiss Mark IX Universarium Star Projector

Harry C. Kendall Planetarium—Portland
www.omsi.edu/visit/planetarium
(503) 797-4000

Fifty-two-foot domed theatre with Digistar 3 projection; presentations on astronomy, space science, and lasers; school programs

Doran Planetarium—Sudbury
laurentian.ca/physics/planetarium/planetarium.html
(705) 675-1151

Programs include Lecture, School, and Specialty series; largest planetarium in northern Ontario

Ontario Science Centre—Toronto
www.ontariosciencecentre.ca
(416) 696-1000

In central Toronto; OMNIMax theatre; kids' sleepovers; summer day camps; home of the RASC Toronto Centre

MacMillan Planetarium—Vancouver
www.hrmacmillanspacecentre.com
(604) 738-7827

Close to downtown Vancouver; special laser shows in summer; numerous programs for school groups of all ages; teacher packages

Centre of the Universe—Victoria
www.hia-iha.nrc-cnrc.gc.ca/cu/main_e.html
(250) 363-8262

Interactive exhibits; Starlab planetarium; multimedia shows; family-friendly weekend events; Plaskett (1.8 m) Telescope

Albert Einstein Planetarium—Washington
www.nasm.si.edu/visit/theaters/planetarium/index.cfm
(877) 932-4629

At National Air and Space Museum; café; IMAX theatre; special exhibits commemorate 100th year of powered flight

Northern Lights—Watson Lake, Yukon
www.northernlightscentre.ca
(867) 536-7827

Canada's only all-dome video planetarium; daily shows; programs concentrate on aurora borealis and northern experience

Aldrin Planetarium—West Palm Beach
www.sfsm.org/planetarium.html
(561) 832-1988

Laser shows; telescopes; exhibits; science camps; Larry the Cat In Space; teachers' programs; birthday party programs

Manitoba Planetarium—Winnipeg
www.manitobamuseum.mb.ca
(204) 956-2830

In central Winnipeg; science centre, museum, and planetarium in one site; school programs; Guide/Scout badge program

SELECTED INTERNET RESOURCES

The World Wide Web is an important source of astronomical information. A selection of Web sites together with a reference to a page number in this Handbook (if any) is given below. A listing of all Web sites mentioned in this Handbook, with URL links to the various sites, is available at:

www.rasc.ca/handbook/links.shtml

URL	Description
www.aavso.org	American Association of Variable Star Observers (p. 270)
www.lpl.arizona.edu/alpo	Association of Lunar and Planetary Observers
www.astrosociety.org	Astronomical Society of the Pacific (p. 19)
www.astronomy.com	*Astronomy* magazine (p. 11)
www.cascaeducation.ca	Canadian Astronomical Society's education Web site (p. 17)
www.space.gc.ca	Canadian Space Agency
www.cleardarksky.com/csk	Clear Sky Clock, by Attila Danko (p. 82)
www.MrEclipse.com	Eclipse photography and safety (p. 132)
heritage.stsci.edu	Hubble Heritage Site, access to HST images
www.cfa.harvard.edu/iau/cbat.html	International Astronomical Union Central Bureau (p. 10); see also www.iau.org
www.darksky.org	International Dark-Sky Association (p. 88)
www.imo.net	International Meteor Organization (p. 234)
www.lunar-occultations.com/iota	International Occultation Timing Association (p. 158)
www.jpl.nasa.gov	Jet Propulsion Laboratory, activities for adults and kids
miac.uqac.uquebec.ca	Meteorites and Impacts Advisory Committee, Canadian Space Agency (p. 236)
cdsads.u-strasbg.fr	NASA Astrophysics Data System (ADS); bibliographic database, access to millions of articles
sunearth.gsfc.nasa.gov/eclipse	NASA eclipse site (p. 133)
nedwww.ipac.caltech.edu	NASA/IPAC Extragalactic Database (p. 304)
spaceflight.nasa.gov	NASA space flight site giving current information on Space Shuttle missions and ISS activities
www.rasc.ca/handbook	*Observer's Handbook* Web site (p. 6)
planetary.org	Planetary Society—contains over 2000 pages of information about space exploration
www.rasc.ca	Royal Astronomical Society of Canada (p. 10)
www.saguaroastro.org	Saguaro Astronomy Club, includes observing list database (p. 91)
www.heavens-above.com	Satellite tracking information, including International Space Station and Space Shuttle
simbad.u-strasbg.fr/simbad	SIMBAD astronomical database
www.skyandtelescope.com	*Sky & Telescope* and Sky Publishing (p. 11)
www.skynewsmagazine.com	*SkyNews*—Canada's astronomy magazine (p. 11)
www.stsci.edu	Space Telescope Science Institute; access to Digitized Sky Survey
www.seds.org	Students for the Exploration and Development of Space
vizier.hia.nrc.ca/viz-bin/VizieR	VizieR service; access to most astronomical catalogues

TEACHING AND THE *OBSERVER'S HANDBOOK*
BY JOHN R. PERCY

You are holding in your hand a valuable resource for teaching astronomy. Every user of this Handbook, whether amateur or professional astronomer or teacher in any setting, at any level, can contribute to education in astronomy; see *JRASC, 96* (October 2002), p. 196, (also found at www.cascaeducation.ca/files/outreach_paper.html) for information on how you can too.

As a result of curriculum renewal in Canada, the United States, and other countries, astronomy is now taught in many elementary and secondary schools; see *JRASC, 96* (June 2002), p. 114. The Canadian Astronomical Society, in partnership with the RASC and other organizations, has now embarked on a major education and public outreach initiative and has created a Canadian astronomy education Web site: www.cascaeducation.ca. The RASC has published *Skyways*, by Mary Lou Whitehorne, an excellent astronomy guide for teachers; a French version, *Explorons l'astronomie*, is also available.

The Night Sky

Teachers should make sure that their students are aware of what can be seen in the night sky, even though "the stars come out at night, but the students don't." THE SKY MONTH BY MONTH section of this Handbook (pp. 92–119) provides an excellent guide. Star charts can be found in many books and magazines (see p. 11) as well as in MAPS OF THE NIGHT SKY (pp. 309–317). (Study the first page of this section to get the most out of these maps.) Make sketches, including the horizon and compass points, to record the appearance and changes of the sky. Observational activities, with good record-keeping procedures (p. 90), can enable students to "learn science by doing science" and may be especially suitable for students in "applied" or technical streams. Students can use sky-simulation software to predict what they might see in the sky, or to explain what they have previously observed and recorded. Even the study of light pollution (pp. 86–88) can be an educational experience; see *JRASC, 96* (February 2002), p. 24, and www.astrosociety.org/education/publications/tnl/44/lightpoll.html.

Seasons, Scale of the Solar System, and the Phases of the Moon

Surveys show that these basic astronomical concepts are misunderstood by most people. One common misconception is that it is hottest in the summer because of the shape of Earth's orbit—many people assume we are closest to the Sun in the summer. Then why are the seasons reversed in the Southern Hemisphere? Even those who know that the seasons are due to the tilt of Earth's axis may think that, because of the tilt, the hemispheres are significantly closer to the Sun during their respective summers.

Other misconceptions relate to a lack of understanding of the scale of the solar system. Assuming a high speed that we are familiar with, say that of a commercial jet plane, how long would it take to travel to the Moon? To the Sun? If a beach ball represents the Sun, the solar system fits in your town, but the next nearest star is another beach ball on the opposite side of Earth! The sections PRINCIPAL ELEMENTS OF THE SOLAR SYSTEM (pp. 22–23), THE BRIGHTEST STARS (pp. 252–261), and THE NEAREST STARS (pp. 262–266) are useful references for constructing such models.

Here is a useful hands-on activity to illustrate phases of the Moon: Choose a day when the Sun and Moon are both visible in the sky (in the afternoon when the Moon is near first quarter or in the morning when the Moon is near last quarter; see THE SKY MONTH BY MONTH (pp.92–119). Hold a ball in your hand so that the Sun shines on it, and extend it toward the Moon. You will see the ball and the Moon illuminated by the Sun in the *same* way—a clear demonstration that the Moon is a spherical, nonluminous body floating in space.

These concepts are so basic that it is worth teaching them correctly, that is, monitoring the students' preconceptions through interviews and discussions, and being absolutely sure that they understand the concepts and can explain them from their understanding—not just from memorization. See also www.learner.org/teacherslab/pup.

The Sun

(1) Track the path of the Sun in the sky during one day and over successive days and weeks. This may be done safely and simply by using the shadow of a pole. Sunrise/sunset data and the changing position of the Sun in the heavens are given on pp. 196–197 and p. 178, respectively. This connects effectively with archaeoastronomy and multicultural astronomy; see www.astrosociety.org/education/publications/tnl/53/multicultural.html.

(2) Using binoculars or a small telescope, project an image of the Sun on a sheet of white cardboard. Observe and record sunspots, and watch the Sun rotate from day to day. Practise setting up such a demonstration ahead of time; then it can be set up very quickly. These observations can be supplemented with daily images of the Sun available on the Internet (see, e.g. sohowww.nascom.nasa.gov). **Warning:** Never observe the Sun directly, especially by looking through binoculars or a telescope. Permanent eye damage could result. When projecting a solar image, use a barrier to prevent anyone from looking directly into the light beam. See the sections FILTERS (pp. 66–69) and VIEWING A SOLAR ECLIPSE—A WARNING (p. 147) in this Handbook.

The Moon

(1) Keep a "Moon journal" as a class project: Observe and record where the Moon is, what shape it is, and when it rises and sets. Note how these variables change over several days and weeks. (Don't forget that the Moon can be visible in the daytime.)

(2) Draw the general appearance of the Moon's surface as seen with your naked eye. Many features, including the regions of the Apollo landing sites, can be identified using the MAP OF MOON on pp. 148–149. A video of one of the Apollo missions is worth showing to a class.

(3) Eclipses: a three-dimensional model, to the correct scale, is a great aid in explaining eclipses and why there is not an eclipse every two weeks. See the ECLIPSES IN 2008 section in this Handbook (pp. 124–143) for information on eclipses that may be visible from your locality this year.

(4) If ocean tides occur in your area, correlate the times and the range of the tide with the Moon's position in your sky, its phases, and distances. Lunar phases, perigees, and apogees are tabulated in THE SKY MONTH BY MONTH (pp.92–119), and an overview of tides appears in the TIDES AND THE EARTH–MOON SYSTEM article in this Handbook (pp. 173–177).

The Planets

(1) Nothing can stimulate student interest like direct experience, so observe the planets when they are visible. See THE SKY MONTH BY MONTH and THE PLANETS FOR 2008 sections (pp. 201–213 for the latter) for the visibility of the planets during the year.

(2) Develop an awareness of Earth as a planet. Study photographs of Earth from space. For a hands-on experience, place an Earth globe in sunlight with its north pole oriented northward. Then rotate and tilt the globe so your locality is at the "top" of the globe (the globe will then be oriented the same way in space as planet Earth). The regions on Earth where the Sun is rising or setting at that moment will be apparent.

Note which pole is experiencing 24 hours of daylight. Slowly turn the globe eastward about its axis (counterclockwise when viewed from the north) to show a sped-up day/night progression.

(3) Use Web sites, videos, and posters to capture the excitement of planetary exploration (see the catalogues in RECOMMENDED READING AND ATLASES on p. 11).

(4) See www.spacegrant.hawaii.edu/class_acts/CratersTe.html for an excellent cratering activity that enables students to study the cratering process in the classroom.

Comets and Asteroids

These are interesting topics, especially as it now appears that collisions between these objects and Earth may explain the extinctions of species such as the dinosaurs. Use the section METEORITE IMPACT CRATERS OF NORTH AMERICA (pp. 239–242) to have students locate nearby impact craters on geographical maps. See THE BRIGHTEST ASTEROIDS (p. 225) for a finder chart to locate a bright asteroid in the night sky (only binoculars are needed). There is a classic demonstration of "Creating a Comet" (out of dry ice and sand) described at www.noao.edu/education/crecipe.html.

Is a Telescope Necessary?

Binoculars and telescopes can be useful but are not essential; much interesting astronomy can be done with the unaided eye. However, binoculars are often available and should be used when helpful. See the section BINOCULARS (pp. 62–65) for a guide to their selection and use. The inexpensive, make-it-yourself *Project STAR* telescopes are highly recommended. See TELESCOPE PARAMETERS (p. 53) and TELESCOPE EXIT PUPILS (pp. 54–57) for a summary of some quantitative aspects of telescopes.

Resources

In addition to the list of reading material below, and the RASC's *Skyways,* you may be able to make use of the following:

(1) See the SELECTED OBSERVATORIES, STAR PARTIES, AND PLANETARIA section in this Handbook (pp. 12–15). Take your students to visit one of these.

(2) The Royal Astronomical Society of Canada is the largest organization of amateur astronomers in Canada. Their 28 Centres across Canada (see the section THE ROYAL ASTRONOMICAL SOCIETY OF CANADA on p. 10) offer a wide variety of activities that might be interesting to you and your students. For example, a member of the RASC might be willing to visit your class and demonstrate a telescope. The Astronomical Society of the Pacific's *Project ASTRO How-To Manual* can facilitate such visits. See www.astrosociety.org/education/astro/project_astro.html.

Astronomical Society of the Pacific, 390 Ashton Ave, San Francisco CA 94112, USA. In addition to their excellent educational material, the ASP publishes a free quarterly teachers' newsletter; download current and back issues from www.astrosociety.org/education/publications/tnl/tnl.html.

Project STAR Hands-on Science Materials, Learning Technologies Inc, 40 Cameron Ave, Somerville MA 02144, USA; (617) 628-1459; www.starlab.com. Unique, high-quality, low-cost materials for introducing students (and teachers) to astronomy.

SkyNews, Box 10, Yarker ON K0K 3N0; (866) 759-0005; www.skynewsmagazine.com. Bimonthly. General astronomy from a Canadian perspective. Included with RASC membership.

The Universe at Your Fingertips, and *More Universe at Your Fingertips,* edited by Andrew Fraknoi et al. Astronomical Society of the Pacific, 390 Ashton Ave, San Francisco CA 94112, USA. Another excellent collection of teaching activities and resources for grades 3–12. See also www.astrosociety.org/education/activities/astroacts.html.

BASIC DATA

TERMINOLOGY AND SYMBOLS

COORDINATE SYSTEMS

Astronomical positions are usually measured in a system based on the *celestial poles* and *celestial equator,* the intersections of Earth's rotation axis and equatorial plane, respectively, and the infinite sphere of the sky. *Right ascension* (RA or α) is measured in hours (h), minutes (m), and seconds (s) of time, eastward along the celestial equator from the vernal equinox (see below). *Declination* (Dec or δ) is measured in degrees (°), minutes ('), and seconds (") of arc, northward (N or +) or southward (S or –) from the celestial equator toward the north or south celestial pole.

Positions can also be measured in a system based on the *ecliptic,* the intersection of Earth's orbital plane and the infinite sphere of the sky. The Sun appears to move eastward along the ecliptic during the year. *Longitude* is measured eastward along the ecliptic from the vernal equinox; *latitude* is measured at right angles to the ecliptic, northward or southward toward the north or south ecliptic pole. The *vernal equinox* is one of the two intersections of the ecliptic and the celestial equator; it is the one at which the Sun crosses the celestial equator moving from south to north.

An object is *in conjunction with the Sun* if it has the same longitude as the Sun and *at opposition* if its longitude differs from that of the Sun by 180°. Mercury and Venus are in *superior* conjunction when they are more distant than the Sun and in *inferior* conjunction when they are nearer than the Sun (see the diagram at the right). An object is *stationary* when its reaches an extreme longitude.

Two *nonsolar* objects are in conjunction if they have the same RA. Generally, but not always, close mutual approaches correspond to conjunctions; following Jean Meeus, we use the term *quasi-conjunction* to denote close (< 5°) nonconjunctional approaches.

If an object crosses the ecliptic moving northward, it is at the *ascending node* of its orbit; if it crosses the ecliptic moving southward, it is at the *descending node.*

Elongation is the geocentric angle between an object and the Sun, or between a satellite and its primary, measured in the plane formed by Earth and the other two bodies.

SYMBOLS

Sun, Moon, and Planets

☉ Sun	☾ Last Quarter	⊕ Earth	♅ Uranus
⏺ New Moon	☾ Moon generally	♂ Mars	♆ Neptune
☺ Full Moon	☿ Mercury	♃ Jupiter	♇ Pluto
☽ First Quarter	♀ Venus	♄ Saturn	

Signs of the Zodiac

♈	Aries....................0°	♌	Leo ....120°	♐	Sagittarius ....240°
♉	Taurus...............30°	♍	Virgo ....150°	♑	Capricornus.....270°
♊	Gemini ....60°	♎	Libra................180°	♒	Aquarius..........300°
♋	Cancer..............90°	♏	Scorpius ....210°	♓	Pisces ....330°

The Greek Alphabet

A, α.......alpha	H, η.......eta	N, ν.......nu	T, τ........tau
B, β ....beta	Θ, θ, ϑ...theta	Ξ, ξ xi	Y, υ.......upsilon
Γ, γ........gamma	I, ι.........iota	O, o ....omicron	Φ, ϕ.......phi
Δ, δ ......delta	K, κ ......kappa	Π, π.......pi	X, χ.......chi
E, ε........epsilon	Λ, λ ......lambda	P, ρ........rho	Ψ, ψ ......psi
Z, ζ........zeta	M, μ ......mu	Σ, σ ....sigma	Ω, ω ......omega

SOLAR-SYSTEM GEOMETRY

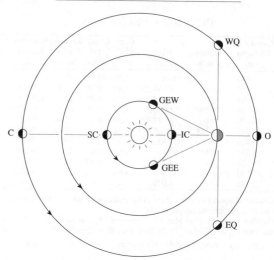

The diagram is a simplified view of our solar system, from the north side. Earth is shown (middle orbit) together with an inferior planet (i.e. Mercury or Venus) and a superior planet (e.g. Mars). Four special geometrical configurations of the inferior planet relative to Earth are shown; in counterclockwise chronological sequence they are inferior conjunction (IC), greatest elongation west (GEW), superior conjunction (SC), and greatest elongation east (GEE). Four special configurations of the superior planet relative to Earth are also shown; in clockwise chronological sequence they are opposition (O), eastern quadrature (EQ), conjunction with the Sun (C), and western quadrature (WQ).

PLANETARY HELIOCENTRIC LONGITUDES FOR 2008

The heliocentric longitude of a planet is the angle between the vernal equinox and the planet, as seen from the Sun. It is measured in the ecliptic plane, in the direction of the orbital motion of the planet (counterclockwise as viewed from the north side of the ecliptic plane). Knowing these heliocentric longitudes and the distances of the planets from the Sun (see p. 23), one can construct a diagram or model showing the relative orientations of the Sun and planets on any date.

UT	Me °	V °	E °	Ma °	J °	S °	U °	N °	P °
Jan. 1.0	308	183	100	96	272	153	348	321	269
Feb. 1.0	104	233	131	111	274	154	348	322	269
Mar. 1.0	227	279	161	124	277	155	349	322	269
Apr. 1.0	318	328	192	138	279	156	349	322	269
May 1.0	116	16	221	151	282	158	349	322	270
Jun. 1.0	239	66	251	165	284	159	350	322	270
Jul. 1.0	330	114	280	178	287	160	350	323	270
Aug. 1.0	139	164	309	192	289	161	350	323	270
Sep. 1.0	250	214	339	206	292	162	351	323	270
Oct. 1.0	346	262	8	220	295	163	351	323	270
Nov. 1.0	159	311	39	236	297	164	351	323	271
Dec. 1.0	258	359	69	251	300	165	352	323	271
Jan. 1.0	5	48	101	269	302	166	352	324	271

PRINCIPAL ELEMENTS OF THE SOLAR SYSTEM

PHYSICAL ELEMENTS

Object (Pronun.)	Equatorial Diameter km	Oblate- ness	Mass Earth=1	Den- sity t/m³	Grav- ity* Earth=1	Escape Speed* km/s	Rotation Period d	Inclina- tion† °	Albedo
Sun	1 392 530	0	332 946.0	1.41	27.9	617.5	25–35‡	– –	
Mercury (mûr'kū–rē)	4 879	0	0.055 274	5.43	0.38	4.2	58.646	0.0	0.11
Venus (vē'nŭs)	12 104	0	0.815 005	5.24	0.90	10.4	243.019	2.6	0.65
Earth (ûrth)	12 756	1/298	1.000 000	5.52	1.00	11.2	0.9973	23.4	0.37
Moon	3 475	0	0.012 300	3.35	0.17	2.4	27.3217	6.7	0.12
Mars (màrz)	6 792	1/148	0.107 447	3.94	0.38	5.0	1.0260	25.2	0.15
Jupiter (jōō'pǐ–tēr)	142 980 ††	1/15.4	317.833	1.33	2.53	59.5	0.4101‡‡	3.1	0.52
Saturn (sàt'ûrn)	120 540 ††	1/10.2	95.163	0.69	1.06	35.5	0.4440	26.7	0.47
Uranus^A (yûr'à–nŭs)	51 120 ††	1/43.6	14.536	1.27	0.90	21.3	0.7183	82.2	0.51
Neptune^B (nĕp'tyōon)	49 530 ††	1/58.5	17.149	1.64	1.14	23.5	0.6712	28.3	0.41
Pluto^C (plōō'tō)	2 390	0	0.002 2	1.8	0.08	1.3	6.3872	57.5	0.3

*At the equator †Inclination of equator to orbital plane ‡Depending on latitude ††At 1 atmosphere (101.325 kPa)
‡‡For the most rapidly rotating part, the equatorial region
^ADiscovered by Sir William Herschel, 1781 Mar. 13 ^BDiscovered by Johann G. Galle, 1846 Sep. 23
^CDiscovered by Clyde Tombaugh, 1930 Feb. 18. In 2007, the IAU reclassified Pluto as a dwarf planet.

Pronunciation guide: à gàgà; ĕ wĕ; ĕ mĕt; ē makēr; ĭ bĭt; ō gō; ōō mōōn; ū ūnite; ŭ sŭn; û ûrn

OSCULATING ORBITAL ELEMENTS FOR 2008

The tables at the right give the orbital elements of the planets and 30 largest main-belt asteroids, the latter provided by Dr. Brian Marsden. At any given time or "epoch," six basic quantities determine each body's elliptical orbit, for example:

(1) the mean distance from the Sun, a, equal to the semimajor axis of the ellipse;
(2) the eccentricity e of the ellipse;
(3) the inclination i of the orbital plane to the ecliptic;
(4) the longitude Ω of the ascending node of the orbital plane on the ecliptic;
(5) the longitude $\tilde{\omega}$ of perihelion;
(6) the body's mean longitude L at the given epoch.

The date of the ecliptic and equinox used to measure the last four quantities must also be specified, and may be different from the given epoch. Other, equivalent parameters may be substituted: the distance q of perihelion in place of a; the argument of perihelion, $\omega = \tilde{\omega} - \Omega$, in place of $\tilde{\omega}$; or the mean anomaly, $M = L - \tilde{\omega}$, or time T of perihelion in place of L. Once six fundamental quantities are known, all other attributes of the orbit of the body, such as the sidereal period P and synodic period S, can be derived.

If the body followed a perfectly elliptical orbit as predicted by classical orbital mechanics, then for a fixed ecliptic and equinox the first five quantities above would be constant over time. However, because of perturbations caused by the gravitational influence of other bodies, the orbits are not perfectly elliptical; hence the orbital elements depend on the epoch. The given *osculating* elements can be used to determine an elliptical orbit that is a close approximation to the actual path of the body for times near the given epoch. Two epochs, corresponding to Jan. 15 and Aug. 21, are provided for the planets; the elements for these epochs can be linearly interpolated to other epochs in 2008 for precision of a few arcseconds (typically $1''$ or $2''$). For the asteroids one epoch, corresponding to Nov. 30, is given, with resulting precision of about $1'$.

HELIOCENTRIC OSCULATING ORBITAL ELEMENTS FOR 2008
REFERRED TO THE MEAN ECLIPTIC AND EQUINOX OF J2000.0

Planet	Epoch Julian Date 245	Mean Distance a au	Eccen-tricity e	Incli-nation i °	Long. of Asc. Node Ω °	Long. of Perihelion $\tilde{\omega}$ °	Long. at Epoch L °	Sidereal Period P a	Synodic Period* S d

Elements are for epochs 2008 Jan. 15 and 2008 Aug. 21 respectively.

Planet	Date	a	e	i	Ω	$\tilde{\omega}$	L	P	S
Mercury	4480.5	0.387 098	0.205 645	7.0045	48.3215	77.4707	25.3112	0.2409	115.88
	4699.5	0.387 098	0.205 639	7.0044	48.3214	77.4723	201.5326	0.2409	115.88
Venus	4480.5	0.723 323	0.006 755	3.3945	76.6579	131.657	205.0346	0.6152	583.90
	4699.5	0.723 327	0.006 754	3.3945	76.6574	131.663	195.9020	0.6152	583.91
Earth†	4480.5	1.000 012	0.016 750	0.0011	173.2	102.9239	113.7208	1.0000	—
	4699.5	0.999 990	0.016 730	0.0011	173.6	102.9945	329.5669	1.0000	—
Mars	4480.5	1.523 725	0.093 332	1.8490	49.5358	336.1384	93.7399	1.8809	779.89
	4699.5	1.523 601	0.093 430	1.8490	49.5327	336.1422	208.5048	1.8807	780.00
Jupiter	4480.5	5.202 082	0.048 932	1.3038	100.5097	14.6813	248.3654	11.8598	398.89
	4699.5	5.202 360	0.048 917	1.3038	100.5097	14.6219	264.9881	11.8607	398.88
Saturn	4480.5	9.536 986	0.053 687	2.4878	113.6337	92.4319	148.3533	29.4491	378.09
	4699.5	9.530 684	0.053 541	2.4880	113.6414	91.7283	155.6680	29.4199	378.10
Uranus	4480.5	19.21728	0.045 892	0.7719	74.0222	172.9104	347.4866	84.2453	369.64
	4699.5	19.23664	0.044 828	0.7719	74.0404	172.7439	350.0710	84.3727	369.63
Neptune	4480.5	30.18150	0.008 445	1.7698	131.7786	18.723	322.2607	165.8126	367.47
	4699.5	30.21292	0.009 462	1.7692	131.7750	15.261	323.6203	166.0716	367.46
Pluto	4480.5	39.80754	0.253 977	17.1147	110.3344	224.9275	251.5376	251.1687	366.71
	4699.5	39.78562	0.253 266	17.1121	110.3380	224.0328	249.9178	250.9613	366.71

*Synodic period = (product of Ps of two planets) ÷ (difference of the Ps). Tabular values are relative to Earth.
† Values are actually for the Earth-Moon barycentre.

Asteroid	Diameter km	Mean Distance a au	Eccen-tricity e	Incli-nation i °	Long. of Asc. Node Ω °	Long. of Perihelion $\tilde{\omega}$ °	Long. at Epoch L °	Sidereal Period P a	Synodic Period* S d

Elements are for epoch Julian Date 245 4800.5 (2008 Nov. 30)

Asteroid	km	a	e	i	Ω	$\tilde{\omega}$	L	P	S
(1) Ceres	957	2.766792	0.079475	10.5857	80.4045	153.3001	137.8454	4.6022	466.66
(2) Pallas	524	2.772650	0.230878	34.8377	173.1321	123.3886	91.3630	4.6168	466.25
(4) Vesta	512	2.361269	0.089055	7.1352	103.9149	253.7702	38.6341	3.6284	504.22
(10) Hygiea	444	3.138648	0.117332	3.8422	283.4507	236.6430	74.6080	5.5605	445.35
(704) Interamnia	329	3.062441	0.150366	17.2910	280.3860	16.1469	136.0989	5.3592	449.05
(511) Davida	326	3.167952	0.185953	15.9376	107.6649	86.0163	113.8030	5.6386	444.00
(15) Eunomia	320	2.643423	0.187649	11.7384	293.2659	31.0992	163.6291	4.2978	476.01
(52) Europa	302	3.094958	0.105853	7.4816	128.7541	112.8156	21.8769	5.4448	447.43
(3) Juno	274	2.672153	0.255933	12.9680	169.9609	57.8943	314.7109	4.3681	473.70
(87) Sylvia	261	3.486031	0.080839	10.8574	73.3110	339.2356	214.2236	6.5087	431.56
(31) Euphrosyne	256	3.148599	0.225332	26.3152	31.2316	93.1713	231.2594	5.5870	444.89
(16) Psyche	239	2.920993	0.139250	3.0960	150.3250	17.8174	278.1046	4.9922	456.75
(88) Thisbe	232	2.767148	0.165347	5.2188	276.7643	313.3587	268.7301	4.6031	466.63
(65) Cybele	230	3.441421	0.107352	3.5513	155.6938	261.0936	289.5185	6.3842	433.10
(324) Bamberga	228	2.685418	0.337405	11.1070	327.9913	11.8572	330.6551	4.4007	472.66
(451) Patientia	225	3.059511	0.077293	15.2216	89.3881	69.4069	190.2617	5.3515	449.19
(19) Fortuna	225	2.443171	0.157950	1.5721	211.2813	33.1648	329.2427	3.8188	494.83
(107) Camilla	223	3.475111	0.077789	10.0497	173.1284	122.8351	231.2635	6.4782	431.93
(48) Doris	222	3.108642	0.074784	6.5555	183.7354	80.8684	183.3097	5.4810	446.77
(45) Eugenia	215	2.720994	0.081644	6.6099	147.9191	233.4814	159.8752	4.4884	469.96
(29) Amphitrite	212	2.554712	0.072951	6.0961	356.4852	59.6936	146.8514	4.0833	483.72
(7) Iris	211	2.384906	0.231427	5.5274	259.7192	45.0155	249.0363	3.6830	501.39
(121) Hermione	209	3.444273	0.135453	7.5994	73.1767	10.8807	5.0012	6.3921	433.00
(423) Diotima	209	3.065677	0.039981	11.2336	69.5189	272.5899	353.2769	5.3677	448.88
(9) Metis	209	2.386203	0.121977	5.5748	68.9614	75.2791	56.2623	3.6860	501.24
(13) Egeria	208	2.576374	0.085880	16.5416	43.2844	124.0467	125.8371	4.1354	481.75
(532) Herculina	207	2.771222	0.178158	16.3139	107.5991	184.2324	76.7696	4.6132	466.35
(94) Aurora	204	3.159887	0.087920	7.9653	2.6997	62.5109	65.1286	5.6170	444.37
(702) Alauda	195	3.192001	0.021716	20.6134	289.9677	282.9227	38.3600	5.7029	442.92
(6) Hebe	190	2.424804	0.202221	14.7540	138.7389	18.2361	193.2309	3.7759	496.84

NATURAL SATELLITES OF THE PLANETS
By Philip D. Nicholson

Of the 168 natural satellites listed in the table, all but 6 orbit the giant planets Jupiter (62), Saturn (60), Uranus (27), and Neptune (13). With a few exceptions, these moons may be divided into three groups, which presumably reflect their different origins. Closest to the planets are small ring moons, 20 km to 200 km in diameter and with strong evolutionary and dynamical connections to the planetary ring systems. Most of these objects were discovered during the *Voyager* flybys of 1979–1989, and all are very difficult to observe from Earth. These include the shepherd satellites Prometheus, Pandora, Cordelia, Ophelia, and Galatea; the co-orbital satellites Janus and Epimetheus; and Pan, which orbits within the Encke gap in Saturn's A-ring.

Next come the larger "regular" satellites in near-circular orbits in or near the planets' equatorial planes, thought to have been formed in situ via accretion in circumplanetary disks at the dawn of the solar system. The dividing line between the first two groups is fuzzy, but the regular satellites may be considered to start beyond about three planetary radii, that is, at Amalthea, Mimas, Puck, and Proteus. This group extends out to Callisto, Iapetus, Oberon, and Proteus but probably does not include Triton, which is now thought to have been captured. There are numerous orbital resonances among the regular satellites, for example, Io:Europa:Ganymede (1:2:4), Mimas:Tethys (1:2), Enceladus:Dione (1:2), and Titan:Hyperion (3:4); the origin of the orbital resonance is generally ascribed to orbital expansion driven by tidal interaction with Jupiter or Saturn. Temporary capture in similar resonances in the past may have been responsible for the anomalously large inclinations of Miranda and (perhaps) Naiad. Tidal energy dissipation within Io is responsible for this moon's spectacular volcanic activity, and similar heating at a lower level may still occur within Europa and Enceladus.

The third and outermost group—and the group whose numbers have increased so much in recent years—comprises the "irregular" satellites. These generally small bodies (2 km to 200 km in diameter, except for 340-km Nereid) move in quite eccentric orbits at large inclinations to the planets' orbital planes. Their orbits are not random; rather, they fall into several more-or-less tight clusters in semimajor axis and inclination: three or four at Jupiter (all but one retrograde) centred on Himalia, Ananke, Pasiphae, and Carme and three at Saturn (one retrograde) centred on Albiorix, Siarnaq, and Phoebe. These clusters are believed to be due to collisional disruptions of a smaller number of original objects captured from heliocentric orbits. The situation at Uranus and Neptune remains unclear, although there are now nine Uranian irregulars (all but one retrograde) and six Neptunians (three retrograde). The orbits of the irregular satellites, along with that of the Earth's Moon, are subject to strong solar gravitational perturbations and thus maintain approximately fixed inclinations to their respective planet's orbital planes rather than to their equators.

In 2006/2007 twelve new irregular satellites of Saturn were reported or discovered, all but one on retrograde orbits. In addition, images from the *Cassini* spacecraft revealed a third small Saturnian satellite, S/2007 S4, orbiting between Mimas and Enceladus. It joins Methone and Pallene, which were discovered by *Cassini* in 2004.

Thirteen previously announced satellites have received permanent numbers and names from the International Astronomical Union. Their designation in previous editions follows in parentheses.

Jupiter: XLIX Kore (2003 J14)
Saturn: XXXV Daphnis (2005 S1), XXXVI Aegir (2004 S10), XXXVII Bebhionn (2004 S11), XXXVIII Bergelmir (2004 S15), XXXIX Bestla (2004 S18), XL Farbauti (2004 S9), XLI Fenrir (2004 S16), XLII Fornjot (2004 S8), XLIII Hati (2004 S14)
Neptune: IX Halimede (2002 N1), X Psamathe (2003 N1), XI Sao (2002 N2), XII Laomedeia (2002 N3), XIII Neso (2002 N4)

TABLE OF NATURAL SATELLITES OF THE PLANETS

Name (Pronunciation)	Diameter km	Mass[A] Pt	Density t/m³	Visual Mag.[B]	Albedo	Mean Dist. from Planet 10³ km	Orbital Period d	Eccentricity	Orbit Incl.[C] °	Discovery
Satellite of Earth										
Moon* (mōōn)	3475.	73 490. (10)	3.34	-12.7	0.11	384.4	27.322	0.0554	5.16	—
Satellites of Mars										
I Phobos* (fō'bŏs)	22.	0.0107 (0.00002)	1.87	11.4	0.07	9.38	0.319	0.0151	1.1	A. Hall, 1877
II Deimos* (dī'mŏs)	12.	0.0022 (0.0002)	2.3	12.5	0.07	23.46	1.262	0.0002	1.8v	A. Hall, 1877
Satellites of Jupiter										
XVI Metis (mē'tĭs)	43.	—	—	17.5	0.06	128.0	0.295	0.0012	0.02	*Voyager 2*, 1979
XV Adrastea (a-drăs'tē-ä)	16.	—	—	18.7	≈0.05	129.0	0.298	0.0018	0.39	*Voyager 1*, 1979
V Amalthea* (ăm-'l-thē'ä)	167.	—	—	14.1	0.09	181.4	0.498	0.0031	0.39	E. Barnard, 1892
XIV Thebe** (thē'be)	99.	—	—	16.0	0.05	221.9	0.675	0.0177	1.07	*Voyager 1*, 1979
I Io*[D] (ī'ō)	3643.	89 330. (10)	3.53	5.0	0.62	421.8	1.769	0.0041	0.04	Galileo, 1610
II Europa*[D] (ū-rō'pä)	3122.	48 000. (10)	3.01	5.3	0.68	671.1	3.551	0.0094	0.47	Galileo, 1610
III Ganymede*[D] (găn'ē-mēd')	5262.	148 200. (10)	1.94	4.6	0.44	1 070.	7.155	0.0011	0.17	Galileo, 1610
IV Callisto* (kä-lĭs'tō)	4820.	107 600. (10)	1.83	5.6	0.19	1 883.	16.689	0.0074	0.19	Galileo, 1610
XVIII Themisto (thē-mĭs'tō)	4.[E]	—	—	21.0	—	7 284.	130.	0.24	43.	C. Kowal, 1975[F]
XIII Leda (lē'dä)	≈20.	—	—	19.5	—	11 165.	241.	0.16	27.	C. Kowal, 1974
VI Himalia*** (hĭm'à-lī-ä)	185.	—	—	14.6	0.03	11 461.	251.	0.16	27.	C. Perrine, 1904
X Lysithea*** (lĭs'ĭ-thē'ä)	≈35.	—	—	18.3	—	11 717.	259.	0.11	28.	S. Nicholson, 1938
VII Elara (e'lär-ä)	85.	—	—	16.3	0.03	11 741.	260.	0.22	26.	C. Perrine, 1905
XLVI Carpo (kär'po)	3.[G]	—	—	23.0	—	16 989.	456.	0.43	51.	S. Sheppard et al., 2003
S/2003 J12	1.[G]	—	—	23.9	—	17 582.	490.	0.51	151.	S. Sheppard et al., 2003

Pronunciation guide:ă tăp; ā cāre; à däte; ä gägä; ĕ wĕ; ē mēt; ĭ bĭt; ī īce; ŏ gŏ; ō hōt; ŏ ŏrb; oo book; ōō mōōn; ŭ cŭte; ŭ ŭp; ū ūrn

For some background on the satellites' names, visit planetarynames.wr.usgs.gov/append7.html.

Visual magnitudes are at mean opposition distance.

* synchronous rotation; ** probably synchronous; *** asynchronous; **** chaotic rotation; (no asterisk) rotation unknown

[A] The numbers in parentheses are possible errors.

[B] Jovian, Saturnian, and Uranian irregular satellites discovered in 1997–2001 are CCD-R magnitudes (675 nm); the solar V–R is 0.53.

[C] Inclinations of inner satellites (those closer than 100 planetary radii) are relative to the planet's *equator*. As customary, inclinations for outer satellites (those beyond Jupiter IV, Saturn VIII, Uranus IV, and Neptune I) are relative to the planet's *orbital plane*. Iapetus is an intermediate case. For our Moon, the inclination relative to Earth's orbital plane is 5°; relative to Earth's equator it varies between 18° and 29° in an 18.61-year cycle. A value >90° indicates retrograde motion.

[D] Laplace resonance; longitudes satisfy L(Io) – 3L(Europa) + 2L(Ganymede) ≈ 180°. Also, the mean motions are such that the three periods are nearly 1:2:4.

[E] Diameters assume an albedo of 0.06.

[F] Initially detected in 1975 and then lost; recovered in 2000 by S. Sheppard and D. Jewitt.

[G] Diameters assume an albedo of 0.04.

TABLE OF NATURAL SATELLITES OF THE PLANETS (continued)

Name (Pronunciation)	Diameter km	Mass[A] Pt	Density t/m^3	Visual Mag.[B]	Albedo	Mean Dist. from Planet 10^3 km	Orbital Period d	Eccentricity	Orbit Incl.[C] °	Discovery
Satellites of Jupiter (continued)										
XXXIV Euporie (ū-pôr'ĭ-ē)	2.[E]	—	—	23.1	—	19 304.	551.	0.14	146.	S. Sheppard et al., 2001
S/2003 J3	2.[G]	—	—	23.4	—	20 221.	584.	0.20	148.	S. Sheppard et al., 2003
S/2003 J18	2.[G]	—	—	23.4	—	20 514.	597.	0.02	146.	B. Gladman et al., 2003
XXXV Orthosie (ôr-thō-sī'ē)	2.[E]	—	—	23.1	—	20 720.	623.	0.28	146.	S. Sheppard et al., 2001
XXXIII Euanthe (ū-an'thē)	3.[E]	—	—	22.8	—	20 797.	620.	0.23	149.	S. Sheppard et al., 2001
XXII Harpalyke (här-pă-lē'kē)	3.[E]	—	—	22.2	—	20 858.	623.	0.23	149.	S. Sheppard et al., 2000
XXVII Praxidike (prăk-sĭ'dĭ-kē)	5.[E]	—	—	21.2	—	20 907.	625.	0.23	149.	S. Sheppard et al., 2000
XXIX Thyone (thī'ō-nē)	3.[E]	—	—	22.3	—	20 939.	627.	0.23	149.	S. Sheppard et al., 2001
S/2003 J16	2.[G]	—	—	23.3	—	20 957.	616.	0.22	149.	B. Gladman et al., 2003
XXIV Iocaste (ī-ō-kăs'tē)	4.[E]	—	—	21.8	—	21 061.	632.	0.22	149.	S. Sheppard et al., 2000
XL Mneme (nē'mē)	2.[G]	—	—	23.3	—	21 069.	620.	0.23	149.	B. Gladman, S. Sheppard, 2003
XXX Hermippe (hêr-mĭp'ē)	4.[E]	—	—	22.1	—	21 131.	634.	0.21	151.	S. Sheppard et al., 2001
XLII Thelxinoe (thĕl-kī'nō-ē)	2.[G]	—	—	23.4	—	21 162.	628.	0.22	151.	S. Sheppard et al., 2004
XLV Helike (hē'lĭ-kē)	4.[G]	—	—	22.6	—	21 263.	635.	0.16	155.	S. Sheppard et al., 2003
XII Ananke*** (ā'nän-kē)	≈30.	—	—	18.8	—	21 276.	630.	0.24	149.	S. Nicholson, 1951
S/2003 J15	2.[G]	—	—	23.5	—	22 627.	690.	0.19	147.	S. Sheppard et al., 2003
XXXII Eurydome (ū-rĭd'ō-mē)	3.[E]	—	—	22.7	—	22 865.	717.	0.28	150.	S. Sheppard et al., 2001
S/2003 J17	3.[E]	—	—	23.4	—	22 922.	714.	0.24	165.	B. Gladman et al., 2003
XLIII Arche (är'kē)	3.[G]	—	—	22.8	—	22 931.	724.	0.26	165.	S. Sheppard et al., 2002
XXXVIII Pasithee (pă-sī'thē)	2.[E]	—	—	23.2	—	23 004.	719.	0.27	165.	S. Sheppard et al., 2001
S/2003 J10	2.[E]	—	—	23.6	—	23 041.	716.	0.43	165.	S. Sheppard et al., 2003
XXI Chaldene (kăl'dē-nē)	3.[E]	—	—	22.5	—	23 100.	724.	0.25	165.	S. Sheppard et al., 2000
XXVI Isonoe (ī-sō'nō-ē)	3.[E]	—	—	22.5	—	23 155.	726.	0.25	165.	S. Sheppard et al., 2000
XXV Erinome (ē-rĭn'ō-mē)	3.[E]	—	—	22.8	—	23 196.	729.	0.27	165.	S. Sheppard et al., 2000
XXXVII Kale (ka'lē)	2.[E]	—	—	23.0	—	23 217.	729.	0.26	165.	S. Sheppard et al., 2001
XXXI Aitne (ā-īt'nē)	3.[E]	—	—	22.7	—	23 229.	730.	0.26	165.	S. Sheppard et al., 2001
XX Taygete (tā-ĭj'ĕ-tē)	4.[E]	—	—	21.9	—	23 280.	732.	0.25	165.	S. Sheppard et al., 2000
S/2003 J9	1.[G]	—	—	23.7	—	23 384.	733.	0.26	165.	S. Sheppard et al., 2003
XI Carme (kär'mē)	≈45.	—	—	17.6	—	23 404.	734.	0.25	165.	S. Nicholson, 1938
XXXVI Sponde (spŏn'dē)	2.[E]	—	—	23.0	—	23 487.	748.	0.31	151.	S. Sheppard et al., 2001
XIX Megaclite (mĕg-ā-klī'tē)	4.[E]	—	—	21.7	—	23 493.	753.	0.42	153.	S. Sheppard et al., 2000
S/2003 J5	4.[G]	—	—	22.4	—	23 495.	739.	0.25	165.	S. Sheppard et al., 2003
S/2003 J19	2.[G]	—	—	23.7	—	23 533.	740.	0.26	165.	B. Gladman et al., 2003
S/2003 J23	2.[G]	—	—	23.5	—	23 563.	732.	0.27	146.	S. Sheppard et al., 2004

TABLE OF NATURAL SATELLITES OF THE PLANETS (continued)

Name (Pronunciation)	Diameter km	Mass[A] Pt	Density t/m³	Visual Mag.[B]	Albedo	Mean Dist. from Planet 10³ km	Orbital Period d	Eccentricity	Orbit Incl.[C] °	Discovery
Satellites of Jupiter (continued)										
XXIII Kalyke (kă-lē'kē)	4.[E]	—	—	21.8	—	23 566.	742.	0.25	165.	S. Sheppard et al., 2000
VIII Pasiphae (pă-sĭf'ă-ē')	≈60.	—	—	17.0	—	23 624.	744.	0.41	151.	P. Melotte, 1908
XLVII Eukelade (ū-kĕ-lă'dē)	4.[G]	—	—	22.6	—	23 661.	746.	0.27	165.	S. Sheppard et al., 2003
S/2003 J4	2.[G]	—	—	23.0	—	23 930.	755.	0.36	150.	S. Sheppard et al., 2003
XXXIX Hegemone (hē-jĕ'mŏ-nē)	3.[G]	—	—	22.8	—	23 947.	740.	0.33	155.	S. Sheppard et al., 2003
XLVIII Cyllene (sĭ-lē'nē)	2.[G]	—	—	23.2	—	23 951.	752.	0.41	150.	S. Sheppard et al., 2003
XLI Aoede (ā-ō'dē)	4.[G]	—	—	22.5	—	23 981.	762.	0.43	158.	S. Sheppard et al., 2003
IX Sinope*** (sĭ-nō'pē)	≈38.	—	—	18.1	—	23 939.	759.	0.25	158.	S. Nicholson, 1914
XLIX Kore	2.[G]	—	—	23.6	—	24 011.	779.	0.34	145.	S. Sheppard et al., 2003
XLIV Kallichore (kă-lĭ-kŏ'rē)	2.[G]	—	—	23.7	—	24 043.	765.	0.26	166.	S. Sheppard et al., 2003
XXVIII Autonoe (ô-tŏn'ō-ē)	3.[E]	—	—	22.0	—	24 046.	761.	0.32	152.	S. Sheppard et al., 2001
XVII Callirrhoe (kă-lĭr'ō-ē)	7.[E]	—	—	20.7	—	24 103.	759.	0.28	147.	J. Scotti, T. Spahr, 1999
S/2003 J2	2.[G]	—	—	23.2	—	29 541.	980.	0.23	161.	S. Sheppard et al., 2003
Satellites of Saturn										
XVIII Pan[H] (păn)	26.	—	—	19.4	≈0.5	133.6	0.575	0.0002	0.007	M. Showalter, 1990
XXXV Daphnis (dăf-nĭs)	7.	—	—	23.4[I]	—	136.5	0.594	≈0.	≈0.	Cassini ISS team, 2005
XV Atlas (ăt'lăs)	20.	—	—	19.0	0.4	137.7	0.602	0.0012	0.01	Voyager 1, 1980
XVI Prometheus**[J] (prŏ-mē'thē-ŭs)	94.	0.19	0.44	15.8	0.6	139.4	0.613	0.002	0.006	Voyager 1, 1980
XVII Pandora**[J] (păn-dôr'ă)	81.	0.15	0.53	16.4	0.5	141.7	0.629	0.004	0.052	Voyager 1, 1980
XI Epimetheus*[K] (ep'ă-mē'thē-ŭs)	120.	0.5 (0.1)	0.61	15.6	0.5	151.4	0.694	0.010	0.35	J. Fountain, S. Larson, 1978
X Janus*[K] (jā'nŭs)	180.	1.9 (0.1)	0.66	14.4	0.6	151.5	0.695	0.007	0.17	A. Dollfus, 1966
I Mimas* (mī'măs)	397.	38. (1)	1.16	12.8	0.6	185.6	0.942	0.0206	1.57	W. Herschel, 1789
XXXII Methone (mĕth-ō'nē)	3.	—	—	25.1[I]	—	194.3	1.010	0.001	0.02	Cassini ISS team, 2004
S/2007 S4	≈2[E]	—	—	≈26	—	197.7	1.037	—	—	Cassini ISS team, 2007
XXXIII Pallene (pă-lā'nē)	4.	—	—	24.5[I]	—	212.3	1.154	0.004	0.18	Cassini ISS team, 2004
II Enceladus* (ĕn-sĕl'ă-dŭs)	499.	65. (2)	1.61	11.8	1.0	238.1	1.370	0.0001	0.01	W. Herschel, 1789
III Tethys* (tē'thĭs)	1060.	627. (5)	0.96	10.3	0.8	294.7	1.888	0.0001	0.168	G. Cassini, 1684
XIII Telesto (tă-lĕs'tō)	25.	—	—	18.5	0.7	294.7	1.888[L]	≈0.	1.16	B. Smith et al., 1980

[H] Orbits within the Encke gap. Discovered in *Voyager* images (1980–81).
[I] Magnitudes are estimated from published diameters, which is the reverse of the practice for irregular satellites.
[J] Prometheus and Pandora are shepherds of the F-ring.
[K] Co-orbital satellites
[L] Telesto librates about the trailing (#5) Lagrangian point of Tethys's orbit.
[M] Calypso librates about the leading (#4) Lagrangian point of Tethys's orbit.

TABLE OF NATURAL SATELLITES OF THE PLANETS (continued)

Name (Pronunciation)	Diameter km	Mass[A] Pt	Density t/m³	Visual Mag.[B]	Albedo	Mean Dist. from Planet 10³ km	Orbital Period d	Eccentricity	Orbit Incl.[C] °	Discovery
Satellites of Saturn (continued)										
XIV Calypso** (kă-lĭp'sō)	19.	—	—	18.7	1.0	294.7	1.888[M]	≈0.	1.47	D. Pascu et al., 1980
IV Dione* (dī-ō'nē)	1120.	1097. (2)	1.46	10.4	0.6	377.4	2.737	0.0002	0.002	G. Cassini, 1684
XII Helene (hĕ-lĕn')	30.	—	—	18.4	0.6	377.4	2.737[N]	≈0.	0.21	P. Laques, J. Lecacheux, 1980
XXXIV Polydeuces (pŏl-i-dū'sēz)	3.5	—	—	24.8[I]	—	377.4	2.737[O]	0.018	0.17	*Cassini* ISS team, 2004
V Rhea* (rē'a)	1530.	2308. (60)	1.23	9.7	0.6	527.1	4.518	0.0009	0.327	G. Cassini, 1672
VI Titan** (tī't'n)	5150.[P]	134570. (20)	1.88	8.4	0.2	1221.9	15.945	0.0288	0.33	C. Huygens, 1655
VII Hyperion*** (hī-pēr'ī-ŏn)	266.	—	0.57	14.4	0.3	1464.1	21.276	0.0175	0.57	W. Bond, G. Bond, W. Lassell, 1848
VIII Iapetus* (ī-ăp'ĕ-tŭs)	1469.	1809	1.09	11.0v	0.08–0.4	3560.8	79.331	0.0284	7.57	G. Cassini, 1671
XXIV Kiviuq (kē-vyook')	14.[E]	—	—	21.9	—	11365.	449.	0.33	46.	B. Gladman et al., 2000
XXII Ijiraq (ē-jē-rāk')	10.[E]	—	—	22.5	—	11442.	451.	0.32	47.	J. Kavelaars et al., 2000
IX Phoebe*** (fē'bē)	213.	8.2	1.63	16.5	0.08	12944.3	548.	0.1644	175.	W. Pickering, 1898
XX Paaliaq (pa-lyak')	19.[E]	—	—	21.2	—	15198.	687.	0.36	45.	B. Gladman et al., 2000
XXVII Skadi (ska'dē)	6.[E]	—	—	23.5	—	15641.	728.	0.27	153.	J. Kavelaars et al., 2000
XXVI Albiorix (ăl'bē-ôr-ĭks)	26.[E]	—	—	20.4	—	16394.	783.	0.48	34.	M. Holman, T. Spahr, 2000
S/2007 S2	5.[E]	—	—	24.4	—	16725.	808.	0.18	174.	S. Sheppard et al., 2007
XXXVII Bebhionn	6.[E]	—	—	24.1	—	17119.	835.	0.47	35.	S. Sheppard, D. Jewitt, 2005
XXIX Siarnaq (syar-nák')	32.[E]	—	—	20.0	—	17531.	896.	0.30	46.	B. Gladman et al., 2000
XXVIII Erriapo (ĕr-rē-ăp'ō)	8.[E]	—	—	22.9	—	17604.	871.	0.47	34.	J. Kavelaars et al., 2000
S/2006 S8 = XLVII Skoll	6.[E]	—	—	24.5	—	17665.	878.	0.46	161.	S. Sheppard et al., 2006
S/2007 S1	7.[E]	—	—	23.9	—	18009.	888.	0.16	46.	S. Sheppard et al., 2007
S/2004 S13	6.[E]	—	—	24.5	—	18057.	906.	0.26	167.	S. Sheppard, D. Jewitt, 2005
S/2006 S4	6.[E]	—	—	24.4	—	18206.	921.	0.33	180.	S. Sheppard et al., 2006
XXI Tarvos (tar'vōs)	13.[E]	—	—	22.0	—	18239.	926.	0.54	33.	J. Kavelaars et al., 2000
S/2004 S19 = XLIV Hyrrokkin	8.[E]	—	—	23.5	—	18437.	932.	0.33	152.	S. Sheppard et al., 2007
XXXI Narvi (när'vē)	5.[E]	—	—	24.1	—	18719.	956.	0.35	135.	S. Sheppard et al., 2003
XXV Mundilfari (mŭnd'ĭl-făr-ē)	6.[E]	—	—	23.7	—	18722.	952.	0.21	167.	B. Gladman et al., 2000
S/2006 S1	6.[E]	—	—	24.6	—	18790.	963.	0.12	156.	S. Sheppard et al., 2006
S/2006 S6	5.[E]	—	—	24.7	—	18811.	965.	0.22	163.	S. Sheppard et al., 2006
S/2007 S3	5.[E]	—	—	24.9	—	18975.	978.	0.19	175.	S. Sheppard et al., 2007
S/2004 S17	4.[E]	—	—	25.2	—	19099.	985.	0.23	167.	S. Sheppard, D. Jewitt, 2005
XXXVIII Bergelmir	6.[E]	—	—	24.2	—	19372.	1007.	0.15	158.	S. Sheppard, D. Jewitt, 2005

[N] Helene librates about the leading (#4) Lagrangian point of Dione's orbit with a period of 769 d.

[O] Polydeuces librates about the trailing (#5) Lagrangian point of Dione's orbit with a period of 792 d.

[P] Titan's cloud-top diameter is 5550 km; as seen in the eyepiece.

TABLE OF NATURAL SATELLITES OF THE PLANETS (continued)

Name (Pronunciation)	Diameter km	Mass[A] Pt	Density t/m³	Visual Mag.[B]	Albedo	Mean Dist. from Planet 10³ km	Orbital Period d	Eccentricity	Orbit Incl.[C] °	Discovery
Satellites of Saturn (continued)										
XXIII Suttungr (sŭt'tŭng)	6.[E]	—	—	23.8	—	19465.	1017.	0.11	176.	B. Gladman et al., 2000
XXXVI Aegir	6.[E]	—	—	24.4	—	19614.	1026.	0.24	167.	S. Sheppard, D. Jewitt, 2005
S/2004 S12	5.[E]	—	—	24.8	—	19906.	1049.	0.40	164.	S. Sheppard, D. Jewitt, 2005
XXXIX Bestla	7.[E]	—	—	23.8	—	19959.	1053.	0.77	148.	S. Sheppard, D. Jewitt, 2005
XXX Thrymr (thrĭm)	6.[E]	—	—	23.8	—	20219.	1092.	0.49	176.	B. Gladman et al., 2000
XL Farbauti	5.[E]	—	—	24.7	—	20291.	1079.	0.21	158.	S. Sheppard, D. Jewitt, 2005
XLIII Hati	6.[E]	—	—	24.4	—	20304.	1080.	0.29	163.	S. Sheppard, D. Jewitt, 2005
S/2004 S7	6.[E]	—	—	24.5	—	20577.	1102.	0.55	166.	S. Sheppard, D. Jewitt, 2005
S/2006 S2 = XLV Kari	7.[E]	—	—	23.9	—	22089.	1231.	0.48	156.	S. Sheppard et al., 2006
S/2006 S3	6.[E]	—	—	24.6	—	22096.	1227.	0.40	158.	S. Sheppard et al., 2006
XLI Fenrir	4.[E]	—	—	25.0	—	22611.	1269.	0.13	163.	S. Sheppard, D. Jewitt, 2005
S/2006 S7 = XLVIII Surtur	5.[E]	—	—	24.8	—	22704.	1297.	0.45	178.	S. Sheppard et al., 2006
S/2006 S5 = XLVI Loge	6.[E]	—	—	24.6	—	23058.	1311.	0.19	168.	S. Sheppard et al., 2006
XIX Ymir (ē'mēr)	16.[E]	—	—	21.6	—	23130.	1315.	0.33	173.	B. Gladman et al., 2000
XLII Fornjot	6.[E]	—	—	24.6	—	23609.	1354.	0.19	168.	S. Sheppard, D. Jewitt, 2005
Satellites of Uranus										
VI Cordelia[Q] (kôr-dēl'yà)	25.[R]	—	—	24.2	—	49.8	0.335	≈0.	0.08	*Voyager 2*, 1986
VII Ophelia[Q] (ō-fēl'yà)	30.[R]	—	—	23.9	—	53.8	0.376	0.01	0.10	*Voyager 2*, 1986
VIII Bianca (bē-äng'kà)	45.[R]	—	—	23.1	—	59.2	0.435	0.001	0.19	*Voyager 2*, 1986
IX Cressida (krĕs'ĭ-dà)	65.[R]	—	—	22.3	—	61.8	0.464	≈0.	0.01	*Voyager 2*, 1986
X Desdemona (dĕz'dà-mō'nà)	60.[R]	—	—	22.5	—	62.7	0.474	0.11	0.11	*Voyager 2*, 1986
XI Juliet (joo'lē-ĕt)	85.[R]	—	—	21.7	—	64.4	0.493	0.001	0.06	*Voyager 2*, 1986
XII Portia (pôr'shà)	110.[R]	—	—	21.1	—	66.1	0.513	≈0.	0.06	*Voyager 2*, 1986
XIII Rosalind (rŏz'à-lĭnd)	60.[R]	—	—	22.5	—	69.9	0.558	≈0.	0.28	*Voyager 2*, 1986
XXVII Cupid (cū'pĭd)	18.	—	—	25.9	—	74.4	0.613	≈0.	≈0.	M. Showalter, J. Lissauer, 2003
XIV Belinda (bà-lĭn'dà)	68.[R]	—	—	22.1	—	75.3	0.624	≈0.	0.03	*Voyager 2*, 1986
XXV Perdita (pûr'dĭ-tà)	26.	—	—	23.6	—	76.4	0.638	0.003	0.07	E. Karkoschka, 1999[S]
XV Puck (pŭk)	155.	—	—	20.4	0.07	86.0	0.762	≈0.	0.32	*Voyager 2*, 1985
XXVI Mab (măb)	24.[R]	—	—	25.4	—	97.7	0.923	0.003	0.13	M. Showalter, J. Lissauer, 2003
V Miranda*[T] (mĭ-răn'dà)	472.	66. (8)	1.2	15.8	0.32	129.9	1.413	0.0013	4.34	G. Kuiper, 1948

[Q] Cordelia and Ophelia are shepherds of the ε-ring.
[R] Diameter assumes the same albedo (0.07) as Puck.
[S] In *Voyager 2* (January 1986) images
[T] Near resonance(?); L(Miranda) – 3L(Ariel) + 2L(Umbriel) drifts slowly (period ≈ 12.5 years).

TABLE OF NATURAL SATELLITES OF THE PLANETS (continued)

Name (Pronunciation)	Diameter km	Mass[A] Pt	Density t/m³	Visual Mag.[B]	Albedo	Mean Dist. from Planet 10³ km	Orbital Period d	Eccentricity	Orbit Incl.[C] °	Discovery
Satellites of Uranus (continued)										
I Ariel*[T] (âr'ē-ĕl)	1158.	1350. (120)	1.7	13.7	0.39	190.9	2.520	0.0012	0.04	W. Lassell, 1851
II Umbriel*[T] (ŭm'brē-ĕl')	1169.	1170. (140)	1.4	14.5	0.21	266.0	4.144	0.0040	0.13	W. Lassell, 1851
III Titania* (tī'tä'nē-ä)	1578.	3520. (90)	1.7	13.5	0.27	436.3	8.706	0.0011	0.079	W. Herschel, 1787
IV Oberon* (ō'bä-rōn)	1523.	3010. (80)	1.6	13.7	0.23	583.5	13.463	0.0014	0.068	W. Herschel, 1787
XXII Francisco (frän'cis-cō)	14.[E]	—	—	25.3	—	4276.	267.	0.15	145.	M. Holman, J. Kavelaars, 2001
XVI Caliban (kā'lĭ-bän)	60.[R]	—	—	22.4	—	7231.	580.	0.16	141.	B. Gladman et al., 1997
XX Stephano (stĕf'ä-nō)	20.[R]	—	—	24.1	—	8004.	677.	0.23	144.	B. Gladman et al., 1999
XXI Trinculo (trĭn'cū-lō)	14.[E]	—	—	25.3	—	8504.	749.	0.22	167.	M. Holman, J. Kavelaars, 2002
XVII Sycorax (sĭk'ō-räks)	120.[R]	—	—	20.8	—	12179.	1288.	0.52	159.	P. Nicholson et al., 1997
XXIII Margaret (mär'gär-ĕt)	15.[E]	—	—	25.2	—	14345.	1687.	0.66	57.	D. Jewitt, S. Sheppard, 2003
XVIII Prospero (prós'pér-ō)	30.[R]	—	—	23.2	—	16256.	1978.	0.44	152.	M. Holman et al., 1999
XIX Setebos (sĕt'ē-bŏs)	35.[R]	—	—	23.3	—	17418.	2225.	0.59	158.	J. Kavelaars et al., 1999
XXIV Ferdinand (fŭr'dĭn-nänd)	16.[E]	—	—	25.0	—	20901.	2887.	0.37	170.	M. Holman, J. Kavelaars, 2001
Satellites of Neptune										
III Naiad (nī'ăd)	66.	—	—	24.6	0.07	48.2	0.294	≈0.	4.74	*Voyager 2*, 1989
IV Thalassa (thä-läs'ä)	82.	—	—	23.9	0.09	50.1	0.311	≈0.	0.21	*Voyager 2*, 1989
V Despina (dĭs-pīn'ä)	150.	—	—	22.5	0.09	52.5	0.335	≈0.	0.07	*Voyager 2*, 1989
VI Galatea (gal'ä-tē'ä)	176.	—	—	22.4	0.08	62.0	0.429	≈0.	0.05	*Voyager 2*, 1989
VII Larissa** (lä-rĭs'ä)	194.	—	—	22.0	0.09	73.5	0.555	0.001	0.20	*Voyager 2*, 1989
VIII Proteus** (prō'tē-ŭs)	420.	—	—	20.3	0.10	117.6	1.122	≈0.	0.039	*Voyager 2*, 1989
I Triton* (trī't'n)	2706.	21400. (50)	2.06	13.5	0.76	354.8	5.877	≈0.	157.	W. Lassell, 1846
II Nereid*** (nerē-īd)	340.	—	—	19.7	0.16	5513.4	360.	0.75	7.23	G. Kuiper, 1949
IX Halimede	50.[E]	—	—	24.4	—	15686.	1875.	0.57	134.	M. Holman, J. Kavelaars, 2002
XI Sao	27.[E]	—	—	25.7	—	22452.	2919.	0.30	48.	M. Holman, J. Kavelaars, 2002
XII Laomedeia	33.[E]	—	—	25.3	—	22580.	2982.	0.48	35.	M. Holman, J. Kavelaars, 2002
XIII Neso	43.[E]	—	—	24.7	—	46570.	8863.	0.53	132.	M. Holman, J. Kavelaars, 2002
X Psamathe (săm'ä-thē)	36.[E]	—	—	25.1	—	46738.	9136.	0.45	137.	D. Jewitt et al., 2003
Satellites of Pluto										
I Charon* (kär'ĕn)	1208.	1620. (90)	1.65	17.3	0.37	19.57	6.387	0.00	0.0[U]	J. Christy, 1978
II Nix (nĭx)	36.[G]	—	—	23.4	—	48.68	24.856	0.02	0.0[U]	H. Weaver, S. Stern, 2005
III Hydra (hī'drä)	36.[G]	—	—	23.3	—	64.78	38.207	0.05	0.2[U]	H. Weaver, S. Stern, 2005

[U] Nix and Hydra orbit in the same plane as the Pluto–Charon binary. Their orbital periods are in the ratio 1:4:6 (Charon:Nix:Hydra). The inclinations are with respect to Pluto's assumed equatorial plane. Most other references give these inclinations with respect to the ecliptic, which are about 96°.

ORBITAL MOTION
By Roy Bishop

Whether you are observing a distant galaxy, the stars in a globular cluster, the waltz of Jupiter's Galilean satellites, or the drift of the Moon during an occultation or merely uttering an expletive as an artificial satellite passes through the field of your camera, an understanding of orbital motion is central to an appreciation of the heavens.

Among early cosmologies were those of **Aristotle** (340 BC) and **Ptolemy** (published as the *Almagest*, c. 150 AD), and the superior heliocentric model proposed by **Copernicus** (*De revolutionibus*, 1543). These attempts at modelling the heavens used complex systems of circles upon circles, of eccentric deferents and epicycles. John Milton, a contemporary of Galileo, wrote the following lines in his epic poem "Paradise Lost" (1674), possibly expressing his discontent with the Ptolemaic and Copernican systems of compounded circles:

> From Man or Angel the great Architect
> Did wisely to conceal, and not divulge
> His secrets to be scann'd by them who ought
> Rather admire; or if they list to try
> Conjecture, he his Fabric of the Heav'ns
> Hath left to thir disputes, perhaps to move
> His laughter at thir quaint Opinions wide
> Hereafter, when they come to model Heav'n
> And calculate the Stars, how they will wield
> The mighty frame, how build, unbuild, contrive
> To save appearances, how gird the Sphere
> With Centric and Eccentric scribbl'd o'er,
> Cycle and Epicycle, Orb in Orb.

Kepler, using observations accumulated by Tycho Brahe, broke with the 2000-year preoccupation with circles when he discovered that the planets move in an elegantly simple way along elliptical paths (*Astronomia nova,* 1609). Although he had discovered *how* the planets move, Kepler was unable to explain quantitatively *why* they move in this way.

Galileo strongly supported the Copernican heliocentric universe (*Dialogue on the Two Chief World Systems,* 1632) and achieved brilliant insights concerning the motion of objects (*Two New Sciences,* 1638); however, he ignored Kepler's ellipses and did not apply his mechanics to the sky.

Newton united the heavens and Earth by showing that the laws governing motions on Earth also apply to the heavens. In his *Principia* (1687), the greatest book in the physical sciences, Newton presented his three laws of motion and the first ever physical force law, his law of gravitation. He used these to explain the motions not only of bodies on Earth, but also of the planets, comets, stars, equinoxes, tides, etc. Newton was the first to realize that the Moon is falling toward Earth just as freely as does an apple, and that the elliptical orbit of the centre of mass of the Earth–Moon system is the path that results (as he described it) as these two bodies free-fall under the action of the Sun's gravitational force.

In popular-level explanations of phenomena involving rotary motion, such as spinning wheels, automobiles on corners, tides, and orbital motion, "centrifugal force" is usually invoked. This is unfortunate because centrifugal force is a fiction, and its use in a popular description of motion obscures understanding.[1]

In the case of orbits, the common misconception is that the inward gravitational force is balanced by an outward "centrifugal force." Newton's view is simpler: There is only one force, the inward pull of gravity. There is *no physical agent* to cause an outward force. (Note that forces cause accelerations, not vice versa.) Also, if there *were* an outward supporting force, the two forces would cancel and, as Galileo realized, the body would then move along a straight line. If you choose a rotating reference frame and then ignore the rotation (mistake no. 1), you have to pretend there is a "centrifugal force" (mistake no. 2) in order to make sense of motions occurring within this frame. The two mistakes effectively cancel, but the description has been made needlessly complicated, and if you do not realize what you have done, you do not understand the motion.

Einstein's general theory of relativity (GTR) of 1915 superseded Newton's description of gravity. The arbiter of which is a good theory and which theory is wrong is nature. Newton's laws are accurate enough for most of NASA's calculations, but they do not work exactly. For example, if the computer programs used in the Global Positioning System (GPS) were based on Newton's gravitation, the system would be a multibillion-dollar boondoggle. Einstein's conception of gravitation is essential to the operation of this satellite-based navigation system. In the case of strong gravitation and/or speeds approaching the speed of light, Newton's laws fail dramatically. The GTR may be wrong too, but so far it has passed all experimental tests. Science does not hie after ultimate explanations or "truth"; its goal is a rational, coherent description of the measurable physical world, a description that has beauty in its simplicity, a description that makes sense. In the courtroom of nature, any aspect of science is falsifiable. Modern technology is making possible increasingly precise tests of general relativity (for instance, see *Sky & Telescope,* July 2004, p. 22).

According to Einstein's GTR, gravitation is not a mysterious force that one mass exerts upon a distant mass; gravitation is the geometry (non-Euclidean) of the 4-dimensional spacetime within which we and the stars exist. Golf balls (if air friction is ignored), satellites, planets, stars, and light follow *geodesics,* the straightest possible, force-free paths through a spacetime whose geometry is shaped by mass–energy. The difficulty in intellectually grasping a non-Euclidean spacetime originates with us. Common sense is inadequate. This is not surprising, given that our common sense is based on the Euclidean, 3-dimensional geometry of straight lines, rectangles, and spheres we learned in the crib by age 2. The underlying cause of our delusion is that our senses and thought processes are constrained by the speed of neuron signals. Compared to light, neuron signals ooze along at a very slow rate, about one ten-millionth the speed of light. Consequently, to us a second of time is brief, light looks instantaneous, relativistic effects seem foreign, and time appears to be independent of space.

Gravitation is geometry. That is why no one has ever felt a force of gravity. Like the centrifugal force, it never did exist. A force of gravity was the glue Newton invented to make his naïve, Euclidean, space-plus-time model of the universe approximate reality. Newton himself was well aware of the unsatisfactory nature of several of his assumptions, far more so than most people who came after him.

When you release a coin from your hand, you see the coin "fall" because the contact force of the ground on your feet (the *only* force you feel) accelerates you the other way. An orbiting astronaut experiences no such force, so he remains beside a released coin. Orbital motion could not be simpler—*no* forces are involved.

What would Milton have written had he been familiar with the conjectures of Newton and Einstein?

---

[1] Brief descriptions of tides in the Newtonian context (without invoking the obfuscating centrifugal force!) and in the context of the general theory of relativity appear on pp. 173 and 177, respectively.

SOME ASTRONOMICAL AND PHYSICAL DATA
BY ROY BISHOP

Many of the numbers listed below are based on measurement. Exceptions include defined quantities (indicated by ≡), quantities calculated from defined quantities (e.g. m/ly, au/pc), and numbers of mathematical origin such as π and conversion factors in angular measure. Of those based on measurement, some are known to only approximate precision and the equal sign is reduced to ≈. Many others are known to quite high precision (the uncertainties occur after the last digit given), and several are from "the 2002 CODATA recommended values of the fundamental physical constants" (see physics.nist.gov/cuu/Constants/index.html). The units (Système International (SI) where possible), symbols, and nomenclature are based on recommendations of the International Astronomical Union and the International Union of Pure and Applied Physics.

LENGTH

1 metre (m) = the distance travelled by light in a vacuum in $(299\,792\,458)^{-1}$ s
1 astronomical unit (au) = $1.495\,978\,715 \times 10^{11}$ m = 499.004 786 4 light-s
1 light-year (ly)   = $9.460\,536 \times 10^{15}$ m (based on average Gregorian year)
                    = 63 239.8 au
1 parsec (pc)   = $3.085\,678 \times 10^{16}$ m = 206 264.8 au = 3.261 631 ly
1 mile*   ≡ 1.609 344 km
1 micron*   ≡ 1 µm   *Indicates deprecated unit;
1 angstrom*   ≡ 0.1 nm   unit on right is preferred

TIME

1 second (s) ≡ 9 192 631 770 periods of the radiation involved in the transition between the two hyperfine levels of the ground state of the ^{133}Cs atom at mean sea level

Day: Mean sidereal (equinox to equinox)   = 86 164.0914 s
         Mean rotation (fixed star to fixed star) = 86 164.0998 s
         Day (d)   ≡ 86 400. s
         Mean solar   = 86 400.0009 s

Month: Draconic (node to node)   = 27.212 221 d
         Tropical (equinox to equinox)   = 27.321 582 d
         Sidereal (fixed star to fixed star)   = 27.321 662 d
         Anomalistic (perigee to perigee)   = 27.554 550 d
         Synodic (new Moon to new Moon) = 29.530 589 d

Year: Eclipse (lunar node to lunar node)   = 346.620 075 d
         Tropical (equinox to equinox) (a)   = 365.242 190 d
         Average Gregorian   ≡ 365.242 5 d
         Average Julian   ≡ 365.25 d
         Sidereal (fixed star to fixed star)   = 365.256 363 d
         Anomalistic (perihelion to perihelion) = 365.259 635 d

EARTH

Mass, $M_E = 5.9742 \times 10^{24}$ kg   Age ≈ 4.6 Ga   Central T ≈ 5000 K to 6000 K
Geocentric gravitational constant, $GM_E = 3.986\,004\,39 \times 10^{14}$ m^3/s^2
Radius: Equatorial, a = 6378.14 km   Polar, b = 6356.75 km
           Mean = $(a^2b)^{1/3}$ = 6371.00 km   Of metallic core = 3475 km
Solar parallax = 8.794 143″ (Earth equatorial radius ÷ 1 au)
1° of latitude = 111.132 95 − 0.559 82 cos 2ϕ + 0.001 17 cos 4ϕ km (at latitude ϕ)
1° of longitude = 111.412 88 cos ϕ − 0.093 50 cos 3ϕ + 0.000 12 cos 5ϕ km

1 knot = 1 nautical mile ($\approx 1'$ of latitude) per hour $\equiv$ 1.852 km/h = 0.51444 m/s
Distance of sea horizon for eye h metres above sea level
   (allowing for refraction) $\approx 3.9h^{1/2}$ km $\approx 2.1h^{1/2}$ nautical miles
Atmospheric pressure: 1 atm $\equiv$ 101.325 kPa (There is $\approx$1 kg of air above 1 cm^2.)
Density of air at sea level (1 atm, 20 °C) = 1.2 kg/m^3
Values of atmospheric refraction for various elevations (assuming 1 atm, 10 °C):
   90°: 0′; 44°: 1′; 26°: 2′; 18°: 3′; 11°: 5′; 6°: 8′; 4°: 12′; 2°: 18′; 0°: 34′
Speed of sound in standard atmosphere = 331 m/s $\approx$ 1 km/3 s $\approx 10^{-6}$ c
Magnetic field at surface $\approx 5 \times 10^{-5}$ T (**B** field comes out of a N-seeking pole)
Magnetic poles: 83°N, 115°W; 65°S, 138°E (as of 2005)
Standard acceleration of gravity $\equiv$ 9.806 65 m/s^2
Meteoritic flux $\approx 1 \times 10^{-15}$ kg/(m^{2}s) $\approx 10^4$ t/a over entire Earth
Obliquity of ecliptic = 23.4393° (2000.0)   Constant of aberration = 20.495 52″
Annual general precession = −50.29″ (2000.0); Precession period $\approx$ 25 800 a
Escape speed from Earth = 11.2 km/s   Mean orbital speed = 29.786 km/s
Escape speed at 1 au from Sun = 42.1 km/s (= $\sqrt{2}$ × orbital speed)

SUN

Mass = 1.9891 × 10^{30} kg   Radius = 696 265 km   Eff. Temp. $\approx$ 5780 K
Output: Power = 3.85 × 10^{26} W, M_{bol} = 4.79
       Luminous intensity = 2.84 × 10^{27} cd, M_v = 4.82
At 1 au outside Earth's atmosphere:
   Energy flux = 1.37 kW/m^2, m_{bol} = −26.78
   Illuminance = 1.27 × 10^5 lx, m_v = −26.75
Inclination of the solar equator on the ecliptic of date = 7.25°
Longitude of ascending node of the solar equator on the ecliptic of date = 76°
Period of rotation at equator $\equiv$ 25.38 d (sidereal), 27.2753 d (mean synodic)
Solar wind speed near Earth $\approx$ 450 km/s (travel time, Sun to Earth $\approx$ 4 d)
Solar velocity = 19.4 km/s toward α = 18.07h, δ = +30° (solar apex)
Location in Milky Way Galaxy: $\approx$ 25 kly from centre, $\approx$ 50 ly N of galactic
   plane, on the inner edge of the Orion arm

MILKY WAY GALAXY

Mass $\approx 10^{12}$ solar masses   Diameter $\approx$ 300 kly (including the galactic halo)
Centre: α = 17h 45.7m, δ = −29°00′; N pole: α = 12h 51m, δ = 27°08′ (2000.0)
Rotation speed at Sun $\approx$ 230 km/s, period $\approx$ 200 Ma
Velocity relative to 3 K background radiation $\approx$ 400 km/s toward $\alpha \approx$ 14h, $\delta \approx$ −30°

CONSTANTS

Speed of light, $c \equiv$ 299 792 458 m/s (This, in effect, defines the metre.)
Planck's constant, h = 6.626 07 × 10^{-34} J·s = 4.135 667 × 10^{-15} eV·s
Gravitational constant, G = 6.672 × 10^{-11} N·m^2/kg^2
Elementary charge, e = 1.602 176 × 10^{-19} C
Constant in Coulomb's law $\equiv 10^{-7}$ c^2 (SI units) (This defines the coulomb.)
Avogadro constant, N_A = 6.022 142 × 10^{26} kmol^{-1}
Boltzmann constant, k = 1.380 65 × 10^{-23} J/K = 8.617 × 10^{-5} eV/K $\approx$ 1 eV/10^{4}K
Stefan-Boltzmann constant, σ = 5.6704 × 10^{-8} W/(m^{2}K^4)
Wien's Law: $\lambda_m T$ = 2.8978 × 10^{-3} m·K (per dλ)
Hubble constant, H = 71 ± 4 km/(s·Mpc)   Age of universe = 13.7 ± 0.2 Ga
−273.15 °C (degree Celsius) = 0 K (kelvin) (lowest thermodynamic temperature)
Volume of ideal gas at 0 °C, 101.325 kPa = 22.4140 m^3/kmol
Water: fusion at 0 °C: 0.333 MJ/kg   vapourization at 100 °C: 2.26 MJ/kg
       specific heat and density (near 20 °C): 4.18 kJ/(kg·C°) and 1.00 t/m^3

MASS AND ENERGY

Mass is a measure of sluggishness of response to a net force. (SI unit: kg)
Weight ($\neq$ mass) is the force required to support a body. (SI unit: N)
   (1 pound-mass* = 0.453 59 kg) (1 pound-force* = 4.4482 N)

1 kilogram (kg) $\equiv$ mass of a platinum-iridium cylinder stored in Paris, France
1 atomic mass unit (u) $\equiv$ 1/12 of the mass of an atom of ^{12}C
$$= 1.660\,539 \times 10^{-27} \text{ kg} = N_A^{-1} = 931.4940 \text{ MeV}$$
1 joule (J) $\equiv$ work done by a force of 1 N acting through a distance of 1 m
   $\approx$ the kinetic energy gained by this Handbook in falling freely 0.4 m
1 electron-volt (eV) $\equiv$ the kinetic energy gained by a particle carrying one unit
   of elementary electrical charge *(e)* in falling through an
   electrical potential difference of one volt (V)
$$= 1.602\,176 \times 10^{-19} \text{ J}$$

Electron mass = $9.109\,38 \times 10^{-31}$ kg = 548.579 91 µu = 0.510 998 9 MeV
Proton mass = $1.672\,622 \times 10^{-27}$ kg = 1.007 276 467 u = 938.2720 MeV
Neutron mass = $1.674\,927 \times 10^{-27}$ kg = 1.008 664 92 u = 939.565 MeV

Some atomic masses: ^1H (1.007 825 u) ^2H (2.014 102 u) ^4He (4.002 603 u)

Thermochemical calorie* (cal) = 4.184 J
1 erg*/s = 10^{-7} J/s = 10^{-7} W
1 BTU*/h = 1054.35 J/h = 0.292 88 W   *Indicates deprecated unit;
1 horsepower* = 745.7 W   unit on right is preferred.
1 eV per event = 23 060 cal/mol
$C + O_2 \rightarrow CO_2 + 4.1$ eV $4\,^1H \rightarrow\,^4He + 26.73$ MeV

Highest cosmic-ray energy (carried by protons) $\approx 10^{20}$ eV
Power output (average) of an adult human $\approx$ 100 W
1 kg of TNT or milkshake releases 4.2 MJ $\approx$ 1000 kcal $\approx$ 1 kWh
Fuel oil: 6.36 GJ/barrel (1 barrel $\equiv$ 42 U.S. gallons = 35.0 Imp. gallons = 159 L)

Relation between rest mass *(m)*, linear momentum *(p)*, total energy *(E)*, kinetic
   energy *(KE)*, and $\gamma \equiv (1 - v^2/c^2)^{-0.5}$, where *c* is the speed of light and *v* is the
   speed of the object: $E = \gamma mc^2 = mc^2 + KE = [(mc^2)^2 + (pc)^2]^{0.5}$

MAGNITUDE RELATIONS (See also p. 50.)

Log of light intensity ratio $\equiv$ 0.4 times magnitude difference
Distance modulus *(D)* $\equiv$ apparent magnitude *(m)* – absolute magnitude *(M)*
Log of distance in ly = 0.2*D* + 1.513 435 (neglecting absorption)
Magnitude of sum of magnitudes m_i is equal to $-2.5 \log \Sigma_i\, 10^{-0.4 m_i}$

Moon's apparent visual magnitude at phase angle *P* degrees (0° = full Moon)
   when at its average distance from Earth: $-12.7 + 0.026\,|P| + (4 \times 10^{-9})P^4$

A light source of apparent visual magnitude *m* provides an illuminance
   E (lux) where $E = 10^{-0.4(m + 13.99)}$ or $m = -13.99 - 2.5 \log E$
A diffuse (matte) surface with albedo *A* subject to illuminance *E* (lux) will have
   luminance *L* (visual surface brightness): $L = AE \div \pi$ (cd/m^2)
To convert luminance *S* (magnitude/arcsecond^2) to luminance *L* (cd/m^2):
   $L = 10^{0.4(12.59-S)}$ or $S = 12.59 - 2.5 \log L$

DOPPLER RELATIONS FOR LIGHT

$\alpha \equiv$ angle between velocity of source and line from source to observer
$\beta \equiv v/c$ $\gamma \equiv (1 - \beta^2)^{-0.5}$
Frequency: $f = f_0\, \gamma^{-1}(1 - \beta \cos \alpha)^{-1}$ $z \equiv (\lambda - \lambda_0)/\lambda_0 = \gamma\,(1 - \beta \cos \alpha) - 1$
For $\alpha = \pi$ radians: $z = (1 + \beta)^{0.5}(1 - \beta)^{-0.5} - 1$ ($\approx \beta$ if $\beta \ll 1$)
$$\beta = [(1 + z)^2 - 1][(1 + z)^2 + 1]^{-1}$$

OPTICAL WAVELENGTH DATA

Bright-adapted (photopic) visible range $\approx 400 - 750$ nm ($L \approx 0.005 - 10^5$ cd/m^2)
Dark-adapted (scotopic) visible range $\approx 400 - 620$ nm ($L \approx 1 - 5000$ µcd/m^2)
Wavelength of peak sensitivity of eye: ≈ 555 nm (photopic), 507 nm (scotopic)
Mechanical equivalent of light: 1 lm $\equiv$ 1/683 W at 540 THz ($\lambda \approx 555$ nm)
   i.e. 1.46 W/klm (A 60-W incandescent light bulb emits about 1 klm = 1000 lm.
   Compared to an optimum light source that delivers all its energy as light
   at 540 THz, a 60-W incandescent light bulb is 1.46/60 $\approx$ 2.4% efficient.)
Colours (representative wavelength, nm):
   violet (420), blue (470), green (530), yellow (580), orange (610), red (660)

Some useful wavelengths (element, spectral designation or colour and/or
(Fraunhofer line)):

H Lyman α	121.6 nm	N$_2^+$ blue†	465.2	Hg yellow	579.1
Ca (K solar)	393.4	Hβ (F solar)*	486.1	Na (D$_2$ solar)	589.0
Ca (H solar)	396.8	O^{++} green*	495.9	Na (D$_1$ solar)	589.6
Hg violet	404.7	O^{++} green*	500.7	O red†	630.0
Hδ (h solar)	410.2	Hg green	546.1	He-Ne laser	632.8
Hγ (g solar)	434.0	O yel.-green†	557.7	O red†	636.4
Hg deep blue	435.8	Hg yellow	577.0	Hα (C solar)	656.3

* Strong contributor to the visual light of gaseous nebulae
† Strong auroral lines

ANGULAR RELATIONS

2π radians = 360° $\pi = 3.141\,592\,653\,589\,793\,2... \approx (113 \div 355)^{-1}$
Number of square degrees on a sphere = 41 253
For 360° = 24 h, 15° = 1 h, 15′ = 1 min, 15″ = 1 s (Earth turns 360° in 86 164.1 s)
Relations between sidereal time t, right ascension α, hour angle h, declination δ,
azimuth A (measured east of north), altitude a, and latitude ϕ:
   $h = t - \alpha$
   $\sin a = \sin \delta \sin \phi + \cos h \cos \delta \cos \phi$
   $\cos \delta \sin h = -\cos a \sin A$
   $\sin \delta = \sin a \sin \phi + \cos a \cos A \cos \phi$
   Annual precession in $\alpha \approx 3.0750 + 1.3362 \sin \alpha \tan \delta$ seconds   (α must be
   Annual precession in $\delta \approx 20.043'' \cos \alpha$ in degrees)

SOME SI SYMBOLS AND PREFIXES

m	metre	N	newton (kg·m/s^2)	a	atto	10^{-18}
kg	kilogram	J	joule (N·m)	f	femto	10^{-15}
s	second	W	watt (J/s)	p	pico	10^{-12}
min	minute	Pa	pascal (N/m^2)	n	nano	10^{-9}
h	hour	t	tonne (10^3 kg)	µ	micro	10^{-6}
d	day	L	litre (10^{-3} m^3)	m	milli	10^{-3}
a	year	Hz	hertz (s^{-1})	c	centi	10^{-2}
A	ampere	C	coulomb (A·s)	h	hecto	10^2
rad	radian	V	volt (J/C)	k	kilo	10^3
mas	milliarcsecond	Wb	weber (V·s)	M	mega	10^6
sr	steradian	T	tesla (Wb/m^2)	G	giga	10^9
K	kelvin (temperature)	lm	lumen	T	tera	10^{12}
ha	hectare (10^4 m^2)	cd	candela (lm/sr)	P	peta	10^{15}
b	barn (10^{-28} m^2)	lx	lux (lm/m^2)	E	exa	10^{18}

THE ELECTROMAGNETIC SPECTRUM
BY ROY BISHOP

The Scottish physicist James Clerk Maxwell (1831–1879) was the first to understand the nature of light. In 1865, with elegant mathematics, Maxwell predicted that light is a self-sustaining electromagnetic wave, a quivering linkage of electric and magnetic fields in which a changing electric field generates a magnetic field, and vice versa, sustaining each other as they travel at a prodigious speed.

Four decades later Albert Einstein (1879–1955) revealed three more remarkable properties of light: (1) unlike water waves and sound waves, electromagnetic waves require no medium whatsoever in which to travel; (2) the speed of electromagnetic waves is the same for all observers, irrespective of any motion of the source of the waves; (3) when electromagnetic waves interact with matter, they do so as if composed of discrete particles, photons, whose individual energy E is proportional to the frequency f of the wave: $E = hf$, where h is Planck's constant (see p. 30).

The product of wavelength λ and wave frequency is the speed of a wave: $\lambda f = c$, where c is the usual symbol for the speed of an electromagnetic wave. The frequency (or photon energy, or wavelength) range of electromagnetic waves is unlimited, but our eyes see only a very narrow slice of this spectrum. Vision has a range of less than an octave, $\lambda \sim 400$ to 750 nm (see p. 32). We are almost blind! Nevertheless, once the physics was understood, the technologies to generate and detect all parts of the electromagnetic spectrum were soon developed. The first step in this direction occurred prior to Maxwell's work, in 1800 when astronomer Sir William Herschel (1738–1822) discovered *infrared* radiation beyond the red end of the visible spectrum.

The diagram at the end of this article summarizes the electromagnetic spectrum. The various named parts of the spectrum overlap to some extent. One part is defined by the source of the radiation rather than by wavelength or photon energy: *gamma rays* refer to electromagnetic radiation emitted by radioactive atomic nuclei. *X-rays* overlap with gamma rays but are produced by sources other than atomic nuclei—an arbitrary distinction based on the historical origins of these two terms. A detector defines another part of the spectrum: *light* is usually restricted to human vision, although occasionally this term is extended to include the adjacent *ultraviolet* portion of the spectrum.

The importance of the particle aspect at high frequencies and of the wave aspect at low frequencies is implied by the names; for instance, gamma **rays** and radio **waves**. Photon energy, not wavelength, dominates the behaviour of gamma rays. At the other end of the spectrum the energy of individual photons is very small, obscuring the granular nature of the radiation, and frequency is usually the measured characteristic of the radiation. Vision operates between these two extremes where *both* particle and wave properties play significant roles. Events in the retina are triggered by individual photons, and wave diffraction is relevant for minimum eye pupil size and the spacing of retinal photoreceptors. For the infrared and microwave regions, wavelength has a convenient range and is usually cited. The transition across the spectrum from photon through wavelength to frequency domination is indicated in the diagram by the range of the units on the left side of each of the three scales.

Photon energy determines how electromagnetic radiation interacts with matter. Chemistry and biology involve changes in atomic and molecular structure, the energies involved being typically a few *electron-volts* (eV) per reaction (see p. 35). Retinal photochemistry operates over a very limited energy range, and thereby determines the narrow visual window on the electromagnetic spectrum. For $\lambda > 750$ nm, the photon energy is insufficient (<1.6 eV) to alter the structure of light-sensing protein molecules in the retina, so we cannot see the infrared. For $\lambda < 400$ nm, the photon energy is high enough (>3.1 eV) to damage these delicate molecules; however, the cornea and lens of the eye absorb that radiation before it can reach the retina. Thus we cannot see the ultraviolet.

Although the energy of an infrared photon is too weak to stimulate vision, infrared photons are readily absorbed by many types of molecules, such as water, causing the molecules to move more rapidly, thereby increasing the temperature of the substance. In this manner, infrared radiation from the Sun, a fire, or a hot stove warms us. Hence infrared is often called heat radiation, although it is *not* heat that is being radiated. The heating is a secondary effect, generated in our bodies subsequent to the absorption of the photons.

Confusion of sensation with electromagnetic radiation also occurs with visible light. For instance, almost invariably we speak of colours as if they were a property of light, or of the bodies emitting the light, rather than being indescribable hue sensations arising in the brain. As Sir Isaac Newton cautioned us three centuries ago: "The rays, to speak properly, are not coloured." The light reflected by a leaf is not green, and neither is the leaf; green exists only in the neuron-based representation of the leaf in the observer's consciousness, and then only if the light is not too dim. The electromagnetic radiation from a leaf is characterized by a particular spatial and spectral distribution of radiant power. A CCD or CMOS chip finds only photons. It is we who create the colour and the brightness. The distinction between our internal visual world and the external physical world is profound but rarely appreciated. It is the distinction between how the world *looks* to us, and how it *is*.

Visual perception aside, what *is* light, a wave or a particle? Light travels like a wave (Maxwell was right) and interacts like a particle (Einstein was right). A detector finds photons, but *where* the detector finds photons is determined by a wave. When a typical backyard telescope is aimed at an average star in the night sky, at any instant there is seldom more than one photon from that star in transit through the telescope. Yet the distribution of light in the star's image at the focal plane is determined by an aperture-filling wave. In the case of a Newtonian telescope with a four-vane spider support for the secondary mirror, in some real sense, each photon passes through all four quadrants of the spider. But it is not that the spider quarters the hapless photon like a cleaver quarters a steak in a butcher shop; whole photons, not quartered photons arrive at the detector. The message of physics revealed during the first half of the last century is that it is simply *wrong* to speak of the path of a photon while in transit to a detector. Light is queerer than we can imagine. Matter is equally queer, for it too displays a wave-particle duality, a duality that is particularly obvious on the subatomic scale. Just as it is wrong to speak of the path of a photon, it is wrong to speak of the path of an electron in an atom—as if, for example, it were in orbit about the nucleus. The wave-particle puzzle is of our own making, for we try to apply naïve concepts abstracted from crude sensory experiences on the macroscopic scale of everyday life to the subatomic world. Pure waves or pure particles never did exist. Reality is more mysterious.

Despite the strange behaviour of electromagnetic radiation, we know how to describe its interaction with matter quantitatively and with astounding accuracy. The theory encompasses the work of Maxwell and Einstein, and was completed in the mid-20th century by Richard Feynman (1918–1988) and Julian Schwinger (1918–1994) of the United States, and Sin-Itiro Tomonaga (1906–1979) of Japan, for which they shared the Nobel Prize in Physics in 1965. The theory is called quantum electrodynamics. With the exception of gravitation and things that go on inside atomic nuclei, quantum electrodynamics appears to describe all phenomena in the physical world—in principle, if not in actuality, in the case of complex systems because of complexity.

THE ELECTROMAGNETIC SPECTRUM

VOYAGES IN OUR SOLAR SYSTEM
By Randy Attwood

During the second half of the 20th century, humankind began its reconnaissance of the solar system. Although people have travelled only as far as the Moon, robotic space probes have been sent to all the planets but one—Pluto—plus a few asteroids and comets. Our understanding of the solar neighbourhood is increasing at a tremendous pace as a result of the improving sophistication of these spacecraft.

The following is a list of some of the important firsts in the short history of the exploration of our solar system. Note that all space missions are not recorded, not even all the space firsts. A short list of upcoming missions to watch for is also included.

Year	Name	Significance
1957	*Sputnik 1*	First artificial satellite of Earth (Oct. 4); USSR
1957	*Sputnik 2*	First living being in Earth orbit (a dog named Laika); USSR
1959	*Luna 1*	First to escape Earth's gravity; USSR
1959	*Luna 2*	First to impact on the Moon; USSR
1959	*Luna 3*	First to image the far side of the Moon; USSR
1961	*Vostok 1*	First human in Earth orbit (Yuri Gagarin, Apr. 12); USSR
1962	*Mariner 2*	First to fly by another planet, Venus; USA
1965	*Mariner 4*	First to fly by Mars and take pictures; USA
1966	*Luna 9*	First soft landing on the Moon; USSR
1966	*Venera 3*	First to impact on another planet, Venus; USSR
1966	*Luna 10*	First to orbit the Moon; USSR
1968	*Apollo 8*	First humans to orbit the Moon; USA (Frank Borman, James Lovell, William Anders, Dec. 24)
1969	*Apollo 11*	First humans to land and walk on the Moon; USA (Neil Armstrong, Edwin Aldrin, Jul. 20)
1970	*Venera 7*	First soft landing on another planet, Venus; USSR
1971	*Mariner 9*	First to orbit another planet, Mars; USA
1971	*Mariner 9*	First close views of outer satellites (Phobos, Deimos); USA
1972	*Apollo 17*	Last 2 of 12 men to walk on the Moon; USA
1973	*Pioneer 10*	First to fly by Jupiter, reach solar escape speed; USA
1974	*Mariner 10*	First to fly by and study Mercury; USA
1975	*Venera 9*	First to return surface pictures of Venus; USSR
1976	*Viking 1*	First to softly land on Mars, return pictures; USA
1979	*Voyager 1*	First close-up study of Jupiter and its moons; USA
1979	*Pioneer 11*	First to fly by Saturn; USA
1980	*Voyager 1*	First close-up study of Saturn and its moons; USA
1985	*ICE*	*International Cometary Explorer;* first to study a comet; USA
1986	*Voyager 2*	First close-up study of Uranus and its moons; USA
1986	*Giotto*	First images taken of a comet nucleus, Halley; ESA
1989	*Voyager 2*	First close-up study of Neptune and its moons; USA
1991	*Galileo*	First flyby, close-up photos of an asteroid, 951 Gaspra; USA
1995	*Ulysses*	First flyby above the Sun's south/north poles; ESA
1995	*Galileo*	First probe into Jupiter's atmosphere; USA
2001	*NEAR Shoemaker*	First to orbit and soft land on an asteroid, Eros; USA
2003	*MOST*	First Canadian space telescope launched into Earth orbit
2004	*Mars Rovers*	First long-range surface exploration of Mars; USA
2004	*Stardust*	First collection and return of cometary material, Wild 2; USA
2004	*Cassini*	First to orbit Saturn; USA
2005	*Huygens*	First to land on Titan; USA/ESA
2005	*Deep Impact*	First to impact on and study the interior of a comet, Tempel 1; USA
2010	*Hayabusa*	First asteroid-sample return mission; Japan (Rendezvous completed in 2005, return delayed due to spacecraft problems; predicted return 2010)
2011	*Dawn**	First spacecraft to orbit an asteroid (Vesta, and Ceres in 2015); USA
2011	*Messenger*	First spacecraft to orbit and study Mercury; USA
2014	*Rosetta*	First to orbit, soft land on a comet; ESA
2015	*New Horizons*	First to fly by Pluto, its moon, Charon, Kuiper Belt Objects (2016–2020); USA

*Mission not yet launched

TABLE OF PRECESSION FOR ADVANCING 50 YEARS

RA for Dec− h m	RA for Dec+ h m	Prec in Dec ′	85° m	80° m	75° m	70° m	60° m	50° m	40° m	30° m	20° m	10° m	0° m	Prec in Dec ′	RA for Dec+ h m	RA for Dec− h m
12 00	0 00	16.7	2.56	2.56	2.56	2.56	2.56	2.56	2.56	2.56	2.56	2.56	2.56	−16.7	12 00	24 00
12 30	0 30	16.6	4.22	3.39	3.10	2.96	2.81	2.73	2.68	2.64	2.61	2.59	2.56	−16.6	11 30	23 30
13 00	1 00	16.1	5.85	4.20	3.64	3.35	3.06	2.90	2.80	2.73	2.67	2.61	2.56	−16.1	11 00	23 00
13 30	1 30	15.4	7.43	4.98	4.15	3.73	3.30	3.07	2.92	2.81	2.72	2.64	2.56	−15.4	10 30	22 30
14 00	2 00	14.5	8.92	5.72	4.64	4.09	3.53	3.22	3.03	2.88	2.76	2.66	2.56	−14.5	10 00	22 00
14 30	2 30	13.3	10.31	6.41	5.09	4.42	3.73	3.37	3.13	2.95	2.81	2.68	2.56	−13.3	9 30	21 30
15 00	3 00	11.8	11.56	7.03	5.50	4.72	3.92	3.50	3.22	3.02	2.85	2.70	2.56	−11.8	9 00	21 00
15 30	3 30	10.2	12.66	7.57	5.86	4.99	4.09	3.61	3.30	3.07	2.88	2.72	2.56	−10.2	8 30	20 30
16 00	4 00	8.4	13.58	8.03	6.16	5.21	4.23	3.71	3.37	3.12	2.91	2.73	2.56	−8.4	8 00	20 00
16 30	4 30	6.4	14.32	8.40	6.40	5.39	4.34	3.79	3.42	3.15	2.94	2.74	2.56	−6.4	7 30	19 30
17 00	5 00	4.3	14.85	8.66	6.57	5.52	4.42	3.84	3.46	3.18	2.95	2.75	2.56	−4.3	7 00	19 00
17 30	5 30	2.2	15.18	8.82	6.68	5.59	4.47	3.88	3.49	3.20	2.96	2.76	2.56	−2.2	6 30	18 30
18 00	6 00	0.0	15.29	8.88	6.72	5.62	4.49	3.89	3.50	3.20	2.97	2.76	2.56	0.0	6 00	18 00
0 00	12 00	−16.7	2.56	2.56	2.56	2.56	2.56	2.56	2.56	2.56	2.56	2.56	2.56	16.7	24 00	12 00
0 30	12 30	−16.6	0.90	1.74	2.02	2.16	2.31	2.39	2.44	2.48	2.51	2.54	2.56	16.6	23 30	11 30
1 00	13 00	−16.1	−0.73	0.93	1.49	1.77	2.06	2.22	2.32	2.39	2.46	2.51	2.56	16.1	23 00	11 00
1 30	13 30	−15.4	−2.31	0.14	0.97	1.39	1.82	2.05	2.20	2.31	2.41	2.49	2.56	15.4	22 30	10 30
2 00	14 00	−14.5	−3.80	−0.60	0.48	1.03	1.60	1.90	2.09	2.24	2.36	2.46	2.56	14.5	22 00	10 00
2 30	14 30	−13.3	−5.19	−1.28	0.03	0.70	1.39	1.75	1.99	2.17	2.31	2.44	2.56	13.3	21 30	9 30
3 00	15 00	−11.8	−6.44	−1.90	−0.38	0.40	1.20	1.62	1.90	2.11	2.27	2.42	2.56	11.8	21 00	9 00
3 30	15 30	−10.2	−7.54	−2.45	−0.74	0.13	1.03	1.51	1.82	2.05	2.24	2.41	2.56	10.2	20 30	8 30
4 00	16 00	−8.4	−8.46	−2.91	−1.04	−0.09	0.89	1.41	1.75	2.00	2.21	2.39	2.56	8.4	20 00	8 00
4 30	16 30	−6.4	−9.20	−3.27	−1.28	−0.27	0.78	1.33	1.70	1.97	2.19	2.38	2.56	6.4	19 30	7 30
5 00	17 00	−4.3	−9.73	−3.54	−1.45	−0.39	0.70	1.28	1.66	1.94	2.17	2.37	2.56	4.3	19 00	7 00
5 30	17 30	−2.2	−10.06	−3.70	−1.56	−0.47	0.65	1.25	1.63	1.92	2.16	2.37	2.56	2.2	18 30	6 30
6 00	18 00	0.0	−10.17	−3.75	−1.59	−0.50	0.63	1.23	1.63	1.92	2.16	2.36	2.56	0.0	18 00	6 00

Precession in right ascension for declination in row immediately below

1₂3

If declination is positive, use inner RA scale; if declination is negative, use outer RA scale and reverse the sign of the precession in declination. To avoid interpolation in this table, which becomes increasingly inaccurate for large |Dec|, precession formulae may be used (see p. 36).

TIME

TIME AND TIME SCALES
By Roy Bishop

Time has been said to be nature's way of keeping everything from happening at once. In 1687, Sir Isaac Newton (1642–1727) perceived time as being separate from and more fundamental than the spinning of changeable planets or the oily mechanisms of clocks: "Absolute, true, and mathematical time, of itself, and from its own nature flows equably without regard to anything external." This is the common sense or intuitive view most people have of time.

Albert Einstein (1879–1955) was the first to understand that time is but an abstraction that does not exist independently of clocks. In his special theory of relativity (1905) Einstein predicted that clocks moving relative to an observer run slower. This is called time dilation or the second-order Doppler effect. For example, relative to a clock fixed beside a road the wristwatch of a person driving past at a speed of 100 km/h loses 0.26 ps per minute (ps = picosecond = 10^{-12} s; see p. 36). A decade later, in his theory of gravitation, the general theory of relativity, Einstein predicted that clocks lower or higher than the observer in a gravitational field run slower or faster, respectively, than the observer's clock. In the case of a lower clock this is called the gravitational redshift. For example, an alarm clock on the floor a metre below your bed loses 3.1 ps per 8-h night relative to a watch on your wrist. These counterintuitive effects are not only real, but in recent years they have found their way into the consumer marketplace in the form of GPS (Global Positioning System) receivers. These handheld units receive signals from orbiting atomic clocks and rely on programs that allow for time dilation and gravitational redshift (see *Physics Today,* May 2002, p. 41). In astronomy the general theory of relativity was mostly ignored until the last few decades of the 20th century, when increasing precision of clocks and advances in theoretical astrophysics and cosmology demanded its use.

As to understanding time, Lord Kelvin (1824–1907) said that you know a physical quantity if you can measure it. Time can indeed be measured, with mind-boggling precision. For those who feel compelled to state "We still don't know what time actually is," perhaps the mystery resides merely in the meaning of this statement.

The essence of time is that isolated material changes occur in invariant ratios one with respect to another. That is, as Sir Hermann Bondi (1919–2005) put it: "Time is that which is manufactured by clocks." Thus, to deal with time, clocks must be devised and units and time scales established. Readers who wish to pursue this topic beyond the brief overview presented here should consult *The Measurement of Time,* by C. Audoin and B. Guinot, Cambridge University Press, 2001, and the *Explanatory Supplement to the Astronomical Almanac,* by P.K. Seidelmann (ed.), University Science Books, 1992. For less-technical descriptions of many aspects of time see *A Matter of Time,* a special edition of *Scientific American* (vol. 16, no. 1, 2006) that includes ten articles from the September 2002 issue of that magazine.

Periodic Time Intervals and Clocks

There are three obvious, natural, periodic time intervals on Earth: the seasonal cycle (year), the cycle of lunar phases (month), and the day–night cycle (day). The cycle of the seasons is called the *tropical year* and contains 365.242 190 days. The cycle of lunar phases is known as the *synodic month* and equals 29.530 589 days. The average day–night (diurnal) cycle is the *mean solar day* and presently contains approximately

86 400.0009 s. Other types of year, month, and day have been defined and are listed along with brief definitions and durations on p. 33.

The problem of accurately subdividing these natural intervals to make time locally available at any moment (i.e. timekeeping) was satisfactorily solved in 1657 by Christiaan Huygens, who invented the first practical pendulum clock. Through successive refinements the pendulum clock reigned supreme for nearly three centuries, until it was surpassed in precision by the quartz oscillator in the 1940s. Within another 20 years the quartz clock was, in turn, superseded by the cesium atomic clock, which, using the technique of *laser cooling* of atomic beams (see *Physics Today,* December 1997, p. 17, February 1998, p. 21, and March 2001, p. 37), today has a precision near 2 in 10^{15} (one second in 16 million years).

Earth's Rotation and Time Scales

Of the three obvious, natural, periodic time intervals on Earth (year, month, and day), the day dominates our lives and determines the various time scales we have created. The day is caused primarily by Earth's rotation on its axis. To count rotations, a reference or fiducial point is required. Four such points are of interest, and three of these are the basis of five time scales:

(1) Earth's rotation relative to the distant stars: Although the distant stars (or better, extragalactic sources) provide a reference frame to determine the "true" period of Earth's rotation (presently about 86 164.0998 s), because of Earth's orbital motion and its rotational precession, this true period is not that of either the solar day or the RA/Dec coordinate grid used to specify astronomical positions. Hence no time scales are based on Earth's true rotational period.

(2) Earth's rotation relative to the equinox: The equator and poles of the RA/Dec celestial coordinate grid are aligned with Earth's mean equator and poles. ("Mean" denotes that small, periodic variations caused by the nutation of Earth's axis have been averaged out. Nutation involves the true pole moving relative to the mean pole with an amplitude of about $9''$ and a variety of short periods up to 18.6 years.) Hence the RA/Dec grid slowly shifts relative to the distant stars as Earth's rotation axis and equator precess, a motion caused primarily by the torques exerted by the Moon and Sun on Earth's equatorial bulge. The other planets make a smaller contribution to this *precession of the equator* and also cause a *precession of the ecliptic.* The sum of these two precessions is called *general precession.* General precession causes the zero point of right ascension (the "Greenwich of the skies," the vernal equinox, or "first point of Aries") to drift westward (retrograde) along the ecliptic about $50''$ per year. As a result, Earth's rotation period relative to the equinox (called the *mean sidereal day,* currently 86 164.0914 s) is 8.4 ms shorter than the time for one rotation (see p. 33). At any longitude on Earth the RA of a star on the meridian (corrected for nutation) is the *Local Mean Sidereal Time* **(LMST)** at that instant. At the Greenwich meridian (0° longitude) this is called *Greenwich Mean Sidereal Time* **(GMST).** LMST may be used to set a telescope on an object of known right ascension. The hour angle of the object equals the sidereal time less the right ascension. LMST may be available from a sidereal clock, or it can be calculated as explained in the middle of p. 49. Because Earth makes one more rotation with respect to the other stars than it does with respect to the Sun during a year, sidereal time gains relative to time scales linked to the Sun (see below) by about 3 min 56 s per day, or 2 h per month.

(3) Earth's rotation relative to the real Sun: A common misconception is that the Sun is highest in the sky and lies on the local north–south meridian at 12:00 noon. However, time based on the position of the Sun in the sky, known as local *apparent solar time* or *sundial time,* can differ by up to an hour or more from civil time (the time that we normally use). There are two reasons for this discrepancy. One reason is that the Sun's eastward annual apparent motion around the sky is far from uniform both because of Earth's elliptical orbit and because of the inclination of the celestial equator to the ecliptic. Thus apparent solar time does not have a uniform rate (see the next paragraph). The second reason for the difference between sundial time and civil time is addressed in the penultimate paragraph of this article.

(4) Earth's rotation relative to the mean Sun: If the Sun is replaced by a fictitious mean sun moving uniformly along the celestial equator, Earth's rotation relative to this mean sun defines *Local Mean (solar) Time* **(LMT)**. Apparent solar time can differ by up to 16 min from LMT depending upon the time of year (see the diagram on p. 178). Small, periodic shifts of Earth's crust relative to the axis of rotation *(polar motion)* affect astronomical time determinations through the resulting east–west shift in the meridian at latitudes away from the equator. LMT at the Greenwich meridian (0° longitude) when corrected for this polar motion is called *Universal Time* **(UT1, or often simply UT)**. UT1 is determined using very-long-baseline interferometry, satellite laser-ranging data, lunar laser-ranging data, and GPS data (via the International GPS Service).

All the above mean time scales (LMST, GMST, LMT, and UT1), being based upon Earth's rotation, are only as uniform as this rotation. By the mid-19th century discrepancies between theory and the observed motion of the Moon indicated that, over the long term, Earth's rotation is slowing down. However, not until clocks became better timekeepers than the spinning Earth (c. 1940, when crystal-controlled clocks exceeded precisions of 1 in 10^{10}) was it realized how complex is the variable rotation of our planet. There are (i) long-, (ii) medium-, and (iii) short-term accelerations:

(i) Over many centuries there is a *secular* slowing caused by tidal friction of about 8 parts in 10^{13} per day (i.e. the day becomes one second longer about every 40 000 years).

(ii) Over a few decades there are *random* accelerations (positive and negative), apparently caused by core–mantle interactions and possibly by changes in ocean currents. These are about 10 times larger than the tidal deceleration and thus completely obscure the latter effect over time intervals of less than a century or so.

(iii) The largest accelerations in Earth's rotation rate are short-term ones: *periodic components* are associated mainly with lunar-induced tides (over two-week and monthly intervals) and seasonal meteorological factors (over semiannual and annual intervals); *nonperiodic* (chaotic) high-frequency variations are associated mainly with the global atmospheric wind and pressure distributions. These short-term accelerations are typically one or two orders of magnitude larger again than the random, decade fluctuations on which they are superimposed (see the article by John Wahr in the June 1986 issue of *Sky & Telescope*, p. 545).

Uniform Time Scales

(1) Based on orbital motion: Although Earth's axial rotation is not sufficiently predictable to serve as a precise clock, the orbital motions of our Moon, Earth, and the other planets are predictable to high accuracy. Through the dynamical equations describing these motions plus extended astronomical observations, a uniform dynamical time scale can be derived. Such a scale, known as *Ephemeris Time* (ET), was for several years (1952–1984) the basis of astronomical ephemerides. The ephemeris second, defined in 1955 as a certain fraction of the tropical year 1900.0, was the fundamental unit of time. Early in the 20th century the UT1 and ET scales coincided, but because Earth's rotation rate has been generally slower than the ET rate, by 1984 UT1 was 54 s behind ET and was losing about half a second per year. From 1985 until 1999 Earth's rotation rate was fairly steady, losing about 0.7 s per year relative to ET (actually TT, see below). During the years 2000–2005 the rotation rate increased (part of the random decade fluctuations) such that by 2005 the annual loss was less than 0.2 s. Beginning in 2006 an abrupt slowing occurred, more than doubling the annual loss.

(2) Based on atomic motion: The quantum nature of matter gives atoms a permanence and stability that macroscopic objects such as quartz crystals, planets, and pendulums do not possess. The idea of an atomic clock was proposed by the Austrian–American physicist Isidor Rabi in 1945. In 1967, the second was given an atomic definition: 9 192 631 770 periods of the radiation involved in the transition between the two hyperfine levels of the ground state of the cesium 133 atom. This is known as the SI (for Système International) second (abbreviation s, *not* sec). The number 9 192 631 770 was chosen so that on the rotating geoid (i.e. for clocks fixed on Earth at mean sea level), the SI second is identical to the older ET second to within the precision of measurement.

The previous sentence implies that clocks on the geoid run at the same rate. What about Earth's rotation? Clocks nearer the equator move faster, so does time dilation not make them run slower relative to clocks at higher latitudes? Ignoring the Moon and Sun, if Earth did not rotate and had an isotropic density distribution, its geoid (mean sea-level surface) would be spherical, and clocks fixed on this geoid would, by symmetry, all run at the same rate (they would all be at rest and have similar positions in Earth's gravitational field). For a rotating Earth the equatorial bulge is such that clocks away from the poles are just enough higher in Earth's gravitational field that the resulting gravitational blueshift exactly cancels the time dilation associated with their rotational speed. This simple, elegant, and convenient result is a consequence of Einstein's principle of equivalence: A body at rest in a gravitational field is equivalent to a body being accelerated in a field-free space. As described by general relativity, gravitation is geometry, not a force, which is why no one has ever felt a force of gravity. The only force acting on Earth-based clocks, or on any stationary Earth-based objects, is the electromagnetic contact force supporting them. Any two nearby clocks located on the same surface perpendicular to the direction of this contact force (the plumb-bob direction) will have identical rates. Thus *all* clocks on the geoid run at the same rate. Whether or not the planet beneath is rotating is immaterial.

Five SI-second-based time scales are in use today. One of these (UTC) merely differs an integal number of seconds from one of the other four and is described in the last section. The fundamental time scale for unambiguously dating events within the solar system and beyond (e.g. planet and interplanetary spacecraft motions, and pulsar signals) is **Barycentric Coordinate Time (TCB)**. TCB is the time base of a non-rotating coordinate system with its origin located at the centre of mass of the solar system, and it is not influenced by the gravitational fields of any bodies in the solar system. It is as if the solar system were not present.

The fundamental time scale for unambiguously dating events in the vicinity of Earth (e.g. motions of Earth-orbiting satellites) is **Geocentric Coordinate Time (TCG)**. TCG is the time base of a non-rotating coordinate system with its origin located at the centre of mass of Earth, and it is not influenced by the gravitational field of Earth. It is as if all bodies of the solar system except Earth were present.

TCG runs at a slower (and slightly variable) rate relative to TCB because of both time dilation associated with Earth's orbital motion, and gravitational redshift associated with Earth's location within the Sun's gravitational well and (to a much lesser extent) the gravitational wells of all the other bodies in the solar system (except Earth). Relative to TCB, TCG loses about 467 ms per year.

One might expect that TCG would be the time scale of choice for Earth-based observers (e.g. for dealing with apparent geocentric ephemerides); however, cesium atomic clocks at Earth's surface are deep within Earth's gravitational well and lose about 22 ms per year relative to TCG. To avoid this inconvenience a second geocentric coordinate time scale has been devised, **Terrestrial Time (TT)**. TT is defined as having a rate exactly $1 - 6.969290134 \times 10^{-10}$ as large as the TCG rate so that the unit of the TT scale is very close to the SI second on the rotating geoid, matching the rate of Earth-based atomic clocks. Thus TT is a derived scale, not fundamental. The TT rate definition is based upon TCG and not the geoid because of uncertainties surrounding the realization of the geoid (the geoid would coincide with Earth's sea surface *if* the waters of the oceans were homogeneous and at rest). TT loses about $22 + 467 = 489$ ms (nearly half a second) per year relative to TCB.

TCB, TCG and TT are theoretical, ideal time scales. Real clocks are needed for measurements. To this end, in 1972 *International Atomic Time* (TAI = Temps Atomique International) was introduced. TAI is based on a weighted average of more than 200 atomic clocks in more than 30 countries and presently is the most precise *achievable* time scale. Not even atomic clocks are perfect time keepers (they drift randomly one with respect to another), so TAI shifts unpredictably relative to the ideal TT rate by about 0.1 µs/year (a few parts in 10^{15}). The TAI scale was set to agree with UT1 on 1958 Jan. 1, which led to the definition that TT be exactly 32.184 s ahead of TAI on 1977 Jan. 1.0 (TAI) to ensure continuity of TT with ET, TT's predecessor for geocentric ephemerides.

TCB, TCG and TT are defined to have had the same reading on 1977 Jan. 1.0 (TAI) at Earth's centre of mass, all three being exactly 32.184 s ahead of TAI at that point in spacetime. At the beginning of 2008 TT is about 0.7 s behind TCG, and 15 seconds behind TCB. TCB, TCG and TT are realized via TAI.

Three time scales no longer in use are associated with the SI second: ET, TDT, and TDB. ET and TDT have been abandoned, and TDB is deprecated. Unfortunately they still appear in some publications so they must be mentioned. *Ephemeris Time* (ET), introduced in section (1) above, was defined and adopted by the International Astronomical Union in the 1950s. The transition from ET to the modern TT took place in three steps: (i) Because of several difficulties surrounding both the original concept of ET and its determination (the most serious being that it ignored relativity), and because atomic clocks had become readily available, in 1984 ET was abandoned in favour of *Terrestrial Dynamical Time* (TDT). The unit of TDT was the SI second on the rotating geoid, and its scale was chosen to agree with the 1984 ET scale. (ii) In 1991 the general theory of relativity was explicitly adopted as the theoretical background for spacetime reference systems. To emphasize that TDT was no longer derived from observations of the dynamical aspects of solar system bodies, TDT was renamed simply Terrestrial Time (TT). (iii) Because of uncertainties surrounding the realization of the geoid (mentioned above), in 2000 TT was redefined in terms of TCG.

In 1976, *Barycentric Dynamical Time* (TDB) was introduced when it became necessary to acknowledge relativistic effects but before the general theory of relativity was accepted by astronomers. It was similar to TCB except its scale unit was adjusted to approximate ET (currently TT). TDB was needlessly complex and confusing; however, it was used extensively by the Jet Propulsion Laboratory for ephemerides in planetary exploration, so was not completely abandoned when TCB was introduced in 1991. This unsatisfactory situation was resolved in 2006 when TDB was redefined by a simple linear relation in terms of TCB. Although redundant and deprecated, TDB is now an alternative way to express TCB, with the minor convenience that it keeps nearly in step with TT at Earth's centre.

(3) Based on pulsars: Millisecond radio pulsars (old, rapidly spinning neutron stars) display extraordinary stability in their rotation. Their stability, after allowing for spin-down, is almost as good as the best atomic clocks. However, uncertainties in

This diagram displays the rate and scale relations between Earth-based time scales that run at or near the SI rate at sea level and that are not longitude dependent.

predicting the spin-down rate of a pulsar and in Earth's motion relative to a pulsar, the elaborate equipment needed to observe a pulsar, and the complex data analysis required all make it unlikely that a pulsar will ever replace cesium clocks as the basis for a uniform time scale. Like quartz crystals, planets, and pendulums, pulsars do not possess the permanence and stability of atoms.

Uniform Time Scales with Steps (to track the mean Sun)

Closely related to UT1 (which follows Earth's variable rotation relative to the mean Sun) is *Coordinated Universal Time* (UTC), introduced in its present form in 1972. UTC, the basis of the world system of civil time, runs at the TAI rate and is offset an integral number of seconds from TAI so that it approximates UT1. When required (usually on Jun. 30 or Dec. 31), "leap seconds" are inserted into (or, if necessary, deleted from) UTC so that the difference UT1 − UTC = ΔUT1 does not exceed ±0.9 s. The most recent leap second occurred on 2005 Dec. 31 (the previous one occurred seven years earlier), making the difference TAI − UTC = ΔAT = 33 s. Hence TT − UTC = 33 s + 32.184 s = 65.184 s exactly during 2007 and probably throughout 2008 (see the diagram above). UTC is readily available via radio time signals and GPS receivers. (Note: The term *Greenwich Mean Time* (GMT) over the years has had three different meanings: the same as UT1, UTC, and mean solar time at the Greenwich meridian with 0 h corresponding to noon. To avoid confusion, the term *Greenwich Mean Time* should not be used.)

Anyone in North America can keep track of Earth's varying rotation by listening to the CHU or WWV radio time signals in which is coded the difference ΔUT1 = (UT1 − UTC) (see TIME SIGNALS on p. 49). Also, see the Web site tf.nist.gov/pubs/bulletin/leapsecond.htm. It is interesting to record ΔUT1 about once a month and use these data to make a graphical display of (TT − UT1) as a function of time over several years. Note that most likely during 2008, TT − UT1 = 65.184 − (UT1 − UTC).

Local Mean (solar) Time (LMT) would suffice for the inhabitants of an isolated village, but with the advent in the 19th century of rapid travel and communication (railways, steamships, and the telegraph), it became essential that clocks over a range of longitudes indicate the same time. To keep these clocks reasonably in phase with the day–night cycle and yet avoid the inconvenience to travellers of a local time that varies continuously with longitude, in 1884, Earth was divided into 24 *Standard Time* zones, adjacent zones generally differing by one hour and each ideally 15° wide (see the time-zone map on p. 51). All clocks within the same zone read the same time. The Canadian railway surveyor and construction engineer Sir Sandford Fleming (1827–1915) was instrumental in establishing this system of standard time zones. The zero zone is centred on the Greenwich meridian (longitude 0°), and, since 1972, standard time in that zone is UTC. Thus the world system of civil time is based on UTC and includes the "leap seconds," which keep UTC near UT1. Depending upon an observer's location within his or her standard time zone, standard time may differ by up to an hour or so from LMT (see the third paragraph on p. 195). This is the second reason why the Sun seldom, if ever, is on the observer's meridian at 12:00 noon, standard time.

Humans generally have an awake/asleep cycle that is delayed by a few hours relative to the day/night cycle. Consequently in higher latitudes during the spring and summer when the Sun rises before humans do, more energy is needed for lighting in the evening than would be the case if the two cycles coincided. To shift the lifestyles of their citizens more in phase with the day/night cycle many countries adopt *Daylight Saving Time,* advancing clocks by one hour during the spring and summer (a better term would be *Energy Saving Time* because it is energy that is being saved, not daylight). For most of Canada and the United States[1] clocks are advanced by one hour at 2:00 local time on the second Sunday in March, and return to standard time at 2:00 local time on the first Sunday in November: *spring ahead, fall back.*

---

[1] Some regions, such as Saskatchewan, southeastern British Columbia, Hawaii, and most of Arizona, do not observe Daylight Saving Time. For more information see webexhibits.org/daylightsaving.

TIME SIGNALS

National time services distribute Coordinated Universal Time (UTC). UTC is coordinated through the Bureau International des Poids et Mesures (BIPM) in Sèvres, France so that most time services are synchronized to a tenth of a millisecond. Radio time signals available in North America include:

CHU Ottawa, Ontario, Canada 3.330, 7.335, 14.670 MHz
WWV Fort Collins, Colorado, USA 2.5, 5, 10, 15, 20 MHz

For CHU, each minute starts at the *beginning* of the tone following the voice announcement, the tone for the 29th second is omitted, and the tones for seconds 31 through 39 have a different sound from the others.

The difference ΔUT1 = UT1 – UTC to the nearest tenth of a second is coded in the signals. If UT1 is ahead of UTC, second markers beginning at the 1-second mark of each minute are doubled, the number of doubled markers indicating the number of tenths of a second UT1 is ahead of UTC. If UT1 is behind UTC, the doubled markers begin at the 9-second point.

Time signals are also available by telephone from the National Research Council in Ottawa. Call (613) 745-1576 for English, and (613) 745-9426 for French; the call may be routed via one or two communications satellite hops, being delayed by 0.25 seconds per hop. Internet time services can be found at time5.nrc.ca/webclock_e.shtml and www.boulder.nist.gov/timefreq.

MEAN SIDEREAL TIME, 2008

The following is the Greenwich Mean Sidereal Time (GMST) in hours on day 0 at 0h UT of each month ("day 0" is the last day of the previous month):

Jan. 6.6029	Apr. 12.5825	Jul. 18.5621	Oct. 0.6074
Feb. 8.6399	May 14.5538	Aug. ...20.5991	Nov. 2.6444
Mar. 10.5455	Jun. 16.5908	Sep. 22.6361	Dec. 4.6157

GMST (in hours) at hour t UT on day d of the month =
GMST at 0h UT on day $0 + 0.065710d + 1.002738t$
LMST (Local Mean Sidereal Time) = GMST – west longitude (or + east longitude)

LMST computed by this method is accurate to ±0.2 s provided t is stated to ±0.1 s or better and the observer's longitude is known to ±1″. Note that t must be expressed in decimal hours UT and longitude in hours, not degrees. Also, to achieve ±0.1 s accuracy in t, the correction ΔUT1 must be applied to UTC. See TIME SIGNALS above.

JULIAN DATE (JD), 2008

The Julian Date (JD) is commonly used by astronomers to refer to the time of astronomical events, because it avoids some of the annoying complexities of the civil calendar. Julian Date 0.0 was the instant of Greenwich mean noon on 4713 Jan. 1 BC (see "The Origin of the Julian Day System" by G. Moyer, *Sky & Telescope,* April 1981).

The Julian day **commences at noon** (12h) UT. To find the Julian Date at any time during 2008, determine the day of the month and time at the Greenwich meridian, convert this to a decimal day, and add it to one of the following numbers according to the month (these numbers are the Julian Dates for 0h UT on the 0th day of each month):

Jan. ...245 4465.5	Apr. ... 245 4556.5	Jul. 245 4647.5	Oct. 245 4739.5
Feb. ...245 4496.5	May ... 245 4586.5	Aug. ..245 4678.5	Nov. ...245 4770.5
Mar. ..245 4525.5	Jun. ...245 4617.5	Sep. ...245 4709.5	Dec. ...245 4800.5

For example, 21:36 EDT on May 18 = 1:36 UT on May 19 = May 19.07 UT = 245 4586.5 + 19.07 = JD 245 4605.57.

The Julian Dates for 0h UT Jan. 0 for the three previous years are 245 0000.5 plus: 3370 (2005), 3735 (2006), and 4100 (2007).

STANDARD TIME ZONES

The map on the following page shows the world system of standard time zones. It was prepared and provided by Her Majesty's Nautical Almanac Office. Over the open oceans, the time zones are uniformly spaced and are bounded by lines of longitude 15° apart. In populated regions, political and other considerations have considerably modified the ideal geometry.

As Earth rotates with sunlight shining from one side, at some line of longitude the day of the week must jump discontinuously ahead by one day (otherwise, Monday would be followed by Monday!). The line chosen for this jump is in the relatively unpopulated central part of the Pacific Ocean and approximates longitude 180°. It is called the International Date Line. A person travelling westward across this line has to advance the calendar date by one day, while an eastward-bound traveller moves back one day on the calendar.

The standard time zones are generally designated by letters of the alphabet. The zero time zone, centred on the longitude 0° meridian passing through the Airy Transit Circle at the Old Royal Observatory in Greenwich, England, is denoted Z. Standard time within this zone is Coordinated Universal Time (UTC). Zones A, B, C,..., M (J excluded), run eastward at one-hour intervals to the International Date Line, while zones N, O, P,..., Y run westward to the same boundary. Zones M and Y are only one-half hour wide. Also, as indicated on the map, there are several partial zones that are one-half hour different from the adjacent main zones.

In North America there are six standard time zones and one partial zone. In terms of their name (and letter designation, hours behind the Greenwich zone, and the west longitude of the reference or standard meridian), these are:

(1)	Newfoundland	(P*, 3 h 30 min, 52.5°)
(2)	Atlantic	(Q, 4 h, 60°)
(3)	Eastern	(R, 5 h, 75°)
(4)	Central	(S, 6 h, 90°)
(5)	Mountain	(T, 7 h, 105°)
(6)	Pacific	(U, 8 h, 120°)
(7)	Alaska	(V, 9 h, 135°)

Note: Caution is advised when relying on the time-zone information given in this map. The zones are drawn based on the best information available as of June 2005 and are subject to change. Also, local jurisdictions, especially those near depicted zone boundaries, often adopt a different time. For current official Canadian and U.S. time zones visit **inms-ienm.nrc-cnrc.gc.ca/en/time_services/time_services_e.php** and **www.time.gov** respectively.

WORLD MAP OF TIME ZONES

ASTRONOMICAL TWILIGHT AND SIDEREAL TIME
By Randall Brooks

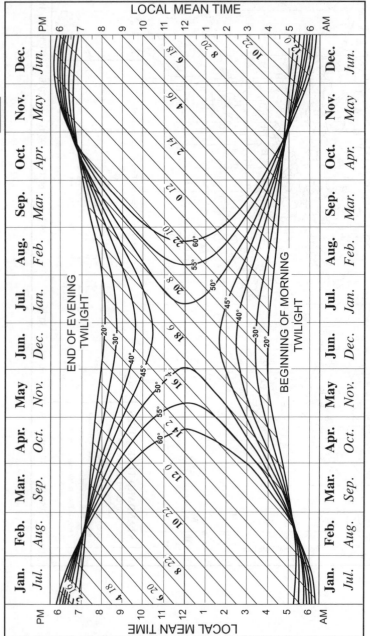

*The diagram gives for any day of the year: (1) the local mean time (LMT) of the end and beginning of astronomical twilight at seven specified latitudes (curved lines); (2) the local mean sidereal time (LMST = right ascension at the observer's meridian) as a function of LMT (diagonal lines). Months and right ascensions shown in **boldface** are for observers in the northern hemisphere, those in italics are for observers in the southern hemisphere.*

OPTICS AND OBSERVING

TELESCOPE PARAMETERS

Equations

Objective: f_o = focal length   *Eyepiece:* f_e = focal length
         D = diameter d_f = diameter of field stop
         FR = focal ratio θ_p = apparent angular field

Whole Instrument: M = angular magnification
         d_p = diameter of exit pupil
         θ_c = actual angular field

$$M \equiv \tan(\theta_p/2)/\tan(\theta_c/2) = f_o/f_e = D/d_p \approx \theta_p/\theta_c \qquad FR = f_o/D \qquad d_f^* \approx f_o\theta_c \approx f_e\theta_p$$

*(θ_c and θ_p must be expressed in radians.)

Performance

D is assumed to be expressed in millimetres.

Light Grasp (LG) is the ratio of the light flux intercepted by a telescope's objective lens or mirror to that intercepted by a human eye having a 7-mm-diameter entrance pupil.

Limiting Visual Magnitude m $\approx 2.7 + 5 \log D$, assuming transparent, dark-sky conditions and magnification $M \geq 1D$. (See *Sky & Telescope, 45,* 401, 1973; *77,* 332, 1989; *78,* 522, 1989).

Smallest Resolvable Angle $\alpha \approx 116/D$ seconds of arc (Dawes's limit). However, atmospheric conditions seldom permit values less than 0.5″.

Useful Magnification Range $\approx 0.2D$ to $2D$. The lower limit ($0.2D$) guarantees that, for most observers, all the light exiting a telescope can reach the retina. (The reciprocal of the coefficient to D is the diameter (in mm) of the telescope's exit pupil. Also, see the next section concerning exit pupils and magnification.) The upper limit ($2D$) is determined by the wave nature of light and the optical limitations of the eye, although atmospheric turbulence usually limits the maximum magnification to 400× or less. For examination of double stars, detection of faint stars, and studying structure in bright nebulae, magnifications of up to $3D$ are sometimes useful.

Values for some common apertures are:

D (mm):	60	100	125	150	200	250	330	444
LG:	73	200	320	460	820	1300	2200	4000
m:	11.6	12.7	13.2	13.6	14.2	14.7	15.3	15.9
α:	1.93″	1.16″	0.93″	0.77″	0.58″	0.46″	0.35″	0.26″
$0.2D$:	12×	20×	25×	30×	40×	50×	66×	89×
$2D$:	120×	200×	250×	300×	400×	500×	660×	890×

TELESCOPE EXIT PUPILS
By Roy Bishop

The performance of a visual telescope is constrained by Earth's atmosphere, the wave aspect of light, the design of the telescope and imperfections in its optical system, and the properties of the human visual system. Telescope and eye meet at the *exit pupil* of the telescope, which is the image of the telescope's objective lens or mirror formed by its eyepiece. When a telescope is pointed at a bright area, such as the daytime sky, the exit pupil appears as a small disk of light hovering in the space just behind the eyepiece. (Insert a small piece of paper in this vicinity to prove that this disk of light *really is* located behind the eyepiece.) Since the exit pupil is the narrowest point in the beam of light emerging from the telescope, it is here that the observer's eye must be located to make optimum use of the light passing through the telescope.

The diagram on p. 56 may be used to display the relation between the diameter of the exit pupil (d_p) of a telescope and the focal lengths (f_e) of various eyepieces. Both d_p and f_e are expressed in millimetres. The numbered scale around the upper right-hand corner of the diagram indicates the focal ratio (FR) of the objective lens or mirror of the telescope. (The FR equals the focal length of the objective divided by its diameter; see p. 53.) To prepare the diagram for a particular telescope, locate the FR of the telescope's objective on the FR scale, and draw a straight diagonal line from there to the origin (the lower left-hand corner). The diagram provides a visual display of the standard relation $d_p = f_e/\text{FR}$. One can see at a glance what range of eyepiece focal lengths is suitable for a particular telescope. Concerning the "AGE" scale on the diagram, see the section Very Low (RFT) Magnifications below.

To determine, for example, the eyepiece focal length required to produce a 3-mm exit pupil on a certain telescope, locate $d_p = 3$ on the ordinate, run horizontally across to the diagonal line corresponding to the FR of that telescope, and from there drop vertically downward to the abscissa to find f_e. This procedure may, of course, be reversed: for a given f_e, find the corresponding d_p.

Magnification Ranges

The ranges H, M, L, and RFT blocked off along the ordinate of the diagram break the d_p scale into four sections, starting at 0.5 mm and increasing by factors of 2. Although this sectioning is somewhat arbitrary, it does correspond closely to what are usually considered to be the high (H), medium (M), low (L), and "richest-field telescope" (RFT) magnification ranges of any visual telescope—and the associated d_p ranges are easy to remember. Note that these magnification ranges are defined by d_p, not by the numerical value of the magnification; for example, a magnification of 100× is "high" for a telescope of aperture $D = 70$ mm, "medium" for $D = 150$ mm, "low" for $D = 300$ mm, "very low (RFT)" for $D = 600$ mm, and "ultra-low" for D larger than 0.8 m.

High Magnifications: In the case of the Moon, the planets, and all but the dimmest stars, the highest useful magnification is the point at which blurring due to diffraction (caused by the wave nature of light) becomes noticeable. This corresponds approximately to $d_p = 0.5$ mm, assuming good optics and negligible atmospheric turbulence (i.e. excellent "seeing"). Higher magnifications will not reveal any more detail in these images and will cause reductions in four desirable features: sharpness, brightness, field of view, and eye relief (the space between the eye and eyepiece). However, for double stars and for some objects requiring the use of averted vision (e.g. faint stars) very high magnifications ($d_p < 0.5$ mm) can sometimes be used to advantage.

Medium Magnifications: A problem with high magnifications is that exit-pupil diameters of about 1 mm and smaller cause "floaters" (mobile debris in the vitreous humour of the eye in front of the retina) to interfere with vision. This problem increases with the age of the observer and with decreasing d_p. To avoid the distraction of floaters, an observer might choose to keep exit-pupil diameters no smaller than 1.5 mm (i.e. in the "medium" magnification range). For this lower limit the diagram indicates a minimum eyepiece focal length of, for example, 7 mm for a FR = 4.5 telescope, 15 mm for a FR = 10 telescope, and 24 mm for a FR = 16 telescope. With this restriction, to achieve a magnification of 250× for observing planets, a telescope would need an aperture of at least $D = M \times d_p = 250 \times 1.5 = 375$ mm. Hence, in addition to providing more light and greater resolution, a large-aperture telescope makes floaters less noticeable and magnifications in the "high" range less necessary.

With magnifications greater than very low (RFT) magnifications and also possibly greater than low magnifications, structure in dim, extended objects, such as galaxies and bright and dark nebulae, will be more easily seen. To see such objects, observers use averted vision, which places the image on the peripheral retina, which is composed primarily of the very sensitive "rod" photoreceptor cells. However, the number of rod cells far exceeds the number of nerve axons available to carry the signals to the visual centres in the brain. To accommodate this limitation and to cope with spontaneous thermal noise in the rod cells, the cells are grouped into detector units of various sizes (analogous to binning of pixels in a CCD chip). Because of the thermal noise, only those signals triggered by almost simultaneous photon hits in several rod cells are allowed to produce a conscious sensation. Thus in very dim light only large retinal detector units receive enough photon hits to respond. As a consequence, our ability to see detail is greatly reduced in dim light. Hence extra magnification helps to reveal structure in galaxies and nebulae.

Low Magnifications: Low magnifications have several advantages over certain other magnification ranges:

(1) For most observers an exit-pupil diameter between 2 mm and 4 mm results in the sharpest optical image because the combined influence of optical aberrations in the eye of the observer (which increase with increasing d_p) and blurring due to diffraction (which decreases with increasing d_p) is at a minimum. Assuming, for example, that the optimum d_p for a "typical observer" is 2.5 mm, then to realize this and achieve a magnification of 250× for observing planets, a telescope needs an aperture of $D = M \times d_p = 250 \times 2.5 = 625$ mm. Once again, the superiority of a large telescope (by amateur standards) is apparent. Another example: the reason for the crisp images provided by Canon's image-stabilized binoculars is that their d_p is in the "low magnification" range, and their optical quality is up to the challenge.

(2) Low magnifications provide greater luminance than high or medium magnifications, enabling the eye to discern contrast variations over a wider range of spatial frequencies.

(3) Viewing is more comfortable than with very low (RFT) magnifications, since the observer can move a bit (move the head and/or scan the field) without cutting into the light beam and dimming the image. As mentioned below, ultra-low magnifications have the same advantage, but light is wasted.

(4) Light entering near the edge of the pupil of the dark-adapted eye is not as effective in stimulating the rod cells in the retina—the "scotopic Stiles-Crawford effect" (see VanLoo and Enoch, *Vision Research, 15* (1975), p. 1005,). Thus low magnifications make more effective use of the light than very low (RFT) magnifications.

(5) Low magnifications provide a darker sky background than very low (RFT) magnifications, producing views that some observers consider to be aesthetically more pleasing.

(text continues overleaf)

EXIT-PUPILS DIAGRAM

Very Low (RFT) Magnifications: Magnifications in the RFT range are useful because they yield wide fields of view, the brightest (greatest luminance) images of extended objects, and for common telescope apertures, the most stars visible in one view (hence the term *richest field*). The lowest magnification that still makes use of the full aperture of a telescope is determined by the point at which the diameter of the telescope's exit pupil matches the diameter of the *entrance pupil* of the observer's eye.

For the dark-adapted eye, the entrance-pupil diameter seldom equals the often-quoted figure of 7 mm, but depends, among other things, upon the age of the observer as indicated by the scale in the upper-left portion of the diagram (see Kadlecová et al., *Nature, 182* (1958), p. 1520; *Sky & Telescope,* May 1992, p. 502). Note that this scale indicates *average* values; the maximum diameter of the entrance pupil of the eye of any *one* individual may differ by up to a millimetre from these values. A horizontal line should be drawn across the diagram corresponding to the maximum diameter of one's own entrance pupil. This line will be an upper bound on d_p in the same sense that the line at $d_p = 0.5$ mm is a lower bound. Note that in daylight, the entrance pupil of the eye has a diameter in the range of 2 mm to 4 mm. Thus for daylight use of telescopes, the upper bound on d_p will be correspondingly reduced.

Ultra-Low Magnifications: If a d_p value larger than the entrance pupil of the eye is used, the iris of the observer's eye will cut off some of the light passing through the telescope to the retina; that is, the iris will have become the light-limiting aperture *(aperture stop)* of the system rather than the edge of the telescope's objective. In this case, the cornea of the eye together with the lenses of the telescope's eyepiece form an image of the observer's iris at the objective of the telescope; to the incoming starlight, a highly magnified image of the iris hovers as an annular skirt covering the outer region of the objective of the telescope! A telescope can be used at such "ultra-low" magnifications, but obviously a telescope of smaller aperture would perform as well. However, ultra-low magnifications have two advantages:

(1) A wider actual field of view, assuming the field stop of the eyepiece will permit this (an eyepiece having a 2-in. barrel diameter is usually necessary).

(2) Ease of alignment of the entrance pupil of the eye with the exit pupil of the telescope, an aspect of viewing that is usually troublesome when these two pupils are nearly the same size. An oversize exit pupil provides "slop," making alignment less critical. This is particularly helpful when using binoculars during activities involving motion, such as boating or bird watching. This is one advantage of using 7×50 ($= M \times D$) binoculars rather than 7×35 binoculars for daytime activities, although less than half of the light entering the larger binoculars can reach the observer's retinas.

Some examples using the diagram:

(1) Consider the common 8-in. Schmidt-Cassegrain telescopes. These have $D = 200$ mm and (usually) FR = 10. The diagram indicates that eyepieces with focal lengths from 5 mm to 55 mm are usable for most observers. With a 32-mm eyepiece, the diagram gives $d_p = 3.2$ mm, in the L magnification range, and the magnification $M = D/d_p = 200/3.2 = 62\times$.

(2) If an observer wishes to use the full aperture of an FR = 4.5 telescope, a 40-mm eyepiece is ruled out. Similarly, a 70-year-old observer should probably not use even a 27-mm eyepiece on such a telescope and should not bother with 7×50 or 11×80 binoculars, unless ease of eye/exit-pupil alignment is the main consideration.

(3) There is no point in using extremely short focal length eyepieces, especially when combined with Barlow lenses, on telescopes having large FRs. This is a common fault (among many others!) with camera/department store "junk telescopes."

MAGNIFICATION AND CONTRAST IN DEEP-SKY OBSERVING
BY LEE JOHNSON AND WILLIAM ROBERTS

One of the main challenges of deep-sky observing is to distinguish faint, extended objects from the light of the background night sky. As we shall see below, the visibility of an object is a function of its apparent size and contrast, where contrast is the ratio of the object's surface brightness (neglecting the contribution of the background sky) to that of the background sky. As an object's apparent size increases, its minimum detectable surface brightness decreases. As the background sky surface brightness decreases, so does an object's minimum detectable surface brightness. This article addresses the consequences for the visibility of faint deep-sky objects and the effect of magnification thereon.

Surface Brightness and Exit Pupils

Table 1 lists the surface brightness (luminance) of three representative deep-sky objects expressed in magnitude per square arcsecond (mag/sq$''$). (For more details on these objects, see, respectively, pp. 298, 288, and 298.) When these surface brightnesses are compared to those of skies corresponding to mountain-top observatories (22 mag/sq$''$), dark country sites (21 mag/sq$''$), sites with magnitude-5 stars visible (19.5 mag/sq$''$), and a suburban setting with magnitude-4 stars visible (18.5 mag/sq$''$), it is clear that the surface brightness of an object can be lower than the sky background, thus leading to very low values of contrast.

TABLE 1—SURFACE BRIGHTNESS OF OBJECTS

Object	m_V	Size $'$	Surface Brightness mag/sq$''$
NGC 7317 (galaxy)	13.6	0.5×0.5	20.7
M97 (planetary nebula)	9.9	3.2×3.2	21.1
Jones 1 (planetary nebula)	12.1	5.5×5.5	24.4

Sizes and magnitudes of deep-sky objects can be found in *The Deep Sky Field Guide to Uranometria 2000.0.* The surface brightnesses of several nebulae are also given in the section GALACTIC NEBULAE, p. 285. For any extended deep-sky object, the surface brightness, S, in mag/sq$''$ can be approximated by

$$S = m_V + 2.5 \log(2827ab),$$

where a and b are, respectively, the object's major and minor diameters in arcminutes ($'$), assuming an elliptical shape. (To convert magnitude per square arcminute to magnitude per square arcsecond, add 8.89.)

The exit pupil of a telescope, which equals (objective diameter)/magnification, determines the image brightness through the telescope (see TELESCOPE EXIT PUPILS, pp. 54–57). When an extended object is magnified to the point that the exit pupil is smaller than the eye's entrance pupil—which is nominally 7 mm—its brightness decreases relative to the naked-eye view. The decrease in brightness is the same for both the object and the background sky. In other words, magnification does not alter contrast. Table 2 shows how the degree to which an object's surface brightness or that of the sky decreases as the exit pupil becomes smaller than 7 mm.

TABLE 2—DIMMING WITH RESPECT TO A 7-MM EXIT PUPIL

Exit Pupil (mm)	7	6	5	4	3	2	1	0.5
Dimming (mag)	0.0	0.3	0.7	1.2	1.8	2.7	4.2	5.7

Human binocular vision has a lower surface-brightness limit of approximately 1 μcd/m², which, when adjusted for monocular vision, is about 27 mag/sq″. When the dimming due to smaller exit pupils, as given in Table 2, is added to the sky brightness, it is apparent that the magnified sky may approach the detection limit of the eye; for example, a 1-mm exit pupil in a 22 mag/sq″ sky lowers the apparent sky brightness to 26.2 mag/sq″, which is near the eye's limit.

The Relation Between Size and Threshold Surface Brightness

Blackwell (*J. Opt. Soc. Am., 36* (1946), p. 624), in a massive World War II study that is still the only one of its kind, analyzed approximately 450000 observations of threshold contrast under varying background illuminations. Table 3, derived from Blackwell's data, which goes down to 26 mag/sq″, gives the minimum detectable surface brightness of an object as the object's apparent size and the brightness of the sky vary. The values are corrected for monocular vision and presuppose a 50% probability of detection; for 90% probability, subtract 0.5 from the entries in the table.

TABLE 3—THRESHOLD SURFACE BRIGHTNESS FOR SIZE AND SKY BRIGHTNESS

Size (′)	Sky Surface Brightness (mag/sq″)							
	26	25	24	23	22	21	20	19
360	26.3	26.0	25.6	25.0	24.4	23.7	23.0	22.3
240	26.1	25.8	25.4	24.8	24.2	23.5	22.8	22.2
120	25.5	25.3	24.9	24.4	23.7	23.1	22.4	21.8
60	24.7	24.5	24.2	23.7	23.1	22.5	21.9	21.3
30	23.8	23.8	23.3	22.8	22.3	21.7	21.1	20.6
15	22.5	22.3	22.0	21.6	21.1	20.6	20.1	19.7

As magnification is increased, one moves up and to the left in the table. For a fixed apparent sky brightness, large objects are more easily detected than small ones of equal surface brightness. In addition, low-surface-brightness objects are more easily seen against darker backgrounds and by using higher magnifications, in agreement with experience. However, note that differences in thresholds from increases in magnification are relatively smaller toward the upper-left portion of the table. With sufficient magnification a point may be reached where a further increase in magnification reduces an object's surface brightness faster than the improvement in threshold brightness due to the increase in size. Thus the object will become more difficult to detect, although the increased magnification makes it easier to see any bright detail within the object.

It is important to note that the values in this table are guidelines only. If Table 3 suggests that the detection of an object is marginal, do not be discouraged; try anyway. Other factors that affect the detection of an object are atmospheric extinction, a telescope's efficiency of light transmission, the differences between the eye's nighttime and daytime response (see FILTERS, pp. 66–69), and the observer's visual acuity. Typically, the cumulative effect of these factors is between −0.5 and +0.5 magnitudes; see Schaefer (*PASP, 102* (1990), pp. 213–215) for further details.

An example using Table 3

(1) Consider NGC 7317 under a 21 mag/sq″ sky. A magnification of 148× with a 445-mm telescope gives a size of 74′ and an exit pupil of 3 mm. The dimming due to a 3-mm exit pupil is 1.8 magnitudes (Table 2), which when added to both the object's and sky's surface brightness results in brightnesses of 22.5 mag/sq″ and 22.8 mag/sq″, respectively. The entry in Table 3 for a sky of surface brightness 23 mag/sq″ and size 60′ gives a threshold surface brightness of 23.7 mag/sq″. This is more than one magnitude dimmer than the brightness of NGC 7317, which should therefore be clearly visible under the specified conditions. A 130-mm telescope with a magnification of 43×, on the other hand, gives a size of 22′ and the same surface brightnesses and exit pupil. From the interpolated value 22.2 in the fourth column of Table 3 we see that the object will likely not be visible in this smaller instrument at this magnification. Alternatively, finding the object brightness in the 23 mag/sq″ column we see that the minimum apparent size is almost 30′, and since 22′ is less than this, the object is unlikely to be seen.

Some examples using Figure 1

Figure 1 is a graphical representation of the data in Table 3, whose columns are depicted as a set of correlative curves. The y-axis represents the minimum apparent size of the object for visibility, and the x-axis is the contrast between the object and the sky. Whereas Table 3 emphasizes the visibility of the object as a function of its brightness and apparent size, Figure 1 emphasizes the visibility of the object as a function of the contrast between it and the sky in relation to its apparent size.

(2) An example with a larger object shows that magnification can be increased without dropping the object below the threshold surface brightness. Consider M97 viewed with a 200-mm aperture under a 20 mag/sq″ sky. The contrast between the object and sky surface brightnesses of 21.1 mag/sq″ and 20 mag/sq″ is 1.1 mag/sq″, which does not change with magnification. A 5-mm exit pupil (40×) gives a sky surface brightness of 20.7 mag/sq″, with a 128′ apparent size. Starting at the 1.1 mag/sq″ point on the x-axis, move vertically to the curve (21 mag/sq″) most closely corresponding to the sky surface brightness and then horizontally to get the minimum apparent object size on the y-axis (40′). Since the apparent size is greater than the minimum, M97 should be visible. If the magnification is increased to 100×, resulting in an exit pupil of 2 mm and apparent size of 320′, the sky brightness changes to 22.7 mag/sq″ and the minimum size to 80′. The object is still visible, but the apparent size is 2.5 times greater, thus resulting in a more detailed view.

The contrast of emission nebulae is a special case and can be increased with bandpass filters (see FILTERS, pp. 66–69). Bandpass filters such as the UHC, OIII, and Hβ increase contrast by passing light near the emission wavelengths and rejecting broad-spectrum light from light pollution and natural skyglow, effectively reducing the sky's surface brightness by about 1.6 magnitudes for the UHC and about 2.6 magnitudes for the OIII and Hβ filters. The visible light from emission nebulae is mainly in the OIII and Hβ wavelengths, which lie close to the peak response of the dark-adapted eye. Filters such as the UHC pass all the light from these lines and do not significantly dim the nebulae. These filters therefore do not require an increase in exit pupils in order to maintain an object's surface brightness. OIII and especially Hβ filters, on the other hand, may pass only a portion of the light from a nebula and result in a dimming of the nebula. Here, the restoration of the object's surface brightness requires an increase in exit pupil and thus a decrease in magnification. The OIII filter passes most of the light from a typical planetary nebula and thus does not require an increase in exit pupil; it is therefore the filter of choice for these objects. The situation for other emission nebulae is not so clear.

(3) Consider viewing the planetary nebula Jones 1 with a 250-mm aperture under a 21 mag/sq″ sky. Exit pupils of 2 mm and smaller reduce the surface brightness below the eye's absolute threshold of 27 mag/sq″; larger exit pupils do not dim the sky sufficiently to make the object visible. A magnification of 50× gives an exit pupil of 5 mm, which results in a contrast of 3.4 mag/sq″, sky brightness of 21.7 mag/sq″, and

an object size of 275'. Figure 1 shows the minimum apparent size to be greater than 360' and that Jones 1 is not visible under these conditions. An OIII filter will reduce the sky surface brightness by 2.6 magnitudes without dimming Jones 1 appreciably and results in a sky surface brightness of 24.3 mag/sq". The contrast is now 0.1 mag/sq", and the minimum apparent size is approximately 70'. The planetary nebula should be visible when viewed with the filter.

FIGURE 1 – CRITICAL SIZE VS. CONTRAST BY SKY BRIGHTNESS

curves are for the indicated **Sky Brightness** (19, 20,..., 26 mag/sq")

Summary

Generally, experienced deep-sky observers select eyepieces that result in exit pupils in the range of 2 mm to 3 mm when viewing a faint deep-sky object. This range of exit pupils corresponds to the middle of Table 3 and to the central sections of the middle curves in Figure 1. Larger exit pupils correspond to the lower right of the table, where small, faint objects may fall below the threshold of visibility; and smaller exit pupils to the upper left, where excessive magnification may dim the object to invisibility. At any fixed apparent size, moving from right to left across the table results in a decrease in threshold brightness, which shows the benefit of observing in increasingly dark skies or with the aid of a filter. The corresponding values for Figure 1 show that the threshold size of an object decreases in relation to the darker skies represented by curves further along the x-axis.

BINOCULARS
BY ROY BISHOP

For an experienced observer, binoculars are indispensable. For a beginning observer, binoculars are preferable to an astronomical telescope. For a beginner unfamiliar with the large-scale features of the sky, who cannot yet identify a dozen constellations on any clear night, a telescope's narrow field of view, confusing image orientations, and unfamiliar controls will quickly cause more frustration than fun. The beginner is at a double disadvantage because he or she also does not know enough about astronomical telescopes to distinguish those that are worthy of the name from the common camera/department-store "junk telescopes"—the $299 wonders with poor optics and wobbly mounts. How many such telescopes are gathering dust in closets, their young owners turned off astronomy and their parents a few hundred dollars poorer? Far better had the same investment been made in a good pair of binoculars. With their ease of use, wide field of view, and unreversed, upright images, binoculars are a great help in finding one's way around the sky, and provide many unique views of the heavens.

Binoculars magnifying 6 to 8 times are ideal for locating planets in the twilight, scanning the constellations, studying the larger dark nebulae and star fields of our galaxy, and viewing bright comets. Binoculars magnifying 10 to 20 times provide the best views of objects spanning a few degrees, such as the Hyades, the Pleiades, the North America Nebula, and the Andromeda Galaxy; they also give the finest view of the slender crescent Moon, or of the full Moon with broken clouds blowing by.

Binoculars permit us to view the universe with both eyes, thereby providing more advantages: an improved sense of reality and depth (although parallax is negligible when viewing the heavens); more relaxed viewing; a complete view in the sense that the blind areas of one eye (associated with blood vessels and the region where the optic nerve attaches to the retina) are compensated by the field provided by the other eye; and dim objects appear brighter when viewed with two eyes.

Sizes: Binocular sizes are specified by numbers, for example, 7 × 50 and 8 × 30. The first number, including the "×," is the angular magnification or "power"; the second number is the diameter of the front (objective) lenses in millimetres. That is, in the notation on p. 53: $M \times D$. Thus the exit pupil diameter is easily calculated from $D \div M$ (e.g. 7 × 35 binoculars have exit pupils of $35 \div 7 = 5$ mm). Another important parameter is field of view. Binoculars have apparent angular field diameters of about 50° when equipped with standard eyepieces, to near 70° with wide-angle eyepieces. The actual field of view on the sky (typically 3° to 10°) equals approximately the apparent field divided by the magnification. Thus the area of sky visible decreases rapidly with higher magnifications.

What is the best binocular size for astronomical use? There is no simple answer. Almost *any* pair of binoculars will show far more than can be seen with the unaided eyes; however, for astronomical use the objective lenses should be at least 30 mm in diameter. Also, small binoculars of high quality are more enjoyable to use than a large pair of low quality. For maximum light transmission and high-contrast images, binoculars with *multicoated* optics are preferable to those with merely *coated* optics (the former give greenish or deep red reflections from their surfaces, the latter bluish or violet).

Caveat emptor! Low-quality binoculars (and telescopes) are common. Images seen through low-quality binoculars are slightly fuzzy (usually not apparent to the inexperienced observer), one's eyes will be strained in trying to compensate for imperfectly aligned optics, and the focusing mechanism is usually flexible and crackling with an excess of grease used to mask poor workmanship. Avoid both zoom (variable magnification) binoculars and binoculars that do not have an adjustable focus—invariably these are of low quality.

Considering that binoculars contain at least 14 pieces of glass with 36 optical surfaces, antireflection coatings on (hopefully) all air-to-glass surfaces, plus two focusing mechanisms and an interpupillary adjustment, it is not surprising that top-quality instruments are in the same price range as video cameras. Such prices buy crisp, high-contrast images, accurately aligned optics, precise, rugged, dust- and moisture-proof construction, and pleasurable service for a lifetime. Nevertheless, there is a big market for $99 binoculars and $299 telescopes, and manufacturers are happy to satisfy the demand. When it comes to optical equipment, quality usually matches price.

Stability: One aspect of binocular use not often appreciated is how much more can be seen if the binoculars are mounted on a stable support, such as a camera tripod. This eliminates the constant jiggling associated with hand-holding and also supports the weight of the instrument. Adapters for attaching binoculars to a tripod are available, although usually it is not difficult to make your own. A recent major advance in binocular design is "image stabilization," an active optical system built into binoculars that compensates for the tremor associated with hand-holding. For example, the Canon company has introduced microprocessor-controlled binocular image stabilization that gives almost tripod-like stability with the convenience of hand-holding. Canon has produced 10 × 30, 10 × 42, 12 × 36, 15 × 45, 15 × 50, and 18 × 50 models, the latter three being particularly impressive for astronomy (see *SkyNews,* July/August 1998, p. 12; and *Sky & Telescope,* July 2000, p. 59).

Rating Binoculars

A frequently cited figure for binocular performance is "Relative Brightness," which equals the square of the diameter (in millimetres) of the instrument's exit pupils. For example, for 7 × 50 binoculars this figure is $(50 ÷ 7)^2 ≈ 51$. Although this is a measure of the surface brightness *(luminance)* of an extended object seen through the binoculars under nighttime conditions, it is a totally inadequate measure of binocular performance on the night sky. For instance, using this figure of merit, large 14 × 100 binoculars have practically the same rating as the unaided eyes (which, when young and in dim light, are effectively 1 × 7 binoculars)!

Since seeing depends upon light, and the amount of light passing through a pair of binoculars depends primarily upon the *area* of the objective lenses (diameter D), a D^2 dependence appears reasonable. However, although the amount of light going into the point images of stars increases as D^2, assuming constant magnification the increase in the luminance of the background sky as D increases leads to a somewhat slower improvement in the visibility of these stars. A similar muted improvement occurs for dim extended images, resulting in an approximately D^1 dependence, rather than D^2.

Also, for constant D the detail that can be seen in the night sky increases with the magnification M. The resulting lower luminance of the background sky allows fainter stars to be seen, and the visibility of structure in extended images improves as M increases because the image is larger and of fixed contrast relative to the sky background.

The simplest figure of merit for the performance of binoculars in low-light conditions that combines both variables is the mathematical product $M × D$ (which happens to look the same as the binocular size specification). In the case of two pairs of binoculars, one having twice the M and twice the D of the other, $M × D$ indicates that "four times as much" should be visible in the larger instrument (e.g. 16 × 60 versus 8 × 30 binoculars). This is to be expected, since in the larger instrument stars will be four times brighter and extended images will have four times the area from which the eyes can glean information, with luminances being the same in both instruments.

For many decades the venerable Carl Zeiss optical company has cited $\sqrt{(M \times D)}$ as a "Twilight Performance Factor" for binoculars, its value said to be proportional to the distance at which various binoculars will show the same detail. This is equivalent to $M \times D$ being proportional to *the amount of detail that can be seen at the same distance*. The latter situation is relevant for astronomy since, unlike a bird or other object on Earth, a star or a galaxy is always at essentially the *same distance* from the observer. $M \times D$ could be called the *visibility factor*.

Binocular Performance Diagram

The diagram on the following page enables one to quickly compare binoculars in terms of their ability to reveal detail in the night sky. The vertical axis is magnification M; the horizontal axis is aperture D. The uniform grid of small dots is a guide to reading the diagram. The five straight lines indicate constant exit-pupil diameters of 3, 4, 5, 6, and 7 mm, as indicated both by numbers and by circles of these diameters near the top ends of the lines. The five curved arcs indicate constant values of $M \times D$ (the visibility factor), increasing by successive powers of 2 toward the upper right (100, 200, 400, 800, and 1600). Each large dot represents a common size of binoculars. The arrows in the lower-right corner indicate the directions on the diagram in which various quantities increase most rapidly.

Each straight line (constant exit-pupil diameter) also corresponds to constant luminance of extended areas, such as the Orion Nebula or the background sky glow, with the luminance being proportional to the square of the exit-pupil diameter (provided the entrance pupils of the observer's eyes are large enough to accommodate the exit pupils of the binoculars). However, exit pupils of 3 to 5 mm ensure that (1) all the light transmitted by the binoculars can enter the dark-adapted eyes no matter what the observer's age; (2) alignment of exit pupils with dark-adapted eye pupils is relatively easy to achieve; (3) the background sky glow will be subdued; and (4) star images will be less distorted by aberrations in the observer's eyes (see TELESCOPE EXIT PUPILS, pp. 54–57).

Examples: Some examples apparent from the diagram: for viewing the night sky 10 × 50 binoculars will show about twice as much detail as 7 × 35s; 11 × 80 and 15 × 60 binoculars are equally capable, as are 8 × 30s and 6 × 42s (assuming one's eye pupils can accommodate the exit pupils of the instrument with the larger D); 10 × 50 binoculars are appreciably better than 7 × 50s for visibility (although, assuming equal apparent angular fields, 7 × 50s will show about twice as much sky area as will 10 × 50s). Canon's image-stabilized 15 × 45 binoculars are nearly equivalent to tripod-mounted 10 × 70s, with the *triple* advantage of smaller size, accommodating observers whose pupils will not open to 7 mm, and not requiring a tripod!

The visibility factor ($M \times D$) is applicable to the usual range of binocular sizes (exit pupils between about 2 mm and 7 mm), but should not be extrapolated indefinitely. For instance, as the magnification is increased on a telescope and the exit pupil approaches 1 mm or less, a point will be reached (dependent upon the darkness of the sky) where the background sky glow is imperceptible. Also, stars will begin to show either seeing disks or diffraction disks. A further increase in M will not cause a noticeable improvement in the visibility of stars, and the perceived contrast between an extended object and the sky will decrease. In addition, the angular size of an extended object must be kept in mind. Once M is increased to the point at which the object fills the field of view of the instrument, the object may not be visible at all! For example, a large, dim comet coma may be visible in 15 × 60 binoculars ($M \times D = 900$) but *invisible* in a 45 × 200 telescope ($M \times D = 9000$).

BINOCULAR PERFORMANCE DIAGRAM

FILTERS
By Roy Bishop

Optical filters reflect and absorb some portion of the incident light. *Neutral-density filters* reflect and absorb light more or less uniformly across the visible spectrum. *Coloured (dye) filters* typically pass only one or two moderately broad portions of the spectrum. *Interference filters* are more selective and typically pass only one or two well-defined, narrow segments of the spectrum. All three types of filter are invaluable in astronomy.

In addition to categorization by physical type, filters may be categorized according to their intended use: lunar and planetary (neutral-density and dye filters), solar (neutral-density and interference filters), and nebular (interference filters).

Lunar and Planetary Filters

As viewed in a telescope, the Moon and the planets Venus, Mars, and Jupiter are often uncomfortably bright. A neutral-density filter, which passes only 13% to 25% of the light, solves this problem while avoiding the loss in resolution that would accompany stopping down the aperture of the telescope to decrease the brightness to the same level. With a less-glaring image, light scattering in the observer's eye is reduced and fine details are easier to see. A neutral-density filter is typically about 26 mm in diameter and is attached to the forward-facing end of an eyepiece.

Dye filters can enhance the visibility of various planetary features. For instance, a red or yellow filter will absorb bluish light scattered by the Martian atmosphere and thereby improve the contrast of features on the surface of Mars. A green filter will increase the visibility of pale red and blue areas in the atmosphere of Jupiter (although the entire image will then appear green). Also, since they absorb an appreciable fraction of the light, dye filters or polarizing filters have the same advantage as a weak neutral-density filter when viewing bright objects.

Solar Filters

A filter is essential when observing the Sun. Solar filters must be designed not only to reduce the brightness of the solar surface to a comfortable level, but to block out the invisible but damaging infrared and ultraviolet radiation. Just because a filter makes the Sun dim enough to view comfortably is no guarantee that it is not transmitting damaging amounts of invisible radiation! This is no place to experiment with do-it-yourself filter designs—use only a proper solar filter from a reputable manufacturer. *Failure to use a proper filter when observing the Sun can cause immediate and irreversible damage to vision.*

A special warning: Heavy atmospheric haze near sunrise or sunset often dims the Sun so that it appears as a dull red disk, not uncomfortably bright to the eye. At such times resist the temptation to view the Sun with a telescope without using a solar filter. The atmosphere at such times is still relatively transparent in the invisible infrared portion of the spectrum, and the great light grasp of a telescope can result in thermal retinal damage! With the unaided eyes the retinal solar image, although just as bright, is much smaller and the eye can better dissipate the heat. Also, with unaided vision, one is less apt to fixate on the Sun for a prolonged period.

For white-light views of the Sun a dark, broad-spectrum, neutral-density solar filter is needed. Aluminized Mylar and metal-coated glass are common designs, although they usually do not attenuate light uniformly across the visible spectrum (i.e. they are not perfect neutral-density filters). Aluminized Mylar gives a bluish colour to the solar image, while metal-coated glass filters usually give an orange colour.

The filter should be 50 mm or more in diameter and must be positioned to cover the *front* of the telescope. Ensure that the filter is *securely attached* so that a gust of wind or a bump cannot dislodge it. (Some small telescopes are sold with a "Sun filter" designed to attach to the eyepiece, just before the observer's eye. Sunlight concentrated by the telescope can overheat and shatter a filter of this design. Such filters should be thrown in the garbage!)

For direct viewing of the Sun (not using binoculars or a telescope) shade #14 (no other shade) rectangular welder's glass may be used; this is available for a few dollars at welding supplies shops. These filters are not suitable for attaching to the front of binoculars or a telescope simply because their poor optical quality results in a fuzzy image.

Red, flame-like prominences at the Sun's limb and much structure in its chromosphere across the solar disk can be seen in hydrogen-alpha (Hα) light, a strong spectral line emitted by atomic hydrogen. This light is totally overwhelmed by the rest of the solar spectrum, so a neutral-density filter will not work. Advances in vacuum thin-film technology have made possible interference filters, filters that operate on the same principle as Fabry-Perot interferometers, involving the interference of multiply reflected beams of light. These filters can be constructed so they are transparent only to light having an extremely narrow range of wavelengths, typically 0.15 to 0.05 nm for solar viewing, although band-passes of up to 1 nm are used in solar-prominence viewers designed to occult the solar disk. If this band-pass is centred on the Hα wavelength (656.3 nm), nearly all the Sun's light will be blocked, leaving an image in Hα light.

Hα filters are expensive, particularly for band-passes near 0.05 nm that are needed for high-contrast images of the solar disk. These filters may be located either in front of the objective of a telescope or between the objective and the eyepiece. In the latter case, because the wavelength of the centre of the narrow band-pass varies with the angle at which light rays enter the filter (a characteristic of interference filters), the focal ratio of the imaging telescope must be near f/20 for 0.15-nm band-pass filters and f/30 or higher for filters with narrower band-passes. Temperature control is usually required to keep the band-pass centred on the Hα wavelength, although some Hα filters are designed to be tilted in order to tune them to the Hα wavelength (the wavelength of peak transmittance is shifted toward shorter wavelengths when the filter is tilted away from 90° incidence).

Hα filters require a broadband "energy-rejection prefilter," located at the front of the telescope. The prefilter has a band-pass of about 100 nm in the red part of the spectrum and blocks essentially all the infrared, ultraviolet, and much of the visible part of the solar radiation from entering the telescope.

Nebular Filters

From the surface of Earth, the night sky is not completely dark. Even in the absence of light pollution (human-made and lunar), the air itself emits a feeble light called airglow. In higher latitudes, aurorae can also contribute to the glow of the atmosphere. Two other components of the light of the night sky are the zodiacal light and background starlight. The diffuse glow from all four sources reduces the contrast of celestial objects and, in the case of dim comets, galaxies, and nebulae, the object may be completely obscured by the brightness of the sky.

Filters transmit only a fraction of the incident light. Thus employing them to see faint objects may seem counterproductive. However, there are objects in the heavens that emit light only at certain wavelengths. This behaviour is characteristic of plasmas — excited gases, matter composed of separate atoms energized either by ultraviolet radiation from nearby hot stars or by collisions such as occur in supernova explosion shock fronts. Such regions are called emission nebulae and include star-forming regions, planetary nebulae, and some supernova remnants. A filter that selectively blocks most of the background sky glow but is transparent to the wavelengths at which such objects emit most of their visible light will darken the sky background without appreciably dimming the object of interest. With narrow-band-pass interference-type filters the effect can be dramatic, improving contrast and revealing details that otherwise are completely invisible. It is the next best thing to observing these objects from above Earth's atmosphere!

Dark-adapted (scotopic) human vision responds to light having wavelengths from approximately 400 to 620 nm. In bright light (photopic vision) the spectral range extends to somewhat longer wavelengths, about 750 nm. For both types of vision the response curve (sensitivity vs. wavelength) is "bell-shaped," the wavelength of maximum sensitivity being in the middle of the visible range—near 507 nm for scotopic vision and 555 nm for photopic vision (see the figure "Nebular Filter Transmission" on the following page). The photopic sensation produced by 555-nm light is green; for scotopic vision colour is not produced, but at photopic levels 507-nm light appears blue-green.

Hydrogen is the predominant element in the universe. Atomic hydrogen, when excited by ultraviolet radiation from a nearby hot star, emits light in the visible spectrum at only four discrete wavelengths: 656, 486, 434, and 410 nm (designated as Hα, Hβ, Hγ, and Hδ, respectively, part of the *Balmer spectrum* of hydrogen). Scotopic vision is blind to 656-nm (Hα) light and relatively insensitive to the less intense 434- and 410-nm light. However, 486 nm (Hβ) lies near the 507-nm peak sensitivity of scotopic vision, and an Hβ ("H-beta") filter having a narrow band-pass at this wavelength will greatly reduce the surrounding sky brightness and reveal Hβ-emitting nebulae.

The classic example is the Horsehead Nebula, a dark, silhouetted column of dust just southeast of the east end of Orion's belt. The surrounding hydrogen gas, excited probably by the nearby hot star ζ Orionis, fluoresces dimly with Hβ light. If the obscuring airglow is blocked by an Hβ filter, the dark Horsehead can distinctly be seen in a telescope having an aperture of 400 mm or greater. However, the number of objects that can be viewed advantageously with an Hβ filter is very limited, apparently because few nebulae emit strongly in Hβ light.

Two other strong nebular emission lines lie at 496 and 501 nm, nearly at the peak sensitivity of scotopic vision. Originally detected in 1864 by the British astronomer William Huggins, the origin of these lines was unknown at that time, and they were attributed to a hypothetical new element, "nebulium." In 1927, the American astrophysicist Ira Bowen identified the lines as due to doubly ionized oxygen (O^{++} or OIII), which glows brightly when very low-density nebular gas is strongly excited (high temperature). A filter that has a narrow band-pass spanning these two wavelengths gives striking views of highly excited nebulae. A good example is the Veil Nebula, a supernova remnant in eastern Cygnus. Through an OIII filter on a dark, transparent night, the direct view of the Veil in a large amateur telescope is more spectacular than any photograph or CCD image. Planetary nebulae (fluorescing, low-density shells of gas surrounding hot central stars) also show up well with an OIII filter; examples include the Helix Nebula, the Owl Nebula (M97), the Dumbbell Nebula (M27), and the Ring Nebula (M57).

Because of their narrow band-passes, Hβ and OIII filters are sometimes called *line filters,* although their band-passes are much wider than that of an Hα filter. Filters encompassing both the Hβ and OIII lines, such as the Lumicon Ultra High Contrast (UHC) filter, are termed *narrowband filters*. These filters also enhance views of many emission nebulae, although with the wider band-pass the sky background is brighter. With a large telescope under dark skies, I find that the single most useful filter is the OIII line filter. With smaller apertures (less than about 200 mm), the narrowband

Lumicon UHC filter (or equivalent filter from other manufacturers) may be preferable since it dims the stars less.

Some other nebulae that are greatly enhanced by OIII and narrowband filters include the Omega or Loon Nebula (M17), the Trifid Nebula (M20), the Lagoon Nebula (M8), the Rosette Nebula, the Eagle Nebula (M16), the North America Nebula, and the Eta Carinae Nebula.

Nebular Filter Transmission

The dotted, dashed, and continuous curves show the transmission versus wavelength characteristic of four interference filters (in descending order in the legend): two line filters, a narrowband filter, and a broadband filter. The bell-shaped curves composed of small open and solid circles show the relative response of bright-adapted (photopic) vision and dark-adapted (scotopic) vision. In ascending sequence above the curves are spectral colours, nebula emission lines, and light-pollution lines (M = mercury, S = high-pressure sodium, and LPS = low-pressure sodium). High-pressure sodium light sources emit an additional broad continuum spectrum that is not shown. The two unlabelled light-pollution lines are strong airglow/auroral lines produced by atomic oxygen. (David Lane used a "Varian Model Cory 50 Conc. UV-Visible Spectrophotometer" owned by the Chemistry Department at Saint Mary's University to obtain the filter curves; he also prepared the diagram.)

Stars emit light across the entire visible spectrum. Thus line filters and narrowband filters impair views of single stars, reflection nebulae, star clusters, and galaxies. Filters with wide band-passes extending from about 450 to 530 nm are called *broadband filters*. Examples are the Lumicon Deep Sky filter, the Orion SkyGlow filter, and the Meade Broadband filter. These decrease the airglow somewhat and block several of the brighter wavelengths emitted by sodium- and mercury-vapour streetlights, without dimming stars and galaxies too much. Thus they provide a modest improvement in the visibility of some objects from light-polluted sites. Because of their wide band-pass and high transmission at the Hα line, they are also useful for photography of emission nebulae. However, under dark skies an unfiltered view is preferable to that through a broadband filter.

LIMITING MAGNITUDES
BY DOUGLAS PITCAIRN

Limiting Visual Magnitudes

One of the many difficulties with visual observing from the surface of our planet is the variability of the atmosphere. In any record of observations it is important to note the condition of the sky. Parameters such as brightness and contrast are greatly affected by the transparency of the sky and the presence of light pollution or aurorae.

One of the simplest ways to quantify local sky conditions is to note the magnitude of the faintest star visible with the unaided eye—the *limiting visual magnitude* (LVM). Although individuals differ in their ability to detect faint stars, these differences are generally small, and for any one observer such observations provide a consistent measure of sky quality.

The chart at the left shows a 9°-wide field in the vicinity of Polaris (the brightest star on the chart) and is useful for observers at latitude 20°N or higher. For orientation, the solid lines mark the beginning of the handle of the Little Dipper, as in the ALL-SKY MAPS on pp. 309–317. Several stars have their visual magnitudes indicated (with decimal points omitted). Using this field to determine your LVM has several advantages: it is always above the horizon in midnorthern latitudes; its altitude does not change with the time of night or year, so the variation of atmospheric extinction with altitude is not a consideration; there are no bright stars or planets in the field to dazzle the eye; the faint stars are quite well spaced and therefore easy to identify; and being a simple field, it can be memorized. Especially note the dashed spiral of descending magnitudes labelled "A" through "F."

Limiting Telescopic Magnitudes

Aperture, telescope design, eyepiece design, magnification, and the quality of optical surfaces are a few of the many variables that will determine the faintest stars visible through a given telescope and eyepiece. By determining an instrument's limiting magnitude—the *limiting telescopic magnitude* (LTM)—you can effectively assess the effect of these variables. The quality of the night sky will also affect the LTM. Therefore, changes in the LVM should be taken into account when determining the LTM. (The relationship between LTM and LVM is complex; readers may explore it using the excellent Web-based calculator at **www.go.ednet.ns.ca/~larry/astro/maglimit.html**.) The LTM is a useful guide when attempting faint targets (Pluto in a 150-mm scope?), comparing the performance of different instruments ("Can my scope see as faint as yours?"), or determining whether a mirror or lens needs cleaning (many people clean their optics too often, assuming that dust degrades optical performance more than it actually does).

To help determine the LTM of your instrument, use the charts on the next page, which show an 8'-wide section of the northwest quadrant of M67 centred at RA 8h 50.1m and Dec +11°53'. This old open cluster lies 8° south-southeast of M44, Cancer's famous Beehive cluster. The accompanying table lists the visual magnitudes and the $B - V$ colour indices of the labelled stars. The diagram was constructed from

STAR	VISUAL	B – V
A	10.60	1.10
B	11.19	0.43
C	11.59	0.42
D	12.01	0.57
E	12.26	0.68
F	12.57	0.59
G	13.04	0.85
H	13.35	0.59
I	13.61	0.59
J	13.96	0.62
K	14.34	0.56
L	14.66	0.67
M	14.96	0.69
N	15.30	0.79
O	15.58	0.84
P	16.06	0.74
Q	16.31	0.99
R	16.62	0.81
S	17.05	1.26
T	17.38	1.17
U	17.64	1.31
V	18.04	1.27
W	18.38	0.76
X	18.69	1.17
Y	19.07	1.56
Z	19.29	0.61
a	19.42	1.34
b	20.10	0.00
c	20.35	0.83
d	20.61	1.55
e	21.03	0.32

"Left-Right Correct" View

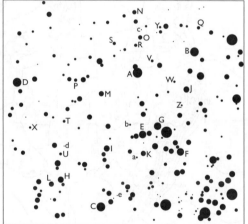
"Mirror Reversed" View

The "left-right correct" chart is for telescopes with an even number of reflecting surfaces (e.g. Newtonian reflectors) and the "mirror-reversed" chart is for telescopes with an odd number of reflecting surfaces (e.g. a refractor with a diagonal). North is at top in both of these charts.

a photograph taken by René Racine of the Université de Montréal, who exposed a 103a-D plate at the f/3.67 focus of the Hale Reflector. The magnitudes are based on work by Racine and Ronald Gilliland of the Space Telescope Science Institute.

Correction for Atmospheric Extinction

Atmospheric extinction varies with altitude above the horizon. To normalize observations to the zenith (altitude 90°), the following values should be added to estimates of faintest visible magnitude obtained using the charts (format: altitude range/**correction**):

18° – 20°/**0.5;** 20° – 24°/**0.4;** 24° – 29°/**0.3;** 29° – 36°/**0.2;** 36° – 52°/**0.1;** 52° – 90°/**0.0**

These corrections are for near sea level and would be reduced at higher elevations. Also, excellent sky conditions are assumed; under less than ideal conditions the corrections are generally larger and can be quite uncertain, especially when the target area is closer to the horizon.

FREQUENCY OF NIGHTTIME CLOUD COVER
By Jay Anderson

APRIL–MAY MEAN NIGHTTIME CLOUD COVER IN PERCENT

The maps on this and the following page are constructed from observations taken from 19 years of satellite observations beginning in 1981. Computer algorithms are used to determine the amount of cloud within a one-degree longitude by one-degree latitude bin for nighttime satellite passages using observations in several infrared wavelengths. The observations suffer from small biases over snow and ice fields and lose some of their reliability at high latitudes in spring. The chart above is an average of April and May observations; that on the following page is for July and August.

In spring the clearest skies can be found in a band stretching from central Mexico north-westward through Arizona and into southern California. In Canada best observing prospects are found over southeast Alberta and southwest Saskatchewan, but the cloud amounts are considerably larger than along the Mexico border. Cloud cover is relatively uniform at Canadian latitudes, a result of the many storm systems that travel along and near the border as warmer weather arrives.

JULY–AUGUST MEAN NIGHTTIME CLOUD COVER IN PERCENT

High cloud frequencies are found along the Atlantic coast, the California shoreline (mostly low cloud and fog), over the higher parts of the Rocky Mountain chain (where cirrus cloudiness is endemic), and, to a lesser extent, over the Appalachians. Resolution of the cloud cover within the narrow valleys of the western mountains is not possible at the scale of the observations, although in April the heavy cloudiness of winter is mostly over.

In July and August the clear springtime skies of the southwestern deserts of the United States give way to an increased cloudiness as the "monsoon season" brings moisture and frequent thunderstorms into Arizona, New Mexico, and Colorado. California's interior retains its reputation as the sunniest location, but clearer skies return to the midwestern plains, extending northward into the Prairie provinces. Almost all regions are clearer than in the April–May chart, although the Appalachians and the Atlantic provinces continue to be among the cloudiest locations. As in the spring, the Cypress Hills area of Alberta and Saskatchewan experiences the most reliable nighttime skies in Canada.

The maps may be used for planning travel to star parties and sunnier climates and to special astronomical events. During April and May, cloud cover is changing rapidly across the centre of the continent, and the average cloudiness shown in the chart at the left is likely too optimistic for April and too pessimistic for May.

STAR-PARTY WEATHER
By Jay Anderson

Have you got a favourite star party? Or do you like to travel from one to another? Here is a set of climatological tables that will let you know how the weather shapes up.

These data are extracted from 20 years of observational data provided by the National Climate Data Center. At each star-party site, the closest location for which cloud-cover data are available was selected, with due regard for similar topographical positioning and climate influences. The tables are a little unfair to some mountain star parties (both on the east and west coast) where the nearest climate station (usually airports) is not particularly close to the star-party site. Some star-party sites and dates also change from year to year, but the most recent information available is included in the tables.

Cloud amounts are observed in eighths of sky cover, known as oktas. "Clear" means no cloud whatsoever. Even the slightest amount will push the observed sky condition to "scattered," defined as 1–4 oktas of cloudiness. "Broken" runs from 5–7 oktas and "overcast" is just that—even the slightest opening in the clouds will turn this category to "broken."

After the month, the first four numbers from left to right, indicate the midnight percentage frequency of the sky being clear, scattered, broken, and overcast. The fifth number (in **bold**) indicates the average cloud cover and is calculated by averaging the frequency of each okta with its corresponding cloud cover.

CANADIAN STAR PARTIES

Name	Location	Month	Clear	Scattered	Broken	Overcast	Average
Tuktoyaktuk Star Party	Tuktoyaktuk, N.W.T.	Jan.	37.6	18.0	13.5	30.9	**46**
Frozen Banana Star Party	Munro Park near Powassan, Ont.	May	28.6	20.8	16.8	33.9	**53**
RASCALS Star Party	Malahat, B.C.	Aug.	30.8	32.1	24.2	13.0	**41**
Rendez-vous des Observateurs du Ciel	Mansonville, Qué.	Jun.	22.0	30.3	22.7	25.0	**51**
Stargazing Manitoulin	Gordon's Park, Manitoulin Island, Ont.	Jul.	29.6	27.9	17.0	25.4	**47**
StarBQ, Eccles Ranch	Caroline, Alta.	Jul.	11.2	44.4	30.0	14.4	**50**
Butterpot Star Party	Butter Pot Prov. Park near St. John's, Nfld.	Jul.	8.9	19.5	19.6	52.0	**73**
Concours Annuel de Fabricants de Téléscopes d'Amateurs	Valleyfield, Qué.	Jul.	18.1	35.5	27.7	18.6	**50**
Astro Atlantik	Mt. Carleton Prov. Park, N.B.	Aug.	41.7	18.8	13.5	26.0	**42**
Manitoulin Star Party	Manitoulin Island, Ont.	Aug.	35.9	26.0	15.7	22.4	**42**
Starfest, River Place Campground	Mount Forest, Ont.	Aug.	22.1	29.8	20.6	27.4	**52**
Saskatchewan Summer Star Party	Cypress Hills, Sask.	Aug.	63.2	19.5	5.3	12.1	**22**
Mt. Kobau Star Party	Mt. Kobau, B.C.	Aug.	34.5	38.7	16.9	10.0	**34**
Nova East	Smileys Prov. Park, Brooklyn, N.S.	Aug.	25.1	23.8	17.6	33.5	**54**
Huronia Star Party	Camp Saulaine, Ivy, Ont.	Sep.	36.5	21.1	17.9	24.5	**44**
Spruce Woods Star Party	Spruce Woods Prov. Park, Man.	Sep.	43.7	22.3	12.8	21.2	**37**

CANADIAN STAR PARTIES (continued)

Name	Location	Month	Midnight percent frequency of...				
			Clear	Scattered	Broken	Overcast	Average
Alberta Star Party	Eccles Ranch, Caroline, Alta.	Sep.	28.7	26.1	21.1	24.2	48
Fall'N'Stars	North of Belleville, Ont.	Sep.	25.0	28.6	19.7	26.7	50
Annual Algonquin Adventure	Algonquin Park, Ont.	Sep.	26.6	26.9	14.1	32.4	51
Northern Prairie Starfest	Black Nugget Lake, Alta.	Sep.	17.2	31.8	28.7	22.3	54
Merritt Star Quest (Fall)	Loon Lake Gravel Pit, Merritt, B.C.	Sep.	41.6	22.7	18.4	17.4	38

AMERICAN STAR PARTIES

Name	Location	Month	Midnight percent frequency of...				
			Clear	Scattered	Broken	Overcast	Average
Deep South Texas Stargaze	Escondido Ranch south of San Antonio, Texas	Jan.	33	11	10	46	57
Cedar Key Winter Star Party	Cedar Key, Fla.	Feb.	41	17	12	30	44
Orange Blossom Special Star Party	Alafia River State Park southeast of Tampa, Fla.	Feb.	36	20	17	27	46
Winter Star Party	Girl Scout Camp Wesumkee, Florida Keys, Fla.	Feb.	30	38	20	12	38
Wagman Winterfest	Deer Lakes Regional Park near Russellton, Pa.	Mar.	23	11	12	54	67
All Arizona Messier Marathon	Farnsworth Ranch near Arizona City, Ariz.	Mar.	53	17	11	20	33
CFAS Astrofest	Seminole Comm. Coll. Star Range near Sanford, Fla.	Mar.	37	20	19	24	44
Kisatchie Star Party	Kisatchie National Forest near Natchitoches, La.	Mar.	36	14	12	38	51
Tennessee Spring Star Party	Fall Creek Falls State Park near Spencer, Tenn.	Mar.	31	11	12	46	58
Death Valley Star Party	Death Valley National Park, Nev.	Mar.-Apr.	58	25	10	7	22
Southern New Mexico Star Party	City of Rocks State Park, N.Mex.	Apr.	56	20	15	10	27
Mid-South Star Gaze	French Camp, Mich.	Apr.	38	16	13	32	47
South Jersey Spring Star Party	Belleplain State Forest, N.J.	Apr.	37	13	12	39	51
Georgia Sky View Party	Indian Springs State Park south of Jackson, Ga.	Apr.	48	13	13	26	40
Riverside Telescope Makers Conference	YMCA Camp Oakes near Big Bear City, Calif.	May	72	16	6	6	15
Northern Arizona Star Party	Prescott, Ariz.	May	59	18	9	11	23
Texas Star Party	Prude Ranch near Fort Davis, Texas	May	54	22	12	12	27
Lake Whitney Star Party	Lake Whitney State Park near Hillsboro, Texas	May	35	21	17	28	47
Desert Sunset Star Party	Three Points, Ariz.	May	71	13	8	8	18
Apollo Rendezvous and Telescope Fair	John Bryan State Park near Yellow Springs, Ohio	Jun.	33	23	17	28	47
North Dakota Star Party	Cross Ranch State Park, N.Dak.	Jun.	29	23	16	32	50
Prineville Reservoir Star Party	Prineville, Ore.	Jun.	36	13	12	39	52

AMERICAN STAR PARTIES (continued)

Name	Location	Month	Clear	Scattered	Broken	Overcast	Average
			Midnight percent frequency of...				
Starconn	Middleton, Conn.	Jun.	27	19	16	38	56
Cherry Springs Star Party	Cherry Springs State Park near Coudersport, Pa.	Jun.	33	20	12	36	51
Grand Canyon Star Party	South Rim, Ariz.	Jun.	65	19	10	5	19
Lowell Star Party	Flagstaff, Ariz.	Jun.	65	19	10	5	19
Wisconsin Observers Weekend (WOW)	Hartman Creek State Park, Wis.	Jun.	38	18	14	30	46
Rocky Mountain Star Stare	Pike's National Forest, Colo.	Jun.	39	24	12	20	36
Craters Star Party	Craters of the Moon National Monument, Idaho	Jun.	38	26	17	19	40
Jersey Starquest	Hope, N.J.	Jun.	34	19	13	19	50
Arkansas Star Party	Devil's Den State Park near Winslow, Ark.	Jul.	56	17	11	16	29
Green Bank Star Quest	Green Bank, W. Va.	Jul.	24	18	22	36	58
Montana Starwatch	Kings Hill, Mont.	Jul.	48	24	16	13	32
Mount Bachelor Star Party	Mount Bachelor Ski Area, Ore.	Jul.	59	9	9	22	32
Nebraska Star Party	Merritt Reservoir, Nebr.	Jul.	43	19	10	28	41
Prairie Grass Stargaze	Jefferson Petroglyphs Historic Site near Jeffers, Minn.	Jul.	38	24	16	23	42
Astronomers Conjunction	Northfield Mountain, Mass.	Jul.	35	18	14	34	50
Table Mountain Star Party	Table Mountain, near Ellensberg, Wash.	Jul.	67	13	10	10	21
Shingletown Star Party	Shingletown, Calif.	Jul.	81	12	5	2	9
Almost Heaven Star Party	southeast of Elkins, W. Va.	Aug.	21	19	20	40	61
Badlands Star Party	North Unit, Theodore Roosevelt National Park, N. Dak.	Aug.	45	25	14	17	34
Weekend Under the Stars	Foxpark west of Laramie, Wyo.	Aug.	39	24	19	18	40
Central Texas Star Party	Canyon of the Eagles Lodge near Burnet, Texas	Aug.	55	22	14	10	27
Indiana Family Star Party	Camp Cullom near Frankfort, Ind.	Aug.	40	21	15	24	42
Northwoods Starfest	Beaver Creek Reserve near Eau Claire, Wis.	Aug.	45	18	13	24	40
Oregon Star Party	Ochoco National Forest, Ore.	Aug.	56	11	9	24	34
Sola Fide Star Party	Austin, Minn.	Aug.	43	19	12	26	41
Stellafane	Breezy Hill, Springfield, Vt.	Aug.	27	20	17	35	55
Astroblast	Two Mile Run County Park, Franklin, Pa.	Sep.	38	19	13	31	46
Astrofest	Kankakee, Ill.	Sep.	36	19	17	28	47
Ark-La-Tex Star Party	west of Nashville, Ark.	Sep.	54	12	9	25	36
Blackwater Falls Astro Weekend	Blackwater Falls State Park, W.Va.	Sep.	33	21	12	34	49
Black Forest Star Party	Cherry Springs State Park, Pa.	Sep.	33	14	11	42	54

AMERICAN STAR PARTIES (continued)

Name	Location	Month	Clear	Scattered	Broken	Overcast	Average
			Midnight percent frequency of...				
Connecticut Star Party	Arunah Hill near near Pittsfield, Mass.	Sep.	33	16	13	39	53
Delmarva No Frills Star Party	Tukahoe State Park near Queen Anne, Md.	Sep.	38	15	13	34	48
Eagles Park Star Party (Fall)	near Montauk State Park, Mo.	Sep.	48	14	11	28	40
Great Lakes Star Gaze	River Valley RV Park, Gladwin, Mich.	Sep.	32	14	14	41	55
Great Plains Star Party	Kansas Astronomy Village south of Kansas City, Kans.	Sep.	49	17	12	23	37
Idaho Star Party	Bruneau Dunes State Park, Idaho	Sep.	57	17	10	16	28
NOVAC Star Gaze	Crockett Park south of Manassas, Va.	Sep.	34	16	14	36	52
Prairie Skies Star Party	Camp Shaw-Waw-Nas-See near Bourbonnais, Ill.	Sep.	45	15	11	30	42
Illinois Dark Skies Star Party	Jim Edgar Panther Creek State Fish and Wildlife Area, Ill.	Sep.	45	16	11	28	41
ScopeOut	Cincinnati, Ohio	Sep.	44	15	12	28	42
South Jersey Fall Star Party	Belle Plain State Forest, N.J.	Sep.	37	19	12	33	47
South Dakota Star Party	near Beresford, S.Dak.	Sep.	44	16	12	28	42
California Star Party (CalStar)	Lake San Antonio, Calif.	Sep.	44	21	14	21	38
Enchanted Skies Star Party	Socorro, N.Mex.	Sep.	53	20	15	13	30
White Sands Star Party	White Sands, N.Mex.	Sep.	40	23	20	17	39
Tennessee Star Party	Camp Nakanawa, Crossville, Tenn.	Sep.	40	21	16	23	42
Astrofest	Vana's Farm near Kankakee, Ill.	Sep.	43	17	11	29	42
All Arizona Star Party	Farnsworth Ranch south of Arizona City, Ariz.	Oct.	66	16	10	9	21
RTMC Nightfall	Palm Canyon Resort, Borrego Springs, Calif.	Oct.	80	9	6	5	12
Mason-Dixon Star Party	Shreveport Airport/Footlight Ranch south of Harrisburg, Pa.	Oct.	42	13	12	34	47
Twin Lakes Star Party	Pennyrile State Forest, Ky.	Oct.	50	10	11	29	40
IC Stars Star Party	IC Stars Ranch near Warrensburg, Mich.	Oct.	53	13	10	25	36
Starry Nights Festival	Yucca Valley, Calif.	Oct.	77	10	8	5	14
Eldorado Star Party	northwest of Sonora, Texas	Oct.	57	16	8	19	30
Mid-Atlantic Star Party (MASP)	near Robbins, S.C.	Oct.	47	12	11	30	42
Okie-Tex Star Party	Kenton, Okla.	Oct.	72	9	7	13	21
Peach State Star Gaze	near Ducktown, Tenn.	Oct.	48	13	10	29	41
Stella-Della-Valley Star Party	Camp Onas near Ottsville, Pa.	Oct.	40	14	11	35	47
Deep South Regional Star Gaze	Camp Ruth Lee north of Baton Rouge, La.	Nov.	47	11	10	33	44
Chiefland Astronomy Village Star Party	Chiefland, Fla.	Nov.	45	16	14	25	40

WEATHER RESOURCES ON THE INTERNET
BY ALLAN RAHILL

Despite public skepticism, weather forecasts are in fact quite accurate, provided they are from informed sources. Specialized weather services—usually involving a fee—are available for aviation, agriculture, forestry, and marine applications. Until recently there was no such service for astronomy, likely because there was no directly related economy. However, the Canada-France-Hawaii Observatory at Mauna Kea has been using a seeing and transparency forecast for more than five years to "queue schedule" observing activities. This marks a new era in which professional observatories are making the best use of weather conditions and changing planned observing activities accordingly.

Similar information has been freely available to amateur and professional astronomers worldwide on the Internet for several years. With light pollution becoming more and more pervasive, amateur astronomers must drive long distances to get to dark skies. They can avoid frustration by using the information and URLs below to plan their observing sessions.

Satellite Images

Many astronomers rely on satellite images to predict nighttime cloud cover. Real-time images are available from GOES satellites for eastern and western America; other satellites such as Meteosat give the same service for Europe and Africa. These satellites give three main types of images: visible, infrared (IR), and water vapour. Visible images are easy to interpret, but they are available only during the day; for nighttime tracking of clouds, IR images are available. Water vapour images do not track clouds; they indicate the total moisture in the air mass. Usually the darkest areas in those images have good correlation with the best sky transparency.

Particularly useful for short-term forecasting are IR satellite loops, which are available at many Web sites. IR images show the radiance emission from Earth and indicate the temperature of the ground and/or clouds. During cold seasons, the ground can be as cold as, if not colder than, the air mass, and single IR satellite images are not very helpful in identifying low-level clouds such as stratocumulus. One way to separate clouds from the ground in these situations is to use a time-lapse loop and look for motion: the ground doesn't move but clouds do. Those in northern latitudes from late fall to early spring should keep this trick in mind.

There are many IR image enhancements available at various Web sites, and you should be aware that many of them do not display *any* low clouds, even with the trick mentioned above. One way to familiarize yourself with low-cloud detection is to compare visible GOES images to IR enhancements in the early morning, when the ground is still cold. In some situations, you may be surprised by the amount of low cloud not displayed in the IR satellite images. By comparing IR and visible images, you can select a Web site that you feel gives accurate images and one that you are comfortable with. I recommend the following Web site for IR satellite images because it provides the ability to zoom into your region, to choose different satellite image enhancements, and to do animation easily:

weather.unisys.com/satellite/sat_ir_hem.html

To make the best use of weather satellite images, you also should be aware of the behaviour of certain types of cloud. Low-level clouds such as stratus usually develop locally and generally move much more slowly than high clouds. These clouds appear during the night and usually get burned off by the Sun during the day. Coastal regions will usually see the low clouds moving inland in the evening and out to sea in the morning.

In addition, cumulus, towering cumulus, and cumulonimbus clouds arise with daytime convective heating if the air mass is unstable. The depth or height of the cloud structure is related to the level of instability and can reach up to 20 000 m for severe thunderstorms. On satellite loops, these clouds appear as clear areas that are gradually filled with clouds during the day and that slowly vanish in the evening. In the summer, some of the most unstable cumulonimbus clouds will survive at night. Even though thunderstorms, associated with cumulonimbus clouds, can be far from your location, cirrus blowoff from these cells may reach you quite quickly, depending on the upper wind direction, and thus ruin your observing session. Satellite and radar loops are good ways to keep track of these thunderstorm lines.

Radar

Remote-controlled observatories, where the operator is not physically present, and star parties, where telescopes are often left set up and exposed, are becoming more popular. When the sky conditions are variable, there is one common worry: is there a fast-moving precipitation band approaching the observing site? The best way to track precipitation in the short term is with radar. The radar network is extensive across the United States; it also covers populated regions of Canada.

Radar images require careful interpretation. During the night, the air cools near the ground and creates a temperature inversion. On some nights with strong inversions, radar signals are refracted, or bent, toward the ground and scattered back to the radar, thus appearing as precipitation on the graphical displays. Similar situations occur in mountainous areas, where higher terrain interrupts the radar signal. A radar loop will help you distinguish these areas: sometimes they are nearly motionless; at other times they shift around in a chaotic jumble. Precipitation moves in a smoother fashion, at times linearly. The best Web sites for access to radar loops for Canada and the United States, respectively, are:

www.weatheroffice.ec.gc.ca/radar/index_e.html
www.intellicast.com (click on "radar")

Weather Forecasts for Astronomy

Cloud Forecasts: Local media and television "experts" cannot always be relied upon when conditions are uncertain. Usually their forecasts cover a large area, and the weather can be quite different within the region. Also, for most people, including many local weather forecasters, skies are considered clear despite thin, high cloudiness that may interfere with observing.

The best forecasts for clouds are from the direct output of numerical models. Weather models are not perfect, but they are surprisingly good at capturing local effects and predicting cloud formation and dissipation. The biggest problem with numerical forecasting is convection (thunderstorms): it is like trying to predict the next bubble in boiling water. Complex thunderstorm cells can be forecast much farther away than they actually appear, leading to poor cloud progression forecasts for regions hundreds of kilometres ahead.

Some weather channels and Web sites use animated forecasts to show cloud progression for the next day, but these animations generally have low resolution and are not very useful for astronomy. The only North American high-resolution cloud forecast I still know of is produced at the Canadian Meteorological Centre (CMC):

www.weatheroffice.ec.gc.ca/astro/clds_vis_e.html

Occasionally, especially in the fall when low clouds (stratocumulus) are omnipresent, a weather balloon can be launched into a cloud hole, and the resulting cloud forecast may be too optimistic for the surrounding regions. To avoid a bad forecast, always compare the cloud cover forecast with the latest satellite picture. In these situations, an old forecast may be a better choice. This is why the most recent old forecast, in addition to the current forecast, is available at this Web site; hourly forecasts are now available.

Sky Transparency Forecasts: For deep-sky observing, sky transparency is critical because it largely determines how dark the sky will be. Aerosols—particles suspended in the atmosphere—and moisture reduce sky transparency and brighten the sky by diffusing the light in the sky. Aerosols include volcanic ash, pollen, sea salts, and smoke from forest fires. Spectacular examples of events that introduced aerosols into the atmosphere are the Mount St. Helens volcanic eruption, which spread roughly 109 tonnes of ash into the atmosphere in 1980, and the more recent large forest fires: in summer 2003 over British Columbia, which spread smoke over large areas, and in 2002 in northern Québec, which spread smoke over all of northeastern North America. Specialized weather numerical models handle aerosol phenomena; Web sites that track aerosol envelopes with up to five-day forecasts across the world are:

jwocky.gsfc.nasa.gov
www.nrlmry.navy.mil/aerosol/#currentaerosolmodeling

Moisture is the only weather element affecting sky transparency that can be forecast with confidence. For many northern-latitude residents, moisture is the most important contributor to reduced sky transparency; despite clear skies, very often high-level ice crystals (extremely thin clouds) are present and can be seen only at sunset and sunrise. In addition, moisture from open waters, vegetation (evapo-transpiration), or moist soil can keep the low-level atmosphere humid.

Over the years, I have compared water-vapour satellite images to various observers' estimates of background sky brightness. The resulting hourly sky transparency forecasts can be found at:

www.weatheroffice.ec.gc.ca/astro/transparence_e.html

There is a good correlation between the darkest areas in water-vapour images and the darkest observed sky conditions. There are some cases where the sky background is brighter than expected due to moisture trapped by a temperature inversion. Based on this observation and others, the forecasts in the previous Web site emphasize humidity near the surface and also near the tropopause (cirrus heights).

Seeing Forecasts: Seeing conditions determine the steadiness of images through a telescope and are relevant for planetary as well as deep-sky observing. When highest resolution is necessary for planetary imaging or visual observing, seeing should be at its best.

Conditions are favourable when the atmosphere is turbulence-free all across the path of the light. The best weather pattern is weak wind circulation at all levels. These conditions occur more frequently over the southeastern United States than any other region of North America, with Atlantic Canada generally having the worst conditions among populated North American regions. Canadian and U.S. central prairies often experience blocking weather systems that give weak upper wind circulation and excellent seeing conditions.

Another pattern for excellent seeing takes place when moderate winds blow from the same direction at all levels, that is, when horizontal and vertical wind shear are weak at all levels. In other words, no jet stream (strong winds reaching 200 km/h–400 km/h at an altitude of 10 km–12 km) or sudden shifts or increase in wind speed with height are present.

At locations downwind from mountains when winds are moderate, it is best to be far away from the mountains, since "gravity waves"—vertical air-mass oscillations caused by the mountains—can downgrade seeing. In general, topography is quite important because rough terrain increases the wind shear in the low-level atmosphere, due to friction and gravity waves.

Temperature variation at the surface also plays a role in seeing conditions. Nights of excellent wind conditions as described above may nevertheless have marginal seeing. On such nights, temperatures quickly and steadily fall, and large telescopes have trouble cooling at the same rate as the surrounding air. This creates what is called "local seeing": thermal heat released from the optics (despite good ventilation) ruins the seeing despite the excellent weather pattern. The opposite is also true: the best planetary observations with a large telescope often take place just before thick clouds roll in or when looking through thin cirrostratus cloud. Under these conditions the temperature usually rises a few degrees before the clouds appear. Thin cirrostratus clouds usually keep the temperature steady, eliminating any negative local seeing effects. Thin clouds also play the role of a neutral-density filter, increasing fine detail and contrast on bright planets. Ground fog can also be associated with excellent seeing conditions (until the fog thickens) if you can keep your optics dry.

Predicting favourable seeing conditions requires the ability to interpret weather charts, something that is difficult for most observers to do. The Canadian weather service now has a seeing forecast, available at their astro-weather Web site, which attempts to simulate wind shears, topography, and temperature effects:

www.weatheroffice.ec.gc.ca/astro/seeing_e.html

Some Tips to Get the Most Out of Your Telescope: "Local seeing" is the term used to describe the effects of heat radiating from the components of a telescope (e.g. its optics) or from the immediate surroundings (e.g. observatory walls and floor, trees, flowing water, neighbouring houses). If the local seeing is bad, the telescopic viewing will be significantly deteriorated. However, in contrast to atmospheric seeing, the effects of local seeing can be controlled.

Tube currents in particular will dramatically deteriorate telescopic images. Mirror-type instruments are more sensitive to such currents than refractors. Large mirrors can take hours to cool down during the night and in fact may never reach full thermal equilibrium. However, the amateur astronomer can accelerate the cooling of the primary mirror by installing one or more battery-type fans behind it. Their use will cool down the mirror to near the ambient temperature in one or two hours. Another approach is to use a high quality but thin primary mirror. Many manufacturers offer 1-inch-thick mirror blanks for mirror diameters up to 16″, in addition to the traditional 2-3-inch-thick mirrors. The thinner mirrors will reach thermal equilibrium 2-3 times faster[*] than the thicker ones. Many amateurs also ventilate the front of their primary mirror with two fans placed on either side of the mirror, separated by 180°. One fan pulls air into the tube while the other pushes it out. Such ventilation has two benefits: it breaks up the thermal boundary layer near the mirror surface (and therefore reduces convective-type turbulence) and it cools the mirror up to 50% more quickly than without the fans[*].

The popular Schmidt-Cassegrain telescopes do not come with cooling fans and they are known to suffer from internal turbulence, especially at large apertures. Only a few advanced amateur astronomers will have the courage to add fans to those telescopes. Any telescope, and particularly the Schmidt-Cassegrain type, should always be brought outside to cool it down at least two hours before the observing session. Better yet is to keep a telescope permanently outside in a backyard observatory.

To minimize the occurrence of poor local seeing, one must avoid all potential sources of heat in the surroundings. For example, concrete structures and buildings or

---

[*]*Sky and Telescope,* June 2004, page 124 (Improving the Thermal Properties of Newtonian Reflectors - Part 2)

houses have the capacity to retain daytime heat and then release it during the night. Even trees during the growing season can release heat at night, and so deteriorate the local seeing for astronomical objects found just above their canopy. Ideally, the amateur should choose an environment free from all these elements. If you are lucky enough to have an observatory, then remember that all the outside walls must be white, since even pale colours will allow the walls to heat up during the day and then create local seeing problems when they release the heat at night.

The local geography can also be used to one's advantage: observing can be better at the top of a hill than at its base. It appears that the local seeing is improved at the top of a hill, due to nighttime katabatic winds that drain air down the slope of the hill to its base. This means that air above the hill must also move downward to replace the air that moved away. This descent creates a dry subsidence inversion which, combined with the cool surface temperature at the top of the hill, stabilizes the air locally. This results in good seeing. Many of my best planetary observations took place on hill tops.

One final tip: near dusk and dawn, if you can spot planets, then there will often be a 20-60 minute window during which the seeing will be one or two notches better than during the night. This seems to be related to large scale tidal motions in the atmosphere that create more stable conditions at those times, but the effect is not well understood. Give it a try in the early morning and the early evening.

The Clear Sky Clock

The Canadian Meteorological Centre's numerical weather forecasts, given in the URLs above, are unique because they are specifically designed for astronomers. In June 2005, these forecasts became official; they can be found in the weather map section of the Environment Canada Web site:

www.weatheroffice.ec.gc.ca/canada_e.html

We took this opportunity to add a few more products for the astronomy community. We added hourly humidity, temperature, and wind forecast images. However, they include 842 forecast images per day, covering all of North America, so it can be a chore to find the one you want. All the above weather forecasts for astronomy can be viewed at a glance for any particular observing site in North America using Attila Danko's excellent Clear Sky Clock:

www.cleardarksky.com/csk

Editor's Note: Attila Danko, a member of the Ottawa Centre of the Royal Astronomical Society of Canada, received the Ken Chilton Prize from the Society in 2005 for his creation of the Clear Sky Clock, which uses the Canadian Meteorological Centre's forecasts for astronomers created by Allan Rahill. Most popular observing locations in North America now have an associated Clock, and many amateur astronomers rely on these forecasts to plan their observing sessions.

POLAR ALIGNMENT
BY RAJIV GUPTA

The charts for the north and south celestial poles on the next pages can be used to align an equatorial mount in either the northern or southern hemisphere. To polar align a mount, that is, to point the polar axis of the mount at the corresponding celestial pole, select a telescope/eyepiece combination for which you know, or have carefully measured, the diameter of the field of view. Depending on the accuracy required (see below), you can use the finderscope, guidescope, or main telescope. Point the chosen telescope in the same direction as the mount's polar axis. Simply adjusting the mount's declination until the setting circle reads 90° is not sufficient; instead, rotate the mount 180° in RA, and check whether the field rotates in the eyepiece without shifting. If not, make adjustments in declination until the amount of shift is minimal. To reduce the shift to an acceptable level, you may have to make further, one-time transverse adjustments, leaving the declination fixed. For example, on a German equatorial mount, shims can be inserted between a mounting ring and the mounting plate.

Next, using one of the charts, adjust the mount's altitude and azimuth so that the starfield seen in the eyepiece is centred at the pole. Circles corresponding to various field diameters are indicated on both charts; you can draw a circle corresponding to your own exact field size using a compass if you prefer.

Precise polar alignment is necessary for long-exposure photography; otherwise, the stars will be elongated as a result of "field rotation." With good guiding on a system that is free of mechanical flexure, the guidestar will remain stationary on the film or imaging CCD chip. However, because of polar misalignment, all other stars will trace tiny arcs about the guidestar. The length of a particular star's arc a depends upon the amount of polar misalignment p (in arcminutes), the length of the exposure t (in hours), the distance d (in millimetres) in the imaging plane between the star and the guidestar, the declination of the guidestar δ (in degrees), and the geometrical circumstances of the exposure. An approximate formula for a (in μm (microns)), assuming the worst possible geometry, is

$$a \approx ptd/(14 \cos \delta).$$

For example, with $p = 5'$, $t = 1$ h, $d = 20$ mm, and $\delta = 20°$, we have $a \approx 7.6$ μm. You can use this formula to determine the value of p needed to keep a within a specified tolerance (such as 10 μm, a good target for high-resolution imaging), and then achieve the required polar-alignment accuracy using the above method. For example, to keep a under 5 μm with $t = 30$ min (0.5 h), $d = 20$ mm, and $\delta = 60°$, the required accuracy is $p \approx (5)(14)(\cos 60°)/(0.5)(20) = 3.5'$. If you need very high polar-alignment accuracy, you may want to shift the mount down by the amount of atmospheric refraction at the altitude of the pole (see p. 30 for some values of atmospheric refraction), so that the mount is aligned on the true pole instead of the refracted pole.

An alternative method for precise polar alignment is the *star drift method,* which involves alternately detecting the drift in declination of two stars near the celestial equator, one near transit and the other rising in the east, and making azimuth and altitude adjustments accordingly. In the northern hemisphere, if the first star drifts north, the mount's axis is pointing west of the true pole; if it drifts south the axis is east of the pole. Also, if the second star drifts north, the axis is pointing too high; if it drifts south the axis is too low. For the southern hemisphere, interchange "north" and "south" in the previous two sentences. The amount of misalignment p (in arcminutes) in terms of the amount of drift d (in arcseconds) and the length of time t the star is observed (in minutes) is given by

$$p \approx 3.8d/t.$$

For example, if a star drifts 10″ in 5 min, the misalignment is $\approx$7.6′; a rate of drift of 1″/min corresponds to a misalignment of $\approx$3.8′.

CHARTS FOR THE NORTH CELESTIAL POLE

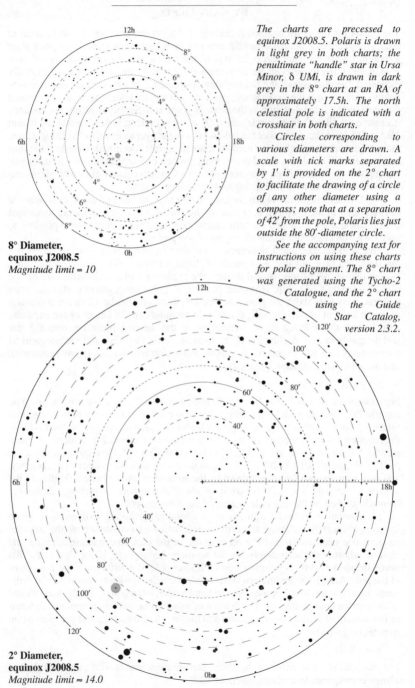

**8° Diameter,
equinox J2008.5**
Magnitude limit = 10

The charts are precessed to equinox J2008.5. Polaris is drawn in light grey in both charts; the penultimate "handle" star in Ursa Minor, δ UMi, is drawn in dark grey in the 8° chart at an RA of approximately 17.5h. The north celestial pole is indicated with a crosshair in both charts.

Circles corresponding to various diameters are drawn. A scale with tick marks separated by 1′ is provided on the 2° chart to facilitate the drawing of a circle of any other diameter using a compass; note that at a separation of 42′ from the pole, Polaris lies just outside the 80′-diameter circle.

See the accompanying text for instructions on using these charts for polar alignment. The 8° chart was generated using the Tycho-2 Catalogue, and the 2° chart using the Guide Star Catalog, version 2.3.2.

**2° Diameter,
equinox J2008.5**
Magnitude limit ≈ 14.0

CHARTS FOR THE SOUTH CELESTIAL POLE

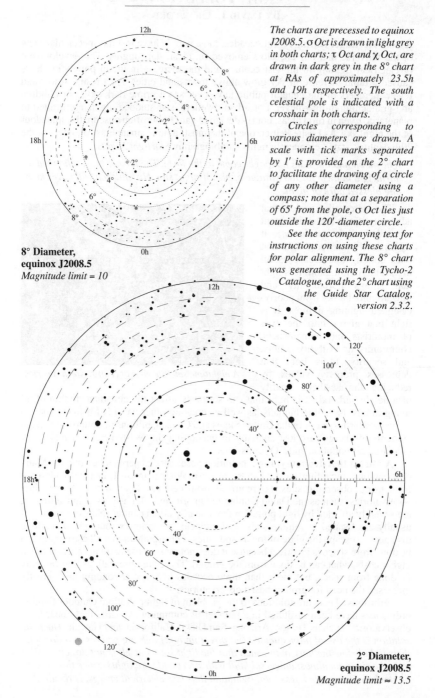

The charts are precessed to equinox J2008.5. σ Oct is drawn in light grey in both charts; τ Oct and χ Oct, are drawn in dark grey in the 8° chart at RAs of approximately 23.5h and 19h respectively. The south celestial pole is indicated with a crosshair in both charts.

Circles corresponding to various diameters are drawn. A scale with tick marks separated by 1′ is provided on the 2° chart to facilitate the drawing of a circle of any other diameter using a compass; note that at a separation of 65′ from the pole, σ Oct lies just outside the 120′-diameter circle.

See the accompanying text for instructions on using these charts for polar alignment. The 8° chart was generated using the Tycho-2 Catalogue, and the 2° chart using the Guide Star Catalog, version 2.3.2.

8° Diameter,
equinox J2008.5
Magnitude limit = 10

2° Diameter,
equinox J2008.5
Magnitude limit ≈ 13.5

LIGHT POLLUTION
By David L. Crawford

A Lost Heritage: During recent decades, most people have lost the spectacular view of the universe that our ancestors enjoyed on clear, dark nights. The development of electrical lighting in the last century and the increase in urban population have caused a rapid increase in sky glow above towns and cities. As a result, fewer and fewer members of the general public have ever see a prime dark sky; our children and grandchildren may never. For urban dwellers, star-studded nights are limited to planetaria. Even in rural areas, poorly designed yard lights often obscure the splendour of the night sky. As Leslie Peltier, one of the most famous amateur astronomers of the 20th century, stated eloquently in his autobiography *Starlight Nights:*

> *The moon and the stars no longer come to the farm. The farmer has exchanged his birthright in them for the wattage of his all-night sun. His children will never know the blessed dark of night.*

The increased sky glow that adversely affects the environment is called *light pollution;* it originates from excess light that does nothing to increase useful nighttime illumination. It is light that sprays horizontally and upward into the sky from poorly-designed lighting fixtures. It is light that glares into the eyes of motorists and homeowners, compromising visibility, safety, and security. It is light that depresses property values by reducing the aesthetic quality

A nighttime satellite view of central North America

of a neighbourhood. It is light that can seriously affect the circadian rhythm of all living things, including humans, as well as creating other hazards for many species (birds, sea turtles, etc.). In the United States and Canada, billions of dollars (plus large amounts of energy) are lost annually in generating this wasted light. It makes for increased air pollution and CO_2 emissions.

A Threat to Astronomy: Light pollution poses special perils to astronomy. Many observations, including most of those of cosmological interest, can be made only from prime observing sites, far removed from centres of population. Some older observatories, such as the David Dunlap in Ontario and Mount Wilson in California, are severely affected by light pollution from nearby urban centres. New observatories usually are located at remote sites, and amateur astronomers routinely drive long distances to escape the glare of towns and cities. The argument that all astronomy can be done from space is incorrect because it does not make sense to do in space, at much higher costs, what can be done from the ground. There are observations that can only be done from space, but more than three decades of space astronomy have greatly increased the need for ground-based observatories.

Solutions: There are solutions to the problem of light pollution: Outdoor lighting ordinances have been instituted in a number of communities, particularly near large observatories, such as Tucson, Arizona, San Diego, California, and Hawaii. *The main solution is the use of fully-shielded (no direct uplight) lighting fixtures that direct all their light below the horizontal, such that the light source itself is not directly visible from the side—an almost universal fault with street and yard lights. Since this puts the light where it is needed, less total light, and thus less electrical energy, is required.*

Inefficient street lighting

The light source makes a difference too; it should be an energy-efficient lamp. Quite a few cities worldwide are realizing substantial savings each year through extensive use of low-pressure sodium (LPS) street lighting. For example, replacing a 175-W mercury-vapour lighting fixture with a fully-shielded, 35-W LPS fixture can get the same amount of useful light, and with none of the glare and light trespass. The energy saving is remarkable, as is the better visibility. In addition to providing light at the lowest cost, LPS lights are nearly monochromatic, with the result that most of their light can be filtered out by astronomers. Low-pressure-sodium lights are especially good for street lighting, parking lot lighting, security lighting, and any application where colour rendering is not important.

Common Types of Outdoor Lights
(in increasing order of efficiency)

Type	Power (W/klm)
incandescent (ordinary bulbs)	60
mercury vapour (violet-white light)	24
metal halide (white)	17
high-pressure sodium (orange-gold)	12
low-pressure sodium (yellow)	8

A full-cutoff, efficient light fixture

Even less light pollution and more savings can be realized by using *no more light than is required, and ordinances usually regulate the maximum amount of light that can be used for different tasks.* Too much light and/or poorly shielded lights can ruin adaptation to night lighting, blinding us just when we need to see. When we go from too bright to too dark or vice versa, "transient adaptation" is impaired, and we have poor visibility for a while. Do not exceed IESNA (Illuminating Engineering Society of North America, www.iesna.org) recommended lighting levels. Overkill never helps; it usually just adds glare, and it always wastes energy. In addition, lights should be used only when necessary (timers are useful for controlling lights). Curfews are usually also included in lighting ordinances. IDA, with the help of IESNA and others, has produced a Model Lighting Ordinance as a help for communities wanting more effective and efficient night lighting.

Another common inclusion in lighting ordinances is the use of lighting zones. Different areas have different requirements for lighting; downtown Toronto is not the same as rural Ontario. In addition, some locales have officially declared themselves to be a Dark-Sky Preserve, a region where lighting is strictly controlled or prohibited. A number of these are located in Canada, and the RASC has been instrumental in helping establish these.

Increased lighting generally gives a perception of greater security, yet there is no statistically significant evidence that more lighting results in less crime. Criminals need light. "Security lights" provide this. Furthermore, security lights may draw attention to a house or business that would otherwise not be noticed and mask any additional light that criminals may need to do their work. Our cities and towns are far more brightly lit than ever, yet there has been little or no reduction in the crime rate. We just see more and more bright and glary lights. Security can best be provided by shielded, motion-activated lights that come on only when triggered by movement nearby. These serve to frighten criminals, alert others that there is a potential problem, and provide glare-free visibility (when properly installed so they are glare-free); they also use insignificant amounts of energy.

Lack of Awareness: The biggest problem in controlling light pollution is lack of awareness rather than resistance. After all, it costs money to light pollute! Unlike the case with many other forms of pollution, simple solutions are available; moreover, *everyone benefits* in applying these solutions. Most people are not yet aware of the expense, the waste, and the harm associated with excess lighting. They put up with distant lights that shine directly into their eyes, not realizing that not only does this do *nothing* to illuminate the area near the light but that it also produces a veiling glare. The pollution usually involves not only the light itself but also other forms of environmental pollution associated with the production of the wasted light: the extraction, transportation, and burning of coal and oil. This general lack of awareness has been summarized nicely by Doug Pitcairn, an astronomy teacher in Nova Scotia:

> *It surprises me how someone who would never think of leaving a plastic bottle on the ground at a picnic site will pay extra money each month to illuminate half the neighbourhood with unnecessary, distracting light.*

Education: Educating the public, government officials, lighting professionals, and astronomers is a major thrust of current programs. These efforts have helped. Most committees in the IESNA and the International Commission on Illumination (CIE) have been addressing these issues, and Recommended Practices and other documents reflect these concerns. As they are issued, one will see them implemented, albeit on a slow time schedule. Astronomers and environmentalists should do all they can to both learn from these documents and to help publicize them and thereby get them into existing practices in our communities.

The International Dark-Sky Association (IDA) has many information sheets available to assist you in educating others — in several languages in addition to English and French — and can provide examples of lighting policies that have been enacted in man communities to enforce high-quality, effective nighttime lighting. For up-to-date information, stay tuned to the IDA Web site and newsletter.

About the International Dark-Sky Association: The IDA is a tax-exempt, nonprofit membership organization dedicated to overcoming this awareness problem. Its goal is to preserve dark skies while at the same time maximizing the quality and efficiency of nighttime outdoor lighting. The IDA needs your help. Membership begins at $30 U.S. per year. To join this effort or to obtain further information on any aspect of the issue, contact the International Dark-Sky Association, 3225 N First Ave, Tucson AZ 85719, USA (phone: (520) 293-3198; fax: (520) 293-3192; email: ida@darksky.org; Web site: www.darksky.org). Plenty of useful information is on the Web site, including images, and content is added regularly. .

Within Canada: The Royal Astronomical Society of Canada has an active Light-Pollution Abatement Committee. See rasc.ca/committees/lpa.shtml to learn about the committee or to contact the chair of the committee. You may also contact the RASC directly (see p. 10). Also, some Centres of the RASC have light-pollution abatement committees and have taken action to address poor lighting practices in their areas.

Editor's Note: The IDA has members in over 70 countries, and its total membership is over 11 000 (with about 250 from Canada). Of these, about 600 are organizational members and about 200 are individual lifetime members. This is still well less than 10% of the community of amateur and professional astronomers. As Daniel Green of the Smithsonian Astrophysical Observatory has put it (see *Sky & Telescope,* May 1998, p. 10): "Where are all the astronomers?" Anyone who values the night sky should support this unique and deserving organization. *You* can help make a difference. Please do!

DEEP-SKY OBSERVING HINTS
BY ALAN DYER

In the 1960s and 1970s, few observers owned telescopes larger than 200-mm aperture. Today, 250-mm to 600-mm Dobsonian-mounted reflectors are commonplace. Using computerized telescopes, observers can now find thousands of objects at the push of a button. As a result, deep-sky observing has soared in popularity.

However, owners of less sophisticated, small-aperture instruments shouldn't think they are shut out of deep-sky viewing. In a dark sky an 80-mm to 100-mm telescope will show all the Messier objects and reveal hundreds of brighter NGC (New General Catalogue) objects. In fact, many large objects are best seen in fast (f/4 to f/6), small-aperture telescopes or in giant 70-mm and 80-mm binoculars. Contrary to popular belief, even slow f-ratio instruments (f/11 to f/16) are useful; their only disadvantage is the difficulty of achieving a low-power wide field. No matter what telescope you use, follow these techniques to get the most out of a night's deep-sky viewing:

- Always plan each night's observing: Prepare a list of a dozen or so objects for the night. Hunt them down on star charts or with computer programs first during the day to become familiar with their location.
- Seek out dark skies; a black sky improves contrast and makes up for lack of aperture.
- To preserve night vision, always use a dim red flashlight for reading charts.
- Avoid prolonged exposure to bright sunlight earlier in the day (such as a day at the beach); it will reduce your ability to dark adapt and make for tired eyes at night.
- Use averted vision; looking to one side of an object places it on a more sensitive part of the retina.
- Another technique for picking out faint objects is to jiggle the telescope (and the image) slightly.
- Don't be afraid to use high power; it often brings out small, faint objects such as planetary nebulae and galaxies and resolves detail in globulars, in small, rich open clusters, and in bright galaxies.
- Use a nebular filter on emission and planetary nebulae (see the section FILTERS on pp. 66–69); even in a dark sky, filters can dramatically enhance the view of these kinds of objects, often making obvious an otherwise elusive nebula.
- Be comfortable; sit down while at the eyepiece and be sure to dress warmly.
- Collimate and clean your optics; a poorly maintained telescope will produce distorted star images, reduce image contrast, and make it more difficult to see faint stars and other threshold objects.
- Don't expect to use analog setting circles; in a portable telescope "dial-type" circles will rarely be accurate.
- Digital setting circles and Go To telescopes can find objects precisely. While they are wonderful observing aids, they can overwhelm observers with thousands of targets, often supplying scant information about each one. When making a list for a night's viewing, books such as the three-volume *Burnham's Celestial Handbook* and the two-volume *Night Sky Observer's Guide* by Keppel and Sanner are still the best guides.
- Don't be in a rush to check off targets; take time to examine each object, and take notes or make drawings. Both will help train your eye to see subtle detail; you'll learn to see the most through your telescope.
- Consider keeping a logbook or journal of your nightly tours of the sky; including eyepiece impressions and drawings provides a record of your improving observing skills that is fun to look back upon in future years. See the section THE OBSERVING LOGBOOK (immediately following) for suggestions on organizing a journal.

THE OBSERVING LOGBOOK
By Paul Markov

There are many good reasons for maintaining an observing logbook: A logbook is useful for recalling the details of previous observations and comparing past observations with current ones; maintaining one will make your observing organized and methodical; and having to describe an object forces you to *look* for more details, thus sharpening your observing skills. Finally, if you are planning to apply for an observing certificate (e.g. the RASC's Explore the Universe, Messier, or Finest NGC Certificate; see p. 286), then a logbook with your observations may be required when submitting your application.

Logbooks can be chronological or sectional. In a chronological logbook all observations are listed sequentially by date, regardless of object type. In a sectional logbook observations are grouped by object type, such as open clusters and galaxies. With either format, you may want to keep a master index of objects for cross referencing to the correct page in your logbook.

What about the book itself? Typical choices are the simple three-ring binder with standard lined paper, spiral bound notebooks, and hardcover record/accounting books. In my opinion, the most practical is the three-ring binder because it allows you to insert auxiliary materials into your logbook with the help of a three-hole punch. With this choice, entering observations out of sequence is never an issue because you can easily rearrange the sheets. Also, should you wish to make a copy of your logbook for safekeeping, it's much easier with loose sheets.

For recording observations, using a preprinted observing form offers these advantages: the fill-in-the-blank fields remind you to record the relevant data; many of these forms have a space for making a drawing of the observed object; and they give your book a neat and organized look. An example of an observing form can be found at www.rasc.ca/handbook/obsform.pdf; you may prefer to design your own observing form by using the fields suggested below. However, you can also use plain lined paper: you will never have to worry about running out of forms, and you will not need different forms for different types of objects.

There are two choices for recording your observations: using full sentences and using acronyms and abbreviations. Using full sentences is the preferred method if you enjoy re-reading your observations from past years, or if you want others to be able to easily read your logbook. But if your intent is to keep a data book for reference purposes only, then acronyms and abbreviations are the recommended choices.

It is useful to record the following information for each observing session: date; time of arrival and departure (if you have travelled somewhere to observe); location; names of other people at the observing site; sky transparency (i.e. clarity of the atmosphere, which is generally noted by faintest visible stellar magnitude; see pp. 70–71); seeing (i.e. the steadiness of the atmosphere: if stars and planets appear to shimmer, that indicates poor seeing; if they appear sharp and steady, that indicates good seeing), and environmental conditions (e.g. temperature, dew, wind, sources of light pollution, snow cover, and mosquitoes). You can also number each observing session sequentially for easy referencing within your logbook.

Be sure to standardize your time/date format. For recording time, choose either the military time or a.m./p.m. format. In addition, use alpha characters to specify the month rather than numbers. For example, use 2008 Aug. 5 instead of 8/5/2008; this will avoid ambiguity in reading the date.

For each object observed, record the following information as a minimum: date and time of observation, object name or designation, type of object, constellation, telescope and magnification used, type of filter (if any), and visual description. Making drawings is highly recommended and adds substantially to the appearance of your logbook. It is also important to record failed observations because these entries will remind you to try again in your next observing session.

If you are able to write neatly while observing, it is best to enter observations directly into your logbook. However, if this proves too difficult given the environmental circumstances, you can record your observations in a temporary notebook and transcribe them into your logbook the next day. An audio recorder can also be used if you are careful to ensure its mechanical integrity while in the field and if you are diligent enough to transcribe the recorded observations into your observing logbook regularly. Below are some suggestions on what to look for when observing deep-sky objects.

All Object Types: What is the shape of the object? What is its size (based on the field of view of your eyepiece)? Is averted vision required to see the object? Does averted vision allow you to see more detail? (If yes, describe the extra detail.) Is the object near (or in the same field of view as) other deep-sky objects or bright stars? What magnification gives the best view of the object? Does a filter improve the view? (See the section FILTERS on pp. 66–69.)

Open Cluster: Is there a greater concentration of stars in a specific part of the cluster? Is it fully resolved into its component stars, or are there any unresolved stars causing the cluster to appear nebulous? How many stars can you see (only if reasonable to count them)? Are there any bright stars within the cluster? Are there any coloured stars? (If so, describe their tints and locations within the cluster.) Does the cluster stand out from the background star field?

Globular Cluster: What is the degree of star concentration (high, medium, low)? How much can be resolved to component stars (none, outer edges, middle, to the core)?

Galaxy: Is it uniform in brightness, or does it have a brighter nucleus? Is it diffuse or stellar? Can any detail or mottling be seen in the arms? Are there any stars visible within the arms?

Emission or Reflection Nebula: Is the brightness even, or are there brighter/darker areas? Are the edges of the nebula well defined? Are there any stars within the nebula? Is there a hint of any colour?

Planetary Nebula: Is it stellar in appearance, or can a disk be seen? Are the edges well defined or diffuse? Are there any brighter/darker areas? Can a central star be seen? Is there a hint of any colour?

Dark Nebula: Is it easy or difficult to discern the dark nebula from the background sky? Are there any stars within the nebula?

Logbooks and Databases

If you enjoy using computers, an electronic database can be a helpful complement to an observing logbook. You can obtain commercially available deep-sky databases that allow you to enter your own observations for any object. These databases are also useful for creating observing lists and planning observing sessions. A highly recommended database, which also happens to be freeware, is the Saguaro Astronomy Club (SAC) deep-sky database, available at **www.saguaroastro.org**. With minimal tweaking, the SAC database can be formatted to accept your own observations.

You can transcribe complete observations from your logbook into the database or simply enter four valuable pieces of information for each observed object: seen (Y/N), date, telescope used, and location. With these fields filled in, in a matter of seconds you can determine which and how many objects you have observed, and the date field for any object will direct you to the correct page in your observing logbook. You can also determine interesting facts such as from which observing location you observed the most objects or which telescope produced the most observations.

THE SKY MONTH BY MONTH

LEFT-HAND PAGES BY
DAVID LANE (TABLES) AND ALAN WHITMAN (TEXT)

INTRODUCTION

In the descriptions on the left-hand monthly pages (pp. 96–118), the right ascension (**RA**), declination (**Dec**) (both for equinox J2000.0), distance from Earth's centre in astronomical units (**Dist**), visual magnitude (**Mag**), and equatorial angular diameter (**Size**) are tabulated for seven planets for 0h UT on the 1st, 11th, and 21st day of each month. The RA, Dec, distance, and diameter of the Sun are also given. **Any stated planet visibility times are in local mean time, which may differ significantly from standard or Daylight Saving Time (see pp. 44, 48).** "Northern observers" and "southern observers" are assumed to be at latitudes 45°N and 30°S, respectively. Unless otherwise stated, descriptions are given first for northern observers and then for southern observers. AT refers to astronomical twilight, NT to nautical twilight, and CT to civil twilight (see p. 200).

Sun

Data concerning the position, transit, orientation, rotation, and activity of the Sun plus times of sunrise and sunset appear on pp. 178–184 and 195–197. For detailed information on this year's solar eclipses, see ECLIPSES IN 2008 on pp. 124–143.

Moon

Conjunctions of the Moon with the naked-eye planets and the bright Messier objects that lie near the ecliptic — the Beehive Cluster (M44), the Lagoon Nebula (M8), M35, and the Pleiades Cluster (M45) — are given in the right-hand monthly tables (pp. 97–119). Only events for which the elongation of the Moon is at least 14° are included, and only selected such events involving the Messier objects are listed. See p. 20 for the definition of conjunction and elongation.

The Moon's phases and perigees and apogees (distances from *Astronomical Tables of the Sun, Moon, and Planets,* by Jean Meeus, 2nd ed., Willmann-Bell, 1995) are also given in the right-hand tables. The phases new Moon, first quarter, full Moon, and last quarter correspond, respectively, to the Moon having a longitude 0°, 90°, 180°, and 270° east of that of the Sun. The age of the Moon is the time since the new phase; first quarter, full, and last quarter phases correspond approximately to 7.4, 14.8, and 22.1 days, respectively. For times of moonrise and moonset, see pp. 151–157.

The Sun's selenographic colongitude (SSC), given on the left-hand monthly pages, indicates the position of the sunrise terminator as it moves across the face of the Moon and provides a method of ascertaining the angle of illumination of features on the Moon's surface. The SSC is the angle of the sunrise terminator measured toward the observer's east (i.e. westward on the Moon) starting from the lunar meridian that passes through the mean centre of the apparent disk. Its value increases by nearly 12.2° per day, or about 0.5° per hour, and is approximately 0°, 90°, 180°, and 270° at the first quarter, full, last quarter, and new phases, respectively. Values of the SSC are given on pp. 96–118 for the beginning of each month.

Selenographic longitude (λ) is measured toward the observer's west (i.e. eastward on the Moon) from the mean central lunar meridian. Thus sunrise will occur at a given point on the Moon when SSC = 360° – λ; values of 360° – λ for several lunar features are listed in the MAP OF MOON on pp. 148–149. The longitude of the sunset terminator differs by 180° from that of the sunrise terminator.

Libration, also given on the left-hand pages, is the apparent rocking motion of the Moon as it orbits Earth. As a consequence, over time, about 59% of the lunar surface can be viewed from Earth (see *Sky & Telescope,* July 1987, p. 60). Libration in longitude (±8°) results from the nearly uniform axial rotation of the Moon combined with its varying orbital speed along its elliptical orbit, while libration in latitude (±7°) is caused by the tilt of the Moon's equator to its orbital plane. A smaller contribution (up to ±1°), called *diurnal libration,* is associated with the shifting of the observer due to Earth's rotation.

When the libration in longitude is positive, more of the Moon's east limb, the limb near Mare Crisium, is exposed to view (in reference to the lunar limbs, *east* and *west* are used in this lunar sense; see also the "E" and "W" labels on the MAP OF MOON). When the libration in latitude is positive, more of the Moon's north limb is exposed to view. The monthly dates of the greatest positive and negative values of the libration in longitude and latitude and the dates of greatest northern and southern declination are given on the left-hand pages.

The lunar graphics on the right-hand pages give the geocentric appearance of the Moon at 0h UT on odd-numbered days of the month. They depict the Moon's phase, size, and libration. A small dot of size proportional to the amount of libration appears near the limb that is exposed. The graphics were prepared by Rajiv Gupta from images provided by Roger Fell using the *Lunar Calculator* computer program written by Alister Ling (see www3.telus.net/public/aling/lunarcal/lunarcal.htm). Lunar libration, phase, and distance data provided by David Lane is generated by custom-made software.

The Moon's orbit is inclined 5°09′ to the ecliptic. The gravitational influences of Earth and the Sun cause (1) the orbital plane to wobble, and (2) the major axis of the orbit to precess. (1) The wobble shifts the line of nodes (see below) westward (retrograde) along the ecliptic with a period of 18.61 years. During 2008, the ascending node regresses from longitude 330.4° to 311.0°, moving from Aquarius into Capricornus over the course of the year. The monthly range of the Moon's declination continues to decrease from its 2006 maximum of ±29°. (Jan. 20 for extreme northern declination of +27°59′, and Feb. 3 for the extreme southern declination of −28°01′.) (2) The precession shifts the perigee point eastward (prograde) with a period of 8.85 years, although the positions of successive perigees fluctuate considerably from the mean motion. The Moon's mean equatorial plane, its mean orbital plane, and the plane of the ecliptic intersect along a common line of nodes, the equator being inclined at 1°32′ to the ecliptic and at 1°32′ + 5°09′ = 6°41′ to the orbit (i.e. the ascending node of the equator on the ecliptic coincides with the descending node of the orbit).

Jupiter's Satellites

The configurations of Jupiter's Galilean satellites, provided by Larry Bogan, are given on the right-hand monthly pages. In these diagrams the vertical double line represents the equatorial diameter of the disk of Jupiter. Time is shown on the vertical scale, successive horizontal lines indicating 0h UT on the various days of the month. The relative east–west positions of the four satellites with respect to the disk of Jupiter are given by the four curves, where I = Io, II = Europa (dashed curve), III = Ganymede, and IV = Callisto. Note the "West–East" orientation given at the top of each diagram; these directions are those of the observer's sky, not Jupiter's limbs, and correspond to the view in an inverting telescope.

Double shadow transits of Jupiter's Galilean satellites that are not within 1.5 months of Jupiter's conjunction with the Sun are listed. Double satellite transits that are not accompanied by a double-shadow event are generally also listed. For more information about the various transits, occultations, and eclipses of Jupiter's Galilean satellites, see PHENOMENA OF THE GALILEAN SATELLITES on pp. 214–220.

Occultations Involving the Moon, Stars, Planets, and Asteroids

Occultations by the Moon of the bright stars that lie near the ecliptic—Aldebaran, Antares, Regulus, and Spica—and of the planets and bright asteroids—Ceres, Pallas, Juno, and Vesta—are given in the right-hand tables. If the elongation of the Moon is less than 14° the event is not listed. Footnotes give areas of visibility; for more details on occultations visible in North America, including several involving members of the Pleiades (M45), see pp. 158–172 and pp. 228–231.

Minima of Algol

Predicted times of mideclipse are based on the formula heliocentric minimum = $245\,2253.567 + 2.867\,321E$ and are expressed as geocentric times for comparison with observations. The first number is the Julian Date for the minimum of 2001 Dec. 10.067, and the second is the period of Algol in days; E is an integer.

Planets

Conjunctions of the planets (except for Pluto) with each other and the bright ecliptic stars and Messier objects are listed in the right-hand tables, with the elongation of the inner planet indicated in parentheses. Only events for which the elongation of the inner planet is greater than 11° are included, and not all events involving the Messier objects are listed. Also included are oppositions, conjunctions with the Sun, greatest elongations, and stationary times. See pp. 20–21 for definitions of these terms, and TABLE OF CONTENTS or the INDEX for the location of more information on each of the planets. The diagrams below and overleaf give an overview of the circumstances of the planets in 2008.

Miscellaneous Entries

The lunation number is the number of times the Moon has circled the Earth since January 1923, based on a series described by Ernest W. Brown in *Planetary Theory*, 1933. Peaks of major meteor showers (see also p. 234), equinoxes and solstices, heliocentric phenomena of the planets, phenomena of the bright asteroids, and a few other events and occasional notes are also given in the right-hand tables.

MAGNITUDES OF NAKED-EYE PLANETS IN 2008

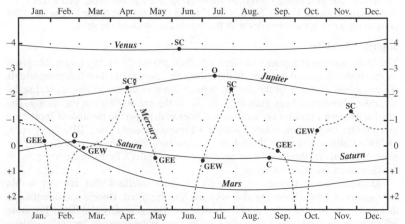

The visual magnitudes of the five, classical (naked-eye) planets during 2008 are given. Oppositions (O), conjunctions (C), superior conjunctions (SC), and greatest elongations east and west (GEE, GEW) are indicated. A diagram explaining these terms is on p. 21.

RIGHT ASCENSIONS OF THE SUN AND PLANETS IN 2008

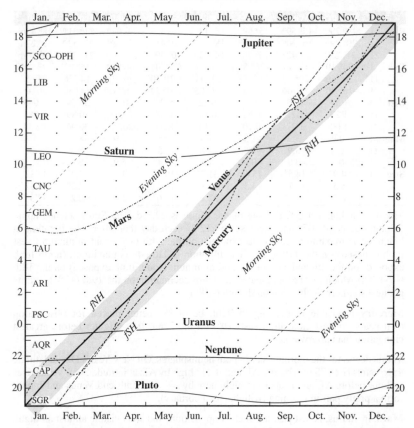

This diagram shows the variation during the year in the right ascension (vertical axis) of the Sun and the planets. The slightly curved, heavy diagonal line represents the Sun; the shaded regions approximately indicate parts of the night sky affected by twilight. The two thin, dashed diagonal lines at the upper left and bottom right represent the boundary between the evening sky and the morning sky.

The diagram may be used to determine in what part of the sky a planet may be found (including in which constellation—note the abbreviations along the vertical axis), when a superior planet is in conjunction with the Sun or at opposition (opposition is approximately where its curve intersects the dashed diagonal lines, and note that, due to retrograde motion, this point is also where the planet's curve has its maximum negative slope), when Mercury and Venus have their various greatest elongations and conjunctions, and when there are conjunctions of planets—that is, when the curves for two planets intersect. For example, note the opposition of Saturn at the end of February, the opposition of Jupiter in late June, the conjunction of Mars with Saturn in the middle of July, the conjunction of Mercury, Venus, and Mars in late September, and the conjunction of Jupiter and Venus in November. Also note that the curves of Mercury and Venus cross five times in one year. This "quintuple" conjuction will not reoccur until 2048.

For observers in midlatitudes, at certain times of the year the ecliptic stands steeply to the horizon in the western evening sky or the eastern morning sky, making apparitions of planets in these parts of the sky favourable from the Northern Hemisphere ("fNH" on the diagram) or favourable from the Southern Hemisphere ("fSH").

For more information on all these events, see the following 24 monthly pages and THE PLANETS FOR 2008 (pp. 201–213).

THE SKY FOR 2008 JANUARY

		Mercury	Venus	Mars	Jupiter	Saturn	Uranus	Neptune	Sun
RA	1	$19^h\,20^m$	$15^h\,59^m$	$5^h\,59^m$	$18^h\,13^m$	$10^h\,42^m$	$23^h\,07^m$	$21^h\,31^m$	$18^h\,43m$
	11	$20^h\,29^m$	$16^h\,50^m$	$5^h\,45^m$	$18^h\,23^m$	$10^h\,41^m$	$23^h\,08^m$	$21^h\,32^m$	$19^h\,27m$
	21	$21^h\,25^m$	$17^h\,42^m$	$5^h\,36^m$	$18^h\,32^m$	$10^h\,39^m$	$23^h\,10^m$	$21^h\,33^m$	$20^h\,10m$
Dec	1	–24° 19′	–18° 27′	+26° 56′	–23° 14′	+10° 01′	–6° 30′	–15° 02′	–23° 05′
	11	–20° 59′	–20° 44′	+26° 58′	–23° 11′	+10° 10′	–6° 22′	–14° 56′	–21° 57′
	21	–15° 40′	–22° 06′	+26° 51′	–23° 05′	+10° 23′	–6° 12′	–14° 50′	–20° 06′
Dist	1	1.37	1.15	0.61	6.22	8.71	20.48	30.79	0.983
	11	1.23	1.21	0.64	6.19	8.58	20.63	30.89	0.983
	21	1.00	1.27	0.70	6.13	8.47	20.77	30.96	0.984
Mag	1	–0.9	–3.9	–1.5	–1.8	0.6	5.9	8.0	
	11	–0.8	–3.9	–1.2	–1.8	0.5	5.9	8.0	
	21	–0.7	–3.9	–0.9	–1.8	0.4	5.9	8.0	
Size	1	4.9″	14.5″	15.4″	31.7″	19.1″	3.4″	2.2″	32′32″
	11	5.5″	13.7″	14.5″	31.8″	19.4″	3.4″	2.2″	32′32″
	21	6.7″	13.1″	13.4″	32.1″	19.6″	3.4″	2.2″	32′31″

Moon—On Jan. 1.0 UT, the age of the Moon is 22.3 d. The Sun's selenographic colongitude is 183.07° and increases by 12.2° each day thereafter. The libration in longitude is maximum (east limb exposed) on the 24th (+6°), and minimum (west limb exposed) on the 11th (–5°). The libration in latitude is maximum (north limb exposed) on the 4th and 31st (+7°), and minimum (south limb exposed) on the 18th (–7°). The Moon reaches its greatest northern declination on the 19th (+28°), and its greatest southern declination on the 6th (–28°).

Mercury is visible in evening twilight, becoming better placed for observation as it nears greatest elongation east (19°) on the 22nd. It is brighter before greatest elongation than afterwards.

Venus decorates the morning sky in both hemispheres. On New Year's Day at latitude 45N Venus rises 75 min before AT, and is 11° high by AT; at latitude 30°S Venus rises an hour before AT, and is also 11° high there by AT. At month-end Venus and Jupiter form a pretty pair in morning twilight (see February).

Mars, in Taurus, is just past its Dec. 24 opposition, and so is visible almost all night. On Jan. 15 it transits about 22:00, passing through the zenith at latitude 30°N, at an altitude of 72° for mid-northern observers, and 33° for mid-southern observers. Mars starts the month moving retrograde (westward) very slowly, is stationary on the 30th, and then resumes direct (eastward) motion.

Jupiter, in Sagittarius all year, was in conjunction with the Sun on Dec. 23, so it is hidden in the solar glare as the year opens. At sunrise on Jan. 15 Jupiter is 9° high in the southeast for mid-northern observers, and 16° up in the east-southeast at latitude 30°S. By the 31st both latitudes see Jupiter rise in a dark sky. (See Venus above.)

Saturn resides in Leo all year. At mid-month it rises in the east-northeast in mid-evening. It transits near 3:00 at these altitudes: 55° at latitude 45°N, 70° at latitude 30°N, and 50° at latitude 30°S. The southern side of the rings is visible.

The tilt of the rings increases from 6.7° on Jan.1 to 9.9° in early May, and then closes to only 0.8° at year-end. The Sun and Earth pass through Saturn's ring-plane in August and September, 2009, respectively.

Time (UT) d h m	JANUARY EVENTS	Jupiter's Satellites West East
Tue. 1	Ceres stationary	
15 15	Algol at minimum	
Wed. 2 23	Earth at perihelion (147 096 448 km)	
Thu. 3 8	Moon at apogee (405 331 km)	
Fri. 4	Mercury at greatest heliocentric lat. S	
7	**Quadrantid meteors peak**	
12 04	Algol at minimum	
Sat. 5 6	Venus 7° N of Moon	
10	**Antares 0.5° N of Moon, occultation†**	
Sun. 6		
Mon. 7 1	Venus 6° N of Antares (38° W)	
8 54	Algol at minimum	
Tue. 8 11 37	**New Moon (lunation 1052)**	
Wed. 9		
Thu. 10 5 43	Algol at minimum	
Fri. 11 1	**Neptune 0.4° N of Moon, occultation‡**	
Sat. 12		
Sun. 13 2 32	Algol at minimum	
Mon. 14		
Tue. 15 19 46	**First Quarter**	
23 21	Algol at minimum	
Wed. 16		
Thu. 17		
Fri. 18 7	**Moon 1.1° N of Pleiades (M45)**	
20 11	Algol at minimum	
Sat. 19 9	Moon at perigee (366 430 km)	
Sun. 20 0	**Mars 1.1° S of Moon, occultation††**	
Mon. 21 17 00	Algol at minimum	
Tue. 22 5	**Mercury greatest elongation E (19°)**	
13 35	**Full Moon**	
23	**Moon 0.3° N of Beehive (M44)**	
Wed. 23	Mercury at ascending node	
4	Mercury 0.3° N of Neptune (18° W)	
Thu. 24 13 49	Algol at minimum	
15	**Regulus 0.7° N of Moon, occultation‡‡**	
Fri. 25 6	Saturn 3° N of Moon	
Sat. 26		
Sun. 27	Mercury at perihelion	
10 39	Algol at minimum	
Mon. 28 7	Mercury stationary	
Tue. 29		
Wed. 30 5 03	**Last Quarter**	
7 28	Algol at minimum	
21	Mars stationary	
Thu. 31 4	Moon at apogee (404 533 km)	

† S S. America, part of Antarctica ‡ S tips of Australia, part of Antarctica, New Zealand
†† N Russia, Arctic regions, NW Tip of N. America
‡‡ S Indonesia, Australasia, part of Antarctica

THE SKY FOR 2008 FEBRUARY

		Mercury	Venus	Mars	Jupiter	Saturn	Uranus	Neptune	Sun
RA	1	21^h 37^m	18^h 40^m	5^h 33^m	18^h 43^m	10^h 37^m	23^h 12^m	21^h 35^m	20^h 55m
	11	20^h 55^m	19^h 33^m	5^h 36^m	18^h 52^m	10^h 34^m	23^h 13^m	21^h 36^m	21^h 36m
	21	20^h 41^m	20^h 25^m	5^h 44^m	19^h 00^m	10^h 31^m	23^h 15^m	21^h 38^m	22^h 15m
Dec	1	−11° 32′	−22° 23′	+26° 40′	−22° 57′	+10° 40′	−6° 00′	−14° 42′	−17° 22′
	11	−13° 38′	−21° 28′	+26° 31′	−22° 48′	+10° 58′	−5° 48′	−14° 35′	−14° 20′
	21	−16° 21′	−19° 30′	+26° 23′	−22° 37′	+11° 16′	−5° 35′	−14° 28′	−10° 54′
Dist	1	0.72	1.34	0.78	6.05	8.38	20.89	31.01	0.985
	11	0.66	1.39	0.86	5.95	8.32	20.98	31.03	0.987
	21	0.77	1.44	0.95	5.84	8.29	21.04	31.02	0.989
Mag	1	1.9	−3.8	−0.6	−1.9	0.4	5.9	8.0	
	11	3.2	−3.8	−0.3	−1.9	0.3	5.9	8.0	
	21	0.6	−3.8	0.0	−1.9	0.2	5.9	8.0	
Size	1	9.3″	12.5″	12.0″	32.6″	19.9″	3.4″	2.2″	32′28″
	11	10.3″	12.0″	10.9″	33.1″	20.0″	3.3″	2.2″	32′25″
	21	8.7″	11.6″	9.9″	33.7″	20.1″	3.3″	2.2″	32′21″

Moon—On Feb. 1.0 UT, the age of the Moon is 23.5 d. The Sun's selenographic colongitude is 200.00° and increases by 12.2° each day thereafter. The libration in longitude is maximum (east limb exposed) on the 21st (+5°), and minimum (west limb exposed) on the 7th (−5°). The libration in latitude is maximum (north limb exposed) on the 28th (+7°), and minimum (south limb exposed) on the 14th (−7°). The Moon reaches its greatest northern declination on the 16th (+28°), and its greatest southern declination on the 2nd (−28°).

There is an **annular solar eclipse** in Antarctica on the 7th; a partial eclipse is visible from New Zealand, southeastern Australia, and adjacent Oceania. There is a **total eclipse of the Moon** on the night of the 20th-21st visible from North and South America, Europe, and Africa (see the ECLIPSES IN 2008 p.124). (See also Venus.)

Mercury is at inferior conjunction on the 6th. It becomes visible to southern observers in morning twilight by mid-month, and reaches greatest elongation west (27°) on Mar. 3. **For the southern hemisphere, late February to mid-March offers the year's best morning apparition.** On Feb. 26 Mercury passes 1.3° north of Venus, but they remain close until late March.

Venus is a morning planet. On the 15th it rises 20 min after AT at latitude 45°N, but at latitude 30°N it rises 15 min before AT. Southern observers see Venus dominating the morning sky, rising 50 min before AT because it is south of the Sun. **Venus passes 0.6° north of magnitude −1.8 Jupiter on the 1st.** The pair is joined on the 4th by the waning crescent Moon with earthshine. (See also Mercury.)

Mars, in Taurus, continues to be well-placed in the northern hemisphere's evening skies. However, its disk is shrinking rapidly this month, and the telescopic observing season is winding down. On the 15th Mars transits about 20:00. At latitude 45°N, Mars sets about 4:00 in the northwest; southern observers see it set near 1:00 in the west-northwest.

Jupiter on the 15th at morning CT is 13° high in the southeast at latitude 45°N, and 22° up at latitude 30°N. At latitude 30°S Jupiter is 36°high in the east as CT begins, having risen shortly after 2:00. (See also Venus.)

Saturn, in Leo, is at opposition on the 24th, when it rises at sunset and sets at sunrise. It transits at midnight at these altitudes: 56° at latitude 45°N, 71° at latitude 30°N, and 49° at latitude 30°S. The rings are inclined about 8° at mid-month.

Time (UT)	FEBRUARY EVENTS	Jupiter's Satellites
d h m		West East

Fri. 1 12	**Venus 0.6° N of Jupiter (32° W)**	
18	**Antares 0.6° N of Moon, occultation†**	
Sat. 2 4 17	Algol at minimum	
Sun. 3		
Mon. 4 6	**Jupiter 4° N of Moon**	
12	**Venus 4° N of Moon**	
Tue. 5 1 06	Algol at minimum	
Wed. 6	Mercury at greatest heliocentric lat. N	
18	Mercury in inferior conjunction	
Thu. 7 3 44	**New Moon** (lunation 1053)	
	annular solar eclipse (p.124)	
21 56	Algol at minimum	
Fri. 8		
Sat. 9		
Sun. 10 18 45	Algol at minimum	
Mon. 11 2	Neptune in conjunction with the Sun	
Tue. 12		
Wed. 13 15 34	Algol at minimum	
Thu. 14 1	Moon at perigee (370 219 km)	
3 33	**First Quarter**	
13	**Moon 1.2° N of Pleiades (M45)**	
Fri. 15	Venus at descending node	
Sat. 16 8	**Mars 1.6° S of Moon**	
12 24	Algol at minimum	
Sun. 17		
Mon. 18 16	Mercury stationary	
Tue. 19 8	**Moon 0.3° N of Beehive (M44)**	
9 13	Algol at minimum	
Wed. 20	Vesta in conjunction with the Sun	
Thu. 21 0	**Regulus 0.7° N of Moon, occultation‡**	
3 30	**Full Moon, total lunar eclipse** (p.124)	
12	Saturn 3° N of Moon	
Fri. 22 6 02	Algol at minimum	
Sat. 23	**Zodiacal Light** visible in N lat. in W	
	after evening twilight for next two weeks	
Sun. 24 10	**Saturn at opposition**	
Mon. 25 2 52	Algol at minimum	
Tue. 26 2	**Mercury 1.3° N of Venus (27° W)**	
Wed. 27 23 41	Algol at minimum	
Thu. 28 1	Moon at apogee (404 443 km)	
Fri 29 2	**Antares 0.6° N of Moon, occultation††**	
2 18	**Last Quarter**	

† Australia, New Zealand, part of Antarctica, S part of S. America
‡ Most of S. America, part of Antarctica
†† Part of Antarctica, S tips of Australia

THE SKY FOR 2008 MARCH

		Mercury	Venus	Mars	Jupiter	Saturn	Uranus	Neptune	Sun
RA	1	21^h 04^m	21^h 11^m	5^h 55^m	19^h 07^m	10^h 29^m	23^h 17^m	21^h 39^m	22^h 49m
	11	21^h 50^m	22^h 00^m	6^h 09^m	19^h 14^m	10^h 26^m	23^h 19^m	21^h 40^m	23^h 26m
	21	22^h 45^m	22^h 47^m	6^h 26^m	19^h 21^m	10^h 23^m	23^h 22^m	21^h 42^m	0^h 02m
Dec	1	–16° 39′	–16° 55′	+26° 16′	–22° 28′	+11° 33′	–5° 23′	–14° 21′	–7° 34′
	11	–14° 38′	–13° 17′	+26° 04′	–22° 16′	+11° 50′	–5° 10′	–14° 14′	–3° 42′
	21	–10° 22′	–9° 04′	+25° 46′	–22° 06′	+12° 06′	–4° 56′	–14° 08′	+0° 15′
Dist	1	0.91	1.48	1.03	5.73	8.30	21.08	30.98	0.991
	11	1.06	1.53	1.13	5.59	8.33	21.09	30.91	0.993
	21	1.18	1.57	1.23	5.44	8.39	21.07	30.82	0.996
Mag	1	0.1	–3.8	0.2	–2.0	0.2	5.9	8.0	
	11	0.0	–3.8	0.4	–2.0	0.3	5.9	8.0	
	21	–0.1	–3.8	0.6	–2.1	0.3	5.9	8.0	
Size	1	7.4″	11.3″	9.1″	34.4″	20.0″	3.3″	2.2″	32′17″
	11	6.4″	10.9″	8.3″	35.3″	20.0″	3.3″	2.2″	32′12″
	21	5.7″	10.6″	7.6″	36.2″	19.8″	3.3″	2.2″	32′07″

Moon—On Mar. 1.0 UT, the age of the Moon is 22.8 d. The Sun's selenographic colongitude is 192.84° and increases by 12.2° each day thereafter. The libration in longitude is maximum (east limb exposed) on the 18th (+5°), and minimum (west limb exposed) on the 5th (–6°). The libration in latitude is maximum (north limb exposed) on the 26th (+7°), and minimum (south limb exposed) on the 12th (–7°). The Moon reaches its greatest northern declination on the 14th (+28°), and its greatest southern declination on the 1st and 28th (–28°).

On the 5th the waning crescent **occults Venus** in daytime for much of North America.

Mercury reaches greatest elongation west (27°) on the 3rd. **For the southern hemisphere, late February to mid-March offers the best morning apparition of the year.** Mercury remains visible throughout March, brightening as its elongation decreases. Northern hemisphere observers will also be able to find Mercury, because it travels in tandem with Venus all month, always within 3° until the 30th. They are in conjunction on the 23rd, when Mercury passes 1.0° south of Venus in the eastern dawn.

Venus is still a morning planet, but it is has faded to magnitude –3.8 this month, and its elongation from the Sun decreases to 22° by the 15th. It then rises during NT at latitude 45°N, and barely before NT at latitude 30°N. Favoured southern observers see it rise 20 min before AT. (See also the Moon and Mercury.)

Mars leaves Taurus for Gemini on the 5th. On the 15th it transits near the end of evening CT. It is then high in the south for northern observers. It sets in the northwest before 3:00 (before 2:00 at latitude 30°N). Southern observers see it transit 34° high in the north, and set in the west-northwest shortly before midnight. On the night of the 29th-30th the fading Red Planet passes 15′ north of third-magnitude Epsilon Geminorum.

Jupiter at mid-month is 10° high in the southeast near AT at latitude 45°N. At latitude 30°N the planet rises at 2:35, and is high enough, at 30°, for useful telescopic observing by CT. Southern observers see it rise an hour after midnight, and it is 60° up as CT begins. On the morning of the 30th the nearby last quarter Moon will provide an opportunity to spot magnitude –2.1 Jupiter in the daytime with the unaided eye.

Saturn is just past its Feb. 24 opposition. It spends March through June near Regulus. On Mar. 15 Saturn transits around 22:48 at 57° altitude at latitude 45°N, 72° high at latitude 30°N, and 48° up at latitude 30°S. It sets in the west-northwest at CT at latitude 45°N, at NT at latitude 30°N, and shortly before AT at latitude 30°S. The rings are inclined about 9° at mid-month.

Time (UT) d h m	MARCH EVENTS	Jupiter's Satellites West East

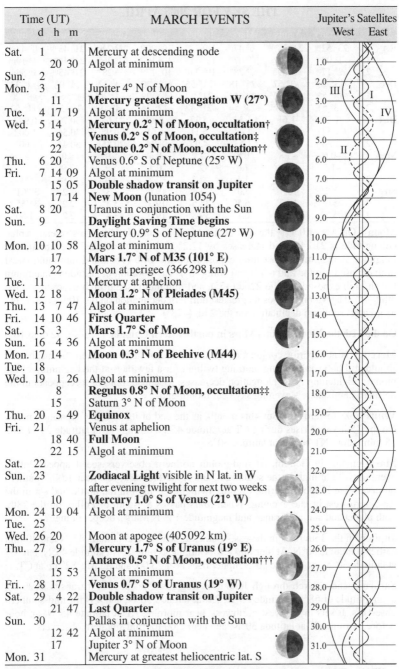

Sat. 1 — Mercury at descending node
    20 30 — Algol at minimum
Sun. 2
Mon. 3 1 — Jupiter 4° N of Moon
    11 — **Mercury greatest elongation W (27°)**
Tue. 4 17 19 — Algol at minimum
Wed. 5 14 — **Mercury 0.2° N of Moon, occultation†**
    19 — **Venus 0.2° S of Moon, occultation‡**
    22 — **Neptune 0.2° N of Moon, occultation††**
Thu. 6 20 — Venus 0.6° S of Neptune (25° W)
Fri. 7 14 09 — Algol at minimum
    15 05 — **Double shadow transit on Jupiter**
    17 14 — **New Moon** (lunation 1054)
Sat. 8 20 — Uranus in conjunction with the Sun
Sun. 9 — **Daylight Saving Time begins**
    2 — Mercury 0.9° S of Neptune (27° W)
Mon. 10 10 58 — Algol at minimum
    17 — **Mars 1.7° N of M35 (101° E)**
    22 — Moon at perigee (366 298 km)
Tue. 11 — Mercury at aphelion
Wed. 12 18 — **Moon 1.2° N of Pleiades (M45)**
Thu. 13 7 47 — Algol at minimum
Fri. 14 10 46 — **First Quarter**
Sat. 15 3 — **Mars 1.7° S of Moon**
Sun. 16 4 36 — Algol at minimum
Mon. 17 14 — **Moon 0.3° N of Beehive (M44)**
Tue. 18
Wed. 19 1 26 — Algol at minimum
    8 — **Regulus 0.8° N of Moon, occultation‡‡**
    15 — Saturn 3° N of Moon
Thu. 20 5 49 — **Equinox**
Fri. 21 — Venus at aphelion
    18 40 — **Full Moon**
    22 15 — Algol at minimum
Sat. 22
Sun. 23 — **Zodiacal Light** visible in N lat. in W after evening twilight for next two weeks
    10 — **Mercury 1.0° S of Venus (21° W)**
Mon. 24 19 04 — Algol at minimum
Tue. 25
Wed. 26 20 — Moon at apogee (405 092 km)
Thu. 27 9 — **Mercury 1.7° S of Uranus (19° E)**
    10 — **Antares 0.5° N of Moon, occultation†††**
    15 53 — Algol at minimum
Fri.. 28 17 — **Venus 0.7° S of Uranus (19° W)**
Sat. 29 4 22 — **Double shadow transit on Jupiter**
    21 47 — **Last Quarter**
Sun. 30 — Pallas in conjunction with the Sun
    12 42 — Algol at minimum
    17 — Jupiter 3° N of Moon
Mon. 31 — Mercury at greatest heliocentric lat. S

† S half of S. America, NW Africa   ‡ E Melanesia, Polynesia, N. America except NE and NW
†† Australia except N, New Zealand, Polynesia, W Mexico
‡‡ New Zealand, E Melanesia, Polynesia, part of Antarctica
††† N Island of New Zealand, Polynesia, S part of S. America, part of Antarctica

THE SKY FOR 2008 APRIL

		Mercury	Venus	Mars	Jupiter	Saturn	Uranus	Neptune	Sun
RA	1	$23^h 52^m$	$23^h 38^m$	$6^h 47^m$	$19^h 27^m$	$10^h 20^m$	$23^h 24^m$	$21^h 43^m$	$0^h 42m$
	11	$1^h 00^m$	$0^h 24^m$	$7^h 07^m$	$19^h 31^m$	$10^h 19^m$	$23^h 26^m$	$21^h 44^m$	$1^h 19m$
	21	$2^h 17^m$	$1^h 09^m$	$7^h 28^m$	$19^h 34^m$	$10^h 17^m$	$23^h 28^m$	$21^h 45^m$	$1^h 56m$
Dec	1	–3° 20′	–3° 57′	+25° 18′	–21° 55′	+12° 20′	–4° 42′	–14° 02′	+4° 34′
	11	+4° 52′	+0° 55′	+24° 42′	–21° 47′	+12° 29′	–4° 30′	–13° 57′	+8° 20′
	21	+13° 51′	+5° 46′	+23° 54′	–21° 42′	+12° 34′	–4° 19′	–13° 53′	+11° 52′
Dist	1	1.29	1.61	1.34	5.27	8.49	21.02	30.70	0.999
	11	1.34	1.64	1.44	5.11	8.61	20.95	30.56	1.002
	21	1.30	1.67	1.53	4.95	8.74	20.85	30.41	1.005
Mag	1	–0.6	–3.8	0.8	–2.2	0.4	5.9	8.0	
	11	–1.5	–3.8	1.0	–2.2	0.4	5.9	7.9	
	21	–1.8	–3.8	1.1	–2.3	0.5	5.9	7.9	
Size	1	5.2″	10.4″	7.0″	37.4″	19.6″	3.3″	2.2″	32′01″
	11	5.0″	10.2″	6.5″	38.6″	19.3″	3.3″	2.2″	31′55″
	21	5.2″	10.0″	6.1″	39.8″	19.0″	3.4″	2.2″	31′50″

Moon—On Apr. 1.0 UT, the age of the Moon is 24.3 d. The Sun's selenographic colongitude is 210.48° and increases by 12.2° each day thereafter. The libration in longitude is maximum (east limb exposed) on the 14th (+6°), and minimum (west limb exposed) on the 2nd (–7°) and 30th (–8°). The libration in latitude is maximum (north limb exposed) on the 22nd (+7°), and minimum (south limb exposed) on the 8th (–7°). The Moon reaches its greatest northern declination on the 10th (+28°), and its greatest southern declination on the 24th (–28°).

On the 12th the **Moon occults Mars in northeastern Canada**. (See No. 92 on p.167)

Mercury is at superior conjunction on the 16th, but in the southern hemisphere it should still be visible during morning twilight for a few days at the beginning of the month, brightening as its elongation decreases. (See also March.) It reappears in the northern hemisphere's evening sky near month-end.

Venus sinks towards the Sun this month, as the end of its morning apparition nears. On the 15th Venus rises during CT at latitude 45°N, during NT at latitude 30°N, and 15 min before NT begins at latitude 30°S.

Mars remains in Gemini. At mid-month northern observers see it appear during evening twilight high in the southwest, and set in the northwest near 1:00. Southern observers see it appear during evening twilight 35° high in the north, and set in the west-northwest in late evening. When Mars passes 5° south of Pollux on the 28th, both planet and star are orange and magnitude 1.2. Is Mars a deeper orange?

Jupiter on the 15th rises in the east-southeast, near 1:30 at latitude 45°N and 40 min earlier at latitude 30°N. At morning CT its altitude is only 21° at latitude 45°N, but 37° at latitude 30°N. At latitude 30°S Jupiter rises near 23:00, and transits 82° up at CT.

Saturn spends March through June near Regulus. On the 15th it transits at 20:40, at an altitude of 58° at latitude 45°N, 73° at latitude 30°N, and 48° for mid-southern observers. It sets in the west-northwest: near morning AT at latitude 45°N, an hour before morning AT at latitude 30°N, and near 2:00 for mid-southern observers

Time (UT)			APRIL EVENTS	Jupiter's Satellites	
d	h	m		West	East

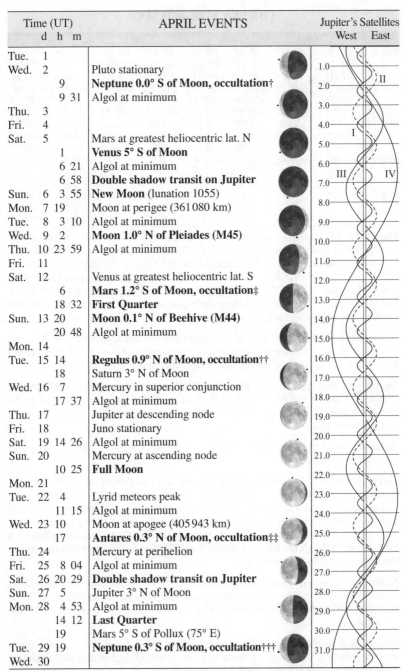

Tue.	1			
Wed.	2		Pluto stationary	
		9	**Neptune 0.0° S of Moon, occultation†**	
		9 31	Algol at minimum	
Thu.	3			
Fri.	4			
Sat.	5		Mars at greatest heliocentric lat. N	
		1	**Venus 5° S of Moon**	
		6 21	Algol at minimum	
		6 58	**Double shadow transit on Jupiter**	
Sun.	6	3 55	**New Moon** (lunation 1055)	
Mon.	7	19	Moon at perigee (361080 km)	
Tue.	8	3 10	Algol at minimum	
Wed.	9	2	**Moon 1.0° N of Pleiades (M45)**	
Thu.	10	23 59	Algol at minimum	
Fri.	11			
Sat.	12		Venus at greatest heliocentric lat. S	
		6	**Mars 1.2° S of Moon, occultation‡**	
		18 32	**First Quarter**	
Sun.	13	20	**Moon 0.1° N of Beehive (M44)**	
		20 48	Algol at minimum	
Mon.	14			
Tue.	15	14	**Regulus 0.9° N of Moon, occultation††**	
		18	Saturn 3° N of Moon	
Wed.	16	7	Mercury in superior conjunction	
		17 37	Algol at minimum	
Thu.	17		Jupiter at descending node	
Fri.	18		Juno stationary	
Sat.	19	14 26	Algol at minimum	
Sun.	20		Mercury at ascending node	
		10 25	**Full Moon**	
Mon.	21			
Tue.	22	4	Lyrid meteors peak	
		11 15	Algol at minimum	
Wed.	23	10	Moon at apogee (405943 km)	
		17	**Antares 0.3° N of Moon, occultation‡‡**	
Thu.	24		Mercury at perihelion	
Fri.	25	8 04	Algol at minimum	
Sat.	26	20 29	**Double shadow transit on Jupiter**	
Sun.	27	5	Jupiter 3° N of Moon	
Mon.	28	4 53	Algol at minimum	
		14 12	**Last Quarter**	
		19	Mars 5° S of Pollux (75° E)	
Tue.	29	19	**Neptune 0.3° S of Moon, occultation†††**	
Wed.	30			

†Central S. America, central Africa, Middle East ‡NE Canada, Greenland, Iceland, N Scandinavia
†† Madagascar, part of Antarctica ‡‡ S half of Australia, New Zealand, Polynesia
††† Indonesia except Sumatra, N Australasia, Hawaiian Islands

THE SKY FOR 2008 MAY

		Mercury	Venus	Mars	Jupiter	Saturn	Uranus	Neptune	Sun
RA	1	3ʰ 36ᵐ	1ʰ 55ᵐ	7ʰ 50ᵐ	19ʰ 36ᵐ	10ʰ 17ᵐ	23ʰ 29ᵐ	21ʰ 46ᵐ	2ʰ 34ᵐ
	11	4ʰ 40ᵐ	2ʰ 42ᵐ	8ʰ 12ᵐ	19ʰ 36ᵐ	10ʰ 17ᵐ	23ʰ 31ᵐ	21ʰ 46ᵐ	3ʰ 13m
	21	5ʰ 17ᵐ	3ʰ 31ᵐ	8ʰ 35ᵐ	19ʰ 35ᵐ	10ʰ 18ᵐ	23ʰ 32ᵐ	21ʰ 46ᵐ	3ʰ 52m
Dec	1	+21° 11′	+10° 26′	+22° 55′	−21° 39′	+12° 36′	−4° 08′	−13° 50′	+15° 05′
	11	+24° 41′	+14° 42′	+21° 44′	−21° 39′	+12° 34′	−3° 59′	−13° 48′	+17° 54′
	21	+24° 42′	+18° 21′	+20° 20′	−21° 42′	+12° 28′	−3° 52′	−13° 47′	+20° 12′
Dist	1	1.13	1.69	1.63	4.79	8.89	20.74	30.25	1.008
	11	0.90	1.71	1.72	4.64	9.05	20.60	30.08	1.010
	21	0.71	1.72	1.80	4.51	9.22	20.45	29.92	1.012
Mag	1	−0.9	−3.8	1.2	−2.4	0.5	5.9	7.9	
	11	0.0	−3.8	1.3	−2.4	0.6	5.9	7.9	
	21	1.4	−3.8	1.4	−2.5	0.6	5.9	7.9	
Size	1	5.9″	9.9″	5.8″	41.1″	18.7″	3.4″	2.2″	31′45″
	11	7.4″	9.7″	5.5″	42.4″	18.4″	3.4″	2.2″	31′40″
	21	9.5″	9.7″	5.2″	43.7″	18.0″	3.4″	2.2″	31′36″

Moon—On May 1.0 UT, the age of the Moon is 24.8 d. The Sun's selenographic colongitude is 216.42° and increases by 12.2° each day thereafter. The libration in longitude is maximum (east limb exposed) on the 12th (+7°), and minimum (west limb exposed) on the 28th (−8°). The libration in latitude is maximum (north limb exposed) on the 19th (+7°), and minimum (south limb exposed) on the 6th (−7°). The Moon reaches its greatest northern declination on the 8th (+28°), and its greatest southern declination on the 22nd (−28°).

On the 6th the Moon reaches its third-closest perigee distance of the year (357 771 km). With New Moon occurring less than a day earlier, large tides will occur. (See TIDES AND THE EARTH–MOON SYSTEM (p.173) and also June and December.)

Mercury reaches greatest elongation east (22°) on the 14th and inferior conjunction on Jun. 7. The first half of May offers the best evening apparition of the year in the northern hemisphere. The planet fades throughout the month, and by the 24th it is a dim 2nd magnitude.

Venus becomes increasingly difficult to see as May progresses, because it is at superior conjunction on June 9.

Mars, having spent two months in Gemini, crosses into Cancer on the 5th. At mid-month, northern observers will find Mars 45° up in the west-southwest during evening twilight, and see it set in the west-northwest near midnight. Southern observers will find the planet 38° high in the north-northwest during evening twilight, and watch it set in the west-northwest near 22:00. **On the night of the 22nd-23rd, magnitude-1.4 Mars drifts through the bright Beehive Star Cluster, M44, a marvellous sight in binoculars or wide-field scopes.**

Jupiter begins its retrograde loop on the 9th. On the 15th it rises in the east-southeast in late evening at mid-northern latitudes, and by mid-evening at latitude 30°S. It transits at 4:02 at these altitudes: only 23° at latitude 45°N, 38° at latitude 30°N, and 82° at latitude 30°S.

Saturn, near Regulus all month, is stationary on the 3rd and then resumes direct (eastward) motion. Observers at latitude 45°N see Saturn 54° high in the south-southwest at the end of evening CT, and watch it set about 45 min before morning AT in the west-northwest. At latitude 30°N it is 71° up at CT, and sets about 75 min after midnight. At latitude 30°S it transits 48° high in the north at AT, and sets just after midnight.

Time (UT)			MAY EVENTS	Jupiter's Satellites	
d	h	m		West	East

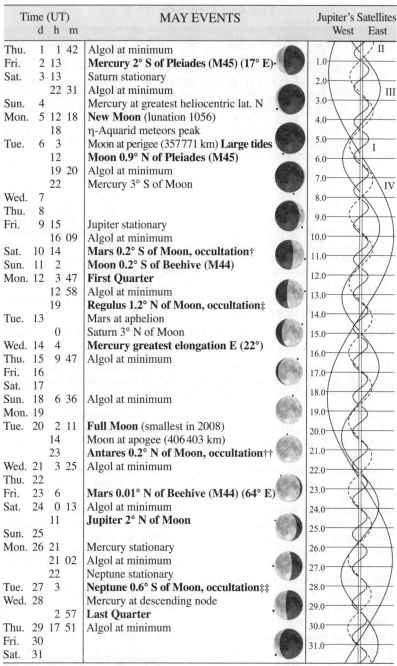

Thu.	1	1 42	Algol at minimum		
Fri.	2	13	**Mercury 2° S of Pleiades (M45) (17° E)**		
Sat.	3	13	Saturn stationary		
		22 31	Algol at minimum		
Sun.	4		Mercury at greatest heliocentric lat. N		
Mon.	5	12 18	**New Moon** (lunation 1056)		
		18	η-Aquarid meteors peak		
Tue.	6	3	Moon at perigee (357771 km) **Large tides**		
		12	**Moon 0.9° N of Pleiades (M45)**		
		19 20	Algol at minimum		
		22	Mercury 3° S of Moon		
Wed.	7				
Thu.	8				
Fri.	9	15	Jupiter stationary		
		16 09	Algol at minimum		
Sat.	10	14	**Mars 0.2° S of Moon, occultation†**		
Sun.	11	2	**Moon 0.2° S of Beehive (M44)**		
Mon.	12	3 47	**First Quarter**		
		12 58	Algol at minimum		
		19	**Regulus 1.2° N of Moon, occultation‡**		
Tue.	13		Mars at aphelion		
		0	Saturn 3° N of Moon		
Wed.	14	4	**Mercury greatest elongation E (22°)**		
Thu.	15	9 47	Algol at minimum		
Fri.	16				
Sat.	17				
Sun.	18	6 36	Algol at minimum		
Mon.	19				
Tue.	20	2 11	**Full Moon** (smallest in 2008)		
		14	Moon at apogee (406403 km)		
		23	**Antares 0.2° N of Moon, occultation††**		
Wed.	21	3 25	Algol at minimum		
Thu.	22				
Fri.	23	6	**Mars 0.01° N of Beehive (M44) (64° E)**		
Sat.	24	0 13	Algol at minimum		
		11	**Jupiter 2° N of Moon**		
Sun.	25				
Mon.	26	21	Mercury stationary		
		21 02	Algol at minimum		
		22	Neptune stationary		
Tue.	27	3	**Neptune 0.6° S of Moon, occultation‡‡**		
Wed.	28		Mercury at descending node		
		2 57	**Last Quarter**		
Thu.	29	17 51	Algol at minimum		
Fri.	30				
Sat.	31				

† N Africa, Europe except N parts, S Asia
‡ Southern S. America, part of Antarctica
†† E part of S. America, S parts of Africa   ‡‡ N half of Africa, SE Europe, W Asia

THE SKY FOR 2008 JUNE

		Mercury	Venus	Mars	Jupiter	Saturn	Uranus	Neptune	Sun
RA	1	5ʰ 19ᵐ	4ʰ 27ᵐ	9ʰ 00ᵐ	19ʰ 33ᵐ	10ʰ 20ᵐ	23ʰ 33ᵐ	21ʰ 46ᵐ	4ʰ 37m
	11	4ʰ 58ᵐ	5ʰ 20ᵐ	9ʰ 23ᵐ	19ʰ 29ᵐ	10ʰ 22ᵐ	23ʰ 33ᵐ	21ʰ 46ᵐ	5ʰ 18m
	21	4ʰ 48ᵐ	6ʰ 14ᵐ	9ʰ 45ᵐ	19ʰ 25ᵐ	10ʰ 24ᵐ	23ʰ 34ᵐ	21ʰ 46ᵐ	5ʰ 59m
Dec	1	+22° 04'	+21° 27'	+18° 35'	−21° 49'	+12° 17'	−3° 46'	−13° 47'	+22° 04'
	11	+19° 02'	+23° 14'	+16° 48'	−21° 58'	+12° 04'	−3° 42'	−13° 49'	+23° 05'
	21	+17° 59'	+23° 54'	+14° 50'	−22° 09'	+11° 47'	−3° 41'	−13° 51'	+23° 26'
Dist	1	0.57	1.73	1.89	4.38	9.40	20.27	29.73	1.014
	11	0.56	1.74	1.97	4.29	9.56	20.11	29.58	1.015
	21	0.65	1.73	2.04	4.22	9.72	19.94	29.43	1.016
Mag	1	4.1	−3.8	1.5	−2.6	0.7	5.9	7.9	
	11	5.1	−3.8	1.6	−2.6	0.7	5.9	7.9	
	21	2.1	−3.8	1.6	−2.7	0.8	5.8	7.9	
Size	1	11.7"	9.6"	4.9"	45.0"	17.7"	3.5"	2.3"	31'33"
	11	12.1"	9.6"	4.7"	46.0"	17.4"	3.5"	2.3"	31'30"
	21	10.4"	9.6"	4.6"	46.7"	17.1"	3.5"	2.3"	31'29"

Moon—On Jun. 1.0 UT, the age of the Moon is 26.5 d. The Sun's selenographic colongitude is 235.02° and increases by 12.2° each day thereafter. The libration in longitude is maximum (east limb exposed) on the 9th (+8°), and minimum (west limb exposed) on the 25th (−7°). The libration in latitude is maximum (north limb exposed) on the 15th (+7°), and minimum (south limb exposed) on the 2nd and 29th (−7°). The Moon reaches its greatest northern declination on the 4th (+28°), and its greatest southern declination on the 18th (−28°).

The four-day-old crescent is paired with Mars on the evening of the 7th (best in eastern North America). On the 23rd the **Moon occults Neptune** for most of North America.

On the 3rd the Moon reaches its second-closest perigee distance of the year (357 251 km). With New Moon that day, extra large tides will occur. (See TIDES AND THE EARTH–MOON SYSTEM (p.173) and also December.)

Mercury, at inferior conjunction on the 7th, reappears in morning twilight during the last ten days of June, brightening as it moves towards greatest elongation west (22°) on Jul. 1. Binoculars will probably be needed to spot Mercury in June; the planet's visibility will improve in early July.

Venus is hidden behind the Sun in June. Venus is in superior conjunction on June 9, when it is occulted by the Sun, marking the midpoint between the Transits of 2004 Jun. 8 and 2012 Jun. 6.

Mars, which began June in Cancer, moves into Leo on the 10th. On the 15th Mars sets in the west-northwest about 23:00 at latitude 45°N, and by mid-evening at latitude 30°S. Mars passes 0.7° north of Regulus on the 30th (the date in North America). They will form a striking matched naked-eye double: bluish Regulus is magnitude 1.4, and orange Mars will be magnitude 1.6. Brighter Saturn, magnitude 0.8, is in the same binocular field of view, only 5° east. (See also the Moon.)

Jupiter is approaching its opposition, which occurs on Jul. 9. On mid-June evenings it rises as NT ends at latitude 45°N, near AT at latitude 30°N, and shortly after AT at latitude 30°S. It transits near 2:00 at the altitudes given in May.

Saturn is still near Regulus. At mid-month northern observers see Saturn in the west-southwest at evening CT: at latitude 45°N it is 33° high, and at 30°N it is 48° up. Southern observers see it 47° up in the north-northwest at CT. Both northern and southern observers watch it set in the west-northwest in late evening. (See also Mars.)

Pluto, in Sagittarius, reaches opposition on June 20. See the finder chart for Pluto on p. 213.

Time (UT) d h m	JUNE EVENTS	Jupiter's Satellites West East
Sun. 1 14 40	Algol at minimum	
17 20	**Double shadow transit on Jupiter**	
Mon. 2		
Tue. 3 13	Moon at perigee (357 251 km) **Large tides**	
19 23	**New Moon** (lunation 1057)	
Wed. 4 11 29	Algol at minimum	
Thu. 5		
Fri. 6		
Sat. 7	Mercury at aphelion	
	Venus at ascending node	
8 17	Algol at minimum	
11	**Moon 0.4° S of Beehive (M44)**	
15	Mercury in inferior conjunction	
Sun. 8 2	**Mars 1.1° N of Moon, occultation†**	
19 54	**Double shadow transit on Jupiter**	
Mon. 9 3	**Regulus 1.4° N of Moon**	
4	Venus in superior conjunction, occulted	
9	Saturn 3° N of Moon	
Tue. 10 5 06	Algol at minimum	
15 04	**First Quarter**	
Wed. 11		
Thu. 12	Juno at opposition	
Fri. 13 1 55	Algol at minimum	
Sat. 14		
Sun. 15 22 44	Algol at minimum	
22 42	**Double shadow transit on Jupiter**	
Mon. 16 18	Moon at apogee (406 228 km)	
Tue. 17 5	**Antares 0.2° N of Moon, occultation‡**	
Wed. 18 17 30	**Full Moon**	
19 32	Algol at minimum	
Thu. 19 15	Mercury stationary	
Fri. 20	Pluto at opposition	
13	**Jupiter 2° N of Moon**	
Sat. 21 0 00	**Solstice**	
16 21	Algol at minimum	
Sun. 22		
Mon. 23 2 40	**Double shadow transit on Jupiter**	
9	**Neptune 0.8° S of Moon, occultation††**	
Tue. 24 13 10	Algol at minimum	
Wed. 25		
Thu. 26 12 10	**Last Quarter**	
Fri. 27	Mercury at greatest heliocentric lat. S	
8	Uranus stationary	
9 58	Algol at minimum	
Sat. 28	Ceres in conjunction with the Sun	
Mon. 30 6 47	Algol at minimum	

† New Zealand
‡ Polynesia, Southern S. America
†† N. America except Alaska, S Greenland

THE SKY FOR 2008 JULY

		Mercury	Venus	Mars	Jupiter	Saturn	Uranus	Neptune	Sun
RA	1	5ʰ 09ᵐ	7ʰ 07ᵐ	10ʰ 08ᵐ	19ʰ 20ᵐ	10ʰ 28ᵐ	23ʰ 34ᵐ	21ʰ 45ᵐ	6ʰ 41m
	11	6ʰ 01ᵐ	8ʰ 00ᵐ	10ʰ 31ᵐ	19ʰ 14ᵐ	10ʰ 31ᵐ	23ʰ 34ᵐ	21ʰ 44ᵐ	7ʰ 22m
	21	7ʰ 20ᵐ	8ʰ 51ᵐ	10ʰ 53ᵐ	19ʰ 09ᵐ	10ʰ 35ᵐ	23ʰ 33ᵐ	21ʰ 43ᵐ	8ʰ 02m
Dec	1	+19° 36′	+23° 24′	+12° 43′	−22° 21′	+11° 28′	−3° 41′	−13° 54′	+23° 06′
	11	+22° 10′	+21° 45′	+10° 28′	−22° 32′	+11° 07′	−3° 43′	−13° 58′	+22° 06′
	21	+22° 53′	+19° 03′	+8° 06′	−22° 43′	+10° 43′	−3° 47′	−14° 03′	+20° 28′
Dist	1	0.82	1.72	2.11	4.17	9.86	19.78	29.30	1.017
	11	1.05	1.71	2.17	4.16	9.99	19.62	29.20	1.017
	21	1.25	1.68	2.23	4.18	10.10	19.48	29.11	1.016
Mag	1	0.5	−3.8	1.6	−2.7	0.8	5.8	7.9	
	11	−0.5	−3.8	1.7	−2.7	0.8	5.8	7.8	
	21	−1.4	−3.8	1.7	−2.7	0.8	5.8	7.8	
Size	1	8.2″	9.7″	4.4″	47.2″	16.9″	3.5″	2.3″	31′28″
	11	6.4″	9.8″	4.3″	47.4″	16.6″	3.6″	2.3″	31′28″
	21	5.4″	9.9″	4.2″	47.2″	16.5″	3.6″	2.3″	31′29″

Moon—On Jul. 1.0 UT, the age of the Moon is 27.2 d. The Sun's selenographic colongitude is 241.66° and increases by 12.2° each day thereafter. The libration in longitude is maximum (east limb exposed) on the 7th (+7°), and minimum (west limb exposed) on the 22nd (−6°). The libration in latitude is maximum (north limb exposed) on the 12th (+7°), and minimum (south limb exposed) on the 26th (−7°). The Moon reaches its greatest northern declination on the 1st and 29th (+28°), and its greatest southern declination on the 15th (−28°).

Mercury is at greatest elongation west (22°) on the 1st, and at superior conjunction on the 29th. It brightens throughout the apparition, making the first half of July a better opportunity for dawn observations than late June was.

Venus slowly reappears from the solar glare during July, and is in the evening sky for the rest of the year. On the 15th Venus sets in the west-northwest about 40 min after sunset.

Mars, in Leo, has a **0.7° conjunction with Saturn on the evening of the 10th** (the date in North America). On the 10th the pair sets late in AT at latitude 45°N, an hour after AT ends at 30°N, and over two hours after AT at 30°S, all in the west-northwest.

Jupiter is at opposition on the 9th when it rises at sunset and sets at sunrise. When it crosses the meridian at midnight, it is at these altitudes: only 23° at latitude 45°N (too low for many memorable views), 38° at latitude 30°N, and 83° at latitude 30°S.

Saturn, in Leo, is down in the west at evening CT on the 15th for northern observers: only 15° up from latitude 45°N, and 24° altitude from 30°N. Southern observers see Saturn 33° high in the northwest at CT. All three latitudes see it set in the west-northwest in mid-evening. (See Mars above.)

Time (UT) d h m	JULY EVENTS	Jupiter's Satellites West East
Tue. 1 4	**Mars 0.7° N of Regulus (49° E)**	
15	Mercury 8° S of Moon	1.0
18	**Mercury greatest elongation W (22°)**	
21	Moon at perigee (359 513 km)	2.0 III
Wed. 2		3.0
Thu. 3 2 19	**New Moon** (lunation 1058)	II
3 36	Algol at minimum	4.0
Fri. 4 7	Earth at aphelion (152 104 136 km)	5.0
21	**Moon 0.5° S of Beehive (M44)**	IV
Sat. 5		6.0
Sun. 6 0 24	Algol at minimum	I
12	Regulus 1.6° N of Moon	7.0
18	Mars 3° N of Moon	
22	Saturn 3° N of Moon	8.0
Mon. 7		9.0
Tue. 8 21 13	Algol at minimum	10.0
Wed. 9 8	**Jupiter at opposition**	
Thu. 10 4 35	**First Quarter**	11.0
Fri. 11	Venus at perihelion	
6	**Mars 0.7° S of Saturn (46° E)**	12.0
18 02	Algol at minimum	13.0
Sat. 12	Juno at opposition	
5	**Mercury 1.9° S of M35 (18° W)**	14.0
Sun. 13		15.0
Mon. 14 4	Moon at apogee (405 452 km)	
12	**Antares 0.3° N of Moon, occultation†**	16.0
14 50	Algol at minimum	17.0
Tue. 15		
Wed. 16		18.0
Thu. 17	Mercury at ascending node	
11 39	Algol at minimum	19.0
12	Jupiter 3° N of Moon	20.0
Fri. 18 7 59	**Full Moon**	
Sat. 19		21.0
Sun. 20 8 28	Algol at minimum	22.0
13	**Neptune 0.9° S of Moon, occultation‡**	
Mon. 21	Mercury at perihelion	23.0
Tue. 22		
Wed. 23 5 16	Algol at minimum	24.0
Thu. 24		25.0
Fri. 25 18 42	**Last Quarter**	
Sat. 26 2 05	Algol at minimum	26.0
Sun. 27 16	**Moon 1.1° N of Pleiades (M45)**	27.0
Mon. 28 20	S. δ-Aquarid meteors peak	
22 53	Algol at minimum	28.0
Tue. 29 20	Mercury in superior conjunction	
23	Moon at perigee (363 883 km)	29.0
Wed. 30		30.0
Thu. 31	Mercury at greatest heliocentric lat. N	
5	Ceres 0.9° N of Moon, occultation††	31.0
19 42	Algol at minimum	

†S half of Australia, New Zealand, Polynesia
‡E Asia, Japan, Alaska, NW part of Canada
††Madagascar, SW Australia

THE SKY FOR 2008 AUGUST

		Mercury	Venus	Mars	Jupiter	Saturn	Uranus	Neptune	Sun
RA	1	8ʰ 58ᵐ	9ʰ 45ᵐ	11ʰ 18ᵐ	19ʰ 03ᵐ	10ʰ 40ᵐ	23ʰ 32ᵐ	21ʰ 42ᵐ	8ʰ 46m
	11	10ʰ 14ᵐ	10ʰ 33ᵐ	11ʰ 41ᵐ	18ʰ 59ᵐ	10ʰ 44ᵐ	23ʰ 31ᵐ	21ʰ 41ᵐ	9ʰ 24m
	21	11ʰ 16ᵐ	11ʰ 18ᵐ	12ʰ 04ᵐ	18ʰ 56ᵐ	10ʰ 49ᵐ	23ʰ 30ᵐ	21ʰ 40ᵐ	10ʰ 01m
Dec	1	+19° 02′	+15° 04′	+5° 22′	−22° 53′	+10° 15′	−3° 53′	−14° 08′	+18° 00′
	11	+12° 31′	+10° 45′	+2° 49′	−23° 00′	+9° 48′	−4° 00′	−14° 14′	+15° 15′
	21	+5° 12′	+5° 57′	+0° 12′	−23° 05′	+9° 21′	−4° 08′	−14° 19′	+12° 06′
Dist	1	1.35	1.65	2.29	4.23	10.20	19.34	29.05	1.015
	11	1.32	1.62	2.33	4.30	10.27	19.24	29.03	1.013
	21	1.23	1.58	2.37	4.40	10.32	19.16	29.03	1.012
Mag	1	−1.9	−3.8	1.7	−2.7	0.8	5.8	7.8	
	11	−0.8	−3.8	1.7	−2.6	0.8	5.8	7.8	
	21	−0.2	−3.8	1.7	−2.6	0.8	5.7	7.8	
Size	1	5.0″	10.1″	4.1″	46.6″	16.3″	3.6″	2.3″	31′31″
	11	5.1″	10.3″	4.0″	45.8″	16.2″	3.6″	2.3″	31′34″
	21	5.5″	10.5″	3.9″	44.8″	16.1″	3.7″	2.3″	31′37″

Moon—On Aug. 1.0 UT, the age of the Moon is 28.9 d. The Sun's selenographic colongitude is 260.59° and increases by 12.2° each day thereafter. The libration in longitude is maximum (east limb exposed) on the 4th (+6°), and minimum (west limb exposed) on the 18th (−5°). The libration in latitude is maximum (north limb exposed) on the 9th (+7°), and minimum (south limb exposed) on the 23rd (−7°). The Moon reaches its greatest northern declination on the 25th (+28°), and its greatest southern declination on the 11th (−28°).

There is a **total solar eclipse** on the 1st. The path begins in the Canadian Arctic Archipelago (Victoria Island through Ellesmere Island), and continues across northernmost Greenland, Siberia, easternmost Kazakhstan, westernmost Mongolia, and northern China. The partial eclipse is visible from eastern Maine, eastern Québec, the Atlantic Provinces, Greenland, and most of Europe and Asia. There is a **partial lunar eclipse** on the 16th visible from parts of every continent except North America (See ECLIPSES IN 2008 p.124).

Mercury was at superior conjunction on Jul. 29, and reaches greatest elongation east (27°) on Sep. 11, fading as its elongation from the Sun increases. By mid-August Mercury becomes visible near Venus in evening twilight. **Between late August and mid-September southern observers have the year's best evening apparition of Mercury.** (See also Venus.)

Venus continues to move away from the Sun this month, becoming better placed in the early evening sky. In mid-August Venus forms a trio with Mercury and Saturn. On the 13th Venus passes only 0.2° south of Saturn. After leaving Saturn behind, Venus and Mercury have a 1.2° conjunction on the 22nd (the date in North America). Then the fleet pair of inner planets reel in Mars in late August, forming a new trio for several weeks, culminating with conjunctions on Sep. 11 and 12. Southern observers have a better view of these events, because of the favourable inclination of the ecliptic to the horizon, and because Venus is well south of the Sun until early December.

Mars, which begins August in Leo, continues eastwards into Virgo on the 9th. On the 14th, at 19:20 PST, Mars passes only 1.6′ from magnitude-3.6 Beta Virginis. Mars is disappearing into the evening twilight for observers at latitude 45°N, who watch it set near the end of NT at mid-month. But, due to the inclination of the ecliptic, observers at latitude 30°S still have Mars 22° up in the west-northwest at the end of NT. (See also Venus.)

Jupiter was at opposition on Jul. 9. In mid-August it transits in mid-evening at these altitudes: only 22° at latitude 45°N, 37° at 30°N, and 83° at 30°S. It sets in the west-southwest near 2:00 at mid-northern latitudes, and an hour before AT at mid-southern.

Saturn is in conjunction with the Sun on Sep. 4. Mid-northern observers may still spot the planet in bright evening twilight early in August, but it drops into the solar glare by mid-month. Southern observers can see it for a few days longer than northerners, near Venus.

Neptune, in Capricornus throughout 2008, reaches opposition on Aug. 15. See the finder chart for Neptune on p. 212.

Time (UT) d h m	AUGUST EVENTS	Jupiter's Satellites West East

Fri. 1 10 12	**New Moon** (lunation 1059)	
	total solar eclipse (p.124)	
Sat. 2	Venus at greatest heliocentric lat. N	
15	**Venus 2° N of Moon**	
22	Regulus 1.7° N of Moon	
Sun. 3 14	Saturn 4° N of Moon	
16 31	Algol at minimum	
Mon. 4 12	Mars 4° N of Moon	
Tue. 5 9 04	**Double shadow transit on Jupiter**	
19	Venus 1.1° N of Regulus (15° E)	
Wed. 6 13 19	Algol at minimum	
Thu. 7		
Fri. 8 20 20	**First Quarter**	
Sat. 9 10 08	Algol at minimum	
Sun. 10	Juno stationary	
19	**Antares 0.4° N of Moon, occultation†**	
20	Moon at apogee (404 556 km)	
Mon. 11		
Tue. 12 6 56	Algol at minimum	
11	**Perseid meteors peak**	
Wed. 13 14	Jupiter 3° N of Moon	
19	**Venus 0.2° S of Saturn (17° E)**	
Thu. 14		
Fri. 15 3 45	Algol at minimum	
8	**Neptune at opposition**	
Sat. 16 0	**Mercury 0.7° S of Saturn (16° E)**	
19	**Neptune 0.8° S of Moon, occultation‡**	
21 16	**Full Moon, partial lunar eclipse** (p.124)	
Sun. 17		
Mon. 18 0 33	Algol at minimum	
Tue. 19 12 55	**Double shadow transit on Jupiter**	
Wed. 20 21 22	Algol at minimum	
Thu. 21		
Fri. 22		
Sat. 23 5	**Mercury 1.3° S of Venus (20° E)**	
18 11	Algol at minimum	
22	**Moon 1.1° N of Pleiades (M45)**	
23 49	**Last Quarter**	
Sun. 24	Mercury at descending node	
Mon. 25		
Tue. 26 4	Moon at perigee (368 696 km)	
14 50	**Double shadow transit on Jupiter**	
14 59	Algol at minimum	
Wed. 27		
Thu. 28	**Zodiacal Light** vis. in N lat. in E before morning twilight for next two weeks	
16	**Moon 0.6° S of Beehive (M44)**	
Fri. 29 11 48	Algol at minimum	
Sat. 30 19 58	**New Moon** (lunation 1060)	
Sun. 31		

† Central S. America, S tips of Africa and Madagascar
‡ NE Africa, E Europe, W and Central Asia

THE SKY FOR 2008 SEPTEMBER

		Mercury	Venus	Mars	Jupiter	Saturn	Uranus	Neptune	Sun
RA	1	12ʰ 12ᵐ	12ʰ 08ᵐ	12ʰ 30ᵐ	18ʰ 54ᵐ	10ʰ 54ᵐ	23ʰ 28ᵐ	21ʰ 39ᵐ	10ʰ 42ᵐ
	11	12ʰ 52ᵐ	12ʰ 52ᵐ	12ʰ 54ᵐ	18ʰ 54ᵐ	10ʰ 59ᵐ	23ʰ 27ᵐ	21ʰ 38ᵐ	11ʰ 18ᵐ
	21	13ʰ 16ᵐ	13ʰ 37ᵐ	13ʰ 18ᵐ	18ʰ 55ᵐ	11ʰ 03ᵐ	23ʰ 25ᵐ	21ʰ 37ᵐ	11ʰ 54ᵐ
Dec	1	−2° 30′	+0° 21′	−2° 42′	−23° 09′	+8° 50′	−4° 18′	−14° 25′	+8° 16′
	11	−8° 22′	−4° 47′	−5° 20′	−23° 10′	+8° 21′	−4° 27′	−14° 30′	+4° 33′
	21	−12° 01′	−9° 47′	−7° 56′	−23° 09′	+7° 53′	−4° 37′	−14° 34′	+0° 42′
Dist	1	1.10	1.54	2.41	4.53	10.34	19.11	29.07	1.009
	11	0.96	1.49	2.44	4.66	10.34	19.09	29.13	1.007
	21	0.80	1.44	2.46	4.81	10.31	19.10	29.22	1.004
Mag	1	0.0	−3.8	1.7	−2.5	0.8	5.7	7.8	
	11	0.2	−3.8	1.7	−2.4	0.9	5.7	7.8	
	21	0.5	−3.8	1.7	−2.4	0.9	5.7	7.8	
Size	1	6.1″	10.8″	3.9″	43.5″	16.1″	3.7″	2.3″	31′42″
	11	7.0″	11.2″	3.8″	42.3″	16.1″	3.7″	2.3″	31′47″
	21	8.4″	11.6″	3.8″	41.0″	16.1″	3.7″	2.3″	31′52″

Moon—On Sep. 1.0 UT, the age of the Moon is 1.2 d. The Sun's selenographic colongitude is 279.30° and increases by 12.2° each day thereafter. The libration in longitude is maximum (east limb exposed) on the 1st and 28th (+5°), and minimum (west limb exposed) on the 14th (−5°). The libration in latitude is maximum (north limb exposed) on the 5th (+7°), and minimum (south limb exposed) on the 19th (−7°). The Moon reaches its greatest northern declination on the 21st (+28°), and its greatest southern declination on the 8th (−28°).

On the 1st there is a glorious grouping of the two-day-old crescent Moon with earthshine, Venus, Mercury, and Mars. The inclination of the ecliptic favours southern observers.

Mercury reaches greatest elongation east (27°) on Sep. 11, and inferior conjunction on Oct. 6. **The southern hemisphere enjoys its best evening apparition of the year between late August and mid-September.** Mercury remains well placed for southerners until near month-end, but the crescent fades to 2nd magnitude. (See also the Moon and Venus.)

Venus forms an evening twilight trio with Mercury and Mars for several weeks, climaxing with conjunctions on the 11th and 12th. Canadians and other northern observers will need a flat horizon to view the trio: at latitude 45°N on the 11th Mercury sets only 10 min after CT ends, and Venus sets 10 min before NT ends. The viewing circumstances are more favourable further south. At latitude 30°N Mercury sets 10 min after NT ends, and Venus sets 10 min later. At latitude 30°S both planets set in a dark sky. (See Mars, the Moon, and also Venus for August.)

Mars, in Virgo, forms a trio with Venus and Mercury during the first half of September, and Venus passes only 0.3° north of Mars on the 11th. Spica makes it a quartet, beginning on the 15th. Unfortunately, northern observers will not get a good view of this show. (See also the Moon and Venus.)

Jupiter in retrograde (westward) motion to begin the month, is stationary on the 8th, and then resumes direct (eastward) motion. On the 15th it transits at 19:13. See August for its culmination altitudes. It sets in the west-southwest, near local midnight for mid-northern observers, and two hours later for mid-southern ones.

Saturn is in conjunction with the Sun on the 4th. During the last ten days of the month northern observers see Saturn reappear rapidly in the dawn. By month-end, it rises in the east before AT. For less favoured southern observers, it is only 6° high in the east-northeast as CT begins on the 30th.

Uranus, in Aquarius all year, is at opposition on the 13th. Uranus is visible with the unaided eye at any good observing site. See the finder chart on p. 211.

Time (UT) d h m	SEPTEMBER EVENTS	Jupiter's Satellites West East

Day	d	h	m	Event
Mon.	1	8	37	Algol at minimum
		21		Venus 5° N of Moon
		23		Mercury 3° N of Moon
Tue.	2	8		Mars 5° N of Moon
		18	40	**Double shadow transit on Jupiter**
Wed.	3			Mercury at aphelion
Thu.	4	2		Saturn in conjunction with the Sun
		5	25	Algol at minimum
Fri.	5			
Sat.	6			
Sun.	7	2	14	Algol at minimum
		3		**Antares 0.3° N of Moon, occultation†**
		14	04	**First Quarter**
		15		Moon at apogee (404 214 km)
Mon.	8	0	12	**Double shadow transit on Jupiter**
		3		Jupiter stationary
Tue.	9			Pluto stationary
		20		Jupiter 3° N of Moon
		23	02	Algol at minimum
Wed.	10			
Thu.	11	4		**Mercury greatest elongation E (27°)**
		4		Mercury 4° S of Venus (26° E)
		20		**Venus 0.3° N of Mars (25° E)**
Fri.	12			Vesta stationary
		19	51	Algol at minimum
		21		Mercury 3° S of Mars (26° E)
Sat.	13	2		**Neptune 0.8° S of Moon, occultation‡**
		2		**Uranus at opposition**
Sun.	14			
Mon.	15	9	13	**Full Moon**
		16	40	Algol at minimum
Tue.	16			
Wed.	17			
Thu.	18	13	28	Algol at minimum
Fri.	19	5		Mercury 4° S of Mars (24° E)
Sat.	20	3		Moon at perigee (368 886 km)
		4		**Moon 1.0° N of Pleiades (M45)**
Sun.	21	10	17	Algol at minimum
Mon.	22	5	04	**Last Quarter**
		15	45	**Equinox**
Tue.	23			Mercury at greatest heliocentric lat. S
Wed.	24	5		Mercury stationary
		7	06	Algol at minimum
		22		**Moon 0.7° S of Beehive (M44)**
Thu.	25			
Fri.	26	15		**Regulus 1.7° N of Moon**
Sat.	27			**Zodiacal Light** vis. in N lat. in E before morning twilight for next two weeks
				Venus at descending node
		3	54	Algol at minimum
		20		Saturn 5° N of Moon
Sun.	28			
Mon.	29	8	12	**New Moon** (lunation 1061)
Tue.	30	0	43	Algol at minimum
		11		**Mercury 1.1° N of Moon**

† E Australasia, Polynesia, SW S. America
‡ N. America except NW part, N tip of S. America, Iceland, United Kingdom

THE SKY FOR 2008 OCTOBER

		Mercury	Venus	Mars	Jupiter	Saturn	Uranus	Neptune	Sun
RA	1	13^h 09^m	14^h 23^m	13^h 43^m	18^h 58^m	11^h 08^m	23^h 24^m	21^h 36^m	12^h 30m
	11	12^h 34^m	15^h 11^m	14^h 09^m	19^h 01^m	11^h 12^m	23^h 23^m	21^h 36^m	13^h 06m
	21	12^h 39^m	16^h 01^m	14^h 36^m	19^h 06^m	11^h 16^m	23^h 21^m	21^h 36^m	13^h 43m
Dec	1	−11° 01′	−14° 25′	−10° 29′	−23° 06′	+7° 26′	−4° 46′	−14° 38′	−3° 12′
	11	−4° 23′	−18° 31′	−12° 56′	−23° 02′	+7° 00′	−4° 54′	−14° 41′	−7° 02′
	21	−2° 13′	−21° 50′	−15° 15′	−22° 55′	+6° 36′	−5° 01′	−14° 43′	−10° 42′
Dist	1	0.67	1.39	2.48	4.96	10.25	19.15	29.34	1.001
	11	0.70	1.33	2.49	5.11	10.18	19.22	29.47	0.998
	21	0.94	1.27	2.50	5.27	10.08	19.31	29.62	0.995
Mag	1	2.6	−3.8	1.6	−2.3	1.0	5.7	7.9	
	11	3.2	−3.8	1.6	−2.2	1.0	5.7	7.9	
	21	−0.4	−3.8	1.6	−2.2	1.0	5.8	7.9	
Size	1	10.0″	12.0″	3.8″	39.7″	16.2″	3.7″	2.3″	31′57″
	11	9.6″	12.5″	3.8″	38.5″	16.3″	3.6″	2.3″	32′03″
	21	7.2″	13.1″	3.7″	37.4″	16.5″	3.6″	2.3″	32′08″

Moon—On Oct. 1.0 UT, the age of the Moon is 1.7 d. The Sun's selenographic colongitude is 285.35° and increases by 12.2° each day thereafter. The libration in longitude is maximum (east limb exposed) on the 24th (+6°), and minimum (west limb exposed) on the 11th (–6°). The libration in latitude is maximum (north limb exposed) on the 2nd and 29th (+7°), and minimum (south limb exposed) on the 16th (–7°). The Moon reaches its greatest northern declination on the 19th (+27°), and its greatest southern declination on the 5th (–27°).

Mercury is at inferior conjunction on the 6th, and reaches greatest elongation west (18°) on the 22nd. The northern hemisphere enjoys its finest morning twilight apparition of the year during the second half of October.

Venus bejewels the evening sky. On the 1st and again on the 31st (the dates in North America) it is joined by twilight's other splendour, the three-day-old crescent Moon with earthshine. By month-end Venus sets after AT, even at latitude 45°N.

Mars, in Virgo, crosses into Libra on the 15th, but few northerners will still see it by then, as it sinks into the solar glare. Even favoured southern observers see Mars only 3° high in the west-southwest at the end of NT. Mars will be in conjunction with the Sun on Dec. 5.

Jupiter on the 15th transits at 17:24 (near sunset for northern observers), at the altitudes given for August. It sets in the west-southwest near 22:00 at mid-northern latitudes, and just after midnight at mid-southern.

Saturn, a morning planet in Leo, rises in the east. At mid-month favoured northern observers see it rise near 3:00; for southern observers it rises near AT. By CT at latitude 30°N it is 30° up, 27° high at latitude 45°N, and only 14° up at latitude 30°S. The planet is unusually faint, only magnitude 1.0 because the rings are only inclined 2.8° from edge-on.

Vesta is at opposition on the 30th, and peaks in brightness at magnitude 6.4 on the 27th.

Time (UT) d h m	OCTOBER EVENTS		Jupiter's Satellites West East
Wed. 1 4	Mars 5° N of Moon		
Thu. 2 2	Venus 5° N of Moon		
21 32	Algol at minimum		
Fri. 3			
Sat. 4 11	**Antares 0.1° N of Moon, occultation†**		
Sun. 5 11	Moon at apogee (404 721 km)		
18 21	Algol at minimum		
Mon. 6 21	Mercury in inferior conjunction		
Tue. 7 7	**Jupiter 2° N of Moon**		
9 04	**First Quarter**		
Wed. 8 1	Draconid meteors peak		
15 09	Algol at minimum		
Thu. 9			
Fri. 10 10	**Neptune 0.9° S of Moon, occultation‡**		
Sat. 11 11 58	Algol at minimum		
Sun. 12	Mercury at ascending node		
Mon. 13			
Tue. 14 8 47	Algol at minimum		
20 02	**Full Moon**		
Wed. 15 5	Mercury stationary		
Thu. 16			
Fri. 17	Mercury at perihelion		
5 36	Algol at minimum		
6	Moon at perigee (363 823 km)		
11	**Moon 0.8° N of Pleiades (M45)**		
Sat. 18			
Sun. 19			
Mon. 20	Mars at descending node		
2 25	Algol at minimum		
Tue. 21 4	Orionid meteors peak		
11 55	**Last Quarter**		
Wed. 22 4	**Moon 0.9° S of Beehive (M44)**		
10	**Mercury greatest elongation W (18°)**		
23 13	Algol at minimum		
Thu. 23 21	**Regulus 1.9° N of Moon**		
Fri. 24			
Sat. 25 8	Saturn 5° N of Moon		
20 02	Algol at minimum		
Sun. 26 12	Venus 3° N of Antares (35° E)		
Mon. 27	Mercury at greatest heliocentric lat. N		
17	Mercury 7° N of Moon		
Tue. 28 16 51	Algol at minimum		
23 14	**New Moon** (lunation 1062)		
Wed. 29	Pallas stationary		
Thu. 30	Vesta at opposition		
Fri. 31 13 40	Algol at minimum		
18	**Antares 0.1° S of Moon, occultation††**		

† S half of Africa, Madagascar, W Australasia
‡ E Asia, Philippines, Japan, W Alaska
†† Central S. America, west tip of Africa

THE SKY FOR 2008 NOVEMBER

		Mercury	Venus	Mars	Jupiter	Saturn	Uranus	Neptune	Sun
RA	1	13ʰ 32ᵐ	16ʰ 58ᵐ	15ʰ 06ᵐ	19ʰ 13ᵐ	11ʰ 21ᵐ	23ʰ 20ᵐ	21ʰ 35ᵐ	14ʰ 26m
	11	14ʰ 32ᵐ	17ʰ 51ᵐ	15ʰ 35ᵐ	19ʰ 20ᵐ	11ʰ 24ᵐ	23ʰ 20ᵐ	21ʰ 35ᵐ	15ʰ 06m
	21	15ʰ 36ᵐ	18ʰ 44ᵐ	16ʰ 04ᵐ	19ʰ 27ᵐ	11ʰ 27ᵐ	23ʰ 19ᵐ	21ʰ 36ᵐ	15ʰ 47m
Dec	1	–7° 31′	–24° 21′	–17° 35′	–22° 45′	+6° 12′	–5° 07′	–14° 43′	–14° 26′
	11	–13° 52′	–25° 28′	–19° 29′	–22° 33′	+5° 53′	–5° 11′	–14° 43′	–17° 26′
	21	–19° 23′	–25° 21′	–21° 07′	–22° 18′	+5° 37′	–5° 13′	–14° 41′	–19° 55′
Dist	1	1.21	1.21	2.50	5.43	9.95	19.45	29.80	0.993
	11	1.37	1.14	2.50	5.56	9.82	19.59	29.98	0.990
	21	1.44	1.08	2.49	5.69	9.67	19.74	30.15	0.988
Mag	1	–0.8	–3.9	1.5	–2.1	1.1	5.8	7.9	
	11	–0.9	–3.9	1.5	–2.1	1.1	5.8	7.9	
	21	–1.2	–4.0	1.4	–2.0	1.1	5.8	7.9	
Size	1	5.5″	13.8″	3.7″	36.3″	16.7″	3.6″	2.2″	32′14″
	11	4.9″	14.6″	3.7″	35.4″	16.9″	3.6″	2.2″	32′19″
	21	4.7″	15.5″	3.8″	34.6″	17.2″	3.5″	2.2″	32′23″

Moon—On Nov. 1.0 UT, the age of the Moon is 3.0 d. The Sun's selenographic colongitude is 303.10° and increases by 12.2° each day thereafter. The libration in longitude is maximum (east limb exposed) on the 20th (+7°), and minimum (west limb exposed) on the 8th (–7°). The libration in latitude is maximum (north limb exposed) on the 25th (+7°), and minimum (south limb exposed) on the 12th (–7°). The Moon reaches its greatest northern declination on the 15th (+27°), and its greatest southern declination on the 1st and 29th (–27°).

Mercury was at greatest elongation west (18°) on Oct. 22, and should still be visible to northern hemisphere observers during bright morning twilight in the first days of November. Mercury is at superior conjunction on Nov. 25.

Venus brightens to magnitude –4.2 during the month, dominating the evening sky since it sets well after full dark. On the last evening of November the two brightest planets have a striking conjunction, as **Venus passes 2° south of magnitude –1.9 Jupiter**, while the three-day-old crescent Moon with earthshine has closed to only 7° away (as seen from the west coast of North America), a scene that will be widely photographed and published. Northern observers will need a flat southwestern horizon to view the trio.

Mars will be in conjunction with the Sun on Dec. 5, and so is hidden in the solar glare.

Jupiter decorates the evening sky, especially at month-end when it joins Venus. (See Venus.) At the end of CT on the 15th, Jupiter is at 32° altitude at latitude 30°N, still high enough for telescopic observing, and at 46° altitude at latitude 30°S. It sets in the west-southwest, during mid-evening in mid-northern latitudes, and late evening at 30°S.

Saturn, in Leo, rises in the east near 1:30 at mid-month. By morning CT its altitude in the southeast is: 47° at latitude 45°N, 55° at latitude 30°N, and 31° at latitude 30°S (in the east-northeast). On the 15th the inclination of the rings is only 1.5° from edge-on.

Time (UT) d h m			NOVEMBER EVENTS	Jupiter's Satellites West	East
Sat.	1		Venus at aphelion	1.0	II
	8		Venus 3° N of Moon		I
Sun.	2		**Daylight Saving Time ends**	2.0	
	5		Moon at apogee (405 724 km)	3.0	
	7		Neptune stationary		III
Mon.	3	10 29	Algol at minimum	4.0	
	22		**Jupiter 1.9° N of Moon**	5.0	IV
Tue.	4				
Wed.	5	4	S. Taurid meteors peak	6.0	
Thu.	6	4 03	**First Quarter**	7.0	
	7 18		Algol at minimum	8.0	
	19		**Neptune 1.1° S of Moon, occultation†**	9.0	
Fri.	7				
Sat.	8			10.0	
Sun.	9	4 07	Algol at minimum	11.0	
Mon.	10			12.0	
Tue.	11				
Wed.	12	0 56	Algol at minimum	13.0	
	4		N. Taurid meteors peak	14.0	
Thu.	13	6 17	**Full Moon**	15.0	
	20		**Moon 0.7° N of Pleiades (M45)**		
Fri.	14	10	Moon at perigee (358 971 km) **Large tides**	16.0	
	21 45		Algol at minimum	17.0	
Sat.	15			18.0	
Sun.	16				
Mon	17	10	Leonid meteors peak	19.0	
	18 34		Algol at minimum	20.0	
Tue.	18	10	**Moon 1.2° S of Beehive (M44)**		
Wed.	19	21 31	**Last Quarter**	21.0	
Thu.	20		Mercury at descending node	22.0	
	15 23		Algol at minimum	23.0	
Fri.	21	18	Saturn 6° N of Moon		
Sat.	22			24.0	
Sun.	23		Venus at greatest heliocentric lat. S	25.0	
	12 12		Algol at minimum	26.0	
Mon.	24				
Tue.	25	17	Mercury in superior conjunction	27.0	
Wed.	26	9 01	Algol at minimum	28.0	
Thu.	27	16 55	**New Moon** (lunation 1063)	29.0	
Fri.	28	0	Uranus stationary		
Sat.	29	5 50	Algol at minimum	30.0	
	17		Moon at apogee (406 480 km)	31.0	
Sun.	30		Mercury at aphelion		

† NE tip of Canada, United Kingdom except SE part, S Scandinavia, Iceland

THE SKY FOR 2008 DECEMBER

		Mercury	Venus	Mars	Jupiter	Saturn	Uranus	Neptune	Sun
RA	1	16ʰ 41ᵐ	19ʰ 35ᵐ	16ʰ 35ᵐ	19ʰ 36ᵐ	11ʰ 29ᵐ	23ʰ 19ᵐ	21ʰ 36ᵐ	16ʰ 29m
	11	17ʰ 50ᵐ	20ʰ 25ᵐ	17ʰ 07ᵐ	19ʰ 44ᵐ	11ʰ 31ᵐ	23ʰ 20ᵐ	21ʰ 37ᵐ	17ʰ 13m
	21	18ʰ 59ᵐ	21ʰ 12ᵐ	17ʰ 39ᵐ	19ʰ 54ᵐ	11ʰ 32ᵐ	23ʰ 20ᵐ	21ʰ 38ᵐ	17ʰ 57m
Dec	1	–23° 21′	–24° 03′	–22° 25′	–22° 00′	+5° 24′	–5° 13′	–14° 39′	–21° 48′
	11	–25° 20′	–21° 39′	–23° 23′	–21° 40′	+5° 16′	–5° 11′	–14° 35′	–23° 00′
	21	–25° 00′	–18° 20′	–23° 57′	–21° 17′	+5° 12′	–5° 07′	–14° 31′	–23° 26′
Dist	1	1.45	1.01	2.48	5.80	9.51	19.91	30.32	0.986
	11	1.40	0.94	2.47	5.90	9.34	20.08	30.48	0.985
	21	1.29	0.87	2.45	5.98	9.18	20.26	30.62	0.984
Mag	1	–1.1	–4.0	1.3	–2.0	1.0	5.8	7.9	
	11	–0.8	–4.1	1.3	–2.0	1.0	5.8	7.9	
	21	–0.7	–4.1	1.3	–1.9	1.0	5.9	7.9	
Size	1	4.6″	16.5″	3.8″	34.0″	17.5″	3.5″	2.2″	32′26″
	11	4.8″	17.8″	3.8″	33.4″	17.8″	3.5″	2.2″	32′29″
	21	5.2″	19.2″	3.8″	33.0″	18.1″	3.5″	2.2″	32′31″

Moon—On Dec. 1.0 UT, the age of the Moon is 3.3 d. The Sun's selenographic colongitude is 308.17° and increases by 12.2° each day thereafter. The libration in longitude is maximum (east limb exposed) on the 18th (+8°), and minimum (west limb exposed) on the 6th (–8°). The libration in latitude is maximum (north limb exposed) on the 22nd (+7°), and minimum (south limb exposed) on the 10th (–7°). The Moon reaches its greatest northern declination on the 12th (+27°), and its greatest southern declination on the 26th (–27°).

There is a daylight occultation of Venus by the Moon on the 1st in the northeastern tip of Canada. While waiting for Venus to reappear, try observing magnitude –1.9 Jupiter with the unaided eye in the daytime, since Jupiter will be less than 2° from the Moon.

On the 12th the Moon reaches its closest perigee distance in 15 years (356 566 km), resulting in extra large tides in areas such as Canada's Bay of Fundy, since it will also be Full Moon (see TIDES AND THE EARTH–MOON SYSTEM, p.173). The Moon's farthest apogee distance (406 601 km) this year occurs on the 26th.

Mercury was at superior conjunction on Nov. 25. It emerges into evening twilight by mid-December, but southern hemisphere observers are favoured until late in the month. Mercury passes 1.3° south of Jupiter on the 30th (the date in North America).

Venus brightens to magnitude –4.4 during December, and continues to dominate the evening sky, setting long after full dark. It begins the month 2° south of Jupiter, but pulls away rapidly, and they are 5° apart by the evening of the 5th. (See also the Moon.)

Mars hides behind the Sun, being in conjunction with our star on the 5th.

Jupiter still sets in a dark sky in the west-southwest at mid-month, but by year-end it is down before twilight ends. (See Venus, Mercury, and the Moon for Jupiter's attractive groupings with twilight's other ornaments this month.)

Saturn, in Leo, rises in the east near midnight at mid-month. Observers at latitude 45°N see it transit 50° near morning AT, while at latitude 30°N it culminates 65° up as NT begins. Southern observers view Saturn 49° high in the northeast as CT begins. By year's end the inclination of the rings has closed to 0.8°.

Time (UT) d h m	DECEMBER EVENTS	Jupiter's Satellites West East
Mon. 1 0	**Venus 2° S of Jupiter (42° E)**	
15	**Jupiter 1.3° N of Moon**	
16	**Venus 0.8° S of Moon, occultation†**	
Tue. 2 2 39	Algol at minimum	
Wed. 3		
Thu. 4	Pallas at opposition	
23 28	Algol at minimum	
Fri. 5 21 26	**First Quarter**	
22	Mars in conjunction with the Sun	
Sat. 6		
Sun. 7 20 17	Algol at minimum	
Mon. 8		
Tue. 9		
Wed. 10 17 06	Algol at minimum	
Thu. 11 8	**Moon 0.7° N of Pleiades (M45)**	
Fri. 12 16 37	**Full Moon** (largest in 2008)	
22	Moon at perigee (356 566 km) **Large tides**	
Sat. 13 13 56	Algol at minimum	
23	**Geminid meteors peak**	
Sun. 14		
Mon. 15 19	**Moon 1.4° S of Beehive (M44)**	
Tue. 16 10 45	Algol at minimum	
Wed. 17		
Thu. 18		
Fri. 19	Vesta stationary	
3	Saturn 6° N of Moon	
7 34	Algol at minimum	
10 29	**Last Quarter**	
Sat. 20	Mercury at greatest heliocentric lat. S	
Sun. 21 12 04	**Solstice**	
Mon. 22	Pluto in conjunction with the Sun	
4 23	Algol at minimum	
8	Ursid meteors peak	
Tue. 23		
Wed. 24		
Thu. 25 1 12	Algol at minimum	
7	**Antares 0.1° S of Moon, occultation‡**	
Fri. 26 18	Moon at apogee (406 601 km)	
Sat. 27 1	**Venus 1.5° S of Neptune (46° E)**	
12 22	**New Moon** (lunation 1064)	
22 02	Algol at minimum	
Sun. 28		
Mon. 29 4	**Mercury 0.7° S of Moon, occultation††**	
9	**Jupiter 0.6° N of Moon, occultation‡‡**	
Tue. 30 18 51	Algol at minimum	
Wed. 31 5	**Mercury 1.3° S of Jupiter (18° E)**	

† NE tip of Canada, Europe, S Scandinavia
‡ S half of Africa, Madagascar, SE Asia   †† E Asia, Japan, N Indonesia
‡‡ Australia except E part, most of Antarctica

ECLIPSES
ECLIPSE PATTERNS
BY ROY BISHOP

Eclipse Seasons

The plane of the Moon's orbit is tilted about 5° to the plane of Earth's orbit, the ecliptic. Since 5° is considerably larger than both the north–south range of lunar parallax for various localities on Earth ($\approx$1.9°) and the angular radii of the Sun and Moon (each $\approx$0.25°), solar eclipses can occur only when the Sun is near (within about

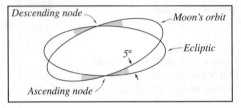

±15° to ±18°) one of the two points at which the Moon's orbit crosses the ecliptic (nodes). Lunar eclipses have a comparable restriction. The *ascending* node is the one at which the Moon crosses to the *north* side of the ecliptic.

The Sun moves eastward along the ecliptic about 1° per day; thus the interval during which an eclipse can occur is at most about (2 × 18°) ÷ 1°/d = 36 d, an *eclipse season*. Since the interval between new moons (29.5 days) is somewhat less, one or two solar eclipses will occur in each eclipse season. Six months later, when the Sun is near the other node, another eclipse season occurs. However, the plane of the Moon's orbit wobbles, making the nodes regress slowly westward along the ecliptic with a period of 18.61 years; thus the two eclipse seasons drift backward through the year, occurring about 19 days earlier each year. *The eclipse seasons of 2008 occur in February and August.*

In a calendar year,
- there can be as many as seven eclipses (solar and lunar combined, as last occurred in 1982) and as few as four (the usual number, as in 2008);
- there can be as many as five solar or lunar eclipses and as few as two;
- the number of total or annular solar eclipses can range from zero to two, the number of total lunar eclipses from zero to three.

In 2008, there are four eclipses: two lunar (one total and one partial) and two solar (one annular and one total).

The Saros

Eclipses of the Sun and Moon recur with various periodicities that are more or less approximate. These periodicities are interesting both as numerical curiosities and because they may be used to predict eclipses. The most famous periodicity, the *Saros,* has been known since ancient times. It is a consequence of a remarkable commensurability between three lunar average periods:

Synodic month *(S)* (new to new)   = 29.530 589 d, 223*S* = 6585.3213 d
Draconic month *(N)* (node to node)   = 27.212 221 d, 242*N* = 6585.3575 d
Anomalistic month *(P)* (perigee to perigee) = 27.554 550 d, 239*P* = 6585.5375 d

Several aspects of this arithmetic are relevant to the pattern of eclipses (for brevity, the following comments are restricted primarily to the case of solar eclipses):

(1) An integer number of Ss (223) ensures a new Moon and hence the possibility of a second solar eclipse.

(2) $242N \approx 223S$ means that the new Moon will be at almost the same position relative to a node, ensuring that an eclipse *will* occur again and that it will occur on Earth's globe about the same distance north or south of the ecliptic plane as did the first eclipse.

(3) The Saros $(223S) = 6585.3213$ d $= 18$ years $+$ *only* 10.3213 d or 11.3213 d (depending on the number of intervening leap years). Thus one Saros later Earth will be at almost the same point in its elliptical orbit and hence at nearly the same distance from the Sun. Moreover, the inclination of Earth toward the Sun (season) will be nearly the same; thus the same latitude region of Earth will be exposed to the eclipse.

(text continues on next page)

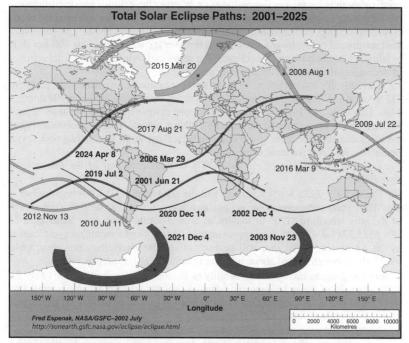

The figure shows the paths of all total solar eclipses, excluding hybrid annular/total eclipses, occurring during the years 2001–2025. There are 15 eclipses, one in each of the years 2001, 2002, 2003, 2006, 2008, 2009, 2010, 2012, 2015, 2016, 2017, 2019, 2020, 2021, and 2024. Because the 25-year period covered by the figure is somewhat longer than the 18-year Saros interval, the first four and last four eclipses, drawn with heavy shading and with labels in bold type, make up four Saros pairs, with Saros numbers 127, 142, 152, and 139, respectively. Note that the members of each pair are both total eclipses, are separated in time by one Saros, have similar path shapes, and occur at similar latitudes; note also that the later member is shifted 120° westward in longitude (see items (2) through (6) of the text explaining these features). The figure was produced by Fred Espenak and is presented here with his permission. For figures showing total solar eclipses, annular eclipses, and hybrid annular/total eclipses for the period 1801–2200, see sunearth.gsfc.nasa.gov/eclipse/SEatlas/SEatlas.html.

(4) $239P \approx 223S$ means that one Saros later the new Moon will be at almost the same point in its elliptical orbit and thus at the same distance from Earth. With the same lunar and solar distances, the type of eclipse (total or annular) will be the same. Since the eclipse will occur near the same geographic latitude (see (2) and (3)), the duration of totality or annularity, or the magnitude of partial eclipse if the eclipse is not central, will be almost the same as it was one Saros earlier.

(5) $242N - 223S = 0.0361$ d $= 0.87$ h. This, together with the 0.55°/h eastward speed of the Moon in its orbit, means that after one Saros the Moon will be about 0.5° west of its former position relative to its node. Thus a Saros series does not last forever; there will be about $36°/0.5° \approx 72$ eclipses in a Saros series (the number ranges from 69 to 87). Furthermore, any one Saros series will last for about $72 \times 18 \approx 1300$ years (the range is 1226 to 1551 years).

A Saros series begins with about 10 partial eclipses of increasing magnitude in the north or south polar region, depending upon whether the eclipses are occurring near the ascending or descending lunar node, respectively. These are followed by about 50 central eclipses (either total or annular), which over many centuries progressively shift southward or northward across Earth (on average an approximate 300-km shift in latitude with each successive eclipse). The series ends with 10 or so partial eclipses of decreasing magnitude in the opposite polar region.

Currently, for solar eclipses, 39 Saros series are running simultaneously, numbers 117 through 155 (for lunar eclipses, 41 Saros series are running, numbers 109 through 149). That is, in any 18-year 11-day interval, one eclipse from each of these 39 (and 41) series takes place, after which the whole pattern repeats. Those series occurring at the lunar ascending node are given odd numbers; those at the descending node, even numbers (vice versa for lunar eclipses).

The eclipse sequence of the year 2008 is similar to that of the four-eclipse year 1990.

(6) The Saros $= 223S = 6585.3213$ d, and the fractional 0.3213 d $\approx$ one-third of a day. Thus each successive solar eclipse in a Saros series will be shifted one-third of the way westward (120° in longitude) around Earth. After three Saros periods $(3 \times 6585.3213$ d $\approx 19\,756$ d, or approximately 54 years and 1 month), a cycle known as the *Exeligmos,* the eclipse will be back at approximately the same geographic longitude, although shifted about 1000 km in latitude. Two examples follow.

    (a) The geographic region of visibility of the total lunar eclipse of 2008 Feb. 21 (no. 26 of Saros 133) which is centred over the western Atlantic is similar to that of the total lunar eclipse of 1990 Feb. 9 (no. 25 of Saros 133) which was centred over India, 120° further east.

    (b) The total solar eclipse of 2024 Apr. 8 (no. 30 of Saros 139), which sweeps northeastward across eastern North America, will be geographically similar to that of 1970 Mar. 7 (no. 27 of Saros 139), which followed the eastern seaboard of North America one Exeligmos earlier. Also, one Saros earlier we had the similar total solar eclipse of 2006 Mar. 29 (no. 29 of Saros 139), which occurred about 120° to the east, across Africa and the Mediterranean (see the figure on the previous page). You, the reader, should now be able to figure out the date, the shape of the path of totality, and the geographic location of solar eclipse no. 28 of Saros 139!

The Metonic Cycle

The sequence of lunar phases and the year repeat their relative pattern at 19-year intervals, a cycle known to astronomers in ancient Babylon and that was discovered independently around 430 BC by Meton, a Greek astronomer. We have

$235S = 235 \times 29.530\,589 = 6939.6884$ d;

19 years = 6939 d or 6940 d (depending on leap years).

Moreover, $255N$ is also very close to 19 years:

$255N = 255 \times 27.212\,221 = 6939.1164$ d.

Thus solar and lunar eclipses also repeat on a 19-year "Metonic" cycle. Since $255N$ is less than $235S$, the Moon does not reach the same phase (new or full for an eclipse) until it has moved eastward relative to the node by

$(235S - 255N) \times 24$ h $\times 0.55°/h = 7.5°$.

Thus a Metonic eclipse series will have only

eclipse season width on the ecliptic $(36°) \div 7.5° \approx 4$ or 5 eclipses;

and the geographic latitude of successive solar eclipses in a series will change substantially (north or south, depending upon whether the Moon is at its ascending node or descending node, respectively).

What about the Moon's position in its orbit relative to its perigee? Using the anomalistic month P (the Moon returns to perigee on average every 27.554 550 d),

$235S \div P = 251.85$, which is *not* near an integer.

Thus in a Metonic series the Moon's distance is not the same from one eclipse to another. Hence the type of solar eclipse (total or annular) will vary within the series.

With only about four eclipses in a series, a mix of eclipse types, and scattered geographic occurrence, a Metonic eclipse series is not as elegant or useful as a Saros series. The main feature of a Metonic eclipse series is that, like lunar phases, the successive eclipses occur on (almost) the *same day* of the year.

Examples of the Metonic cycle for a lunar phase, lunar eclipses, and two recent Western Hemisphere total solar eclipses are given below. The numbers in parentheses are Saros numbers.

Full Moon	Lunar Eclipses	Solar Eclipses
1951 Mar. 23	1932 Feb. 22 (no eclipse)	1960 Feb. 26 (no eclipse)
1970 Mar. 23	1951 Feb. 21 Penumbral (103)	**1979** Feb. 26 Total (120)
1989 Mar. 22	1970 Feb. 21 Partial (113)	**1998** Feb. 26 Total (130)
2008 Mar. 21	1989 Feb. 20 Total (123)	2017 Feb. 26 Annular (140)
2027 Mar. 22	**2008** Feb. 21 Total (133)	2036 Feb. 27 Partial (150)
2046 Mar. 22	2027 Feb. 20 Penumbral (143)	2055 Feb. 27 (no eclipse)
2065 Mar. 22	2046 Feb. 20 (no eclipse)	

ECLIPSES IN 2008
By Fred Espenak

Two central solar and two lunar eclipses occur in 2008 as follows:

Feb. 7:   Annular solar eclipse
Feb. 21:   Total lunar eclipse
Aug. 1:   Total solar eclipse
Aug. 16:   Partial lunar eclipse

Predictions for the eclipses are summarized in Figures 1 through 6 (pp. 138–143). World maps show the regions of visibility for each eclipse. The lunar eclipse diagrams also include the path of the Moon through Earth's shadows. Contact times for each principal phase are tabulated along with the magnitudes and geocentric coordinates of the Sun and Moon at greatest eclipse.

Annular Solar Eclipse of February 7

The first solar eclipse of 2008 occurs at the Moon's ascending node in Capricornus. An annular eclipse will be visible from a wide track, which traverses Antarctica and southern regions of the Pacific Ocean. A partial eclipse will be seen within the much larger path of the Moon's penumbral shadow, which includes the southeastern third of Australia, all of New Zealand, and most of Antarctica (Figure 1, p. 138).

The annular path begins in Antarctica at 03:20 UT when the Moon's antumbral shadow meets Earth and forms a 581–kilometre wide corridor near the base of the continent's peninsula region. Traveling westward, the shadow quickly crosses Antarctica and turns north as it heads into the Pacific. Greatest eclipse[1] takes place at 03:55:05 UT, when the eclipse magnitude[2] will reach 0.9650. At this instant, the annular duration is 2 minutes 12 seconds, the path width is 444 kilometres, and the Sun is 16° above the featureless horizon of the open ocean. The central track continues north before gradually curving to the east where it ends at local sunset at 04:31 UT. During its 1 hour 10 minute flight across our planet, the Moon's antumbra travels approximately 5600 kilometres and covers 0.59% of Earth's surface area. Path coordinates and central line circumstances are presented in Table 1 (p. 134).

The most unusual characteristic of this eclipse is that it begins and ends along Earth's sunset terminator. Most eclipse paths travel from west to east, however, the 2008 annular eclipse path begins by running east to west and slowly turns north before curving west to east near its terminus.

Partial phases of the eclipse are visible primarily from eastern Australia, New Zealand, and the South Pacific. Local circumstances for a number of cities are listed in Table 2. All times are given in Universal Time. The Sun's altitude and azimuth, the eclipse magnitude and obscuration are all given at the instant of maximum eclipse.

This is the 60th eclipse of Saros 121. The series began with the first of six partial eclipses on 944 Apr. 25. The first central eclipse was total in the Northern Hemisphere on 1070 Jul. 10. It was followed by 41 more total eclipses before the series produced two hybrid eclipses in 1827 and 1845. The first annular eclipse of the series occurred on 1863 Nov. 11. The series will produce 11 annular eclipses, the last of which is 2044 Feb. 28. This means there are only two more central eclipses after the 2008 eclipse. The series terminates on 2206 Jun. 07, after nine more partial eclipses. Complete details for Saros 121 may be found at: sunearth.gsfc.nasa.gov/eclipse/SEsaros/SEsaros121.html.

---

[1] The instant of greatest eclipse occurs when the distance between the Moon's shadow axis and Earth's geocentre reaches a minimum.

[2] Eclipse magnitude is defined as the fraction of the Sun's diameter occulted by the Moon.

Total Lunar Eclipse of February 21

The first lunar eclipse of 2008 is perfectly placed for observers throughout most of the Americas as well as western Europe. The eclipse occurs at the Moon's descending node, midway between perigee and apogee. During the eclipse, Saturn lies about 3° northeast of the Moon and shines brightly ($m_V = +0.2$) because it is near opposition.

The Moon's orbital trajectory takes it through the southern half of Earth's umbral shadow. Although the eclipse is not central, the total phase still lasts nearly 25 minutes. The Moon's path through Earth's shadow as well as a map illustrating worldwide visibility of the event are shown in Figure 2 (p. 139). The timings of the major phases of the eclipse are listed below.

Penumbral eclipse begins:	0:36:35 UT
Partial eclipse begins:	1:43:19 UT
Total eclipse begins:	3:01:10 UT
Greatest eclipse:	3:26:05 UT
Total eclipse ends:	3:50:57 UT
Partial eclipse ends:	5:08:47 UT
Penumbral eclipse ends:	6:15:39 UT

At the instant of greatest eclipse (03:26 UT) the Moon lies near the zenith for observers in French Guiana. At this time, the umbral magnitude peaks at 1.1062 as the Moon's northern limb passes 7.2 arc-minutes south of the shadow's central axis. In contrast, the Moon's southern limb lies 3.3 arc-minutes from the southern edge of the umbra and 38.4 arc-minutes from the shadow centre. Thus, the northern half of the Moon will appear much darker than the southern half because it lies deeper in the shadow. Since the Moon samples a large range of umbral depths during totality, its appearance will change dramatically with time. It is not possible to predict the exact brightness distribution in the umbra, so observers are encouraged to estimate the Danjon value at different times during totality (see Danjon Scale of Lunar Eclipse Brightness below). Note that it may also be necessary to assign different Danjon values to different portions of the Moon (i.e. north vs. south).

During totality, the spring constellations are well placed for viewing so a number of bright stars can be used for magnitude comparisons. Regulus ($m_V = +1.40$) is 3° northwest of the eclipsed Moon, while Procyon ($m_V = -0.05$) is 40° to the west, Spica ($m_V = +0.98$) is 51° to the southeast, and Arcturus ($m_V = -0.05$) is 58° to the northeast. Alphard or Alpha Hya ($m_V = +1.99$) is 23° to the southwest, and Saturn ($m_V = +0.2$) is just 3° to the northeast of the Moon.

The entire event is visible from South America and most of North America. Observers along North America's west coast miss the early stages of the partial eclipse because it begins before moonrise. Alaskans in Anchorage and Fairbanks experience moonrise during totality but bright evening twilight will make it difficult for sourdoughs to view the event. Western Europe and northwest Africa also see the entire eclipse. Further to the east (east Africa and central Asia), the Moon sets before the eclipse ends. None of the eclipse is visible from eastern Asia or Australia.

Table 3 (p. 135) lists predicted umbral immersion and emersion times for 20 well-defined lunar craters. The timing of craters is useful in determining the atmospheric enlargement of Earth's shadow (see Crater Timings During Lunar Eclipses below).

Total Solar Eclipse of August 1

On Friday, Aug. 1, a total eclipse of the Sun is visible from a narrow corridor that traverses half the Earth. The path of the Moon's umbral shadow begins in Canada and extends across northern Greenland, the Arctic, central Russia, Mongolia, and China, where it will end at sunset [Espenak and Anderson 2006]. A partial eclipse is seen within the much broader path of the Moon's penumbral shadow, which includes northeastern North America, most of Europe, and Asia (Figure 3, p. 140).

The path of totality begins in northern Canada, where the Moon's umbral shadow first touches down in the territory of Nunavut at 09:23 UT (Figure 4, p. 141). Along the sunrise terminator in Queen Maud Gulf, the duration is 1 min 30 s from the centre of the 206-km-wide path. Traveling over 0.6 km/s, the umbra quickly sweeps north across southern Victoria Island, Prince of Wales Island, and northern Somerset Island. The shadow's northern limit clips the southeastern corner of Cornwallis Island and just misses the high-Arctic town of Resolute. The nearly 200 residents of this isolated settlement will witness a partial eclipse of magnitude of 0.997 at 09:26 UT with the Sun 7° above the horizon.

Continuing on its northeastern trajectory, the umbra crosses Devon Island and reaches the southern coast of Ellesmere Island. The central line cuts across Nares Strait as the shadow straddles Ellesmere Island and Greenland. Canada's remote outpost Alert, the northernmost permanently inhabited place on Earth, lies near the northern limit of the eclipse track and experiences 43 s totality with the Sun at 16° altitude at 09:32 UT.

After crossing northern Greenland, the track passes between Franz Josef Land and Svalbard. By the time the central line reaches the northern coast of Novaya Zemlya (10:00 UT), the duration is 2 min 23 s with the Sun at 31°. The track crosses its northern island and the Kara Sea before reaching the Yamal Peninsula and the Russian mainland.

The instant of greatest eclipse occurs at 10:21:07 UT (latitude 65° 39′ N, longitude 72° 18′ E), when the axis of the Moon's shadow passes closest to the centre of Earth (gamma = +0.8307, where gamma is the minimum distance of the Moon's shadow axis from Earth's centre in units of equatorial Earth radii). Totality reaches its maximum duration of 2 min 27 s, the Sun's altitude is 34°, the path width is 237 km and the umbra's velocity is 0.507 km/s.

During the next hour, the Moon's umbra works its way across central Asia (Figure 5, p. 142). The shadow gradually picks up speed and its course changes from south-southeast to nearly east at its terminus. Novosibirsk, Russia's third most-populous city, lies only 18 km from the central line. The midpoint of Novosibirsk's 2 min 18 s total eclipse occurs at 10:45 UT with the Sun's altitude at 30°. Three and a half minutes later, Barnaul is plunged into a 2 min 16 s total eclipse.

The centre of the track follows the China–Mongolia border for several hundred kilometres, while the central duration and the Sun's altitude both decrease. From Altay, China, the total eclipse begins at 10:59 UT and lasts 1 min 25 s with the Sun 25° above the horizon. Across the border, western Mongolia is very sparsely populated, and the Altan Mountains bring cloudiness to the area. Ten minutes later, the umbra just misses Hami, China, where a deep partial eclipse of magnitude 0.998 occurs at 11:10 UT. This region in northwest China is noteworthy because it offers some of the most promising weather prospects along the entire eclipse path. Its position between the Gobi Desert to the east and the Talikmakan Desert to the west spares it from the monsoon systems that affect much of Southeast Asia during the summer months.

During the final ten minutes of the umbra's track, it quickly sweeps across northern China as the duration of totality and the Sun's altitude decrease. The major city of Xi'an straddles the southern limit where maximum eclipse occurs with the Sun just 4° above the horizon. From the central line 106 km to the north, the duration of totality still lasts 1 min 35 s. Seconds later, the axis of the Moon's shadow lifts off Earth and the central eclipse ends (11:20 UT). Over the course of 2 hours, the Moon's umbra travels along a path approximately 10 200 km long and covers 0.4% of Earth's surface area. Path coordinates and central line circumstances are presented in Table 4 (pp. 135–136).

Partial phases of the eclipse are visible from most of Asia, northern Europe, and northern Canada. Local circumstances for a number of cities are listed in Table 5 (pp. 136–137). All times are given in Universal Time. The Sun's altitude and azimuth, the eclipse magnitude and obscuration are all given at the instant of maximum eclipse.

This is the 47th eclipse of Saros 126. The series began with the first of eight partial eclipses on 1179 Mar. 10. The first central eclipse was annular in the Southern Hemisphere on 1305 May 24. It was followed by 27 more annular eclipses before the series produce 3 hybrid eclipses in 1828, 1846, and 1864. The first total eclipse of the series occurred on 1882 May 17. The series will produce ten total eclipses, the last of which is 2044 Aug. 23. Thus, there are only two more central eclipses after the 2008 eclipse. The series terminates on 2459 May 03, after a long string of 23 partial eclipses. Complete details for Saros 126 may be found at sunearth.gsfc.nasa.gov/eclipse/SEsaros/SEsaros126.html

Partial Lunar Eclipse of August 28

The last eclipse of 2008 is a partial lunar eclipse at the Moon's ascending node in Capricornus. It is visibile primarily from the Eastern Hemisphere as well as eastern South America (Figure 6, p. 143). Greatest eclipse takes place at 21:10:06 UT, when the eclipse magnitude will reach 0.8076. The timings of the major phases of the eclipse are listed below.

Penumbral eclipse begins:	18:24:49 UT
Partial eclipse begins:	19:36:07 UT
Greatest eclipse:	21:10:09 UT
Partial eclipse ends:	22:44:16 UT
Penumbral eclipse ends:	23:55:25 UT

The Moon's trajectory takes it through the northern umbral shadow, resulting in a partial eclipse that lasts 94 minutes. At mid-eclipse the Moon's northern limb passes 5.9 arc-minutes outside the umbra's northern edge. The Moon's southern edge is then 16.5 arc-minutes from the shadow's centre.

Table 6 (p. 137) lists predicted umbral immersion and emersion times for 17 well-defined lunar craters. The timing of craters is useful in determining the atmospheric enlargement of Earth's shadow (see Crater Timings During Lunar Eclipses below).

Solar Eclipse Figures

For each solar eclipse, an orthographic projection map of Earth shows the path of penumbral (partial) and umbral (total and annular) eclipse. North is to the top in all cases, and the daylight terminator is plotted for the instant of greatest eclipse. An asterisk (*) indicates the subsolar point[3] on Earth.

The limits of the Moon's penumbral shadow delineate the region of visibility of the partial eclipse. This irregular or saddle-shaped region often covers nearly half the daylight hemisphere of Earth and consists of several distinct zones, or limits. At the northern and/or southern boundaries lie the limits of the penumbra's path. Partial eclipses have only one of these limits, as do central eclipses when the Moon's shadow axis falls no closer than about 0.45 radii from Earth's centre. Great loops at the western and eastern extremes of the penumbra's path identify the areas where the eclipse begins/ends at sunrise and sunset, respectively. If the penumbra has both a northern and southern limit, the rising and setting curves form two separate closed loops. Otherwise, the curves are connected in a distorted figure 8. Bisecting the "eclipse begins/ends" loops is the curve of maximum eclipse at sunrise (western loop) and sunset (eastern loop). The points P1 and P4 mark the coordinates where the penumbral shadow first contacts (partial eclipse begins) and last contacts (partial eclipse ends) Earth's surface. If the penumbral path has both a northern and southern limit, then points P2 and P3 are also plotted. These correspond to the coordinates where the penumbral shadow cone becomes internally tangent to Earth's disk.

---

[3] The subsolar point is the geographic location where the Sun appears directly overhead (zenith).

A curve of maximum eclipse is the locus of all points where the eclipse is at maximum at a given time, and is plotted at each half-hour Universal Time. The points generally run between the penumbral limits in the north/south direction, or from the "maximum eclipse at sunrise and sunset" curves to one of the limits. If the eclipse is central (i.e. total or annular), the curves of maximum eclipse run through the outlines of the umbral shadow, plotted at 10-min intervals. The curves of constant eclipse magnitude delineate the locus of all points where the magnitude at maximum eclipse is constant. These curves run exclusively between the curves of maximum eclipse at sunrise and sunset. Furthermore, they are parallel to the northern/southern penumbral limits and the umbral paths of central eclipses. In fact, the northern and southern limits of the penumbra can be thought of as curves of constant magnitude of 0.0. The adjacent curves are for magnitudes of 0.2, 0.4, 0.6, and 0.8. For total eclipses, the northern and southern limits of the umbra are curves of constant magnitude of 1.0. Umbral path limits for annular eclipses are curves of maximum eclipse magnitude.

Greatest eclipse is defined as the instant when the axis of the Moon's shadow passes closest to Earth's centre. Although greatest eclipse differs slightly from the instants of greatest magnitude and greatest duration (for total eclipses), the differences are negligible. The point on Earth's surface intersected by the axis at greatest eclipse is marked by an asterisk symbol. For partial eclipses, the shadow axis misses Earth entirely, so the point of greatest eclipse lies on the day/night terminator and the Sun appears on the horizon.

Data pertinent to the eclipse appear with each map. At the top are listed the instant of ecliptic conjunction of the Sun and Moon (i.e. New Moon) and the instant of greatest eclipse, expressed in Terrestrial Dynamical Time and Universal Time. The eclipse magnitude is defined as the fraction of the Sun's diameter obscured by the Moon at greatest eclipse. For central eclipses (total or annular), the magnitude is replaced by the geocentric ratio of diameters of the Moon and the Sun. Gamma is the minimum distance of the Moon's shadow axis from Earth's centre in Earth radii at greatest eclipse. The Saros series of the eclipse is listed, followed by the member position. The first member number identifies the sequence position of the eclipse in the Saros, while the second is the total number of eclipses in the series.

In the upper left and right corners are the geocentric coordinates of the Sun and the Moon, respectively, at the instant of greatest eclipse. They are:

R.A.   Right ascension
Dec.   Declination
S.D.   Apparent semi-diameter
H.P.   Horizontal parallax

To the lower left in the figures are exterior/interior contact times of the Moon's penumbral shadow with Earth, which are defined as follows:

P1   Instant of first exterior tangency of penumbra with Earth's limb
     (partial eclipse begins)
P2   Instant of first interior tangency of penumbra with Earth's limb
P3   Instant of last interior tangency of penumbra with Earth's limb
P4   Instant of last exterior tangency of penumbra with Earth's limb
     (partial eclipse ends)

Not all eclipses have P2 and P3 penumbral contacts. They are only present in cases where the penumbral shadow falls completely within Earth's disk. For central eclipses, the lower right corner lists exterior/interior contact times of the Moon's umbral shadow with Earth's limb, which are defined as follows:

U1   Instant of first exterior tangency of umbra with Earth's limb
     (umbral [total/annular] eclipse begins)
U2   Instant of first interior tangency of umbra with Earth's limb

U3   Instant of last interior tangency of umbra with Earth's limb
U4   Instant of last exterior tangency of umbra with Earth's limb
      (umbral [total/annular] eclipse ends)

At bottom centre are the geographic coordinates of the position of greatest eclipse, along with the local circumstances at that location (i.e. Sun altitude, Sun azimuth, path width, and duration of totality/annularity). At bottom left are a list of parameters used in the eclipse predictions, while bottom right gives the Moon's geocentric libration (optical + physical) at greatest eclipse.

Lunar Eclipse Figures

Each lunar eclipse has two diagrams associated with it along with data pertinent to the eclipse. The top figure shows the path of the Moon through Earth's penumbral and umbral shadows. Above this figure are listed the instant of ecliptic conjunction of the Moon with the point 180° from the Sun (i.e. Full Moon) and the instant of greatest eclipse, expressed in Terrestrial Dynamical Time and Universal Time. The penumbral and umbral magnitudes are defined as the fraction of the Moon's diameter immersed in the two shadows at greatest eclipse. The radii of the penumbral and umbral shadows, P. Radius and U. Radius, are also listed. Gamma is the minimum distance in Earth radii of the Moon's centre from Earth's shadow axis at greatest eclipse, and Axis is the same parameter expressed in degrees. The Saros series of the eclipse is listed, followed by a pair of numbers. The first number identifies the sequence position of the eclipse in the Saros; the second is the total number of eclipses in the series.

In the upper left and right corners are the geocentric coordinates of the Sun and the Moon, respectively, at the instant of greatest eclipse, defined as in the solar-eclipse diagrams.

To the lower left are the semi, or half, durations of the penumbral, umbral (partial), and total eclipses. Below them are the Sun/Moon ephemerides used in the predictions, followed by the extrapolated value of ΔT (the difference between Terrestrial Dynamical Time and Universal Time). To the lower right are the contact times of the Moon with Earth's penumbral and umbral shadows, defined as follows:

P1   Instant of first exterior tangency of Moon with penumbra
      (penumbral eclipse begins)
U1   Instant of first exterior tangency of Moon with umbra
      (partial umbral eclipse begins)
U2   Instant of first interior tangency of Moon with umbra
      (total umbral eclipse begins)
U3   Instant of last interior tangency of Moon with umbra
      (total umbral eclipse ends)
U4   Instant of last exterior tangency of Moon with umbra
      (partial umbral eclipse ends)
P4   Instant of last exterior tangency of Moon with penumbra
      (penumbral eclipse ends)

The bottom figure is a cylindrical equidistant projection map of Earth that shows the regions of visibility for each stage of the eclipse. In particular, the moonrise/moonset terminator is plotted for each contact and is labelled accordingly. The point where the Moon is in the zenith at greatest eclipse is indicated by an asterisk. Observers in the region that is completely unshaded will observe the entire eclipse, while those in the darkly shaded area will witness no eclipse. Observers in the remaining lightly shaded areas will experience moonrise or moonset while the eclipse is in progress. Those in the shaded zones east of the asterisk will witness moonset before the eclipse ends, and those in the shaded zones west will witness moonrise after the eclipse has begun.

Shadow Diameters and Lunar Eclipses

To compensate for Earth's atmosphere when calculating the circumstances for lunar eclipses, Chauvenet [1891] introduced an empirical enlargement of 1/50 to the diameters of the umbral and penumbral shadows. This rule has been employed by many of the national institutes in their official eclipse predictions (including the author's work at NASA). However, the French astonomer André-Louis Danjon [1951] pointed out a flaw in this method because it applies the same relative correction to the umbra and penumbra instead of using the same absolute correction. From eclipse observations, Danjon proposed to enlarge Earth's diameter by 1/85 to compensate for the atmosphere. The umbral and penumbral shadow diameters are then calculated based on this modified geometry. The French almanac *Connaissance des Temps* has used the Danjon rule in its eclipse predictions since 1951. The resulting umbral and penumbral eclipse magnitudes are approximately 0.005 and 0.026 magnitudes smaller, respectively, than predictions using the traditional 1/50 rule.

Beginning in 2007, we use the Danjon rule in calculating lunar eclipse circumstances.

Danjon Scale of Lunar Eclipse Brightness

The Moon's appearance during a total lunar eclipse can vary enormously from one eclipse to the next. Obviously, the geometry of the Moon's path through the umbra plays an important role. Not as apparent is the effect that Earth's atmosphere has on total eclipses. Although the physical mass of Earth blocks all direct sunlight from the umbra, the planet's atmosphere refracts some of the Sun's rays into the shadow. Earth's atmosphere contains varying amounts of water (clouds, mist, precipitation) and solid particles (meteoric dust, organic debris, volcanic ash). This material significantly filters and attenuates the sunlight before it is refracted into the umbra. For instance, large or frequent volcanic eruptions dumping huge quantities of ash into the atmosphere are often followed by very dark, red eclipses for several years. Extensive cloud cover along Earth's limb also tends to darken the eclipse by blocking sunlight.

Danjon proposed a useful five-point scale for evaluating the visual appearance and brightness of the Moon during total lunar eclipses. L values for various luminosities are defined as follows:

$L = 0$ Very dark eclipse
(Moon almost invisible, especially at mid-totality)
$L = 1$ Dark eclipse, grey or brownish in colouration
(details distinguishable only with difficulty)
$L = 2$ Deep red or rust-coloured eclipse
(very dark central shadow, while outer umbra is relatively bright)
$L = 3$ Brick-red eclipse
(umbral shadow usually has a bright or yellow rim)
$L = 4$ Very bright copper-red or orange eclipse
(umbral shadow has a bluish, very bright rim)

The assignment of an L value to lunar eclipses is best done with the naked eye, binoculars, or a small telescope near the time of mid-totality. It is also useful to examine the Moon's appearance just after the beginning and just before the end of totality. The Moon is then near the edge of the shadow, providing an opportunity to assign an L value to the outer umbra. In making any evaluations, the instrumentation used and the time should both be recorded. Also note any variations in colour and brightness in different parts of the umbra, as well as the apparent sharpness of the shadow's edge. Pay attention to the visibility of lunar features within the umbra. Notes and sketches made during the eclipse are often invaluable in recalling important details, events, and impressions.

Crater Timings During Lunar Eclipses

In 1702, Pierre de La Hire made a curious observation about Earth's umbra. In order to accurately predict the duration of a lunar eclipse, he found it necessary to increase the radius of the shadow about 1% more than is warranted by geometric considerations. Although the effect is clearly related to Earth's atmosphere, it is not completely understood, since the shadow enlargement seems to vary from one eclipse to the next. The enlargement can be measured through careful timings of lunar craters as they enter and exit the umbra.

Such observations are best made using a low-power telescope and a clock or watch synchronized with radio time signals. Timings should be made to a precision of 0.1 min. Record the instant when the most abrupt gradient at the umbra's edge crosses the apparent centre of the crater. In the case of large craters such as Tycho and Copernicus, record the times when the shadow touches the two opposite edges of the crater. The average of these times is equal to the instant of crater bisection.

As a planning guide, Tables 3 and 6 list 20 well-defined craters with predicted umbral immersion and emersion times during the two lunar eclipses of 2008. You should be thoroughly familiar with these features before viewing an eclipse in order to prevent confusion and misidentification. The four umbral contacts with the Moon's limb can also be used in determining the shadow's enlargement. However, these events are less distinct and therefore difficult to time accurately. Observers are encouraged to make crater timings and to send their results to *Sky & Telescope* (Sky Publishing Corporation, 90 Sherman Street, Cambridge MA 02140–3264, USA) for analysis.

Note that all predictions presented here use Danjon's rule of shadow enlargement (see Shadow Diameters and Lunar Eclipses). In particular, the diameter of the umbral shadow has been calculated assuming an enlargement of Earth's radius of 1/85 to account for the opacity of the terrestrial atmosphere. The effects of Earth's oblateness have also been included.

Eclipse Altitudes and Azimuths

The altitude a and azimuth A of the Sun or Moon during an eclipse depend on the time and the observer's geographic coordinates. They are calculated as follows:

$$h = 15 (GST + UT - \alpha) + \lambda$$
$$a = \arcsin [\sin \delta \sin \phi + \cos \delta \cos h \cos \phi]$$
$$A = \arctan [-(\cos \delta \sin h)/(\sin \delta \cos \phi - \cos \delta \cos h \sin \phi)]$$

where

h = hour angle of Sun or Moon
a = altitude
A = azimuth
GST = Greenwich Sidereal Time at 0:00 UT
UT = Universal Time
α = right ascension of Sun or Moon
δ = declination of Sun or Moon
λ = observer's longitude (east +, west −)
ϕ = observer's latitude (north +, south −)

During the eclipses of 2008, the values for GST and the geocentric right ascension and declination of the Sun or the Moon (at greatest eclipse) are as follows:

Eclipse	Date	GST	α	δ
Annular solar	2008 Feb. 7	9.111	21.346	−15.516
Total lunar	2008 Feb. 21	10.029	10.247	10.469
Total solar	2008 Aug. 1	20.693	8.798	17.866
Partial lunar	2008 Aug. 16	21.708	21.762	−12.925

Two Web-based tools can be used to calculate the local circumstances for all solar and lunar eclipses visible from any location. They are the Javascript Solar Eclipse Explorer and the Javascript Lunar Eclipse Explorer. The URLs for these tools are:

sunearth.gsfc.nasa.gov/eclipse/JSEX/JSEX-index.html
sunearth.gsfc.nasa.gov/eclipse/JLEX/JLEX-index.html

Eclipses In 2009

Next year (2009), there will be two central solar and four lunar eclipses:

2009 Jan. 26:	Annular solar eclipse
2009 Feb. 9:	Penumbral lunar eclipse
2009 Jul. 7:	Penumbral lunar eclipse
2009 Jul.22:	Total solar eclipse
2009 Aug. 6:	Penumbral lunar eclipse
2009 Dec. 31:	Partial lunar eclipse

A full report on these eclipses will be published next year in the *Observer's Handbook 2009*.

NASA Solar Eclipse Bulletins

Special bulletins containing detailed predictions and meteorological data for future solar eclipses of interest are prepared by Fred Espenak and Jay Anderson and are published through NASA's Publication series. The bulletins are provided as a public service to both the professional and lay communities, including educators and the media. A list of currently available bulletins and an order form can be found at:

sunearth.gsfc.nasa.gov/eclipse/SEpubs/RPrequest.html

The most recent bulletin of the series covers the total solar eclipse of 2008 Aug. 1, which is visible from northern Canada, Russia, Mongolia, and China. Single copies of the eclipse bulletins are available at no cost by sending a 9 × 12-in. self-addressed envelope stamped with postage for 11 oz. (310 g). Please print the eclipse year on the envelope's lower left corner. Use stamps only, since cash and cheques cannot be accepted. Requests from outside the United States and Canada may include ten international postal coupons. Mail requests to: Fred Espenak, NASA's Goddard Space Flight Center, Code 693, Greenbelt MD 20771, USA.

The NASA eclipse bulletins are also available over the Internet, including out-of-print bulletins. Using a Web browser, they can be read or downloaded through the World Wide Web from the GSFC/SDAC (Solar Data Analysis Centre) eclipse page:

umbra.nascom.nasa.gov/eclipse/index.html

Eclipse Web Sites

The URL of the NASA Eclipse home page is:

sunearth.gsfc.nasa.gov/eclipse/eclipse.html

The site features predictions and maps for all solar and lunar eclipses well into the 21st century, with special emphasis on upcoming eclipses. Special pages are devoted to the total solar eclipses of 2008, 2009, and 2010 featuring detailed path maps, tables, graphs, and meteorological data are included. A world atlas of solar eclipses provides maps of all central eclipse paths from 2000 BC to AD 3000. Additional catalogues list every solar and lunar eclipse over a 5000-year period.

Detailed information on solar and lunar eclipse photography and tips on eclipse observing and eye safety may be found at:

www.MrEclipse.com

Acknowledgments

All eclipse predictions were generated on an Apple G4 iMac computer using algorithms developed from the *Explanatory Supplement* (1974) with additional algorithms from Meeus, Grosjean, and Vanderleen (1966). The solar coordinates used in the eclipse predictions are based on VSOP87 [P. Bretagnon and G. Francou, 1988]. The lunar coordinates are based on ELP-2000/82 [M. Chapront-Touzé and J. Chapront, 1983]. For lunar eclipses, the diameter of the umbral and penumbral shadows were calculated using Danjon's rule of enlarging Earth's radius by 1/85 to compensate for the opacity of the terrestrial atmosphere; corrections for the effects of oblateness have also been included. Text and table composition was done on a Macintosh using Microsoft Word. Additional figure annotation was performed with Claris MacDraw Pro.

All calculations, diagrams, tables, and opinions presented in this paper are those of the author, and he assumes full responsibility for their accuracy.

This publication is available electronically through the Internet along with additional information and updates at:

sunearth.gsfc.nasa.gov/eclipse/OH/OH2008.html

References

Bretagnon P. and Francou G., "Planetary Theories in rectangular and spherical variables: VSOP87 solution," *Astron. and Astrophys.,* vol. 202, no. 309 (1988).

Chapront-Touzé, M and Chapront, J., "The Lunar Ephemeris ELP 2000," *Astron. and Astrophys.,* vol. 124, no. 1, pp 50-62 (1983).

Chauvenet, W., *Manual of Spherical and Practical Astronomy, Vol. 1,* 1891, Dover edition, 1961.

Danjon, A., "Les éclipses de Lune par la pénombre en 1951," *L'Astronomie, 65,* 51–53, Feb. 1951.

Espenak, F., *Fifty Year Canon of Solar Eclipses: 1986–2035,* Sky Publishing Corp., Cambridge, Mass., 1988.

Espenak, F., *Fifty Year Canon of Lunar Eclipses: 1986–2035,* Sky Publishing Corp., Cambridge, Mass., 1989.

Espenak, F. and Anderson, J., *Total Solar Eclipse of 2008 August 01,* NASA TP–2007-214149, Goddard Space Flight Center, Greenbelt, MD, 2007.

Espenak, F. and Meeus, J., *Five Millennium Canon of Solar Eclipses: –2000 to +3000 (2000 BCE to 3000 CE),* NASA TP–2006-214141, Goddard Space Flight Center, Greenbelt, MD, 2006.

Explanatory Supplement to the Astronomical Ephemeris and the American Ephemeris and Nautical Almanac, Her Majesty's Nautical Almanac Office, London, 1974.

Littmann, M., Willcox, K., and Espenak, F., *Totality—Eclipses of the Sun,* Oxford University Press, New York, 1999.

Meeus, J., Grosjean, C.C., and Vanderleen, W., *Canon of Solar Eclipses,* Pergamon Press, New York, 1966.

Meeus, J. and Mucke, H., *Canon of Lunar Eclipses: –2002 to +2526,* Astronomisches Buro, Wien, 1979.

TABLE 1—PATH OF THE ANTUMBRAL SHADOW FOR ANNULAR SOLAR ECLIPSE OF 2008 FEBRUARY 7

Universal Time	Northern Limit Lat.	Northern Limit Long.	Southern Limit Lat.	Southern Limit Long.	Central Line Lat.	Central Line Long.	Sun Alt °	Path Width km	Central Duration
Limits	73°43'S	064°28'W	71°49'S	080°58'W	72°57'S	072°32'W	0	581	02m14s
03:24	80°00'S	091°21'W	———	———	73°38'S	073°41'W	1	574	02m14s
03:26	80°26'S	103°19'W	———	———	77°21'S	088°00'W	6	519	02m14s
03:28	80°19'S	114°01'W	———	———	78°16'S	099°08'W	8	496	02m13s
03:30	79°51'S	123°00'W	75°06'S	092°46'W	78°26'S	109°00'W	10	479	02m13s
03:32	79°08'S	130°12'W	76°00'S	102°56'W	78°10'S	117°26'W	11	467	02m13s
03:34	78°18'S	135°54'W	76°06'S	111°16'W	77°37'S	124°25'W	12	457	02m13s
03:36	77°22'S	140°24'W	75°47'S	118°12'W	76°54'S	130°05'W	13	450	02m13s
03:38	76°23'S	143°52'W	75°14'S	123°55'W	76°04'S	134°39'W	14	445	02m13s
03:40	75°22'S	146°39'W	74°32'S	128°37'W	75°09'S	138°19'W	14	441	02m12s
03:42	74°20'S	148°51'W	73°43'S	132°26'W	74°12'S	141°17'W	15	438	02m12s
03:44	73°18'S	150°36'W	72°50'S	135°34'W	73°13'S	143°40'W	15	436	02m12s
03:46	72°16'S	152°01'W	71°54'S	138°07'W	72°13'S	145°35'W	16	436	02m12s
03:48	71°14'S	153°07'W	70°57'S	140°11'W	71°12'S	147°09'W	16	436	02m12s
03:50	70°12'S	154°00'W	69°58'S	141°52'W	70°11'S	148°23'W	16	437	02m12s
03:52	69°10'S	154°41'W	68°58'S	143°14'W	69°10'S	149°23'W	16	439	02m12s
03:54	68°08'S	155°12'W	67°57'S	144°18'W	68°08'S	150°09'W	16	442	02m12s
03:56	67°06'S	155°35'W	66°56'S	145°09'W	67°06'S	150°45'W	16	446	02m12s
03:58	66°05'S	155°50'W	65°54'S	145°47'W	66°05'S	151°11'W	16	451	02m12s
04:00	65°04'S	155°58'W	64°52'S	146°13'W	65°03'S	151°28'W	16	456	02m12s
04:02	64°03'S	156°00'W	63°49'S	146°29'W	64°01'S	151°37'W	16	463	02m11s
04:04	63°01'S	155°56'W	62°46'S	146°36'W	62°59'S	151°38'W	16	470	02m11s
04:06	62°00'S	155°47'W	61°41'S	146°33'W	61°56'S	151°33'W	15	477	02m11s
04:08	60°58'S	155°33'W	60°36'S	146°20'W	60°53'S	151°20'W	15	486	02m11s
04:10	59°56'S	155°13'W	59°29'S	145°57'W	59°49'S	151°01'W	14	495	02m11s
04:12	58°53'S	154°48'W	58°20'S	145°23'W	58°44'S	150°34'W	14	506	02m11s
04:14	57°50'S	154°16'W	57°09'S	144°36'W	57°37'S	149°54'W	13	516	02m11s
04:16	56°46'S	153°39'W	55°54'S	143°32'W	56°29'S	149°14'W	12	527	02m11s
04:18	55°40'S	152°54'W	54°32'S	142°03'W	55°19'S	148°17'W	11	539	02m12s
04:20	54°32'S	152°00'W	52°59'S	139°49'W	54°05'S	147°07'W	10	550	02m12s
04:22	53°22'S	150°55'W	50°27'S	134°10'W	52°46'S	145°34'W	9	560	02m12s
04:24	52°08'S	149°36'W	———	———	51°16'S	143°26'W	7	568	02m12s
04:26	50°48'S	147°57'W	———	———	49°19'S	139°42'W	3	571	02m12s
Limits	45°47'S	137°35'W	50°00'S	132°40'W	47°46'S	135°21'W	0	565	02m13s

TABLE 2—LOCAL CIRCUMSTANCES FOR ANNULAR SOLAR ECLIPSE OF 2008 FEBRUARY 7

Geographic Location		Eclipse Begins h:m	Max. Eclipse h:m	Eclipse Ends h:m	Sun Alt °	Sun Azm °	Ecl. Mag.	Ecl. Obs.
ANTARCTICA	South Pole	02:11	03:12	04:14	16	135	0.849	0.797
	McMurdo Station	02:22	03:28	04:33	25	322	0.824	0.767
AUSTRALIA	Adelaide	04:07	04:27	04:46	63	309	0.025	0.005
	Brisbane	04:19	05:00	05:39	47	277	0.141	0.062
	Canberra	03:48	04:39	05:27	53	293	0.205	0.107
	Geelong	03:37	04:27	05:13	57	306	0.176	0.086
	Hobart	03:19	04:19	05:16	53	309	0.298	0.185
	Launceston	03:24	04:22	05:17	54	307	0.273	0.162
	Melbourne	03:39	04:28	05:15	56	304	0.181	0.089
	Newcastle	03:56	04:47	05:34	50	286	0.210	0.111
	Southport	04:16	04:59	05:40	47	277	0.156	0.071
	Sydney	03:53	04:44	05:32	51	288	0.216	0.116
	Wollongong	03:50	04:43	05:31	51	289	0.219	0.118
FIJI	Suva	04:37	05:26	06:10	18	259	0.318	0.203
FRENCH POLYNESIA	Papeete	04:26	04:35s	—	0	254	0.126	0.052
NEW ZEALAND	Auckland	03:47	04:52	05:51	30	272	0.574	0.470
	Christchurch	03:29	04:37	05:40	33	281	0.628	0.532
	Wellington	03:36	04:43	05:44	31	277	0.627	0.531

All times are Universal Time.
"s" indicates eclipse in progress at sunset.

TABLE 3—CRATER IMMERSION AND EMERSION TIMES
FOR THE TOTAL LUNAR ECLIPSE OF 2008 FEBRUARY 21

Immersion	Crater Name	Emersion	Crater Name
01:48	Grimaldi	04:06	Grimaldi
01:49	Aristarchus	04:07	Billy
01:54	Kepler	04:07	Tycho
01:56	Billy	04:09	Campanus
02:00	Pytheas	04:19	Kepler
02:02	Copernicus	04:22	Aristarchus
02:03	Timocharis	04:27	Copernicus
02:05	Plato	04:30	Pytheas
02:11	Campanus	04:36	Timocharis
02:14	Aristoteles	04:42	Dionysius
02:15	Eudoxus	04:42	Manilius
02:16	Manilius	04:44	Plato
02:20	Menelaus	04:46	Menelaus
02:24	Dionysius	04:47	Goclenius
02:24	Plinius	04:49	Plinius
02:27	Tycho	04:51	Eudoxus
02:34	Proclus	04:52	Aristoteles
02:38	Taruntius	04:53	Langrenus
02:42	Goclenius	04:55	Taruntius
02:48	Langrenus	04:59	Proclus

All times are Universal Time. The size of the umbral shadow was computed assuming an increase in Earth's radius of 1/85 due to the terrestrial atmosphere.

TABLE 4—PATH OF THE UMBRAL SHADOW FOR
TOTAL SOLAR ECLIPSE OF 2008 AUGUST 1

Universal Time	Northern Limit Lat.	Long.	Southern Limit Lat.	Long.	Central Line Lat.	Long.	Sun Alt. °	Path Width km	Central Duration
Limits	68°44′N	105°22′W	67°49′N	101°02′W	68°17′N	103°08′W		206	1m30s
09:24	69°24′N	104°13′W	75°42′N	82°12′W	73°58′N	91°30′W	7	213	1m41s
09:27	77°09′N	87°54′W	78°57′N	68°51′W	78°18′N	78°27′W	12	217	1m49s
09:30	80°32′N	75°34′W	81°03′N	53°56′W	80°59′N	64°36′W	16	219	1m55s
09:33	82°52′N	60°02′W	82°18′N	36°31′W	82°45′N	47°27′W	18	221	2m00s
09:36	84°19′N	38°56′W	82°47′N	17°36′W	83°39′N	26°42′W	21	222	2m04s
09:39	84°47′N	13°27′W	82°36′N	0°14′E	83°43′N	5°13′W	22	223	2m08s
09:42	84°21′N	9°56′E	81°54′N	15°02′E	83°07′N	13°02′E	24	224	2m11s
09:45	83°19′N	26°57′E	80°53′N	26°28′E	82°05′N	26°43′E	26	224	2m14s
09:48	82°00′N	38°29′E	79°42′N	35°10′E	80°51′N	36°38′E	27	225	2m16s
09:51	80°34′N	46°30′E	78°26′N	41°53′E	79°30′N	43°58′E	28	226	2m18s
09:54	79°06′N	52°20′E	77°06′N	47°10′E	78°06′N	49°32′E	29	227	2m20s
09:57	77°37′N	56°48′E	75°46′N	51°27′E	76°41′N	53°56′E	30	228	2m22s
10:00	76°09′N	60°21′E	74°25′N	55°01′E	75°17′N	57°31′E	31	229	2m23s
10:03	74°41′N	63°16′E	73°04′N	58°01′E	73°53′N	60°30′E	32	230	2m24s
10:06	73°15′N	65°44′E	71°43′N	60°38′E	72°29′N	63°04′E	32	231	2m25s
10:09	71°49′N	67°53′E	70°23′N	62°55′E	71°07′N	65°18′E	33	232	2m26s
10:12	70°24′N	69°47′E	69°04′N	64°58′E	69°45′N	67°17′E	33	233	2m27s
10:15	69°01′N	71°30′E	67°45′N	66°49′E	68°23′N	69°05′E	33	234	2m27s
10:18	67°38′N	73°04′E	66°26′N	68°32′E	67°02′N	70°44′E	33	236	2m27s
10:21	66°15′N	74°32′E	65°08′N	70°06′E	65°42′N	72°15′E	34	237	2m27s
10:24	64°53′N	75°54′E	63°50′N	71°35′E	64°22′N	73°41′E	33	238	2m27s
10:27	63°32′N	77°12′E	62°32′N	73°00′E	63°03′N	75°03′E	33	240	2m27s
10:30	62°11′N	78°28′E	61°15′N	74°21′E	61°43′N	76°22′E	33	241	2m26s
10:33	60°50′N	79°41′E	59°57′N	75°39′E	60°24′N	77°38′E	33	243	2m25s
10:36	59°29′N	80°53′E	58°39′N	76°56′E	59°05′N	78°52′E	32	244	2m24s
10:39	58°07′N	82°05′E	57°21′N	78°12′E	57°45′N	80°06′E	32	245	2m23s
10:42	56°45′N	83°18′E	56°03′N	79°27′E	56°25′N	81°20′E	31	247	2m22s
10:45	55°23′N	84°31′E	54°44′N	80°43′E	55°04′N	82°35′E	30	248	2m20s
10:48	54°00′N	85°46′E	53°24′N	82°00′E	53°43′N	83°51′E	29	249	2m18s

TABLE 4—PATH OF THE UMBRAL SHADOW FOR
TOTAL SOLAR ECLIPSE OF 2008 AUGUST 1 (continued)

Universal Time	Northern Limit Lat.	Northern Limit Long.	Southern Limit Lat.	Southern Limit Long.	Central Line Lat.	Central Line Long.	Sun Alt. °	Path Width km	Central Duration
10:51	52°36′N	87°04′E	52°04′N	83°18′E	52°21′N	85°09′E	28	250	2m16s
10:54	51°10′N	88°25′E	50°42′N	84°40′E	50°57′N	86°31′E	27	251	2m14s
10:57	49°43′N	89°52′E	49°19′N	86°05′E	49°31′N	87°57′E	26	252	2m12s
11:00	48°13′N	91°26′E	47°53′N	87°36′E	48°04′N	89°29′E	25	252	2m09s
11:03	46°39′N	93°08′E	46°25′N	89°14′E	46°33′N	91°09′E	23	251	2m06s
11:06	45°02′N	95°03′E	44°54′N	91°01′E	44°59′N	93°00′E	21	250	2m02s
11:09	43°18′N	97°16′E	43°18′N	93°02′E	43°19′N	95°06′E	19	247	1m58s
11:12	41°24′N	99°57′E	41°35′N	95°21′E	41°32′N	97°34′E	16	243	1m54s
11:15	39°12′N	103°31′E	39°42′N	98°12′E	39°30′N	100°43′E	13	236	1m48s
11:18	36°03′N	109°53′E	37°28′N	102°01′E	36°59′N	105°20′E	8	224	1m40s
Limits	34°15′N	114°35′E	32°45′N	113°14′E	33°30′N	113°54′E		200	1m28s

TABLE 5—LOCAL CIRCUMSTANCES FOR
TOTAL SOLAR ECLIPSE OF 2008 AUGUST 1

Geographic Location		Eclipse Begins h:m	Max. Eclipse h:m	Eclipse Ends h:m	Sun Alt. °	Sun Azm. °	Ecl. Mag.	Ecl. Umbral Obs. Durat.
AFGHANISTAN	Kabul	10:16	11:19	12:17	37	267	.616	.529
ARMENIA	Jerevan	9:46	10:45	11:41	59	230	.341	.229
AUSTRIA	Vienna	8:58	9:45	10:32	56	146	.195	.102
AZERBAIJAN	Baku	9:48	10:51	11:50	55	239	.428	.317
BELARUS	Minsk	8:55	9:58	11:01	54	173	.442	.333
BELGIUM	Brussels	8:39	9:24	10:11	46	126	.209	.112
CANADA	Halifax	———	9:03 r	9:23		64	.238	.135
	Québec	———	9:27 r	9:32		63	.069	.022
	St. John's	———r	8:43	9:24	5	68	.317	.205
CHINA	Beijing	10:17	11:10	———s	3	291	.916	.901
	Chengdu	10:33	11:28	———s	6	288	.913	.898
	Chongqing	10:34	11:28	———s	3	289	.911	.895
	Harbin	10:07	10:57	———s		296	.816	.774
	Nanjing	10:28	11:01 s	———		292	.633	.548
	Shanghai	10:28	10:48 s	———		291	.391	.278
	Shenyang	10:13	11:03 s	———		295	.862	.833
	Shuicheng	10:39	11:33	———s	3	289	.850	.817
	Tianjin	10:18	11:11	———s	2	292	.922	.909
	Wuhan	10:31	11:16 s	———		291	.855	.823
	Xi'an	10:27	11:21	——— s	4	289	.999	1.000
CZECH REPUBLIC	Praha	8:51	9:41	10:31	53	143	.236	.134
DENMARK	København	8:38	9:36	10:35	48	143	.385	.273
ENGLAND	London	8:33	9:18	10:05	43	119	.218	.119
FINLAND	Helsinki	8:45	9:50	10:55	47	167	.576	.483
FRANCE	Paris	8:42	9:21	10:01	46	121	.143	.064
GEORGIA	Tbilisi	9:41	10:43	11:40	59	228	.377	.265
GERMANY	Berlin	8:44	9:38	10:33	51	143	.300	.190
HUNGARY	Budapest	9:03	9:50	10:38	58	153	.197	.103
ICELAND	Reykjavík	8:15	9:11	10:09	27	104	.585	.493
INDIA	Bombay	10:57	11:47	12:33	26	281	.379	.267
IRAN	Tehran	10:04	11:03	11:58	54	250	.364	.252
IRAQ	Baghdad	10:12	11:00	11:45	61	245	.199	.104
IRELAND	Dublin	8:25	9:12	10:01	38	113	.267	.160
KAZAKHSTAN	Alma-Ata	10:01	11:06	12:06	33	264	.840	.806
KOREA, SOUTH	Seoul	10:18	10:39 s	———	0	293	.408	.295
KYRGYZSTAN	Frunze	10:00	11:05	12:06	34	263	.808	.766
MONGOLIA	Ulaanbaatar	10:04	11:00	11:53	13	282	.888	.867
MYANMAR	Yangon	10:58	11:48	———s	4	288	.588	.494

All times are Universal Time.
"r" indicates eclipse in progress at sunrise; "s" indicates eclipse in progress at sunset.

TABLE 5—LOCAL CIRCUMSTANCES FOR
TOTAL SOLAR ECLIPSE OF 2008 AUGUST 1 (continued)

Geographic Location		Eclipse Begins h:m	Max. Eclipse h:m	Eclipse Ends h:m	Sun Alt °	Sun Azm °	Ecl. Mag.	Ecl. Umbral Obs.Duration	
NETHERLANDS	Amsterdam	8:36	9:25	10:16	46	128	.257	.152	
NORWAY	Oslo	8:33	9:34	10:36	44	143	.495	.390	
PAKISTAN	Lahore	10:25	11:27	12:23	31	273	.636	.553	
POLAND	Warsaw	8:52	9:50	10:48	54	158	.345	.233	
ROMANIA	Bucureşti	9:20	10:07	10:54	63	172	.183	.093	
RUSSIA	Gorki	9:07	10:16	11:22	50	204	.653	.575	
	Kazan	9:13	10:22	11:28	48	214	.696	.627	
	Moscow	9:02	10:09	11:15	52	193	.578	.485	
	Novosibirsk	9:41	10:45	11:45	30	258	1.038	1.000	2m18s
	Omsk	9:35	10:41	11:44	36	248	.935	.927	
	Perm	9:16	10:24	11:30	44	223	.802	.759	
	St. Petersburg	8:50	9:56	11:02	48	177	.607	.519	
	Volgograd	9:22	10:29	11:32	55	215	.512	.409	
SCOTLAND	Glasgow	8:24	9:16	10:10	38	118	.344	.231	
SVALBARD	Svalbard	8:41	9:43	10:45	29	163	.939	.932	
SWEDEN	Stockholm	8:40	9:42	10:46	47	155	.513	.411	
TAJIKISTAN	Dusanbe	10:06	11:11	12:11	38	263	.674	.599	
UKRAINE	Kiev	9:05	10:07	11:07	57	181	.386	.273	
UZBEKISTAN	Taşkent	10:00	11:06	12:06	38	260	.721	.657	

All times are Universal Time.

TABLE 6—CRATER IMMERSION AND EMERSION TIMES
FOR THE PARTIAL LUNAR ECLIPSE OF 2008 AUGUST 16

Immersion	Crater Name	Emersion	Crater Name
19:43	Grimaldi	21:28	Aristarchus
19:47	Billy	21:35	Timocharis
19:54	Campanus	21:39	Pytheas
19:59	Tycho	21:43	Grimaldi
20:03	Kepler	21:43	Kepler
20:11	Aristarchus	21:49	Copernicus
20:14	Copernicus	21:53	Billy
20:22	Pytheas	21:57	Manilius
20:32	Dionysius	21:58	Menelaus
20:34	Timocharis	22:01	Plinius
20:35	Manilius	22:07	Proclus
20:38	Goclenius	22:09	Campanus
20:41	Menelaus	22:11	Dionysius
20:44	Langrenus	22:18	Taruntius
20:45	Plinius	22:22	Tycho
20:49	Taruntius	22:30	Goclenius
20:57	Proclus	22:33	Langrenus

All times are Universal Time. The size of the umbral shadow was computed assuming an increase in Earth's radius of 1/85 due to the terrestrial atmosphere

FIGURE 1—ANNULAR SOLAR ECLIPSE OF 2008 FEBRUARY 7

Ecliptic Conjunction = 03:45:36.0 TD (= 03:44:30.6 UT)
Greatest Eclipse = 03:56:10.5 TD (= 03:55:05.1 UT)

Eclipse Magnitude = 0.9650   Gamma = -0.9570

Saros Series = 121   Member = 60 of 71

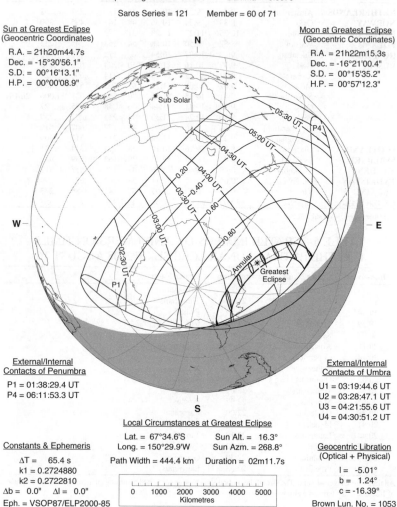

Sun at Greatest Eclipse
(Geocentric Coordinates)

R.A. = 21h20m44.7s
Dec. = -15°30'56.1"
S.D. = 00°16'13.1"
H.P. = 00°00'08.9"

Moon at Greatest Eclipse
(Geocentric Coordinates)

R.A. = 21h22m15.3s
Dec. = -16°21'00.4"
S.D. = 00°15'35.2"
H.P. = 00°57'12.3"

External/Internal
Contacts of Penumbra

P1 = 01:38:29.4 UT
P4 = 06:11:53.3 UT

External/Internal
Contacts of Umbra

U1 = 03:19:44.6 UT
U2 = 03:28:47.1 UT
U3 = 04:21:55.6 UT
U4 = 04:30:51.2 UT

Local Circumstances at Greatest Eclipse

Lat. = 67°34.6'S	Sun Alt. = 16.3°	
Long. = 150°29.9'W	Sun Azm. = 268.8°	
Path Width = 444.4 km	Duration = 02m11.7s	

Constants & Ephemeris

ΔT = 65.4 s
k1 = 0.2724880
k2 = 0.2722810
Δb = 0.0" Δl = 0.0"
Eph. = VSOP87/ELP2000-85

Geocentric Libration
(Optical + Physical)

l = -5.01°
b = 1.24°
c = -16.39°

Brown Lun. No. = 1053

0 1000 2000 3000 4000 5000
Kilometres

F. Espenak, NASA's GSFC - 2007 Jun 01

http://sunearth.gsfc.nasa.gov/eclipse/eclipse.html

See pp. 127–129 for an explanation of this figure.

FIGURE 2—TOTAL LUNAR ECLIPSE OF 2008 FEBRUARY 21

Ecliptic Conjunction = 03:31:36.3 TD (= 03:30:30.9 UT)
Greatest Eclipse = 03:27:08.7 TD (= 03:26:03.3 UT)

| Penumbral Magnitude = 2.1451 | P. Radius = 1.2339° | Gamma = -0.3992 |
| Umbral Magnitude = 1.1062 | U. Radius = 0.6948° | Axis = 0.3801° |

Saros Series = 133   Member = 26 of 71

Sun at Greatest Eclipse
(Geocentric Coordinates)

R.A. = 22h15m30.0s
Dec. = -10°48'31.3"
S.D. = 00°16'10.5"
H.P. = 00°00'08.9"

Moon at Greatest Eclipse
(Geocentric Coordinates)

R.A. = 10h14m48.5s
Dec. = +10°28'07.7"
S.D. = 00°15'34.2"
H.P. = 00°57'08.5"

Eclipse Semi-Durations

Penumbral = 02h49m32s
Umbral = 01h42m44s
Total = 00h24m53s

ΔT = 65.4 s
Rule = CdT (Danjon)
Eph. = VSOP87/ELP2000-85

F. Espenak, NASA's GSFC - 2007 May 31
http://sunearth.gsfc.nasa.gov/eclipse/eclipse.html

Eclipse Contacts

P1 = 00:36:34 UT
U1 = 01:43:17 UT
U2 = 03:01:09 UT
U3 = 03:50:55 UT
U4 = 05:08:46 UT
P4 = 06:15:38 UT

See p. 129 for an explanation of this figure.

FIGURE 3—TOTAL SOLAR ECLIPSE OF 2008 AUGUST 1

Ecliptic Conjunction = 10:13:38.3 TD (= 10:12:32.8 UT)
Greatest Eclipse = 10:22:11.8 TD (= 10:21:06.3 UT)

Eclipse Magnitude = 1.0394   Gamma = 0.8307

Saros Series = 126   Member = 47 of 72

Sun at Greatest Eclipse
(Geocentric Coordinates)

R.A. = 08h47m54.1s
Dec. = +17°51'56.4"
S.D. = 00°15'45.5"
H.P. = 00°00'08.7"

Moon at Greatest Eclipse
(Geocentric Coordinates)

R.A. = 08h49m08.8s
Dec. = +18°38'01.6"
S.D. = 00°16'14.1"
H.P. = 00°59'34.8"

External/Internal
Contacts of Penumbra

P1 = 08:04:05.8 UT
P4 = 12:38:25.4 UT

External/Internal
Contacts of Umbra

U1 = 09:21:06.9 UT
U2 = 09:24:09.9 UT
U3 = 11:18:26.9 UT
U4 = 11:21:25.1 UT

Local Circumstances at Greatest Eclipse

Lat. = 65°39.3'N   Sun Alt. =   33.5°
Long. = 072°18.4'E   Sun Azm. = 235.2°
Path Width = 237.0 km   Duration = 02m27.1s

Constants & Ephemeris

ΔT =   65.5 s
k1 = 0.2724880
k2 = 0.2722810
Δb = 0.0" Δl = 0.0"
Eph. = VSOP87/ELP2000-85

Geocentric Libration
(Optical + Physical)

l =   4.22°
b = -1.02°
c = 14.02°
Brown Lun. No. = 1059

0	1000	2000	3000	4000	5000
Kilometres

F. Espenak, NASA's GSFC - 2007 Jun 01
http://sunearth.gsfc.nasa.gov/eclipse/eclipse.html

See pp. 127–129 for an explanation of this figure.

FIGURE 4—TOTAL SOLAR ECLIPSE OF 2008 AUGUST 1
PATH OF THE ECLIPSE THROUGH CANADA AND GREENLAND

FIGURE 5—TOTAL SOLAR ECLIPSE OF 2008 AUGUST 1
PATH OF THE ECLIPSE THROUGH ASIA

Adapted from "Total Solar Eclipse of 2008 August 01,"
NASA/TP—2007—214149, Espenak & Anderson

FIGURE 6—PARTIAL LUNAR ECLIPSE OF 2008 AUGUST 16

Ecliptic Conjunction = 21:17:32.4 TD (= 21:16:26.9 UT)
Greatest Eclipse = 21:11:11.6 TD (= 21:10:06.1 UT)

Penumbral Magnitude = 1.8367   P. Radius = 1.2141°   Gamma = 0.5646
Umbral Magnitude = 0.8076   U. Radius = 0.6876°   Axis = 0.5301°

Saros Series = 138   Member = 29 of 83

Sun at Greatest Eclipse
(Geocentric Coordinates)

R.A. = 09h46m37.2s
Dec. = +13°24'18.2"
S.D. = 00°15'47.9"
H.P. = 00°00'08.7"

Moon at Greatest Eclipse
(Geocentric Coordinates)

R.A. = 21h45m41.8s
Dec. = -12°55'29.3"
S.D. = 00°15'21.1"
H.P. = 00°56'20.6"

Ecliptic

P4
U4
Greatest
U1
P1

Earth Umbra

Earth Penumbra

Eclipse Semi-Durations

Penumbral = 02h45m18s
Umbral = 01h34m05s

| 0 | 15 | 30 | 45 | 60 |
Arc-Minutes

Eclipse Contacts

P1 = 18:24:46 UT
U1 = 19:36:04 UT
U4 = 22:44:14 UT
P4 = 23:55:23 UT

ΔT = 65.5 s
Rule = CdT (Danjon)
Eph. = VSOP87/ELP2000-85

F. Espenak, NASA's GSFC - 2007 May 31
http://sunearth.gsfc.nasa.gov/eclipse/eclipse.html

See p. 129 for an explanation of this figure.

WEATHER FOR THE 2008 SOLAR ECLIPSE
By Jay Anderson

2008 AUGUST 1 TOTAL SOLAR ECLIPSE

In spite of a wide-ranging track that takes it from the melting snow and ice of the Canadian Archipelago to the deserts of northern China, this eclipse samples only a few of the climatologies that the globe offers. The high northern latitudes of its early track are depressingly cloudy—though loaded with adventure—and the global weather prospects are saved only by a small area of inviting sunshine statistics in southern Siberia and the bordering regions of China.

North of the Arctic Circle

While those of us who live in southern Canada often welcome the clear, dry skies (though not the temperatures) of an Arctic outbreak for its astronomical benefits, the region north of the Arctic Circle is actually better known for the disheartening cloudiness of its climatology. This is especially true of the summer months, when cold ocean waters clash with warm and humid southerly winds, bringing a high frequency of low-level cloud. Figure 1, a graph of the mean cloudiness along the central axis of the eclipse track, shows that the high latitude cloudiness exceeds 80% over most of the region, and more than 90% near Svalbard. Table 1, a catalogue of surface-based observations, crowns Ny-Alesund on Spitzbergen Island with the lowest measurements of sunshine, only 18% of the maximum possible in this land of perpetual summer daylight.

For those inclined to opt for adventure rather than eclipse, the start of the track near Cambridge Bay, Canada, offers the best chances for an Arctic Circle expedition. In this area, the percent of possible sunshine—the best measure of the true probability of seeing the eclipse—averages 34%. Farther north, at Resolute, average cloud cover has climbed over 80% and sunshine probability has dropped to 22%, a trend that continues to Grise Fiord and beyond.

Expeditions into Canadian Arctic sites should allow sufficient time for flight delays due to weather—in this part of the world, a delay often means another day, not another hour. Fog is especially prevalent, and sudden blizzards may bring visibilities too low for aircraft to operate. Temperatures in the continuous daylight typically reach a few degrees above freezing during the warmest hours.

From Alert to the Russian archipelago of Novaya Zemlya, the track does not make a significant landfall and so expeditions near Svalbard or Franz Josef Land must be ship-based. After passing its peak near Svalbard, cloudiness begins to decline steadily, making the area between the Russian coast and Novaya Zemlya the most promising for a ship-borne expedition. Even with mobility, the search for openings in the cloud will be a challenge, though at any given date, satellite images of the area usually show large breaks somewhere in the overcast. A little luck will be most welcome.

Siberia

Figure 1 shows that the trend of cloudiness is steadily downward for the latter half of the shadow track, except for occasional upward blips where mountain ranges promote the formation of clouds. From the Arctic coast to Novosibirsk, average cloudiness drops by nearly 20%, reaching a minimum of about 44% in the foothills of the Altai Mountains that separate Russia and China. The percent of possible sunshine increases to 54% at Novosibirsk. This city, Russia's third-largest, will be a popular destination for eclipse-seekers. On Novo's southwestern suburbs, the 100-km-long Ob Reservoir provides a convenient observing location, as the cool waters of the lake will suppress the development of convective clouds and help to increase the chances of sunshine. Sites can be chosen on either the north or south shore, according to the onshore wind of the day. Photographers will find skies that are wonderfully transparent when clouds are absent.

Other than Nadym, opportunities for eclipse sites are very limited to the north of Novosibirsk. Destinations to the south, however, are a different story. Cloudiness continues to decline right up to the slopes of the Altai Mountains that separate Russia and China, and a major highway more-or-less straddles the central line. Barnaul, some 200 km south of Novosibirsk, basks in 57% of the sunshine possible in August. Sites closer to the Chinese border fare even better, until, about 500 km from Novosibirsk, the foothills of the Altai Mountains begin. The weather associated with the mountains forms a prominent bulge in the trend of cloudiness depicted in Figure 1.

Northern China

Once across the Altai mountains, the eclipse track descends into the dry and sunny climate of northern China. This region is too far north to be greatly affected by the monsoon circulation that saturates central and southern China in August, and the track passes between two great deserts—the Gobi and the Taklimakan—that lend their influences to the climatology. It is a dry and rocky region, interrupted by lush fields wherever water is available. The steep drop in cloudiness that began north of the Russian coast resumes with even more intensity once the Altai Mountains have been left behind. Satellite measurements place the lowest cloud cover for the entire track on the central line between the cities of Hami and Jiuquan.

Surface observations give Hami the nod for the greatest amount of sunshine—a generous but not overwhelming 76% of the maximum possible; Jiuquan lags slightly at 67%. Cloud observations from the local weather stations confirm this difference, but the statistics must be used with caution, as neither city is actually on the central axis of the path. At Hami, the middle of the shadow lies 150 km to the east, on a broad plateau beyond a range of glaciated 4000-m mountains. The mountains create a favourable climate for the development of convective clouds every afternoon, and any passing weather disturbance will tend to bring heavier cloud and rain to the peaks.

Fortunately, the plateau beyond the mountains (known as the Barkol grasslands) enjoys a more hospitable eclipse climatology, and the satellite-based cloud graph gives the region's cloud prospects "two thumbs up." The convective clouds that form on the mountain or the cloud that comes across the mountains in association with large-scale weather systems tends to dissipate as it leaves the mountain slopes and descends onto the grassland. Eclipse sites should be chosen to avoid the immediate lee of the mountain, but instead get far enough to the east to gain maximum advantage from this descending flow. A favourite destination seems to be the town of Yiwu, but a better site would be to head right to the central line, a farther 30 km or so. The average cloud amount for Yiwu is about 9% higher than at Hami, and only 3% above that for Jiuquan. Mountains in the vicinity of Jiuquan are lower than those near Hami, and the extra terrain-induced cloudiness is probably small. All-in-all, destinations near Hami and near Jiuquan are likely to have the same prospects for success.

Beyond Jiuquan, cloud and weather conditions deteriorate quickly. The monsoon season is well entrenched over central China in early August, and the percent of possible sunshine drops by 20% at Xian. Even when skies are relatively sunny, the atmosphere near major cities is filled with a brown haze of humidity and industrial pollution. At Xian, the evening Sun disappears while still 10° high, and the low altitude eclipse is likely to be totally invisible. To the north of Xian, on the central line, visibility may be better, but the higher frequency of cloudy skies across this part of China greatly reduces the chances for a successful view of the eclipse.

WEATHER STATISTICS FOR
TOTAL SOLAR ECLIPSE OF 2008 AUGUST 1

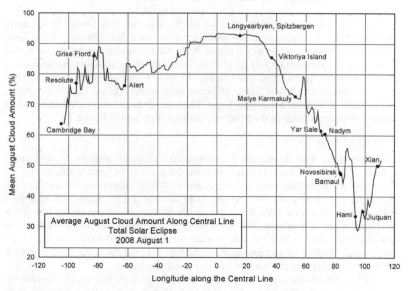

Figure 1: A graph of average cloud cover along the central line of the eclipse in percent, derived from 20 years of satellite observations. Longitudes of places on or near the central line are indicated. Cloud data from ISCCP.

TABLE 1—CLOUD AND SUNSHINE STATISTICS FOR SELECTED LOCATIONS ALONG THE TRACK FROM SURFACE OBSERVATIONS

Geographic Location		Percentage of Possible Sunshine	Clear	Few	Scattered	Broken	Overcast	Obscured	Partly Obscured	Calculated Mean Cloud Cover (%)
CANADA	Cambridge Bay	34	9.5	15.1	11.6	37.8	24.6	1.4	0.0	62
	Resolute Bay	22	1.9	12.7	8.8	23.4	43.0	10.0	0.2	77
	Grise Fiord		5.8	19.8	3.4	22.2	43.0	4.3	1.4	71
	Alert	32	1.6	22.9	5.3	32.7	34.7	2.9	0.0	69
SVALBARD	Nye-Alesund	18	0.9	10.8	7.7	36.5	40.5	3.6	0.0	77
	Longyearbyen		0.5	8.9	8.0	66.9	15.3	0.4	0.0	71
RUSSIA	Novy Port		5.0	7.2	6.1	52.3	28.3	1.1	0.0	73
	Nadym		3.9	6.7	5.5	56.9	26.5	0.5	0.0	73
	Novosibirsk	54	7.2	13.9	8.7	27.9	42.2	0.0	0.0	70
	Barnaul	57	6.3	13.8	10.9	58.7	10.1	0.2	0.0	62
	Kos-Agac		0.8	7.0	10.9	40.9	40.3	0.0	0.0	77
MONGOLIA	Hovd	67	6.2	20.7	14.1	50.5	8.4	0.0	0.0	56
CHINA	Altay	73	3.9	35.5	5.2	53.7	1.6	0.0	0.0	51
	Hami	76	9.3	43.4	5.4	39.8	1.8	0.3	0.0	42
	Yiwu		3.6	33.2	9.7	50.9	2.7	0.0	0.0	51
	Jiuquan	66	11.9	34.3	5.1	48.3	15.4	0.0	0.0	48
	Luochuan		2.7	25.9	7.7	48.3	15.4	0.0	0.0	60
	Xian	54	17.2	19.7	5.2	30.8	27.1	0.0	0.0	56

VIEWING A SOLAR ECLIPSE—A WARNING

Solar eclipses are among the most widely publicized and observed celestial events. It is essential to be aware of the visual danger associated with a solar eclipse. The safety rule is simple but not widely appreciated: **Never look at the surface of the Sun, either directly with the unaided eyes or through binoculars or a telescope.** To do so one risks permanent partial blindness, and this can occur almost instantly in the case of telescopic viewing. Viewing our Sun is just as dangerous on any clear day, but at the time of an eclipse people have a reason to want to look at it—and often resort to dangerous methods.

A direct view of the Sun is safe only if a suitable filter is used in a proper manner. In the case of binoculars or a telescope, the filter must be one that attaches *securely* to the *front* end of the instrument, never one that attaches to the eyepiece end (the heat developed near the eyepiece can shatter such a filter).

Filters specifically designed for solar viewing include aluminized Mylar and glass filters plated with a slightly transparent, metallic film. Such filters may be purchased at telescope supply stores. Shade #14 (no other shade) rectangular welder's glass may be used; however, since these filters are of low optical quality, they are useful only for views not involving binoculars or a telescope. All of these are commercial items and cannot be replaced with ordinary household items. For example, layers of photographic colour film, coloured glass, stacked sunglasses, crossed polarizers, smoked glass, or photographic neutral-density filters must never be used. Although one may devise a combination that dims the *visible* sunlight to a comfortable level, the makeshift filter may be quite transparent in the infrared part of the solar spectrum, and this invisible radiation will damage the retina of the observer's eye. For the same reason, one must never rely on clouds or heavy atmospheric haze to dim the solar image when using a telescope. Two layers of fully exposed and developed, silver-based, black and white photographic film provides adequate protection, but many modern films, including all colour films, are based on dyes that do not provide protection in the infrared. Thus it is best to avoid using filters made of photographic film.

One of the simplest, safest, and least known ways to observe the partial phases of a solar eclipse is *pinhole mirror projection*. Take a small pocket mirror and, with masking tape, cover all but a small section of the mirror's surface. The shape and size of the small opening are not critical, but a square about 6 mm on a side works well. Prop the mirror up on a sunny windowsill and orient the mirror so the reflected sunlight shines on the ceiling or a wall of the room—but not directly into anyone's eyes! The spot of light on the viewing surface will be a *pinhole image* of the solar disk. The mirror has a great advantage over the usual "pinhole-in-a-box arrangement" in that the image can be aimed across a substantial distance to a convenient viewing screen. The greater the projection distance, the larger, but dimmer, the Sun's image. The size of the mirror aperture should be adjusted for the best compromise between image brightness and image sharpness. With this simple device the progress of a solar eclipse can be viewed in complete safety by a group of children in a darkened room.

A sharper and brighter image of the solar disk may be projected onto a white viewing screen placed 30 or 40 cm behind the eyepiece of binoculars or a small telescope (the telescope aperture should be stopped down to about 50 mm in order to limit the intensity of sunlight passing through the instrument, and the viewing screen should be shielded from direct sunlight). However, one must *not* look through the instrument when aiming it, and, especially if children are present, a physical barrier should be used to prevent anyone from attempting to look into the eyepiece. If the telescope has a finderscope, it should be either covered or removed.

THE MOON

MAP OF MOON
By Roy Bishop

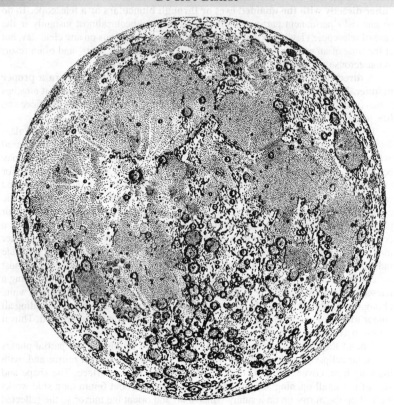

Maria	
LS	Lacus Somniorum (Lake of Dreams) (330°)
MC	Mare Crisium (Sea of Crises) (300°)
MFe	Mare Fecunditatis (Sea of Fertility) (310°)
MFr	Mare Frigoris (Sea of Cold) (0°)
MH	Mare Humorum (Sea of Moisture) (40°)
MI	Mare Imbrium (Sea of Rains) (20°)
MNe	Mare Nectaris (Sea of Nectar) (325°)
MNu	Mare Nubium (Sea of Clouds) (15°)
MS	Mare Serenitatis (Sea of Serenity) (340°)
MT	Mare Tranquillitatis (Sea of Tranquillity) (330°)
MV	Mare Vaporum (Sea of Vapours) (355°)
OP	Oceanus Procellarum (Ocean of Storms) (50°)
SA	Sinus Aestuum (Seething Bay) (8°)
SI	Sinus Iridum (Bay of Rainbows) (32°)
SM	Sinus Medii (Central Bay) (0°)
SR	Sinus Roris (Bay of Dew) (60°)

Lunar Probes

2 *Luna 2*, First to reach Moon (1959–9–13) (0°)
7 *Ranger 7*, First close pictures (1964–7–31) (21°)
9 *Luna 9*, First soft landing (1966–2–3) (64°)
11 *Apollo 11*, First men on Moon (1969–7–20) (337°)
12 *Apollo 12* (1969–11–19) (23°)
14 *Apollo 14* (1971–2–5) (17°)
15 *Apollo 15* (1971–7–30) (356°)
16 *Apollo 16* (1972–4–21) (344°)
17 *Apollo 17* (1972–12–11) (329°)

Angles in parentheses equal $360° - \lambda$, where λ is the selenographic longitude of the centre of the feature. 0° marks the mean centre of the lunar disk, and the angles increase toward the observer's east (i.e. westward on the Moon). These angles facilitate locating the feature on the accompanying map, and may be correlated with the Sun's selenographic colongitude (see THE SKY MONTH BY MONTH (pp. 92–119)) to determine the optimum times for viewing the feature.

MAP OF MOON (continued)

Craters

21 Albategnius (356°)
22 Alphonsus (3°)
23 Arago (338°)
24 Archimedes (4°)
25 Aristarchus (47°)
26 Aristillus (358°)
27 Aristoteles (342°)
28 Arzachel (2°)
29 Atlas (315°)
31 Autolycus (358°)
32 Bessel (342°)
33 Bullialdus (22°)
34 Cassini (355°)
35 Catharina (336°)
36 Clavius (15°)
37 Cleomedes (304°)
38 Cook (311°)
39 Copernicus (20°)
41 Cyrillus (336°)
42 Delambre (342°)

43 Endymion (305°)
44 Eratosthenes (11°)
45 Eudoxus (343°)
46 Fracastorius (326°)
47 Furnerius (299°)
48 Gassendi (40°)
49 Grimaldi (68°)
51 Halley (354°)
52 Hercules (321°)
53 Herschel (2°)
54 Hevelius (66°)
55 Hipparchus (354°)
56 Julius Caesar (345°)
57 Kepler (38°)
58 Langrenus (299°)
59 Lansberg (27°)
61 Longomontanus (21°)
62 Macrobius (314°)
63 Maginus (6°)
64 Manilius (351°)
65 Maskelyne (330°)
66 Maurolycus (345°)

67 Mersenius (49°)
68 Newcomb (316°)
69 Petavius (298°)
71 Piccolomini (327°)
72 Plato (10°)
73 Plinius (336°)
74 Posidonius (330°)
75 Ptolemaeus (2°)
76 Reinhold (23°)
77 Ross (338°)
78 Schickard (55°)
79 Schiller (40°)
81 Snellius (304°)
82 Stevinus (305°)
83 Taruntius (313°)
84 Theophilus (333°)
85 Timocharis (13°)
86 Tycho (11°)
87 Wilhelm (20°)

Mountains

A Alpine Valley (356°)
B Alps Mts. (359°)
E Altai Mts. (336°)
F Apennine Mts. (2°)
G Carpathian Mts. (24°)
H Caucasus Mts. (352°)
K Haemus Mts. (349°)
M Jura Mts. (34°)
N Pyrenees Mts. (319°)
R Rheita Valley (312°)
S Riphaeus Mts. (27°)
V Spitzbergen (5°)
W Straight Range (20°)
X Straight Wall (8°)
Y Taurus Mts. (319°)
Z Teneriffe Mts. (13°)

UNIVERSAL TIME OF NEW MOON DATES

2008			2009		
Jan.	8.5	May	5.5	Aug. 30.8	Jan.	26.3	May	24.5	Sep.	18.8

2008						2009					
Jan.	8.5	May	5.5	Aug.	30.8	Jan.	26.3	May	24.5	Sep.	18.8
Feb.	7.2	Jun.	3.8	Sep.	29.3	Feb.	25.1	Jun.	22.8	Oct.	18.2
Mar.	7.7	Jul.	3.1	Oct.	29.0	Mar.	26.7	Jul.	22.1	Nov.	16.8
Apr.	6.2	Aug.	1.4	Nov.	27.7	Apr.	25.1	Aug.	20.4	Dec.	16.5
				Dec.	27.5						

These dates will be useful for planning observing sessions, determining favourable dates for observing very thin lunar crescents, and setting Moon dials on clocks. The dates are indicated to lower precision in the calendar on the inside back cover.

TIMES OF MOONRISE AND MOONSET
BY RAJIV GUPTA

The table on pp. 152–157 gives the times of moonrise and moonset for locations ranging from 20°N to 60°N latitude. Dates of New Moon and Full Moon are given in **bold** and *italic* respectively. The table may be interpolated linearly for nontabular latitudes and can be extrapolated beyond the 20° and 60° limits a few degrees without significant loss of accuracy. "Rise" and "Set" correspond to the upper limb of the Moon appearing at the horizon for an observer at sea level. The times are local mean time (LMT) for the Greenwich meridian (i.e. UT at 0° longitude). Because of the relatively rapid eastward motion of the Moon, unlike the sunrise and sunset table, for observers not near 0° longitude the times cannot be read directly as LMT; the table must be interpolated according to the observer's longitude. Also, to convert from the observer's LMT to standard time, the observer's longitude correction relative to his or her standard meridian must be applied. After it is prepared for a given location, the chart at the right enables the sum of these two corrections to be determined in one step.

To prepare the **Moonrise/Moonset Correction Diagram,** first mark your longitude on the *West or East Longitude* scale. Draw a diagonal line from this mark to the 0,0 point. Next, the *Correction in minutes* axis (which is subdivided at two-minute intervals) must be labelled. As a guide, the first three divisions have been tentatively labelled 0, ±2, ±4 *(use + if you are west of the prime meridian in Greenwich, England, − if east);* but, to these numbers must be added your longitude correction relative to your standard meridian (see the third paragraph on p. 195). As an aid both for labelling and for reading the chart, the vertical lines at 10-min intervals are wider. **Examples:** For Toronto, which is 4.5° W of its standard meridian of 75°W, the longitude correction is +18 min, so an observer in Toronto would label the Correction axis 18, 20, 22, 24,...; an observer in Boston (longitude correction −16) would label the axis −16, −14, −12,...; an observer in Hong Kong (east longitude, longitude correction +24) would label the axis 24, 22, 20,...; an observer in Vienna (longitude correction −6) would label the axis −6, −8, −10,....

The chart is now ready for use on any day from your position. Interpolating for nontabular latitudes, from the table obtain today's time for the event (moonrise, or moonset) and tomorrow's time if you are west of Greenwich, yesterday's time if east, enter the difference on the *Tabular Delay* axis, and run horizontally across to meet the diagonal line. The correction, to the nearest minute, can then be read directly below off the Correction axis. This correction is applied to the tabular "today's time" and results in the standard time of the event for your position. **Example:** The latitude of Toronto is 44°N. Interpolating the 40°N and 45°N entries, the table gives for 44°N a moonset time of 21:10 on May 6 and 22:25 on May 7. The Correction corresponding to a 75-min Tabular Delay, when the chart is prepared for Toronto as described above, is +35 min; hence the time of moonset is 21:10 + 35 min = 21:45 EST May 17 or 22:45 EDT May 6.

Note: Due to a difference in height between the observer and the actual horizon, the observed time may differ by several minutes from the predicted time.

MOONRISE/MOONSET CORRECTION DIAGRAM

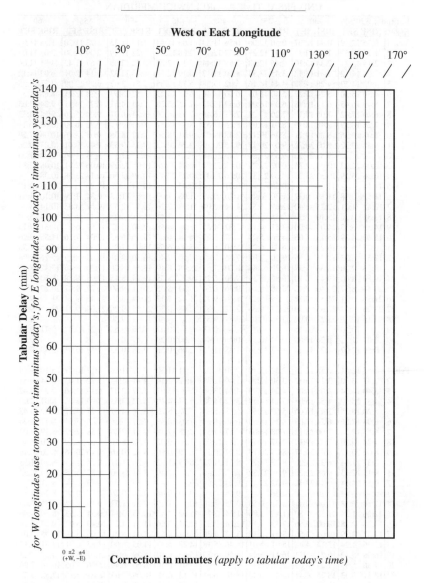

West or East Longitude

10° 30° 50° 70° 90° 110° 130° 150° 170°

Tabular Delay (min)

for W longitudes use tomorrow's time minus today's; for E longitudes use today's time minus yesterday's

0 ±2 ±4
(+W, –E)

Correction in minutes *(apply to tabular today's time)*

MOONRISE AND MOONSET, 2008 JANUARY, FEBRUARY
UNIVERSAL TIME AT GREENWICH MERIDIAN

Latitude:	+20°		+30°		+35°		+40°		+45°		+50°		+55°		+60°	
Event:	RISE	SET	RISE	SET	RISE	SET	RISE	SET	RISE	SET	RISE	SET	RISE	SET	RISE	SET
Jan. 1	0:35	12:19	0:44	12:07	0:50	12:00	0:56	11:53	1:03	11:44	1:12	11:33	1:23	11:20	1:38	11:03
2	1:24	12:53	1:39	12:37	1:47	12:27	1:57	12:17	2:08	12:04	2:22	11:49	2:39	11:30	3:03	11:04
3	2:15	13:31	2:34	13:10	2:46	12:58	2:58	12:44	3:14	12:28	3:32	12:08	3:57	11:42	4:31	11:06
4	3:08	14:12	3:31	13:48	3:45	13:34	4:00	13:17	4:19	12:58	4:43	12:33	5:14	12:01	6:02	11:12
5	4:02	14:59	4:28	14:32	4:44	14:16	5:02	13:58	5:23	13:35	5:51	13:07	6:29	12:29	7:32	11:25
6	4:56	15:50	5:24	15:22	5:40	15:05	6:00	14:46	6:23	14:23	6:53	13:53	7:34	13:11	8:48	11:58
7	5:49	16:45	6:17	16:18	6:33	16:02	6:52	15:43	7:15	15:20	7:44	14:51	8:25	14:11	9:34	13:03
8	6:40	17:42	7:05	17:17	7:20	17:03	7:37	16:46	7:58	16:26	8:24	16:01	9:00	15:26	9:54	14:33
9	7:26	18:39	7:48	18:19	8:01	18:07	8:15	17:53	8:33	17:37	8:54	17:17	9:22	16:50	10:02	16:11
10	8:08	19:36	8:26	19:21	8:36	19:12	8:48	19:02	9:01	18:50	9:17	18:35	9:38	18:16	10:06	17:50
11	8:48	20:32	9:00	20:22	9:07	20:17	9:15	20:10	9:24	20:02	9:35	19:53	9:49	19:41	10:07	19:26
12	9:24	21:27	9:31	21:23	9:35	21:21	9:40	21:18	9:45	21:15	9:51	21:11	9:58	21:06	10:08	21:00
13	10:00	22:23	10:01	22:24	10:02	22:25	10:03	22:27	10:04	22:28	10:05	22:29	10:06	22:31	10:08	22:34
14	10:36	23:19	10:32	23:27	10:29	23:31	10:26	23:37	10:23	23:42	10:19	23:50	10:14	23:58	10:08	—
15	11:14	—	11:04	—	10:58	—	10:51	—	10:43	—	10:34	—	10:23	—	10:08	0:10
16	11:55	0:18	11:39	0:32	11:30	0:40	11:20	0:49	11:08	1:00	10:53	1:13	10:34	1:29	10:10	1:51
17	12:42	1:21	12:21	1:40	12:09	1:51	11:54	2:04	11:38	2:20	11:17	2:39	10:51	3:03	10:14	3:38
18	13:35	2:26	13:10	2:50	12:55	3:04	12:38	3:21	12:17	3:41	11:51	4:05	11:17	4:39	10:24	5:30
19	14:35	3:33	14:07	4:00	13:51	4:16	13:32	4:35	13:09	4:58	12:40	5:27	11:59	6:07	10:51	7:15
20	15:40	4:39	15:13	5:06	14:56	5:23	14:37	5:42	14:14	6:05	13:45	6:35	13:04	7:16	11:55	8:26
21	16:47	5:39	16:22	6:05	16:07	6:20	15:50	6:38	15:30	6:59	15:04	7:25	14:30	8:01	13:36	8:56
22	17:51	6:33	17:31	6:55	17:20	7:08	17:06	7:22	16:50	7:40	16:30	8:01	16:03	8:29	15:26	9:08
23	18:53	7:20	18:38	7:37	18:29	7:46	18:20	7:57	18:08	8:10	17:54	8:26	17:36	8:46	17:12	9:13
24	19:50	8:00	19:41	8:12	19:36	8:19	19:30	8:26	19:23	8:35	19:14	8:45	19:04	8:58	18:50	9:14
25	20:44	8:37	20:40	8:43	20:38	8:46	20:36	8:50	20:34	8:55	20:31	9:00	20:27	9:07	20:22	9:15
26	21:35	9:11	21:37	9:12	21:39	9:12	21:40	9:12	21:42	9:13	21:44	9:13	21:46	9:14	21:49	9:15
27	22:26	9:44	22:33	9:39	22:37	9:36	22:42	9:33	22:48	9:30	22:55	9:26	23:04	9:21	23:15	9:14
28	23:16	10:16	23:28	10:07	23:36	10:01	23:44	9:55	23:54	9:48	—	9:39	—	9:28	—	9:14
29	—	10:50	—	10:36	—	10:27	—	10:18	—	10:07	0:06	9:53	0:21	9:37	0:41	9:14
30	0:07	11:27	0:24	11:08	0:34	10:57	0:46	10:44	1:00	10:29	1:17	10:11	1:38	9:48	2:09	9:16
31	0:59	12:07	1:21	11:44	1:33	11:30	1:48	11:15	2:06	10:56	2:28	10:33	2:57	10:03	3:39	9:19
Feb. 1	1:52	12:51	2:18	12:25	2:32	12:10	2:50	11:52	3:11	11:30	3:37	11:03	4:13	10:27	5:10	9:29
2	2:47	13:40	3:14	13:12	3:30	12:56	3:49	12:37	4:12	12:14	4:41	11:44	5:22	11:03	6:34	9:51
3	3:40	14:34	4:08	14:06	4:24	13:49	4:44	13:30	5:07	13:07	5:37	12:37	6:19	11:56	7:33	10:42
4	4:31	15:30	4:58	15:04	5:14	14:49	5:32	14:31	5:54	14:10	6:22	13:43	7:00	13:06	8:01	12:05
5	5:20	16:28	5:43	16:06	5:57	15:53	6:13	15:38	6:32	15:20	6:56	14:57	7:27	14:27	8:12	13:43
6	6:04	17:26	6:24	17:09	6:35	16:59	6:48	16:47	7:03	16:33	7:21	16:16	7:45	15:54	8:17	15:24
7	6:45	18:24	7:00	18:12	7:08	18:05	7:17	17:57	7:28	17:48	7:41	17:36	7:58	17:22	8:19	17:03
8	7:24	19:20	7:32	19:14	7:37	19:11	7:43	19:07	7:50	19:02	7:58	18:56	8:07	18:49	8:20	18:40
9	8:00	20:17	8:03	20:17	8:05	20:17	8:07	20:17	8:10	20:16	8:12	20:16	8:16	20:16	8:20	20:16
10	8:37	21:14	8:34	21:20	8:33	21:23	8:31	21:27	8:29	21:32	8:26	21:37	8:24	21:44	8:20	21:53
11	9:15	22:13	9:06	22:25	9:01	22:32	8:56	22:40	8:49	22:49	8:41	23:00	8:32	23:15	8:20	23:33
12	9:55	23:14	9:41	23:32	9:32	23:42	9:23	23:54	9:12	—	8:59	—	8:43	—	8:21	—
13	10:40	—	10:20	—	10:08	—	9:55	—	9:40	0:08	9:21	0:26	8:57	0:48	8:24	1:19
14	11:30	0:18	11:06	0:41	10:51	0:55	10:35	1:10	10:15	1:29	9:51	1:52	9:19	2:23	8:31	3:09
15	12:26	1:24	11:59	1:50	11:43	2:06	11:24	2:24	11:02	2:46	10:33	3:14	9:54	3:53	8:50	4:56
16	13:28	2:28	13:00	2:56	12:43	3:13	12:24	3:32	12:01	3:56	11:31	4:25	10:49	5:07	9:37	6:20
17	14:32	3:29	14:06	3:56	13:51	4:12	13:33	4:30	13:11	4:52	12:44	5:21	12:06	5:59	11:05	7:01
18	15:36	4:24	15:14	4:48	15:01	5:01	14:46	5:18	14:28	5:37	14:05	6:00	13:35	6:31	12:51	7:17
19	16:38	5:12	16:21	5:31	16:11	5:42	15:59	5:55	15:45	6:10	15:29	6:28	15:07	6:52	14:37	7:23
20	17:36	5:55	17:24	6:09	17:18	6:17	17:10	6:26	17:01	6:36	16:50	6:49	16:36	7:05	16:18	7:26
21	18:31	6:33	18:25	6:41	18:22	6:46	18:18	6:51	18:13	6:58	18:08	7:05	18:01	7:15	17:52	7:27
22	19:24	7:07	19:23	7:11	19:23	7:12	19:23	7:14	19:23	7:17	19:22	7:19	19:22	7:22	19:21	7:27
23	20:15	7:41	20:20	7:39	20:23	7:37	20:26	7:36	20:30	7:34	20:35	7:32	20:41	7:29	20:49	7:26
24	21:06	8:14	21:16	8:06	21:22	8:02	21:29	7:57	21:37	7:51	21:47	7:45	21:59	7:37	22:15	7:26
25	21:57	8:48	22:12	8:35	22:21	8:28	22:32	8:20	22:44	8:10	22:58	7:59	23:17	7:45	23:43	7:26
26	22:49	9:23	23:09	9:06	23:21	8:56	23:34	8:45	23:50	8:31	—	8:15	—	7:55	—	7:27
27	23:42	10:02	—	9:40	—	9:28	—	9:13	—	8:56	0:10	8:35	0:36	8:08	1:13	7:29
28	—	10:44	0:06	10:19	0:20	10:05	0:36	9:48	0:56	9:27	1:21	9:02	1:54	8:28	2:45	7:36
29	0:36	11:31	1:03	11:04	1:18	10:48	1:37	10:29	1:59	10:06	2:27	9:37	3:07	8:58	4:13	7:51

MOONRISE AND MOONSET, 2008 MARCH, APRIL
UNIVERSAL TIME AT GREENWICH MERIDIAN

Latitude:	+20°		+30°		+35°		+40°		+45°		+50°		+55°		+60°	
Event:	RISE	SET	RISE	SET	RISE	SET	RISE	SET	RISE	SET	RISE	SET	RISE	SET	RISE	SET
Mar. 1	1:29	12:22	1:57	11:54	2:14	11:38	2:33	11:18	2:57	10:55	3:27	10:25	4:09	9:43	5:23	8:28
2	2:21	13:17	2:49	12:50	3:05	12:34	3:24	12:15	3:46	11:53	4:15	11:24	4:56	10:45	6:03	9:38
3	3:10	14:14	3:36	13:50	3:50	13:36	4:07	13:19	4:28	12:59	4:53	12:35	5:28	12:01	6:20	11:10
4	3:56	15:11	4:18	14:52	4:30	14:40	4:44	14:27	5:01	14:11	5:22	13:51	5:49	13:26	6:28	12:49
5	4:39	16:09	4:55	15:55	5:05	15:46	5:16	15:37	5:29	15:25	5:45	15:11	6:04	14:53	6:31	14:29
6	5:18	17:07	5:30	16:58	5:36	16:53	5:44	16:47	5:52	16:40	6:03	16:32	6:15	16:22	6:32	16:08
7	5:56	18:05	6:02	18:02	6:05	18:00	6:09	17:58	6:13	17:56	6:18	17:54	6:24	17:50	6:32	17:46
8	6:34	19:03	6:34	19:06	6:33	19:08	6:33	19:11	6:33	19:13	6:33	19:16	6:33	19:20	6:32	19:25
9	7:12	20:03	7:06	20:13	7:02	20:18	6:58	20:25	6:53	20:32	6:48	20:41	6:41	20:52	6:32	21:07
10	7:53	21:05	7:40	21:21	7:33	21:30	7:25	21:41	7:16	21:53	7:05	22:08	6:51	22:28	6:33	22:54
11	8:37	22:10	8:19	22:31	8:09	22:44	7:57	22:58	7:43	23:15	7:26	23:37	7:05	—	6:36	—
12	9:26	23:16	9:03	23:42	8:50	23:57	8:35	—	8:16	—	7:54	—	7:24	0:05	6:42	0:46
13	10:22	—	9:55	—	9:39	—	9:21	0:14	9:00	0:36	8:32	1:02	7:55	1:39	6:56	2:37
14	11:22	0:22	10:54	0:50	10:37	1:06	10:18	1:25	9:55	1:48	9:25	2:18	8:44	2:59	7:32	4:10
15	12:25	1:24	11:58	1:51	11:42	2:07	11:24	2:26	11:02	2:49	10:33	3:18	9:54	3:58	8:48	5:04
16	13:28	2:20	13:05	2:45	12:51	2:59	12:35	3:16	12:15	3:36	11:51	4:01	11:19	4:35	10:29	5:25
17	14:29	3:09	14:10	3:30	13:59	3:42	13:47	3:56	13:31	4:12	13:13	4:32	12:48	4:58	12:14	5:34
18	15:28	3:52	15:14	4:08	15:06	4:17	14:57	4:28	14:46	4:40	14:33	4:55	14:17	5:13	13:54	5:37
19	16:23	4:31	16:14	4:42	16:10	4:48	16:04	4:54	15:58	5:02	15:50	5:12	15:41	5:24	15:29	5:39
20	17:15	5:06	17:13	5:12	17:11	5:14	17:09	5:18	17:07	5:22	17:05	5:26	17:02	5:32	16:58	5:39
21	18:06	5:40	18:09	5:40	18:11	5:40	18:13	5:39	18:15	5:39	18:18	5:39	18:21	5:39	18:25	5:39
22	18:57	6:13	19:05	6:07	19:10	6:04	19:15	6:01	19:22	5:57	19:29	5:52	19:39	5:46	19:51	5:39
23	19:48	6:46	20:01	6:35	20:09	6:29	20:18	6:23	20:28	6:15	20:41	6:05	20:57	5:54	21:19	5:39
24	20:40	7:21	20:58	7:06	21:09	6:57	21:21	6:47	21:35	6:35	21:53	6:21	22:16	6:03	22:48	5:39
25	21:33	7:58	21:55	7:39	22:08	7:27	22:23	7:14	22:42	6:58	23:04	6:39	23:34	6:15	—	5:41
26	22:27	8:39	22:52	8:16	23:07	8:02	23:25	7:46	23:46	7:27	—	7:03	—	6:32	0:19	5:46
27	23:20	9:24	23:47	8:58	—	8:42	—	8:24	—	8:03	0:13	7:35	0:50	6:58	1:49	5:58
28	—	10:13	—	9:46	0:04	9:29	0:23	9:10	0:46	8:47	1:15	8:17	1:56	7:36	3:07	6:25
29	0:12	11:06	0:40	10:39	0:56	10:22	1:15	10:03	1:38	9:41	2:08	9:11	2:49	8:30	4:00	7:20
30	1:02	12:01	1:28	11:36	1:43	11:21	2:01	11:03	2:22	10:43	2:49	10:16	3:26	9:40	4:25	8:43
31	1:48	12:57	2:11	12:36	2:24	12:23	2:40	12:08	2:58	11:51	3:21	11:29	3:52	11:00	4:35	10:17
Apr. 1	2:31	13:54	2:50	13:37	3:01	13:27	3:13	13:16	3:28	13:02	3:46	12:46	4:09	12:24	4:40	11:55
2	3:11	14:51	3:25	14:39	3:33	14:32	3:42	14:25	3:53	14:16	4:05	14:05	4:21	13:51	4:42	13:32
3	3:49	15:48	3:58	15:42	4:03	15:39	4:08	15:35	4:14	15:30	4:22	15:25	4:31	15:18	4:43	15:09
4	4:27	16:46	4:30	16:46	4:31	16:46	4:33	16:46	4:35	16:47	4:37	16:47	4:40	16:47	4:44	16:48
5	5:05	17:46	5:02	17:52	5:00	17:56	4:58	18:00	4:55	18:05	4:52	18:11	4:49	18:19	4:44	18:29
6	5:45	18:48	5:36	19:01	5:30	19:09	5:24	19:17	5:17	19:27	5:09	19:40	4:58	19:55	4:45	20:16
7	6:29	19:54	6:13	20:13	6:05	20:24	5:54	20:37	5:43	20:52	5:29	21:10	5:11	21:35	4:47	22:09
8	7:18	21:02	6:57	21:26	6:45	21:40	6:31	21:57	6:14	22:16	5:54	22:41	5:28	23:14	4:52	—
9	8:13	22:11	7:48	22:38	7:33	22:54	7:16	23:12	6:55	23:35	6:30	—	5:55	—	5:04	0:04
10	9:13	23:16	8:46	23:44	8:30	—	8:11	—	7:48	—	7:19	0:04	6:39	0:43	5:32	1:50
11	10:17	—	9:50	—	9:34	0:00	9:15	0:19	8:53	0:42	8:24	1:11	7:44	1:52	6:36	3:00
12	11:22	0:15	10:57	0:41	10:43	0:56	10:26	1:13	10:06	1:34	9:40	2:01	9:06	2:36	8:13	3:30
13	12:24	1:07	12:04	1:29	11:52	1:42	11:38	1:57	11:22	2:14	11:02	2:35	10:35	3:03	9:58	3:43
14	13:23	1:52	13:08	2:09	12:59	2:19	12:49	2:31	12:37	2:44	12:22	3:00	12:04	3:20	11:39	3:48
15	14:18	2:32	14:08	2:44	14:03	2:51	13:56	2:59	13:49	3:08	13:40	3:19	13:28	3:32	13:13	3:50
16	15:11	3:08	15:06	3:14	15:04	3:18	15:01	3:23	14:58	3:28	14:54	3:34	14:49	3:41	14:43	3:51
17	16:02	3:41	16:03	3:43	16:03	3:44	16:04	3:45	16:05	3:46	16:06	3:47	16:07	3:49	16:09	3:51
18	16:52	4:14	16:58	4:10	17:02	4:08	17:06	4:06	17:11	4:03	17:17	4:00	17:24	3:56	17:34	3:51
19	17:42	4:46	17:54	4:38	18:00	4:33	18:08	4:27	18:17	4:21	18:28	4:13	18:41	4:03	18:59	3:51
20	18:33	5:21	18:50	5:07	18:59	4:59	19:10	4:50	19:23	4:40	19:39	4:28	19:59	4:12	20:27	3:52
21	19:26	5:57	19:47	5:39	19:59	5:28	20:13	5:16	20:30	5:02	20:50	4:45	21:18	4:23	21:57	3:54
22	20:19	6:37	20:44	6:15	20:58	6:02	21:15	5:47	21:35	5:29	22:00	5:07	22:34	4:39	23:27	3:58
23	21:13	7:20	21:39	6:55	21:55	6:40	22:14	6:23	22:36	6:02	23:04	5:36	23:44	5:01	—	4:08
24	22:05	8:08	22:33	7:41	22:49	7:25	23:08	7:06	23:31	6:43	—	6:15	—	5:35	0:50	4:28
25	22:55	8:59	23:22	8:32	23:38	8:15	23:56	7:56	—	7:33	0:00	7:04	0:41	6:23	1:52	5:13
26	23:42	9:53	—	9:27	—	9:11	—	8:53	0:18	8:32	0:46	8:05	1:24	7:27	2:26	6:26
27	—	10:47	0:06	10:25	0:20	10:11	0:37	9:55	0:56	9:37	1:21	9:13	1:53	8:42	2:41	7:55
28	0:25	11:43	0:46	11:24	0:58	11:13	1:11	11:00	1:27	10:45	1:47	10:27	2:13	10:03	2:48	9:29
29	1:06	12:38	1:22	12:24	1:31	12:16	1:41	12:07	1:53	11:56	2:08	11:43	2:27	11:26	2:52	11:03
30	1:44	13:33	1:54	13:25	2:01	13:20	2:08	13:14	2:16	13:08	2:25	13:00	2:38	12:50	2:53	12:37

MOONRISE AND MOONSET, 2008 MAY, JUNE
UNIVERSAL TIME AT GREENWICH MERIDIAN

Latitude: Event:	+20° RISE SET	+30° RISE SET	+35° RISE SET	+40° RISE SET	+45° RISE SET	+50° RISE SET	+55° RISE SET	+60° RISE SET
May 1	2:20 14:29	2:26 14:26	2:29 14:25	2:32 14:23	2:36 14:21	2:41 14:19	2:47 14:16	2:54 14:12
2	2:57 15:26	2:57 15:30	2:56 15:32	2:56 15:34	2:56 15:37	2:56 15:40	2:55 15:44	2:55 15:49
3	3:36 16:27	3:29 16:37	3:26 16:42	3:21 16:49	3:17 16:56	3:11 17:05	3:04 17:17	2:56 17:32
4	4:17 17:31	4:05 17:47	3:58 17:57	3:50 18:07	3:40 18:20	3:29 18:35	3:16 18:55	2:58 19:21
5	5:04 18:40	4:46 19:01	4:35 19:14	4:23 19:28	4:09 19:46	3:52 20:07	3:31 20:36	3:01 21:18
6	5:57 19:50	5:34 20:16	5:20 20:31	5:05 20:49	4:46 21:10	4:23 21:37	3:53 22:14	3:10 23:12
7	6:57 20:59	6:31 21:27	6:15 21:43	5:57 22:02	5:35 22:25	5:07 22:54	4:30 23:35	3:30 —
8	8:03 22:04	7:35 22:30	7:19 22:46	7:00 23:04	6:37 23:26	6:08 23:53	5:28 —	4:20 0:43
9	9:10 23:00	8:44 23:24	8:29 23:37	8:11 23:53	7:50 —	7:24 —	6:47 0:30	5:49 1:29
10	10:15 23:49	9:53 —	9:41 —	9:26 —	9:08 0:11	8:47 0:34	8:18 1:05	7:35 1:48
11	11:17 —	11:00 0:08	10:50 0:19	10:39 0:31	10:26 0:46	10:10 1:03	9:49 1:26	9:20 1:56
12	12:14 0:31	12:03 0:45	11:56 0:53	11:49 1:02	11:40 1:12	11:29 1:24	11:16 1:40	10:58 2:00
13	13:08 1:09	13:02 1:17	12:58 1:22	12:55 1:27	12:50 1:33	12:45 1:41	12:38 1:50	12:29 2:01
14	13:59 1:43	13:58 1:46	13:58 1:48	13:58 1:50	13:58 1:52	13:57 1:55	13:57 1:58	13:56 2:02
15	14:49 2:16	14:54 2:14	14:56 2:12	15:00 2:11	15:03 2:09	15:08 2:08	15:13 2:05	15:21 2:02
16	15:39 2:48	15:49 2:41	15:54 2:37	16:01 2:32	16:09 2:27	16:18 2:21	16:30 2:13	16:45 2:03
17	16:29 3:22	16:44 3:10	16:53 3:03	17:03 2:55	17:14 2:46	17:29 2:35	17:47 2:21	18:11 2:03
18	17:21 3:57	17:40 3:41	17:52 3:31	18:05 3:20	18:20 3:07	18:39 2:51	19:04 2:32	19:40 2:05
19	18:14 4:36	18:37 4:15	18:51 4:03	19:07 3:49	19:26 3:32	19:49 3:12	20:21 2:46	21:09 2:09
20	19:07 5:18	19:33 4:54	19:49 4:40	20:07 4:23	20:28 4:03	20:56 3:39	21:33 3:06	22:35 2:17
21	20:00 6:04	20:28 5:38	20:44 5:22	21:03 5:04	21:25 4:42	21:54 4:14	22:35 3:36	23:44 2:34
22	20:51 6:55	21:18 6:27	21:34 6:11	21:52 5:52	22:15 5:29	22:43 5:00	23:22 4:20	— 3:11
23	21:39 7:47	22:04 7:21	22:18 7:06	22:35 6:47	22:55 6:25	23:21 5:58	23:55 5:19	0:26 4:15
24	22:23 8:42	22:44 8:18	22:57 8:04	23:11 7:48	23:29 7:28	23:50 7:04	— 6:30	0:46 5:40
25	23:03 9:36	23:21 9:16	23:31 9:05	23:42 8:51	23:56 8:35	— 8:15	0:17 7:49	0:56 7:12
26	23:41 10:30	23:54 10:15	— 10:06	— 9:56	— 9:44	0:12 9:29	0:33 9:10	1:00 8:44
27	— 11:24	— 11:14	0:01 11:08	0:09 11:01	0:19 10:53	0:30 10:43	0:44 10:31	1:03 10:15
28	0:17 12:18	0:25 12:13	0:29 12:10	0:33 12:07	0:39 12:03	0:45 11:59	0:54 11:54	1:04 11:46
29	0:53 13:13	0:55 13:14	0:56 13:14	0:57 13:15	0:58 13:16	1:00 13:16	1:02 13:17	1:05 13:19
30	1:29 14:10	1:25 14:17	1:23 14:21	1:21 14:25	1:18 14:31	1:15 14:37	1:11 14:45	1:05 14:55
31	2:08 15:11	1:58 15:24	1:53 15:31	1:47 15:40	1:39 15:50	1:31 16:02	1:20 16:18	1:07 16:38
Jun. 1	2:51 16:16	2:36 16:34	2:27 16:45	2:17 16:58	2:05 17:13	1:51 17:32	1:33 17:56	1:10 18:29
2	3:40 17:25	3:19 17:49	3:07 18:03	2:53 18:19	2:37 18:38	2:17 19:03	1:51 19:35	1:16 20:25
3	4:37 18:36	4:12 19:02	3:57 19:18	3:40 19:37	3:20 19:59	2:54 20:27	2:20 21:07	1:29 22:11
4	5:41 19:44	5:13 20:11	4:57 20:27	4:38 20:46	4:16 21:08	3:47 21:37	3:08 22:16	2:02 23:20
5	6:49 20:46	6:22 21:11	6:06 21:25	5:48 21:42	5:26 22:02	4:58 22:27	4:19 23:01	3:15 23:51
6	7:58 21:40	7:34 22:01	7:20 22:13	7:04 22:26	6:45 22:42	6:21 23:02	5:49 23:28	5:00 —
7	9:03 22:26	8:44 22:42	8:33 22:51	8:21 23:01	8:06 23:13	7:48 23:27	7:24 23:45	6:50 0:03
8	10:04 23:07	9:51 23:17	9:43 23:22	9:34 23:29	9:24 23:37	9:12 23:46	8:56 23:57	8:34 0:08
9	11:01 23:43	10:53 23:48	10:49 23:50	10:44 23:53	10:38 23:57	10:31 —	10:22 —	10:11 0:11
10	11:54 —	11:52 —	11:51 —	11:49 —	11:48 —	11:46 0:01	11:43 0:06	11:40 0:12
11	12:45 0:17	12:48 0:16	12:50 0:16	12:52 0:15	12:55 0:15	12:58 0:14	13:02 0:14	13:07 0:13
12	13:35 0:50	13:44 0:44	13:49 0:41	13:54 0:37	14:01 0:33	14:09 0:27	14:18 0:21	14:31 0:13
13	14:26 1:23	14:39 1:12	14:47 1:06	14:56 0:59	15:06 0:51	15:19 0:41	15:35 0:29	15:57 0:14
14	15:17 1:58	15:35 1:42	15:46 1:33	15:58 1:23	16:12 1:11	16:30 0:57	16:53 0:39	17:25 0:15
15	16:09 2:35	16:31 2:15	16:45 2:04	17:00 1:51	17:18 1:35	17:40 1:17	18:10 0:52	18:54 0:19
16	17:03 3:16	17:28 2:53	17:43 2:39	18:00 2:23	18:21 2:05	18:47 1:41	19:24 1:10	20:21 0:25
17	17:56 4:01	18:23 3:35	18:39 3:20	18:57 3:02	19:20 2:41	19:49 2:14	20:29 1:37	21:36 0:39
18	18:48 4:51	19:15 4:23	19:31 4:07	19:49 3:48	20:12 3:26	20:41 2:57	21:20 2:17	22:27 1:09
19	19:36 5:43	20:02 5:16	20:17 5:00	20:34 4:42	20:55 4:20	21:22 3:51	21:57 3:12	22:52 2:06
20	20:22 6:37	20:44 6:13	20:58 5:58	21:13 5:41	21:31 5:21	21:53 4:55	22:22 4:20	23:04 3:26
21	21:03 7:32	21:22 7:11	21:33 6:58	21:45 6:44	21:59 6:27	22:17 6:06	22:39 5:38	23:10 4:57
22	21:42 8:26	21:56 8:10	22:04 8:00	22:13 7:49	22:23 7:35	22:36 7:19	22:52 6:58	23:13 6:29
23	22:18 9:20	22:27 9:08	22:32 9:01	22:37 8:53	22:44 8:44	22:52 8:33	23:02 8:19	23:14 8:00
24	22:53 10:13	22:56 10:06	22:58 10:03	23:00 9:58	23:03 9:53	23:06 9:47	23:10 9:40	23:15 9:30
25	23:27 11:06	23:26 11:05	23:24 11:05	23:23 11:04	23:22 11:03	23:20 11:02	23:18 11:01	23:16 11:00
26	— 12:01	23:56 12:05	23:52 12:08	23:47 12:11	23:42 12:15	23:35 12:19	23:27 12:25	23:17 12:32
27	0:04 12:58	— 13:08	— 13:15	— 13:22	— 13:30	23:53 13:40	23:38 13:52	23:19 14:09
28	0:44 13:59	0:31 14:15	0:23 14:25	0:15 14:36	0:05 14:49	— 15:04	23:53 15:25	23:23 15:53
29	1:29 15:04	1:10 15:26	0:59 15:38	0:47 15:53	0:33 16:11	0:15 16:32	— 17:01	23:32 17:44
30	2:20 16:12	1:57 16:38	1:43 16:53	1:27 17:11	1:09 17:32	0:46 17:59	0:16 18:36	23:53 19:34

MOONRISE AND MOONSET, 2008 JULY, AUGUST
UNIVERSAL TIME AT GREENWICH MERIDIAN

Latitude:	+20°	+30°	+35°	+40°	+45°	+50°	+55°	+60°
Event: RISE SET	RISE SET	RISE SET	RISE SET	RISE SET	RISE SET	RISE SET	RISE SET	RISE SET
Jul. 1	3:19 17:21	2:53 17:49	2:37 18:05	2:19 18:24	1:57 18:46	1:30 19:16	0:52 19:56	— 21:03
2	4:25 18:26	3:58 18:53	3:42 19:08	3:23 19:26	3:00 19:48	2:31 20:15	1:51 20:52	0:44 21:50
3	5:34 19:25	5:09 19:48	4:54 20:01	4:37 20:17	4:16 20:35	3:49 20:57	3:13 21:27	2:16 22:09
4	6:43 20:16	6:21 20:34	6:09 20:44	5:55 20:56	5:38 21:10	5:16 21:27	4:48 21:48	4:08 22:17
5	7:47 21:00	7:32 21:12	7:22 21:20	7:12 21:28	6:59 21:37	6:44 21:48	6:25 22:02	5:58 22:21
6	8:48 21:39	8:38 21:46	8:32 21:50	8:25 21:54	8:17 21:59	8:08 22:05	7:56 22:13	7:41 22:22
7	9:44 22:15	9:39 22:16	9:37 22:17	9:34 22:18	9:31 22:19	9:27 22:20	9:22 22:21	9:16 22:23
8	10:37 22:49	10:38 22:45	10:39 22:42	10:40 22:40	10:41 22:37	10:42 22:33	10:44 22:29	10:46 22:24
9	11:29 23:22	11:35 23:13	11:39 23:08	11:44 23:02	11:49 22:55	11:55 22:47	12:03 22:37	12:13 22:24
10	12:20 23:57	12:32 23:43	12:38 23:35	12:46 23:26	12:56 23:15	13:07 23:03	13:21 22:47	13:40 22:26
11	13:11 —	13:28 —	13:38 —	13:49 23:52	14:02 23:38	14:18 23:21	14:39 22:58	15:07 22:28
12	14:04 0:34	14:25 0:15	14:37 0:05	14:51 —	15:08 —	15:29 23:43	15:57 23:15	16:37 22:33
13	14:57 1:14	15:21 0:51	15:36 0:38	15:52 0:23	16:12 0:05	16:38 —	17:12 23:38	18:06 22:44
14	15:50 1:58	16:17 1:32	16:33 1:17	16:51 1:00	17:13 0:39	17:42 0:13	18:21 —	19:27 23:07
15	16:43 2:45	17:10 2:18	17:26 2:02	17:45 1:44	18:08 1:21	18:37 0:53	19:17 0:13	20:26 23:54
16	17:33 3:37	17:59 3:10	18:14 2:54	18:32 2:35	18:54 2:12	19:21 1:43	19:59 1:03	20:59 —
17	18:19 4:31	18:43 4:06	18:57 3:51	19:13 3:33	19:32 3:12	19:56 2:45	20:27 2:08	21:14 1:09
18	19:03 5:26	19:22 5:04	19:34 4:51	19:47 4:36	20:03 4:17	20:22 3:54	20:47 3:24	21:21 2:39
19	19:42 6:21	19:58 6:03	20:06 5:53	20:17 5:40	20:28 5:26	20:43 5:08	21:00 4:45	21:24 4:13
20	20:19 7:16	20:29 7:02	20:35 6:55	20:42 6:46	20:50 6:35	20:59 6:23	21:11 6:07	21:26 5:45
21	20:54 8:09	20:59 8:01	21:02 7:57	21:06 7:51	21:09 7:45	21:14 7:38	21:20 7:28	21:27 7:16
22	21:29 9:02	21:29 9:00	21:29 8:58	21:28 8:57	21:28 8:55	21:28 8:53	21:28 8:50	21:27 8:46
23	22:05 9:56	21:59 9:59	21:55 10:01	21:52 10:03	21:47 10:06	21:42 10:08	21:36 10:12	21:28 10:17
24	22:42 10:52	22:31 11:01	22:24 11:06	22:17 11:12	22:09 11:18	21:58 11:27	21:46 11:37	21:29 11:51
25	23:24 11:50	23:07 12:05	22:58 12:13	22:47 12:23	22:34 12:34	22:18 12:48	21:58 13:06	21:32 13:30
26	— 12:52	23:50 13:12	23:37 13:24	23:23 13:37	23:05 13:53	22:44 14:13	22:17 14:39	21:38 15:15
27	0:11 13:57	— 14:21	— 14:36	— 14:53	23:47 15:13	23:21 15:38	22:46 16:12	21:52 17:04
28	1:06 15:04	0:40 15:31	0:25 15:47	0:08 16:06	— 16:28	— 16:57	23:33 17:36	22:26 18:43
29	2:07 16:09	1:40 16:36	1:23 16:52	1:05 17:11	0:42 17:34	0:13 18:02	— 18:41	23:40 19:46
30	3:13 17:10	2:47 17:34	2:31 17:49	2:13 18:06	1:50 18:26	1:22 18:51	0:43 19:24	— 20:14
31	4:21 18:03	3:58 18:24	3:44 18:36	3:28 18:49	3:09 19:06	2:45 19:25	2:13 19:50	1:24 20:25
Aug. 1	5:27 18:50	5:09 19:06	4:58 19:14	4:46 19:24	4:31 19:36	4:13 19:50	3:49 20:07	3:16 20:31
2	6:30 19:32	6:17 19:42	6:10 19:47	6:01 19:53	5:51 20:00	5:39 20:09	5:24 20:20	5:03 20:33
3	7:29 20:10	7:22 20:14	7:18 20:16	7:13 20:18	7:08 20:21	7:02 20:25	6:54 20:29	6:43 20:34
4	8:25 20:45	8:23 20:44	8:23 20:43	8:22 20:42	8:21 20:40	8:20 20:39	8:19 20:37	8:17 20:35
5	9:18 21:20	9:23 21:13	9:25 21:09	9:28 21:04	9:31 20:59	9:36 20:53	9:41 20:45	9:47 20:35
6	10:10 21:54	10:20 21:42	10:26 21:36	10:32 21:28	10:40 21:19	10:49 21:08	11:01 20:54	11:16 20:36
7	11:03 22:31	11:18 22:14	11:26 22:04	11:36 21:53	11:48 21:40	12:02 21:25	12:20 21:05	12:45 20:38
8	11:55 23:10	12:15 22:49	12:26 22:37	12:39 22:23	12:55 22:06	13:14 21:46	13:39 21:19	14:15 20:42
9	12:49 23:53	13:12 23:28	13:26 23:14	13:42 22:57	14:01 22:37	14:25 22:13	14:57 21:40	15:45 20:50
10	13:42 —	14:08 —	14:24 23:57	14:42 23:38	15:03 23:16	15:31 22:48	16:09 22:10	17:11 21:07
11	14:35 0:39	15:03 0:12	15:19 —	15:38 —	16:01 —	16:30 23:35	17:10 22:54	18:20 21:44
12	15:26 1:29	15:53 1:02	16:09 0:46	16:28 0:27	16:50 0:04	17:18 —	17:57 23:54	19:02 22:50
13	16:14 2:23	16:39 1:56	16:54 1:41	17:11 1:22	17:31 1:00	17:56 0:32	18:30 —	19:22 —
14	16:59 3:18	17:21 2:54	17:33 2:40	17:47 2:24	18:04 2:04	18:25 1:39	18:53 1:06	19:31 0:16
15	17:40 4:13	17:57 3:53	18:07 3:42	18:19 3:28	18:32 3:12	18:48 2:52	19:08 2:26	19:36 1:49
16	18:19 5:08	18:31 4:53	18:38 4:44	18:46 4:34	18:55 4:22	19:06 4:08	19:20 3:49	19:38 3:24
17	18:55 6:03	19:02 5:53	19:06 5:47	19:10 5:41	19:15 5:33	19:22 5:24	19:29 5:12	19:39 4:57
18	19:30 6:57	19:32 6:53	19:32 6:50	19:33 6:47	19:35 6:44	19:36 6:40	19:37 6:35	19:40 6:28
19	20:06 7:51	20:02 7:53	19:59 7:54	19:57 7:54	19:54 7:55	19:50 7:57	19:46 7:58	19:40 8:00
20	20:43 8:47	20:33 8:54	20:28 8:58	20:22 9:03	20:14 9:08	20:06 9:15	19:55 9:23	19:41 9:34
21	21:24 9:45	21:09 9:58	21:00 10:05	20:50 10:14	20:38 10:24	20:24 10:36	20:07 10:51	19:44 11:12
22	22:09 10:46	21:49 11:04	21:37 11:15	21:23 11:27	21:07 11:42	20:48 12:00	20:23 12:23	19:49 12:56
23	23:00 11:49	22:36 12:12	22:21 12:26	22:05 12:42	21:45 13:00	21:20 13:24	20:48 13:56	19:59 14:43
24	23:58 12:54	23:31 13:21	23:15 13:36	22:56 13:54	22:34 14:16	22:06 14:44	21:27 15:22	20:24 16:25
25	— 13:59	— 14:26	— 14:42	23:59 15:01	23:36 15:24	23:07 15:53	22:27 16:33	21:20 17:40
26	1:01 14:59	0:33 15:25	0:17 15:40	— 15:58	— 16:19	— 16:46	23:48 17:22	22:53 18:18
27	2:06 15:54	1:41 16:17	1:27 16:30	1:09 16:45	0:49 17:02	0:23 17:24	— 17:53	— 18:34
28	3:12 16:43	2:51 17:00	2:39 17:10	2:25 17:22	2:08 17:36	1:47 17:52	1:20 18:13	0:41 18:41
29	4:15 17:26	3:59 17:38	3:50 17:45	3:40 17:53	3:28 18:02	3:13 18:13	2:54 18:27	2:28 18:44
30	5:14 18:05	5:05 18:11	4:59 18:15	4:53 18:19	4:45 18:24	4:36 18:30	4:25 18:37	4:10 18:46
31	6:11 18:41	6:07 18:42	6:05 18:42	6:02 18:43	5:59 18:44	5:56 18:45	5:51 18:46	5:46 18:47

MOONRISE AND MOONSET, 2008 SEPTEMBER, OCTOBER
UNIVERSAL TIME AT GREENWICH MERIDIAN

Latitude:	+20°		+30°		+35°		+40°		+45°		+50°		+55°		+60°	
Event:	RISE	SET	RISE	SET	RISE	SET	RISE	SET	RISE	SET	RISE	SET	RISE	SET	RISE	SET
Sep. 1	7:06	19:16	7:07	19:11	7:08	19:09	7:10	19:06	7:11	19:03	7:13	18:59	7:15	18:54	7:18	18:47
2	7:59	19:51	8:06	19:41	8:11	19:36	8:15	19:29	8:21	19:22	8:28	19:13	8:37	19:02	8:48	18:48
3	8:52	20:27	9:05	20:12	9:12	20:04	9:20	19:54	9:30	19:43	9:42	19:29	9:57	19:12	10:18	18:50
4	9:45	21:06	10:03	20:46	10:13	20:35	10:25	20:22	10:39	20:07	10:56	19:49	11:18	19:25	11:48	18:53
5	10:39	21:47	11:01	21:24	11:13	21:10	11:28	20:55	11:46	20:36	12:08	20:13	12:37	19:43	13:20	18:59
6	11:33	22:32	11:58	22:06	12:13	21:51	12:30	21:33	12:50	21:12	13:17	20:45	13:52	20:09	14:49	19:12
7	12:26	23:21	12:53	22:54	13:09	22:37	13:28	22:19	13:50	21:56	14:19	21:27	14:59	20:47	16:06	19:39
8	13:18	—	13:45	23:46	14:01	23:30	14:20	23:11	14:43	22:49	15:12	22:20	15:52	21:40	16:59	20:33
9	14:07	0:13	14:33	—	14:48	—	15:06	—	15:27	23:49	15:54	23:23	16:30	22:48	17:27	21:51
10	14:53	1:07	15:16	0:42	15:29	0:27	15:45	0:10	16:03	—	16:26	—	16:56	—	17:40	23:22
11	15:35	2:02	15:54	1:40	16:05	1:28	16:18	1:13	16:33	0:55	16:51	0:33	17:14	0:04	17:46	—
12	16:15	2:57	16:29	2:40	16:37	2:30	16:47	2:18	16:58	2:04	17:11	1:48	17:27	1:26	17:49	0:56
13	16:52	3:52	17:01	3:40	17:06	3:33	17:12	3:25	17:19	3:15	17:27	3:04	17:38	2:49	17:51	2:30
14	17:28	4:47	17:32	4:40	17:34	4:36	17:36	4:32	17:39	4:27	17:42	4:20	17:47	4:13	17:52	4:02
15	18:04	5:42	18:02	5:41	18:01	5:40	18:00	5:40	17:59	5:39	17:57	5:38	17:55	5:37	17:53	5:35
16	18:42	6:38	18:34	6:43	18:30	6:46	18:25	6:49	18:19	6:53	18:13	6:57	18:04	7:03	17:54	7:10
17	19:22	7:36	19:09	7:47	19:01	7:54	18:53	8:01	18:43	8:09	18:31	8:19	18:16	8:32	17:56	8:49
18	20:07	8:38	19:48	8:54	19:37	9:04	19:25	9:15	19:10	9:28	18:53	9:44	18:31	10:05	18:00	10:33
19	20:57	9:42	20:34	10:03	20:20	10:16	20:04	10:31	19:46	10:48	19:23	11:10	18:53	11:39	18:09	12:21
20	21:53	10:47	21:26	11:13	21:11	11:28	20:53	11:45	20:31	12:06	20:04	12:33	19:27	13:09	18:29	14:07
21	22:54	11:52	22:27	12:19	22:11	12:35	21:52	12:54	21:29	13:17	21:00	13:46	20:21	14:26	19:14	15:32
22	23:58	12:54	23:33	13:20	23:17	13:36	23:00	13:54	22:38	14:16	22:11	14:43	21:35	15:21	20:36	16:20
23	—	13:49	—	14:13	—	14:27	—	14:43	23:54	15:02	23:32	15:25	23:02	15:56	22:18	16:41
24	1:03	14:39	0:40	14:58	0:27	15:09	0:12	15:22	—	15:37	—	15:55	—	16:19	—	16:51
25	2:05	15:23	1:48	15:37	1:37	15:45	1:26	15:54	1:12	16:05	0:55	16:18	0:34	16:34	0:04	16:55
26	3:04	16:02	2:52	16:11	2:46	16:16	2:38	16:21	2:28	16:28	2:17	16:36	2:03	16:45	1:45	16:57
27	4:01	16:38	3:55	16:42	3:51	16:44	3:47	16:46	3:42	16:48	3:37	16:51	3:29	16:54	3:20	16:59
28	4:55	17:13	4:55	17:11	4:54	17:10	4:54	17:09	4:54	17:07	4:53	17:05	4:53	17:03	4:52	17:00
29	5:48	17:48	5:53	17:41	5:56	17:36	6:00	17:32	6:04	17:26	6:08	17:19	6:14	17:11	6:22	17:01
30	6:41	18:24	6:52	18:11	6:58	18:04	7:05	17:56	7:13	17:46	7:22	17:35	7:35	17:21	7:51	17:02
Oct. 1	7:35	19:02	7:50	18:44	7:59	18:34	8:09	18:23	8:22	18:09	8:36	17:53	8:55	17:33	9:21	17:05
2	8:28	19:42	8:48	19:21	9:00	19:08	9:14	18:54	9:30	18:37	9:50	18:16	10:16	17:48	10:53	17:10
3	9:23	20:26	9:46	20:01	10:00	19:47	10:16	19:30	10:36	19:10	11:00	18:45	11:33	18:11	12:23	17:20
4	10:16	21:13	10:43	20:47	10:58	20:31	11:16	20:13	11:38	19:50	12:05	19:22	12:44	18:44	13:46	17:41
5	11:09	22:04	11:36	21:37	11:52	21:21	12:11	21:02	12:33	20:40	13:02	20:11	13:42	19:31	14:49	18:24
6	11:59	22:57	12:25	22:31	12:41	22:16	12:59	21:58	13:21	21:36	13:48	21:09	14:26	20:32	15:26	19:32
7	12:46	23:51	13:10	23:28	13:24	23:14	13:40	22:58	14:00	22:39	14:24	22:16	14:56	21:44	15:45	20:57
8	13:29	—	13:49	—	14:01	—	14:15	—	14:32	23:46	14:52	23:27	15:17	23:03	15:54	22:28
9	14:09	0:45	14:25	0:26	14:35	0:15	14:45	0:02	14:58	—	15:13	—	15:33	—	15:58	—
10	14:46	1:39	14:58	1:25	15:05	1:16	15:12	1:07	15:21	0:55	15:31	0:41	15:44	0:24	16:01	0:00
11	15:23	2:33	15:29	2:24	15:33	2:19	15:37	2:12	15:41	2:05	15:47	1:57	15:54	1:46	16:03	1:32
12	15:59	3:28	16:00	3:24	16:00	3:22	16:01	3:19	16:01	3:17	16:02	3:13	16:03	3:09	16:04	3:03
13	16:36	4:23	16:31	4:26	16:28	4:27	16:25	4:28	16:21	4:30	16:17	4:32	16:12	4:34	16:05	4:37
14	17:16	5:22	17:05	5:30	16:59	5:34	16:52	5:40	16:44	5:46	16:34	5:53	16:23	6:03	16:07	6:15
15	18:00	6:23	17:43	6:37	17:34	6:45	17:23	6:54	17:11	7:05	16:56	7:19	16:37	7:36	16:11	7:59
16	18:49	7:27	18:28	7:47	18:15	7:59	18:01	8:12	17:44	8:27	17:23	8:47	16:56	9:12	16:19	9:48
17	19:45	8:35	19:20	8:59	19:05	9:13	18:48	9:29	18:27	9:49	18:01	10:14	17:27	10:47	16:35	11:39
18	20:46	9:42	20:19	10:09	20:03	10:25	19:45	10:43	19:22	11:05	18:54	11:33	18:15	12:12	17:11	13:15
19	21:51	10:47	21:25	11:13	21:09	11:29	20:51	11:47	20:30	12:10	20:02	12:37	19:24	13:16	18:23	14:17
20	22:56	11:45	22:33	12:10	22:20	12:24	22:04	12:41	21:45	13:00	21:21	13:25	20:50	13:57	20:02	14:46
21	23:59	12:37	23:41	12:57	23:30	13:09	23:17	13:23	23:02	13:39	22:44	13:58	22:20	14:24	21:47	14:59
22	—	13:22	—	13:38	—	13:47	—	13:57	—	14:09	—	14:23	23:50	14:41	23:28	15:05
23	0:59	14:02	0:46	14:12	0:38	14:18	0:29	14:25	0:19	14:33	0:06	14:42	—	14:53	—	15:08
24	1:56	14:39	1:48	14:44	1:43	14:47	1:38	14:50	1:32	14:53	1:25	14:58	1:16	15:03	1:04	15:10
25	2:50	15:14	2:47	15:13	2:46	15:13	2:44	15:13	2:43	15:12	2:40	15:12	2:38	15:12	2:34	15:11
26	3:42	15:48	3:45	15:42	3:47	15:39	3:49	15:35	3:51	15:31	3:54	15:26	3:58	15:20	4:03	15:12
27	4:34	16:23	4:43	16:12	4:48	16:06	4:53	15:59	5:00	15:51	5:08	15:41	5:17	15:29	5:30	15:14
28	5:27	16:59	5:40	16:44	5:48	16:35	5:57	16:25	6:08	16:13	6:21	15:58	6:37	15:40	6:59	15:16
29	6:20	17:39	6:38	17:19	6:49	17:07	7:01	16:54	7:16	16:38	7:33	16:19	7:57	15:55	8:29	15:21
30	7:14	18:21	7:36	17:58	7:49	17:44	8:04	17:28	8:22	17:09	8:45	16:46	9:15	16:15	9:59	15:30
31	8:08	19:07	8:33	18:42	8:48	18:26	9:05	18:09	9:26	17:47	9:52	17:21	10:28	16:44	11:25	15:47

MOONRISE AND MOONSET, 2008 NOVEMBER, DECEMBER
UNIVERSAL TIME AT GREENWICH MERIDIAN

Latitude:	+20°		+30°		+35°		+40°		+45°		+50°		+55°		+60°	
Event:	RISE	SET	RISE	SET	RISE	SET	RISE	SET	RISE	SET	RISE	SET	RISE	SET	RISE	SET
Nov. 1	9:01	19:57	9:28	19:30	9:44	19:14	10:02	18:56	10:24	18:33	10:52	18:05	11:31	17:26	12:36	16:21
2	9:52	20:49	10:19	20:23	10:34	20:07	10:52	19:49	11:14	19:27	11:42	19:00	12:21	18:22	13:23	17:20
3	10:40	21:42	11:04	21:18	11:19	21:04	11:36	20:47	11:56	20:28	12:22	20:03	12:56	19:30	13:47	18:39
4	11:23	22:35	11:45	22:15	11:58	22:03	12:13	21:49	12:30	21:32	12:52	21:12	13:20	20:45	14:00	20:06
5	12:04	23:28	12:22	23:12	12:32	23:03	12:44	22:52	12:58	22:39	13:15	22:23	13:37	22:03	14:06	21:36
6	12:42	—	12:55	—	13:03	—	13:12	23:55	13:22	23:47	13:34	23:36	13:49	23:22	14:10	23:05
7	13:17	0:21	13:26	0:10	13:31	0:03	13:36	—	13:43	—	13:50	—	14:00	—	14:12	—
8	13:53	1:14	13:56	1:08	13:58	1:04	14:00	1:00	14:02	0:55	14:05	0:50	14:09	0:43	14:13	0:33
9	14:29	2:07	14:26	2:07	14:25	2:07	14:24	2:06	14:22	2:06	14:20	2:05	14:18	2:04	14:15	2:03
10	15:06	3:03	14:59	3:08	14:54	3:11	14:49	3:15	14:43	3:19	14:36	3:24	14:28	3:29	14:17	3:37
11	15:48	4:02	15:35	4:13	15:27	4:20	15:18	4:27	15:08	4:36	14:56	4:46	14:40	4:59	14:20	5:16
12	16:35	5:06	16:16	5:23	16:05	5:32	15:53	5:44	15:38	5:57	15:20	6:13	14:57	6:34	14:26	7:03
13	17:29	6:13	17:06	6:35	16:52	6:48	16:36	7:03	16:17	7:21	15:54	7:43	15:23	8:12	14:39	8:55
14	18:30	7:23	18:04	7:48	17:48	8:03	17:30	8:21	17:09	8:42	16:42	9:09	16:04	9:45	15:06	10:43
15	19:37	8:31	19:10	8:58	18:54	9:14	18:36	9:32	18:14	9:54	17:46	10:23	17:07	11:01	16:05	12:04
16	20:44	9:35	20:20	10:00	20:06	10:15	19:49	10:32	19:29	10:53	19:04	11:18	18:31	11:53	17:39	12:46
17	21:51	10:31	21:31	10:52	21:19	11:05	21:05	11:20	20:49	11:37	20:29	11:58	20:03	12:26	19:26	13:04
18	22:53	11:19	22:38	11:36	22:29	11:46	22:20	11:57	22:08	12:10	21:54	12:26	21:36	12:46	21:11	13:13
19	23:51	12:02	23:42	12:14	23:36	12:20	23:30	12:28	23:23	12:37	23:14	12:47	23:04	13:00	22:49	13:17
20	—	12:40	—	12:46	—	12:50	—	12:54	—	12:59	—	13:04	—	13:11	—	13:20
21	0:46	13:15	0:42	13:16	0:40	13:17	0:38	13:18	0:35	13:18	0:31	13:19	0:27	13:20	0:21	13:22
22	1:39	13:49	1:40	13:45	1:41	13:43	1:42	13:40	1:44	13:37	1:45	13:33	1:47	13:29	1:50	13:23
23	2:31	14:24	2:37	14:14	2:41	14:09	2:46	14:03	2:51	13:56	2:58	13:48	3:06	13:38	3:16	13:25
24	3:22	14:59	3:34	14:45	3:41	14:37	3:49	14:28	3:59	14:17	4:10	14:04	4:24	13:48	4:43	13:27
25	4:15	15:37	4:31	15:19	4:41	15:08	4:52	14:56	5:06	14:42	5:22	14:24	5:43	14:02	6:12	13:31
26	5:08	16:19	5:29	15:56	5:41	15:43	5:55	15:28	6:12	15:11	6:33	14:49	7:01	14:20	7:41	13:39
27	6:02	17:04	6:26	16:38	6:40	16:24	6:57	16:07	7:17	15:46	7:42	15:20	8:16	14:46	9:08	13:53
28	6:55	17:52	7:21	17:25	7:37	17:10	7:55	16:52	8:17	16:30	8:44	16:02	9:22	15:23	10:24	14:21
29	7:47	18:43	8:13	18:17	8:29	18:01	8:47	17:43	9:09	17:21	9:37	16:53	10:16	16:15	11:19	15:12
30	8:35	19:36	9:01	19:11	9:16	18:57	9:33	18:40	9:54	18:20	10:20	17:54	10:55	17:19	11:50	16:25
Dec. 1	9:20	20:29	9:43	20:08	9:57	19:55	10:12	19:40	10:30	19:23	10:53	19:01	11:23	18:32	12:06	17:50
2	10:02	21:22	10:21	21:04	10:32	20:54	10:45	20:42	11:00	20:28	11:18	20:11	11:42	19:49	12:14	19:18
3	10:40	22:14	10:55	22:01	11:03	21:53	11:13	21:44	11:24	21:34	11:38	21:22	11:55	21:06	12:18	20:46
4	11:15	23:05	11:25	22:57	11:31	22:52	11:38	22:47	11:46	22:41	11:55	22:33	12:06	22:24	12:21	22:12
5	11:50	23:56	11:55	23:54	11:58	23:52	12:01	23:50	12:05	23:48	12:10	23:46	12:15	23:42	12:23	23:38
6	12:24	—	12:24	—	12:24	—	12:24	—	12:24	—	12:24	—	12:24	—	12:24	—
7	12:59	0:49	12:54	0:52	12:51	0:54	12:48	0:55	12:44	0:57	12:39	1:00	12:33	1:03	12:26	1:07
8	13:38	1:45	13:27	1:53	13:21	1:58	13:14	2:03	13:06	2:10	12:56	2:17	12:44	2:27	12:29	2:40
9	14:21	2:44	14:05	2:58	13:55	3:06	13:45	3:15	13:32	3:26	13:17	3:40	12:58	3:57	12:33	4:19
10	15:10	3:48	14:49	4:07	14:37	4:19	14:23	4:32	14:06	4:47	13:45	5:07	13:19	5:32	12:42	6:07
11	16:08	4:56	15:43	5:20	15:28	5:34	15:11	5:50	14:51	6:10	14:25	6:35	13:51	7:08	13:00	7:58
12	17:12	6:06	16:46	6:32	16:30	6:48	16:11	7:06	15:49	7:28	15:21	7:56	14:43	8:34	13:41	9:36
13	18:22	7:14	17:56	7:40	17:41	7:56	17:23	8:14	17:02	8:35	16:35	9:02	15:59	9:40	15:01	10:38
14	19:32	8:15	19:10	8:39	18:57	8:53	18:42	9:09	18:24	9:28	18:01	9:51	17:32	10:22	16:48	11:07
15	20:38	9:10	20:21	9:29	20:12	9:40	20:00	9:52	19:47	10:07	19:30	10:25	19:09	10:48	18:40	11:20
16	21:41	9:56	21:29	10:10	21:23	10:18	21:15	10:27	21:07	10:37	20:56	10:50	20:43	11:05	20:25	11:26
17	22:39	10:38	22:33	10:46	22:30	10:50	22:26	10:56	22:22	11:02	22:17	11:09	22:11	11:18	22:02	11:29
18	23:34	11:15	23:34	11:18	23:34	11:19	23:34	11:21	23:34	11:23	23:34	11:25	23:34	11:28	23:34	11:32
19	—	11:50	—	11:47	—	11:46	—	11:44	—	11:42	—	11:40	—	11:37	—	11:33
20	0:26	12:25	0:32	12:17	0:35	12:12	0:39	12:07	0:43	12:01	0:48	11:54	0:54	11:46	1:02	11:35
21	1:19	13:00	1:29	12:47	1:35	12:40	1:42	12:32	1:51	12:22	2:01	12:10	2:13	11:56	2:30	11:37
22	2:11	13:37	2:26	13:20	2:35	13:10	2:46	12:59	2:58	12:45	3:13	12:29	3:32	12:08	3:58	11:41
23	3:04	14:17	3:23	13:56	3:35	13:44	3:48	13:29	4:04	13:13	4:24	12:52	4:50	12:25	5:27	11:47
24	3:57	15:01	4:20	14:37	4:34	14:22	4:50	14:06	5:09	13:46	5:33	13:21	6:06	12:48	6:54	11:59
25	4:50	15:48	5:16	15:22	5:31	15:06	5:49	14:48	6:10	14:27	6:38	13:59	7:15	13:22	8:15	12:22
26	5:43	16:39	6:09	16:12	6:25	15:56	6:43	15:38	7:05	15:16	7:34	14:48	8:12	14:09	9:17	13:05
27	6:32	17:31	6:58	17:06	7:13	16:51	7:31	16:34	7:52	16:13	8:19	15:46	8:56	15:10	9:54	14:13
28	7:19	18:25	7:42	18:02	7:56	17:49	8:12	17:33	8:31	17:15	8:55	16:52	9:27	16:21	10:13	15:36
29	8:01	19:18	8:21	18:59	8:33	18:48	8:47	18:35	9:03	18:20	9:22	18:01	9:48	17:37	10:23	17:04
30	8:40	20:10	8:56	19:55	9:06	19:47	9:16	19:37	9:29	19:26	9:44	19:12	10:03	18:55	10:28	18:31
31	9:16	21:01	9:28	20:51	9:34	20:46	9:42	20:39	9:51	20:32	10:01	20:23	10:14	20:12	10:31	19:57

OCCULTATIONS BY THE MOON
BY DAVID W. DUNHAM

The Moon often passes between Earth and a star, an event called an *occultation*. During an occultation, a star suddenly disappears as the east limb of the Moon crosses the line between the star and the observer. The star reappears from behind the west limb some time later. Because the Moon moves through an angle about equal to its own diameter every hour, the longest time for an occultation is about an hour. The time is shorter if the occultation is not central. Solar eclipses are actually occultations: the star being occulted by the Moon is the Sun.

Since observing occultations is rather easy, amateur astronomers should try this activity. The slow, majestic drift of the Moon in its orbit is an interesting part of such observations, and the disappearance or reappearance of a star at the Moon's limb is a remarkable sight, particularly when it occurs as a *graze* near the Moon's northern or southern limb. During a graze, a star may disappear and reappear several times in succession as mountains and valleys in the Moon's polar regions drift by it. On rarer occasions the Moon occults a planet. During 2008 the planets Venus and Mars, and the second-magnitude star σ Sagittarii (Nunki), are occulted. Also occulted are several stars in the Pleiades and Praesepe star clusters.

Lunar occultation and graze observations refine our knowledge of the shape of the lunar profile and the fundamental star coordinate system. These observations complement those made by other techniques, such as Clementine laser ranging and photographs. Improved knowledge of the lunar profile is useful in determinations of the Sun's diameter from solar eclipse records. Occultation observations are also useful for detecting double stars and measuring their separations. Binaries with separations as small as 0.02″ have been discovered visually during grazes. Doubles with separations in this range are useful for filling the gap between doubles that can be directly resolved and those whose duplicity has been discovered spectroscopically.

Observations

The **International Lunar Occultation Centre (ILOC)** analyzes lunar occultation observations and is the world clearinghouse for such observations. Anyone interested in pursuing a systematic program of lunar occultation observations should write to the ILOC, Geodesy and Geophysics Division, Hydrographic Department, Tsukiji 5-3-1, Chuo-ku, Tokyo 104-0045, Japan, email iloc@jodc.go.jp, for their booklet *Guide to Lunar Occultation Observations*. ILOC's Web site is www1.kaiho.mlit.go.jp/KOHO/iloc/obsrep.

Observers in North America should also contact the **International Occultation Timing Association (IOTA)**, 26920 136th Pl. SE, Kent, WA 98042, USA; email: business@occultations.org. IOTA provides predictions and coordination services for occultation observers. Detailed predictions for any grazing occultation are available ($1.50 U.S. each; free by email); instructions explaining the use of predictions are also available ($5 U.S.; free at iota.jhuapl.edu/ocmangrz.htm). Annual membership in IOTA is $30 U.S. in North America, $35 U.S. overseas. Less expensive online rates are available. Membership includes free graze predictions, descriptive materials, and a subscription to *Occultation Newsletter* (available separately for $20 U.S. in North America, $25 overseas). IOTA's administrative Web site is www.occultations.org, and its site for predictions, updates, observations, and other technical information is www.lunar-occultations.com/iota, which includes more predictions than can be given here.

For observers in the southwestern Pacific (New Zealand, Australia, Papua New Guinea, and nearby areas), the Royal Astronomical Society of New Zealand

(RASNZ) provides occultation data (total lunar, lunar grazing, planetary, and Jupiter's satellites), plus comprehensive instructions for new observers. See the RASNZ Web page: occsec.wellington.net.nz/sitemap.htm.

The main information required in a lunar occultation observation is the time of the event and the observer's location. Supplementary data include the seeing conditions, telescope size, timing method, estimate of the observer's reaction time and the accuracy of the timing, and whether or not the reaction-time correction has been applied. The timing should be accurate to 0.5 s or better (a shortwave radio time signal and audio recorder provide a simple, permanent time record, but a video record provides higher accuracy). The observer's longitude, latitude, and altitude should be reported to the nearest tenth of an arcsecond and 10 m, respectively, and should be accurate to at least 0.5″ or 16 m. These can be determined from either GPS measurements (10 min of position averaging and an unobstructed view of the sky above 15° altitude are needed) or a suitable topographical map. For Canada, the maps are available from the Policy and Product Promotion Office, Centre for Topographic Information, Natural Resources Canada, 615 Booth St, Room 180, Ottawa ON K1A 0E9. For the United States (except Alaska), write to USGS Information Services (Product Sales), PO Box 25286, Denver CO 80225, asking for an index to topographical maps in the desired state, or call (303) 202-4200. For Alaska, write to US Geological Survey, Map Sales, 4230 University Dr, Room 101, Anchorage AK 99508-4664, or phone (907) 786-7011. Parts of USGS maps can be viewed and printed at www.topozone.com. Detailed imagery and maps are available at other Web sites, such as www.terraserver.com and Google Earth. IOTA is exploiting these resources for predictionss, but they are not accurate enough for reporting lunar occultation observations. IOTA's online observing manual, found at www.poyntsource.com/IOTAmanual/Preview.htm is very useful.

Observers are encouraged to learn how to videotape occultations in order to obtain reliable and accurate timings. Inexpensive yet sensitive video cameras are now available. Visual timings must be accurate to ±0.2 s to be good enough for further improvement of the lunar profile and other parameters, except for grazes, where ±0.5 s is adequate. Information about videotaping occultations is on IOTA's technical Web site given above.

Pages 164–172 give tables of occultation predictions and a table and maps of northern or southern limits for grazing occultations.

STANDARD STATIONS

1000 km

1. TOTAL OCCULTATION PREDICTIONS

PREDICTIONS BY THE INTERNATIONAL LUNAR OCCULTATION CENTRE, JAPAN

The total occultation predictions, as given in the tables on pp. 164–166, are for the 18 standard stations identified on the map on the previous page; the longitudes and latitudes of these stations are given in the table headings.

The predictions are limited to stars of magnitude 5.0 and brighter. The first five columns give for each occultation the date, the Zodiacal Catalogue (ZC) number of the star, its magnitude, the phenomenon, and the elongation of the Moon from the Sun in degrees. Under each station are given the Universal Time of the event, factors A and B (see below), and the position angle P (from the north point, eastward around the Moon's limb to the point of occurrence of the phenomenon). If no data are given for an occultation for a given station, the reason is specified. If A and B give an unrealistic representation, as in the case of near grazes, they are omitted.

The terms A and B are for determining corrections to the times of the events for stations within 300 km of the standard stations. If Lo* and La* represent the longitude and latitude of the standard station, and Lo and La those of the observer, then for the observer,

UT of event = UT of event at the standard station + A(Lo − Lo*) + B(La − La*),

where Lo, etc., are expressed in degrees, and A and B are in minutes of time per degree. Longitude measured *west* of Greenwich is assumed to be *positive* (which is opposite to the IAU convention and that used by IOTA's *Occult* software). Due regard must be paid to the algebraic signs of the terms. To convert UT to the standard time of the observer, see the section STANDARD TIME ZONES on pp. 50–51.

As an example, consider the occultation of ZC 3126 (ι Capricorni) on 2008 Jan. 10 as seen from Saint John, New Brunswick. For Saint John, Lo = 66.05° and La = 45.27°. The nearest standard station is Halifax, for which Lo* = 63.60° and La* = 44.60°. Therefore, the UT of the disappearance at the dark limb (DD) is:

21:12.1 − 0.6 × (66.05° − 63.60°) min + 0.1 × (45.27° − 44.60°) min = 21:10.7.

The elongation of the Moon is 28°, which corresponds to the waxing crescent phase (between new Moon and first quarter). The position angle of disappearance is approximately 46°. Note that at Halifax, the Sun will still be above the horizon, so bright twilight might hinder observation at Saint John.

The number of events observable from any location increases *rapidly* as predictions are extended to fainter stars. Observers who wish to pursue such work can obtain software or more extensive lists from Walter Robinson, 515 W Kump, Bonner Springs KS 66012–1439, USA, by providing accurate geographical coordinates and a long, self-addressed envelope (with postage); or, better, email webmaster@lunar-occultations.com.

2. GRAZE PREDICTIONS AND DATA ON OCCULTED STARS

BY EBERHARD RIEDEL AND DAVID W. DUNHAM

(A) GRAZE PREDICTIONS

The table on pp. 166–168 lists lunar grazing occultation predictions for much of North America for 2008. The events are limited to stars of magnitude 6.5 or brighter (paths for stars down to magnitude 7.5 are shown when the Moon is 20% or less sunlit and to 9.5 during lunar eclipses) that will graze the limb of the Moon when it is at a favourable elongation from the Sun and at least as high above a land horizon in degrees as the star's magnitude (e.g. a third-magnitude star is included only if its altitude is at least 3°). The star's USNO reference number is the ZC number, unless the number is prefixed with an X. In the latter case, the star is not in the ZC and its number is from the XZ catalogue, a more extensive catalogue of zodiacal stars prepared originally at the U.S. Naval Observatory but now updated by David Herald in Australia.

The maps on pp. 169–172 show the predicted graze tracks. The maps are "false" projections, since the latitude and longitude scales are both linear. This makes it much easier for measuring coordinates or plotting locations with known coordinates than is possible with any other type of projection. The longitude scale is compressed by a factor of cos 50°. The maps are not detailed enough for locating oneself in the 2- or 3-km-wide zone where multiple disappearances of the star may occur. To obtain detailed predictions of any graze for plotting on larger-scale maps of your region, write to (or email) IOTA (see p. 158). For grazes of very bright stars, IOTA overlays the predicted limit line on the very detailed maps and imagery of maps.google.com, available at www.fingerlakessynthetics.com/occultations/GrazeMaps.html, but further corrections are needed based on the predicted lunar profile and the observer's height above sea level.

Each track is keyed to the sequential number in the table. The computer-drawn number appears at the east and west ends of the track and is aligned parallel to it. Some overlapping numbers have been omitted for legibility; in these cases, check the other end of the track for the number. Conditions are represented by three different types of lines:

solid line = dark limb, night
dashed line = bright limb, night
dotted line = dark or bright limb, day

Thicker lines are drawn for first-magnitude stars and planets. Many tracks begin and/or end with the letter A, B, or S: A denotes that the Moon is at a low altitude, B that the bright limb interferes, and S that sunlight or twilight interferes. The tick marks along the tracks indicate multiples of 10 min of every hour. For example, if the time for the west end of the track is 3:16.2, the tick marks proceeding eastward correspond to 3:20, 3:30, etc. Time always increases from west to east along the path. *The time ticks, track numbers, and the A, B, and S letters are on the side of the limit with an occultation,* that is north of southern limits and south of northern limits. The locations for the North American standard stations for lunar total occultation predictions are indicated by asterisks on the graze maps (see the map on p. 159). For grazes of planets, a *partial occultation* of the object will occur at the northern or southern limit. The line plotted is the centre of the partial occultation zone, typically several kilometres wide.

(B) NAMES OF OCCULTED STARS

The stars that are occulted by the Moon are stars that lie along the zodiac; hence they are known by their number in the ZC compiled by James Robertson and published in the *Astronomical Papers Prepared for the Use of the American Ephemeris and Nautical Almanac, Vol. 10,* Part 2 (U.S. Government Printing Office, Washington, 1940). Robertson's ZC has been out of print for several years. In 1986, Isao Sato, a member of the Lunar Occultation Observers Group in Japan, republished the ZC. This new edition is based on the epoch J2000 and includes much new data, particularly on double stars. Since stars are not usually recognized by their ZC numbers, the equivalent Bayer designations or Flamsteed numbers of the stars occulted during the year are given in the table on p. 162. The ZC and XZ (now version XZ80Q) catalogues, updated in 2005 by D. Herald using *HIPPARCOS*, Tycho-2, and UCAC-2 data, are available on IOTA's Web site.

ZC	Name	ZC	Name	ZC	Name
68	51 Psc	1117	57 Gem	1944	75 Vir
233	101 Psc	1178	82 Gem	1967	83 Vir
244	104 Psc	1187	84 Gem	2263	1 Sco
341	23 Ari	1224	μ Cnc	2268	2 Sco
370	26 Ari	1277	η Cnc	2276	4 Sco
518	7 Tau	1282	35 Cnc	2287	π Sco
529	11 Tau	1292	38 Cnc	2383	τ Sco
536	16 Tau (Celaeno)	1299	ε Cnc	2554	X Sgr
537	17 Tau (Electra)	1302	42 Cnc	2721	φ Sgr
538	18 Tau	1310	δ Cnc (Asellus Australis)	2750	σ Sgr (Nunki)
539	19 Tau (Taygeta)	1331	X Cnc	2809	ψ Sgr
541	20 Tau (Maia)	1371	81 Cnc	2861	51 Sgr
542	21 Tau (Asterope)	1375	π Cnc	2864	52 Sgr
543	22 Tau	1434	ψ Leo	3069	20 Cap
545	23 Tau (Merope)	1439	18 Leo	3071	21 Cap
552	η Tau (Alcyone)	1448	21 Leo	3079	θ Cap (Tsin)
560	27 Tau (Atlas)	1466	ν Leo	3126	ι Cap (Tae)
561	28 Tau (Pleione)	1486	31 Leo	3173	42 Cap
616	44 Tau	1549	48 Leo	3177	44 Cap
890	136 Tau	1611	65 Leo	3206	μ Cap (Kuh)
1030	ε Gem (Mebsuta)	1635	75 Leo	3252	37 Aqr
1055	37 Gem	1637	76 Leo	3334	67 Aqr
1061	39 Gem	1652	79 Leo	3467	13 Psc
1062	40 Gem	1685	υ Leo	3494	λ Psc
1070	ω Gem	1759	FG Vir	3512	22 Psc
1094	49 Gem	1800	21 Vir	X07994	RT Cap
1099	52 Gem				

(C) OCCULTED STARS KNOWN TO BE DOUBLE

In the table below are data on double stars for which graze predictions are given. This information is from DSFILE, a comprehensive file of zodiacal double-star data compiled by Don Stockbauer, Henk Bulder, Mitsuru Sôma, David Herald, and David Dunham; most of the data for the ZC stars are in the Sato ZC catalogue. The successive columns give the USNO reference number of the star, the number of the graze track, the double-star code (d), the magnitudes of the brighter (A) and dimmer (B) components, the separation in arcseconds, and the position angle (PA) of B from A measured eastward from north. If the star is triple, the third component's magnitude is given under C, and its separation and PA from A are given in the last columns. XZ numbers are given for the last four non-ZC stars.

The parameters are given for the epoch of the occultation, computed from orbital elements when available or from extrapolations from a long series of observations. If there is little change in the available observations, the last-observed separation and PA are used. Components fainter than magnitude 11.5 are not listed, and some very close doubles whose parameters are not known, generally with separations less than 0.2″, are also not listed. The latter include spectroscopic binaries (code J, U, or sometimes V) and visual occultation doubles (most codes K and X, and many Vs).

The codes have the following meanings:

A, C, or G.. visual double
B or V........close double, usually discovered by occultation
D...............primary of wide pair; secondary has separate catalogue entry
E...............secondary star of wide pair
F...............prediction is for the following component of a visual double
H...............triple, with close occultation pair and third visual component; prediction uses a mean position
I................data for B component computed from orbital elements, but B component is itself a close double, with data for C component referred to B rather than A
K...............possible double from occultation
L...............close triple star (only two stars often listed because inner pair is often spectroscopic)
M...............mean position (centre of light) of a close pair is used by the ZC and/or XZ catalogue

N............... northern component of nearly equal double star
O............... orbital elements available and used to calculate the separation and PA
Q............... = O, but A component may be close double (if triple, C-component data are computed from
                orbital elements)
R............... triple; close pair = O and C component also has orbit relative to centre of close pair
S .... southern component of nearly equal double star
T............... visual triple star
W............... = A or C, but A component is a spectroscopic binary
X............... probable double from occultation
Y............... triple, K or X (B component) and A or C (C component)
Z............... triple, O (B component) and V (C component)

Some close pairs have rapid orbital motion so the current PA is unknown.

USNO	Graze #	d	A	B	Sep. "	PA °	C	Sep. "	PA °
68	28	Y	6.2	6.9	0.03	233	8.0	0.1	266
163	55	A	7.2	10.2	8.6	197			
311	57, 168	V	6.6	9.0	0.03	287			
438	178	O	7.4	7.5	0.5	272			
470	33, 170	D	6.8	10.4	42.6	35			
518	5, 34, 151, 208	O	6.6	6.7	0.7	351			
539	6, 78, 135, 179, 211, 264	V	4.6	6.1	0.01				
548	9, 140, 184	K	6.8	9.8	0.3	173			
552	182, 267	K	3.0	4.6	0.03	207			
701	14, 35, 152	W	8.0	8.0	0.1		7.4	4.4	10
746	83, 187	A	6.8	8.3	20.5	205			
750	188	O	7.1	8.4	0.3	352			
771	60	T	6.1	9.1	0.28	90	8.6	11.8	27
773	61, 189	C	7.1	8.7	14.0	352			
844	214	M	6.6	6.6	1.1	139			
885	16, 85	Y	5.9	7.2	0.01	270	12.0	15.0	232
890	15, 17, 86	V	4.8	6.3	0.05	270			
906	88	L	7.3	8.0	0.04	333	8.3	0.04	153
909	89	T	6.2	8.2	0.0	194	12.4	242.5	242
909	18, 89	T	6.2	8.2	0.03	194	12.4	240.9	242
1013	39	O	7.1	8.7	0.7	292			
1144	243	A	6.6	8.4	11.5	178			
1178	105	T	6.8	7.3	0.3	45	13.5	4.0	34
1261	126	C	7.2	9.2	37.5	191			
1293	107	M	6.8	9.9	0.5	226			
1298	108	A	6.5	9.0	20.5	54	8.8	63.2	342
1321	144, 222	O	7.5	7.5	0.3	76			
1371	271	O	7.2	7.2	0.1	298			
1611	249	M	5.6	9.7	2.7	104			
1688	274	A	6.3	10.5	5.2	279			
1759	21	Y	7.3	7.3	0.1	50	11.6	74.4	195
1944	252	C	5.6	11.2	85.6	110	13.5	18.9	320
2164	197	C	6.8	12.5	10.3	200			
2268	279	H	5.6	5.6	0.1	90	7.1	2.2	270
2287	116, 162	W	3.4	4.6			12.2	50.4	132
2405	281	M	6.6	10.1	2.0	13			
2750	146, 253	Y	2.9	2.9	0.1	90	9.5	9.0	244
2864	165, 204	A	4.7	9.2	2.4	174			
3071	237	V	6.8	8.2	0.4	77			
X09881	217	V	7.7	8.4	0.3	69			
X10792	124	A	7.1	9.8	13.8	310			
X15425	43	M	9.1	9.8	4.4	225			
X15947	231	M	7.6	8.1	2.0	335			

TABLE OF TOTAL LUNAR OCCULTATION PREDICTIONS

DATE	ZC	MAG	PH	ELG °	HALIFAX 63.6°W, 44.6°N TIME (UT)	A m	B m	P °	MONTRÉAL 73.6°W, 45.5°N TIME (UT)	A m	B m	P °	TORONTO 79.4°W, 43.7°N TIME (UT)	A m	B m	P °
Jan. 10	3126	4.3	DD	28	21:12.1	−0.6	0.1	46	Before Sunset				Before Sunset			
18	539	4.4	DD	123	6:59.2	0.5	−1.6	113	7:02.0	0.4	−2.1	123	7:9.4	0.7	−2.9	139
20	890	4.5	DD	149	6:36.1	−1.5	0.5	43	6:21.9	−1.4	−0.2	59	6:14.5	−1.4	−0.5	73
Apr. 9	539	4.4	DD	41	1:50.2	0.2	−0.9	81	1:50.9	0.1	−1.2	90	1:53.9	0.1	−1.5	101
9	541	4.0	DD	41	After Moonset				2:06.7	0.4	−1.7	114	2:12.8	0.5	−2.2	128
29	3126	4.3	RD	278	7:27.7	−1.0	1.4	276	Before Moonrise				Before Moonrise			
Jun. 30	539	4.4	DD	320	6:40.8			347	No Occultation				No Occultation			
30	539	4.4	RD	320	6:44.5			338	No Occultation				No Occultation			
30	537	3.8	RD	320	6:51.0	0.4	1.4	244	6:56.1	0.4	1.2	254	Before Moonrise			
30	552	3.0	DB	320	7:03.1	−0.3	0.5	128	7:03.1	0.1	0.8	113	Before Moonrise			
30	545	4.3	RD	320	No Occultation				7:05.3			187	Before Moonrise			
30	541	4.0	RD	320	7:13.8	0.0	1.0	282	7:14.7	0.1	0.8	294	Before Moonrise			
30	552	3.0	RD	321	7:31.6	0.8	2.4	196	7:40.3	0.6	1.9	212	7:40.7	0.6	1.7	216
Sep. 20	537	3.8	RD	242	2:00.4	0.3	1.6	236	2:05.0	0.4	1.4	246	2:4.9	0.4	1.3	249
20	539	4.4	RD	242	2:05.7			313	No Occultation				No Occultation			
20	552	3.0	DB	242	No Occultation				2:17.4	−0.3	0.6	125	2:15.4	0.0	0.6	121
20	541	4.0	RD	242	2:27.9	−0.2	1.3	272	2:27.8	−0.1	1.0	285	2:26.0	0.0	0.9	289
20	552	3.0	RD	242	No Occultation				2:48.4	0.8	2.4	199	2:48.6	0.7	2.1	204
Oct. 7	2721	3.3	DD	86	No Occultation				1:17.8			133	1:06.9	−2.6	−2.2	124
22	1310	4.2	RD	279	4:56.2	0.1	1.8	254	4:59.4	0.2	1.4	266	Before Moonrise			
Nov. 3	2809	4.9	DD	65	22:29.6	−1.3	−0.3	61	22:16.8	−1.3	0.3	46	Before Sunset			
30	2750	2.1	DD	34	19:28.7			144	18:57.1	−2.5	−0.6	125	18:44.1	−2.3	−0.3	124
30	2750	2.1	RB	34	19:54.6			179	19:53.2	−1	1.0	204	19:44.5	−1.4	1.2	208
Dec. 11	539	4.4	DD	160	8:00.6	−0.6	−0.1	49	7:53.3	−0.8	−0.3	58	7:49.4	−0.9	−0.6	69
11	537	3.8	DD	160	7:51.2	0.1	−2.3	126	7:49.5	0.0	−3.1	136	7:58.7			159
11	541	4.0	DD	160	8:09.0	−0.3	−0.9	74	8:04.1	−0.5	−1.1	81	8:3.0	−0.6	−1.3	92
11	552	3.0	DD	161	8:55.0	0.8	−2.7	141	9:01.9			161	No Occultation			
11	552	3.0	RB	161	9:24.7	−0.5	0.4	211	9:16.1			191	No Occultation			
24	2287	3.0	DB	329	After Moonset				17:29.3	−1.2	−0.9	71	17:23.0	−1.5	−0.7	70

DATE	ZC	MAG	PH	ELG °	WINNIPEG 97.2°W, 49.9°N TIME (UT)	A m	B m	P °	EDMONTON 113.4°W, 53.6°N TIME (UT)	A m	B m	P °	VANCOUVER 123.1°W, 49.2°N TIME (UT)	A m	B m	P °
Jan. 18	539	4.4	DD	123	6:56.2	0.1	−3.6	139	6:38.8	−0.6	−3.7	136	No Occultation			
20	890	4.5	DD	149	5:46.1	−1.6	0.1	70	5:23.8	−1.4	1.2	63	5:05.3	−1.4	1.0	77
26	1685	4.5	RD	229	Bright Twilight				13:38.8	−0.1	−2.2	355	13:44.7	−0.6	−2.1	337
Apr. 9	539	4.4	DD	41	1:42.0	−0.4	−1.7	101	Before Sunset				Before Sunset			
9	541	4.0	DD	41	2:03.5	0.1	−2.7	130	Before Sunset				No Occultation			
Jun. 30	560	3.8	RD	321	8:20.9	0.8	1.9	19	8Before Moonrise				Before Moonrise			
Jul. 6	1442	5.0	DD	41	3:32.8			198	No Occultation				No Occultation			
Aug. 14	2864	4.7	DD	150	No Occultation				7:39.7	−1.6	−1.3	104	7:27.8	−1.9	−0.8	97
Sep. 20	552	3.0	RD	243	3:09.9	0.5	1.5	231	Before Moonrise				Before Moonrise			
20	560	3.8	RD	243	3:26.0			179	3:47.9	0.7	1.6	208	Before Moonrise			
Oct. 3	2287	3.0	RB	52	No Occultation				20:44.2	−0.1	−0.4	343	20:40.9	−0.5	0.2	319
7	2721	3.3	DD	86	0:23.1	−1.8	−0.2	93	Before Sunset				Before Sunset			
17	537	3.8	RD	216	No Occultation				10:13.9			195	9:41.1			167
17	539	4.4	RD	216	11:13.7	−1.1	−0.9	263	10:50.8	−1.3	−0.8	274	10:38.3	−1.6	0.1	262
17	541	4.0	RD	216	11:26.1	−1.2	0.0	238	11:6.4	−1.2	0.1	247	10:50.9	−1.4	1.1	235
20	1030	3.2	RD	253	3:47.2	0.7	1.6	236	Before Moonrise				Before Moonrise			
Nov. 6	3079	4.2	DD	90	After Moonset				4:27.1	−0.7	−0.6	61	4:20.7	−1.0	−0.2	58
16	1030	3.2	RD	226	Bright Twilight				13:07.5	−1.1	−1.0	266	12:55.5	−1.8	0.5	240
18	1310	4.2	RD	252	No Occultation				11:53.0			1	11:57.6	−1.1	−1.7	328
30	2750	2.1	DD	33	18:16.3	−1.2	0.8	118	Before Moonrise				Before Moonrise			
Nov. 30	2750	2.1	RB	34	19:22.8	−1.6	1.2	225	Before Moonrise				Before Moonrise			
Dec. 11	537	3.8	DD	160	7:24.9	−0.9	−3.6	137	6:54.9	−1.4	−1.8	119	6:48.4	−2.1	−3.1	135
11	539	4.4	DD	160	7:28.3	−1.2	0.0	59	7:09.9	−1.2	1.1	47	6:52.8	−1.4	1.0	59
11	541	4.0	DD	160	7:40.7	−1.1	−0.9	84	7:19.4	−1.3	−0.1	74	7:06.3	−1.5	−0.1	86
24	2287	3.0	DB	329	16:49.8	−1.9	0.0	61	16:20.2	−1.8	0.8	70	15:59.2	−1.6	1.1	87
24	2287	3.0	RD	330	17:55.8	−1.7	−1.5	319	17:27.8	−1.3	−0.5	319	17:16.2	−1.4	−0.1	308

DATE	ZC	MAG	PH	ELG °	MASSACHUSETTS 72.5°W, 42.5°N TIME (UT)	A m	B m	P °	WASHINGTON, DC 77.0°W, 38.9°N TIME (UT)	A m	B m	P °	CHICAGO 87.7°W, 41.9°N TIME (UT)	A m	B m	P °
Jan. 18	539	4.4	DD	123	7:08.0	0.6	−2.3	132	7:25.8			165	No Occultation			
20	890	4.5	DD	149	6:24.3	−1.3	−0.4	67	6:21.1	−1.2	−0.9	85	6:04.0	−1.5	−0.8	89
Apr. 9	539	4.4	DD	41	1:54.4	0.2	−1.2	96	2:00.7	0.3	−1.6	112	1:57.8	0.1	−1.9	116
9	541	4.0	DD	41	2:11.3	0.6	−1.8	122	2:22.5	1.0	−2.7	143	2:24.1			152
11	890	4.5	DD	68	No Occultation				1:12.2			34	0:50.8	−2.3	1.6	44

TABLE OF TOTAL LUNAR OCCULTATION PREDICTIONS (continued)

DATE	ZC	MAG	PH	ELG °	MASSACHUSETTS (cont) 72.5°W, 42.5°N TIME (UT)	A m	B m	P °	WASHINGTON, DC (cont) 77.0°W, 38.9°N TIME (UT)	A m	B m	P °	CHICAGO (cont) 87.7°W, 41.9°N TIME (UT)	A m	B m	P °
Jun. 30	541	4.0	RD	320	7:12.1	0.1	0.8	288	Before Moonrise				Before Moonrise			
30	552	3.0	RD	321	7:33.8	0.7	2.0	205	7:30.1	0.8	2.0	203	Before Moonrise			
Sep. 20	539	4.4	RD	242	1:58.3			329	Before Moonrise				No Occultation			
20	537	3.8	RD	242	2:00.3	0.4	1.4	241	Before Moonrise				Before Moonrise			
20	552	3.0	DB	242	2:16.7			135	2:14.6			138	Before Moonrise			
20	541	4.0	RD	242	2:24.7	0.0	1.0	279	2:21.4	0.1	0.9	278	Before Moonrise			
20	552	3.0	RD	242	2:39.7 188	2	34.7		185:2 51.1	0.7	1.8		211:			
Oct. 3	2287	3.0	DD	52	No Occultation				No Occultation				20:57.8			18
3	2287	3.0	RB	52	No Occultation				No Occultation				21:01.9			13
7	2721	3.3	DD	86	No Occultation				No Occultation				0:48.6	-2.6	-1.3	113
17	539	4.4	RD	216	Bright Twilight				Bright Twilight				11:28.8	-1.2	-0.2	242
17	541	4.0	RD	217	Bright Twilight				Bright Twilight				11:33.8	-1.5	1.5	211
22	1310	4.2	RD	279	4:54.7	0.3	1.6	256	Before Moonrise				Before Moonrise			
Nov. 3	2809	4.9	DD	65	22:17.5	-1.5	0.3	52	Before Sunset				Before Sunset			
30	2750	2.1	DD	34	19:02.8	-2.9	-1.3	132	18:54.1			136	18:26.9	-1.9	0.0	126
30	2750	2.1	RB	34	19:50.2	-0.7	1.7	195	19:39.4			193	19:28.9	-1.8	1.6	212
Dec. 11	539	4.4	DD	160	7:55.5	-0.7	-0.6	66	7:54.9	-0.7	-0.9	82	7:42.8	-1.1	-0.8	81
11	537	3.8	DD	160	8:00.0 151				No Occultation				No Occultation			
11	541	4.0	DD	160	8:08.0	-0.4	-1.2	89	8:11.2	-0.4	-1.6	105	8:00.2	-0.7	-1.7	105
24	2287	3.0	DB	330	17:33.4	-1.2	-1.0	76	17:30.4	-1.6	-0.8	79	17:09.8	-2.0	-0.4	70
24	2287	3.0	RD	330	After Moonset				After Moonset				18:26.5	-1.7	-1.9	303

DATE	ZC	MAG	PH	ELG °	MIAMI 80.3°W, 25.8°N TIME (UT)	A m	B m	P °	ATLANTA 84.3°W, 33.8°N TIME (UT)	A m	B m	P °	AUSTIN 97.8°W, 30.2°N TIME (UT)	A m	B m	P °
Jan. 20	890	4.5	DD	149	6:36.8	-0.6	-2.1	129	6:18.3	-1.2	-1.5	110	6:09.5	-1.2	-3.1	142
Feb. 28	2263	4.8	RD	262	7:36.7	1.0	-3.0	354	No Occultation				7:36.4	0.2	-0.8	326
Apr. 9	539	4.4	DD	41	No Occultation				2:15.1	0.9	-3.0	143	No Occultation			
11	890	4.5	DD	68	1:04.3	-1.4	-0.8	92	0:53.5	-1.8	-0.2	72	Before Sunset			
26	2721	3.3	RD	243	5:26.2	-0.2	-0.4	308	Before Moonrise				Before Moonrise			
May 20	2287	3.0	DD	186	After Moonset				After Moonrise				10:4.5	-1.0	-0.2	64
Jun. 9	1486	4.6	DD	72	3:49.3	-0.5	-0.3	70	3:48.4			43	3:31.8	-1.2	-0.9	83
Oct. 3	2287	3.0	DD	52	20:47.5	-3.4	0.8	68	20:43.8	-3.6	1.8	50	19:55.4	-2.6	0.9	85
3	2287	3.0	RB	53	22:11.6	-2.7	-2.4	317	21:40.3	-2.1	-3.0	339	21:20.4	-2.0	-1.4	317
7	2721	3.3	DD	86	No Occultation				No Occultation				0:34.0	-3.8	-1.9	127
Nov. 30	2750	2.1	DD	33	No Occultation				18:42.7			149	No Occultation			
30	2750	2.1	RB	34	No Occultation				19:14.3			186	No Occultation			
Dec. 11	539	4.4	DD	160	8:13.8	-0.1	-2.6	133	7:55.7	-0.8	-1.6	106	7:52.0	-1.0	-3.5	135
11	541	4.0	DD	160	No Occultation				8:19.7	-0.1	-2.9	134	No Occultation			
24	2263	4.8	RD	327	Bright Twilight				Bright Twilight				12:30.1			228
24	2287	3.0	DB	330	17:36.8	-2.2	-1.2	103	17:20.8	-2.1	-0.7	84	16:48.4	-2.8	-0.3	92
24	2287	3.0	RD	330	19:00.3	-1.0	-0.7	261	18:46.1	-1.5	-1.5	285	18:25.3	-2.3	-1.3	287

DATE	ZC	MAG	PH	ELG °	KANSAS CITY 94.5°W, 39.0°N TIME (UT)	A m	B m	P °	DENVER 105.0°W, 39.8°N TIME (UT)	A m	B m	P °	NEW MEX., ARIZ. 109.0°W, 34.0°N TIME (UT)	A m	B m	P °
Jan. 20	890	4.5	DD	149	5:56.5	-1.6	-1.2	105	5:37.5	-1.8	-1.1	110	5:40.3	-1.9	-2.6	135
Feb. 3	2617	4.7	RD	317	Bright Twilight				13:00.3	-1.0	0.8	289	12:50.9	-1.1	1.1	272
Apr. 9	539	4.4	DD	41	2:06.2	0.4	-3.0	138	2:08.9			156	No Occultation			
May 20	2287	3.0	DD	186	10:06.2	-0.4	0.1	44	10:03.2			125	9:52.2	-1.3	0.9	41
20	2287	3.0	RD	186	After Moonset				10:30.2			346	10:42.6	-2.3	-3.3	329
Jun. 9	1486	4.6	DD	72	3:33.1			49	3:12.5	-1.8	-0.8	74	3:12.0	-1.6	-1.2	95
Sep. 10	2809	4.9	DD	120	After Moonset				No Occultation				7:26.8	0.9	1.9	12
Oct. 3	2287	3.0	DD	52	20:17.6	-3.3	2.0	54	19:50.2	-2.2	1.6	74	19:35.7	-1.6	0.8	96
3	2287	3.0	RB	52	21:11.2	-1.1	-2.0	342	20:58.2	-1.1	-0.9	328	20:56.9	-1.6	-0.5	309
7	2721	3.3	DD	86	0:33.7	-2.7	-0.8	110	Before Sunset				Before Sunset			
Oct. 17	539	4.4	RD	216	11:18.6	-1.6	0.9	225	11:02.0	-1.7	1.3	224	10:37.9			191
Nov. 6	3079	4.2	DD	90	No Occultation				4:56.6			120	No Occultation			
18	1310	4.2	RD	253	Bright Twilight				12:36.5	-1.2	-2.1	321	12:40.6	-1.8	-1.4	298
30	2750	2.1	DD	33	18:15.9	-1.4	-0.3	135	18:05.3	-0.5	-0.6	144	No Occultation			
30	2750	2.1	RB	34	19:09.8	-2.2	2.3	208	18:48.2	-2.4	3.0	206	No Occultation			
Dec. 11	539	4.4	DD	160	7:38.0	-1.2	-1.2	96	7:22.0	-1.6	-1.0	96	7:24.2	-1.9	-2.4	121
11	541	4.0	DD	160	8:00.6	-0.8	-2.4	122	7:47.4	-1.3	-2.7	126	No Occultation			
24	2263	4.8	RD	327	12:54.9	-1.5	1.2	269	Before Sunset				No Occultation			
24	2287	3.0	DB	329	16:55.6	-2.4	-0.1	75	16:29.6	-2.5	0.4	80	16:17.8	-2.5	0.2	95
24	2287	3.0	RD	330	18:18.9	-2.0	-1.7	303	17:55.5	-2.1	-1.3	306	17:53.3	-2.5	-1.1	295

DB/DD = Disappearance at Bright/Dark limb; RB/RD = Reappearance at Bright/Dark limb
See p. 160 for additional explanation of these tables.

TABLE OF TOTAL LUNAR OCCULTATION PREDICTIONS (continued)

			ELG	LOS ANGELES 118.3°W, 34.1°N				N. CALIFORNIA 122.0°W, 38.0°N				HONOLULU 157.9°W, 21.3°N			
DATE	ZC	MAG	PH	°	TIME (UT)	A m	B m	°	TIME (UT)	A m	B m	°	TIME (UT)	A m	B m	°
Jan. 0	1815	4.8	RD	272	No Occultation				No Occultation				12:42.5	-0.7	-0.9	314
4	2263	4.8	RD	317	No Occultation				No Occultation				15:34.0	-1.2	0.7	272
20	890	4.5	DD	149	5:20.3	-2.3	-2.6	137	5:05.6	-2.1	-0.9	118	Before Sunset			
26	1685	4.5	RD	230	14:21.7	-0.8	-2.3	324	14:09.8	-0.9	-2.2	325	No Occultation			
Feb. 18	1170	3.7	DD	144	No Occultation				No Occultation				7:03.3	-2.6	-0.2	102
28	2287	3.0	RD	263	No Occultation				No Occultation				11:17.8	-0.4	0.2	288
Apr. 17	1685	4.5	DD	148	After Moonset				After Moonset				13:37.3	-0.5	-0.8	89
May 20	2287	3.0	DD	186	9:36.3			36	No Occultation				7:41.6	-0.8	-0.8	133
20	2287	3.0	RD	186	10:17.8			342	No Occultation				9:05.3	-2.6	0.1	278
23	2721	3.3	RD	218	Bright Twilight				Bright Twilight				13:18.3	-3.3	-0.1	271
24	2864	4.7	RD	228	Bright Twilight				Bright Twilight				11:39.9	-2.5	1.7	240
Jun. 16	2263	4.8	DD	155	After Moonset				After Moonset				12:37.5	-1.0	-0.3	75
Aug. 13	2721	3.3	DD	140	After Moonset				9:05.1	-1.4	-1.7	102	7:57.3	-3.1	0.2	84
14	2864	4.7	DD	150	No Occultation				7:46.0			126	6:09.5	-2.1	-1.1	126
Sep. 12	3079	4.2	DD	144	After Moonset				After Moonset				11:04.6	-1.1	0.6	55
Oct. 3	2287	3.0	DD	51	19:24.9	-0.8	0.5	112	19:24.5	-0.7	0.7	108	No Occultation			
3	2287	3.0	RB	52	20:43.0	-1.4	0.2	294	20:39.2	-1.1	0.3	297	No Occultation			
7	2750	2.1	DD	88	After Moonset				After Moonset				5:05.3	-2.7	0.6	68
7	2750	2.1	RB	89	After Moonset				After Moonset				6:40.7	-1.7	0.3	246
17	541	4.0	RD	215	No Occultation				No Occultation				9:05.5			182
17	539	4.4	RD	216	10:24.1	-1.4	4.0	200	10:29.4	-1.7	2.1	222	9:11.2	-0.5	2.0	225
Nov. 6	3079	4.2	DD	90	4:42.0	-2.8	-2.5	111	4:27.7	-1.9	-0.9	87	Before Sunset			
18	1310	4.2	RD	252	12:21.4	-2.2	-0.5	284	12:11.7	-1.9	-0.6	292	No Occultation			
Dec. 11	539	4.4	DD	160	7:04.0	-2.4	-1.9	118	6:51.1	-2.1	-0.5	98	5:33.3	-1.5	0.4	97
11	541	4.0	DD	160	No Occultation				7:22.7	-2.4	-3.7	135	No Occultation			
24	2287	3.0	DB	329	15:57.1	-1.9	0.2	108	15:51.9	-1.7	0.5	105	No Occultation			
24	2287	3.0	RD	330	17:30.5	-2.4	-0.5	290	17:20.7	-2.1	-0.3	293	No Occultation			

DB/DD = Disappearance at Bright/Dark limb; RB/RD = Reappearance at Bright/Dark limb
See p. 138 for additional explanation of these tables.

TABLE OF GRAZING LUNAR OCCULTATION PREDICTIONS

The table below lists lunar grazing occultation predictions for much of North America for 2008. The eight maps on pp. 169–172 show the graze tracks (see the descriptive text on pp. 160–163). For each graze is given:

No. .... a chronological sequential number used on the maps
Date .... the date
USNO d ... the star's USNO (U.S. Naval Observatory) reference number (see the bottom of p. 139) and its duplicity code (in the **"d"** column — see section (C) on pp. 141–142 concerning double stars)
m .... its visual magnitude
%sl .... the percent of the Moon sunlit (+ for waxing, – for waning, E for lunar eclipses)
L .... whether the track is a northern (N) or southern (S) limit
W.U.T. ..... the Universal Time at the west end of the track
Lo., La. ..... the longitude and latitude of the west end of the track

No.	Date	USNO d	m	%sl	L	W.U.T.	Lo.	La.	No.	Date	USNO d	m	%sl	L	W.U.T.	Lo.	La.
1	Jan. 5	2383	2.8	9–	S	12:57.4	–60	55	16	20	885 Y	5.6	92+	N	5:15.7	–94	40
2	12	3385	6.7	20+	S	23:20.2	–85	24	17	20	890 V	4.6	92+	N	6:30.3	–77	55
3	16	244	6.7	52+	S	1:13.2	–125	45	18	20	909 T	6.0	93+	N	9:11.9	–126	55
4	17	387 V	6.9	64+	N	4:17.8	–78	49	19	26	1637	5.9	86–	S	2:05.4	–71	47
5	18	518 O	6.0	74+	N	2:57.2	–59	51	20	26	1652 U	5.4	85–	S	4:20.1	–105	23
6	18	539 V	4.3	76+	S	6:39.7	–130	52	21	27	1759 Y	6.6	77–	S	8:00.5	–130	47
7	18	543 K	6.4	76+	S	7:06.8	–130	51	22	29	1967	5.5	58–	S	8:12.8	–121	28
8	18	529 J	6.1	76+	N	5:36.5	–106	22	23	Feb. 1	2320	7.0	30–	S	8:54.6	–82	34
9	18	548 K	6.8	77+	S	7:31.1	–130	54	24	4	X26388	7.4	7–	S	13:49.0	–103	44
10	18	538 V	5.7	76+	N	7:14.4	–81	55	25	9	3357	6.9	4+	S	1:19.0	–110	28
11	18	555	6.4	77+	N	8:22.3	–98	55	26	9	X31099	7.2	4+	S	2:16.8	–124	26
12	18	571 J	6.8	78+	N	9:38.2	–120	55	27	10	3489 A	7.4	9+	S	0:27.4	–94	20
13	18	574 K	6.8	78+	N	9:56.0	–116	55	28	11	68 Y	5.8	17+	S	1:01.8	–107	31
14	19	701 H	6.5	84+	S	1:20.8	–102	20	29	11	X820	7.3	18+	N	5:03.6	–121	55
15	20	890 V	4.6	92+	S	5:19.6	–130	29	30	11	197 K	7.0	25+	S	23:39.4	–93	49

TABLE OF GRAZING LUNAR OCCULTATION PREDICTIONS (continued)

No.	Date	USNO d	m	%sl	L	W.U.T.	Lo.	La.	No.	Date	USNO d	m	%sl	L	W.U.T.	Lo.	La.
31	Feb. 12	233 X	6.2	29+	N	6:56.7	-130	55	105	May 10	1178 T	6.3	29+	N	5:09.5	-130	47
32	13	370 K	6.1	40+	N	6:46.6	-99	55	106	11	1292	6.7	38+	N	2:09.6	-109	31
33	13	470 D	6.8	47+	S	23:35.9	-87	37	107	11	1293 M	6.8	38+	N	2:18.4	-103	44
34	14	518 O	6.0	52+	N	9:06.1	-130	44	108	11	1298 A	6.4	38+	N	2:27.6	-112	34
35	15	701 H	6.5	64+	N	9:42.1	-130	51	109	11	1299 V	6.3	38+	N	2:32.1	-109	41
36	16	797 J	6.3	70+	N	0:47.7	-73	46	110	11	1297 K	6.8	38+	N	2:33.3	-98	53
37	16	840 V	6.3	73+	N	7:11.8	-96	55	111	11	1302 V	6.8	38+	N	2:35.3	-116	30
38	17	994 X	6.6	81+	S	1:26.8	-113	34	112	11	1303	6.8	38+	N	2:44.1	-114	36
39	17	1013 O	7.0	82+	N	5:01.7	-130	39	113	11	1312	6.8	40+	N	4:58.5	-119	55
40	18	1155	6.4	90+	N	5:40.6	-103	55	114	11	1310	3.9	40+	S	5:14.1	-78	55
41	18	1157	6.2	90+	N	6:22.6	-92	55	115	13	1516	6.6	59+	N	2:13.6	-106	38
42	19	1277	5.3	95+	S	3:11.3	-130	37	116	20	2287 W	2.9	100-	N	9:21.8	-130	39
43	21	X15425 M	8.8	100E	N	3:15.8	-130	47	117	22	2554 V	4.5	95-	N	11:42.1	-114	20
44	21	X15465	9.4	100E	N	3:51.1	-130	36	118	24	2861 J	5.6	84-	N	12:03.7	-130	42
45	21	1508	7.8	100E	N	4:25.1	-130	42	119	28	3334	6.4	48-	N	6:40.0	-86	27
46	25	1918	6.8	84-	S	6:20.1	-68	55	120	Jun. 1	336	7.4	8-	N	10:54.2	-113	30
47	26	2046	7.0	74-	S	10:49.0	-130	44	121	2	X4273	7.3	3-	N	9:54.4	-77	20
48	28	2263 V	4.6	58-	N	7:12.6	-92	36	122	6	1097	6.9	7+	N	1:29.7	-85	43
49	28	2261	6.6	58-	S	7:33.7	-91	39	123	6	1099	5.8	7+	N	1:43.4	-98	32
50	28	X21904	7.0	56-	S	12:36.5	-122	55	124	6	X10792 A	7.3	8+	N	2:18.9	-92	47
51	29	2406	6.0	48-	S	9:06.6	-74	52	125	7	1250	5.8	15+	N	3:16.4	-116	39
52	Mar. 5	3126	4.3	6-	N	11:52.6	-100	23	126	7	1261 C	7.3	16+	N	4:56.2	-117	55
53	5	Venus		5-	S	20:55.3	-75	20	127	9	1486 A	4.4	34+	N	3:12.7	-106	51
54	5	Venus		5-	N	20:05.1	-130	23	128	11	1685 K	4.3	54+	N	0:21.1	-84	24
55	10	163 A	7.2	7+	N	1:03.0	-102	48	129	12	1778	7.0	64+	N	2:03.4	-59	55
56	10	177	6.9	8+	N	3:35.5	-130	41	130	14	1993 X	6.6	81+	N	1:18.7	-92	30
57	11	311 V	6.6	15+	N	3:25.7	-130	47	131	20	2809 Q	4.9	98-	N	9:36.1	-83	20
58	13	616	5.4	35+	N	4:34.5	-130	33	132	23	3173 J	5.2	82-	N	5:21.7	-103	32
59	14	756	6.6	44+	N	0:07.5	-87	48	133	23	3196	6.3	81-	N	11:35.8	-108	20
60	14	771 T	6.0	45+	N	2:02.5	-117	32	134	24	X30825	7.0	72-	N	10:10.5	-130	43
61	14	773 C	7.0	45+	N	2:42.6	-81	55	135	30	539 V	4.3	11-	N	6:40.2	-70	41
62	15	958 V	6.7	58+	N	4:35.7	-87	55	136	30	542	5.8	11-	N	6:50.8	-68	37
63	15	994 X	6.6	60+	N	9:00.1	-130	45	137	30	545	4.1	11-	S	6:50.9	-74	42
64	16	1094	7.0	67+	N	0:43.4	-96	50	138	30	543 K	6.4	11-	N	6:57.4	-71	40
65	16	1117 K	5.0	69+	N	5:48.9	-122	55	139	30	541 V	3.9	11-	N	7:15.2	-93	54
66	19	1466 V	5.3	92+	N	1:18.1	-105	41	140	30	548 K	6.8	11-	N	7:24.8	-81	45
67	27	2370	6.9	73-	S	10:02.2	-129	48	141	30	560 U	3.6	11-	S	7:58.7	-93	44
68	27	2383	2.8	72-	S	13:31.3	-130	50	142	30	574 K	6.8	11-	N	8:56.6	-81	20
69	Apr. 1	3069	6.3	26-	N	11:12.9	-110	34	143	30	X5148	7.5	10-	N	10:49.6	-116	24
70	2	3206	5.1	17-	N	12:48.9	-129	37	144	Jul. 5	1321 O	6.9	5+	N	2:16.5	-103	33
71	4	3467	6.4	4-	N	12:03.0	-105	24	145	5	X13516	7.2	6+	N	3:22.7	-107	47
72	8	387 V	6.9	5+	N	0:24.5	-84	42	146	17	2750 Y	2.0	99+	N	3:52.3	-130	22
73	9	X4688 C	7.1	11+	N	0:02.1	-78	42	147	23	X31988	7.0	77-	N	5:23.9	-109	24
74	9	X4741	7.5	11+	N	0:59.3	-95	31	148	25	233 X	6.2	55-	N	8:21.8	-130	38
75	9	537 U	3.7	12+	S	1:54.9	-76	55	149	26	370 K	6.1	44-	N	8:17.1	-127	29
76	9	X4785	7.5	11+	N	1:50.8	-108	34	150	26	387 V	6.9	43-	N	11:44.8	-130	40
77	9	538 V	5.7	12+	N	2:06.4	-108	52	151	27	518 O	6.0	32-	N	10:07.3	-117	20
78	9	539 V	4.3	12+	S	2:09.1	-115	42	152	28	701 H	6.5	21-	N	10:17.6	-112	20
79	9	541 V	3.9	12+	S	2:15.5	-114	49	153	29	X7674	7.0	12-	N	12:09.4	-126	20
80	9	555	6.4	12+	N	3:12.9	-124	52	154	29	X7698	7.1	12-	N	12:34.4	-130	24
81	9	571 J	6.8	13+	N	4:37.4	-130	47	155	30	1046	7.0	5-	N	10:56.8	-119	45
82	9	574 K	6.8	13+	N	4:53.8	-130	48	156	30	1049	6.8	5-	N	11:24.1	-129	49
83	10	746 A	7.0	22+	N	5:59.1	-130	39	157	Aug. 3	1497 X	7.4	3+	N	1:46.4	-103	23
84	10	X7674	7.0	29+	N	23:38.0	-68	52	158	5	1717	7.4	16+	N	3:34.7	-126	34
85	11	885 Y	5.6	30+	N	0:12.4	-85	27	159	7	1918	6.8	32+	N	1:06.6	-90	33
86	11	890 V	4.6	30+	N	0:57.3	-94	47	160	9	2154	6.7	53+	S	5:14.9	-130	49
87	11	X7872	7.0	31+	N	1:54.3	-107	39	161	10	2276	5.6	62+	N	3:53.9	-120	55
88	11	906 L	6.6	32+	N	3:47.1	-94	55	162	10	2287 W	2.9	63+	N	6:38.5	-123	20
89	11	909 T	6.0	32+	N	3:58.3	-130	43	163	12	X23748	6.8	78+	N	1:34.1	-102	26
90	12	1061	6.2	41+	N	1:33.1	-99	49	164	14	2861 J	5.6	93+	S	7:59.7	-115	20
91	12	1062 K	6.4	42+	N	1:59.0	-92	55	165	14	2864 A	4.6	93+	S	7:48.9	-130	28
92	12	Mars		44+	S	6:37.8	-77	55	166	19	3494	4.5	94-	N	9:16.4	-88	20
93	13	1200	6.9	53+	N	1:49.3	-107	34	167	21	177	6.9	80-	N	2:40.5	-80	21
94	14	1322	6.4	63+	N	0:13.4	-65	55	168	22	311 V	6.6	70-	N	3:47.4	-81	20
95	14	1340	6.6	64+	N	3:21.5	-126	48	169	22	341	6.8	68-	N	10:33.2	-91	20
96	14	1343	6.3	65+	N	3:49.8	-130	53	170	23	470 D	6.8	58-	N	8:06.5	-130	42
97	15	1434	5.4	73+	N	0:21.8	-87	31	171	26	994 X	6.6	24-	N	9:52.1	-103	20
98	17	1635 V	5.2	89+	N	1:07.4	-66	55	172	28	X12989	7.5	7-	N	12:09.3	-127	36
99	17	1637	5.9	89+	N	2:35.1	-58	55	173	28	1282	6.5	7-	N	12:15.1	-130	50
100	17	1652 U	5.4	90+	N	4:11.5	-130	41	174	Sep. 9	2643	6.7	64+	N	4:51.6	-92	20
101	25	2583 K	5.8	80-	N	7:48.9	-87	28	175	10	2804	5.8	74+	S	5:43.3	-119	20
102	May 1	3385	6.7	22-	N	9:21.1	-88	54	176	13	3177 K	5.9	94+	S	2:58.5	-130	37
103	9	1049	6.8	20+	N	7:10.1	-130	54	177	18	302 K	6.2	89-	N	10:11.7	-106	20
104	10	1157	6.2	27+	N	1:13.5	-99	22	178	19	438 O	6.8	81-	S	8:41.9	-69	52

TABLE OF GRAZING LUNAR OCCULTATION PREDICTIONS (continued)

No.	Date	USNO d	m	%sl	L	W.U.T.	Lo.	La.	No.	Date	USNO d	m	%sl	L	W.U.T.	Lo.	La.
179	Sep. 20	539 V	4.3	73–	N	1:51.7	–79	40	231	Oct. 24	X15947 M	7.1	20–	S	10:50.1	–123	48
180	20	542	5.8	73–	N	2:02.9	–77	37	232	25	1649	6.0	12–	S	9:40.1	–91	45
181	20	543 K	6.4	73–	N	2:09.7	–79	40	233	25	X17263	7.0	12–	S	13:13.7	–124	55
182	20	552 K	2.9	73–	S	2:20.1	–82	33	234	Nov. 2	X23748	6.8	15+	S	2:33.9	–130	35
183	20	541 V	3.9	73–	N	2:27.8	–100	54	235	5	X47994 P	7.0	40+	S	4:54.9	–125	20
184	20	548 K	6.8	73–	N	2:38.0	–89	45	236	5	3057	6.7	47+	S	21:54.7	–76	46
185	20	571 J	6.8	72–	N	3:59.3	–80	20	237	6	3071 V	6.1	48+	S	2:41.0	–79	20
186	20	574 K	6.8	72–	N	4:15.5	–89	20	238	6	3079	4.1	50+	S	4:41.1	–130	22
187	21	746 A	7.0	61–	N	6:04.3	–87	20	239	6	3173 J	5.2	57+	S	21:20.3	–64	37
188	21	750 O	6.9	61–	S	7:51.2	–54	47	240	7	3196	6.3	58+	S	2:26.8	–103	20
189	21	773 C	7.0	60–	N	10:03.7	–130	20	241	8	X30825	7.0	68+	S	1:09.9	–120	35
190	23	1099	5.8	37–	N	9:25.1	–130	36	242	16	1030	3.1	85–	S	12:23.2	–130	46
191	23	1097	6.9	37–	N	9:36.3	–130	51	243	17	1144 A	6.6	78–	S	5:33.1	–99	46
192	23	1097	6.9	37–	S	9:48.4	–82	28	244	17	1167	6.2	77–	S	10:05.2	–130	43
193	24	1224	5.3	27–	N	7:12.9	–98	48	245	18	1276	6.5	68–	S	5:14.5	–86	38
194	24	1242	6.9	26–	S	10:13.0	–103	47	246	18	1310	3.9	66–	N	11:39.1	–112	55
195	24	1250	5.8	25–	N	12:40.5	–130	53	247	19	1413	6.8	56–	S	10:32.4	–90	55
196	26	1486 A	4.4	9–	S	13:11.8	–130	29	248	19	1422	6.7	55–	S	11:13.9	–130	34
197	Oct. 2	2164 C	6.5	12+	S	23:40.6	–87	26	249	21	1611 M	5.6	35–	S	06:48.5	–82	46
198	4	2297	7.0	20+	S	0:14.0	–94	31	250	22	1727	6.9	25–	S	09:21.8	–103	34
199	5	2554 V	4.5	36+	N	22:48.8	–78	35	251	22	1743	6.6	23–	S	14:28.0	–123	55
200	6	2583 K	5.8	38+	S	3:06.7	–130	20	252	24	1944 C	5.5	10–	S	10:52.8	–99	31
201	6	2721 X	3.2	46+	S	23:42.4	–130	22	253	30	2750 Y	2.0	8+	S	18:13.2	–119	42
202	7	2740	6.3	48+	S	4:39.1	–130	26	254	Dec. 4	3152	6.6	31+	S	1:01.3	–84	20
203	7	2861 J	5.6	55+	S	23:40.5	–88	22	255	5	3270	5.8	40+	S	1:11.6	–80	20
204	8	2864 A	4.6	55+	S	0:00.2	–98	46	256	5	3367	6.3	49+	S	20:50.7	–70	50
205	11	3252	6.6	83+	S	2:42.1	–109	20	257	6	3507 V	6.5	61+	S	23:31.1	–89	20
206	12	3367	6.3	90+	S	2:53.4	–77	20	258	7	X31988	7.0	61+	S	0:32.7	–113	35
207	12	3380 K	5.9	91+	S	4:06.6	–130	34	259	7	3512	5.6	62+	S	2:22.2	–91	20
208	17	518 O	6.0	92–	N	5:12.9	–88	20	260	9	233 X	6.2	82+	S	2:00.6	–123	20
209	17	537 U	3.7	91–	S	9:25.3	–130	47	261	10	370 K	6.1	90+	S	1:52.7	–83	20
210	17	536 V	5.5	91–	S	9:31.2	–123	38	262	11	536 V	5.5	97+	S	6:48.8	–130	35
211	17	539 V	4.3	91–	S	9:46.6	–122	30	263	11	537 U	3.7	97+	S	6:53.1	–130	46
212	17	541 V	3.9	91–	S	9:55.6	–128	36	264	11	539 V	4.3	97+	S	7:02.3	–130	27
213	17	542	5.8	91–	S	10:03.7	–125	27	265	11	541 V	3.9	97+	S	7:24.7	–130	34
214	19	844 M	5.8	76–	N	2:11.2	–81	35	266	11	545	4.1	97+	S	8:29.2	–72	55
215	19	912	7.0	72–	S	13:30.0	–130	37	267	11	552 K	2.9	97+	S	8:28.4	–117	55
216	20	1030	3.1	65–	S	3:15.2	–88	42	268	11	561 K	5.0	97+	S	9:24.3	–105	55
217	20	X9881 V	6.8	64–	N	5:27.1	–116	44	269	11	560 U	3.6	97+	S	9:32.4	–83	55
218	20	1046	7.0	64–	N	5:36.5	–106	25	270	14	1070	5.2	97–	S	3:51.3	–130	37
219	20	1049	6.8	64–	N	6:01.5	–114	29	271	16	1371 O	6.5	82–	S	7:32.9	–130	44
220	20	1055	5.7	64–	N	7:32.3	–130	44	272	16	1375	5.4	82–	S	8:53.6	–130	31
221	21	1187	7.0	53–	N	6:33.8	–117	48	273	18	X16670	7.0	59–	S	15:06.7	–114	55
222	22	1321 O	6.9	41–	N	7:02.8	–105	47	274	19	1688 A	6.4	52–	S	5:46.4	–79	52
223	22	1327	6.9	41–	S	8:17.7	–106	41	275	20	1788	6.8	41–	S	7:38.9	–85	54
224	22	1331	6.3	40–	S	9:12.6	–117	38	276	20	1800	5.5	40–	S	10:53.9	–116	55
225	22	1335	6.2	40–	S	9:56.0	–126	34	277	24	2256 K	7.0	8–	S	11:36.6	–62	54
226	23	1422	6.7	31–	S	5:12.5	–62	49	278	24	2263 V	4.6	8–	S	12:11.4	–105	33
227	23	1439	5.7	30–	S	9:08.5	–120	52	279	24	2268 H	4.5	8–	N	12:57.9	–119	30
228	23	1448	6.9	29–	S	10:42.4	–130	24	280	24	2276	5.6	8–	S	14:58.8	–118	52
229	24	1549 K	5.1	21–	N	8:12.5	–88	39	281	25	2405 M	6.6	4–	S	12:43.1	–95	34
230	24	1555	7.4	20–	S	10:30.6	–118	40									

GRAZING OCCULTATION MAPS

JANUARY 1 – FEBRUARY 15

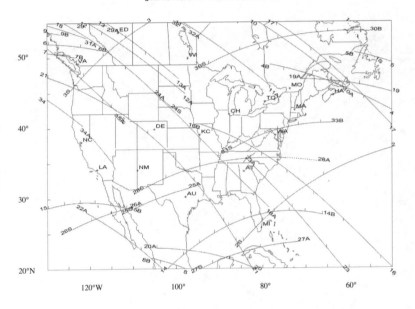

FEBRUARY 16 – MARCH 15

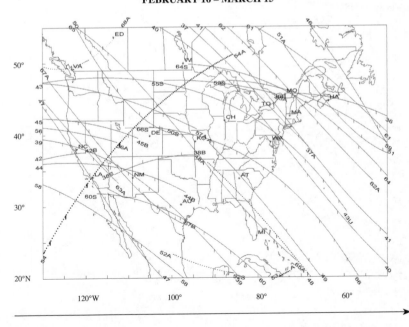

GRAZING OCCULTATION MAPS (continued)

MARCH 16 – MAY 15

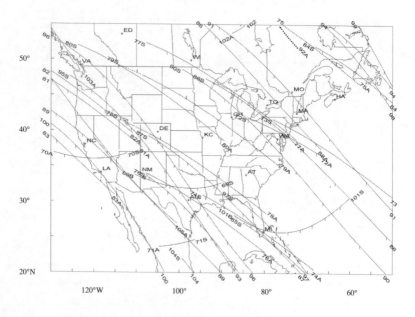

MAY 16 – JUNE 30

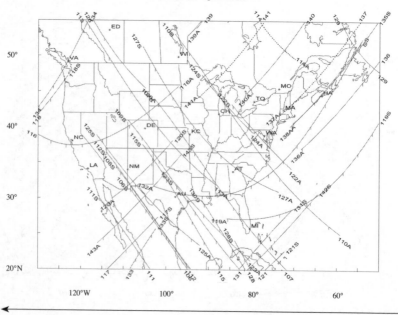

GRAZING OCCULTATION MAPS (continued)

JULY 1 – AUGUST 31

SEPTEMBER 1 – OCTOBER 14

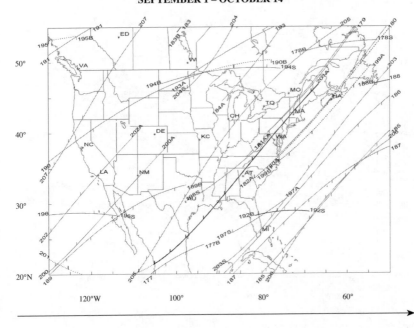

GRAZING OCCULTATION MAPS (continued)

OCTOBER 15 – NOVEMBER 25

NOVEMBER 26 – DECEMBER 31

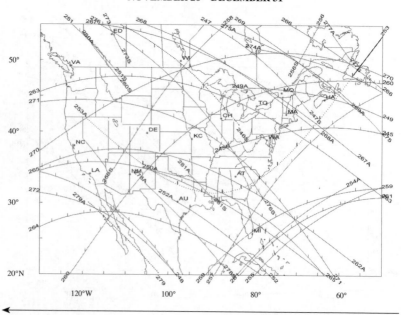

TIDES AND THE EARTH–MOON SYSTEM
BY ROY BISHOP

The tidal aspect of gravitation produces some of the most interesting phenomena in the universe, from the structure of interacting galaxies, such as M51, to the volcanoes of Io, the fragmentation of Comet Shoemaker-Levy 9 by Jupiter in 1992, the synchronous rotation of our Moon, and the pulse of the seas on our planet. Perhaps because they occur at our feet, the tides of the oceans are often overlooked when considering the heavens; yet the pulse of the tides is the heartbeat of a greater universe beyond Earth.

Newtonian Tides

Tides were known to the ancients, but an understanding of their origin came only three centuries ago with the publication of Newton's *Principia* (1687). In the Newtonian context, the decrease of the force of gravity with distance causes the tides. The Moon exerts a force on Earth, and Earth responds by accelerating toward the Moon; however, the waters on the hemisphere facing the Moon, being closer to the Moon, accelerate more and fall ahead of Earth. Similarly, Earth itself accelerates more than the waters on the other hemisphere and falls ahead of these waters; the Moon is yanking Earth out from under the waters on the more distant hemisphere, leaving these waters behind. Thus two tidal bulges are produced, one on the side of Earth facing the Moon and one on the side facing away from the Moon. Because the Moon is quite far from Earth (about 60 Earth radii), these two tidal bulges are essentially equal in size.

Note that the waters directly under the Moon and the waters farthest from the Moon do not rise up because of the slightly larger and smaller, respectively, lunar gravity at these two locations; all that results from the Moon's action on the waters at these two points is a slight decrease in the pressure on the floor of the sea. The two tidal bulges form because the variation in the Moon's gravity causes the *surrounding* waters on each hemisphere to flow horizontally across Earth's surface into these regions:

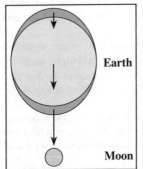

In order of decreasing length, the arrows indicate the force per unit mass (acceleration) produced by the Moon's gravity on the near side, centre, and far side of Earth. It is the resulting horizontal flow of the water across Earth's surface toward the two points nearest and farthest from the Moon that produces the two tidal bulges (indicated by heavy shading).

As Earth rotates on its axis, the orientation of these two bulges in relation to the Moon remains fixed; hence the rise and fall of the oceans on Earth. If Earth had no rigidity, the entire planet would flex freely in the same fashion, and there would be virtually no water tides. The very existence of the ocean tides indicates that on a time scale of several hours our planet displays considerable rigidity.

Because of the Moon's orbital motion, it transits on average 50.47 min later each day. Thus on successive days, high tides recur about 50 min later; or for the many regions experiencing two high tides daily, these tides recur at intervals of 12 h 25 min.

The Sun exerts a gravitational force 180 times stronger than that exerted by the Moon on Earth; however, because the Moon is so much closer, the *variation* in the Moon's force across Earth's diameter is about 2.2 times larger than the variation in the Sun's force. As described above, it is this variation that produces tides; thus the pair of bulges raised by the Moon is considerably larger than the pair raised by the Sun. As the Moon goes through its monthly cycle of phases, these two pairs of tidal bulges get in and out of step, combining in step to produce *spring tides* (no connection with the season) when the Moon is new or full (syzygy) and out of step to produce *neap tides* when the Moon is at first or last quarter (quadrature).

Another factor having a substantial influence on tidal ranges is the elliptical shape of the Moon's orbit. The Moon is only 9% to 12% closer at perigee than at apogee; however, because the *variation* in its gravitational force varies inversely as the cube of its distance (the force itself varies inversely as the square of the distance), the Moon's tidal influence is 31% to 49% greater at perigee than at apogee. Because the Sun tidally influences the shape of the Moon's orbit, exceptionally close perigees coincide with full or new Moon, and the resulting extreme tides are known as *perigean spring tides*. If the lunar orbit were fixed in orientation, such tides would recur at half-year intervals; however, the major axis of the lunar orbit rotates prograde with a period of 8.85 years, making the average interval between perigean spring tides about 23 days longer than half a year (206 days).

The extreme range of a spring tide, or of a perigean spring tide, occurs a day or two after the astronomical influences peak. The variation in the range of the tides at a given locality is determined both by the energy being put into the tides and by the energy being lost through friction with the seabed. As long as the input is greater than the loss, the tide range will increase even though the input may have peaked and already be decreasing. Hence the tide range is greatest not when the astronomical factors are greatest, but a day or two later when the decreasing input equals the increasing loss. At that point the energy in the tides is at a maximum.

Influences on the Tides

Many astronomical factors influence the tides. These can be sorted according to the periods they produce. In ascending order, the periods of the more important components are as follows:

(1) semidiurnal, 12 h 00 min (two solar-induced tidal bulges, as described above);

(2) semidiurnal, 12 h 25 min (two lunar-induced tidal bulges, as described above);

(3) diurnal, 24 h 00 min (the usual nonzero declination of the Sun shifts the pair of solar tidal bulges out of Earth's equatorial plane, resulting in a tidal component with a one-day period);

(4) diurnal, 24 h 50 min (the usual nonzero declination of the Moon shifts the pair of lunar tidal bulges out of Earth's equatorial plane, resulting in a tidal component with a one-day period; this is the dominant tide in some areas, such as parts of the southern coast of Canada's Gulf of St. Lawrence);

(5) semimonthly, 13.66 days (variation in the Moon's declination);

(6) semimonthly, 14.77 days (spring–neap cycle, described above);

(7) monthly, 27.55 days (perigee–apogee cycle, described above);

(8) semiannual, 182.62 days (variation in the Sun's declination);

(9) semiannual, 206 days (perigean spring cycle, described above);

(10) annual, 365.26 days (perihelion–aphelion cycle);

(11) 8.85 years (prograde precession of the lunar perigee); and

(12) 18.61 years (retrograde precession of the nodes of the lunar orbit).

In addition to astronomical factors, the tides on Earth are strongly influenced by the sizes, boundaries, and depths of ocean basins and inlets and by Earth's rotation, winds, and barometric pressure fluctuations. Using Newton's gravitation and laws of motion, the French physicist Pierre-Simon Laplace (1749–1827) developed the dynamical theory of the tides on the rotating Earth (*Mécanique Céleste,* 1799), but because of the complexity of the tides the full application of his theory was not possible until the advent of the digital computer in the last third of the 20th century.

Tides typically have ranges (vertical high to low) of a metre or two, but there are regions in the oceans where the various influences conspire to produce virtually no tides at all and others where the tides are greatly amplified. Among the latter regions are the Sea of Okhotsk, the Gulf of Alaska, the northern coast of Australia, the English Channel, and in Canada, Ungava Bay in northern Québec and the Bay of Fundy between New Brunswick and Nova Scotia. The tidal ranges in these regions are of the order of 10 m.

Fundy Tides

Only two localities on Earth sometimes have a vertical tide range exceeding 16 m (52 ft.), and both are in Canada: Minas Basin, the eastern extremity of the Bay of Fundy in Nova Scotia, and Leaf Basin, a remote inlet on the southwestern side of Ungava Bay in northern Québec. The current best data give Minas Basin a slight edge; however, several years of tide gauge data continuing through the year 2015 are needed to determine which site, if either (to the precision that measurements can be made), has the greater tide range. (In 2015, the 18.61-year lunar cycle will next have its peak effect on the tides; see below.)

The primary cause of the immense tides of Fundy is a resonance of the Bay of Fundy/Gulf of Maine system. The system is effectively bounded at its outer end by the edge of the continental shelf with its approximately 40:1 increase in depth. The system has a natural period of approximately 13 hours, a Q-value[1] of about 5, and is driven near resonance, not directly by the Moon, but by the dominant semidiurnal tides of the Atlantic Ocean. Like a father pushing his daughter on a swing, the gentle Atlantic tidal pulse pushes the waters of the Bay of Fundy/Gulf of Maine basin at nearly the optimum frequency to cause a large oscillation. The seventh Astronomer Royal, G.B. Airy (1801–1892), first developed the theory of the behaviour of tides in restricted arms of the ocean such as the Fundy system.

Fundy tides are unique in that they respond more to the perigee–apogee influence than they do to the spring–neap influence. That is because the lunar tidal period (12.4 hours) is closer to the system's resonant period than is the solar tidal period (12.0 hours). Although the variation in the Moon's distance is not obvious when viewing the Moon directly, near the head of the Bay of Fundy the 3-m to 6-m *increase* in the vertical tidal range makes it obvious when the Moon is near perigee, clear skies or cloudy!

The most dramatic view of the vertical range of Fundy tides is at the Minas Basin Pulp & Power Company wharf in the town of Hantsport, Nova Scotia. Remarkably, this site is practically unknown; it is not advertised, and no special provisions have been made to accommodate spectators.

Perhaps the most awesome display of the tides on our planet occurs at Cape Split, Nova Scotia, on the southern side of the entrance to Minas Basin. (Cape Split may be reached by a pleasant two-hour walk along a popular hiking trail from the village of Scots Bay.) Here, at the time of the midpoint of an incoming tide, for a considerable

---

[1] The Q-value, or quality-value, of an oscillator indicates its efficiency. A large Q means low energy loss per cycle and a well-defined resonant frequency. A Q of 5 is relatively small, indicative of considerable damping in the Fundy system, yet it is large enough to make these tides among the highest on Earth.

distance the forest on the towering cliffs is filled with a hollow roar produced by the turbulence of the waters surging over the submarine ridges below. The currents exceed 8 knots (4 m/s), and the flow in the deep, 5-km-wide channel on the north side of Cape Split equals the combined flow of all the streams and rivers of Earth ($\approx$4 km^3/h). Three hours later the spectacle pauses and then begins flowing in the opposite direction.

The highest of the high tides in the Bay of Fundy occur when a perigean spring high tide coincides with a low barometric-pressure storm system sweeping northward across New Brunswick, accompanied by hurricane-force southerly winds over the Gulf of Maine and the Bay of Fundy. The close Moon, the in-phase solar tide, the reduced air pressure above the water, and the wind drag pushing more water into the Bay of Fundy (the last two effects are called a storm surge) all contribute to an especially high tide. An additional favourable influence is if all this occurs near an equinox, for then the axis of the tidal bulges of the spring tide is at a right angle to Earth's rotation axis, optimizing the tidal range (if the axes were parallel there would be no tidal cycle). This right-angle-axes enhancement of the tides is strengthened in those years when the declination range of the Moon ($\pm$18° to $\pm$29°) is near a minimum, a situation that recurs with the 18.61-year period of the retrograde motion of the nodes of its orbit. (The declination range was at its $\pm$18° minimum in 1959, 1978, and 1997 and will be again in 2015. See p. 93 for the shift in the longitude of the ascending node of the Moon's orbit during 2008.) Furthermore, since perihelion occurs in January, the highest tides of all tend to occur just prior to the March equinox or after the September equinox. The infamous Bay of Fundy "Saxby gale" of 1869 Oct. 5 was a time when all seven of these factors approximately coincided (perigee, spring tide, low pressure, south wind, equinox, minimum declination range, and perihelion enhancement). Since weather is unpredictable, so, too, is the next major tidal flood in the Bay of Fundy.

Paradoxically, the large tides of Fundy protect its shores from flooding associated with most storm surges, since the normal variation in its high tide levels is already several metres. Only those rare storm surges that happen to coincide with a perigean spring high tide will be a problem. In contrast, shorelines with small tides are much more susceptible to storm surges.

Sea level is slowly increasing in the Bay of Fundy region. This is bringing the resonant period of the Fundy/Gulf of Maine system closer to the lunar tidal period which, in turn, is causing Fundy tides to gradually become even larger (by a few centimetres per decade).

Tidal Friction

Tidal friction, which occurs primarily in shallow seas around the margins of the oceans, transforms Earth's rotational kinetic energy into heat at a rate of about 3.5 TW, comparable to humankind's total rate of energy use. Approximately 1% of this energy transformation occurs in the Bay of Fundy, and, since 1984, a tiny portion of this (20 MW peak) is being turned into commercial electric power at the Annapolis Basin tidal power plant in Nova Scotia. The only other large-scale tidal power installation is in France on the Rance estuary (240 MW peak).

Tidal friction also transfers angular momentum from Earth to the Moon, lengthening the day and increasing the size of the orbit of the Moon. The day is lengthening by about 1 s every 40 000 years—imperceptible on a human time scale but of profound significance to Earth's rotation over a few billion years. (For example, 900 million years ago, when Earth was already 80% of its present age, there were about 480 18-hour days in a year.) The Moon is receding about 3.8 cm per year, with the result that about one billion years from now total solar eclipses will cease. Presently we are well into the transitional phase: Annular eclipses already outnumber total solar eclipses. New moons occur, on average, almost one day earlier each successive month; however, because of the increasing size of the lunar orbit, in about 300 million years the lunar (synodic) month will have lengthened to equal the average calendar month (although the average month will then contain only about twenty-eight 26-hour days).

If the Sun does not first incinerate our planet, there will come a day that is as long as the lunar month (each then equal to about 40 present days), and a more distant Moon will stand stationary in the sky, as does Earth now in the lunar sky. But this situation will not endure, for solar tides will still be present and will reduce the angular momentum of the Earth–Moon system, causing the Moon to approach Earth once more.

General Relativity and Tides

Einstein's theory of gravitation, general relativity, superseded Newton's theory nearly a century ago, yet descriptions of the tides almost invariably ignore Einstein (as has this article to this point). The reasons for using the older, wrong theory are: (1) Newton's theory describes the gentle tides on Earth to high accuracy; (2) the mathematics involved is much simpler than that of general relativity; (3) the Newtonian description of the tides is compatible with cultivated common sense. Because of this last reason, Newton's concepts regarding motion and gravitation form the essential foundation for anyone attempting to understand the tides. One must climb up on Newton's towering shoulders before it is possible to focus clearly on Einstein.

As mentioned in the section ORBITAL MOTION (see pp. 31–32), Newton's Euclidean universe with its force of gravity never did exist. Although Newton's ideas are more than adequate for describing the tides on Earth, for some purposes, such as the Global Positioning System (GPS), Newton's concepts of space, time, and gravitation are inadequate. We inhabit an Einsteinian universe, a universe in which gravitation is a manifestation of the structure of spacetime, the four-dimensional stage of our existence in which space and time are interwoven. The geometry of spacetime is curved by the mass–energy of matter, and the curvature tells matter how to move.

The Moon's mass alters the structure of spacetime at its location, and this distortion propagates outward, becoming more dilute with the volume encompassed according to the inverse cube of the distance. At Earth, the distortion results in the waters of the oceans following slightly different paths through spacetime than does the rigid planet beneath, producing the characteristic egglike shape of the tidal effect. The tidal heartbeat is that of the very fabric of spacetime. The tides at our feet carry a profound message.

References

For more information, see the superb introduction *The Tides* by E.P. Clancy, Anchor Books, Doubleday and Co., 1969 (now, unfortunately, out of print). For a detailed account of the evolution of our understanding of the tides see *Tides, A Scientific History,* by D.E. Cartwright, Cambridge University Press, 1999. (Note, however, that neither Clancy nor Cartwright mentions general relativity.) For a popular account of general relativity, see *A Journey into Gravity and Spacetime,* by J.A. Wheeler, Scientific American Library, 1990. An article dealing specifically with the tides of Fundy and tidal power installations has been written by Christopher Garrett (*Endeavour, 8* (1984), No. 2, pp. 58–64). The major astronomical factors influencing the tides (the phases, perigees, and apogees of the Moon) are tabulated in THE SKY MONTH BY MONTH section (pp. 97–119) of this Handbook. These may be perused to determine days favourable for large tides. For information on tides in Canadian waters see www.lau.chs-shc.gc.ca, a Web site of the Canadian Hydrographic Service.

THE SUN

EPHEMERIS FOR THE SUN

Sundial Correction

The **Greenwich Transit** time in the table overleaf may be used to calculate the sundial correction at the observer's position. For example, to find the correction at Halifax on 2008 Aug. 10, determine the following: At Greenwich the Sun transits at 12:05:35 on Aug. 8 and at 12:04:57 on Aug. 12. Thus, to the nearest min, on Aug. 10 at both Greenwich and Halifax the Sun will transit at 12:05 local mean solar time (LMT), or 12:19 Atlantic Standard Time (AST) since Halifax has a longitude correction of +14 min (see the 3rd paragraph on p. 195). Thus a 5-min correction must be added to the reading of a simple sundial to obtain LMT, an additional 14 min must be added to obtain AST, and a further 1 hour for Atlantic Daylight Time (ADT).

A figure accurate to a second or two can be obtained by interpolating for longitude. The interpolated transit time at Greenwich for Aug. 10 is 12:05:16, the daily change in time being −9.5 s. Adjusting this for the longitude of Halifax:

12 h 5 min 16 s − (9.5 s × 4 h 14 min ÷ 24 h) = 12 h 5 min 14 s.

Thus the sundial correction is 5 min 14 s. To find the standard time of the Sun's transit to the nearest second or two, the observer's longitude must be known to 10″ or better. For example, suppose an observer in Halifax is at longitude 63°25′30″W, or 4 h 13 min 42 s W of Greenwich. The time of transit will be 12:05:14 + 13 min 42 s = 12:18:56 AST or 13:18:56 ADT.

Orientation of the Sun

The table overleaf gives three angles that specify the orientation of the Sun.

P is the position angle of the axis of rotation, measured eastward in the observer's sky from the north point on the disk. Note that P varies between +26° (solar north pole tilted eastward) and −26° (tilted westward) during the year. This tilt is associated mainly with the inclination of the ecliptic in the observer's sky, with a smaller contribution from the Sun's 7.2° inclination to the ecliptic (the longitude of the ascending node of the solar equator on the ecliptic is 76°).

B_0 is the heliographic latitude of the centre of the disk, and is the result of the Sun's 7.2° inclination to the ecliptic. Note that positive values of B_0 correspond to the solar equator passing south of the centre of the disk, with the solar north pole being tipped toward the observer.

L_0 is the heliographic longitude of the centre of the disk measured from Carrington's solar prime meridian in the direction of rotation. L_0 decreases about 13° per day. The dates during the year when $L_0 = 0°$ are given in the table below. The rotation period of the Sun depends upon heliographic latitude. The synodic and sidereal periods of rotation at the solar equator are 27.2753 days and 25.38 days, respectively.

Commencement (UT) of Numbered Synodic Solar Rotations

No.*	Commences	No	Commences	No	Commences	No	Commences
2065	'07 Dec. 29.05	2069	Apr. 16.34	2073	Aug. 3.20	2077	Nov. 20.29
2066	'08 Jan. 25.39	2070	May 13.58	2074	Aug. 30.43	2078	Dec. 17.61
2067	Feb. 21.73	2071	Jun. 9.79	2075	Sep. 26.70	2079	'09 Jan. 13.94
2068	Mar. 20.06	2072	Jul. 6.99	2076	Oct. 23.99		

*Based on R.C. Carrington's Greenwich photoheliocentric series in which rotation No. 1 commenced 1853 Nov. 9.

EPHEMERIS FOR THE SUN, 2008

Date 0h UT	Apparent RA (2008) h m	Dec ° '	Greenwich Transit UT	Orientation P	B₀	L₀	Date 0h UT	Apparent RA (2008) h m	Dec ° '	Greenwich Transit UT	Orientation P	B₀	L₀
Jan. 1	18 43.2	−23 04	12:03:19	+2.4	−2.9	321.2	**Sep.** 1	10 42.1	+8 13	11:59:52	+21.2	+7.2	339.3
5	19 00.8	−22 42	12:05:10	+0.4	−3.4	268.5	5	10 56.6	+6 45	11:58:33	+22.1	+7.2	286.4
9	19 18.4	−22 13	12:06:54	−1.5	−3.9	215.8	9	11 11.0	+5 15	11:57:11	+23.0	+7.2	233.6
13	19 35.8	−21 37	12:08:31	−3.4	−4.3	163.1	13	11 25.4	+3 44	11:55:46	+23.8	+7.2	180.8
17	19 53.0	−20 54	12:09:56	−5.3	−4.7	110.5	17	11 39.7	+2 12	11:54:20	+24.4	+7.2	128.0
21	20 10.0	−20 05	12:11:10	−7.2	−5.1	57.8	21	11 54.0	+0 39	11:52:55	+25.0	+7.1	75.2
25	20 26.8	−19 10	12:12:13	−8.9	−5.4	5.1	25	12 08.4	−0 55	11:51:31	+25.5	+7.0	22.4
29	20 43.5	−18 09	12:13:02	−10.7	−5.8	312.5	29	12 22.8	−2 28	11:50:10	+25.8	+6.8	329.6
Feb. 2	20 59.9	−17 03	12:13:39	−12.3	−6.0	259.8	**Oct.** 3	12 37.3	−4 01	11:48:54	+26.1	+6.6	276.8
6	21 16.1	−15 52	12:14:03	−13.9	−6.3	207.1	7	12 51.9	−5 34	11:47:42	+26.2	+6.4	224.0
10	21 32.1	−14 37	12:14:14	−15.4	−6.6	154.5	11	13 06.6	−7 05	11:46:38	+26.3	+6.1	171.3
14	21 49.8	−13 18	12:14:13	−16.8	−6.8	101.8	15	13 21.4	−8 34	11:45:41	+26.2	+5.8	118.5
18	22 03.4	−11 56	12:13:59	−18.2	−6.9	49.1	19	13 36.3	−10 02	11:44:53	+26.0	+5.6	65.8
22	22 18.8	−10 30	12:13:35	−19.4	−7.1	356.4	23	13 51.5	−11 27	11:44:16	+25.6	+5.2	13.0
26	22 34.0	−9 02	12:13:00	−20.6	−7.2	303.8	27	14 06.8	−12 50	11:43:50	+25.2	+4.8	320.2
Mar. 1	22 49.0	−7 32	12:12:16	−21.6	−7.2	251.1	31	14 22.3	−14 09	11:43:36	+24.6	+4.4	267.5
5	23 04.0	−5 59	12:11:25	−22.6	−7.2	198.4	**Nov.** 4	14 38.0	−15 25	11:43:34	+23.9	+4.0	214.8
9	23 18.8	−4 26	12:10:27	−23.4	−7.2	145.7	8	14 54.0	−16 37	11:43:46	+23.1	+3.6	162.0
13	23 33.5	−2 52	12:09:23	−24.2	−7.2	93.0	12	15 10.1	−17 44	11:44:11	+22.1	+3.2	109.3
17	23 48.2	−1 17	12:08:16	−24.8	−7.1	40.2	16	15 26.5	−18 46	11:44:50	+21.0	+2.7	56.5
21	0 02.8	+0 18	12:07:04	−25.3	−7.0	347.5	20	15 43.1	−19 43	11:45:42	+19.8	+2.2	3.8
25	0 13.7	+1 29	12:06:10	−25.6	−6.9	308.0	24	15 59.9	−20 35	11:46:47	+18.5	+1.7	311.1
29	0 31.9	+3 26	12:04:39	−26.0	−6.7	242.0	28	16 17.0	−21 20	11:48:05	+17.1	+1.2	258.4
Apr. 2	0 46.5	+4 59	12:03:28	−26.2	−6.5	189.2	**Dec.** 2	16 34.2	−21 59	11:49:33	+15.6	+0.7	205.6
6	1 01.1	+6 31	12:02:19	−26.3	−6.2	136.5	6	16 51.6	−22 31	11:51:12	+14.0	+0.2	152.9
10	1 15.7	+8 01	12:01:13	−26.2	−6.0	83.7	10	17 09.1	−22 55	11:52:58	+12.3	−0.3	100.2
14	1 30.5	+9 28	12:00:12	−26.1	−5.7	30.1	14	17 26.7	−23 13	11:54:50	+10.5	−0.8	47.5
18	1 45.3	+10 53	11:59:16	−25.8	−5.3	338.0	18	17 44.4	−23 23	11:56:47	+8.7	−1.3	354.8
22	2 00.2	+12 15	11:58:27	−25.4	−5.0	285.2	22	18 02.2	−23 26	11:58:46	+6.8	−1.8	302.1
26	2 15.3	+13 34	11:57:44	−24.9	−4.6	232.4	26	18 20.0	−23 22	12:00:45	+4.9	−2.3	249.4
30	2 30.5	+14 49	11:57:10	−24.2	−4.2	179.5	30	18 37.7	−23 09	12:02:43	+3.0	−2.8	196.8
May 4	2 45.8	+16 01	11:56:44	−23.5	−3.8	126.6							
8	3 01.3	+17 08	11:56:28	−22.6	−3.4	73.8							
12	3 16.9	+18 11	11:56:21	−21.7	−3.0	20.1							
16	3 32.7	+19 08	11:56:22	−20.6	−2.5	328.0							
20	3 48.6	+20 01	11:56:33	−19.4	−2.1	275.1							
24	4 04.7	+20 48	11:56:51	−18.1	−1.6	222.1							
28	4 20.9	+21 29	11:57:18	−16.8	−1.1	169.2							
Jun. 1	4 37.2	+22 05	11:57:53	−15.3	−0.6	116.3							
5	4 53.6	+22 34	11:58:34	−13.8	−0.2	63.4							
9	5 10.2	+22 57	11:59:19	−12.2	+0.3	10.4							
13	5 26.7	+23 13	12:00:08	−10.5	+0.8	317.5							
17	5 43.4	+23 23	12:00:59	−8.8	+1.3	264.5							
21	6 00.0	+23 26	12:01:51	−7.0	+1.8	211.6							
25	6 16.6	+23 23	12:02:43	−5.2	+2.2	158.6							
29	6 33.2	+23 13	12:03:32	−3.4	+2.7	105.7							
Jul. 3	6 49.8	+22 57	12:04:18	−1.6	+3.1	52.7							
7	7 06.2	+22 34	12:04:59	+0.2	+3.6	359.8							
11	7 22.6	+22 05	12:05:34	+2.0	+4.0	306.8							
15	7 38.8	+21 30	12:06:01	+3.8	+4.4	253.9							
19	7 54.9	+20 49	12:06:19	+5.5	+4.7	201.0							
23	8 10.9	+20 02	12:06:29	+7.2	+5.1	148.1							
27	8 26.7	+19 11	12:06:30	+8.9	+5.4	95.2							
31	8 42.3	+18 14	12:06:21	+10.6	+5.7	42.2							
Aug. 4	8 57.8	+17 12	12:06:03	+12.1	+6.0	349.3							
8	9 13.2	+16 06	12:05:35	+13.6	+6.3	296.4							
12	9 28.5	+14 55	12:04:57	+15.1	+6.5	243.6							
16	9 43.3	+13 41	12:04:11	+16.4	+6.7	190.7							
20	9 58.2	+12 24	12:03:16	+17.7	+6.9	137.8							
24	10 13.0	+11 03	12:02:14	+19.0	+7.0	85.0							
28	10 27.6	+9 39	12:01:05	+20.1	+7.1	32.1							

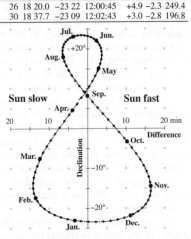

The bowling-pin-shaped analemma depicts the drift of apparent solar time or sundial time relative to local mean time (horizontal axis) and the changing declination of the Sun (vertical axis) during 2008. For points to the left of the vertical axis ("Sun slow") the Sun transits after 12:00 local mean time. To the right ("Sun fast"), the Sun transits before 12:00 local mean time. For each month, a heavy dot marks day 1 with medium dots for days 5, 9, 13, 17, 21, 25, and 29. See pp. 43–44 for further details.

SOLAR ACTIVITY
By Ken Tapping

Following its peak in 2000, Solar Activity Cycle 23*, continues its decline. The plot of monthly means shown in the Figure suggests that we are not yet at the activity minimum, although we could be very close to it. The activity peak of Cycle 23 was a low one. The only weaker maximum was that of Cycle 20. In general shape, Cycle 23 closely resembles Cycle 20, which also had a long, slow, drawn-out decay. If Cycle 23 continues to behave like Cycle 20, we might not see the next solar minimum until late 2007, or in the first half of 2008.

The figure shows solar activity as represented by the adjusted 10.7-cm solar microwave flux activity index (see p. 184) from 1950 to the present. The plotted values are averaged values of the index over each solar (≈27-day) rotation. The ≈11-year activity cycle is clearly evident, as are the dramatic resurgence of activity during 2001 the resurgences of activity during the Cycle's decline, and that we might not reach the minimum of this Cycle until 2008.

Solar activity is fundamentally a magnetic phenomenon. Deep below the photosphere, differential rotation and convection cause the solar material to move in a complex manner. The density of this material is high enough for its movement to drag the magnetic fields along with it. This generates electric currents, which in turn produce magnetic fields. The result is a complex system of subphotospheric "magnetic flux ropes." The penetration of sections of these flux ropes through the photosphere and into the chromosphere and corona gives rise to the many observed forms of solar activity. Above the photosphere the situation is strikingly different: the density is much lower, and the magnetic fields trap and confine the ionized gas of the solar atmosphere, supporting loops and filaments and forming the diverse menagerie of photospheric, chromospheric, and coronal structures with which we are familiar, such as sunspots, active regions, complexes of activity, and systems of loops. Changing emissions in the X-ray and ultraviolet wavelengths, and at radio wavelengths, are due to the changing amount of trapped plasma and the strengths of the magnetic fields containing them. The Sun's total energy output is also affected by magnetic activity, fortunately only slightly.

The organization of the subphotospheric magnetic fields gives rise to a consistent pattern in the magnetic configuration of active regions. Each region is magnetically bipolar, with the bipoles arranged east–west on the disk. All bipoles lying in the same hemisphere are arranged with the same magnetic polarity leading (facing in the direction in which the region appears to move as it is carried across the disk by solar rotation—westward in the observer's sky). In the other hemisphere the leading and following magnetic polarities are reversed.

---

*The numbering system for solar activity cycles was started by Rudolph Wolf, who arbitrarily designated the activity maximum of 1750 as that of Cycle 1.

Exceptions do occur. Regions are sometimes formed that have a magnetic orientation perpendicular to or even the reverse of the norm for that hemisphere. Such regions usually try to move into the conventional orientation but are impeded by the magnetic linkages formed with their surroundings. These regions tend to produce flares as potential energy builds up in their magnetic structures and is subsequently released catastrophically.

The "conventional" magnetic configurations for active regions reverse on alternate activity cycles. For example, during Cycle 22, active regions in the northern solar hemisphere were oriented with their "negative" (i.e. south-seeking) magnetic polarity ends leading and "positive" (north-seeking) ends following, with the reverse situation in the southern hemisphere. In Cycle 23 this arrangement is reversed. A *magnetic* activity cycle, which is probably a more realistic description of the rhythms of solar activity, is equal to two of Wolf's activity cycles and takes about 22 years to complete.

Active regions are not isolated phenomena; they occur in complexes, comprising several active regions at various stages of development, together with the network of elements remaining from decayed regions. This localization of activity gives rise to a rotational modulation of the 10.7-cm flux as active region clusters are carried across the disk and disappear around the west limb. To smooth out this modulation in long-term studies of solar activity, the data are averaged over solar rotations rather than by month. Active regions can persist for one or more solar rotations and the complexes for a dozen or so.

The large-scale organization of solar magnetic activity is also apparent in the spatial distribution of active regions during the solar cycle. The first activity of the new cycle is marked by the formation of active regions at high latitudes. As activity builds toward the maximum of the cycle, the number of active regions increases, and they tend to form at lower latitudes. As the activity wanes toward the next minimum, the number of regions decreases, but the average latitude continues to decrease until the last activity of the cycle is located near the equator. Then, as the new cycle starts, new active regions form at high latitudes.

The formation of a new active region begins with the emergence through the photosphere into the overlying chromosphere and corona of magnetic loops. This is heralded by the appearance of small pores, about 1000 km across, which coalesce and spread into a patch of magnetic flux that may exceed 50 000 km in length. The average magnetic field strength in such patches is of the order of 0.01 T (100 gauss). The emergence of these magnetic fields modifies the spatial and density structure of the chromosphere, giving rise to enhanced emission in the calcium and magnesium II K spectral lines. These bright patches (called plage), which stand out prominently in filtergrams, are the most conspicuous aspect of active regions. In some areas of the new active region, magnetic field strengths reach or exceed 0.1 T. These magnetic fields are strong enough to impede the transfer of energy from within the Sun, leading to these patches being cooler (3000 K) compared with the surrounding photosphere, which has a temperature of about 6000 K. Although actually quite hot and shining quite brightly, in contrast with their hotter surroundings these flux concentrations appear as dark spots: sunspots. As a region grows, one or more large spots form at the leading end, and a scattering of smaller ones form at the trailing end. Sunspots are a prominent feature of active regions and are the aspect of solar activity that has been longest known.

The growth of the new active region continues through repeated episodes of magnetic flux emergence. In general, the size is directly proportional to the total magnetic flux in the region. Growth stops when the emergence of new magnetic flux ceases. Soon after, the region starts to decay. This proceeds partly by the resubmergence of magnetic flux and partly by fragmentation. The spots disappear, and eventually, all that remains is a large area of magnetic flux arranged in a network pattern, blending in slowly with the remains of other decayed active regions.

Repeated episodes of magnetic-flux emergence, together with motions of the footpoints, which are the photospheric anchors of magnetic loops, lead to the magnetic field overactive regions becoming complex and tangled and storing enormous amounts of energy. The relaxation of these fields is an important aspect of the evolution and dissipation of active regions. In some cases, this can occur noncatastrophically; otherwise, stresses increase until various plasma instabilities allow rapid relaxation and reconnection of the magnetic fields and a rapid release of the stored energy. These energy releases are known as flares.

The Solar Wind and Aurorae

The solar atmosphere is not stable. It is constantly flowing outward as a stream of particles and magnetic fields—the *solar wind*. The flow is strongest where the magnetic loops are very large and impose the least drag on the outwardly flowing particles. Because of their lower coronal densities, these regions produce a lower flux of X-rays and appear in X-ray images as dark patches, known as "coronal holes." The solar wind is not homogeneous or steady; its speed, density, and direction can change according to the positions of coronal holes and the nature of current solar activity.

The solar wind profoundly changes Earth's magnetic field. The wind pressure pushes the field out of its dipole shape into a long teardrop. The magnetic geometry in the tail of the drop makes it the site of many plasma instabilities. The flow of the solar wind over the boundary of Earth's magnetic field (the magnetopause) excites many types of waves, which move along Earth's magnetic field lines and which can be detected on the ground at high magnetic latitudes. Increases in the density or velocity of the solar wind change the pressure equilibrium between the solar wind and the magnetosphere, producing fluctuations in the strength and direction of the magnetic field lines at ground level. If the fluctuations are strong enough, the events are referred to as magnetic storms and substorms. These can disrupt any human activity that involves connected metal networks covering large geographical areas, especially at high magnetic latitudes.

Complex interactions between the solar wind and Earth's magnetic field lead to an accumulation of trapped particles in the magnetosphere. During magnetic storms, instabilities and waves excited in the magnetosphere by the solar wind accelerate some of the trapped particles downward along Earth's magnetic field into increasingly dense atmosphere, where they collide with the atmospheric constituents, exciting them with sufficient energy to produce light. These displays are called aurorae, or the northern and southern lights: *aurora borealis* and *aurora australis,* respectively. Views from space show that aurorae fall in a rough circle (the auroral oval), centred around the magnetic pole, that is, in a definite band of magnetic latitudes. As activity increases, the auroral oval expands, covering lower and lower magnetic latitudes. It also becomes increasingly distorted. During the period of very high activity in March 1989, auroral displays were seen as far south as the Caribbean.

Aurorae occur in many forms and can be steady, moving, or rapidly pulsating, depending upon the nature of the particle streams causing them. Aurorae can appear green or red, although if they are faint, the eye cannot respond in colour and they appear grey. The greenish colour is due to spectral lines from oxygen (558 nm) and a range of lines from nitrogen covering the band 391 nm to 470 nm. Under highly disturbed conditions, red spectral-line emissions at 630 nm and 636 nm and in a series of bands between 650 nm and 680 nm can also be seen. The green emissions are produced at a height of about 110 km; the red, 630-nm and 636-nm emissions, due

AURORAL FORMS

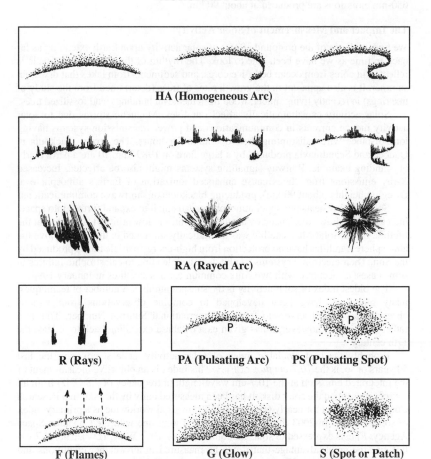

The above sketches illustrate standard auroral forms. This simplified classification was devised for visual observers during the International Geophysical Year over five decades ago (1957–58). Although there is great variety in auroral patterns, the sketches emphasize fundamental features and minimize variations that depend on the location of the observer. The light of the aurora is emitted by the upper fringes of Earth's atmosphere (heights of 100 to 400 km) as it is bombarded by electrons of the solar wind (solar wind protons contribute a smaller amount of energy). The modification of the trajectories of these particles by Earth's magnetic field restricts activity to high latitudes, producing the "aurora borealis" in the Northern Hemisphere and the "aurora australis" in the Southern Hemisphere. The wavelengths of four atmospheric molecular and atomic emission lines that can contribute strongly to auroral light are included in the list on p. 39. Whether aurorae appear coloured depends on their luminance—light that is too faint will not activate colour vision and appears white. When the luminance is sufficiently great, the relative contributions of blue, green, and red emission lines can result in a variety of auroral hues.

to atomic oxygen, originate at heights between 200 km and 400 km; the 650-nm to 680-nm emissions are produced at about 90 km.

The Impact and Measurement of Solar Activity

We find evidence of the profound effects of solar activity upon Earth extending as far back in time as we have been able to look. The rhythm of the solar activity cycle is reflected in cores from ocean beds, ice cores, and sediments from lakes that dry up in summer. It is also apparent in the growth rates of trees (determined from the study of tree rings) in recently living timber, wood from medieval buildings, and fossilized trees.

Solar activity can dramatically affect our lives. Magnetic storms due to solar activity induce currents in communications and power transmission systems having long-distance wires, disrupting their operation for hours. The power blackouts in Québec and Scandinavia produced by a large flare on 1989 Mar. 10 are a particularly outstanding example. Railway signalling systems might also be affected. Increased X-ray emissions from flares cause enhanced ionization of Earth's atmosphere at D-region heights (about 90 km), producing blackouts of shortwave communications.

Solar activity heats the upper atmosphere, causing it to expand further into space, increasing the drag experienced by artificial satellites in low orbits. It is ironic that the lifetime of the Solar Max satellite was dramatically shortened in this way. Above the atmosphere, satellites have no protection from high-energy particle fluxes produced by the Sun. Their electronic systems can be damaged, leading to catastrophic failures in some cases, as occurred with two Anik communications satellites in January 1994.

The oldest index of solar activity is the sunspot number. A number of techniques, many empirical, have been developed to combine observations from various observatories and observers to form the International Sunspot Number. This is a rather poor index; however, it has given us a database extending back to at least the 17th century.

Probably the best available index of solar activity, at least covering the last 50 years or so, is the *10.7-cm flux,* or $F_{10.7}$. This index is an objective measurement of the integrated emission at the 10.7-cm wavelength (a frequency of 2.8 GHz) from all sources present on the solar disk. It has been measured daily by the National Research Council of Canada for nearly 60 years and is now used worldwide as a primary index of solar activity. In 2003 the program became a joint one with the Canadian Space Agency. $F_{10.7}$ is expressed in solar flux units (1 sfu = 10^{-22} W·m^{-2}Hz^{-1}). The 10.7-cm flux has the great advantage that it can be measured in all weather conditions and requires no human involvement or "interpretation." When quiet, the Sun produces a 10.7-cm flux of 64 sfu, due to free-free thermal emission from the quiet solar corona. The 10.7-cm flux can be used as an objective proxy for other activity-related quantities. The strength of the radio emission constituting $F_{10.7}$ is modulated by the annual variation in the distance between Earth and Sun. When considering solar-driven phenomena at the Earth and in near-Earth space, this is not important, so the "Observed" value of the flux may be applicable. On the other hand, when considering solar activity this modulation has to be removed from the data. In such instances, the "Adjusted" flux, which is scaled to an Earth–Sun distance of 1 au, should be used.

We are a long way from understanding the nature and the extent of the effects solar activity has upon Earth. Some correlations, like that between the length of miniskirts and solar activity, are probably spurious; others might not be. As we exploit our environment more fully, we become increasingly sensitive to things that might affect it, even slightly.

RAINBOWS, HALOS, SUNDOGS, PILLARS, CORONAE, GLORIES, AND HEILIGENSCHEIN
BY ROY BISHOP

Sunlight, and more rarely moonlight, interacting with water drops or ice crystals in the sky can result in aerial patterns displaying remarkable symmetry. The patterns cited in the heading, to which this brief account is restricted, are the more common ones. For more extensive treatments, including a dozen relatively rare patterns involving ice crystals, see the book by Greenler in the references and the Web sites listed there. For comprehensive accounts of the history and physics of the rainbow, see the books by Boyer, and Lee and Fraser.

In order of increasing angular distance from the Sun, ice crystals produce coronae, pillars, halos, and sundogs. (Other small particles, including water drops, also produce coronae.) In the half of the sky opposite the Sun, water drops produce rainbows and, surrounding the antisolar point, glories. The heiligenschein is not an atmospheric phenomenon, but like the glory is a bright area in the vicinity of the antisolar point.

Since the rainbow is the most famous, most beautiful, and most complex of these apparitions, I begin with rainbows and devote the greater part of this article to them. Also, if you understand the rainbow, it is easy to understand halos, sundogs, and pillars.

Rainbows
The rainbow has challenged natural philosophers over the centuries, including Aristotle, Roger Bacon, Theodoric of Freiberg, René Descartes, Sir Isaac Newton, Edmund Halley, Thomas Young, George Airy, and Gustav Mie. It was Descartes (1596–1650) who first understood the basic geometry of the rainbow, and it was Newton (1642–1727) who first understood the origin of the colours of the rainbow. In 1803, 1838, and 1908 Young, Airy, and Mie, respectively, gave successively more accurate treatments of the influence of the wave nature of light on the structure of the rainbow. Recently, Alistair Fraser and Raymond Lee, using the power of the computer, provided additional insights concerning the physics of the rainbow. A few poets, including Keats and Goethe, have derided science for analyzing the rainbow, but understanding only deepens one's admiration for the beauty and subtle nature of this phantom.

The Shape of a Raindrop: The shape of a raindrop is relevant for rainbows. Surface tension arising from molecular attraction shrinks raindrops into the shape with the least surface area per unit volume—a sphere. (Raindrops resemble teardrops only after they have crashed against a surface such as a windowpane.) Aerodynamic forces deform large raindrops into a hamburger-bun shape with the short axis vertical, but an average raindrop is essentially spherical.

The Origin of the Rainbow: Sunlight is refracted and reflected by a raindrop (see Figure 1). The *primary* rainbow involves two refractions (where the light ray enters and leaves the drop) and *one* internal reflection. A portion of a ray that enters a drop head-on is deviated through 180° by the internal reflection, but when the ray is shifted off-centre, the reflection produces a smaller deviation. When the ray is shifted 86% of the way toward grazing the drop (as in Figure 1), because of the increasing refraction a *minimum angle of deviation* of approximately 138° is reached. This *stationary* angle concentrates some of the light leaving a raindrop after one reflection near this direction. Dispersion associated with the two refractions makes the minimum angle

FIGURE 1 *The path of a ray of sunlight interacting with a spherical raindrop is displayed. The ray is shown entering the drop at 86% of the drop radius from head-on entry, causing ray P, exiting after one internal reflection, to be at a minimum angle of deviation of 138° and contributing to the primary rainbow. Ray (S) exiting after two internal reflections is close to but not at the minimum deviation for the secondary rainbow (231°); the ray entering the drop must be shifted closer to grazing incidence (to 95% of the drop radius) before a minimum deviation of 231°*

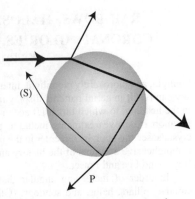

is attained. *Rays undergoing three or more reflections within the drop are not shown, and neither is chromatic dispersion in the three rays exiting the drop. The widths of the various rays give an approximate indication of their relative intensities.*

FIGURE 2 *Two raindrops are shown, greatly magnified, each with a ray of sunlight striking it such that the exiting ray is at the minimum angle of deviation and heading toward the observer. The drop with one internal reflection is contributing light to the observer's primary rainbow, and the drop with two internal reflections is contributing to the observer's secondary rainbow. Other drops (not shown) located along the rays P and S contribute*

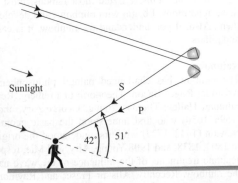

in the same fashion to the two rainbows, and the whole array has rotational symmetry about the dashed line, the extended shadow of the observer's head. The observer, looking from the apices of these conical shells, sees two, circular, coloured bands of light.

vary with wavelength, resulting in a spectrum. This interplay of sunlight with single raindrops in the sky is symmetric about an axis extending from the Sun through the eye of the observer; thus the circular arc of a rainbow is centred on that axis. To look at the primary rainbow, the observer's eyes must be turned toward 138° + 180° = 318° or 42° from the antisolar point, the shadow of the observer's head (see Figure 2).

To Predict Where a Rainbow Might Appear: If the Sun is shining where you are, with the Sun at your back extend your arms together straight out in front of you, splay your fingers and thumbs horizontally, and touch the tips of your thumbs together. Close one eye and align the tip of one little finger with the shadow of your head. As you tilt your hands, the tip of the other little finger will trace out the location of the primary rainbow in the sky. (A double hand-span at arm's length subtends approximately 40°, about the same as the 42° angular radius of the primary rainbow.)

Rainbows: None, Semicircular, and Circular: Don't expect to see a rainbow in the sky at midday in tropical latitudes, or at midday in spring or summer at higher latitudes. The Sun has to be less than 42° above the horizon for the top of the primary rainbow to be above the horizon (see Figure 2). At sunrise or sunset the antisolar centre of a rainbow is at the horizon, resulting in a semicircular rainbow that meets the horizon at 90°. From an airplane, or by spraying a garden hose, it is possible to see a complete circular rainbow at any time of day, provided there are many water drops and sunlight in the entire region 42° from the antisolar point.

A Rainbow Is Not a Bow: Angle, not distance, determines which raindrops send rainbow light to an observer's eye. Hence, the raindrops contributing to a rainbow lie in a conical shell with its tip at the observer's eye, and its axis coinciding with the extended shadow of the observer's head (see Figure 2). Only those parts of the conical shell having both raindrops and sunlight contribute to the rainbow. Thus, in spatial extent, a rainbow is like an immense, mouse-nibbled, ice-cream cone (sans ice cream). From the perspective of the observer located at the tip of this fragmented conical shell, a rainbow *looks* like a section of a flat circular arc or bow, but the only place a flat bow exists is on the observer's retina. Despite how rainbows are sometimes depicted in art and advertising, a rainbow cannot be viewed obliquely (it always appears circular), and it always has the same immense angular size. (Its 84° diameter spans almost one-quarter of the entire horizon.)

Your Rainbow: A rainbow is located at a particular angle relative to the Sun–observer axis (see Figure 2). When the observer moves, the axis moves, and the rainbow moves. The observer's shadow moves too, but a rainbow is subtler than a shadow; you can see someone else's shadow, but you cannot see their rainbow. Each observer has his or her own private rainbow. Although an observer's eyes image different rainbows, the two rainbows are in the same parallel direction, so when the images fuse, the observer sees one rainbow at infinity. Obviously a rainbow is not an object in the normal sense of the word; it is a pattern of light specific to the observer. Unlike the case of a normal object like a tree, there are as many rainbows as there are observers.

The Secondary Rainbow: If conditions are favourable (lots of rain and sunlight, and a dark sky background), a secondary rainbow will be visible. The *secondary* rainbow involves *two* internal reflections in each raindrop (see Figure 1). A light ray that enters a drop head-on is deviated through 360° by the two internal reflections, but when the ray is shifted off-centre the reflections produce a smaller deviation. When the ray is shifted 95% of the way toward grazing the drop, because of the increasing refraction a minimum angle of deviation of approximately 231° is reached. This stationary angle concentrates some of the light leaving a raindrop after two reflections near this direction. Dispersion associated with the two refractions makes the minimum angle vary with wavelength, resulting in a spectrum. To look at the secondary rainbow, the observer's eyes must be turned toward 231° + 180° = 411° or 51° from the antisolar point (see Figure 2). Thus the secondary rainbow lies (51° – 42°) = 9° outside of the primary rainbow (9° is about one fist-width at arm's length).

Width of the Secondary Rainbow: A light ray contributing to the secondary rainbow enters a raindrop closer to the edge of the raindrop than does a light ray contributing to the primary rainbow. Consequently, the amount of refraction and associated spectral dispersion are greater. The additional reflection from the curved inner surface of the raindrop further increases the dispersion, making the spectrum of the secondary bow about 60% wider than that of the primary bow (after taking the 0.5° diameter of the Sun into account).

Reversed Spectra: A light ray contributing to the primary rainbow enters the side of a raindrop nearest the convex side of the rainbow, is deviated through 138°, and exits near the opposite side of the drop heading toward the observer (see Figure 2). Long wavelengths are refracted least, emerging at a steeper angle to the rainbow axis, so the convex side of the primary rainbow appears red. A light ray contributing to the secondary rainbow is deviated through 231°. To reach the observer, the ray must rotate through the raindrop in the *opposite* sense to the path followed by the primary rainbow ray. Long wavelengths are refracted least, emerging at a shallower angle to the rainbow axis, so the concave side of the secondary rainbow appears red. Thus the spectral sequences are reversed, with the red of both bows bordering upon the space that is between the bows.

Alexander's Dark Band: With a raindrop-mandated minimum deviation of 138° for the light of the primary rainbow and 231° in the opposite sense for the light of the secondary rainbow, there is a 138° + 231° − 360° = 9° gap into which the light contributing to the two rainbows cannot enter. Thus the sky between the bows is darker than elsewhere, a feature called *Alexander's Dark Band* after Alexander of Aphrodisias, a Greek philosopher who drew attention to it c. 200 AD. The "dark" band is only moderately darker than the region beneath the primary rainbow because of three sources of light between the bows: skylight, external reflections off raindrops (see Figure 1), and diffraction of light waves by the raindrops.

The Tertiary Rainbow: Edmund Halley (1656–1742) first calculated that light rays exiting a raindrop after *three* reflections have a minimum angle of deviation of 318°, placing the *tertiary* rainbow only 42° from the Sun. For at least 2000 years people had been looking for a tertiary rainbow in the vicinity of the primary and secondary rainbows. They had been looking in the wrong part of the sky! The luminance (surface brightness) of the secondary rainbow is less than that of the primary, and the luminance of the tertiary rainbow is less than that of the secondary because of three effects: (1) Light rays contributing to successively higher-order rainbows strike raindrops closer to grazing incidence, causing a greater fraction of the light to reflect without entering the drops. (2) Some light exits the drops at each internal reflection leaving less for higher-order rainbows. (3) Rainbow width increases as the order increases, spreading the light over a greater area. There is little hope of seeing the faint tertiary rainbow because it is overwhelmed by two sources of white light in that region of the sky (see Figure 1): (1) *Most* of the sunlight entering raindrops passes through without being internally reflected and illuminates the sunward half of the sky. (The lack of a stationary angle in the deviation of these bright, unreflected rays is why there is no "zero-order" rainbow.) (2) Sunlight externally reflected from raindrops. The quaternary rainbow, fainter again than the tertiary, also occurs in the bright sunward half of the sky, about 44° from the Sun. Higher-order rainbows also occur, but only the primary and secondary bows are visible in the sky.

Banding Beneath: The concave side of a primary rainbow may display two or three narrow bands, called *supernumerary bows* or *supernumerary arcs*. They are caused by the interference of two emerging parallel light rays that have entered a raindrop slightly nearer to and farther from grazing incidence than a ray that undergoes minimum deviation. The two paths have different lengths causing interference. Similar pairs of rays emerging at various angles produce the supernumerary bow pattern. British physicist Thomas Young (1773–1829) was the first to present this explanation, although more accurate descriptions involving diffraction were later provided by British astronomer George Airy (1801–1892), German physicist Gustav Mie (1868–1957), and Canadian meteorologist Alistair Fraser (in 1983).

Hamburger Buns and a Pot of Gold: The hamburger-bun distortion of raindrops with increasing drop size has the greatest effect on the top part of a rainbow because light rays in that region traverse a vertical cross section of a raindrop. The distortion has two consequences for the rainbow:

First, the distortion substantially increases the minimum deviation angle such that light from large raindrops of various diameters is spread into a white haze beneath the primary rainbow. Only spherical drops (diameters of about 0.5 mm and smaller) contribute to the upper part of a rainbow, often causing it to be less bright and its colours less vivid than in the lower part of the bow (assuming the Sun is low in the sky so the lower part of the rainbow is at a steep angle to the horizon). In the lower part, drops of all sizes present circular cross sections to light rays that are redirected toward the observer. Thus *all* drops contribute to the lower part of the rainbow, making it the brightest part when there is a heavy rainfall with a wide range of drop sizes. As Lee and Fraser surmise in their book *The Rainbow Bridge,* the bright glow of vivid colours near the end of the rainbow may be the origin of the pot of gold myth.

Second, the distortion-induced modification in the shift of the position of supernumerary bows with drop size causes distinct supernumerary bows to occur only for raindrops having diameters in the range of about 0.4 to 0.8 mm, and only in the upper part of a rainbow. The contributions of larger and smaller drops are blurred due to overlap. A bright rainbow *without* supernumerary bows typically involves a heavy rain shower during which there is a wide range of drop diameters. Drops in the 0.4 to 0.8 mm range are present, but the bright area beneath the primary rainbow caused by larger raindrops obscures their otherwise distinct supernumerary bows.

Beware of Sunglasses: The reflection that rainbow light undergoes inside a raindrop occurs very near *Brewster's angle* at which light reflected from a nonmetallic surface becomes 100% polarized (named in honour of Scottish physicist Sir David Brewster (1781–1868), who discovered this phenomenon). Thus the light of a rainbow is almost 100% polarized. The direction of polarization (the direction of the electric field) is tangent to the bow, which for the upper part of a rainbow has the same orientation as that of partially polarized light reflecting from the dash of a car, a highway, or a body of water. Polarizing sunglasses are designed to block polarized light from the latter three sources and will obliterate a rainbow!

Rainbows at Night: Observations of lunar rainbows are rare. The Moon is bright enough to produce a noticeable rainbow only when it is near its full phase. Also, people are usually indoors at night, and when they do step outside it is often into a light-polluted environment, which rules out any chance of seeing a lunar rainbow. Even when conditions are favourable, few people would notice a lunar rainbow because it is too dim to activate colour vision and therefore appears white.

Not a Good Spectrum: The rainbow is often cited as the paragon of a white light spectrum. However, five factors make the rainbow spectrum inferior to that produced by a laboratory spectroscope. (1) The minimum property of the stationary angle that produces a rainbow means that light of each wavelength is spread over larger angles, resulting in some overlap of the spectral colours. (2) The Sun is not a point source of light. The 0.5° spread of its rays smears the rainbow spectrum. (3) Sunlight reflected from the front of the raindrops and skylight from behind dilutes the colours making them less saturated. (4) The increase in the minimum angle of deviation associated with aerodynamic drop distortion (significant for drop diameters of 0.5 mm and larger) causes additional spectral smearing in the upper part of a rainbow. (5) Diffraction broadening results in further overlap of the spectral colours, particularly for small raindrops. In the case of fog or cloud (drop diameters in the range 0.01 to 0.1 mm), diffraction broadening causes the various colours to overlap sufficiently to produce a white rainbow, called a *fogbow.* Also known as a *cloudbow,* it may sometimes be seen from an airplane, a large white arc moving along on a cloud layer below the airplane.

Fog and Flashlight: A dark, foggy night provides an opportunity to see the stationary angle that is the key to a primary rainbow. Place a bright, well-collimated flashlight on the ground with its beam directed vertically upward into the fog. Step back a short distance and examine the vertical shaft of light. Look for a bright patch about 40° from the zenith. Fog droplets at that position preferentially redirect the light downward toward your eyes. Diffraction causes the stationary angle to deviate somewhat from the nominal 42° produced by larger drops. Diffraction broadening may make the faint patch of light from the secondary bow undetectable. It will be located about 54° from the zenith, below the fragment of the primary bow.

Rainbow Light on the Moon: The greater part of Earth's albedo is due to clouds. An observer on the Moon would see Earth brighten noticeably for several hours when the Sun–Earth–Moon angle is near 40° and the cloud droplets provide a 2°-diameter fragment of a cloudbow. At this point the Moon is in its crescent phase, about 3 days from new, and earthshine will be enhanced. At Sinus Iridum, the Bay of Rainbows, twice each lunar night the plains and surrounding mountains are bathed in the light of a tattered fragment of a white primary rainbow enveloping Earth.

We Are Part of the Rainbow: Although rain and sunlight have been part of Earth's environment for four billion years, coloured rainbows occurred quite recently with the appearance of animals possessing colour vision. Our visual world with its brightness and colours occurs within our skull. Nevertheless, by some feat of mental projection we think that our visual world coincides spatially with the external world. Thus we confuse the neural rainbow with the external rainbow, and naively attribute the indescribable colours of the former to the latter. Three centuries ago Sir Isaac Newton, aware of this overpowering illusion, wrote: "The rays to speak properly are not coloured. In them there is nothing else than a certain power and disposition to stir up a sensation of this or that colour." Yet, even today, most people regard the cone cells of the retina as "colour receptors," as if colours existed in the external world. They speak of "the true colours of moonbows and nebulae revealed by time-exposure photographs," unaware that they are attributing a unique property of the neural photograph in their brain to the external photograph in their hands, and subsequently to moonbows and nebulae in the sky. The eye does not detect the colours of the rainbow; the brain creates them. *We* are part of the rainbow, its most beautiful part.

Halos

Under normal conditions of temperature and pressure, the wave and statistical properties of electrons impose hexagonal crystalline structure on water ice. When sunlight interacts with ice crystals in the frosty sky, it translates the atomic architecture into macroscopic aerial patterns of striking symmetry.

Small ice crystals suspended in the air can have a variety of shapes, including multi-crystalline fragments in which the sixfold symmetry is not obvious, rods that resemble pieces of a hexagonal pencil (unsharpened), flat six-sided plates, and snowflakes with their elegant symmetry.

Alternate sides of a hexagonal ice crystal form a 60° prism (see Figure 3). Light passing through this prism is deviated by the two refractions, the angle of deviation being a minimum (about 22°) when the passage is symmetric, with equal refractions at the two surfaces. As in the case of minimum deviation in a water drop, a significant fraction of the light passing through randomly oriented 60° ice prisms is deviated by approximately 22°, enhancing the brightness at that angle.

Adjacent sides of a hexagonal crystal form a 120° prism, but light cannot pass through such a prism; the light undergoes total internal reflection at the second surface. Opposite sides of a hexagonal crystal are parallel and, like a windowpane, provide no net deviation. End faces of the crystal form 90° prisms with the sides; light passing through a 90° ice prism undergoes a minimum deviation of about 46° when the passage is symmetric.

Crystals having lengths about equal to their widths (called "blocks"; see Figure 3) assume random orientations as they fall. Consequently, the refraction of light rays toward an observer by blocks has symmetry about the Sun–observer axis, and the observer sees a *halo* of light in the sky, centred on the Sun and having an angular

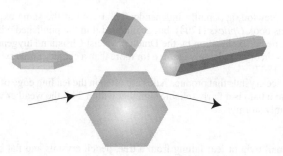

FIGURE 3 *The bottom diagram shows a light ray undergoing a net minimum deviation of 22° when it refracts symmetrically through alternate sides of a hexagonal ice crystal (in effect, a 60° ice prism). The top three diagrams show hexagonal ice crystals having, from left-to-right, increasing length-to-width ratios: a plate, a block, and a pencil. When falling, aerodynamic forces cause the plate and the pencil to orient horizontally, as shown. The block can have any orientation. Plates produce sundogs (refraction) and pillars (reflection). Blocks produce halos (refraction). Pencils produce pillars (reflection) and tangent arcs (refraction).*

FIGURE 4 *A schematic diagram of a 22° halo with sundogs, and a corona and pillar adjacent to the Sun low near the horizon in the centre. Hexagonal ice crystals are in the sky: plates (refraction/sundogs, reflection/pillar); blocks (refraction/halo); and both types of crystal (diffraction/corona). The absence of an upward-curving tangent arc at the top of the halo indicates that pencil crystals are not present.*

radius of 22° (about one hand-span from the Sun at arm's length). See Figure 4. More rarely, refraction in 90° block prisms results in an immense but fainter 46° halo, concentric with the 22° halo. Like the rainbow, a halo is not a circular hoop but a fragmented conical structure seen from its apex. Moonlight can also produce halos, particularly if the Moon is bright, near its full phase.

Because the 22° stationary angle of deviation is a minimum, the halo has a relatively sharp inner edge and a diffuse outer edge, the sky being brighter on the convex side of the halo. Because the deviation is least at the red end of the spectrum, the inner edge of a halo may appear reddish; however, ice crystals are not as optically perfect as raindrops, so the spectral colours of halos are not as pronounced as in rainbows.

The first person to understand the geometry of the 22° halo (i.e. minimum deviation in 60° ice prisms) was the French scientist Edme Mariotte (1620–1684).

Sir Isaac Newton, apparently independently, arrived at the same explanation when writing his book *Opticks* (1704), but abandoned it in the published editions in favour of an erroneous explanation by the Dutch physicist Christian Huygens (1629–1695). Mariotte's theory was largely ignored for more than a century until revived by Thomas Young in 1807.

The ice crystals that produce halos are often in the leading edge of a low-pressure system, so a halo is a fairly reliable sign that within 24 h the weather will be overcast and possibly stormy.

Sundogs

Like a small twig or leaf falling from a tree, pencil crystals and flat crystals such as snowflakes and plates are dynamically stable when oriented horizontally as they fall, maximizing air resistance (see Figure 3). If ice crystals in the air are predominately plates, only those crystals at the same altitude as the Sun can refract light to the observer (provided the Sun is low in the sky), resulting in two bright spots 22° on either side of the Sun (see Figure 4). Called *sundogs* or *parhelia,* under favourable conditions these spots can be almost too bright to look at. Although sundogs appear as spots in the sky, the contributing 60° ice prisms lie along the arms of a 44° "V" with the observer's eye at its vertex.

Rays passing nonsymmetrically through 60° plate prisms are deviated more than 22°, resulting in tails or smearing of the sundogs away from the Sun (see Figure 4). Also, like the 22° halo, sundogs often display a hazy spectrum with red on their sunward side.

Sundogs (or *moondogs,* if the Moon is the light source) may appear singly or in pairs (plate crystals) and may be accompanied by a 22° halo (blocks in addition to plates). Or only a 22° halo may be present (only blocks, or if plates are also present the Sun is too high in the sky for its rays to access the 60° prisms of these horizontally oriented crystals). If the Sun is moderately high in the sky (altitude ~30°), thick plates can still result in sundogs, but the skew rays involved displace the sundogs somewhat farther than 22° from the Sun.

Pillars

In cold weather when the Sun or Moon is near or just below the horizon, a vertical column or *pillar* of light sometimes is seen, extending upward from the Sun or Moon (see Figure 4). On winter nights, tall narrow pillars sometimes extend into the sky, the light sources being unshielded streetlights, often not in direct line of sight. Pillars (also known as *snow pillars*) are caused by plate crystals and/or snowflakes with their mirror-like faces oriented horizontally in the air. Reflections from pencil crystals can also produce pillars. *All* these miniature mirrors throughout the sky reflect light, but only those lying near the vertical plane passing through the light source and an observer reflect light toward the observer; hence the observer sees a vertical pillar. The crystals producing the pillar are located between the light source and the observer.

When sundogs accompany a Sun pillar, plate crystals provide at least some of the mirrors causing the pillar. When a short, upward-curving arc tangent to the top of a 22° halo accompanies a Sun pillar, reflections off the sides of pencil crystals contribute to the pillar, the *tangent arc* being due to refraction in the 60° prisms of the horizontally oriented pencils.

Coronae

In the presence of thin, high cloud, hazy bright rings may closely surround the Sun or Moon, a pattern called a *corona* (not to be confused with the solar corona, the hot outer atmosphere of the Sun itself). Lying within several diameters of the Sun or Moon (see Figure 4), a corona often displays pale colours, including a reddish outer border—the reverse of the refraction-based reddish *inner* border of halos and sundogs. The red-reversal indicates that the corona is caused not by refraction but by diffraction scattering of light waves.

The scattering bodies are usually cloud droplets but can be small ice crystals or even pollen grains. The smaller the scattering bodies, the larger the corona; the more uniform their size, the more obvious the ring structure. Thin clouds passing near the Sun or Moon may display a colourful iridescence associated with evaporation-induced variations in drop size, although in the case of the Sun the display may be too bright to view. Very small particles, such as are injected high into the atmosphere by volcanic eruptions, result in a large corona called a *Bishop's Ring.*

When cloud droplets are involved, a corona is caused by light rays that graze the sides of the water drops without entering the drops, and by rays that pass directly through the drops. The theory describing diffraction scattering is complex, and it is not possible to give a simple explanation of the structure and size of the corona. Note that the corona involves scattering of each light ray by only one drop; scattering by multiple drops eliminates the iridescence and structure of the corona.

Glories

The *glory* resembles the corona and is also caused by diffraction scattering of light waves by fog or cloud droplets; however, the glory occurs on the opposite side of the sky, surrounding the antisolar point. Like the corona, the angular size of the glory (seldom more than a few degrees) varies inversely with the size of the scattering drops. Despite the similarity of the corona and the glory, it is easy to remember which is which: the corona is in the same part of the sky as the solar corona (assuming the Sun, not the Moon, to be the light source of the corona).

Usually seen from an airplane on a cloud layer below, the glory appears as a ring-like pattern of hazy colours centred on the observer's position in the shadow of the airplane. If the cloud layer is sufficiently far from the plane, the plane's shadow (then penumbral only) will not be visible. Mountain climbers sometimes see a glory in a cloud (fog) layer below them. If the fog is close, the climber's shadow, distorted by perspective, will appear to the climber as a dark cavity in the fog with its head centred in the glory, a strange apparition called *the spectre of the Brocken* after a mountain in Germany where the phenomenon has often been observed.

In religious art, the rings or disks of light surrounding the heads of saintly figures were likely inspired by observations of the glory, and possibly the heiligenschein (see below). Certainly it flatters an observer to see an aureole surrounding the shadow of one's own head and not those of others!

The glory involves scattering of a light ray by one drop, whereas a white cloud involves scattering of a light ray by more than one drop—which is why clouds are otherwise white. As in the case of the corona, the theory describing the glory is complex, and it is not possible to give a simple explanation of the structure and size of the glory. Light waves moving along the surface of small water drops and reflections within the drops are both involved.

Heiligenschein

Heiligenschein (German for "holy light") refers to a diffuse colourless glow surrounding the shadow of the observer's head when that shadow is projected on a rough surface or on vegetation covered in dewdrops. Unlike the patterns described above, the heiligenschein is not an atmospheric phenomenon; however, like the glory it surrounds the antisolar point so it should be mentioned.

A rough surface appears brightest when viewed in the antisolar direction because the shadows associated with the roughness are hidden behind the objects casting the shadows. For example, on a sunny day a person walking past shrubbery or a field of grass will see a glowing aura surrounding the shadow of his or her head. A forest viewed from an airplane displays a bright patch surrounding the shadow of the airplane. In the case of vegetation covered in dewdrops, the spherical drops redirect the incident light back from whence it came, enhancing the brightness associated with hidden shadows. Tiny glass spheres imbedded in highway-marker paint or on automobile license plates do the same. If the Moon had a perfectly diffuse matte surface, at full phase it would provide π times more light than at quarter phase when it is half illuminated; however, because of heiligenschein, at full phase the Moon provides more than ten times as much light—the multitude of shadows on the lunar surface are hidden, and impact-produced glass beads littering the lunar surface redirect sunlight toward Earth.

None of these apparitions—rainbows, halos, sundogs, pillars, coronae, glories, and heiligenschein—are objects in the normal sense of the word. They are patterns of light specific to the individual observer. Anyone who understands them will find the world to be a more interesting place.

References
Benn, C.R., "Rainbows, Haloes, and Earthshine," *The Observatory 114*, No. 1120 (1994), p. 115.
Boyer, C.B., *The Rainbow: From Myth to Mathematics,* Princeton University Press, 1987.
Fraser, A.B., "Why Can the Supernumerary Bows Be Seen in a Rain Shower?" *J. Opt. Soc. Am. 73* (1983), p. 1626.
Greenler, R., *Rainbows, Halos, and Glories,* Cambridge University Press, 1980.
Lee, R.L., Jr., "Mie Theory, Airy Theory, and the natural rainbow," *Appl. Opt. 37* (1998), p. 1506.
Lee, R.L., Jr. and Fraser, A.B., *The Rainbow Bridge,* Pennsylvania State University Press, 2001.
Minnaert, M., *Light and Colour in the open air,* Bell and Sons, 1940.
Newton, I., *Opticks* (4th ed. 1730), Dover Publications, 1952.
Nussenzveig, H.M., "The Theory of the Rainbow," *Sci. Am. 236* (4) (1977), p. 116.
Shapiro, A.E., "Newton and Huygens' Explanation of the 22° Halo," *Centaurus 24* (1980), p. 273.
Walker, J., "Rainbows in a Water Drop," *Sci. Am.,* July 1977, p. 138.
Walker, J., "Mysteries of Rainbows," *Sci. Am.,* June 1980, p. 174.
Wright, W.D., *The Rays are not Coloured,* Adam Hilger Ltd., London, 1967.

Web sites:
www.atoptics.co.uk
www.meteoros.de/haloe.htm
www.philiplaven.com/index1.html

TIMES OF SUNRISE AND SUNSET
BY RAJIV GUPTA

The table on the following two pages gives the times of sunrise and sunset at four-day intervals for locations ranging from 20° to 60° north latitude. "Rise" and "set" correspond to the upper limb of the Sun appearing at the horizon for an observer at sea level. The times are local mean time (LMT) for the Greenwich meridian (i.e. UT at 0° longitude), although for North American observers the stated values may be read directly as LMT at the observer's position with an error less than 1 min. The table may be interpolated linearly for both nontabular latitudes and dates, and can be extrapolated beyond the 20° and 60° latitude limits a few degrees without significant loss of accuracy.

It is a common misconception that extreme values for sunrise and sunset times occur on the shortest and the longest days of the year. This is not the case and is due to the tilt of Earth's spin axis to the axis of its orbit and to Earth's varying speed along its elliptical orbit (as Kepler described in his second law). At midnorthern latitudes, the earliest sunset occurs early in December and the latest sunrise in early January whereas the shortest day (in the sense of hours of daylight) is Dec. 21 or 22. For more information see *Sky & Telescope*, December 1988, p. 674 and July 1972, p. 20, and an article by Terence Hicks in *JRASC, 88*, p. 86, February 1994.

The standard time of an event at a particular location must take account of the observer's longitude relative to his or her standard meridian (see STANDARD TIME ZONES on pp. 50–51). The table below lists the latitude and the longitude correction (in minutes of time) for a number of cities in Canada and the United States. For example, to find the time of sunrise at Boston on 2008 May 18: the latitude is 42°, and from the table the time of sunrise at 0° longitude is 4:37 UT (after interpolating for latitude). Thus, at Boston, the time of sunrise will be approximately 4:37 LMT. Boston is in the Eastern time zone (E) and is 16 minutes of time east of the standard meridian for this zone (75°W). Thus, sunrise in Boston will occur at 5:21 EDT (Eastern Daylight Time). The longitude correction for any location may be found by converting the difference between the longitude of the place and that of its standard meridian to time (1° = 4 minutes of time), the correction being + if the place is west of its standard meridian, – if east. **Note**: Due to a difference in height between the observer and the actual horizon, the observed time may differ by several minutes from the predicted time.

Canadian Cities				American Cities	
Belleville	44° +10E	Québec	47° −15E	Atlanta	34° +37E
Calgary	51° +36M	Regina	50° +58C	Boston	42° −16E
Charlottetown	46° +12A	Resolute	75° +20C	Chicago	42° −10C
Corner Brook	49° +22N	Rimouski	48° −26E	Cincinnati	39° +38E
Edmonton	54° +34M	Saint John	45° +24A	Denver	40° 0M
Halifax	45° +14A	St. John's	48° +1N	Fairbanks	65° +50A
Hamilton	43° +20E	Sarnia	43° +29E	Flagstaff	35° +27M
Kelowna	50° −3P	Saskatoon	52° +67C	Kansas City	39° +18C
Kingston	44° +6E	Sudbury	47° +24E	Los Angeles	34° −7P
Kitchener	43° +22E	Thunder Bay	48° +57E	Miami	26° +21E
London	43° +25E	Toronto	44° +18E	Minneapolis	45° +13C
Moncton	46° +19A	Vancouver	49° +12P	New Orleans	30° 0C
Montréal	46° −6E	Victoria	48° +13P	New York	41° −4E
Niagara Falls	43° +16E	Whitehorse	61° +60P	San Francisco	38° +10P
Ottawa	45° +3E	Windsor, Ont.	42° +32E	Seattle	48° +9P
Pangnirtung	66° +23A	Winnipeg	50° +29C	Tucson	32° +24M
Prince George	54° +11P	Yellowknife	62° +38M	Washington	39° +8E

SUNRISE AND SUNSET, 2008 JANUARY–JUNE
UNIVERSAL TIME AT GREENWICH MERIDIAN

Latitude:	+20°		+30°		+35°		+40°		+45°		+50°		+55°		+60°	
Event:	RISE	SET	RISE	SET	RISE	SET	RISE	SET	RISE	SET	RISE	SET	RISE	SET	RISE	SET
Jan. -1	6:34	17:31	6:55	17:10	7:07	16:57	7:21	16:43	7:38	16:27	7:59	16:06	8:25	15:40	9:03	15:02
3	6:36	17:33	6:56	17:12	7:08	17:00	7:22	16:47	7:38	16:30	7:58	16:10	8:25	15:44	9:02	15:07
7	6:37	17:36	6:57	17:15	7:09	17:04	7:22	16:50	7:38	16:34	7:57	16:15	8:23	15:50	8:58	15:14
11	6:37	17:38	6:57	17:19	7:08	17:07	7:21	16:54	7:37	16:39	7:56	16:20	8:20	15:56	8:54	15:22
15	6:38	17:41	6:57	17:22	7:08	17:11	7:20	16:58	7:35	16:44	7:53	16:26	8:16	16:03	8:49	15:30
19	6:38	17:43	6:56	17:25	7:07	17:15	7:19	17:03	7:33	16:49	7:50	16:32	8:12	16:10	8:42	15:40
23	6:38	17:46	6:55	17:29	7:05	17:19	7:16	17:08	7:30	16:54	7:46	16:38	8:07	16:17	8:35	15:49
27	6:37	17:49	6:53	17:32	7:03	17:23	7:13	17:12	7:26	17:00	7:41	16:45	8:00	16:25	8:27	16:00
31	6:36	17:51	6:51	17:36	7:00	17:27	7:10	17:17	7:22	17:05	7:36	16:51	7:54	16:34	8:18	16:10
Feb. 4	6:35	17:53	6:49	17:39	6:57	17:31	7:06	17:22	7:17	17:11	7:30	16:58	7:46	16:42	8:08	16:20
8	6:33	17:55	6:46	17:43	6:54	17:35	7:02	17:27	7:12	17:17	7:24	17:05	7:39	16:50	7:58	16:31
12	6:31	17:58	6:43	17:46	6:50	17:39	6:58	17:32	7:06	17:23	7:17	17:12	7:30	16:59	7:48	16:42
16	6:29	17:59	6:40	17:49	6:46	17:43	6:53	17:36	7:01	17:28	7:10	17:19	7:22	17:07	7:37	16:52
20	6:27	18:01	6:36	17:52	6:41	17:47	6:47	17:41	6:54	17:34	7:03	17:26	7:13	17:16	7:26	17:03
24	6:24	18:03	6:32	17:55	6:37	17:51	6:42	17:45	6:48	17:40	6:55	17:33	7:04	17:24	7:15	17:13
28	6:21	18:04	6:28	17:58	6:32	17:54	6:36	17:50	6:41	17:45	6:47	17:39	6:54	17:32	7:03	17:23
Mar. 3	6:18	18:06	6:23	18:01	6:27	17:58	6:30	17:54	6:34	17:51	6:39	17:46	6:44	17:40	6:52	17:33
7	6:15	18:07	6:19	18:03	6:21	18:01	6:24	17:59	6:27	17:56	6:30	17:53	6:34	17:48	6:40	17:43
11	6:12	18:09	6:14	18:06	6:16	18:05	6:18	18:03	6:19	18:01	6:22	17:59	6:24	17:56	6:28	17:53
15	6:08	18:10	6:10	18:09	6:10	18:08	6:11	18:07	6:12	18:06	6:13	18:05	6:14	18:04	6:16	18:03
19	6:05	18:11	6:05	18:11	6:05	18:11	6:05	18:11	6:05	18:12	6:04	18:12	6:04	18:12	6:04	18:13
23	6:01	18:12	6:00	18:13	5:59	18:14	5:58	18:15	5:57	18:17	5:56	18:18	5:54	18:20	5:52	18:23
27	5:58	18:13	5:55	18:16	5:54	18:18	5:52	18:19	5:50	18:22	5:47	18:25	5:44	18:28	5:40	18:32
31	5:54	18:14	5:50	18:18	5:48	18:21	5:45	18:24	5:42	18:27	5:38	18:31	5:34	18:36	5:27	18:42
Apr. 4	5:51	18:15	5:46	18:21	5:42	18:24	5:39	18:28	5:35	18:32	5:30	18:37	5:23	18:44	5:15	18:52
8	5:47	18:16	5:41	18:23	5:37	18:27	5:33	18:32	5:27	18:37	5:21	18:43	5:13	18:51	5:03	19:02
12	5:44	18:17	5:36	18:26	5:32	18:30	5:26	18:36	5:20	18:42	5:13	18:50	5:04	18:59	4:51	19:12
16	5:41	18:19	5:32	18:28	5:26	18:34	5:20	18:40	5:13	18:47	5:05	18:56	4:54	19:07	4:40	19:21
20	5:38	18:20	5:28	18:31	5:22	18:37	5:15	18:44	5:06	18:52	4:57	19:02	4:44	19:15	4:28	19:31
24	5:35	18:21	5:24	18:33	5:17	18:40	5:09	18:48	5:00	18:57	4:49	19:08	4:35	19:23	4:17	19:41
28	5:33	18:23	5:20	18:36	5:12	18:43	5:04	18:52	4:54	19:02	4:41	19:15	4:26	19:30	4:05	19:51
May 2	5:30	18:24	5:16	18:38	5:08	18:46	4:59	18:56	4:48	19:07	4:34	19:21	4:17	19:38	3:54	20:01
6	5:28	18:26	5:13	18:41	5:04	18:50	4:54	19:00	4:42	19:12	4:27	19:27	4:09	19:46	3:44	20:11
10	5:26	18:27	5:10	18:43	5:00	18:53	4:49	19:04	4:37	19:17	4:21	19:33	4:01	19:53	3:34	20:21
14	5:24	18:29	5:07	18:46	4:57	18:56	4:46	19:08	4:32	19:22	4:15	19:38	3:54	20:00	3:24	20:30
18	5:23	18:30	5:05	18:48	4:54	18:59	4:42	19:11	4:28	19:26	4:10	19:44	3:47	20:07	3:15	20:40
22	5:22	18:32	5:03	18:51	4:52	19:02	4:39	19:15	4:24	19:30	4:05	19:49	3:41	20:14	3:06	20:49
26	5:21	18:34	5:01	18:53	4:50	19:05	4:36	19:18	4:20	19:34	4:01	19:54	3:35	20:20	2:59	20:57
30	5:20	18:35	5:00	18:56	4:48	19:08	4:34	19:21	4:18	19:38	3:57	19:59	3:30	20:26	2:52	21:05
Jun. 3	5:20	18:37	4:59	18:58	4:47	19:10	4:32	19:24	4:15	19:41	3:54	20:03	3:27	20:31	2:46	21:11
7	5:20	18:38	4:58	19:00	4:46	19:12	4:31	19:27	4:14	19:44	3:52	20:06	3:24	20:35	2:41	21:17
11	5:20	18:39	4:58	19:01	4:46	19:14	4:31	19:29	4:13	19:47	3:51	20:09	3:21	20:38	2:38	21:22
15	5:21	18:41	4:59	19:03	4:46	19:16	4:31	19:31	4:13	19:49	3:50	20:11	3:20	20:41	2:36	21:25
19	5:21	18:42	4:59	19:04	4:46	19:17	4:31	19:32	4:13	19:50	3:50	20:13	3:20	20:43	2:36	21:27
23	5:22	18:43	5:00	19:05	4:47	19:18	4:32	19:33	4:14	19:51	3:51	20:13	3:21	20:43	2:36	21:28
27	5:23	18:43	5:01	19:05	4:48	19:18	4:33	19:33	4:15	19:51	3:53	20:13	3:23	20:43	2:39	21:27

SUNRISE AND SUNSET, 2008 JULY–DECEMBER
UNIVERSAL TIME AT GREENWICH MERIDIAN

Latitude:	+20°	+30°	+35°	+40°	+45°	+50°	+55°	+60°
Event:	RISE SET	RISE SET	RISE SET	RISE SET	RISE SET	RISE SET	RISE SET	RISE SET
Jul. 1	5:24 18:43	5:03 19:05	4:50 19:18	4:35 19:33	4:17 19:50	3:55 20:12	3:26 20:42	2:43 21:25
5	5:26 18:44	5:04 19:05	4:52 19:17	4:37 19:32	4:20 19:49	3:58 20:11	3:29 20:39	2:47 21:21
9	5:27 18:43	5:06 19:04	4:54 19:16	4:40 19:31	4:23 19:47	4:02 20:08	3:34 20:36	2:53 21:16
13	5:29 18:43	5:08 19:03	4:56 19:15	4:42 19:29	4:26 19:45	4:06 20:05	3:39 20:32	3:00 21:10
17	5:30 18:42	5:10 19:02	4:59 19:13	4:46 19:26	4:30 19:42	4:10 20:01	3:45 20:27	3:08 21:03
21	5:32 18:41	5:13 19:00	5:02 19:11	4:49 19:24	4:34 19:39	4:15 19:57	3:51 20:21	3:16 20:55
25	5:33 18:40	5:15 18:58	5:04 19:08	4:52 19:20	4:38 19:35	4:20 19:52	3:57 20:15	3:25 20:46
29	5:34 18:38	5:17 18:55	5:07 19:05	4:56 19:16	4:42 19:30	4:26 19:46	4:04 20:08	3:34 20:37
Aug. 2	5:36 18:36	5:20 18:52	5:10 19:02	5:00 19:12	4:47 19:25	4:31 19:40	4:11 20:00	3:44 20:27
6	5:37 18:34	5:22 18:49	5:13 18:58	5:03 19:08	4:51 19:20	4:37 19:34	4:18 19:52	3:53 20:17
10	5:39 18:32	5:25 18:46	5:16 18:54	5:07 19:03	4:56 19:14	4:43 19:27	4:26 19:44	4:03 20:06
14	5:40 18:29	5:27 18:42	5:19 18:49	5:11 18:58	5:01 19:08	4:49 19:20	4:33 19:35	4:13 19:55
18	5:41 18:26	5:29 18:38	5:22 18:44	5:15 18:52	5:06 19:01	4:55 19:12	4:41 19:26	4:22 19:44
22	5:42 18:23	5:32 18:34	5:25 18:40	5:18 18:46	5:10 18:54	5:00 19:04	4:48 19:16	4:32 19:32
26	5:43 18:20	5:34 18:29	5:28 18:34	5:22 18:40	5:15 18:47	5:06 18:56	4:56 19:06	4:41 19:20
30	5:44 18:17	5:36 18:24	5:31 18:29	5:26 18:34	5:20 18:40	5:12 18:48	5:03 18:57	4:51 19:09
Sep. 3	5:45 18:13	5:38 18:20	5:34 18:24	5:30 18:28	5:25 18:33	5:18 18:39	5:11 18:47	5:00 18:57
7	5:46 18:10	5:40 18:15	5:37 18:18	5:34 18:21	5:29 18:26	5:24 18:30	5:18 18:37	5:10 18:44
11	5:47 18:06	5:43 18:10	5:40 18:12	5:37 18:15	5:34 18:18	5:30 18:22	5:25 18:26	5:19 18:32
15	5:47 18:02	5:45 18:05	5:43 18:07	5:41 18:08	5:39 18:10	5:36 18:13	5:33 18:16	5:28 18:20
19	5:48 17:59	5:47 18:00	5:46 18:01	5:45 18:02	5:44 18:03	5:42 18:04	5:40 18:06	5:38 18:08
23	5:49 17:55	5:49 17:55	5:49 17:55	5:49 17:55	5:49 17:55	5:49 17:55	5:48 17:55	5:47 17:56
27	5:50 17:51	5:51 17:50	5:52 17:49	5:53 17:48	5:53 17:48	5:54 17:46	5:55 17:45	5:57 17:44
Oct. 1	5:51 17:48	5:53 17:45	5:55 17:44	5:56 17:42	5:58 17:40	6:00 17:38	6:03 17:35	6:06 17:32
5	5:52 17:44	5:56 17:40	5:58 17:38	6:00 17:35	6:03 17:33	6:07 17:29	6:11 17:25	6:16 17:20
9	5:53 17:41	5:58 17:36	6:01 17:33	6:04 17:29	6:08 17:25	6:13 17:21	6:18 17:15	6:25 17:08
13	5:54 17:38	6:01 17:31	6:04 17:27	6:09 17:23	6:13 17:18	6:19 17:12	6:26 17:05	6:35 16:56
17	5:56 17:35	6:03 17:27	6:08 17:22	6:13 17:17	6:19 17:11	6:26 17:04	6:34 16:56	6:45 16:44
21	5:57 17:32	6:06 17:23	6:11 17:17	6:17 17:11	6:24 17:05	6:32 16:56	6:42 16:46	6:55 16:33
25	5:59 17:29	6:09 17:19	6:15 17:13	6:21 17:06	6:29 16:58	6:39 16:49	6:50 16:37	7:05 16:22
29	6:00 17:27	6:12 17:15	6:18 17:08	6:26 17:01	6:35 16:52	6:45 16:42	6:58 16:28	7:15 16:11
Nov. 2	6:02 17:25	6:15 17:12	6:22 17:05	6:30 16:56	6:40 16:46	6:52 16:35	7:06 16:20	7:26 16:01
6	6:04 17:23	6:18 17:09	6:26 17:01	6:35 16:52	6:46 16:41	6:58 16:28	7:15 16:12	7:36 15:51
10	6:06 17:22	6:21 17:06	6:30 16:58	6:40 16:48	6:51 16:36	7:05 16:22	7:23 16:05	7:46 15:41
14	6:08 17:20	6:24 17:04	6:34 16:55	6:44 16:44	6:57 16:32	7:12 16:17	7:31 15:58	7:56 15:32
18	6:11 17:20	6:28 17:02	6:38 16:53	6:49 16:41	7:02 16:28	7:18 16:12	7:38 15:51	8:06 15:24
22	6:13 17:19	6:31 17:01	6:41 16:51	6:53 16:39	7:07 16:25	7:24 16:08	7:46 15:46	8:16 15:16
26	6:16 17:19	6:34 17:00	6:45 16:49	6:58 16:37	7:12 16:22	7:30 16:04	7:53 15:41	8:25 15:09
30	6:18 17:19	6:38 17:00	6:49 16:48	7:02 16:35	7:17 16:20	7:36 16:01	8:00 15:37	8:34 15:04
Dec. 4	6:21 17:20	6:41 17:00	6:52 16:48	7:06 16:35	7:22 16:19	7:41 15:59	8:06 15:34	8:41 14:59
8	6:23 17:21	6:44 17:00	6:56 16:48	7:09 16:35	7:26 16:18	7:46 15:58	8:11 15:32	8:48 14:56
12	6:26 17:22	6:47 17:01	6:59 16:49	7:13 16:35	7:29 16:18	7:50 15:58	8:16 15:31	8:54 14:54
16	6:28 17:24	6:49 17:02	7:01 16:50	7:16 16:36	7:32 16:19	7:53 15:59	8:20 15:32	8:58 14:53
20	6:30 17:25	6:51 17:04	7:04 16:52	7:18 16:38	7:35 16:21	7:56 16:00	8:23 15:33	9:02 14:54
24	6:32 17:28	6:53 17:06	7:06 16:54	7:20 16:40	7:37 16:23	7:57 16:02	8:24 15:35	9:03 14:56
28	6:34 17:30	6:55 17:09	7:07 16:56	7:21 16:42	7:38 16:26	7:58 16:05	8:25 15:38	9:03 15:00
32	6:35 17:32	6:56 17:11	7:08 16:59	7:22 16:46	7:38 16:29	7:59 16:09	8:25 15:43	9:02 15:05

MIDNIGHT TWILIGHT AND MIDNIGHT SUN
BY ROY BISHOP

Astronomers generally desire dark skies, free of moonlight and man-made light pollution. As mentioned on p. 200, the beginning or end of *astronomical twilight* corresponds to the centre of the Sun being 18° below the horizon. At that point the amount of sunlight scattered by the upper layers of Earth's atmosphere is negligible; that is, it is less than the combined illuminance (about 2×10^{-3} lux) from starlight, airglow, and zodiacal light, the three main contributors to the light of the "dark" night sky.

For observers in countries at high latitudes (e.g. the United Kingdom, Norway, southern Argentina and Chile, and most of Canada), around the time of the summer solstice the Sun always lies less than 18° below the horizon, and the sky does not get dark at night. This "midnight twilight" phenomenon can be displayed in a graph as a function of latitude and time of year.

The following diagram indicates the brightness of the sky at local midnight at any time of the year for any latitude north of 45°N or south of 45°S. Below the lower curve the natural sky is dark. Between the two curves twilight prevails. Above the upper curve the Sun is in the sky. Place names in roman type (left-hand side) are in the Northern Hemisphere; place names in *italic* type (right-hand side) are in the *Southern Hemisphere*. On the horizontal axis use the roman-type months for the former, *italic*-type months for the latter. The diagram is simplified slightly in that the months are assumed to be of equal duration, and the seasonal pattern of months and summer solstices for Earth's two hemispheres are assumed to be identical except for a 6-month phase shift.

The latitude of the Arctic and Antarctic Circles (90° subtract the obliquity of the ecliptic = 66°34′) is indicated by the dashed line. This line is *not* tangent to the Midnight Sun curve because at midnight on the summer solstice at either the Arctic or the Antarctic Circle the Sun is above the horizon. Atmospheric refraction raises the apparent Sun about 34′ above the true Sun. Also, rise/set is defined as the top limb of the Sun at a sea-level horizon; thus the 16′ semidiameter of the Sun must also be taken into account. To see the top limb of the Sun on the horizon at local midnight on the summer solstice, an observer must be 34′ + 16′ = 50′ south of the Arctic Circle (or north of the Antarctic Circle), at latitude 65°44′.

By running a horizontal line across the chart at a selected latitude, the reader can determine the approximate dates when midnight twilight and, possibly, midnight Sun begin and end for any locality at north or south latitudes above 48.6°, the lower limit for midnight twilight on the summer solstice. (Remarkably, when rounded to the nearest degree, the latter figure is the latitude of the longest east–west international border: the 2000-km-long 49th parallel between the United States and western Canada.)

Some examples: The diagram shows that at Grise Fiord (a hamlet on the stunning south coast of Ellesmere Island, and Canada's most northerly community) the sky is never dark from about Mar. 10 until early October, and the midnight Sun lasts from late April until mid-August. Note that Cape Horn at midnight is bathed in dim Antarctic twilight from early November until early February. Even at the latitude of Vancouver there is a period of almost a month each year when the sky never gets astronomically dark—although the natural night sky is obliterated *every* night near any town or city unless there is an electrical power failure! Finally, note that Earth's poles are astronomically dark for less than three months of the year.

MIDNIGHT TWILIGHT AND MIDNIGHT SUN DIAGRAM

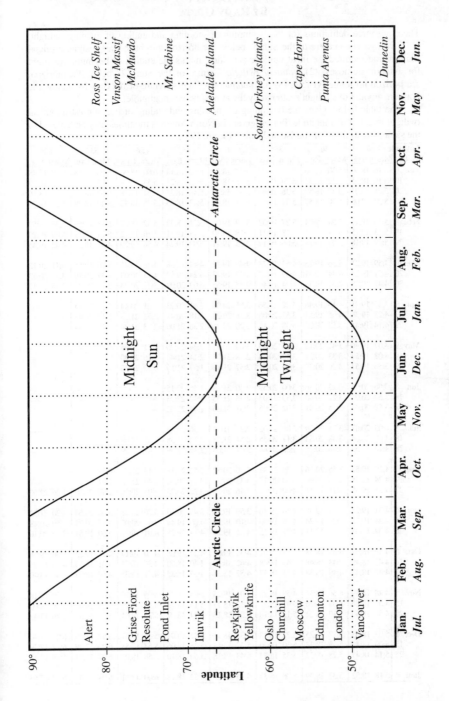

TWILIGHT
By Rajiv Gupta

There are three definitions for the beginning of morning and ending of evening twilight: (1) *Civil twilight*—centre of the Sun 6° below the horizon, brightest stars visible, artificial illumination required for most outdoor activities, marks the ending or beginning of night for aviation purposes; (2) *Nautical twilight*—centre of the Sun 12° below the horizon, sea horizon no longer visible; (3) *Astronomical twilight*—centre of the Sun 18° below the horizon, amount of sunlight scattered by the atmosphere is negligible.

The table below gives the beginning of morning and ending of evening astronomical twilight in UT at 0° longitude. For observers in North America the times may be handled in the same way as those of sunrise and sunset (see p. 195).

Latitude:	+20°		+30°		+35°		+40°		+45°		+50°		+55°		+60°	
M–E:	Morn.	Eve.	Morn.	Eve.	Morn.	Eve.	Morn.	Eve.	Morn.	Eve.	Morn.	Eve.	Morn.	Eve.	Morn.	Eve.
Jan. 0	5:16	18:50	5:30	18:36	5:37	18:29	5:44	18:21	5:52	18:14	6:00	18:06	6:08	17:58	6:18	17:48
10	5:19	18:55	5:32	18:42	5:39	18:36	5:45	18:30	5:52	18:23	5:59	18:16	6:07	18:09	6:15	18:00
20	5:21	19:01	5:32	18:50	5:38	18:44	5:43	18:39	5:49	18:34	5:54	18:28	6:00	18:22	6:06	18:16
30	5:20	19:06	5:30	18:57	5:34	18:53	5:38	18:49	5:42	18:45	5:45	18:42	5:49	18:39	5:52	18:35
Feb. 9	5:18	19:11	5:24	19:04	5:27	19:02	5:29	19:00	5:31	18:58	5:32	18:57	5:33	18:56	5:33	18:57
19	5:13	19:15	5:17	19:11	5:18	19:11	5:18	19:10	5:18	19:11	5:16	19:12	5:14	19:15	5:09	19:20
29	5:07	19:18	5:07	19:18	5:06	19:19	5:05	19:21	5:02	19:24	4:58	19:29	4:51	19:35	4:42	19:45
Mar.10	4:59	19:21	4:56	19:25	4:53	19:28	4:49	19:32	4:44	19:38	4:36	19:45	4:26	19:56	4:11	20:12
20	4:51	19:24	4:44	19:31	4:39	19:37	4:32	19:43	4:24	19:52	4:13	20:03	3:57	20:19	3:35	20:42
30	4:41	19:28	4:31	19:38	4:24	19:46	4:15	19:55	4:03	20:07	3:47	20:23	3:26	20:45	2:55	21:17
Apr. 9	4:32	19:31	4:18	19:46	4:08	19:56	3:56	20:08	3:41	20:23	3:21	20:44	2:52	21:14	2:06	22:02
19	4:23	19:36	4:05	19:54	3:53	20:06	3:38	20:22	3:18	20:41	2:52	21:08	2:13	21:48	0:51	23:19
29	4:14	19:41	3:52	20:03	3:38	20:18	3:20	20:36	2:56	21:00	2:23	21:34	1:26	22:34	—	—
May 9	4:07	19:46	3:41	20:12	3:25	20:29	3:03	20:51	2:34	21:20	1:51	22:05	—	—	—	—
19	4:02	19:52	3:33	20:21	3:13	20:40	2:48	21:06	2:14	21:40	1:16	22:40	—	—	—	—
29	3:58	19:57	3:26	20:29	3:05	20:51	2:37	21:19	1:57	21:59	0:30	23:33	—	—	—	—
Jun. 8	3:56	20:02	3:23	20:36	3:00	20:59	2:30	21:29	1:45	22:15	—	—	—	—	—	—
18	3:57	20:06	3:22	20:40	2:59	21:04	2:28	21:35	1:40	22:23	—	—	—	—	—	—
28	3:59	20:07	3:25	20:41	3:02	21:05	2:31	21:36	1:44	22:22	—	—	—	—	—	—
Jul. 8	4:03	20:07	3:31	20:39	3:08	21:02	2:39	21:31	1:56	22:13	—	—	—	—	—	—
18	4:08	20:04	3:38	20:34	3:17	20:55	2:51	21:21	2:13	21:58	1:01	23:08	—	—	—	—
28	4:14	19:59	3:46	20:26	3:28	20:44	3:04	21:08	2:32	21:39	1:41	22:29	—	—	—	—
Aug. 7	4:19	19:52	3:55	20:16	3:39	20:32	3:19	20:52	2:52	21:18	2:13	21:56	0:51	23:12	—	—
17	4:24	19:44	4:03	20:04	3:50	20:17	3:33	20:34	3:11	20:56	2:40	21:25	1:51	22:13	—	—
27	4:28	19:35	4:11	19:51	4:00	20:02	3:46	20:16	3:28	20:33	3:05	20:56	2:30	21:30	1:26	22:30
Sep. 6	4:31	19:25	4:18	19:38	4:10	19:46	3:59	19:57	3:45	20:10	3:26	20:28	3:00	20:54	2:20	21:32
16	4:34	19:15	4:25	19:24	4:18	19:30	4:10	19:38	4:00	19:48	3:46	20:02	3:27	20:21	2:59	20:48
26	4:37	19:05	4:31	19:11	4:27	19:15	4:21	19:20	4:14	19:28	4:04	19:37	3:50	19:51	3:30	20:10
Oct. 6	4:39	18:57	4:37	18:58	4:35	19:01	4:32	19:04	4:27	19:08	4:20	19:14	4:11	19:23	3:58	19:36
16	4:42	18:49	4:43	18:48	4:43	18:48	4:42	18:49	4:40	18:50	4:36	18:54	4:31	18:59	4:23	19:06
26	4:45	18:43	4:49	18:38	4:51	18:37	4:52	18:36	4:52	18:35	4:51	18:35	4:50	18:37	4:47	18:40
Nov. 5	4:48	18:39	4:56	18:31	4:59	18:28	5:02	18:25	5:04	18:22	5:06	18:20	5:08	18:19	5:09	18:18
15	4:53	18:36	5:03	18:26	5:07	18:22	5:12	18:17	5:16	18:13	5:20	18:09	5:24	18:04	5:29	18:00
25	4:58	18:36	5:10	18:24	5:15	18:18	5:21	18:13	5:27	18:07	5:33	18:01	5:39	17:54	5:46	17:47
Dec. 5	5:03	18:38	5:17	18:25	5:23	18:18	5:30	18:11	5:37	18:04	5:44	17:57	5:52	17:49	6:01	17:40
15	5:09	18:42	5:23	18:28	5:30	18:20	5:37	18:13	5:45	18:06	5:53	17:58	6:02	17:49	6:12	17:39
25	5:14	18:47	5:28	18:32	5:35	18:25	5:43	18:18	5:50	18:10	5:58	18:02	6:07	17:53	6:18	17:43
Jan. 4	5:18	18:52	5:32	18:39	5:38	18:32	5:45	18:25	5:52	18:18	6:00	18:11	6:08	18:02	6:17	17:53

PLANETS AND SATELLITES

THE PLANETS FOR 2008
BY TERENCE DICKINSON

INTRODUCTION

Planetary observing is perhaps the most widely accessible and diversified category of amateur astronomical pursuits. Planets can be seen on almost any clear night of the year. Indeed, in heavily light-polluted cities they are sometimes the *only* celestial objects visible. With dark skies ever more remote from population centres, planetary observing is returning—partly by default—to take its place as an important part of the amateur astronomer's repertoire.

But a factor more important than sky conditions is needed to explain the expanding interest in planetary observing. There is a widespread recognition among amateur astronomers that high-quality optics are essential for good views of the planets; the increased commercial availability of such instruments—especially previously unavailable systems such as apochromatic refractors and Maksutov-Newtonians—means that planetary observing is more accessible than ever.

Planetary observing divides into three distinct categories, each with its opportunities and limitations. *Unaided-eye* observing consists of detecting, identifying, and monitoring the night-to-night and week-to-week motion and visibility of the six brightest planets. *Binoculars* add Neptune along with the Galilean satellites of Jupiter and the crescent phase of Venus. Binoculars are ideal for tracking planetary motion against the backdrop of stars, many of which are too faint for naked-eye detection. But it is only through *telescopic* observing that the planets reveal their uniqueness, and this section concentrates on that aspect. For a listing of unaided-eye highlights such as conjunctions, see THE SKY MONTH BY MONTH section on pp. 92–119.

Urban and suburban locales unsuited for many aspects of astronomy can be perfectly acceptable for telescopic planetary observing. Atmospheric turbulence—seeing—is often no worse, and sometimes better, in urban areas. However, observers should avoid using telescopes on pavement, balconies, or immediately beside a house or substantial building due to the heat radiated to the surrounding atmosphere from these structures. Also, avoid looking over these objects if possible. A typical grassed backyard is fine in most instances. For optimum performance all telescopes (except small refractors) require from ten minutes to an hour to cool to outside temperature when taken outdoors. Hazy but otherwise cloudless nights are usually just as good as, and sometimes better than, clear skies for steady telescopic images of planets.

More than any other class of telescopic observing, planetary observing is most affected by seeing. Many nights are rendered useless for planet watching by ever-present ripples and undulations in Earth's atmosphere. Planets within 15° of the horizon are virtually always afflicted (as many observers of Mars noted in the summer of 2001 from Canadian latitudes). Minimum altitude for expectations of reasonable seeing is 25°. A further problem with low-altitude planetary targets is dispersion associated with atmospheric refraction. Refraction causes celestial objects to appear displaced to higher altitudes. Since the effect is wavelength-dependent (being less for longer wavelengths), for planets at low altitudes this produces a red fringe on the lower side of the planet and a green (or blue) fringe on the upper; the effect also introduces undesirable chromatic smearing to the whole image. Thomas Dobbins explained possible fixes for the problem in an article in *Sky & Telescope* (August 2003,

p. 124). Within a few months, Adirondack Video Astronomy introduced a commercial Planetary Atmospheric Dispersion Corrector (*Sky & Telescope,* November 2003, p. 60) that has caught the interest of some planetary observers.

Regardless of the type of telescope used for planetary observing, optical quality is far more critical than aperture. In no other type of observing are the effects of less-than-perfect optics more apparent. Other factors that can significantly degrade a telescope's planetary performance include a large *central obstruction* in the optical system (all Schmidt-Cassegrains, Maksutov-Cassegrains, and Newtonians with secondary mirror diameters exceeding 25% of their apertures), *secondary mirror supports* (most Newtonians), *chromatic aberration* (most achromatic refractors over 90 mm), *internal air currents* (all types, refractors least), optical component *cooldown time* (mostly aperture-dependent, telescopes over 200 mm can take hours), *improperly light-baffled optics,* and *dirty optics.*

In the remarks below, when a planetary phenomenon is stated as being visible in a certain minimum aperture, good seeing and a moderate level of observer experience are assumed. When a specific minimum aperture is cited, an unobstructed optical system (i.e. a refractor) is assumed. Somewhat larger apertures are often required if centrally obstructed systems are used or the observer is inexperienced.

Editor's Note: The tables and figures that appear in this section were prepared by the editor or other contributors; the editor assumes full responsibility for their accuracy.

MERCURY

Of the five planets visible to the unaided eye, Mercury is by far the most difficult to observe and is seldom conveniently located for either unaided eye or telescopic observation. The problem for observers is Mercury's tight orbit, which constrains the planet to a small zone on either side of the Sun as viewed from Earth. When Mercury is east of the Sun we may see it as an evening "star" low in the west just after sunset. When it is west of the Sun we might view Mercury as a morning "star" in the east before sunrise. But due to the celestial geometry of the tilt of Earth's axis and Mercury's orbit, we get much better views of Mercury at certain times of the year.

From midlatitudes, the best time to see the planet in the *evening* sky is within a month or two of the spring equinox and in the *morning* sky within a month or two of the fall equinox. (This applies to both northern and southern latitudes, although the respective seasons are six months out of phase.) Binoculars are of great assistance in searching for the planet about 30 min to an hour after sunset or before sunrise during the periods when it is visible. The planet's brightness, which varies by more than two magnitudes, is a more important factor influencing its visibility than its angular distance from the Sun during any particular elongation. Mercury's true colour is almost pure white, but absorption from Earth's atmosphere within 15° of the

MERCURY—MOST FAVOURABLE VIEWS IN 2008 FROM NORTHERN LATITUDES: MAY (Morning); OCTOBER (Evening)

Date 0h UT	Mag.	Angular Diameter "	Percent Illuminated	Elongation from Sun °	Apparent RA (2008) h m	Dec ° '
May 4	−0.7	6.3	66	18	3 58	+22 41
9	−0.2	7.1	51	21	4 29	+24 19
14	+0.3	8.0	37	22	4 55	+25 01
Oct. 21	−0.5	7.2	49	18	12 39	−2 16
26	−0.8	6.3	70	18	13 00	−4 07
31	−1.9	5.6	83	15	13 27	−6 56

horizon, where Mercury is most easily seen, usually imparts a yellow or ochre hue to the planet.

Telescopic observers will find the rapidly changing phases of Mercury of interest. The planet zips from gibbous to crescent phase in about three weeks during each of its evening elongations. The phases are accessible to users of 75-mm or larger telescopes; the 30% phase can be detected at 50×. Large apertures (over 200 mm) rarely offer an advantage due to the crippling effects of poor seeing at lower altitudes, especially following sunset when the planet is most frequently observed. Experienced planetary observers often report their most satisfying telescopic observations of Mercury in the morning sky. Near favourable western elongations, the planet may be easily located at least an hour before sunrise, then followed to higher altitudes into the daytime sky. Seeing often remains steady more than an hour after sunrise by which time the planet may be 30° above the horizon. Under such conditions the phase is sharply defined, and the small disk takes on a unique appearance, paler than Venus, with a vaguely textured surface. Surface details, although suspected in moments of fine seeing, are always elusive. Contrasts between the planet's surface features are lower than on the lunar surface, although in other respects the two bodies are similar.

VENUS

Venus is the only world in the solar system that closely resembles Earth in size and mass. It also comes nearer to Earth than any other planet, at times approaching as close as 0.27 au. Despite the fundamental similarity, surface conditions on Earth and Venus differ greatly. The clouds and haze that cloak the planet are highly reflective, making Venus the brightest natural celestial object in the nighttime sky apart from our Moon. Whenever it is visible, it is readily recognized. Because its orbit is within that of Earth's, Venus is never separated from the Sun by an angle greater than 47°, more than sufficient for the dazzling object to dominate the morning or evening sky.

Like Mercury, Venus exhibits phases, although they are much more easily detected in small telescopes because of Venus's greater size. When it is far from us on the other side of its orbit, we see the planet nearly fully illuminated, but because of its distance it appears small—about 10″ in diameter. As Venus moves closer to Earth, the phase decreases (we see less of the illuminated portion of the planet), but the diameter increases until it is a thin slice nearly a minute of arc in diameter. It takes Venus several months to move from one of these extremes to the other, compared to just a few weeks for Mercury.

Overall, this is an unfavourable year for Venus observation, primarily because superior conjunction occurs near the middle of the year (June 9), which creates the double whammy of placing the planet at its most remote from Earth, as well as limiting it to months of flirting with solar glare.

As the year opens, Venus is prominent in the southeast morning sky for northern hemisphere observers, less favourable for southern observers. Visibility declines as Venus approaches the horizon during January and February. By April it is lost in twilight. The brilliant planet reappears in the western evening sky in the southern hemisphere in August, but remains very difficult for northern observers to locate until November when it creeps above the southwest horizon at dusk. Not until December do northern observers see the brightest planet displaying its charms in a dark sky.

For dates late in the year when Venus is favourably positioned, the following information will be useful: on Nov. 15, Venus is a 74% illuminated disk 15″ in apparent diameter; Dec. 1, 69%, 17″; Dec. 15, 64%, 18″; Dec. 31, 58%, 21″.

When Venus is about a 20% crescent, even rigidly held, good-quality binoculars can be used to distinguish that the planet is not spherical or a point source. The new image-stabilized binoculars beautifully display the crescent Venus. A 60-mm refractor should be capable of revealing the shape of all but the gibbous and full phases. Experienced observers prefer to observe Venus during the daytime, and indeed the planet is bright enough to be seen with the unaided eye if one knows where to look.

Because of Venus's high surface brightness (about 40 times greater than Jupiter's), Venus can accommodate the highest magnifications a telescope can deliver. The author has used magnifications over 4× per millimetre of aperture on occasion and regularly employs 1.5× to 3× per millimetre on the planet, particularly in bright twilight when the sky is moderately dark but Venus is still high enough to avoid low-altitude seeing degradation. Venus's cloud-shrouded surface appears to most observers to be featureless no matter what type of telescope is used or what the planet's phase. Broad streaks and splotches in the clouds, revealed in blue-filtered and ultraviolet images of Venus, may be vaguely detected telescopically using a violet filter (#38A or #47), although sketches of these features seldom match among different observers.

MARS

Mars is often considered the most interesting planet to observe with the unaided eye. It moves rapidly among the stars—its motion can often be detected after an interval of less than a week—and it varies in brightness over a far greater range than any other outer planet. Mars can be distinguished by its pale orange-red colour, a hue that originates with rust-coloured dust covering much of the planet. As 2008 opens, Mars is a brilliant magnitude −1.5, very conspicuously decorating the winter sky between Auriga and Gemini, but officially just inside the Taurus boundary. During January and February, Mars declines to magnitude +0.1 as it remains in Taurus, between the bull's horns. In early March it moves into Gemini for two months. In early May, at a much less prominent magnitude +1.2, Mars enters Cancer. By late June, the red planet is in Leo, passing Regulus on Jul. 1 and Saturn on Jul. 10. Thereafter it is buried in twilight glow until emerging on the morning sky late in the year.

In August 2003, Mars made its closest approach to Earth in recorded history, at a distance of 0.373 au. Observers reported a wealth of surface detail visible in telescopes as small as 100-mm aperture. At its most recent close approach, on 2007 Dec. 19, the red planet was considerably more distant at 0.589 au from Earth. Our neighbour world's apparent diameter at closest approach in December was 15.9″ compared to 25.1″ in 2003.

As 2008 begins, the red planet's apparent size is still a respectable 15.4″, but by mid-January Earth begins to rapidly pull away from Mars, reducing its apparent diameter to 12″ by Feb. 1, and 9″ by Mar. 1. For telescopic observers, a Martian disk less than 9″ in diameter can still offer interesting detail in moments of good seeing, but realistically the prime observing window closes by mid-February.

Although telescopic observers at midnorthern latitudes are faced with a smaller apparent diameter of Mars than at previous close-approach apparitions earlier in this decade, this is somewhat offset by the planet's high declination. Through February, observers at 45°N latitude will see Mars about 70° above the horizon when at the meridian. This high opposition altitude for Mars from mid-northern latitudes will not be repeated until 2022.

Mars—2008		
Date		**Equatorial Diameter**
UT	Mag.	″
Jan. 1.0	−1.5	15.4
Jan. 15.0	−1.1	14.1
Feb. 1.0	−0.6	12.2
Feb. 15.0	−0.2	10.3
Mar. 1.0	+0.1	9.1
Apr. 1.0	+0.8	7.0
May 1.0	+1.2	5.7
Jun. 1.0	+1.5	5.0
Jul. 1.0	+1.6	4.4
Aug. 1.0	+1.7	4.2
Sep. 1.0	+1.7	3.9
Oct. 1.0	+1.6	3.8
Nov. 1.0	+1.5	3.7
Dec. 1.0	+1.3	3.8
Dec. 31.0	+1.3	3.9

OPPOSITIONS OF MARS, 2001–2014

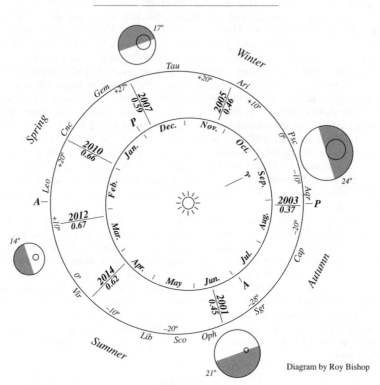

Diagram by Roy Bishop

The above diagram represents the orbits of Earth and Mars as viewed from the north ecliptic pole. Straight lines link simultaneous positions of the two planets for seven successive oppositions of Mars, beginning with that of the year 2001. The separation of the two planets (in astronomical units) at the various oppositions is indicated beside each of the connecting lines. The months inside of Earth's orbit indicate the position of Earth during the year (both planets orbit counterclockwise). For each orbit, two tick marks labelled A and P indicate the aphelion point and the perihelion point, respectively. The direction of the vernal equinox is shown (toward the late September position of Earth). Around the orbit of Mars is indicated its declination (ranges between +27° and –28°) and the constellation in which Mars resides when at opposition.

Four views of Mars are shown—at its two equinoxes and two solstices. These views show the portion of Mars illuminated by the Sun, the location and approximate size of its north polar cap, and the apparent size of Mars (labelled in arcseconds) for oppositions occurring at these points in its orbit. The seasons of the Martian northern hemisphere are indicated around the outer margin of the diagram, and are very nearly one season ahead of those on Earth at the same orbital position. (For the southern hemisphere of Mars, the season and the configuration of the south polar cap are the same as those of the diametrically opposite view.) Note that the maximum angular diameter Mars can attain (25") occurs near its perihelion, at a late-August opposition.

As an example of the information that can be read from this diagram: the 2005 opposition of Mars occurred in early November with Mars 0.46 au from Earth. Mars was about 20" in angular diameter and located near declination +15° in Aries. It was midwinter in the northern hemisphere of Mars, with a large north polar cap beginning to show at the northern limb and a small south polar cap possibly visible near the southern limb.

Although high elevation above the horizon does not make up for the smaller apparent size of Mars this year, planetary observers should be aware that during the observing window around a nearly identical opposition half a century ago, in 1960/61, members of the Toronto and Montreal Centres of the RASC experienced views of Mars that became legendary for good seeing and contrast and clarity of detail. Many pencil sketches of Mars made by observers using 10-20-cm refractors and Newtonian telescopes at both Centres were combined to produce excellent global maps of Mars.

In moments of excellent seeing, observers using 20-cm or larger telescopes of good optical quality will glimpse an overwhelming amount of fine detail on Mars when the disk is above 10″ in diameter (i.e. before mid-February). The planet's chief characteristic is peach-coloured desert with darker greyish zones, which are also deserts of varying size and prominence. The clarity of the surface features varies depending on the regional transparency of the Martian atmosphere. In addition to local dust storms, ice clouds and haze can lower contrast across large areas of the disk. But when the Martian air is clear, and the seeing conditions on Earth permit, the subtle colour and fine detail of the planet's surface are exquisite and compelling in a telescope.

The region within a few degrees latitude of the equator of Mars will be at the centre of the Martian disk throughout the prime observing window. The Martian southern-hemisphere autumn equinox occurred on 2007 Dec. 9. This means that the south polar cap will be near its minimum size and probably undetectable in smaller telescopes. The north polar cap will be near maximum size and likely hidden under an extensive bluish haze called the north polar hood until sometime in January. After that, the north polar hood will gradually break up, exposing the white, mainly frozen carbon dioxide north polar cap. At times during this apparition, the north polar cap should be the most prominent Martian feature. (More Mars observing suggestions and strategies for the prime observing window were given on pages 173-75 of the 2007 Handbook.)

JUPITER

Jupiter, the solar system's largest planet, is a colossal ball of hydrogen and helium without any solid surface comparable to land masses on Earth. Jupiter likely has a small rocky core encased in a thick mantle of metallic hydrogen which is enveloped by a massive atmospheric cloak topped by a quilt of multicoloured clouds. These clouds are the visible surface of Jupiter—a realm of constant change characterized by alternating dark belts and brighter zones. The zones are ammonia ice-crystal clouds, the belts mainly ammonium hydrosulphide clouds. Frequently, the belts intrude on the zones with dark rifts or loops called festoons.

The equatorial region of Jupiter's clouds rotates 5 min faster than the rest of the planet: 9 h 50 min compared to 9 h 55 min. This means constant interaction as one region slips by the other at about 400 km/h. It also means that there are basically two rotational systems from the viewpoint of week-to-week telescopic observation. (See Jupiter—Table of Daily Central Meridians, 2008 on p. 208 for daily longitudes of Jupiter's regions System I and System II.) Jupiter's rapid rotation also makes the great globe markedly bulged at the equator.

Two dark belts, the North Equatorial Belt and the South Equatorial Belt, are obvious in the smallest telescopes. (Although in 2007, for the first time in more than a decade, the SEB dramatically disrupted and faded, before partially recovering its intensity later in the year.) Larger instruments reveal several more narrow dark belts along with the famous Great Red Spot, a salmon-coloured oval vortex observed for centuries on the south edge of the South Equatorial Belt. Historically, the Red Spot has varied from being blatantly obvious to nearly invisible. For example, in 2007 it was detectable with a 100-mm aperture but could hardly be described as prominent because it closely matched its surroundings in hue and contrast. In 2008, observers should find the Red Spot near longitude 120° in System II. (See Jupiter—Daily Central Meridians and Time of Transit of Great Red Spot on the following pages for instructions to determine when the Great Red Spot crosses Jupiter's central meridian.)

The smallest of telescopes will reveal Jupiter's four large satellites, three of which are larger than Earth's Moon (see. p. 25). They provide a never-ending fascination for amateur astronomers. The satellites have the following mean opposition apparent diameters and magnitudes: Io 1.2″, 5.0; Europa 1.0″, 5.3; Ganymede 1.7″, 4.6; and Callisto 1.6″, 5.6. Under good conditions a 150-mm telescope reveals the size differences as well as colour variations among the satellites; a smaller instrument reveals differences in brightness.

For the configurations of the Galilean satellites see the right side of the pages in the THE SKY MONTH BY MONTH section on pp. 97–119. Sometimes the satellites are paired on either side of the belted planet; frequently one is missing—either behind Jupiter, in the planet's shadow, or in front of Jupiter. In the latter case the satellite usually blends in against Jupiter's bright clouds and is difficult to see (more on this below).

Jupiter—2008		
Date		**Equatorial Diameter**
UT	**Mag.**	″
Jan. 1.0	−1.8	31.7
Feb. 1.0	−1.9	32.5
Mar. 1.0	−2.0	34.3
Apr. 1.0	−2.1	37.3
May 1.0	−2.4	41.2
Jun. 1.0	−2.6	45.0
Jul. 1.0	−2.7	47.2
Aug. 1.0	−2.7	46.6
Sep. 1.0	−2.5	43.5
Oct. 1.0	−2.3	39.8
Nov. 1.0	−2.1	36.3
Dec. 1.0	−2.0	34.0
Jan. 1.0	−1.9	32.6

Even more interesting are the occasions when one of the satellites casts its shadow on the disk of the planet. (See PHENOMENA OF THE GALILEAN SATELLITES on pp. 214–220.) The tiny black shadow can be particularly evident if it is cast on one of the bright zones of Jupiter. This phenomenon sometimes is evident in a 60-mm refractor under good seeing conditions. On rarer occasions, *two* shadows are cast on the face of Jupiter. These "double shadow transits" appear in bold type in the table on pp. 215–220 and are included in the right-hand pages of THE SKY MONTH BY MONTH section on pp. 97–119.

The satellite umbral shadows vary significantly in size from one to another. Mean opposition angular diameters are Io 0.9″, Europa 0.6″, Ganymede 1.1″, and Callisto 0.5″. The enormous contrast between the dark shadows and the bright Jovian clouds makes these tiny features visible even though they are smaller than the nominal resolution limit of a small telescope. Furthermore, the satellites' penumbral shadows are quite large, especially Callisto's, which adds a few tenths of an arcsecond to their effective visual diameters.

When the Galilean satellites transit the disk of Jupiter, they are seldom visible in telescopes under 100 mm and are best seen near the planet's limb when entering or leaving the disk. Tracking a satellite transit completely across Jupiter is a challenging observation. Each satellite has a characteristic appearance when superimposed on the Jovian cloudscape. Europa is bright white, similar to the brightest Jovian clouds. When traversing a white cloud zone in the central sector of Jupiter, Europa is usually invisible, however, it stands out well when near the limb or against a dark belt. Callisto, the darkest satellite, is best seen in the reverse circumstances. When seen against a pale zone this greyish satellite can be mistaken for a satellite shadow, but it is often lost against a dark belt. Ganymede is intermediate in surface brightness, but because of its great size, it is the easiest of the four to track completely across Jupiter's face. Io, innermost of the Galilean satellites, is also the most frequently seen in transit. It is generally easier to follow over typical cloud features, being slightly brighter

JUPITER—DAILY CENTRAL MERIDIANS AND TIME OF TRANSIT OF GREAT RED SPOT

The table on the next page can be used to calculate the longitude of the central meridian of the observed disk of Jupiter during the months February–November (when Jupiter is well placed for observation). System I is the most rapidly rotating region between the middle of the North Equatorial Belt and the middle of the South Equatorial Belt. System II applies to the rest of the planet. The rotation rate of System I is 36.577 ± 0.008 °/h and that of System II is 36.259 ± 0.008 °/h. These figures, together with the closest tabular value, can be used to determine the longitude of a system's central meridian for any given date and time (UT) of observation. **Example:** At 1:00 ADT Aug. 8 = 4:00 UT Aug. 8 the longitude of the central meridian of System I is

$$263.2 + (36.577 \times 4) = 409.5°;$$

putting this angle in the range 0°–360° by subtracting 360° leaves a longitude of 49.5°, accurate to about 0.1°.

The table may also be used to determine when the Great Red Spot (GRS) (near longitude 120° in System II) will cross the central meridian of the disk of Jupiter. **Example:** Suppose an observer in Winnipeg is viewing Jupiter on the evening of Apr. 30 (time zone: CDT, −5 h) . At 0h UT May 1 (19h CDT Apr. 30) the table gives approximately 262° for the longitude of the central meridian in System II. A further rotation of 360° − 262° + 120° = 218° will bring the GRS to the central meridian, which will require 218° ÷ 36.259°/h = 6.01 h = 6 h 1 min. Thus the GRS will transit at 6:01 UT May 1 = 1:01 CDT May 1. Note that the GRS slowly drifts in longitude, so the 120° figure is only a guide. By timing a transit of the GRS and using the table, you can update its longitude.

than Europa and also probably due to its slightly greater diameter. Near opposition, a transiting satellite often appears adjacent to its own shadow. These events are especially worth a look. While the three inner satellites experience a transit/shadow transit and an occultation/eclipse during each revolution of Jupiter, these events only occur for distant Callisto when the tilt of the Jovian system is relatively closed. A new series of mutual events involving Callisto begins in early 2008, with such events situated very near the poles of the giant planet.

Jupiter's other satellites are photographic objects for large instruments.

As 2008 opens, Jupiter is too close to the Sun for observation. On Feb. 1, as it enters the morning sky, it is less than one degree from Venus, in Sagittarius. Jupiter remains in Sagittarius for the entire year, reaching opposition on Jul. 9. The giant planet descends into evening twilight in late December.

SATURN

Saturn is the telescopic showpiece of the night sky. The chilling beauty of the ringed orb floating in a field of black is something no photographs or descriptions can adequately duplicate. Any telescope magnifying more than 30× will show the rings. The view is exquisite in 100-mm to 200-mm instruments. The rings consist of billions of particles—largely water ice—that range from microscopic specks to flying boulders the size of houses. The reason "rings" is plural is that gaps and brightness differences define hundreds of distinct rings. However, from Earth only the three most prominent components—known simply as rings A, B, and C—can be distinguished visually. (See the diagram Saturn—Main Ring Features Visible from Earth on p. 210.)

The Cassini Division, a gap between rings A and B discovered in 1675, is visible in small telescopes when the ring system is well inclined to our view. The Cassini Division is a region less densely populated with ring particles than adjacent rings. Ring B, the brightest, overpowers ring C to such an extent that ring C, also known as the *crepe ring,* is seen only with difficulty in small telescopes. A Saturn phenomenon easily seen with backyard telescopes is the shadow of the planet on the rings. From

(text continues on p. 210)

JUPITER — TABLE OF DAILY CENTRAL MERIDIANS, 2008

FEBRUARY Date 0h UT	Sys I	Sys II	APRIL Date 0h UT	Sys I	Sys II	JUNE Date 0h UT	Sys I	Sys II	AUGUST Date 0h UT	Sys I	Sys II	OCTOBER Date 0h UT	Sys I	Sys II
0	137.5	274.0	1	43.0	74.0	1	317.9	243.5	1	237.5	57.6	1	147.1	221.8
1	295.2	64.1	2	200.9	224.3	2	116.0	33.9	2	35.5	208.0	2	304.8	11.9
2	93.0	214.2	3	358.7	14.5	3	274.0	184.3	3	193.4	358.3	3	102.5	162.0
3	250.7	4.3	4	156.6	164.8	4	72.0	334.7	4	351.4	148.6	4	260.3	312.1
4	48.4	154.4	5	314.5	315.0	5	230.0	125.1	5	149.4	299.0	5	58.0	102.3
5	206.2	304.5	6	112.4	105.3	6	28.1	275.5	6	307.3	89.3	6	215.8	252.4
6	3.9	94.7	7	270.3	255.5	7	186.1	65.9	7	105.3	239.6	7	13.5	42.5
7	161.7	244.8	8	68.1	45.8	8	344.1	216.3	8	263.2	30.0	8	171.2	192.6
8	319.4	34.9	9	226.0	196.0	9	142.2	6.7	9	61.2	180.3	9	329.0	342.7
9	117.2	185.0	10	23.9	346.3	10	300.2	157.1	10	219.1	330.6	10	126.7	132.8
10	274.9	335.1	11	181.8	136.6	11	98.2	307.5	11	17.1	120.9	11	284.4	282.9
11	72.7	125.2	12	339.7	286.8	12	256.3	97.9	12	175.0	271.2	12	82.1	73.0
12	230.4	275.3	13	137.6	77.1	13	54.3	248.3	13	332.9	61.5	13	239.9	223.1
13	28.2	65.5	14	295.5	227.4	14	212.3	38.7	14	130.9	211.8	14	37.6	13.1
14	185.9	215.6	15	93.4	17.6	15	10.4	189.1	15	288.8	2.1	15	195.3	163.2
15	343.7	5.7	16	251.3	167.9	16	168.4	339.5	16	86.7	152.4	16	353.0	313.3
16	141.4	155.9	17	49.2	318.2	17	326.5	130.0	17	244.6	302.7	17	150.7	103.4
17	299.2	306.0	18	207.2	108.5	18	124.5	280.4	18	42.6	93.0	18	308.4	253.5
18	97.0	96.1	19	5.1	258.8	19	282.5	70.8	19	200.5	243.3	19	106.1	43.5
19	254.7	246.3	20	163.0	49.1	20	80.6	221.2	20	358.4	33.6	20	263.8	193.6
20	52.5	36.4	21	320.9	199.4	21	238.6	11.6	21	156.3	183.8	21	61.5	343.7
21	210.3	186.5	22	118.8	349.6	22	36.7	162.0	22	314.2	334.1	22	219.2	133.8
22	8.0	336.7	23	276.8	139.9	23	194.7	312.4	23	112.1	124.4	23	16.9	283.8
23	165.8	126.8	24	74.7	290.2	24	352.8	102.8	24	270.0	274.6	24	174.6	73.9
24	323.6	277.0	25	232.6	80.5	25	150.8	253.2	25	67.9	64.9	25	332.3	223.9
25	121.4	67.1	26	30.6	230.9	26	308.8	43.7	26	225.7	215.1	26	130.0	14.0
26	279.1	217.3	27	188.5	21.2	27	106.9	194.1	27	23.6	5.4	27	287.7	164.1
27	76.9	7.4	28	346.4	171.5	28	264.9	344.5	28	181.5	155.6	28	85.4	314.1
28	234.7	157.6	29	144.4	321.8	29	63.0	134.9	29	339.4	305.9	29	243.1	104.2
29	32.5	307.7	30	302.3	112.1	30	221.0	285.3	30	137.2	96.1	30	40.7	254.2
									31	295.1	246.4	31	198.4	44.3

MARCH Date 0h UT	Sys I	Sys II	MAY Date 0h UT	Sys I	Sys II	JULY Date 0h UT	Sys I	Sys II	SEPTEMBER Date 0h UT	Sys I	Sys II	NOVEMBER Date 0h UT	Sys I	Sys II
1	190.3	97.9	1	100.3	262.4	1	19.0	75.7	1	93.0	36.6	1	356.1	194.3
2	348.1	248.1	2	258.2	52.7	2	177.1	226.1	2	250.8	186.8	2	153.8	344.4
3	145.9	38.2	3	56.2	203.1	3	335.1	16.5	3	48.7	337.0	3	311.5	134.4
4	303.7	188.4	4	214.2	353.4	4	133.2	166.9	4	206.5	127.3	4	109.1	284.5
5	101.5	338.6	5	12.1	143.7	5	291.2	317.3	5	4.4	277.5	5	266.8	74.5
6	259.3	128.7	6	170.1	294.0	6	89.2	107.8	6	162.2	67.7	6	64.5	224.6
7	57.1	278.9	7	328.0	84.4	7	247.3	258.2	7	320.0	217.9	7	222.1	14.6
8	214.9	69.1	8	126.0	234.7	8	45.3	48.6	8	117.9	8.1	8	19.8	164.6
9	12.7	219.3	9	284.0	25.1	9	203.3	199.0	9	275.7	158.3	9	177.5	314.7
10	170.5	9.4	10	82.0	175.4	10	1.4	349.4	10	73.5	308.5	10	335.1	104.7
11	328.3	159.6	11	239.9	325.7	11	159.4	139.8	11	231.4	98.7	11	132.8	254.7
12	126.1	309.8	12	37.9	116.1	12	317.4	290.2	12	29.2	248.9	12	290.5	44.8
13	284.0	100.0	13	195.9	266.4	13	115.4	80.6	13	187.0	39.1	13	88.1	194.8
14	81.8	250.2	14	353.9	56.8	14	273.5	230.9	14	344.8	189.2	14	245.8	344.8
15	239.6	40.4	15	151.9	207.2	15	71.5	21.3	15	142.6	339.4	15	43.4	134.9
16	37.4	190.6	16	309.8	357.5	16	229.5	171.7	16	300.4	129.6	16	201.1	284.9
17	195.3	340.8	17	107.8	147.9	17	27.5	322.1	17	98.2	279.8	17	358.8	74.9
18	353.1	131.0	18	265.8	298.2	18	185.5	112.5	18	256.0	69.9	18	156.4	224.9
19	150.9	281.2	19	63.8	88.6	19	343.6	262.9	19	53.8	220.1	19	314.1	15.0
20	308.8	71.4	20	221.8	239.0	20	141.6	53.3	20	211.6	10.3	20	111.7	165.0
21	106.6	221.6	21	19.8	29.3	21	299.6	203.6	21	9.4	160.4	21	269.4	315.0
22	264.4	11.8	22	177.8	179.7	22	97.6	354.0	22	167.2	310.6	22	67.0	105.0
23	62.3	162.0	23	335.8	330.1	23	255.6	144.4	23	324.9	100.7	23	224.7	255.1
24	220.1	312.2	24	133.8	120.4	24	53.6	294.8	24	122.7	250.9	24	22.3	45.1
25	18.0	102.4	25	291.8	270.8	25	211.6	85.1	25	280.5	41.0	25	180.0	195.1
26	175.8	252.7	26	89.8	61.2	26	9.6	235.5	26	78.3	191.1	26	337.6	345.1
27	333.7	42.9	27	247.9	211.6	27	167.6	25.9	27	236.0	341.3	27	135.3	135.1
28	131.5	193.1	28	45.9	2.0	28	325.6	176.2	28	33.8	131.4	28	292.9	285.2
29	289.4	343.3	29	203.9	152.4	29	123.5	326.6	29	191.5	281.5	29	90.6	75.2
30	87.3	133.6	30	1.9	302.7	30	281.5	116.9	30	349.3	71.7	30	248.2	225.2
31	245.1	283.8	31	159.9	93.1	31	79.5	267.3						

one to four months before or after opposition the shadow falling on the rings is very apparent, often giving the scene a powerful three-dimensional aura. The shadow is not easily seen in the weeks near opposition, at which point the shadow is cast straight back from our line of sight.

In addition to the rings, Saturn has a family of at least 61 satellites (see pp. 27–29). Titan, the largest, is easily seen in any telescope as an 8th-magnitude object orbiting Saturn in about 16 days. At east and west elongation Titan appears about five ring diameters from the planet. Telescopes over 60 mm in aperture should reveal 10th-magnitude Rhea at less than two ring diameters from Saturn. The satellite Iapetus has the peculiar property of being five times brighter at western elongation (magnitude 10.1) than at eastern elongation (11.9). One side of the satellite has the reflectivity of snow while the other resembles dark rock. When brightest, Iapetus is located about 12 ring diameters west of the parent planet. Of the remaining satellites, Tethys and Dione may be glimpsed in a 150-mm telescope, but the others require larger apertures. (See CONFIGURATIONS OF SATURN'S BRIGHTEST SATELLITES on pp. 221–224.)

SATURN—MAIN RING FEATURES VISIBLE FROM EARTH

EARTH
(to same scale)

$1.00 = 60\,330$ km $= 9.74''$ (at mean opposition distance)

1.23

1.52

1.95

2.02   RADII

2.26

Diagram by Roy Bishop

SATURN'S RING SYSTEM—MAIN STRUCTURAL REGIONS

Ring	Radius**	Discoverer
D	1.11 – 1.23	*Voyager 1* (1980)
C*	1.23 – 1.52	W.C. & G.P. Bond, W.R. Dawes (1850)
B*	1.52 – 1.95 ⎱	⎰ Galileo (1610), C. Huygens (1659),
A*	2.02 – 2.26 ⎰	⎱ G.D. Cassini (1675)
F	2.33	*Pioneer 11* (1979)
G	2.8	*Voyager 1* (1980)
E	3. – 8.	W.A. Feibelman (1966)

*Visible from Earth; also, the E ring can be detected when Saturn's ring system appears edge-on.
**In units of Saturn's equatorial radius (60 330 km)

Saturn—2008			
Date		**Equatorial**	**Ring**
		Diam.	**Incl.**
UT	**Mag.**	"	°
Jan.	1.0	+0.6	19.1	−6.7
Feb.	1.0	+0.4	19.8	−7.5
Mar.	1.0	+0.2	20.0	−8.5
Apr.	1.0	+0.4	19.6	−9.6
May	1.0	+0.6	18.6	−9.9
Jun.	1.0	+0.7	17.7	−9.6
Jul.	1.0	+0.8	16.8	−8.6
Aug.	1.0	+0.8	16.3	−7.0
Sep.	1.0	+0.8	16.1	−5.3
Oct.	1.0	+1.0	16.2	−3.6
Nov.	1.0	+1.1	16.7	−2.1
Dec.	1.0	+1.1	17.5	−1.1
Jan.	1.0	+1.0	18.5	−0.8

The disk of Saturn appears about one-sixth the area of Jupiter through the same telescope with the same magnification. In telescopes less than 75-mm aperture, probably no features will ever be seen on the cloud deck of the planet other than the shadow cast by the rings. As the size of the telescope is increased, the pale equatorial region, a dusky equatorial band, and the darker polar regions become evident. Saturn has a belt system like Jupiter's, but it is much less active and the contrast is reduced. In addition, it is partially obscured by the ring passing in front of the planet. Seldom in telescopes less than 100 mm in aperture do more than one or two belts come into view.

Saturn is at opposition in Leo on Feb. 24, and spends the entire year in that constellation. The Earthbound observer's view of the tilt of Saturn's rings varies from edge-on to "wide open" (about 27°) and back twice during each 29.5-year revolution of the planet. They were open to their maximum extent in 2003, and will be edge-on in 2009. In 2008 the ring tilt varies between 10° and 1°.

URANUS

At magnitude 5.7–5.9, Uranus can be seen with the unaided eye under a clear, dark sky. However, it is much more easily located with binoculars. A 75-mm telescope will reveal its small, greenish, featureless disk.

Unlike the three other giant planets, the axis of Uranus is tipped almost parallel to the plane of the solar system. This means that we view Uranus nearly pole-on

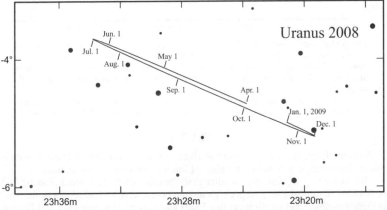

The finder chart above, provided by David Lane, shows the path of Uranus in Aquarius during the nine-month period April–December 2008. Coordinates are for equinox J2000.0, and the magnitude limit is approximately 9.0. Tick marks are drawn along the path at the beginning of each month. The brightest star in the chart, 5.6-magnitude 96 Aqr near the Dec. 1 position, will be within 5 arcminutes of slightly-dimmer Uranus for the three weeks around its stationary point on Nov. 28.

Along the five-month retrograde portion of its track, from Jun. 27 to Nov. 28 and centred at its Sep. 13 opposition, Uranus ranges between 5.7 and 5.8 in magnitude.

at certain points in its 84-year orbit. The southern (and counterclockwise turning) hemisphere of Uranus is now angled slightly toward Earth. Its south pole appeared nearest to (and slightly south of) the centre of its disk in 1985. Uranus has at least 27 satellites (see pp. 29–30), all smaller than Earth's Moon, none of which can be detected in small or moderate-sized telescopes.

Uranus is at opposition in Aquarius on Sep. 13, when it is magnitude 5.7 and 3.7″ in apparent diameter. Use the chart on the previous page to locate this distant planet.

NEPTUNE

Neptune is an 8th-magnitude binocular object—an easy target in 7 × 50 or larger glasses—but seeing the planet as a disk rather than a point of light is a different matter. Magnifications over 200× are usually necessary, and even then Neptune is just a tiny bluish dot with no hard edge due to limb darkening. Neptune's large satellite, Triton, can be seen by an experienced observer using a 300-mm telescope. Triton varies between 8″ and 17″ from Neptune.

In 2008, Neptune is in Capricornus and may be easily identified using the chart below. At opposition on Aug. 15, Neptune is magnitude 7.8 and 2.3″ in diameter.

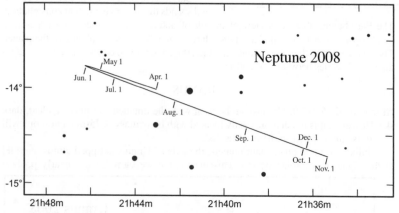

The finder chart above, provided by David Lane, shows the path of Neptune in Capricornus during the eight-month period April–December 2008. Coordinates are for equinox J2000.0, and the magnitude limit is approximately 9.0. Tick marks are drawn along the path at the beginning of each month. The brightest star in the chart is 5th-magnitude 42 Cap, near the Aug. 1 position.

Along the five-month retrograde portion of its track, from May 26 to Nov. 2 and centred at its Aug. 15 opposition, Neptune ranges between 7.8 and 7.9 in magnitude.

PLUTO

In 2006 the International Astronomical Union formally reclassified Pluto as a dwarf planet. Nonetheless it remains an object of interest for amateur astronomers.

Besides being significantly smaller than the other eight traditional planets, Pluto is different in almost every respect. Its unique characteristics include its orbit, which is highly-inclined and so elliptical that Pluto was closer to the Sun than was Neptune from 1980 through 1999. Pluto was near perihelion throughout those years and as bright as it ever gets. At that time, a few observers (with good optics, transparent skies, steady seeing, and high magnifications) succeeded in sighting Pluto with telescopes as small as 100-mm refractors.

In 2008 opposition is on Jun. 19, when Pluto is at magnitude 13.9 in northeastern Sagittarius. It can be identified using the chart overleaf and a 200-mm or larger telescope.

FINDER CHART FOR PLUTO
By Ian Cameron

This chart uses the astrometric UCAC2 catalogue. The UCAC2 lists CCD magnitudes that are somewhat between V and R magnitudes. Uranometria 2000 stars (Chart 339 in Vol. 2) are indicated in light gray and the Tirion 2000 stars (Chart 15 in 1st edition), in dark gray.

The relatively bright star 6 Sgr is located near Pluto's Feb. 10 position. (mag. 6.6 according to UCAC2) Open cluster NGC 6507 is located south, just off chart centre, and Barnard 84a is found near the Nov. 11 position of Pluto. Pluto is at opposition at magnitude 13.9 on Jun. 19.

The chart limiting magnitude is 14.5 according to the UCAC2. The chart is generated using the open source Generic Mapping Tools (GMT4) under MacOS 10.4.10.

PHENOMENA OF THE GALILEAN SATELLITES

The table on the following pages gives the various transits, occultations, and eclipses of the four great satellites of Jupiter during February–November 2008. Jupiter is not well-placed for observing during the first and last month since it is in conjunction with the Sun on Dec. 23. Double shadow transits and satellite transits are indicated in **bold.**

Since the satellite phenomena are not instantaneous but take up to several minutes, the predicted times are for the middle of each event. The predictions were generated by the Institut de Mécanique Céleste et de Calcul des Ephémérides in Paris.

Satellites are denoted using the standard designations: I = Io; II = Europa; III = Ganymede; IV = Callisto. Events are denoted using the following abbreviations:

Ec = eclipse; Oc = occultation; Tr = transit of satellite; Sh = transit of shadow; I = ingress; E = egress; D = disappearance; R = reappearance

The general motion of the satellites and the successive phenomena are shown in the diagram at right, which is a view of Jupiter and the orbit of one of its satellites looking down from the north side. Satellites move from east to west across the face of the planet and from west to east behind it (here "east" and "west" are used in the sense of the observer's sky, not in the Jovian sense). Before opposition, shadows fall to the west and after opposition, to the east (as in the diagram).

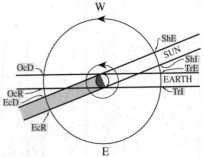

The sequence of phenomena for the outer satellite shown in the diagram, counterclockwise beginning at the lower right, is transit ingress (TrI), transit egress (TrE), shadow ingress (ShI), shadow egress (ShE), occultation disappearance (OcD), occultation reappearance (OcR), eclipse disappearance (EcD), and eclipse reappearance (EcR). The actual sequence will depend on the actual Sun–Jupiter–Earth angle and the size of the satellite's orbit.

Over three-quarters of the phenomena listed will not be visible from any one location because they occur when Jupiter is near or below the horizon or when daylight interferes. In practice, an observer usually knows when Jupiter will be conveniently placed in the night sky; if not, he or she can check THE SKY MONTH BY MONTH section (pp. 96–119) for this information. The table can then be scanned to see if there are any events during the intended observing period. For example, an observer in Halifax would know that Jupiter is well placed near midnight in early July, with opposition occurring on Jul. 9. If planning to observe from Jul. 7 22:00 to Jul. 8 2:00 ADT (3 h behind UT), he or she could scan the table for events in the interval Jul. 8 1:00 to 5:00 UT and find that there are four events, beginning at 22:25 ADT with the ingress of Io's shadow, closely followed at 22:27 by a transit of Io. Just over two hours later Io's shadow egresses at 0:41 (Jul. 8) followed by the end of Io's transit a few minutes later. The configuration of the four Galilean satellites during that night is given in the diagram on the right-hand side of p. 109 in the THE SKY MONTH BY MONTH section.

A total of 2003 events (363 eclipse, 363 occultation, 638 transit, and 639 shadow) appear in the table, an average of one event every 4 h 23 min.

SATELLITES OF JUPITER, UT OF 2008 GEOCENTRIC PHENOMENA

FEBRUARY

Day	Time	Sat	Ph		Day	Time	Sat	Ph		Day	Time	Sat	Ph
0	2:33	II	EcD			11:48	I	ShE		20	3:17	I	EcD
	6:32	II	OcR			12:37	I	TrE			5:19	IV	TrI
	16:04	I	EcD			18:25	II	EcD			6:28	I	OcR
	18:59	I	OcR			22:44	II	OcR			7:56	IV	TrE
	19:13	III	ShI		11	6:55	I	EcD		21	0:25	I	ShI
	21:52	III	TrI			9:59	I	OcR			1:21	I	TrI
	22:03	III	ShE			13:18	III	EcD			2:39	I	ShE
1	0:48	III	TrE			13:38	IV	EcD			3:36	I	TrE
	13:13	I	ShI			15:26	IV	EcR			10:17	II	EcD
	13:52	I	TrI			16:11	III	EcR			14:54	II	OcR
	15:26	I	ShE			16:35	III	OcD			21:45	I	EcD
	16:07	I	TrE			19:35	III	OcR		22	0:58	I	OcR
	21:39	II	ShI			21:06	IV	OcD			7:09	III	ShI
	23:01	II	TrI			23:36	IV	OcR			10:02	III	ShE
2	0:20	II	ShE		12	4:03	I	ShI			11:00	III	TrI
	1:42	II	TrE			4:52	I	TrI			14:01	III	TrE
	10:33	I	EcD			6:17	I	ShE			18:54	I	ShI
	13:29	I	OcR			7:07	I	TrE			19:51	I	TrI
3	2:54	IV	ShI			13:33	II	ShI			21:07	I	ShE
	4:26	IV	ShE			15:13	II	TrI			22:05	I	TrE
	7:41	I	ShI			16:13	II	ShE		23	5:26	II	ShI
	8:22	I	TrI			17:54	II	TrE			7:22	II	TrI
	9:13	IV	TrI		13	1:23	I	EcD			8:06	II	ShE
	9:55	I	ShE			4:29	I	OcR			10:03	II	TrE
	10:37	I	TrE			22:32	I	ShI			16:14	I	EcD
	11:27	IV	TrE			23:22	I	TrI			19:28	I	OcR
	15:50	II	EcD		14	0:45	I	ShE		24	13:22	I	ShI
	19:56	II	OcR			1:36	I	TrE			14:21	I	TrI
4	5:01	I	EcD			7:42	II	EcD			15:36	I	ShE
	7:59	I	OcR			12:07	II	OcR			16:35	I	TrE
	9:20	III	EcD			19:52	I	EcD			23:34	II	EcD
	15:10	III	OcR			22:59	I	OcR		25	4:17	II	OcR
5	2:09	I	ShI		15	3:10	III	ShI			10:42	I	EcD
	2:52	I	TrI			6:03	III	ShE			13:57	I	OcR
	4:23	I	ShE			6:39	III	TrI			21:14	III	EcD
	5:07	I	TrE			9:39	III	TrE		26	0:09	III	EcR
	10:57	II	ShI			17:00	I	ShI			1:15	III	OcD
	12:25	II	TrI			17:52	I	TrI			4:18	III	OcR
	13:38	II	ShE			19:14	I	ShE			7:51	I	ShI
	15:07	II	TrE			20:06	I	TrE			8:50	I	TrI
	23:30	I	EcD		16	2:50	II	ShI			10:04	I	ShE
6	2:39	I	OcR			4:36	II	TrI			11:05	I	TrE
	20:38	I	ShI			5:31	II	ShE			18:43	II	ShI
	21:22	I	TrI			7:18	II	TrE			20:45	II	TrI
	22:52	I	ShE			14:20	I	EcD			21:23	II	ShE
	23:37	I	TrE			17:29	I	OcR			23:26	II	TrE
7	5:08	II	EcD		17	11:28	I	ShI		27	5:11	I	EcD
	9:20	II	OcR			12:22	I	TrI			8:27	I	OcR
	17:58	I	EcD			13:42	I	ShE		28	2:19	I	ShI
	20:59	I	OcR			14:36	I	TrE			3:20	I	TrI
	23:11	III	ShI			20:59	II	EcD			4:33	I	ShE
8	2:02	III	ShE		18	1:31	II	OcR			5:34	I	TrE
	2:16	III	TrI			8:49	I	EcD			7:31	IV	EcD
	5:14	III	TrE			11:58	I	OcR			9:37	IV	EcR
	15:06	I	ShI			17:16	III	EcD			12:51	IV	EcD
	15:52	I	TrI			20:10	III	EcR			16:59	IV	OcD
	17:20	I	ShE			20:56	III	OcD			17:39	II	OcR
	18:07	I	TrE			23:57	III	OcR			19:50	IV	OcR
9	0:15	II	ShI		19	5:57	I	ShI			23:39	I	EcD
	1:49	II	TrI			6:52	I	TrI		29	2:57	I	OcR
	2:55	II	ShE			8:11	I	ShE			11:07	III	ShI
	4:31	II	TrE			9:06	I	TrE			14:01	III	ShE
	12:26	I	EcD			16:08	II	ShI			15:19	III	TrI
	15:29	I	OcR			17:59	II	TrI			18:21	III	TrE
10	9:35	I	ShI			18:48	II	ShE			20:47	I	ShI
	10:22	I	TrI			20:41	II	TrE			21:50	I	TrI
						20:46	IV	ShI			23:01	I	ShE
						22:38	IV	ShE					

MARCH

Day	Time	Sat	Ph		Day	Time	Sat	Ph
1	0:04	I	TrE			11:38	I	ShI
	8:01	II	ShI			12:46	I	TrI
	10:07	II	TrI			12:54	III	OcR
	10:41	II	ShE			13:52	I	ShE
	12:48	II	TrE			15:01	I	TrE
	18:07	I	EcD			23:53	II	ShI
	21:26	I	OcR		12	2:11	II	TrI
2	15:16	I	ShI			2:33	II	ShE
	16:19	I	TrI			4:52	II	TrE
	17:30	I	ShE			8:58	I	EcD
	18:34	I	TrE			12:23	I	OcR
3	2:09	II	EcD		13	6:06	I	ShI
	7:02	II	OcR			7:16	I	TrI
	12:36	I	EcD			8:20	I	ShE
	15:56	I	OcR			9:30	I	TrE
4	1:12	III	EcD			18:01	II	EcD
	4:08	III	EcR			23:07	II	OcR
	5:32	III	OcD		14	3:26	I	EcD
	8:37	III	OcR			6:52	I	OcR
	9:44	I	ShI			19:03	III	ShI
	10:49	I	TrI			21:59	III	ShE
	11:58	I	ShE			23:47	III	TrI
	13:03	I	TrE		15	0:35	I	ShI
	21:18	II	ShI			1:45	I	TrI
	23:28	II	TrI			2:48	I	ShE
	23:58	II	ShE			2:52	III	TrE
5	2:10	II	TrE			3:59	I	TrE
	7:04	I	EcD			13:10	II	ShI
	10:25	I	OcR			15:31	II	TrI
6	4:13	I	ShI			15:50	II	ShE
	5:18	I	TrI			18:13	II	TrE
	6:26	I	ShE			21:54	I	EcD
	7:33	I	TrE		16	1:21	I	OcR
	15:26	II	EcD			1:25	IV	EcD
	20:24	II	OcR			3:47	IV	EcR
7	1:33	I	EcD			12:24	IV	OcD
	4:55	I	OcR			15:30	IV	OcR
	14:41	IV	ShI			19:03	I	ShI
	15:05	**III**	**ShI**			20:14	I	TrI
	16:50	IV	ShE			21:17	I	ShE
	18:00	III	ShE			22:29	I	TrE
	19:34	III	TrI		17	7:19	II	EcD
	22:38	III	TrE			12:29	II	OcR
	22:41	I	ShI			16:23	I	EcD
	23:48	I	TrI			19:50	I	OcR
8	0:55	I	ShE		18	9:09	III	EcD
	1:01	IV	TrI			12:07	III	EcR
	2:02	I	TrE			13:31	I	ShI
	3:55	IV	TrE			13:59	III	OcD
	10:35	II	ShI			14:43	I	TrI
	12:50	II	TrI			15:45	I	ShE
	13:15	II	ShE			16:58	I	TrE
	15:31	II	TrE			17:07	III	OcR
	20:01	I	EcD		19	2:27	II	ShI
	23:24	I	OcR			4:51	II	TrI
9	17:09	I	ShI			5:07	II	ShE
	18:17	I	TrI			7:33	II	TrE
	19:23	I	ShE			10:51	I	EcD
	20:31	I	TrE			14:19	I	OcR
10	4:44	II	EcD		20	8:00	I	ShI
	9:46	II	OcR			9:12	I	TrI
	14:29	I	EcD			10:14	I	ShE
	17:53	I	OcR			11:27	I	TrE
11	5:11	III	EcD			20:36	II	EcD
	8:08	III	EcR		21	1:49	II	OcR
	9:48	III	OcD			5:19	I	EcD
						8:48	I	OcR
						23:01	III	ShI

SATELLITES OF JUPITER, UT OF 2008 GEOCENTRIC PHENOMENA (cont)

MARCH (cont)

22	1:58	III	ShE
	2:28	I	ShI
	3:41	I	TrI
	3:58	III	TrI
	4:42	I	ShE
	5:56	I	TrE
	7:04	III	TrE
	15:44	II	ShI
	18:11	II	TrI
	18:24	II	ShE
	20:53	II	TrE
	23:48	I	EcD
23	3:17	I	OcR
	20:57	I	ShI
	22:10	I	TrI
	23:10	I	ShE
24	0:25	I	TrE
	8:36	IV	ShI
	9:54	II	EcD
	10:59	IV	ShE
	15:10	II	OcR
	18:16	I	EcD
	20:09	IV	TrI
	21:46	I	OcR
	23:17	IV	TrE
25	13:07	III	EcD
	15:25	I	ShI
	16:06	III	EcR
	16:39	I	TrI
	17:39	I	ShE
	18:08	III	OcD
	18:54	I	TrE
	21:16	III	OcR
26	5:02	II	ShI
	7:30	II	TrI
	7:41	II	ShE
	10:12	II	TrE
	12:44	I	EcD
	16:15	I	OcR
27	9:53	I	ShI
	11:08	I	TrI
	12:07	I	ShE
	13:23	I	TrE
	23:12	II	EcD
28	4:30	II	OcR
	7:13	I	EcD
	10:44	I	OcR
29	2:59	III	ShI
	4:22	**I**	**ShI**
	5:37	I	TrI
	5:57	III	ShE
	6:36	I	ShE
	7:52	I	TrE
	8:05	III	TrI
	11:12	III	TrE
	18:19	II	ShI
	20:49	II	TrI
	20:58	II	ShE
	23:31	II	TrE
30	1:41	I	EcD
	5:13	I	OcR
	22:50	I	ShI
31	0:06	I	TrI
	1:04	I	ShE
	2:21	I	TrE
	12:29	II	EcD
	17:50	II	ShI
	20:09	I	EcD
	23:41	I	OcR

APRIL

1	17:04	III	EcD
	17:19	I	ShI
	18:35	I	TrI
	19:21	IV	EcD
	19:33	I	ShE
	20:05	III	EcR
	20:50	I	TrE
	21:56	IV	EcR
	22:12	III	OcD
2	1:22	III	OcR
	7:10	IV	OcD
	7:36	II	ShI
	10:08	II	TrI
	10:15	II	ShE
	10:29	IV	OcR
	12:49	II	TrE
	14:38	I	EcD
	18:10	I	OcR
3	11:47	I	ShI
	13:04	I	TrI
	14:01	I	ShE
	15:18	I	TrE
4	1:47	II	EcD
	7:09	II	OcR
	9:06	I	EcD
	12:39	I	OcR
5	6:15	I	ShI
	6:58	**III**	**ShI**
	7:32	I	TrI
	8:29	I	ShE
	9:47	I	TrE
	9:57	III	ShE
	12:10	III	TrI
	15:18	III	TrE
	20:53	II	ShI
	23:25	II	TrI
	23:32	II	ShE
6	2:07	II	TrE
	3:34	I	EcD
	7:07	I	OcR
7	0:44	I	ShI
	2:01	I	TrI
	2:58	I	ShE
	4:16	I	TrE
	15:05	II	EcD
	20:28	II	OcR
	22:03	I	EcD
8	1:36	I	OcR
	19:12	I	ShI
	20:29	I	TrI
	21:02	III	EcD
	21:26	I	ShE
	22:44	I	TrE
9	0:03	III	EcR
	2:13	III	OcD
	5:24	III	OcR
	10:09	II	ShI
	12:43	II	TrI
	12:49	II	ShE
	15:24	II	TrE
	16:31	I	EcD
	20:04	I	OcR
10	2:32	IV	ShI
	5:09	IV	ShE
	13:41	I	ShI
	14:35	IV	TrI
	14:58	I	TrI
	15:55	I	ShE
	17:13	I	TrE
	17:54	IV	TrE
11	4:22	II	EcD
	9:46	II	OcR
	10:59	I	EcD
	14:32	I	OcR
12	8:09	I	ShI
	9:26	I	TrI
	10:23	I	ShE
	10:57	III	ShI
	11:41	I	TrE
	13:56	III	ShE
	16:09	III	TrI
	19:18	III	TrE
	23:26	II	ShI
13	2:00	II	TrI
	2:06	II	ShE
	4:41	II	TrE
	5:27	I	EcD
	9:01	I	OcR
14	2:37	I	ShI
	3:55	I	TrI
	4:52	I	ShE
	6:10	I	TrE
	17:40	II	EcD
	23:04	II	OcR
	23:56	I	EcD
15	3:29	I	OcR
	21:06	I	ShI
	22:23	I	TrI
	23:20	I	ShE
16	0:38	I	TrE
	1:00	III	EcD
	4:02	III	EcR
	6:11	III	OcD
	9:22	III	OcR
	12:43	II	ShI
	15:16	II	TrI
	15:23	II	ShE
	17:58	II	TrE
	18:24	I	EcD
	21:57	I	OcR
17	15:34	I	ShI
	16:51	I	TrI
	17:48	I	ShE
	19:06	I	TrE
18	6:58	II	EcD
	12:21	II	OcR
	12:52	I	EcD
	13:17	IV	EcD
	16:04	IV	EcR
	16:25	I	OcR
19	1:11	IV	OcD
	4:39	IV	OcR
	10:03	I	ShI
	11:19	I	TrI
	12:17	I	ShE
	13:34	I	TrE
	14:55	III	ShI
	17:56	III	ShE
	20:05	III	TrI
	23:15	III	TrE
20	2:00	II	ShI
	4:32	II	TrI
	4:40	II	ShE
	7:14	II	TrE
	7:21	I	EcD
	10:53	I	OcR
21	4:31	I	ShI
	5:47	I	TrI
	6:45	I	ShE
	8:03	I	TrE
	20:16	II	EcD
22	1:39	II	OcR
	1:49	I	EcD
	5:21	I	OcR
	22:59	I	ShI
23	0:16	I	TrI
	1:14	I	ShE
	2:31	I	TrE
	4:58	III	EcD
	8:01	III	EcR
	10:04	III	OcD
	13:17	III	OcR
	15:17	II	ShI
	17:47	II	TrI
	17:57	II	ShE
	20:17	I	EcD
	20:29	II	TrE
	23:49	I	OcR
24	17:28	I	ShI
	18:44	I	TrI
	19:42	I	ShE
	20:59	I	TrE
25	9:34	II	EcD
	14:46	I	EcD
	14:55	II	OcR
	18:17	I	OcR
26	11:56	I	ShI
	13:11	I	TrI
	14:11	I	ShE
	15:27	I	TrE
	18:53	III	ShI
	20:29	**IV**	**ShI**
	21:54	III	ShE
	23:18	IV	ShE
	23:56	III	TrI
27	3:07	III	TrE
	4:34	II	ShI
	7:02	II	TrI
	7:14	II	ShE
	8:11	IV	TrI
	9:14	I	EcD
	9:44	II	TrE
	11:39	IV	TrE
	12:45	I	OcR
28	6:25	I	ShI
	7:39	I	TrI
	8:39	I	ShE
	9:54	I	TrE
	22:52	II	EcD
29	3:42	I	EcD
	4:11	I	OcR
	7:12	I	OcR
30	0:53	I	ShI
	2:07	I	TrI
	3:08	I	ShE
	4:22	I	TrE
	8:56	III	EcD
	12:01	III	EcR
	13:54	III	OcD
	17:07	III	OcR
	17:50	II	ShI
	20:16	II	TrI
	20:31	II	ShE
	22:10	I	EcD
	22:58	II	TrE

MAY

1	1:40	I	OcR
	19:21	I	ShI
	20:35	I	TrI
	21:36	I	ShE
	22:50	I	TrE
2	12:10	II	EcD
	16:39	I	EcD
	17:26	II	OcR
	20:07	I	OcR
3	13:50	I	ShI
	15:03	I	TrI
	16:05	I	ShE
	17:18	I	TrE
	22:50	III	ShI
4	1:53	III	ShE
	3:43	III	TrI
	6:54	III	TrE
	7:07	II	ShI
	9:30	II	TrI
	9:48	II	ShE
	11:07	I	EcD
	12:12	II	TrE
	14:35	I	OcR
5	7:13	IV	EcD
	8:18	I	ShI
	9:30	I	TrI
	10:12	IV	EcR
	10:33	I	ShE
	11:45	I	TrE
	18:19	IV	OcD
	21:54	IV	OcR
6	1:28	II	EcD
	5:35	I	EcD
	6:41	II	OcR
	9:02	I	OcR
7	2:47	I	ShI
	3:58	I	TrI
	5:01	I	ShE
	6:13	I	TrE
	12:54	III	EcD
	16:00	III	EcR
	17:39	III	OcD
	20:24	II	ShI
	20:52	III	OcR
	22:43	II	TrI
	23:04	II	ShE
8	0:04	I	EcD
	1:25	II	TrE
	3:30	I	OcR
	21:15	I	ShI
	22:25	I	TrI
	23:30	I	ShE
9	0:41	I	TrE
	14:46	II	EcD
	18:32	I	EcD
	19:55	II	OcR
	21:57	I	OcR
10	15:44	I	ShI
	16:53	I	TrI
	17:58	I	ShE
	19:08	I	TrE
11	2:49	III	ShI
	5:53	III	ShE
	7:26	III	TrI
	9:40	II	ShI
	10:38	III	TrE

SATELLITES OF JUPITER, UT OF 2008 GEOCENTRIC PHENOMENA (cont)

MAY (cont)

Date	Time	Sat	Phen
	11:55	II	TrI
	12:21	II	ShE
	13:00	I	EcD
	14:38	II	TrE
	16:24	I	OcR
12	10:12	I	ShI
	11:20	I	TrI
	12:27	I	ShE
	13:35	I	TrE
13	4:04	II	EcD
	7:29	I	EcD
	9:09	II	OcR
	10:51	I	OcR
	14:26	IV	ShI
	17:27	IV	ShE
14	0:52	IV	TrI
	4:25	IV	TrE
	4:40	I	ShI
	5:47	I	TrI
	6:55	I	ShE
	8:03	I	TrE
	16:52	III	EcD
	19:59	III	EcR
	21:19	III	OcD
	22:57	II	ShI
15	0:33	III	OcR
	1:07	II	TrI
	1:38	II	ShE
	1:57	I	EcD
	3:50	II	TrE
	5:19	I	OcR
	23:09	I	ShI
16	0:14	I	TrI
	1:24	I	ShE
	2:30	I	TrE
	17:22	II	EcD
	20:25	I	EcD
	22:21	II	OcR
	23:46	I	OcR
17	17:37	I	ShI
	18:42	I	TrI
	19:52	I	ShE
	20:57	I	TrE
18	6:47	III	ShI
	9:53	III	ShE
	11:04	III	TrI
	12:14	II	ShI
	14:17	III	TrE
	14:19	II	TrI
	14:54	I	EcD
	14:55	II	ShE
	17:01	II	TrE
	18:13	I	OcR
19	12:06	I	ShI
	13:09	I	TrI
	14:21	I	ShE
	15:24	I	TrE
20	6:40	II	EcD
	9:22	I	EcD
	11:34	II	OcR
	12:39	I	OcR
21	6:34	I	ShI
	7:36	I	TrI
	8:49	I	ShE
	9:51	I	TrE
	20:50	III	EcD
	23:57	III	EcR
22	0:54	III	OcD
	1:11	IV	EcD
	1:30	II	ShI
	3:30	II	TrI
	3:50	I	EcD
	4:08	III	OcR
	4:12	II	ShE
	4:20	IV	EcR
	6:12	II	TrE
	7:06	II	OcR
	10:32	IV	OcD
	14:10	IV	OcR
23	1:03	I	ShI
	2:03	I	TrI
	3:18	I	ShE
	4:18	I	TrE
	19:58	II	EcD
	22:19	I	EcD
24	0:46	II	OcR
	1:33	I	OcR
	19:31	I	ShI
	20:29	I	TrI
	21:46	I	ShE
	22:45	I	TrE
25	10:46	III	ShI
	13:53	III	ShE
	14:39	III	TrI
	14:47	II	ShI
	16:40	II	TrI
	16:47	I	EcD
	17:28	II	ShE
	17:52	III	TrE
	19:23	II	TrE
	20:00	I	OcR
26	13:59	I	ShI
	14:56	I	TrI
	16:15	I	ShE
	17:12	I	TrE
27	9:17	II	EcD
	11:15	I	EcD
	13:58	II	OcR
	14:26	I	OcR
28	8:28	I	ShI
	9:23	I	TrI
	10:43	I	ShE
	11:39	I	TrE
29	0:48	III	EcD
	3:56	III	EcR
	4:04	II	ShI
	4:25	III	OcD
	5:44	I	EcD
	5:50	II	TrI
	6:45	II	ShE
	7:39	III	OcR
	8:33	II	TrE
	8:53	I	OcR
30	2:56	I	ShI
	3:50	I	TrI
	5:12	I	ShE
	6:06	I	TrE
	8:24	IV	ShI
	11:35	IV	ShE
	16:36	IV	TrI
	20:12	IV	TrE
	22:34	II	EcD
31	0:12	I	EcD
	3:08	II	OcR
	3:20	I	OcR
	21:25	I	ShI
	22:16	I	TrI
	23:41	I	ShE

JUNE

Date	Time	Sat	Phen
1	0:32	I	TrE
	14:45	III	ShI
	17:20	**II**	**ShI**
	17:53	III	ShE
	18:08	III	TrI
	18:40	I	EcD
	18:59	II	TrI
	20:02	II	ShE
	21:22	III	TrE
	21:42	II	TrE
	21:46	I	OcR
2	15:53	I	ShI
	16:43	I	TrI
	18:09	I	ShE
	18:59	I	TrE
3	11:53	II	EcD
	13:09	I	EcD
	16:13	I	OcR
	16:19	II	OcR
4	10:22	I	ShI
	11:10	I	TrI
	12:38	I	ShE
	13:26	I	TrE
5	4:46	III	EcD
	6:37	II	ShI
	7:37	I	EcD
	8:08	II	TrI
	9:19	II	ShE
	10:39	I	OcR
	10:51	II	TrE
	11:07	III	OcR
6	4:50	I	ShI
	5:36	I	TrI
	7:06	I	ShE
	7:52	I	TrE
7	1:11	II	EcD
	2:05	I	EcD
	5:05	I	OcR
	5:29	II	OcR
	19:10	IV	EcD
	22:29	IV	EcR
	23:19	I	ShI
8	0:02	I	TrI
	1:35	I	ShE
	1:50	IV	OcD
	2:19	I	TrE
	5:30	IV	OcR
	18:44	III	ShI
	19:54	**II**	**ShI**
	20:34	I	EcD
	21:17	II	TrI
	21:34	III	TrI
	21:52	III	ShE
	22:36	II	ShE
	23:31	I	OcR
9	0:00	II	TrE
	0:48	III	TrE
	17:47	I	ShI
	18:29	I	TrI
	20:03	I	ShE
	20:45	I	TrE
10	14:30	II	EcD
	15:02	I	EcD
	17:58	I	OcR
	18:39	II	OcR
11	12:16	I	ShI
	12:55	I	TrI
	14:32	I	ShE
	15:11	I	TrE
12	8:45	III	EcD
	9:10	III	ShI
	9:31	I	EcD
	10:25	II	TrI
	11:53	II	ShE
	12:24	I	OcR
	13:08	II	TrE
	14:31	III	OcR
13	6:44	I	ShI
	7:21	I	TrI
	9:00	I	ShE
	9:38	I	TrE
14	3:48	II	EcD
	3:59	I	EcD
	6:50	I	OcR
	7:47	II	OcR
15	1:13	I	ShI
	1:48	I	TrI
	3:29	I	ShE
	4:04	I	TrE
	22:27	I	EcD
	22:27	II	ShI
	22:42	**II**	**ShI**
	23:33	II	TrI
16	0:56	III	TrI
	1:10	II	ShE
	1:16	I	OcR
	1:52	III	ShE
	2:16	II	TrE
	2:24	IV	ShI
	4:10	III	TrE
	5:45	IV	ShE
	7:30	IV	TrI
	11:08	IV	TrE
	19:42	I	ShI
	20:14	I	TrI
	21:58	I	ShE
	22:30	I	TrE
17	16:56	II	EcD
	17:07	II	EcD
	19:42	I	OcR
	20:57	II	OcR
18	14:10	I	ShI
	14:40	I	TrI
	16:26	I	ShE
	16:56	I	TrE
19	11:24	I	EcD
	11:44	II	ShI
	12:40	II	TrI
	12:44	III	EcD
	14:08	I	OcR
	14:27	II	ShE
	15:24	II	TrE
	17:52	III	OcR
20	8:39	I	ShI
	9:06	I	TrI
	10:55	I	ShE
	11:23	I	TrE
21	5:53	I	EcD
	6:24	II	EcD
	8:34	I	OcR
	10:05	II	OcR
22	3:07	I	ShI
	3:32	I	TrI
	5:24	I	ShE
	5:49	I	TrE
23	0:21	I	EcD
	1:01	II	ShI
	1:47	II	TrI
	2:40	**III**	**ShI**
	3:00	I	OcR
	3:44	II	ShE
	4:15	III	TrI
	4:31	II	TrE
	5:52	III	ShE
	7:29	III	TrE
	21:36	I	ShI
	21:58	I	TrI
	23:52	I	ShE
24	0:15	I	TrE
	13:09	IV	EcD
	18:49	I	EcD
	19:43	II	EcD
	20:05	IV	OcR
	21:26	I	OcR
	23:13	II	OcR
25	16:04	I	ShI
	16:25	I	TrI
	18:21	I	ShE
	18:41	I	TrE
26	13:18	I	EcD
	14:18	II	ShI
	14:54	II	TrI
	15:52	I	OcR
	16:43	III	EcD
	17:01	II	ShE
	17:38	II	TrE
	21:11	III	OcR
27	10:33	I	ShI
	10:51	I	TrI
	12:49	I	ShE
	13:07	I	TrE
28	7:46	I	EcD
	9:01	II	EcD
	10:18	I	OcR
	12:21	II	OcR
29	5:02	I	ShI
	5:17	I	TrI
	7:18	I	ShE
	7:33	I	TrE
30	2:15	I	EcD
	3:35	II	ShI
	4:01	II	TrI
	4:44	I	OcR
	6:18	II	ShE
	6:40	III	ShI
	6:45	II	TrE
	7:33	III	TrI
	9:52	III	ShE
	10:47	III	TrE
	23:30	I	ShI
	23:43	I	TrI

JULY

Date	Time	Sat	Phen
1	1:47	I	ShE
	1:59	I	TrE
	20:43	I	EcD
	22:20	II	EcD
	23:10	I	OcR

SATELLITES OF JUPITER, UT OF 2008 GEOCENTRIC PHENOMENA (cont)

Day	Time	Sat	Phen	Day	Time	Sat	Phen	Day	Time	Sat	Phen	Day	Time	Sat	Phen	Day	Time	Sat	Phen
JULY (cont)				13	8:45	I	TrI		23:21	I	TrI	3	0:54	II	EcR		12:25	II	OcD
2	1:29	II	OcR		8:51	I	ShI		23:43	I	ShI		13:59	I	TrI		15:21	IV	OcR
	17:59	I	ShI		11:01	I	TrE	24	1:38	I	TrE		14:36	I	ShI		16:51	II	EcR
	18:09	I	TrI		11:07	I	ShE		2:00	I	ShE		16:16	I	TrE		19:15	IV	EcD
	20:15	I	ShE	14	5:55	I	OcD		20:31	I	OcD		16:52	I	ShE		23:07	IV	EcR
	20:24	IV	ShI		8:19	I	EcR		23:10	I	EcR	4	11:09	I	OcD	14	4:39	I	TrI
	20:25	I	TrE		8:28	II	TrI		23:49	II	TrI		14:02	I	EcR		5:28	I	ShI
	21:51	IV	TrI		8:43	II	ShI	25	0:35	II	ShI		15:13	II	TrI		6:55	I	TrE
	23:55	IV	ShE		11:12	II	TrE		2:33	II	TrE		16:27	II	ShI		7:45	I	ShE
3	1:28	IV	TrE		11:27	II	ShE		3:19	II	ShE		17:56	II	TrE	15	1:48	I	OcD
	15:12	I	EcD		14:07	III	TrI		7:03	III	OcD		19:11	II	ShE		4:54	I	EcR
	16:52	II	ShI		14:40	III	ShI		11:54	III	EcR	5	0:04	III	TrI		6:40	II	TrI
	17:08	II	TrI		17:21	III	TrE		17:48	I	TrI		2:30	IV	TrI		8:20	II	ShI
	17:36	I	OcR		17:54	III	ShE		18:12	I	ShI		2:38	III	ShI		9:24	II	TrE
	19:35	II	ShE	15	3:11	I	TrI		20:04	I	TrE		3:17	III	TrE		11:04	II	ShE
	19:52	II	TrE		3:20	I	ShI		20:28	I	ShE		5:55	III	ShE		17:14	III	OcD
	20:42	III	EcD		5:27	I	TrE	26	14:58	I	OcD		6:05	IV	TrE		20:27	III	OcR
4	0:27	III	OcR		5:36	I	ShE		17:39	I	EcR		8:26	I	TrI		20:38	III	EcD
	12:28	I	ShI	16	0:21	I	OcD		18:38	II	OcD		8:30	IV	ShI		23:06	I	TrI
	12:35	I	TrI		2:47	I	EcR		22:17	II	EcR		**9:04**	**I**	**ShI**		23:56	III	EcR
	14:44	I	ShE		3:14	II	OcD	27	12:14	I	TrI		10:42	I	TrE		23:57	I	ShI
	14:51	I	TrE		6:21	II	EcR		12:41	I	ShI		11:21	I	ShE	16	1:22	I	TrE
5	9:40	I	EcD		21:37	I	TrI		14:30	I	TrE		12:16	IV	ShE		2:13	I	ShE
	11:38	II	EcD		21:48	I	ShI		14:57	I	ShE	6	5:35	I	OcD		20:15	I	OcD
	12:02	I	OcR		23:53	I	TrE		20:57	IV	OcD		8:31	I	EcR		23:23	I	EcR
	14:36	II	OcR	17	0:05	I	ShE	28	0:35	IV	OcR		10:05	II	OcD	17	1:36	II	OcD
6	6:56	I	ShI		18:47	I	OcD		1:12	IV	EcD		14:14	II	EcR		6:09	II	EcR
	7:01	I	TrI		21:16	I	EcR		4:56	IV	EcR	7	2:53	I	TrI		17:33	I	TrI
	9:13	I	ShE		21:35	II	TrI		9:24	I	OcD		3:33	I	ShI		18:26	I	ShI
	9:17	I	TrE		22:00	II	ShI		12:07	I	EcR		5:09	I	TrE		19:49	I	TrE
7	4:09	I	EcD	18	0:18	II	TrE		12:56	II	TrI		5:50	I	ShE		20:42	I	ShE
	6:09	II	ShI		0:44	II	ShE		13:52	II	ShI	8	0:02	I	OcD	18	14:42	I	OcD
	6:14	II	TrI		3:45	III	OcD		15:40	II	TrE		2:59	I	EcR		17:52	I	EcR
	6:27	I	OcR		7:53	III	EcR		16:36	II	ShE		4:21	II	TrI		19:50	II	TrI
	8:52	II	ShE		16:03	I	TrI		20:43	III	TrI		5:44	II	ShI		21:37	II	ShI
	8:58	II	TrE		16:17	I	ShI		22:39	III	ShI		7:05	II	TrE		22:34	II	TrE
	10:39	III	ShI		18:19	I	TrE		23:56	III	TrE		8:29	II	ShE	19	0:22	II	ShE
	10:50	III	TrI		18:34	I	ShE	29	1:54	III	ShE		13:47	III	OcD		6:58	III	TrI
	13:52	III	ShE	19	12:02	IV	TrI		6:40	I	TrI		19:55	III	EcR		10:11	III	TrE
	14:03	III	TrE		13:13	I	OcD		7:09	I	ShI		21:19	I	TrI		10:38	III	ShI
8	1:25	I	ShI		14:26	IV	ShI		8:56	I	TrE		22:02	I	ShI		12:00	I	TrI
	1:27	I	TrI		15:37	IV	TrE		9:26	I	ShE		23:35	I	TrE		12:55	I	ShI
	3:41	I	ShE		15:44	I	EcR	30	3:50	I	OcD	9	0:18	I	ShE		13:56	III	ShE
	3:43	I	TrE		16:21	II	OcD		6:36	I	EcR		18:28	I	OcD		14:16	I	TrE
	22:37	I	EcD		18:05	IV	ShE		7:47	II	OcD		21:28	I	EcR		15:11	I	ShE
9	0:53	I	OcR		19:40	II	EcR		11:36	II	EcR		23:15	II	OcD	20	9:08	I	OcD
	0:57	II	EcD	20	10:29	I	TrI	31	1:07	I	TrI	10	3:32	II	EcR		12:20	I	EcR
	3:45	II	OcR		10:46	I	ShI		1:38	I	ShI		15:46	I	TrI		14:47	II	OcD
	19:53	I	TrI		12:45	I	TrE		3:23	I	TrE		16:31	I	ShI		19:28	II	EcR
	19:54	I	ShI		13:02	I	ShE		3:55	I	ShE		18:02	I	TrE	21	6:27	I	TrI
	22:09	I	TrE	21	7:39	I	OcD		22:16	I	OcD		18:47	I	ShE		7:24	I	ShI
	22:10	I	ShE		10:13	I	EcR	**AUGUST**				11	12:55	I	OcD		8:43	I	TrE
10	17:04	I	OcD		10:42	II	TrI	1	1:05	I	EcR		15:57	I	EcR		9:40	I	ShE
	19:21	I	EcR		11:17	II	ShI		2:04	II	TrI		17:30	II	TrI		17:38	IV	TrI
	19:21	II	TrI		13:25	II	TrE		3:09	II	ShI		19:02	II	ShI		21:12	IV	TrE
	19:26	II	ShI		14:01	II	ShE		4:48	II	TrE		20:14	II	TrE	22	2:34	IV	ShI
	22:05	II	TrE		17:24	III	TrI		5:54	II	ShE		21:47	II	ShE		3:35	I	OcD
	22:10	II	ShE		18:39	III	ShI		10:23	III	OcD	12	3:29	III	TrI		6:27	IV	ShE
11	0:29	III	OcD		20:38	III	TrE		15:54	III	EcR		6:38	III	ShI		6:49	I	EcR
	3:54	III	EcR		21:54	III	ShE		19:33	I	TrI		6:42	III	TrE		9:01	II	TrI
	6:40	IV	OcR	22	4:55	I	TrI		20:07	I	ShI		9:55	III	ShE		10:55	II	ShI
	10:46	IV	EcR		5:14	I	ShI		21:49	I	TrE		10:13	I	TrI		11:45	II	TrE
	14:19	I	TrI		7:12	I	TrE		22:23	I	ShE		11:00	I	ShI		13:40	II	ShE
	14:22	I	ShI		7:31	I	ShE	2	16:42	I	OcD		12:28	I	TrE		20:44	III	OcD
	16:35	I	TrE	23	2:05	I	OcD		19:33	I	EcR		13:16	I	ShE		23:58	III	OcR
	16:39	I	ShE		4:42	I	EcR		20:55	II	OcD	13	7:21	I	OcD	23	0:38	III	EcD
12	11:30	I	OcD		5:30	II	OcD							10:25	I	EcR		0:54	I	TrI
	13:50	I	EcR		8:59	II	EcR							11:43	IV	OcD		1:52	I	ShI
	14:05	II	OcD																	
	17:02	II	EcR																	

SATELLITES OF JUPITER, UT OF 2008 GEOCENTRIC PHENOMENA (cont)

AUGUST (cont)

```
        3:10  I   TrE
        3:57  III EcR
        4:08  I   ShE
       22:02  I   OcD

24  1:18  I   EcR
    3:59  II  OcD
    8:47  II  EcR
   19:22  I   TrI
   20:21  I   ShI
   21:37  I   TrE
   22:37  I   ShE

25 16:30  I   OcD
   19:47  I   EcR
   22:12  II  TrI

26  0:13  II  ShI
    0:56  II  TrE
    2:58  II  ShE
   10:31  III TrI
   13:44  III TrE
   13:49  I   TrI
   14:39  III ShI
   14:50  I   ShI
   16:04  I   TrE
   17:06  I   ShE
   17:57  III ShE

27 10:57  I   OcD
   14:15  I   EcR
   17:11  II  OcD
   22:06  II  EcR

28  8:16  I   TrI
    9:19  I   ShI
   10:32  I   TrE
   11:35  I   ShE

29  5:24  I   OcD
    8:44  I   EcR
   11:24  II  TrI
   13:31  II  ShI
   14:08  II  TrE
   16:16  II  ShE

30  0:19  III OcD
    2:44  I   TrI
    3:17  IV  OcD
    3:33  III OcR
    3:48  I   ShI
    4:37  III EcD
    4:59  I   TrE
    6:04  I   ShE
    6:56  IV  OcR
    7:57  III EcR
   13:19  IV  EcD
   17:18  IV  EcR
   23:51  I   OcD

31  3:13  I   EcR
    6:24  II  OcD
   11:24  II  EcR
   21:11  I   TrI
   22:17  I   ShI
   23:27  I   TrE
```

SEPTEMBER

```
1   0:33  I   ShE
   18:19  I   OcD
   21:42  I   EcR

2   0:37  II  TrI
    2:49  II  ShI
    3:20  II  TrE
```

```
        5:34  II  ShE
       14:09  III TrI
       15:39  I   TrI
       16:45  I   ShI
       17:22  III TrE
       17:54  I   TrE
       18:40  III ShI
       19:01  I   ShE
       21:58  III ShE

3  12:46  I   OcD
   16:10  I   EcR
   19:38  II  OcD

4   0:43  II  EcR
   10:06  I   TrI
   11:14  I   ShI
   12:22  I   TrE
   13:30  I   ShE

5   7:14  I   OcD
   10:39  I   EcR
   13:50  II  TrI
   16:07  II  ShI
   16:33  II  TrE
   18:52  II  ShE

6   3:58  III OcD
    4:34  I   TrI
    5:43  I   ShI
    6:49  I   TrE
    7:12  III OcR
    7:59  I   ShE
    8:37  III EcD
   11:57  III EcR

7   1:41  I   OcD
    5:08  I   EcR
    8:51  II  OcD
    9:39  IV  TrI
   13:15  IV  TrE
   14:01  II  EcR
   20:40  IV  ShI
   23:02  I   TrI

8   0:12  I   ShI
    0:38  IV  ShE
    1:17  I   TrE
    2:28  I   ShE
   20:09  I   OcD
   23:37  I   EcR

9   3:03  II  TrI
    5:25  II  ShI
    5:47  II  TrE
    8:10  II  ShE
   17:30  I   TrI
   17:51  III TrI
   18:41  I   ShI
   19:45  I   TrE
   20:57  I   ShE
   21:04  III TrE
   22:40  III ShI

10  1:59  III ShE
   14:37  I   OcD
   18:06  I   EcR
   22:06  II  OcD

11  3:20  II  EcR
   11:58  I   TrI
   13:10  I   ShI
   14:13  I   TrE
   15:25  I   ShE

12  9:05  I   OcD
   12:34  I   EcR
   16:18  II  TrI
```

```
       18:43  II  ShI
       19:01  II  TrE
       21:28  II  ShE

13  6:26  I   TrI
    7:39  I   ShI
    7:42  III OcD
    8:41  I   TrE
    9:54  I   ShE
   10:57  III OcR
   12:37  III EcD
   15:59  III EcR

14  3:33  I   OcD
    7:03  I   EcR
   11:21  II  OcD
   16:39  II  EcR

15  0:54  I   TrI
    2:07  I   ShI
    3:09  I   TrE
    4:23  I   ShE
   19:48  IV  OcD
   22:01  I   OcD
   23:29  IV  OcR

16  1:32  I   EcR
    5:32  II  TrI
    7:24  IV  EcD
    8:01  II  ShI
    8:16  II  TrE
   10:46  II  ShE
   11:29  IV  EcR
   19:22  I   TrI
   20:36  I   ShI
   21:37  I   TrE
   21:38  III TrI
   22:52  I   ShE

17  0:51  III TrE
    2:41  III ShI
    6:00  III ShE
   16:29  I   OcD
   20:01  I   EcR

18  0:37  II  OcD
    5:57  II  EcR
   13:50  I   TrI
   15:05  I   ShI
   16:05  I   TrE
   17:21  I   ShE

19 10:57  I   OcD
   14:30  I   EcR
   18:48  II  TrI
   21:19  II  ShI
   21:32  II  TrE

20  0:04  II  ShE
    8:18  I   TrI
    9:34  I   ShI
   10:33  I   TrE
   11:31  III OcD
   11:49  I   ShE
   14:46  III OcR
   16:38  III EcD
   20:00  III EcR

21  5:25  I   OcD
    8:59  I   EcR
   13:53  II  OcD
   19:16  II  EcR

22  2:47  I   TrI
    4:03  I   ShI
    5:02  I   TrE
    6:18  I   ShE
   23:53  I   OcD
```

```
23  3:27  I   EcR
    8:04  II  TrI
   10:37  II  ShI
   10:48  II  TrE
   13:23  II  ShE
   21:15  I   TrI
   22:32  I   ShI
   23:30  I   TrE

24  0:47  I   ShE
    1:29  III TrI
    2:39  IV  TrI
    4:43  III TrE
    6:19  IV  TrE
    6:41  III ShI
   10:01  III ShE
   14:46  IV  ShI
   18:22  I   OcD
   18:51  IV  ShE
   21:56  I   EcR

25  3:10  II  OcD
    8:34  II  EcR
   15:44  I   TrI
   17:00  I   ShI
   17:59  I   TrE
   19:16  I   ShE

26 12:50  I   OcD
   16:25  I   EcR
   21:20  II  TrI
   23:55  II  ShI

27  0:04  II  TrE
    2:41  II  ShE
   10:12  I   TrI
   11:29  I   ShI
   12:27  I   TrE
   13:45  I   ShE
   15:25  III OcD
   18:41  III OcR
   20:39  III EcD

28  0:02  II  EcR
    7:19  I   OcD
   10:54  I   EcR
   16:27  II  OcD
   21:53  II  EcR

29  4:41  I   TrI
    5:58  I   ShI
    6:56  I   TrE
    8:14  I   ShE

30  1:47  I   OcD
    5:23  I   EcR
   10:38  II  TrI
   13:14  II  ShI
   13:22  II  TrE
   16:00  II  ShE
   23:09  I   TrI
```

OCTOBER

```
1   0:27  I   ShI
    1:24  I   TrE
    2:42  I   ShE
    5:25  III TrI
    8:39  III TrE
   10:41  III ShI
   14:02  III ShE
   20:16  I   OcD
   23:52  I   EcR

2   5:45  II  OcD
   11:11  II  EcR
   13:16  IV  OcD
   17:01  IV  OcR
```

```
       17:38  I   TrI
       18:56  I   ShI
       19:53  I   TrE
       21:11  I   ShE

3   1:29  IV  EcD
    5:40  IV  EcR
   14:45  I   OcD
   18:20  I   EcR
   23:55  II  TrI

4   2:32  II  ShI
    2:39  II  TrE
    5:18  II  ShE
   12:07  I   TrI
   13:25  I   ShI
   14:22  I   TrE
   15:40  I   ShE
   19:23  III OcD
   22:39  III OcR

5   0:39  III EcD
    4:03  III EcR
    9:13  I   OcD
   12:49  I   EcR
   19:03  II  OcD

6   0:30  II  EcR
    6:36  I   TrI
    7:54  I   ShI
    8:51  I   TrE
   10:09  I   ShE

7   3:42  II  TrI
    7:18  I   EcR
   13:14  II  TrI
   15:51  II  ShI
   15:58  II  TrE
   18:37  II  ShE

8   1:05  I   TrI
    2:22  I   ShI
    3:20  I   TrE
    4:38  I   ShE
    9:25  III TrI
   12:39  III TrE
   14:42  III ShI
   18:03  III ShE
   22:11  I   OcD

9   1:47  I   EcR
    8:22  II  OcD
   13:48  II  EcR
   19:34  I   TrI
   20:51  I   ShI
   21:49  I   TrE
   23:07  I   ShE

10 16:40  I   OcD
   20:16  I   EcR
   20:35  IV  TrI

11  0:20  IV  TrE
    2:32  II  TrI
    5:09  II  ShI
    5:17  II  TrE
    7:55  II  ShE
    8:52  IV  ShE
   13:03  IV  ShE
   14:03  I   TrI
   15:20  I   ShI
   16:18  I   TrE
   17:35  I   ShE
   23:25  III OcD

12  2:42  III OcR
    4:40  III EcD
    8:04  III EcR
```

SATELLITES OF JUPITER, UT OF 2008 GEOCENTRIC PHENOMENA (cont)

OCTOBER (cont)

```
        11:09  I   OcD
        14:45  I   EcR
        21:41  II  OcD

13  3:06  II  EcR
     8:32  I   TrI
     9:49  I   ShI
    10:47  I   TrE
    12:04  I   ShE

14  5:38  I   OcD
     9:14  I   EcR
    15:52  II  TrI
    18:28  II  ShI
    18:36  II  TrE
    21:14  II  ShE

15  3:01  I   TrI
     4:18  I   ShI
     5:16  I   TrE
     6:33  I   ShE
    13:29  III TrI
    16:44  III TrE
    18:42  III ShI
    22:05  III ShE

16  0:07  I   OcD
     3:43  I   EcR
    11:01  II  OcD
    16:25  II  EcR
    21:30  I   TrI
    22:47  I   ShI
    23:45  I   TrE

17  1:02  I   ShE
    18:37  I   OcD
    22:11  I   EcR

18  5:11  II  TrI
     7:46  II  ShI
     7:56  II  TrE
    10:33  II  ShE
    15:59  I   TrI
    17:15  I   ShI
    18:14  I   TrE
    19:31  I   ShE

19  3:30  III OcD
     6:48  III OcR
     7:37  IV  TrD
     8:40  III EcD
    11:29  IV  OcR
    12:05  III EcR
    13:06  I   OcD
    16:40  I   EcR
    19:35  IV  EcD
    23:51  IV  EcR

20  0:21  II  OcD
     5:43  II  EcR
    10:28  I   TrI
    11:44  I   ShI
    12:44  I   TrE
    14:00  I   ShE

21  7:35  I   OcD
    11:09  I   EcR
    18:32  II  TrI
    21:05  II  ShI
    21:17  II  TrE
    23:52  II  ShE

22  4:58  I   TrI
     6:13  I   ShI
     7:13  I   TrE
     8:29  I   ShE
    17:37  III TrI
    20:54  III TrE
    22:43  III ShI
```

```
23  2:05  I   OcD
     2:07  III ShE
     5:38  I   EcR
    13:42  II  OcD
    19:01  II  EcR
    23:27  I   TrI

24  0:42  I   ShI
     1:42  I   TrE
     2:57  I   ShE
    20:34  I   OcD

25  0:07  I   EcR
     7:53  II  TrI
    10:23  II  ShI
    10:38  II  TrE
    13:10  II  ShE
    17:57  I   TrI
    19:11  I   ShI
    20:12  I   TrE
    21:26  I   ShE

26  7:39  III OcD
    10:58  III OcR
    12:40  III EcD
    15:03  I   OcD
    16:05  III EcR
    18:36  I   EcR

27  3:02  II  OcD
     8:19  II  EcR
    12:26  I   TrI
    13:39  I   ShI
    14:41  I   TrE
    15:21  IV  TrI
    15:55  I   ShE
    19:13  IV  TrE

28  3:00  IV  ShI
     7:16  IV  ShI
     9:33  I   OcD
    13:05  I   EcR
    21:14  II  TrI
    23:42  II  ShI
    23:59  II  TrE

29  2:29  II  ShE
     6:55  I   TrI
     8:08  I   ShI
     9:11  I   TrE
    10:24  I   ShE
    21:49  III TrI

30  1:06  III TrE
     2:44  III ShI
     4:03  I   OcD
     6:08  III ShE
     7:34  I   EcR
    16:24  II  OcD
    21:38  II  EcR

31  1:25  I   TrI
     2:37  I   ShI
     3:40  I   TrE
     4:53  I   ShE
    22:32  I   OcD
```

NOVEMBER

```
1   2:02  I   EcR
    10:35  II  TrI
    13:00  II  ShI
    13:21  II  TrE
    15:48  II  ShE
    19:55  I   TrI
    21:06  I   ShI
    22:10  I   TrE
    23:21  I   ShE

2  11:52  III OcD
    15:11  III OcR
    16:40  III EcD
    17:02  I   OcD
    20:07  III EcR
    20:31  I   EcR

3   5:45  II  OcD
    10:56  II  EcR
    14:24  I   TrI
    15:35  I   ShI
    16:40  I   TrE
    17:50  I   ShE

4  11:31  I   OcD
    15:00  I   EcR
    23:58  II  TrI

5   2:19  II  ShI
     2:44  II  TrE
     2:45  IV  OcD
     5:07  II  ShE
     6:44  IV  OcR
     8:54  I   TrI
    10:03  I   ShI
    11:09  I   TrE
    12:19  I   ShE
    13:41  IV  EcD
    18:03  IV  EcR

6   2:03  III TrI
     5:21  III TrE
     6:01  I   OcD
     6:44  III ShI
     9:29  I   EcR
    10:09  III ShE
    19:07  II  OcD

7   0:14  II  EcR
     3:24  I   TrI
     4:32  I   ShI
     5:39  I   TrE
     6:48  I   ShE

8   0:31  I   OcD
     3:58  I   EcR
    13:20  II  TrI
    15:38  II  ShI
    16:06  II  TrE
    18:26  II  ShE
    21:53  I   TrI
    23:01  I   ShI

9   0:09  I   TrE
     1:17  I   ShE
    16:08  III OcD
    19:01  I   OcD
    19:28  III OcR
    20:41  III EcD
    22:27  I   EcR

10  0:08  III EcR
     8:29  II  OcD
    13:32  II  EcR
    16:23  I   TrI
    17:30  I   ShI
    18:39  I   TrE
    19:46  I   ShE

11 13:31  I   OcD
    16:56  I   EcR

12  2:43  II  TrI
     4:57  II  ShI
     5:29  II  TrE
     7:45  II  ShE
    10:53  I   TrI
    11:58  I   ShI
```

```
    13:08  I   TrE
    14:14  I   ShE

13  6:19  III TrI
     8:01  I   OcD
     9:39  III TrE
    10:44  III ShI
    10:49  IV  TrI
    11:25  I   EcR
    14:10  III ShE
    14:50  IV  TrE
    21:07  IV  ShI
    21:51  II  OcD

14  1:29  IV  ShE
     2:50  II  EcR
     5:23  I   TrI
     6:27  I   ShI
     7:38  I   TrE
     8:43  I   ShE

15  2:31  I   OcD
     5:53  I   EcR
    16:06  II  TrI
    18:15  II  ShI
    18:53  II  TrE
    21:04  II  ShE
    23:53  I   TrI

16  0:56  I   ShI
     2:08  I   TrE
     3:12  I   ShE
    20:27  III OcD
    21:01  I   OcD
    23:49  III OcR

17  0:22  I   EcR
     0:42  III EcD
     4:10  III EcR
    11:14  II  OcD
    16:08  II  EcR
    18:23  I   TrI
    19:25  I   ShI
    20:38  I   TrE
    21:41  I   ShE

18 15:31  I   OcD
    18:51  I   EcR

19  5:30  II  TrI
     7:34  II  ShI
     8:17  II  TrE
    10:23  II  ShE
    12:53  I   TrI
    13:53  I   ShI
    15:08  I   TrE
    16:09  I   ShE

20 10:01  I   OcD
    10:39  III TrI
    13:20  I   EcR
    13:59  III TrE
    14:44  III ShI
    18:11  III ShE

21  0:37  II  OcD
     5:26  II  EcR
     7:23  I   TrI
     8:22  I   ShI
     9:38  I   TrE
    10:38  I   ShE
    22:29  IV  OcD

22  2:36  IV  OcR
     4:31  I   OcD
     7:48  IV  EcD
     7:49  I   EcR
    12:13  IV  EcR
```

```
    18:53  II  TrI
    20:53  II  ShI
    21:40  II  TrE
    23:42  II  ShE

23  1:53  I   TrI
     2:51  I   ShI
     4:08  I   TrE
     5:07  I   ShE
    23:01  I   OcD

24  0:48  III OcD
     2:18  I   EcR
     4:11  III OcR
     4:43  III EcD
     8:11  III EcR
    14:00  II  OcD
    18:43  II  EcR
    20:23  I   TrI
    21:20  I   ShI
    22:38  I   TrE
    23:36  I   ShE

25 17:31  I   OcD
    20:47  I   EcR

26  8:18  II  TrI
    10:12  II  ShI
    11:05  II  TrE
    13:01  II  ShE
    14:53  I   TrI
    15:48  I   ShI
    17:08  I   TrE
    18:05  I   ShE

27 12:02  I   OcD
    15:01  III TrI
    15:16  I   EcR
    18:23  III TrE
    18:45  III ShI
    22:12  III ShE

28  3:23  II  OcD
     8:01  II  EcR
     9:23  I   TrI
    10:17  I   ShI
    11:39  I   TrE
    12:33  I   ShE

29  6:32  I   OcD
     9:44  I   EcR
    21:42  II  TrI
    23:31  II  ShI

30  0:30  II  TrE
     2:20  II  ShE
     3:53  I   TrI
     4:46  I   ShI
     6:09  I   TrE
     6:51  IV  TrI
     7:02  I   ShE
    11:00  IV  TrE
    15:15  IV  ShI
    19:42  IV  ShE
```

**JUPITER
NEAR
CONJUNCTION**

CONFIGURATIONS OF SATURN'S BRIGHTEST SATELLITES
BY LARRY D. BOGAN

The diagrams on the following three pages give the relative locations of Saturn's five brightest satellites for January through July plus November and December 2008. The names and magnitudes of these satellites, in order of increasing distance from Saturn, are Enceladus 11.8, Tethys 10.3, Dione 10.4, Rhea 9.7, and Titan 8.4.

The curves in the diagrams show the elongations of the satellites from Saturn for day 0.0 UT to day 32.0 UT for each month. The dashed curves represent Enceladus and Dione, the first and third out from Saturn. The narrow, central, vertical band represents the disk of Saturn, and the wider band the outer edge of Saturn's A ring.

At the top of each monthly diagram is a scale drawing of Saturn, its rings, and the orbits of four of the five brightest satellites as seen through an inverting telescope (in the Northern Hemisphere). South is up. Because of the small size of the scale drawing, no orbit is shown for Enceladus, the innermost satellite. Due to its faintness and proximity to the bright rings, Enceladus is best seen when near a maximum elongation, but even then good seeing, good optics, and an aperture of at least 250 mm are required.

During 2008, we see Saturn and its satellites from south of the ring plane. The tilt for 2008 varies between −9.9° and −0.8° during the year. The direction of motion of the satellites is clockwise as viewed with a telescope having an even number (0, 2, 4, …) of reflections in its optics.

A particular configuration of the satellites may be determined by drawing a horizontal line across the monthly curves at the time (UT) of interest. The intersection of this line with the curves gives the relative elongations of the satellites. Project these elongations onto the drawing of the orbits at the top of the diagram. The east side of the A ring vertical band has been extended up to the drawing to facilitate transfer of each elongation. A millimetre scale, a pair of dividers, or a strip of paper on which to mark enables one to do this quickly and accurately.

The direction of the orbital motion of a satellite determines on which side of its orbit (north or south) a satellite is located. A satellite *moving right* (east) will be *above* (south of) Saturn in the scale drawing, and a satellite *moving left* (west) will be *below* (north of) Saturn in the drawing. The January diagram shows an example configuration for Jan. 3 at 23:30 EST (Jan. 4 at 4h30 UT).

Greatest Elongations and Conjunctions for Iapetus

The magnitude of Iapetus varies from 10.1 (western elongation) to 11.9 (eastern elongation), comparable to those of the satellites, plotted here. Its orbit is about 2.9 times the size of Titan's and is tilted 15° to Saturn's ring plane; its period is 79 days and is easiest to find every 40 days when it is at conjunction with Saturn. The table below lists times (UT) of greatest elongations and conjunctions during 2008.

Eastern Elong.		Inferior Conj.		Western Elong.		Superior Conj.	
						Jan. 1	8.1h
Jan.. 21	21.7h	Feb. 10	7.7h	Feb. 29	2.0h	Mar. 19	13.2h
Apr. 8	15.8h	Apr. 28	17.5h	May 17	13.7h	Jun. 6	17.8h
Jun. 27	9.5h	Jul. 17	23.0h	Aug. 6	10.5h	Aug. 26	21.1h
Sep. 17	0.7h	Oct. 7	6.6h	Oct. 27	2.9h	Nov. 16	6.0h
Dec. 7	6.6h	Dec. 26	18.8h	—		—	

Note: Three freeware computer programs that display the configurations of Saturn's satellites are (1) *The Planets* (Java) by Benden Murphy (www.cpac.freeserve.co.uk/docs/solar.htm), (2) *Meridian* (Windows) by Claude Duplessis (www.merid.cam.org/meridian/index.html), and (3) *SATSAT2* (DOS) by Dan Bruton (www.midnightkite.com/dansoftware.html).

CONFIGURATIONS OF SATURN'S SATELLITES
2008 JANUARY–MARCH

CONFIGURATIONS OF SATURN'S SATELLITES
2008 APRIL–JUNE

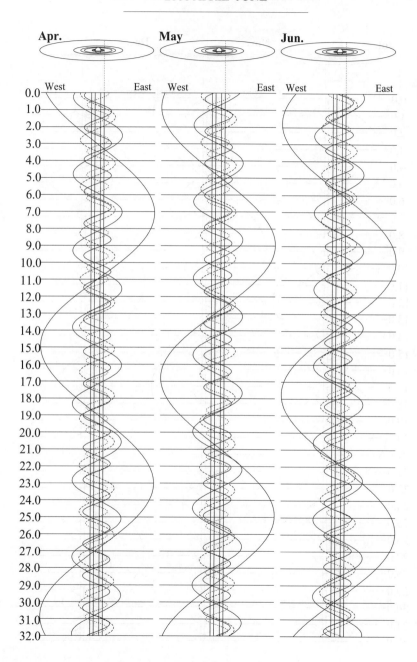

CONFIGURATIONS OF SATURN'S SATELLITES
2008 JULY, NOVEMBER–DECEMBER

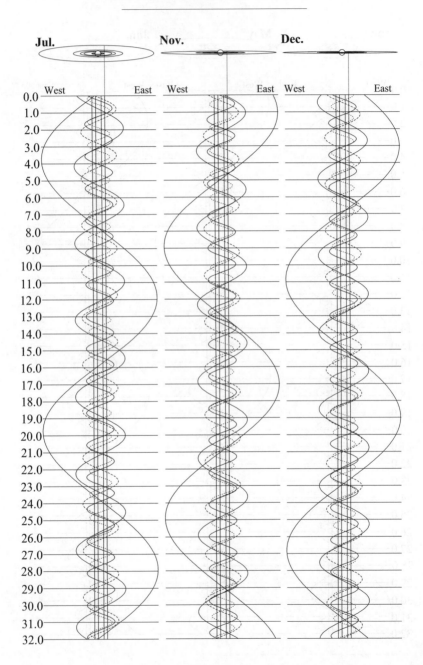

ASTEROIDS

THE BRIGHTEST ASTEROIDS

The following two pages contain ephemerides for asteroids (identified by number and name) that will be brighter than or equal to visual magnitude 10.0 and more than 90° from the Sun during 2008. The positions are based on TT, which differs by about one minute from UT (see TIME AND TIME SCALES on pp. 42–48). "Mag" is visual magnitude. These data were derived from current osculating elements.

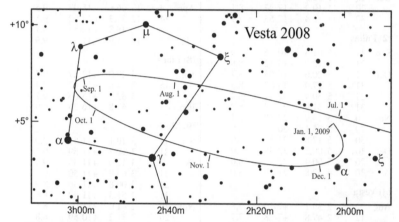

Charts displaying the motion of each asteroid can be produced by using the ephemerides provided and an appropriate star atlas, or on a computer by using a planetarium program. For example, the chart above, provided by David Lane, shows the path of (4) Vesta between late June and late December. The labelled stars in the left half of the chart are in Cetus, those in the right half are in Pisces.

The coordinates in the chart are for equinox J2000.0, and the chart magnitude limit is 8.0; Vesta remains brighter than this limit during the depicted period. Tick marks along the path indicate Vesta's position on the given dates. The "pentagon" of stars in Cetus can be found just above the 3 h mark on the SEPTEMBER ALL-SKY MAP on p 314 and the NOVEMBER ALL-SKY MAP on p. 315. The pentagon is drawn as a "square" but the fifth star is plotted.

Vesta brightens to visual magnitude 6.4 when at opposition on Oct. 30, and will then be bright enough to be seen with the naked eye from a dark site. It will have an angular diameter of about 0.4″.

Ceres was the first asteroid discovered (on the first day of the 19th century), hence its designation (1) Ceres. It was originally classified as a planet, as were the next three asteroids, (2) Pallas, (3) Juno, and (4) Vesta. For most of the 19th century, Vesta was thought to be larger than Ceres due to its greater brightness. Ceres is, in fact, the larger of the two, being almost twice the diameter of Vesta. It is Vesta's higher albedo (0.42 compared to 0.11 for Ceres) that makes Vesta the brighter of the two despite its smaller size.

See p. 23 for a listing of the diameters and current osculating orbital elements of the 30 largest main-belt asteroids.

EPHEMERIDES FOR THE BRIGHTEST ASTEROIDS IN 2008
By Brian Marsden

Date 0h TT	RA (2000) h m	Dec ° '	Mag.	Date 0h TT	RA (2000) h m	Dec ° '	Mag.
(1) Ceres				**(6) Hebe (continued)**			
Jan. 5	2 35.8	+9 56	8.3	Mar. 5	8 56.9	+19 07	9.7
15	2 37.8	+10 51	8.4	15	8 52.7	+20 07	9.9
25	2 42.3	+11 53	8.5				
				(7) Iris			
Nov. 30	10 52.0	+17 23	8.4	Mar. 15	13 23.7	−16 42	9.9
Dec. 10	11 02.0	+17 18	8.2	25	13 15.7	−16 02	9.7
20	11 10.2	+17 27	8.1	Apr. 4	13 06.6	−15 07	9.5
30	11 16.4	+17 53	7.9	14	12 57.3	−14 02	9.5
				24	12 48.8	−12 53	9.7
(2) Pallas				May 4	12 41.9	−11 47	9.9
Sep. 11	5 01.5	−10 36	8.9				
21	5 12.0	−13 12	8.8	**(8) Flora**			
Oct. 1	5 20.6	−16 03	8.7	Jan. 5	3 20.0	+12 27	9.2
11	5 27.0	−19 05	8.5	15	3 24.6	+13 43	9.4
21	5 30.9	−22 11	8.4	25	3 32.3	+15 04	9.7
31	5 31.9	−25 12	8.2	Feb. 4	3 42.8	+16 26	9.9
Nov. 10	5 29.9	−27 58	8.1				
20	5 25.1	−30 17	8.0	**(9) Metis**			
30	5 17.8	−31 57	8.0	Sep. 11	3 10.1	+11 51	9.9
Dec. 10	5 09.2	−32 48	8.0	21	3 12.7	+11 59	9.7
20	5 00.4	−32 47	8.0	Oct. 1	3 12.0	+11 59	9.4
30	4 52.8	−31 54	8.0	11	3 07.9	+11 50	9.2
				21	3 00.8	+11 36	8.9
(4) Vesta				31	2 51.3	+11 20	8.6
Aug. 2	2 39.1	+7 15	7.8	Nov. 10	2 41.0	+11 06	8.5
12	2 47.8	+7 28	7.7	20	2 31.2	+10 59	8.8
22	2 54.6	+7 30	7.6	30	2 23.5	+11 04	9.1
Sep. 1	2 59.1	+7 19	7.4	Dec. 10	2 18.7	+11 24	9.3
11	3 01.0	+6 57	7.2	20	2 17.5	+11 58	9.6
21	3 00.1	+6 25	7.1	30	2 19.6	+12 46	9.8
Oct. 1	2 56.3	+5 44	6.9				
11	2 49.8	+4 58	6.7	**(11) Parthenope**			
21	2 41.2	+4 12	6.5	Jun. 23	21 31.2	−14 00	10.0
31	2 31.3	+3 31	6.4	Jul. 3	21 30.7	−14 27	9.8
Nov. 10	2 21.5	+3 03	6.6	13	21 27.2	−15 10	9.5
20	2 12.8	+2 50	6.8	23	21 21.1	−16 08	9.3
30	2 06.1	+2 55	7.0	Aug. 2	21 13.1	−17 14	8.9
Dec. 10	2 02.0	+3 17	7.2	12	21 04.4	−18 21	9.0
20	2 00.7	+3 55	7.4	22	20 56.2	−19 21	9.3
30	2 02.1	+4 47	7.6	Sep. 1	20 49.9	−20 08	9.6
				11	20 46.3	−20 40	9.8
(5) Astraea							
Mar. 5	13 32.5	−2 56	10.0	**(15) Eunomia**			
15	13 28.7	−1 52	9.8	Jan. 5	7 32.7	+23 29	8.3
25	13 22.3	−0 38	9.6	15	7 21.3	+22 59	8.3
Apr. 4	13 14.4	+0 36	9.4	25	7 10.8	+22 26	8.7
14	13 06.2	+1 41	9.6	Feb. 4	7 02.5	+21 50	8.9
24	12 58.9	+2 28	9.9	14	6 57.1	+21 15	9.2
				24	6 55.0	+20 41	9.4
(6) Hebe				Mar. 5	6 55.8	+20 09	9.7
Jan. 5	9 44.4	+10 00	9.6	15	6 59.5	+19 38	9.9
15	9 38.8	+11 18	9.4				
25	9 31.0	+12 52	9.2	**(27) Euterpe**			
Feb. 4	9 21.8	+14 34	8.9	Dec. 20	9 37.7	+15 14	10.0
14	9 12.3	+16 16	9.1	30	9 38.4	+15 25	9.8
24	9 03.7	+17 49	9.4				

EPHEMERIDES FOR THE BRIGHTEST ASTEROIDS IN 2008 (cont)

Date 0h TT	RA (2000) h m	Dec ° '	Mag.
(29) Amphitrite			
Jan. 5	2 52.7	+25 06	9.8
15	2 56.3	+24 56	10.0
(41) Daphne			
Mar. 15	13 46.2	−3 48	9.9
25	13 44.5	−1 21	9.6
Apr. 4	13 40.6	+1 19	9.4
14	13 35.3	+3 57	9.3
24	13 29.8	+6 16	9.5
May 4	13 25.3	+8 04	9.7
14	13 22.8	+9 14	10.0
(43) Ariadne			
Sep. 1	23 01.4	+1 10	9.8
11	22 51.8	+0 12	9.8
(216) Kleopatra			
Sep. 11	23 08.4	+12 36	10.0
21	23 01.7	+10 53	9.9
Oct. 1	22 56.2	+8 55	10.0

PLANETARY AND ASTEROIDAL OCCULTATIONS
By David W. Dunham and James Starr

As planets, satellites, asteroids, and comets move across the sky, they occasionally pass directly between an observer and a distant star, thereby producing an *occultation*. Astronomers have learned much about various solar system bodies by carefully monitoring the changing apparent brightness of stars during the immersion and emersion phases of occultations. If the occulting body does not have an atmosphere, the occultation is virtually instantaneous; if there is an atmosphere, it causes the star's disappearance and reappearance to occur gradually. If a planet has rings or other debris in its environs, the extent and degree of transparency of this material can be precisely mapped. The rings of Uranus, the ring arcs of Neptune, and the atmosphere of Pluto were all discovered by occultation observations. In addition, if an occultation is observed at several appropriately distributed sites, it is often possible to determine the size and shape of the occulting body more accurately than by other Earth-based techniques.

Amateur astronomers can sometimes make important contributions to occultation observing campaigns. This is particularly true for asteroid occultations, for which the event path across Earth is often very narrow and uncertain in location (due to uncertainties in both the star's position and the ephemeris of the asteroid). By recording the times of the star's disappearance and reappearance as seen from several sites (i.e. by noting the edges of the asteroid's shadow as it sweeps across Earth), the asteroid's profile can be directly determined. Often timings of adequate accuracy can be made by visual observers using modest telescopes.

When observing an occultation, it is important that an observer know his or her location to within a fraction of a kilometre. Geographic longitude and latitude as well as the altitude of an observing site can be determined with a GPS receiver, from a high-quality topographic map, or from some map Web sites. If observations are to be of maximum value, the times of immersion and emersion must be determined as accurately as possible—certainly to better than 0.5 s, and better than 0.2 s for the shortest events (those less than about 10 s in duration). Photoelectric equipment with high-speed digital recording systems is well suited for this work. Attaching a low-light-level video camera to a telescope is a less expensive method for accurately timing these events. Visual observers equipped with audio recorders and shortwave time-signal receivers can also make useful contributions. Even simple measurements of the duration of an occultation made with an ordinary stopwatch can be of value. CCD observers should be aware that most of these systems are incapable of timing accuracies better than about 2 s; hence visual observation may be better. A trick that some CCD observers have used is to turn off the telescope clock drive shortly before the predicted time and let the images trail. The occultation will appear as a break in the trail that can be measured to a few tenths of a second if the moment the drive is turned off is accurately timed.

Occultation observations are coordinated in North America by the International Occultation Timing Association (IOTA). IOTA member or not, IOTA wants to inform you and others in your area able to locate stars to 11th magnitude of last-minute prediction updates. Please email the longitude and latitude (or location from the nearest town) of convenient observing sites, telescope size(s), and an indication of whether you are mobile to dunham@starpower.net. Individuals interested in joining IOTA should refer to OCCULTATIONS BY THE MOON, p. 158, for membership information.

More information is in the *Solar System Photometry Handbook* (Willmann-Bell, Inc., 1983), *Sky & Telescope* (usually the February issue), and occasional papers in the *Astronomical Journal, Icarus,* and other scientific journals.

Observations of asteroidal and planetary occultations, *including* negative observations, should be sent to reports@asteroidoccultation.com and to Jan Manek, Stefanik Observatory, Petrin 205, 118 46 Praha (Prague) 1, Czech Republic (email: jmanek@mbox.vol.cz; copy positive observations to dunham@starpower.net) for analysis and publication by IOTA. When reporting timings, describe your geographic longitude, latitude, and altitude (to the nearest second of arc and 30 m, respectively), telescope size, timing method, the start and end time of observation, an estimate of the observer's reaction-time (if applicable) and the accuracy of the timing, and whether the reaction-time correction has been applied. For reporting, the forms at www.asteroidoccultation.com/observations/NA are preferred. Much useful information is at www.asteroidoccultation.com/observations.

The following two-page table of predictions of asteroidal and planetary satellite occultations visible from North America for 2008 is based on predictions by Edwin Goffin, Scott Donnell, Steve Preston, and David Herald.

The successive columns in the table list (1) the date and central time of the event; (2) the name of the occulting body; (3) the apparent magnitude of the asteroid or planet; (4) the catalogue number of the occulted star; (5) the apparent visual magnitude of the star; (6) the right ascension and (7) declination of the star; (8) the expected magnitude change from the combined brightness; (9) the predicted maximum duration of the occultation in seconds; and (10) the approximate region from which the occultation is predicted to be visible. Due to uncertainties in the catalogue positions of the stars and the ephemerides of the asteroids from which these predictions are derived, the exact region of visibility of an occultation cannot be derived until CCD observations link the star and asteroid to the new *HIPPARCOS* reference frame, usually a few weeks prior to the event.

Note that the times are mostly geocentric; for specific locations in North America, the time may be many minutes earlier. Within a few weeks of each event, improved predictions and the latest path maps may be obtained from Steve Preston's asteroidal occultation Web site: www.asteroidoccultation.com. Much other useful information, including interactive maps to zoom in on the path, circumstances for dozens of stations in and near the path, and lists of stars that can be used to prepoint telescopes to the target stars are at www.poyntsource.com/New/Global.htm. See also the *2008 Planetary Occultation Supplement to Occultation Newsletter* available from IOTA.

Notes regarding some of the events in the table:

Feb. 9: (602) Marianna may have an unusual dumbbell shape according to observations of an occultation observed on 2006 Mar. 12.

Mar. 9: (45) Eugenia has two satellites, 13-km Petit-Prince about 1 200 km away, and 6-km S/2004 (45) 1 about 215 km across, but closer to Eugenia. The path of the occultation by Petit-Prince might be predicted before the event, but for now, observers throughout Mexico and the USA should plan to monitor this bright star for the possibility of a secondary occultation. The star is ZC 741, possibly a close double based on lunar occultation observations, but the duplicity was not confirmed by the *HIPPARCOS* satellite. IOTA plans a major expedition to Baja California; Kerry Coughlin, BajaKerry@gmail.com, is the local coordinator.

Apr. 5: Observers throughout the eastern half of North America should watch for a possible occultation by the 9-km satellite, about 1 200 km from 223-km (107) Camilla. The path for the satellite occultation might be predicted before the event.

Jul. 12: Jupiter's diameter will be 47″. The event will be easier to monitor in wavelengths where Jupiter is faint, such as in the near-infrared methane absorption bands.

Aug. 16: (1) Ceres, the largest main-belt asteroid, is a target of the *Dawn* mission.

Aug. 24: The star may be a close double according to a lunar occultation observation by Henk Bril in 1991.

Sep. 12: The combination of a nearly naked-eye star (easy with binoculars) and wide path crossing North America from coast to coast makes this the best asteroidal occultation of the year. Observers far from the path throughout the continent are encouraged to monitor the star for a possible occultation by a satellite of Metis. The star is ZC 462 and possibly a close double from a lunar occultation observation, but *HIPPARCOS* found the star to be single. IOTA will hold its annual meeting in the Lewis Center in Apple Valley, California, within the path for this event during the weekend following it.

Sep. 26: (216) Kleopatra is an elongated dumbbell-shaped asteroid, the largest "metallic" M-class object.

Nov. 19: The star will disappear on the dark side of Venus's 15″ 73% sunlit disk; about 4″ will separate the disappearing star from Venus's bright terminator. The star has a 10.4-magnitude companion 4.4″ away in PA 177°.

Nov. 23: A secondary occultation video recorded by Roger Venable during a 2004 occultation by (98) Ianthe indicates that the asteroid may have a small satellite.

Dec. 25: It will take a quarter of a second for the edge of the asteroid to cover the 0.0012″ disk of the spectral type M0 red star, and longer for a non-central event.

IOTA SELECTED LIST OF NORTH AMERICAN OCCULTATIONS BY SOLAR SYSTEM OBJECTS FOR THE YEAR 2008

Date	UT	Occulting Body	(Mag.)	Star	RA (2000) h m s	Dec ° ' "	ΔMag.	Dur. s	Nominal Path
Jan. 2	12:31	24 Themis	11.2	UCAC 238791508	08 39 51	+19 33 02	0.6	15.2	Southern Mississippi to Washington
4	11:10	432 Pythia	12.9	SAO 81028	09 49 21	+25 12 36	3.4	5.3	New England to Greenland
5	0:39	95 Arethusa	12.0	TYC 1280-01141-1	04 51 02	+15 28 51	1.1	18.2	Labrador to northern Mexico
12	5:01	70 Panopaea	12.9	TYC 2501-00817-1	09 46 49	+30 34 24	2.0	10.4	South Carolina to southern California
14	9:10	747 Winchester	14.7	PPM 199373	16 10 24	-04 53 46	4.3	5.5	North Carolina
17	2:22	76 Freia	12.3	TYC 1307-00201-1	05 49 11	+20 28 10	1.9	24.1	Newfoundland to Oregon
18	11:40	420 Bertholda	14.7	PPM 264071	15 18 23	-21 03 46	5.0	5.0	Southern California to Yucatan
20	6:40	526 Jena	14.1	SAO 78471	06 32 25	+21 26 37	5.4	4.3	Southern New England to Aleutians
22	2:08	13 Egeria	11.9	PPM 144355	01 11 58	+07 06 39	2.0	9.4	Baja Norte to Newfoundland
23	11:55	275 Sapientia	13.1	UCAC2 31013763	12 59 56	-02 27 09	1.9	9.9	Central Baja to Florida Keys
29	8:07	444 Gyptis	12.6	PPM 146968	03 50 51	+08 43 03	1.6	9.9	Washington to Montana
Feb. 4	1:42	13 Egeria	12.0	TYC 0614-01142-1	01 25 45	+09 26 21	1.0	19.8	British Columbia to Nunavut
9*	8:05	602 Marianna	13.3	TYC 2329-00867-1	02 46 37	+32 52 06	2.8	7.8	Vancouver Island
15	3:36	385 Ilmatar	13.3	SAO 74989	01 52 10	+24 07 03	6.4	6.2	Baja Sur to southern Mexico
26	23:48	739 Mandeville	12.0	SAO 80393	08 44 27	+19 57 51	2.6	3.6	Northern Florida
28	1:29	469 Argentina	12.2	SAO 98982	12 00 15	+11 34 31	3.8	10.3	Cuba to southern Mexico
Mar. 3	11:56	140 Siwa	12.8	SAO 119158	04 57 22	+04 38 00	3.5	11.2	Ontario to Nunavut
9*	5:38	45 Eugenia	13.1	SAO 94227	06 39 53	+17 09 13	7.4	8.8	North of Hawaii to central Mexico
11	7:04	735 Marghanna	14.9	SAO 41242	18 04 24	+42 14 50	5.9	12.2	Central Greenland to central Mexico
13	13:48	19 Fortuna	12.6	HIP 88508	12 12 42	-22 26 19	2.7	7.7	Hawaii
14	12:29	337 Devosa	11.5	SAO 138648	03 39 00	-02 28 22	4.1	6.0	Central Mexico to north of Hawaii
15	1:28	241 Germania	13.5	SAO 76045	12 55 01	+20 54 56	6.9	6.0	Northern Mexico to Puerto Rico
24	8:38	769 Tatjana	13.5	TYC 4950-00135-1	13 48 20	-00 20 57	2.5	5.6	North Carolina to Bering Sea
Apr. 5*	2:24	107 Camilla	12.1	TYC 4970-00691-1	14 24 17	+00 16 26	1.8	8.0	Labrador
16	4:56	259 Aletheia	11.8	PPM 160597			1.3	16.5	Nova Scotia to southern British Columbia
May 13	2:50	29 Amphitrite	11.0	TYC 1871-02127-1	05 57 34	+27 54 02	1.4	16.7	Saskatchewan to Kentucky
23	3:52	712 Boliviana	13.0	UCAC2 27151963	18 22 19	-13 04 41	2.0	5.0	Nova Scotia to eastern Québec
30	7:23	1048 Feodosia	12.8	UCAC2 16456789	17 54 04	-36 20 10	2.2	13	Michigan to southern Mexico
Jun. 1	9:11	5 Astraea	10.9	SAO 119636	12 51 46	+02 11 57	1.6	7.4	West coast of North America
7	7:23	127 Johanna	12.8	TYC 7427-01593-1	19 14 37	-33 20 29	1.8	24.2	New England to southern Mexico
12	11:39	47 Aglaja	11.7	UCAC2 19792163	19 46 47	-29 00 59	1.0	13.1	Northern California to Hawaii
16	4:42	345 Tercidina	12.0	UCAC2 28226955	17 47 13	-10 07 45	1.3	24.7	Nova Scotia to Saskatchewan
18	7:21	19 Fortuna	10.5	SAO 186418	18 10 54	-21 12 25	1.9	8.9	Central Florida to central Baja

* See the note for this event at the bottom of p. 229.

IOTA SELECTED LIST OF NORTH AMERICAN OCCULTATIONS BY SOLAR SYSTEM OBJECTS FOR THE YEAR 2008 (continued)

Date	UT	Occulting Body	(Mag.)	Star	RA (2000) h m s	Dec ° ' "	(Mag.)	ΔMag.	Dur. s	Nominal Path
Jun. 22	1:30	712 Boliviana	12.5	PPM 233813	17 57 47	−11 02 21	10.2	2.4	9.6	Georgia
22	8:34	283 Emma	12.8	TYC 6882−00571−1	19 07 29	−27 37 03	11.0	2.1	14.0	Central Ontario to Washington
29	10:42	404 Arsinoë	12.7	TYC 6945−01027−1	21 14 51	−26 33 20	11.2	1.8	11.2	Louisiana to southwestern Mexico
Jul. 1	4:01	387 Aquitania	11.8	TYC 0899−00029−1	13 44 54	+12 34 28	10.3	1.8	7.4	Québec to east of North Carolina
4	7:28	9 Metis	11.0	UCAC2 34040192	01 56 02	+06 38 09	11.3	0.6	6.7	Northern Florida to southeastern Georgia
12*	7:44	Jupiter	−2.6	SAO 187846	19 13 39	−22 33 58	7.9	0.0	8850	Americas, Pacific, eastern Australia
Aug. 2	3:03	165 Loreley	13.0	TYC 6755−00957−1	14 53 15	−27 15 45	10.8	2.4	11.7	Southern Arizona to Wisconsin
16*	11:24	1 Ceres	8.8	SAO 79926	08 05 28	+24 11 26	8.7	0.8	18.7	Southern Mexico and Guatemala
17	10:14	245 Vera	11.5	UCAC2 24991607	22 30 30	−18 09 07	10.9	1.1	7.9	Minnesota to southern California
24*	4:49	111 Ate	11.7	SAO 145886	22 08 03	−07 57 00	9.7	2.2	11.1	Eastern Nunavut to Vancouver Island
25	8:15	479 Caprera	13.9	TYC 6307−00488−1	19 37 14	−19 26 26	10.8	3.2	10.4	Western Wyoming to southern California
Sep. 12*	6:39	9 Metis	9.9	SAO 93320	03 10 39	+11 52 21	6.0	4.0	44.4	Southern California to Labrador
12	6:58	654 Zelinda	12.8	TYC 2426−00545−1	06 35 11	+32 21 32	11.2	1.8	4.6	Wyoming to southeastern Nunavut
13	10:43	58 Concordia	12.5	TYC 5247−00786−1	23 29 44	−04 44 43	11.0	1.7	7.5	Iowa to southern California
18	5:28	205 Martha	13.5	SAO 145256	21 16 39	−01 36 28	6.6	6.8	10.4	Northwest Territories to northern British Columbia
22	10:06	236 Honoraria	13.5	TYC 1315−00364−1	06 18 21	+16 02 44	10.1	3.4	4.6	Southern Baja California to Miami
26*	11:18	216 Kleopatra	10.0	SAO 127869	22 58 30	+09 49 32	7.7	2.4	12.5	Northern Manitoba to northern British Columbia
Oct. 9	5:49	268 Adorea	13.8	TYC 5810−00213−1	22 19 17	−12 45 09	10.8	3.1	23.0	Southern Georgia to southern Mexico
10	6:41	225 Henrietta	13.9	PPM 146426	03 18 05	+06 30 00	10.4	3.5	8.8	Labrador, eastern USA, southern Mexico
11	1:04	64 Angelina	11.5	SAO 109083	00 14 29	+03 28 11	9.2	2.5	4.4	Southern Florida to southern Mexico
27	7:05	270 Anahita	12.6	TYC 1880−01064−1	06 37 16	+23 09 43	10.5	4.3	14.2	Labrador to Seattle
Nov. 16	9:18	583 Klotilde	13.9	SAO 96841	07 23 17	+19 11 55	9.6	4.3	22.8	Baffin Island, eastern USA, Cuba, Panama
19*	23:26	Venus	−4.1	SAO 187073	18 38 15	−25 25 17	8.1	0.0	314	Southeastern USA, Caribbean, S. America
20	8:50	906 Repsolda	15.4	SAO 81515	10 47 02	+20 34 53	9.1	6.3	3.7	Newfoundland to southern California
23*	6:50	98 Ianthe	13.5	SAO 99697	11 36 57	+10 30 38	8.4	5.2	3.8	Ohio to New England
Dec. 6	2:25	361 Bononia	13.1	PPM 92011	02 49 56	+27 36 22	10.4	2.8	15.3	SE Nunavut to Vancouver Island
10	3:39	1021 Flammario	12.7	TYC 5849−00120−1	00 32 08	−18 52 18	11.4	1.5	6.5	Baja Sur to northern Ontario
11	8:00	135 Hertha	11.8	SAO 93103	02 47 24	+19 50 39	9.2	2.6	15.2	North Carolina to southern California
17	11:15	176 Iduna	12.3	TYC 4780−00383−1	05 47 34	−07 27 46	11.3	1.4	10.0	Texas to Hawaii
18	5:10	402 Chloe	12.1	TYC 0735−02090−1	06 15 49	+10 47 26	9.9	2.3	5.1	Nova Scotia to British Columbia
19	6:52	487 Venetia	11.7	SAO 96531	07 08 16	+18 00 33	9.5	2.3	5.9	Southern New England to British Columbia
25*	13:52	740 Cantabia	13.8	SAO 99284	10 46 35	+13 35 07	9.3	4.5	13.0	Central California to Colorado
29	1:21	267 Tirza	16.0	SAO 147044	00 02 00	−05 12 50	8.5	7.5	2.4	Newfoundland to Baja Sur

*See the note for this event at the bottom of p. 229.

METEORS, COMETS, AND DUST

METEORS

BY MARGARET CAMPBELL–BROWN AND PETER BROWN

A *meteor* (from the Greek *meteoros,* meaning high in the air) is the light, heat, ionization, and, occasionally, sound phenomena produced when a solid body (a *meteoroid*) collides with molecules in Earth's upper atmosphere. These collisions heat the surface of the object; then at a height typically between 120 km and 80 km the meteoroid begins to ablate, or lose mass. Typically, ablation takes the form of vapourization, although melting and quasicontinuous fragmentation may also contribute. It is these ablated meteoric atoms that collide with air molecules to produce atomic excitations, or ionization, leading to the emission of light we see in the night sky. Typical visual meteors are produced by meteoroids the size of a small pebble, although the relationship between mass–brightness and velocity is complex (Figure 1). The faintest meteors visible to the naked eye are due to meteoroids the size of the tip of a ballpoint pen; the brightest meteors are due to meteoroids whose diameters roughly match the thickness of a pen.

Larger and low-velocity meteoroids are favoured to pass through Earth's atmosphere, although rarely as a single monolithic body. When these ponderable masses reach the ground, they are called *meteorites.* At the other extreme, very small meteoroids (micrometres in size) efficiently radiate heat from their surface and do not reach ablation temperatures; such particles reach Earth's surface without having been fully ablated, although most are heated many hundreds of degrees.

Meteoroids can be divided broadly into two groups: stream and sporadic meteoroids. *Stream* meteoroids follow similar orbits around the Sun, many of which can be linked to a particular parent object, in most cases a comet. When Earth intersects the orbit of a stream, a meteor shower occurs. Since all the meteoroids in a stream move along nearly identical orbits, their paths in the atmosphere are parallel. This creates a perspective effect: the meteor trails on the celestial sphere appear to radiate from a fixed location, called the meteor *radiant. Sporadic* meteoroids, in contrast, are much more loosely associated and are not part of tightly grouped streams.

Meteor showers are named for the constellation from which they appear to radiate. When several showers have radiants in the same constellation, nearby bright stars are used in naming. The Quadrantid shower is named for the obsolete constellation Quadrans Muralis, but now has a radiant in Boötes.

The sporadic complex as seen at Earth, however, is structured and shows definite directionalities as well as annual variations in activity levels. Sporadic meteor radiants are concentrated in six major source regions throughout the sky. These sources are in fixed locations with respect to the Sun. Variations in the strengths of these sources throughout the year have been observed; it is the elevation of these sources at a particular location plus the intrinsic strength of each source at a given time of the year that determine the average background sporadic rate. Figure 2 shows the expected sporadic rate as a function of the altitude of the apex of Earth's way throughout the year. The apex is the instantaneous direction of travel of Earth around the Sun; it is the point on the ecliptic that transits at 6:00 apparent solar time (see pp. 36–37). The altitude of the apex for a given time of year, latitude ϕ, and apparent solar time t approximately equals the sum $\pm 23.5 \sin(\lambda - 90) + (90 - |\phi|) \sin(t/24 \times 360)$, where λ is the solar longitude and $\pm$ is the sign of ϕ (except if the sum lies outside the range -90 to $+90$).

In general, meteoroid streams are formed when particles are ejected from comets as they approach the Sun. The parent objects of many showers have been identified from the similarity of the orbits of the object and the stream. Cometary associations include the η-Aquarids and Orionids, which are derived from 1P/Halley, the Leonids, which originate from 55P/Tempel-Tuttle, and the Perseids, from 109P/Swift-Tuttle. One asteroid is known to be associated with a stream: 3200 Phaethon and the Geminid stream, while 2003 EH1 has been tentatively linked to the Quadrantid shower. All of these particles have orbits that coincide closely with that of the parent object, but their orbits are gradually shifted through radiative effects and planetary perturbations. Such effects lead to a broadening of the stream over time, resulting in an increased duration of the meteor shower as seen from Earth—older streams tend to be more long-lived—and eventually transform stream meteoroids into sporadic meteoroids.

The visual strength of a meteor shower is measured by its Zenithal Hourly Rate (ZHR), defined as the number of meteors a single average observer would see if the radiant were directly overhead and the sky dark and transparent with a limiting stellar magnitude of +6.5 (conditions that are rarely met in reality). A more physical measure is the flux of a meteoroid stream, measured in numbers of meteors of absolute brightness (referenced to a range of 100 km) brighter than +6.5 per square kilometre per second perpendicular to the radiant direction. While an observer will tend to see the largest number of meteors by looking at the shower radiant, the most useful counts are obtained by looking some distance away from the radiant.

Most data on meteor showers are currently gathered visually by amateur observers. It is crucial to observe from a dark-sky location with a clear view of the sky, and to allow at least 20 min before the start of observations to allow dark adaptation of the eyes. One should choose an area of the sky to observe, preferably with an elevation greater than 40°. The limiting magnitude should be carefully recorded for each session, along with the UT and the centre of the field of view of the observer. The most basic

FIGURE 1 *Magnitude as a function of velocity for meteoroids of different sizes. Uncertainties in the mass scale are largest at high velocities and small masses, and may be as large as an order of magnitude in mass at the extremes.*

FIGURE 2 *The observed visual rate of sporadic meteors as a function of various elevations of the apex of Earth's way throughout the year. The equivalent hourly rate (like ZHR) is measured for a sky with a limiting stellar magnitude of +6.5. The position of the apex is 90° west of the Sun along the ecliptic plane. Total meteor rates on a given night may be somewhat higher due to contributions from minor showers. Data courtesy of the International Meteor Organization and R. Arlt.*

observations should include an estimate of the brightness of the meteor, the time of observation, and a shower association (based on the radiant and apparent speed of the meteor). Information on collecting and reporting scientifically useful observations can be found at the International Meteor Organization's Web site, www.imo.net.

TABLE OF METEOR SHOWERS FOR 2008

The table lists the major visual showers as well as those detectable by radio/radar methods during the day. The Moon is favourable for two of the stronger nighttime showers of the year, namely the Quadrantids and the Eta Aquarids. The Perseids may experience slightly heightened activity in the 6-8 hours prior to the normal maximum in 2008 from more recent ejections from the parent comet 109P/Swift-Tuttle, though the magnitude of that increase is uncertain. There is also a likelihood that the Taurids will be unusually active this year, with enhanced activity for brighter stream members noticable in late October through early November.

Shower	Max Date UT	λ 2000	D	ZHR	θ ×10⁻⁶	R	Moon %	r	RA h m	Dec °	v km/s
Quadrantid	Jan. 4 7h	283.16	0.6	120	8.4	✓	15–	2.1	15 20	+49	43
Lyrid	Apr. 22 4h	32.3	1.3	20	4.6	✓	97–	2.9	18 10	+34	48
η-Aquarid	May 5 18h	45.5	5	60	6.4	>03	0	2.4	22 30	–2	66
S. δ-Aquarid	Jul. 28 20h	126	8	20	6.2	>23	17–	3.2	22 44	–16	43
Perseid	Aug. 12 11h	140.0	2	90	6.0	✓	81+	2.1	3 08	+58	60
Draconid	Oct. 8 1h	195	<0.1	?	?	✓	55+	2.6	17 28	+54	23
Orionid	Oct. 21 4h	208	2	20	2.2	>23	53–	2.4	6 20	+16	67
S. Taurid	Nov. 5 4h	223	15	10	1.0	✓	40+	2.3	3 34	+14	31
N. Taurid	Nov. 12 4h	230	15	15	1.4	✓	97+	2.3	4 00	+22	30
Leonid	Nov. 17 10h	235.3	1	15	1.9	>00	77–	2.5	10 12	+22	71
Geminid	Dec. 13 23h	262.2	1	120	11.0	✓	97–	2.3	7 28	+33	36
Ursid	Dec. 22 8h	270.7	0.5	10	2.2	✓	22–	3.0	14 36	+75	35
Arietid	Jun. 9 2h	78.5	20	≈60	–	day	–	–	2 52	+26	41
ζ-Perseid	Jun. 13 19h	83	23	≈40	–	day	–	–	4 24	+25	29
β-Taurid	Jun. 27 10h	96	20	≈25	–	day	–	–	5 36	+20	30
D Sextantid	Sep. 29 22h	187	7	≈20	–	day	–	–	10 20	–2	33

The column **Max Date** lists the date and hour (in Universal Time) when Earth intersects the densest part of the stream, based on the solar longitude λ (J2000.0) given in the third column.

The fourth column, *D*, gives the duration of the shower in days, which is the total number of days for which the activity level is over half the maximum activity.

The **ZHR**, or Zenithal Hourly Rate, is given for the peak of the shower. The θ column gives the meteoroid flux at the time of maximum (see text for explanation).

The *R* column gives the local times for which the radiant is above the horizon for an observer at 45°N latitude (and therefore meteors from the shower are visible); a ✓ symbol indicates that the radiant is up throughout the night hours, while "day" indicates that the shower is not visible at night.

The **Moon** column gives the percent illumination of the Moon at the time of the shower peak (+ for waxing, – for waning). The population index, *r*, at the time of the maximum is a measure of the size distribution of particles in the stream. A larger *r* value indicates an excess of small particles, while smaller *r* values indicate larger numbers of brighter meteors. A shower with a higher *r* value will therefore suffer more from background light such as moonlight or light pollution. Sporadic meteors at observable visual magnitudes have an *r* value near 3.0.

The **RA** and **Dec** are given in the next two columns: They give the position in the sky of the radiant at the time of the shower peak. The position of the radiant will vary from these values away from the time of the peak; tables published by the International Meteor Organization in their annual shower calendar provide details of radiant drift. The last column, *v*, gives the apparent atmospheric speed of the meteors in the shower.

RADIO DETECTION OF METEORS
By Philip Gebhardt

The term *meteor* applies not only to the streak of light produced by a meteoroid, but also to the column of ionized atoms and molecules along the path behind the meteoroid. These meteor trails are capable of scattering radio signals from terrestrial stations. Radio detection rates tend to be higher than visual observation rates because particles down to 10^{-5} kg can be detected visually, while particles down to 10^{-10} kg can be detected by radio. Assuming a density of 1 t/m^3, these mass limits correspond to diameters of about 3 mm and 0.06 mm, respectively.

Two types of meteor trails exist: *underdense* and *overdense;* they are determined by the density of free electrons. Reradiated signals from underdense trails (fewer than 2×10^{14} electrons per metre) rise above the receiver noise almost instantaneously and then decay exponentially. The duration of many meteor bursts is about a second or less. Reflected signals from overdense trails may have higher amplitude and longer duration, but destructive interference due to reflection from different parts of the trail can produce fluctuations in the signal.

Data for selected meteor showers appear in the Table of Meteor Showers on the previous page. These data are for visual observations and should only be considered as guidelines for radio purposes. The sporadic meteor rate (visual and radio) peaks about 6:00 local time (i.e. on the advancing side of Earth in its orbit) and is minimum near 18:00. The rate will vary from a few per hour for off-peak times for sporadic meteors to several hundred per hour during a very active shower. Unlike visual observation, radio detection of sporadic meteors or shower meteors can be undertaken in daylight and during inclement weather. Four daytime showers are listed in the Table of Meteor Showers. Frequencies between 20 MHz and 150 MHz are typically used for meteor detection. Both amplitude and duration of meteor bursts are frequency-dependent—they decrease with increasing frequency. At the lower frequencies, however, galactic as well as human-made noise (particularly in urban areas) become limiting factors. Also, as the wavelength becomes comparable to the width of the meteor trail, the echo strength decreases.

The commercial FM broadcast band (88 MHz to 108 MHz) provides a good introductory opportunity for meteor detection. The abundance of over-the-horizon stations transmitting 24 hours a day ensures that a meteor burst can be heard from a suitably positioned meteor regardless of the time of day.

The technique involves listening on a frequency not used by a local FM station. A receiver with a digital frequency readout is therefore an asset. Frequencies throughout North America are assigned at 200-kHz intervals between 88.1 MHz and 107.9 MHz. Alternatively, a TV set (channels 2 through 6) can be used, provided the set is connected to an antenna rather than through cable TV. Long bursts can be heard from WWV (20 MHz, Fort Collins, Colorado) or CHU (14.670 MHz, Ottawa, Ontario), provided there is no ionospheric propagation between the station and your receiving site. In all cases, an outdoor antenna is preferable. It is also possible to listen using the FM radio in your car. Note that other means of signal propagation may be heard, but only meteor signals have their characteristic fast rise-time and short duration.

Further information can be found on the following Web sites:

www.imo.net/calendar/2008
www.spaceweather.com/glossary/nasameteorradar.html
www.iap-kborn.de/radar/Radars/Skiymet/sky_main.htm

Also see *Sky & Telescope, 94* (December 1997), No. 6, p. 108.

FIREBALLS
By Alan Hildebrand

Exceptionally bright meteors (above magnitude –5) that are spectacular enough to light up a wide area and attract public attention are generally referred to as *fireballs*. The main reasons to report the observation of a fireball are the following: (1) to assist with meteorite recovery; (2) to help provide orbital information for recovered meteorites; (3) to rule out other catastrophic events, such as airplane crashes and satellite re-entries; and (4) to help calibrate infrasound arrays deployed to monitor the Comprehensive Test Ban Treaty.

Rapid recovery of freshly fallen meteorites—as well as careful handling and storage—before they have been exposed too long to the terrestrial atmosphere is highly desirable. This allows meteorite researchers to study water-soluble minerals (such as salt), organic phases, and physical properties (such as porosity and seismic velocities). Rapid recovery is also essential for the study of short-lived radioactive isotopes induced by space exposure.

Fireballs no brighter than magnitude –6 can produce small meteorites. A slow fireball with or without terminal breakup is a good candidate for dropping meteorites. A delayed sonic boom associated with a fireball indicates that it is relatively nearby and often that it has penetrated into the lower atmosphere with an associated meteorite fall.

The scientific value of a meteorite is significantly greater when its prefall orbit is known. Under favourable circumstances, visual data can be used to obtain an approximate atmospheric trajectory, which, coupled with satellite or video observations, can be used to derive a prefall orbit.

The Meteorites and Impacts Advisory Committee (MIAC) of the Canadian Space Agency maintains an informative Web site: miac.uqac.uquebec.ca. The preferred method for submitting fireball reports is via the Web:

Canada (only): miac.uqac.uquebec.ca/MIAC/fireball.htm
United States (AMS): www.amsmeteors.org/fireball/report.html
Global (IMO): www.imo.net/fireball/report.html
North American Meteor Network (NAMN):
    visual: www.namnmeteors.org/fireball_form.html
    photographic: www.namnmeteors.org/photo_form.html

Reports of fireballs seen over Canada can also be faxed to the Canadian Fireball Reporting Centre at (403) 284-0074. Reports should include the following information (making notes immediately, at least of the precise time, is recommended):

(1) The name, telephone number/email, and address of the observer(s).
(2) The time of occurrence (and uncertainty in this time); an accurate time is required to search instrumental databases.
(3) The location of the observer at the time the fireball was seen (preferably in precise longitude and latitude).
(4) The beginning and ending points of the fireball, in terms of either right ascension and declination or azimuth and elevation. Indicate whether the true beginning was observed and whether the ending point was blocked by an object on the horizon.
(5) An estimate of the apparent magnitude; or compare the fireball brightness to that of the Moon. Was the ground lit up?
(6) The duration of the fireball and the persistent train (if any).
(7) A qualitative description of the event (e.g. colour, flares, fragmentation, dust clouds persisting after the fireball, and sound). If sound was heard, report the time delay between the fireball and the arrival of the sound or the precise time of the sound arrival as well as that of the fireball.
(8) The existence of any video, audio, or photographic records.

METEORITE IDENTIFICATION
BY RICHARD K. HERD

Meteorites are rocks from space that have fallen on Earth. Some have lain for many thousands of years before discovery. Fossil meteorites are found in ancient strata; others are recent arrivals. Those observed to traverse Earth's atmosphere, and recovered based on those observations, are called meteorite *falls*. Those with no record of arrival are meteorite *finds* when recognized. Meteorites are named for where they are found. Over 25 000 meteorites are known worldwide: 18 000 are from Antarctica and a few thousand from deserts in Africa and Asia. See *The Cambridge Encyclopedia of Meteorites* by O.R. Norton, Cambridge University Press, 2002, and *Meteorites from A to Z* (2nd ed) by M.R. Jensen et al., published by Michael R. Jensen, 2004.

Often there is confusion over when and where meteorites have fallen or have been preserved, and also over what they are and look like, even though Web sites now provide ready access to meteorite research, photos, and data. All are significantly different than Earth rocks. Samples sent to experts for identification, even by other scientists, are usually "meteorwrongs"—terrestrial rocks or minerals, human-made slag, metals, alloys, or concrete—that rarely resemble meteorites. Over 60 identified meteorites are known in Canada. There have been three falls since 1994: Tagish Lake, British Columbia, 2000 Jan. 18; Kitchener, Ontario, 1998 Jul. 12; and St-Robert, Québec, 1994 Jun. 14.

Meteorites probably begin as streams of fragments *(meteoroids)* that are debris from collisions between larger objects. The calculated orbits of several falls intersect the asteroid belt; their ultimate origin in space and time may be elsewhere. About 30 meteorites have come from the Moon. The petrological and isotopic evidence is compelling that a similar number are from Mars, blasted off the surface by impacts. Based on the meteorites' reflectance spectra or density, links have been suggested between other types or groups of meteorites and specific asteroids or asteroid types or comets, but the provenance of most is uncertain. Yet they are an unparalleled source of information about our solar system, from its primitive beginnings to the present. Many preserve presolar mineral grains; some contain primordial compounds made in other stars, yielding information about the origin of the universe. To prepare for space exploration, they are scientifically invaluable. Meteorite researchers are called *meteoriticists*. The Meteoritical Society (**www.meteoriticalsociety.org**) sets international research standards.

Popular ideas about when and where meteorites fall are connected with the observation of *meteors,* the brief streaks of light produced when high-speed, interplanetary particles enter Earth's upper atmosphere. Sporadic meteors and *meteor showers* do not produce meteorites; their fragile cometary debris fragments are reduced to dust high in the atmosphere. Earth collects over 100 tonnes of cosmic dust debris per day. In contrast, stronger, larger space rocks can survive a fiery passage through the atmosphere and result in meteorites. These first appear as bright *fireballs,* are slowed to terminal speeds by atmospheric friction, and cease to show a bright trail long before they reach Earth's surface. Fireballs, which may seem very close, are usually quite high in the atmosphere, 50 km or more from the observer. Even if an extraterrestrial object does reach the surface, it is likely to plunge into the 70% that is water or to be lost among forests, jungles, or mountainous regions. In only uncommonly recorded cases have meteorites struck or landed within a few metres of humans (see "Possible Hazards of Meteorite Falls" by C.E. Spratt, *JRASC, 85* (October 1991), p. 263). Rare meteoroids of masses exceeding 100 tonnes are not slowed appreciably by Earth's atmosphere and produce impact craters. The larger impacts may have dramatically altered the history of life on our planet, but they do not result in meteorites—the kinetic energy is sufficiently high to vapourize the impacting body completely and to deform and melt the target area in a fraction of a second. Crater diameters are typically 10 times the diameter of the impacting body. Glassy *tektites* found scattered over several continents may be evidence of such impacts, but they do not have meteorite compositions or characteristics.

Meteorites are divided into three groups that vary widely both in appearance and properties: *stones* or *stony meteorites (aerolites), stony-irons (siderolites),* and *irons* or *iron meteorites (siderites).* All usually contain metallic nickel-iron compounds (with traces of other metals) and are mildly to strongly magnetic. Those that have lain on Earth's surface for long periods may be rusted almost beyond recognition; some require laboratory tests to confirm their identity. Specimens generally have a quite soft, dull black to brown fusion crust; more prevalent on stones and stony-irons, it may have partially flaked off. Meteorites only rarely contain bubble-like cavities; they are never almost perfectly spherical and smooth. During atmospheric entry, only their surface is affected. Surfaces of irons and stony-irons are dimpled rather than bulbous. They rust easily so there may be no bright metal showing. Stony meteorites do not show protuberances; weathered varieties are rusty, even on broken surfaces. Fresh stony meteorites may have a whitish rock interior, with bright metal specks. Their crusts are black or smoky grey, varying from quite glassy to dull; telltale lines and bubbled patches orient their flight through the air. More metallic samples may also be oriented.

Stones are the most abundant; they resemble some terrestrial rocks but are denser. Most (called *chondrites*) consist of spheres of silicate minerals (called *chondrules*) visible on broken, cut, or polished surfaces and scattered grains of metal. Chondrites are the oldest, most primitive, and least altered meteorites. Rare stony meteorites without chondrules are called *achondrites;* these are thought to be melt products from chondrites, samples of younger volcanic planetary surfaces. In August 1996, NASA scientists announced the discovery of fossil and chemical evidence of bacterial life in an ancient achondrite from Mars, but other scientists disagree. This controversy has resulted in renewed interest in missions to Mars and in finding water and life on Mars and elsewhere, even in extreme conditions on Earth. Irons and stony-irons are dense, with up to equal amounts of silicates and iron, and are often irregular in shape. They are thought to be core/mantle material of planets formed by melting chondrites.

Rare *carbonaceous chondrites* are grey to black, some resembling charcoal with silicate inclusions. The dark colour is from iron oxides and sulphides. They contain a few percent carbon in very fine-grained carbonates, carbides, graphite, diamonds, and primitive organic molecules, detectable mainly by isotopic analyses. They may have had biologically significant roles in providing seeds for the origin of life. They probably come from comet nuclei or similar ice-rich asteroids. Their organic molecules originate in interstellar space as coatings on dust. The study of interplanetary and interstellar dust particles has become important in deciphering the origins of meteorites and, therefore, of our solar system and everything in it. We are all composed of recycled stardust.

The Geological Survey of Canada (GSC) maintains the National Meteorite Collection of about 2700 specimens of 1100 different meteorites, identifies meteorites, and supports research on them. It also offers to pay the owner a minimum of $500 for the first specimen of any new Canadian meteorite. Should you find a suspected meteorite, you may forward it to Geological Survey of Canada, Natural Resources Canada, Attention: Meteorite Identification, 601 Booth St, Ottawa ON K1A 0E8 (telephone: (613) 992-4042; fax: (613) 943-1286; email: herd@nrcan.gc.ca). The specimen will be examined and reported on free of charge. If it is too large for mailing, a description of its appearance (or a photograph) and its exact location should be sent. The GSC also makes available a free brochure on meteorites, with pictures of meteorites and comparative nonmeteorites. Write to the GSC's Publication Office at the above address. Meteorites of Canadian origin are subject to the provisions of the Cultural Property Export and Import Act and may not be exported from Canada without a permit.

METEORITE IMPACT CRATERS OF NORTH AMERICA
BY JOHN SPRAY AND JASON HINES

Earth has endured the hypervelocity impact of planetary materials since its inception 4.57 Ga ago, just like any other planet in our solar system. However, in contrast to the Moon, Mercury, Mars, and many asteroids, the Earth shows relatively few impact craters on its surface. On Earth, currently 174 are proven; see the Earth Impact Database, 2007 at www.unb.ca/passc/ImpactDatabase. The Moon's surface is saturated with craters, as is Mercury's, and 42 000 craters have been catalogued on Mars. Our inventory is limited because Earth (like Venus) is an active planet. This means that most craters are destroyed or buried due to plate tectonics, volcanic activity, and weathering. Of the 174 known craters on Earth, 57 are known from North America (see the following table), 29 of which are in Canada, 27 in the United States, and 1 in Mexico (see the map at the end of this section.) This total thus represents about a third of the world inventory. North American craters range in diameter from as small as 170 m, for the largest of the Odessa crater field (Texas), up to ~250 km for Sudbury (Ontario).

The principal criteria for determining if a geological feature is an impact structure formed by the hypervelocity impact of a meteorite or comet are listed below. Criteria are divided into *megascopic* (overview—bird's eye/satellite scale), *macroscopic* (can be seen easily with the naked eye), and *microscopic* (requires a microscope to see) features:

1. Presence of shatter cones that are *in situ* (macroscopic evidence);
2. Presence of multiple planar deformation features (PDFs) in minerals within *in situ* lithologies (microscopic evidence);
3. Presence of high-pressure mineral polymorphs within *in situ* lithologies (microscopic evidence and requiring proof via X-ray diffraction, etc.). Examples include the high-pressure polymorphs of SiO_2 coesite and stishovite.
4. Morphometry. On some planetary bodies, such as the Moon and Mars, we rely on the shape of the impact structure to determine its presence and type. This is a megascopic quality (i.e. too big to be seen unaided by the human eye, thus requiring remote sensing, etc.). On Earth, recognizing impact structures solely by their morphometry is complicated by two factors: (a) weathering, erosion, burial processes, and tectonic deformation; and (b) certain terrestrial features having comparable shape (e.g. volcanoes, salt diapirs, glacigenic features), *such that a circular structure alone is not sufficient to claim impact structure status*;
5. Presence of an impact-melt sheet and/or dikes, and impact-melt breccias that were generated due to hypervelocity impact (macroscopic). Melt sheets may be overlain by so-called fallback breccias (referred to as "suevite" by some workers), and material blasted out of the crater may form ejecta blankets about the original central cavity. For large impact events, ejecta can be distributed globally;
6. Pseudotachylyte—is a rock generated by faulting at either microscopic or macroscopic scales. Some peudotachylytes are associated with endogenic seismic faulting (e.g. earthquakes due to isostatic rebound and plate tectonics), so they are not exclusively impact generated; however, in association with features 1-3 above, they can be a contributory criterion.

In terms of relative importance, criteria 1–3 above are definitive, with contributory evidence being added by 4–6. For well-preserved buried structures, as revealed by detailed geophysical techniques (especially seismic data), some workers consider this as strong evidence in favour of an impact origin. Normally, buried craters are verified by drilling and sampling for evaluation using criteria 1–3 above.

TABLE OF METEORITE IMPACT CRATERS OF NORTH AMERICA

#	Name, Location	Lat. (N) ° '	Long. (W) ° '	Diam. km	Age* Ma	Surface Expression	Visible Geologic Features
1	Ames, Oklahoma, USA	36 15	98 12	16.	470. (30)	buried 3 km	none
2	Avak, Alaska, USA	71 15	156 38	12.	3–95.	buried 30 m	none
3	Barringer (Meteor) Crater, Arizona, USA	35 02	111 01	1.2	0.049 (0.003)	rimmed polygonal crater	fragments of meteorite, highly shocked sandstone
4	Beaverhead, Montana, USA	44 36	113 00	60.	≈600.	oval area of crushed sandstone, and shatter cones	shatter cones
5	Brent, Ontario	46 05	78 29	3.8	396. (20)	sediment-filled shallow depression	fracturing
6	Calvin, Michigan, USA	41 50	85 57	8.5	450. (10)	buried 400 m	none
7	Carswell, Saskatchewan	58 27	109 30	39.	115. (10)	discontinuous circular ridge	shatter cones, breccia, impact melt
8	Charlevoix, Québec	47 32	70 18	54.	342. (15)	semicircular trough, central peak	breccia, shatter cones, impact melt
9	Chesapeake Bay, Virginia, USA	37 17	76 01	90.	35.5 (0.3)	buried 400–500 m, ring structure	none
10	Chicxulub, Mexico	21 20	89 30	170.	64.98 (0.05)	buried 1 km, ring of sink holes	none (related to the K/T mass extinction event)
11	Clearwater East, Québec	56 05	74 07	26.	290. (20)	circular lake	sedimentary float
12	Clearwater West, Québec	56 13	74 30	36.	290. (20)	island ring in circular lake	impact melt, breccias
13	Cloud Creek, Wyoming, USA	43 07	106 45	7.	190. (30)	buried 1.1 km	none
14	Couture, Québec	60 08	75 20	8.	430. (25)	circular lake	breccia float
15	Crooked Creek, Missouri, USA	37 50	91 23	7.	320. (80)	oval area of disturbed rocks, shallow marginal depression	breccia, shatter cones
16	Decaturville, Missouri, USA	37 54	92 43	6.	<300.	slight oval depression	breccia, shatter cones
17	Deep Bay, Saskatchewan	56 24	102 59	13.	99. (4)	circular bay	sedimentary float
18	Des Plaines, Illinois, USA	42 03	87 52	8.	<280.	buried, 15–100 m	none
19	Eagle Butte, Alberta	49 42	110 30	10.	<65.	minor structural disturbance	shatter cones
20	Elbow, Saskatchewan	50 59	106 43	8.	395. (25)	buried, small mound	none
21	Flynn Creek, Tennessee, USA	36 17	85 40	3.8	360. (20)	sediment-filled shallow depression with small central peak	breccia, shatter cones
22	Glasford, Illinois, USA	40 36	89 47	4.	<430.	buried 350 m	none
23	Glover Bluff, Wisconsin, USA	43 58	89 32	8.	<500.	disturbed dolomite exposed	shatter cones
24	Gow, Saskatchewan	56 27	104 29	5.	<250.	lake and central island	breccia, impact melt
25	Haughton, Nunavut	75 22	89 41	23.	39.	shallow circular depression	shatter cones, breccia
26	Haviland, Kansas, USA	37 35	99 10	0.015	<0.001	excavated depression	fragments of meteorite
27	Holleford, Ontario	44 28	76 38	2.4	550. (100)	sediment-filled shallow depression	sedimentary fill
28	Île Rouleau, Québec	50 41	73 53	4.	<300.	island is central peak of submerged structure	shatter cones, breccia dykes
29	Kentland, Indiana, USA	40 45	87 24	13.	<97.	central peak exposed in quarries, rest buried	breccia, shatter cones, disturbed rocks

* Numbers in parentheses are possible errors.

TABLE OF METEORITE IMPACT CRATERS OF NORTH AMERICA (cont)

#	Name, Location	Lat. (N) ° '	Long. (W) ° '	Diam. km	Age* Ma	Surface Expression	Visible Geologic Features
30	La Moinerie, Québec	57 26	66 37	8.	400. (50)	lake-filled depression	breccia float
31	Manicouagan, Québec	51 23	68 42	100.	214. (1)	circumferential lake, central peak	impact melt, breccia
32	Manson, Iowa, USA	42 35	94 33	35.	73.8 (0.3)	none, central elevation buried 30 m	none
33	Maple Creek, Saskatchewan	49 48	109 06	6.	<75.	buried, small mound	disturbed rocks
34	Marquez, Texas, USA	31 17	96 18	12.7	58. (2)	circular area of disturbed rock	shatter cones
35	Middlesboro, Kentucky, USA	36 37	83 44	6.	<300.	circular depression	disturbed rocks
36	Mistastin, Labrador	55 53	63 18	28.	36.4 (4)	elliptical lake and central island	breccia, impact melt
37	Montagnais, Nova Scotia	42 53	64 13	45.	50.5 (0.8)	none, under water (115 m) and sediment	none
38	New Québec, Québec	61 17	73 40	3.4	1.4 (0.1)	rimmed, circular lake	raised rim, impact melt
39	Newporte, North Dakota, USA	48 58	101 58	3.2	<500.	none, buried 3 km	none
40	Nicholson, NWT	62 40	102 41	12.5	<400.	irregular lake with islands	breccia
41	Odessa, Texas, USA	31 45	102 29	0.17	<0.05	sediment-filled depression with very slight rim, 4 others buried & smaller	fragments of meteorite
42	Pilot, NWT	60 17	111 01	6.	445. (2)	circular lake	fracturing, breccia float
43	Presqu'île, Québec	49 43	74 48	24.	<500.	none, heavily eroded	shatter cones
44	Red Wing, North Dakota, USA	47 36	103 33	9.	200. (25)	none, buried 1.5 km	none
45	Rock Elm, Wisconsin, USA	44 43	92 14	6.	<505.	circular rim depression, central dome	shatter cones, breccia
46	St. Martin, Manitoba	51 47	98 32	40.	220. (32)	none, partially buried	impact melt
47	Serpent Mound, Ohio, USA	39 02	83 24	8.	<320.	circular area of disturbed rock, slight central peak	breccia, shatter cones
48	Sierra Madera, Texas, USA	30 36	102 55	13.	<100.	central hills, annular depression, outer ring of hills	breccia, shatter cones
49	Slate Islands, Ontario	48 40	87 00	30.	≈450.	islands are central peak of submerged structure	shatter cones, breccia dykes
50	Steen River, Alberta	59 30	117 38	25.	91. (7)	none, buried 200 m	none
51	Sudbury, Ontario	46 36	81 11	250.	1850. (3)	deformed elliptical basin	breccia, impact melt, shatter cones, breccia dykes
52	Upheaval Dome, Utah, USA	38 26	109 54	10.	<170.	circular area of disturbed rock	breccia dykes
53	Viewfield, Saskatchewan	49 35	103 04	2.5	190. (20)	buried 1 km	none
54	Wanapitei, Ontario	46 45	80 45	7.5	37. (1.2)	lake-filled depression	breccia float
55	Wells Creek, Tennessee, USA	36 23	87 40	12.	200. (100)	basin with central hill, inner and outer annular valleys, ridges	breccia, shatter cones
56	West Hawk Lake, Manitoba	49 46	95 11	2.4	351. (20)	circular lake	none
57	Wetumpka, Alabama, USA	32 31	86 10	6.5	81. (1.5)	arcuate outer ridge, central depression	breccia

*Numbers in parentheses are possible errors.

MAP OF NORTH AMERICAN METEORITE IMPACT STRUCTURES

Of the 170 plus impact structures identified on Earth, 57 are in North America (29 in Canada, 27 in the United States, and 1 in Mexico). These are identified on the above map; the numbers correspond to the listing in the table on the previous pages. Although the oceans cover 70% of Earth, only two impact structures have been identified on the seafloor (#37 and Mjølnir, in the Barents Sea). Also, with the exception of structure #51, all of those shown occurred within approximately the last 10% of Earth's history. Evidence of many earlier craters has been erased by geologic processes. It is possible, however, to calculate a terrestrial cratering rate by focusing only on geologically stable areas of Earth (known as cratons), with low erosion and sedimentation rates. One such area is the North American craton. These rate calculations indicate that Earth has received at least 10 000 impacts sufficient to result in craters greater than 20 km in diameter over the last 3.5 billion years. Very early in Earth history, the cratering rate was even higher, perhaps as high as 100 times the current rate. Doubtless some of these impacts have had profound influence upon the evolution of life on this planet. For example, Chicxulub (#10), the very large structure in Mexico, is linked to a major extinction event 65 million years ago. Some impact craters are the source of considerable economic resources: in North America, hydrocarbons are extracted from #1, 2, 6, 34, 39, 44, 48, 50, 53; #7 produces uranium; and #51 is the site of a world-class nickel and copper mining camp.

COMETS IN 2008
By Brian G. Marsden

Listed below are the periodic comets expected at perihelion in 2008. The orbital elements are given with sufficient precision to allow an ephemeris computation good to about 1′. The angular elements are referred to the ecliptic and mean equinox J2000.0.

Comet	Perihelion Date T TT	Dist. q au	Eccen. e	Rev. Per. P a	Arg. Peri. ω °	Asc. Node Ω °	Incl. i °
8P	Jan. 27.02	1.0271	0.8199	13.6	207.51	270.34	54.98
46P	Feb. 2.42	1.0575	0.6581	5.4	356.35	82.18	11.74
110P	Feb. 3.49	2.4885	0.3125	6.9	167.80	287.75	11.68
P/2000 U6	Feb. 7.32	2.1379	0.4338	7.3	11.72	24.34	19.38
44P	Feb. 18.28	2.1064	0.4283	7.1	58.07	286.60	5.90
P/2001 Q5	Feb. 20.99	2.1555	0.3961	6.7	8.27	335.26	10.71
P/2000 B3	Feb. 26.03	1.7087	0.5742	8.0	130.64	352.06	11.12
113P	Mar. 23.41	2.1285	0.4230	7.1	49.85	14.47	5.78
26P	Mar. 23.69	1.1167	0.6330	5.3	1.72	211.71	22.36
16P	Apr. 12.59	1.4666	0.5627	6.1	219.47	159.38	4.26
139P	Apr. 19.41	3.4028	0.2465	9.6	165.52	242.45	2.33
124P	Apr. 27.21	1.4686	0.5423	5.7	181.37	1.35	31.34
11P	May 4.58	1.5536	0.5449	6.3	163.90	240.53	13.55
183P	May 9.12	3.8940	0.1358	9.6	161.68	5.84	18.73
P/2003 KV2	May 18.25	1.0604	0.6299	4.9	188.79	66.39	25.55
173P	May 18.52	4.2145	0.2611	13.6	29.83	100.57	16.50
86P	May 20.00	2.3012	0.3660	6.9	179.15	72.58	15.45
146P	May 21.38	1.4175	0.6480	8.1	316.83	53.57	23.08
148P	May 22.74	1.7027	0.5379	7.1	6.68	89.81	3.68
P/1998 VS24	May 24.67	3.4226	0.2421	9.6	244.37	159.18	5.03
180P	May 26.71	2.4687	0.3576	7.5	94.91	84.75	16.91
79P	May 28.45	1.2305	0.5940	5.3	253.28	307.84	2.89
51P	Jun. 19.42	1.6877	0.5445	7.1	269.19	83.76	5.43
15P	Jun. 22.56	0.9700	0.7214	6.5	347.48	13.82	6.81
33P	Jul. 20.36	2.1697	0.4619	8.1	18.98	66.57	22.38
19P	Jul. 22.47	1.3548	0.6245	6.9	353.38	75.44	30.32
P/2001 R1	Aug. 5.18	1.3450	0.6117	6.4	24.96	35.30	7.03
6P	Aug. 14.99	1.3535	0.6128	6.5	178.12	138.94	19.51
P/1997 V1	Aug. 27.43	3.2721	0.3334	10.9	133.79	234.81	12.12
61P	Sep. 6.10	2.1080	0.4265	7.0	221.62	163.12	6.01
147P	Sep. 22.96	2.7564	0.2759	7.4	346.88	93.74	2.37
7P	Sep. 26.63	1.2533	0.6349	6.4	172.33	93.42	22.31
187P	Oct. 6.30	3.6933	0.1705	9.4	131.96	112.00	13.73
P/2001 CV8	Oct. 11.35	2.1600	0.4442	7.7	151.60	359.89	9.04
172P	Oct. 12.84	2.2405	0.3618	6.6	179.00	40.09	11.52
P/2001 J1	Nov. 6.85	0.9441	0.7572	7.7	271.18	200.67	10.15
P/1999 XN120	Nov. 12.51	3.3041	0.2108	8.6	161.61	285.45	5.03
150P	Nov. 26.00	1.7677	0.5459	7.7	245.67	272.43	18.50
P/2001 TU80	Dec. 9.59	1.9403	0.4706	7.0	355.03	109.11	6.58
85P	Dec. 16.36	1.1475	0.7753	11.5	53.58	343.45	4.22
57P	Dec. 25.99	1.7238	0.5003	6.4	115.30	188.83	2.85

For an explanation of these elements, see p. 22; the elements are for an epoch within 20 days of perihelion.

The returns of 6P/d'Arrest, 8P/Tuttle, 26P/Grigg-Skjellerup, 61P/Shajn-Schaldach, 86P/Wild, 110P/Hartley, 124P/Mrkos, 173P/Mueller, 183P/Korlević- Jurić, P/1997 V1 (Larsen), P/1999 XN120 (Catalina), P/2000 B3 (LINEAR), P/2001 TU80 (LINEAR-NEAT), and P/2003 KV2 (LINEAR) are favourable, and those of 79P/du Toit-Hartley, 85P/Boethin, 139P/Väisälä-Oterma, 172P/Yeung, 180P/NEAT, and 187P/LINEAR are fair. The returns of 7P/Pons-Winnecke, 15P/Finlay, 16P/Brooks, 19P/Borrelly, 44P/Reinmuth, 46P/Wirtanen, 51P/Harrington, 113P/Spitaler, 146P/Shoemaker-LINEAR, 147P/Kushida-Muramatsu, 150P/LONEOS, P/1998 VS24 (LINEAR), P/2000 U6 (Tichý), P/2001 CV8 (LINEAR), P/2001 J1 (NEAT), P/2001 Q5 (LINEAR-NEAT), and P/2001 R1 (LONEOS) are poor, and those of 11P/Tempel-Swift-LINEAR, 33P/Daniel, 57P/du Toit-Neujmin-Delporte, and 148P/Anderson-LINEAR are very poor.

For current ephemerides for all comets listed here, visit

www.cfa.harvard.edu/iau/Ephemerides/Comets

OBSERVING COMETS
By David H. Levy

Each comet has its own unique, changing appearance. Observationally, comets are very much like deep-sky objects. Even in large telescopes an observer can confuse a comet with a galaxy or a diffuse planetary nebula. Comets near a telescope's limit are virtually impossible to spot without an accurate position extracted from a detailed atlas like *Uranometria* or *Millennium*. It is difficult to define a telescope's limiting magnitude for comets because the more diffuse a comet, the more difficult it is to find. Typically, under a dark sky a 150-mm telescope will catch a 9th-magnitude comet, a 200-mm telescope will see 10th, and a 400-mm should capture a 13th-magnitude comet.

If you are sure you have discovered a comet, follow the procedure in REPORTING OF ASTRONOMICAL DISCOVERIES, p. 10. For more information on comet observing and hunting, read *David Levy's Guide to Observing and Discovering Comets* (Cambridge, 2003).

Magnitude Estimates

The brightness of the coma can be estimated using a variety of methods, the most common of which is the "In-Out" method:

(1) Study the coma until you are familiar with its "average" brightness, an easy process if the coma is of uniform brightness but rather difficult if there is a strong central condensation.

(2) With the help of a variable-star chart or some source in which star magnitudes are listed, find a comparison star at approximately the same altitude as the comet.

(3) Defocus the star to the size of the in-focus coma.

(4) Compare the star's out-of-focus brightness with that of the coma.

Repeat the last three steps with a second star, or more if needed, until an interpolation can be made.

Physical Characteristics

An estimate of a comet's magnitude is more useful if an estimate of the coma diameter is made at the same time. An observer seeing a 3′ coma, for example, will estimate much brighter than one who sees only a 1′ coma at the same time. The simplest way of estimating coma size is to draw the coma with the embedded and surrounding field stars and then compare the drawing to an atlas, using its scale to determine the size.

A nightly measurement of a comet's degree of condensation is a good way of studying its changing behaviour. A comet undergoing an outburst of dust from its nucleus might begin its display by showing almost overnight the development of an increased condensation. Use an integer scale from 0 to 9, where 0 means a diffuse coma with absolutely uniform brightness, 3 means a diffuse coma with gradually increasing brightness toward the centre, 6 involves a definite central condensation, and 9 refers to an almost stellar image.

Because of the changing Earth–Sun–comet geometry and the changing activity in a comet, the length and position angle of a tail should be measured. A rough way to measure the length of a tail is to sketch it and compare with a detailed atlas, as with the coma. Observers can also measure the position angle using an atlas and a protractor.

Visual Comet Hunting

The key ingredient to a successful comet search is perseverance, especially in this time of automated searches. The chances for a visual discovery have plummeted in the last few years. Although there are stories of people finding comets very quickly (Mark Whitaker discovered Comet Whitaker-Thomas 1968 V after three nights of comet hunting), these are the exception. Don Machholz searched for some 1700 hours for each of his first two comets, and I spent more than 917 hours before my first discovery. In contrast, neither Alan Hale nor Tom Bopp was comet hunting when they independently discovered what later became the Great Comet of 1997.

It is important to know the sky well before beginning a comet search program, but it is more important to know the difference between the fuzzy appearances of comets compared to galaxies, nebulae, and clusters. Observing all the objects in Messier's Catalogue (see pp. 286–289) provides an excellent education in what these distant objects look like, and observing as many known comets as possible is good preparation for recognizing an interloper. Generally, comets lack the bilateral symmetry of spiral galaxies and the mottled appearance of globular clusters. More important, they usually have unsharp edges, fading off into space so that it is often difficult to tell where the comet ends and the sky begins.

Although most comet hunters still use traditional star atlases to check their suspects, some are moving into a new mode of comet hunting. These hunters have attached encoders to their telescopes that allow an instant reading of the suspect's position in right ascension and declination. If the telescope has been properly set up, this approach is faster. However, a sense of the nature of the fuzzy object in the field of view is still important since thousands of nonstellar objects dot the sky.

Comets may appear at any time, but they are usually found within 90° of the Sun. Good areas to search are in the evening western sky during the week after full Moon and in the morning eastern sky before dawn around new Moon. Although comet hunters differ in their approaches to searching, one way is to use an altazimuth mount and make horizontal sweeps. In the western sky, begin near the end of evening twilight at the horizon, sweep across, then return to the point of origin, move upward about half a field of view and sweep again, etc. In the morning reverse the process.

In June 2006 the author captured this image of Comet 73P Schwassmann-Wachmann 3b and 3c using a 250-mm lens and a Meade Pictor CCD camera. Fragments 3b (left) and 3c (right) are seen in the image, which is a combination of four separate 90-second exposures.

Photographic and Electronic Comet Hunting

While still possible, it is now very difficult to discover comets photographically because the sky is so well covered by the professional surveys. With film and a wide-angle camera like a Schmidt camera, take photographs of selected areas of sky, then repeat these exposures after at least 45 min. Using a stereomicroscope or a blink microscope, it is then possible to spot moving objects. Through a stereomicroscope, the comet will appear to "float" above or "sink" below the stellar background. If a blink microscope is used, the comet will appear to jump back and forth.

Using a CCD, take at least three images of each field, then examine either visually or using a moving-object detection program. Visual inspection is like blinking, so moving objects appear to move steadily through the three pictures, then jump back and begin moving again.

Finally, it is possible to discover comets over the Internet. Since images from the SOHO spacecraft are made available soon after they are taken, amateur astronomers can scan these images for Sun-grazing comets. RASC member Michael Boschat won the 2001 Ken Chilton Prize for his discoveries of several SOHO comets in this way.

Designation of Comets

At the International Astronomical Union's 22nd General Assembly in The Hague in 1994, Commission 20 of the IAU approved a resolution that changes the way comets are designated. Under the old system, a comet was designated according to its order of discovery or recovery in a given year (e.g. 1982i, Comet Halley, was the ninth comet to appear in 1982). After cometary information was complete for a given year, each comet also received a Roman numeral designation based on the order of perihelion passage (e.g. Halley at its last return was also known as 1986 III). Although the new designation went into effect in January 1995, it is retroactive to every comet for which a reasonable orbit is available.

Under the new system, a comet is assigned only one designation which is similar, although not identical, to the provisional designation system for asteroids. With this system the year is divided into periods called *half-months* beginning with A (the first half of January) and concluding with Y (the last half of December), omitting the letter I. In addition, there is a letter indicating the comet's status: C for a long-period comet, P for a "periodic comet" (defined as having a period of less than 200 years), X for a comet for which a reasonable orbit cannot be computed, and D for a disappeared comet. Once the orbit of a periodic comet is well known, that comet receives a permanent number according to the order in which the comet's periodicity was recognized. Thus Comet Hale-Bopp, as the first comet to be found in the O part of 1995, is labelled C/1995 O1. Comet Shoemaker-Levy 9 was 1993e; its new designation as the second comet to be found in the F part of 1993 is D/1993 F2. The new designation for Comet Halley is 1P/Halley.

When a comet becomes well known, the vast majority of scientists, press, and public ignore the official designation, preferring instead to use more easily remembered names. Our experience with comets Hale-Bopp and Hyakutake (C/1996 B2) showed clearly that people were more comfortable with proper names. However, with 2 comets named Hyakutake, more than 200 named SOHO, and more than 50 named LINEAR, we need to become familiar with the official designation in order to separate one comet from another.

A handful of comets are named not for their discoverers but for the persons who computed their orbits. The most famous of these is P/Halley, which has been well observed since at least 240 BC. It was finally identified as a comet appearing every 76 years or so by Sir Edmund Halley in 1705. Two others are 2P/Encke and 27P/Crommelin.

In the event that the cometary nature of an object is established after it was originally given an asteroidal designation, the original designation remains. When Gene and Carolyn Shoemaker and I discovered Asteroid 1990 UL3 using the Palomar 18-in. telescope, for example, its orbit appeared to be more cometary than asteroidal. A few weeks after discovery, Steve Larson and I took a series of images through the Kuiper 61-in. telescope that clearly showed a tail, and the identification was changed to periodic comet Shoemaker-Levy 2. The mixed designation C/1990 UL3 applies.

Editor's Note: David Levy is the discoverer of 22 comets: 9 by visual searches and 13 photographically at Palomar under the combined name Shoemaker-Levy.

INTERPLANETARY DUST
BY ROY BISHOP

Outside of the astronomical community it is not generally realized that the inner solar system contains a vast cloud of dust. The particles in this cloud are concentrated near the plane of the ecliptic and toward the Sun, their spatial particle density in the ecliptic falling off somewhat more rapidly than the reciprocal of their distance from the Sun. Measurements from spacecraft indicate that the cloud extends well beyond the orbit of Mars but is negligible in the vicinity of Jupiter's orbit and beyond.

The particles composing the cloud have a continuum of sizes, from pebble-sized clumps down to specks with diameters comparable to the wavelength of visible light and smaller. The smaller particles are the more numerous, although the mass distribution appears to peak near 10^{-8} kg, corresponding to a particle diameter of a few tenths of a millimetre. The total mass of the cloud is small, amounting to perhaps 10^{-14} of the mass of the solar system. It is as if the satellites of Mars had been pulverized and spread throughout the inner solar system.

Like the planetary system, the interplanetary dust cloud is not static; its particles generally move in orbits about the Sun. In addition, the particles undergo continual fragmentation due to collisions, sputtering associated with bombardment by the solar wind, electrostatic bursting, and sublimation. This progression toward smaller and smaller sizes is of crucial significance for the cloud, since particles with diameters appreciably less than a tenth of a millimetre have a sufficiently large surface-to-volume ratio that the radiation pressure of sunlight has a significant effect upon their motion—aberration of sunlight results in a small backward force that slows the dust particles (the Poynting–Robertson Effect), and they slowly spiral inward toward the Sun. During a total solar eclipse in 1983, instruments carried by a balloon detected a ringlike concentration of dust only a couple of solar diameters from the Sun. Its inner edge apparently marks the point at which solar heat vapourizes the infalling particles. The resulting tiny gas molecules, like the smallest particles of dust, are blown out of the solar system by the dominant radiation pressure and interactions with the solar wind.

Because of the above-mentioned influences on the sizes and motions of the dust particles, the estimated mean life of a cloud particle is about 10^4 years. Since this is much less than the age of the solar system, it is obvious that the cloud must be in a dynamic equilibrium—that is, it must be gaining new material as it loses the old. Part of the coma and tail of a comet is the result of significant quantities of dust ejected from its nucleus, and it is generally assumed that comets provide a sizeable fraction of the supply of new dust to the cloud. Since comet nuclei are believed to consist of the undifferentiated matter from which the solar system formed, much of the dust of the interplanetary cloud is most likely composed of this same low-density, fragile, primitive material. IRAS (Infrared Astronomical Satellite) data indicate that collisions of asteroids are also a significant source of dust, but it is not yet known whether comets or asteroids provide the greater input of dust to the cloud.

To an observer on Earth the most noticeable aspect of the dust cloud is meteors—larger particles of the cloud that encounter Earth at high speeds and vapourize in the upper atmosphere. In addition, sunlight scattered by the dust cloud appears as a faint (fortunately!) glow in the vicinity of the ecliptic. This glow is brightest toward the Sun, is due primarily to particles with diameters between a few micrometres and a millimetre, and is referred to as the *zodiacal light*. A slight brightening in the sky opposite the Sun, called the *Gegenschein* (German for "counterglow"), is due to a phase effect (analogous to full moon) and also, possibly, to a concentration of dust at the L3 Lagrangian point of the Earth–Sun system. The integrated visual magnitude of the dust is about −8.5, making it the brightest solar system object in the sky after the Sun and Moon. As astronomical objects the zodiacal light and the Gegenschein are unusual in that they can be seen only with the unaided eye. Because of their large angular sizes and indistinct borders, both are invisible in binoculars or a telescope.

The Zodiacal Light

Poetic references to the zodiacal light go back several centuries (e.g. see *The Observatory, 108* (1988), p. 181). The 19th-century poet Edward FitzGerald is noted for his translation of the famous poem "Rubaiyat" by the Persian Omar Khayyam. In one of the stanzas Khayyam's reference to the morning was altered by FitzGerald into haunting references to the zodiacal light: "Dreaming when Dawn's Left Hand was in the Sky" (in midnorthern latitudes the zodiacal light and the first glow of the early autumn dawn combine to produce a large, glowing, ghostly figure having an upraised left arm); and "Before the phantom of False morning died" (the zodiacal light soon vanishes in the glow of the true dawn).

When conditions are favourable, the zodiacal light is indeed a mysterious and beautiful sight. Because the zodiacal light is brightest nearest the Sun, it is best seen within half an hour following the end of evening twilight and in the half hour prior to the beginning of morning twilight (for times of twilight, see p. 167), and when the ecliptic is at a steep angle relative to the horizon. In the tropics the ecliptic is always at a steep angle to the horizon. In midnorthern latitudes the optimum geometry occurs in the evening western sky in February and March, and in the morning eastern sky in September and October. The zodiacal light appears as a huge, softly radiant pyramid of white light with its base near the horizon and its axis centred on the zodiac. In its brightest parts it exceeds the luminance of the central Milky Way.

Despite its brightness, most people have not seen the zodiacal light. As mentioned above, certain times of night and year are more favourable than others. In addition, moonlight, haze, or light pollution rule out any chance of seeing this phenomenon. Even with a dark, transparent sky the inexperienced observer may confuse the zodiacal light with twilight and thus ignore it, or may not notice it because he or she is expecting a much smaller object.

The Gegenschein

The zodiacal light extends all around the zodiac with a shallow minimum in brightness some 120° to 150° from the Sun; nevertheless, this "zodiacal band" or "light bridge" is exceedingly faint and is visible only from high-altitude sites having very dark, transparent skies. However, the slight brightening in the vicinity of the antisolar point can be seen from most dark observing sites, provided the air is transparent.

The Gegenschein is very faint. Haze, moonlight, bright nearby stars, planets, or light pollution will hide it completely. Most observers, including experienced ones, have not seen it. The Gegenschein is sufficiently faint that, except from high-altitude sites with very dark skies, a person will not notice it without making a special effort to *look* for it. It is a ghostly apparition best seen near midnight, and in midnorthern latitudes, in the autumn or winter when the antisolar point is nearest the zenith. To avoid interference from bright stars or the Milky Way, the periods late September to early November and late January to early February are best. At these times the Gegenschein is in Pisces and Cancer, respectively. It appears as a faint yet distinct, somewhat elliptical glow perhaps 10° in diameter. The luminance of the Gegenschein is about 10^{-4} cd/m^2, some 10 orders of magnitude dimmer than the brightest light the human eye can tolerate.

Don't determine the antisolar point before you look—imagination is too powerful. Find the antisolar point by locating the Gegenschein, and *then* check your star charts!

STARS

CONSTELLATIONS—NAMES AND ABBREVIATIONS

Nominative & Pronunciation	Genitive & Pronunciation	Abbr.	Meaning
Andromeda, ăn-drŏm′ē-dà	Andromedae, ăn-drŏm′ē-dē′	And	Daughter of Cassiopeia
Antlia, ănt′lĭ-à	Antliae, ănt′lē-ē′	Ant	The Air Pump
Apus, ā′pŭs	Apodis, ăp′ă-dĭs	Aps	Bird of Paradise
Aquarius, à-kwâr′ē-ŭs	Aquarii, à-kwâr′ē-ī′	Aqr	The Water-bearer
Aquila, à-kwĭl′à	Aquilae, à-kwĭl′ē	Aql	The Eagle
Ara, ā′rà	Arae, ā′rē	Ara	The Altar
Aries, âr′ēz	Arietis, à-rī′ē-tĭs	Ari	The Ram
Auriga, ô-rī′gà	Aurigae, ô-rī′jē	Aur	The Charioteer
Bootes, bō-ō′tēz	Bootis, bō-ō′tĭs	Boo	The Herdsman
Caelum, sē′lŭm	Caeli, sē′lī	Cae	The Chisel
Camelopardalis kà-mĕl′ō-pàr′dà-lĭs	Camelopardalis kà-mĕl′ō-pàr′dà-lĭs	Cam	The Giraffe
Cancer, kăn′sēr	Cancri, kăn′krē	Cnc	The Crab
Canes Venatici kā′nēz vē-năt′ĭ-sī	Canum Venaticorum kā′nŭm vē-năt′ĭ-kôr′ŭm	CVn	The Hunting Dogs
Canis Major, kā′nĭs mā′jēr	Canis Majoris, kā′nĭs mā-jôr′ĭs	CMa	The Big Dog
Canis Minor, kā′nĭs mī′nēr	Canis Minoris, kā′nĭs mī-ñôr′ĭs	CMi	The Little Dog
Capricornus, kăp′rĭ-kôr-nŭs	Capricorni, kăp′rĭ-kôr-nī	Cap	The Goat
Carina, kà-rī′-nà	Carinae, kà-rī′-nē	Car	The Keel
Cassiopeia, kăs′ĭ-ō-pē′yà	Cassiopeiae, kăs′ĭ-ō-pē′yē	Cas	The Queen
Centaurus, sĕn-tôr′ŭs	Centauri, sĕn-tôr′ī	Cen	The Centaur
Cepheus, sē′fē-ŭs	Cephei, sē′fē-ī′	Cep	The King
Cetus, sē′tŭs	Ceti, sē′tī	Cet	The Whale
Chamaeleon, kà-mē′lē-ŭn	Chamaeleontis, kà-mē′lē-ŏn′tĭs	Cha	The Chameleon
Circinus, sûr′sĭ-nŭs	Circini, sûr′sĭ-nī	Cir	The Compasses
Columba, kō-lŭm′bà	Columbae, kō-lŭm′bē	Col	The Dove
Coma Berenices kō′mà bĕr′ĕ-nī′sēz	Comae Berenices kō′mē bĕr′ĕ-nī′sēz	Com	Berenice's Hair
Corona Australis kō-rō′nà ôs-trā′lĭs	Coronae Australis kō-rō′nē ôs-trā′lĭs	CrA	The Southern Crown
Corona Borealis kō-rō′nà bôr′ē-ăl′ĭs	Coronae Borealis kō-rō′nē bôr′ē-ăl′ĭs	CrB	The Northern Crown
Corvus, kôr′vŭs	Corvi, kôr′vī	Crv	The Crow
Crater, krā′tēr	Crateris, krā-tēr′ĭs	Crt	The Cup
Crux, krŭks	Crucis, kroo′sĭs	Cru	The Cross
Cygnus, sĭg′nŭs	Cygni, sĭg′nī	Cyg	The Swan
Delphinus, dĕl-fī′nŭs	Delphini, dĕl-fī′nī	Del	The Dolphin
Dorado, dō-rà′dō	Doradus, dō-rà′dŭs	Dor	The Swordfish
Draco, drā′kō	Draconis, drā′kō′nĭs	Dra	The Dragon
Equuleus, ē-kwoo′lē-ŭs	Equulei, ē-kwoo′lē-ī′	Equ	The Little Horse
Eridanus, ē-rĭd′à-nŭs	Eridani, ē-rĭd′à-nī′	Eri	The River
Fornax, fôr′năks	Fornacis, fôr-nās′ĭs	For	The Furnace
Gemini, jĕm′ĭ-nī	Geminorum, jĕm′ĭ-nôr′ŭm	Gem	The Twins
Grus, grŭs	Gruis, groo′ĭs	Gru	The Crane (bird)
Hercules, hûr′kū-lēz	Herculis, hûr′kū-lĭs	Her	The Son of Zeus
Horologium, hŏr′ō-lō′jĭ-ŭm	Horologii, hŏr′ō-lō′jĭ-ī	Hor	The Clock
Hydra, hī′drà	Hydrae, hī′drē	Hya	The Water Snake (♀)
Hydrus, hī′drŭs	Hydri, hī′drī	Hyi	The Water Snake (♂)
Indus, ĭn′dŭs	Indi, ĭn′dī	Ind	The Indian

CONSTELLATIONS — NAMES AND ABBREVIATIONS (continued)

Nominative & Pronunciation	Genitive & Pronunciation	Abbr.	Meaning
Lacerta, là-sûr′tà	Lacertae, là-sûr′tē	Lac	The Lizard
Leo, lē′ō	Leonis, lē′ō′nĭs	Leo	The Lion
Leo Minor, lē′ō mī′nēr	Leonis Minoris lē′ō′nĭs mī-nôr′ĭs	LMi	The Little Lion
Lepus, lē′pŭs	Leporis, lĕp′ôr–ĭs	Lep	The Hare
Libra, lē′brà	Librae, lē′brē	Lib	The Balance
Lupus, lōō′pŭs	Lupi, lōō′pī	Lup	The Wolf
Lynx, lĭnks	Lyncis, lĭn′sĭs	Lyn	The Lynx
Lyra, lī′rà	Lyrae, lī′rē	Lyr	The Lyre
Mensa, mĕn′sà	Mensae, mĕn′sē	Men	The Table
Microscopium mī′krō-skō′pē–ŭm	Microscopii mī′krō-skō′pē–ī′	Mic	The Microscope
Monoceros, mō–nŏs′ēr–ŏs	Monocerotis, mō–nŏs′ēr–ō′tĭs	Mon	The Unicorn
Musca, mŭs′kà	Muscae, mŭs′ē	Mus	The Fly
Norma, nôr′mà	Normae, nôr′mē	Nor	The Square
Octans, ŏk′tănz	Octantis, ŏk′tăn′tĭs	Oct	The Octant
Ophiuchus, ō′fē–ū′kŭs	Ophiuchi, ō′fē–ū′kī	Oph	The Serpent-bearer
Orion, ō–rī′ŏn	Orionis, ôr′ē–ō′nĭs	Ori	The Hunter
Pavo, pā′vō	Pavonis, pà–vō′nĭs	Pav	The Peacock
Pegasus, pĕg′à–sŭs	Pegasi, pĕg′à–sī	Peg	The Winged Horse
Perseus, pûr′sē–ŭs	Persei, pûr′sē–ī′	Per	Rescuer of Andromeda
Phoenix, fē′nĭks	Phoenicis, fē–nī′cĭs	Phe	The Phoenix
Pictor, pĭk′tēr	Pictoris, pĭk–tor′ĭs	Pic	The Painter
Pisces, pī′sēz	Piscium, pĭsh′ē–ŭm	Psc	The Fishes
Piscis Austrinus, pī′sĭs ôs–trī′nŭs	Piscis Austrini, pī′sĭs ôs–trī′nī	PsA	The Southern Fish
Puppis, pŭp′ĭs	Puppis, pŭp′ĭs	Pup	The Stern
Pyxis, pĭk′sĭs	Pyxidis, pĭk′sĭ–dĭs	Pyx	The Compass
Reticulum, rē–tĭk′–ū–lŭm	Reticuli, rē–tĭk′–ū–lī	Ret	The Reticle
Sagitta, sà–jĭt′à	Sagittae, sà–jĭt′ē	Sge	The Arrow
Sagittarius, săj′ĭ–târ′ē–ŭs	Sagittarii, săj′ĭ–târ′ē–ī′	Sgr	The Archer
Scorpius, skôr′pē–ŭs	Scorpii, skôr′pē–ī′	Sco	The Scorpion
Sculptor, skŭlp′tēr	Sculptoris, skŭlp′tôr′ĭs	Scl	The Sculptor
Scutum, skū′tŭm	Scuti, skōō′tī	Sct	The Shield
Serpens, sûr′pĕnz	Serpentis, sûr–pĕn′tĭs	Ser	The Serpent
Sextans, sĕks′tănz	Sextantis, sĕks–tăn′tĭs	Sex	The Sextant
Taurus, tôr′ŭs	Tauri, tôr′ī	Tau	The Bull
Telescopium tĕl′à–skō′pē–ŭm	Telescopii, tĕl′à–skō′pē–ī	Tel	The Telescope
Triangulum, trī–ăng′gū–lŭm	Trianguli, trī–ăng′gū–lī′	Tri	The Triangle
Triangulum Australe trī–ăng′gū–lŭm ôs–trā′lē	Trianguli Australis trī–ăng′gū–lī′ ôs–trā′lĭs	TrA	The Southern Triangle
Tucana, tōō–kăn′à	Tucanae, tōō–kăn′ē	Tuc	The Toucan
Ursa Major, ûr′sǎ mā′jēr	Ursae Majoris, ûr′sē mà–jôr′ĭs	UMa	The Great Bear
Ursa Minor, ûr′sǎ mī′nēr	Ursae Minoris, ûr′sē mī–nôr′ĭs	UMi	The Little Bear
Vela, vē′là	Velorum, vē–lôr′ŭm	Vel	The Sails
Virgo, vûr′gō	Virginis, vûr′jĭn–ĭs	Vir	The Maiden
Volans, vō′lănz	Volantis, vō–lăn′tĭs	Vol	The Flying Fish
Vulpecula, vŭl–pĕk′ū–là	Vulpeculae, vŭl–pĕk′ū–lē′	Vul	The Fox

ā dāte; ǎ tǎp; â câre; à gàgà; ē wē; ĕ mĕt; ē makēr; ī īce; ĭ bĭt; ō gō; ŏ hŏt; ô ôrb; ōō mōōn; ū ūnite; ŭ ŭp; û ûrn

In terms of area (based on the official IAU boundaries), of the 88 constellations the 3 largest are Hydra (1303 square degrees), Virgo (1294), and Ursa Major (1280); the 3 smallest: Sagitta (80), Equuleus (72), and Crux (68). A complete list of the areas of the constellations appears in the 1972 edition of *The Handbook of the British Astronomical Association,* and was reproduced in the June 1976 issue of *Sky & Telescope* (p. 408).

FINDING LIST OF SOME NAMED STARS

Name & Pronunciation	Con.	RA	Name & Pronunciation	Con.	RA
Acamar, ā′kà-màr	θ Eri	2	Gienah, jē′nà	γ Crv	12
Achernar, ā′kēr-nàr	α Eri	1	Hadar, hăd′ar	β Cen	14
Acrux, ā′krŭks	α Cru	12	Hamal, hăm′al	α Ari	2
Adara, à-dā′rà	ε CMa	6	Kaus Australis,	ε Sgr	18
Al Na'ir, ăl-nâr′	α Gru	22	kôs ôs-trā′lĭs		
Albireo, ăl-bĭr′ē-ō	β Cyg	19	Kochab, kō′kăb	β UMi	14
Alcor, ăl-kôr′	80 UMa	13	Markab, màr′kăb	α Peg	23
Alcyone, ăl-sī′ō-nē	η Tau	3	Megrez, me′grēz	δ UMa	12
Aldebaran,	α Tau	4	Menkar, mĕn′kàr	α Cet	3
ăl-dĕb′à-ràn			Menkent, mĕn′kĕnt	θ Cen	14
Alderamin,	α Cep	21	Merak, mē′răk	β UMa	11
ăl-dĕr′à-mĭn			Merope, mĕr′ō-pē	23 Tau	3
Algeiba, ăl-jē′bà	γ Leo	10	Miaplacidus,	β Car	9
Algenib, ăl-jē′nĭb	γ Peg	0	mī′à-plăs′ĭ-dŭs		
Algol, ăl′gŏl	β Per	3	Mintaka, mĭn-tà′kà	δ Ori	5
Alioth, ăl′ĭ-ŏth	ε UMa	12	Mira, mī′rà	ο Cet	2
Alkaid, ăl-kād′	η UMa	13	Mirach, mī′răk	β And	1
Almach, ăl′măk	γ And	2	Mirfak, mir′făk	α Per	3
Alnilam, ăl-nī′lăm	ε Ori	5	Mizar, mi′zàr	ζ UMa	13
Alphard, ăl′fàrd	α Hya	9	Nunki, nŭn′kē	σ Sgr	18
Alphecca, ăl-fĕk′à	α CrB	15	Peacock, pē′kŏk	α Pav	20
Alpheratz, ăl-fē′răts	α And	0	Phecda, fĕk′dà	γ UMa	11
Altair, ăl-târ′	α Aql	19	Polaris, pō-lâr′ĭs	α UMi	2
Ankaa, ăn′kà	α Phe	0	Pollux, pŏl′ŭks	β Gem	7
Antares, ăn-tā′rēs	α Sco	16	Procyon, prō′sĭ-ŏn	α CMi	7
Arcturus, ark-tū′rŭs	α Boo	14	Pulcherrima,	ε Boo	14
Atria, ā′trĭ-a	α TrA	16	pŭl-kĕr′ĭ-mà		
Avior, ă-vĭ-ôr′	ε Car	8	Rasalgethi,	α Her	17
Bellatrix, bĕ-lā′trĭks	γ Ori	5	ràs′ăl-jē′thē		
Betelgeuse, bĕt′ĕl-jūz	α Ori	5	Rasalhague, ràs′ăl-hāg	α Oph	17
Canopus, kà-nō′pŭs	α Car	6	Regulus, rĕg′ū-lŭs	α Leo	10
Capella, kàp-pĕl′à	α Aur	5	Rigel, rī′gĕl	β Ori	5
Caph, kăf	β Cas	0	Rigil Kentaurus,	α Cen	14
Castor, kàs′tēr	α Gem	7	rī′jĭl kĕn-tô′rŭs		
Cor Caroli, kôr kăr′ō-lī	α CVn	12	Sabik, sā′bĭk	η Oph	17
Deneb, dĕn′ĕb	α Cyg	20	Scheat, shē′ăt	β Peg	23
Denebola, dĕ-nĕb′ō-la	β Leo	11	Schedar, shĕd′àr	α Cas	0
Diphda, dĭf′dà	β Cet	0	Shaula, shô′là	λ Sco	17
Dubhe, dŭb′ē	α UMa	11	Sirius, sĭr′ĭ-ŭs	α CMa	6
Elnath, ĕl′năth	β Tau	5	Spica, spī′kà	α Vir	13
Eltanin, ĕl-tā′nĭn	γ Dra	17	Suhail, sŭ-hāl′	λ Vel	9
Enif, ĕn′ĭf	ε Peg	21	Thuban, thōō′ban	α Dra	14
Fomalhaut, fō′măl-ôt	α PsA	22	Vega, vē′gà	α Lyr	18
Gacrux, gà′krŭks	γ Cru	12	Zubenelgenubi,	α Lib	14
Gemma, jĕm′à	α CrB	15	zōō-bĕn′ĕl-jĕ-nū′bē		

Key to pronunciation on p. 250

THE BRIGHTEST STARS
By Robert F. Garrison and Toomas Karmo

In the following table the 314 brightest stars (allowing for variability) are listed. Data for visual doubles are for the brighter component (A); the last column describes the companion(s). Where the double is too close to be resolved conveniently, data are for combined light (AB).

Apparent Visual Magnitude (V): Apparent magnitudes, with "v" appended for variables, are from *HIPPARCOS*. (For variables, these data are occasionally in mild conflict with published magnitude ranges.) The photoelectric system is from H.L. Johnson and W.W. Morgan, *Ap. J., 117* (1953). The (yellow) *V* filter corresponds roughly to the response of the eye. The probable error of a *V* value is at most 0.03.

Colour Index (B−V): Since *B* on this system is the brightness of a star through a blue filter, the difference *B−V*, here taken from *HIPPARCOS*, measures apparent colour (as possibly reddened by interstellar dust; although, in general, *B−V* and spectral type are well correlated). The probable error of a *B−V* value is at most 0.02.

Spectral Classification (**MK Type**): The "temperature type" (O, B, A, F, G, K, M) is given first, followed by a finer subtype (0–9) and a "luminosity class" (Roman numerals I–V, with "a" or "b" added occasionally to indicate slightly brighter or fainter stars within the class). O stars are hottest, M stars coolest; Ia stars are the most luminous supergiants, III stars are giants, and V stars are dwarfs. (V stars form the largest class in the cosmos, comprising the main sequence.) Other MK symbols include "e" for hydrogen emission; "f" for broad, nonhydrogen emission in hot stars; "m" for strong metallic absorption; "n" or "nn" for unusually broad absorption (a signature of rotation); "p" for peculiarities; "s" for a mixture of broad and sharp lines; and ":" for a minor uncertainty. The types are the best available from Garrison's unpublished spectrograms and the literature. Where a single star (e.g. α CMa A) is given two types (e.g. A0 and A1), with the second type flagged "m", the first is the type that best characterizes the hydrogen lines, the second the type that best characterizes the metal lines.

Parallax (π): Parallaxes, in milliarcseconds (mas), are from *HIPPARCOS*.

Absolute Visual Magnitude (Mᵥ) and *Distance in Light-Years (D):* Absolute magnitudes and distances are determined from parallaxes, except where a colon follows the absolute magnitude; in these cases, both quantities are determined from a calibration of the spectral classification. Corrections are made for interstellar absorption, by comparing, under an unpublished intrinsic-colour calibration from Garrison, spectral classification with *B−V*.

Proper Motion (μ) and *Position Angle* (**PA**): Proper motion and PA are derived from D. Hoffleit and C. Jaschek, *Bright Star Catalogue,* Yale, 1982. Proper motion is the absolute value of the vector resultant from BSC individual-coordinate proper motions. PA is the direction of the proper motion, as an angle measured from north through east.

Radial Velocity (**RV**): Radial velocities are from BSC. "SB" indicates a spectroscopic binary, an unresolved system whose duplicity is revealed by periodic Doppler oscillations in its spectrum and for which an orbit is generally known. If the lines of both stars are detectable, "SB2" is used; "+" and "−" indicate, respectively, motion away from and toward the observer. "V" indicates a variable velocity in a star not observable as a spectroscopic binary. (In most "V" cases the orbit is unknown.)

Remarks: Remarks include data on variability and spectra, particulars on any companions, and traditional names. Our principal source for variability ranges is P.N. Kholopov et al., *Combined General Catalogue of Variable Stars,* 4.1 ed., 1998 (online as VizieR GCVS4). Our sources for traditional names include BSC and M.E. Bakich, *Cambridge Guide to the Constellations,* Cambridge University Press, 1995. Navigation-star names are **bold.**

TABLE OF BRIGHTEST STARS

Star Name	RA (2007.5) h m	Dec ° ′	V	B–V	MK Type	π mas	Mv	D ly	μ ″/yr	PA °	RV km/s	Remarks
Sun	—	—	−26.75	0.63	G2 V	—	4.8	8 lm	—	—	varies	**Sun**
α And	0 08.8	+29 08	2.07	−0.04	B9p IV: (HgMn)	34	−0.5	97	0.209	139	−12 SB	**Alpheratz**
β Cas	0 09.6	+59 11	2.28v	0.38	F2 III	60	1.2	54	0.555	109	+11 SB	**Caph** var: 2.25–2.31, 0.10 d
γ Peg	0 13.6	+15 14	2.83v	−0.19	B2 IV	10	−2.4	300	0.008	176	+4 SB	**Algenib** var: 2.78–2.89, 0.15 d
β Hyi	0 26.1	−77 13	2.82	0.62	G1 IV	134	3.4	24	2.255	82	+23	
α Phe	0 26.7	−42 16	2.40	1.08	K0 IIIb	42	−0.3	77	0.442	152	+75 SB	**Ankaa**
δ And A	0 39.7	+30 54	3.27	1.27	K3 III	32	0.9	101	0.161	122	−7 SB	
α Cas	0 40.9	+56 35	2.24	1.17	K0 IIIa	14	−2.5	230	0.058	117	−4 V?	**Schedar**
β Cet	0 44.0	−17 57	2.04	1.02	K0 III	34	−1.0	96	0.234	81	13	**Diphda**
η Cas A	0 49.6	+57 51	3.46	0.59	G0 V	168	4.6	19	1.218	115	+9 SB	**Achird** B: 7.51, K4 Ve, 13″
γ Cas	0 57.2	+60 45	2.15v	−0.05	B0 IVnpe (shell)	5	−5.0	600	0.026	90	−7 SB	**Cih** var: 1.6–3.0; B: 8.8, 2″
β Phe AB	1 06.4	−46 41	3.32	0.88	G8 III	16	0.3:	150	0.030	279	−1	AB similar in light, spectrum, 1″
η Cet	1 09.0	−10 09	3.46	1.16	K1.5 III CN1	28	−0.1	120	0.250	122	12	
β And	1 10.2	+35 40	2.07	1.58	M0 IIIa	16	−1.9	200	0.210	121	+3 V	**Mirach**
δ Cas	1 26.3	+60 16	2.66v	0.16	A5 IV	33	0.2	99	0.303	99	+7 SB	**Ruchbah** ecl.? 2.68–2.76, 759 d
γ Phe	1 28.7	−43 17	3.41v	1.54	K7 IIIa	14	−1.6	230	0.204	184	+26 SB	irreg. var.: 3.39–3.49
α Eri	1 38.0	−57 12	0.45	−0.16	B3 Vnp (shell)	23	−2.9	144	0.108	105	+16 V	**Achernar**
τ Cet	1 44.4	−15 54	3.49	0.73	G8 V	274	5.7	12	1.921	296	−16	
α Tri	1 53.5	+29 37	3.42	0.49	F6 IV	51	1.8	64	0.230	177	−13 SB	**Mothallah**
ε Cas	1 54.9	+63 42	3.35	−0.15	B3 IV:p (shell)	7	−2.5	400	0.036	114	−8 V	**Segin**
β Ari	1 55.1	+20 51	2.64	0.16	A4 V	55	1.3	60	0.145	138	−2 SB	**Sheratan**
α Hyi	1 59.0	−61 32	2.86	0.29	F0n III–IV	46	1.1	71	0.271	83	+1 V	
γ And A	2 04.4	+42 22	2.10	1.37	K3 IIb	9	−3.0	350	0.066	136	−12 SB	**Almach** B: 5.4, B9 V, 10″; C: 6.2, A0 V: BC0.3″
α Ari	2 07.6	+23 30	2.01	1.15	K2 IIIab	49	0.5	66	0.238	127	−14 SB	**Hamal** calcium weak?
β Tri	2 10.0	+35 01	3.00	0.14	A5 IV	26	0.1	120	0.153	104	+10 SB2	
ο Cet A	2 19.7	−2 57	6.47v	0.97	M5–10 IIIe	8	3.0	400	0.232	183	+64 V	**Mira** LPV, 2–10; B: VZ Cet, 9.5v, Bpe, 0.5″
α UMi A	2 40.6	+89 18	1.97v	0.64	F5–8 Ib	8	−4.1	400	0.046	95	−17 SB	**Polaris** low-amp. Cep., 4.0 d; B: 8.2, F3 V, 19″
γ Cet AB	2 43.7	+3 16	3.47	0.09	A2 Va	40	1.3	82	0.203	224	−5 V	**Kaffaljidhmah** A: 3.57; B: 6.23, 3″
θ Eri A	2 58.5	−40 16	3.28	0.17	A5 IV	28	−0.3	100	0.065	294	+12 SB2	**Acamar** B: 4.35, A1 Va, 8″
α Cet	3 02.7	+4 07	2.54	1.63	M2 III	15	−1.7	220	0.075	189	−26	**Menkar**
γ Per	3 05.3	+53 32	2.91	0.72	G8 III + A2 V	13	−0.8:	200	0.002	180	+3 SB	composite spectrum
ρ Per	3 05.7	+38 52	3.32v	1.53	M4 II	10	−1.3	320	0.165	128	+4 SB	semiregular var.: 3.3–4.0
β Per	3 08.7	+40 59	2.09v	0.00	B8 V + F:	35	−0.5	93	0.004	124	+4 SB	**Algol** ecl.: 2.12–3.39, 2.9 d; composite
α Per	3 24.9	+49 53	1.79	0.48	F5 Ib	6	−4.9	600	0.033	131	−2 V	**Mirfak** in open cluster
δ Per	3 43.5	+47 49	3.01	−0.12	B5 IIIn	6	−3.1	500	0.042	139	+4 SB	
δ Eri	3 43.6	−9 44	3.52	0.92	K0 IV	111	3.4	29	0.752	352	−6	**Rana**

TABLE OF BRIGHTEST STARS (continued)

Star Name	RA (2007.5) h m	Dec ° ′	V	B−V	MK Type	π mas	Mv	D ly	μ ″/yr	PA °	RV km/s	Remarks	
γ Hyi	3 47.1	−74 13	3.26	1.59	M2 III	15	−1.0	210	0.128	24	16		
η Tau	3 47.9	+24 08	2.85	−0.09	B7 IIIn	9	−1.6:	400	0.048	157	+10 V?	in Pleiades	Alcyone
ζ Per A	3 54.6	+31 54	2.84	0.27	B1 Ib	3	−6.0	1000	0.011	146	+20 SB	B: 9.16, B8 V, 13″	
ε Per A	3 58.4	+40 02	2.90	−0.20	B0.5 IV	6	−3.4	500	0.029	145	+1 SB2	B: 7.39, B9.5 V, 9″	
γ Eri	3 58.4	−13 29	2.97	1.59	M1 IIIb	15	−1.6	220	0.124	153	62	calcium, chromium weak	Zaurak
λ Tau A	4 01.1	+12 31	3.41v	−0.10	B3 V	9	−2.3	400	0.011	218	+18 SB2	ecl.: 3.37−3.91, 4.0 d; B: A4 IV	
α Ret A	4 14.5	−62 27	3.33	0.92	G8 II−III	20	−0.5	160	0.068	43	+36 SB?		
ε Tau	4 29.1	+19 12	3.53	1.01	K0 III	21	0.1	160	0.114	108	39	in Hyades	Ain
θ² Tau	4 29.1	+15 53	3.40	0.18	A7 III	22	0.2	150	0.105	103	+40 SB	in Hyades	
α Dor AB	4 34.2	−55 02	3.30	−0.08	A0p V: (Si)	19	0.2	180	0.051	89	26	A: 3.8; B: 4.3, B9 IV; 0.3″; orbit 12 y	
α Tau A	4 36.4	+16 31	0.87v	1.54	K5 III	50	−0.8	65	0.200	161	+54 SB	irregular var.: 0.75−0.95	Aldebaran
π³ Ori	4 50.2	+6 58	3.19	0.48	F6 V	125	3.7	26	0.463	88	+24 SB2		Tabit
ι Aur	4 57.5	+33 11	2.69v	1.49	K3 II	6	−3.6	500	0.018	167	18	var.: 2.63−2.78	Hasseleh
ε Aur A	5 02.5	+43 50	3.03v	0.54	A9 Iae + B	2	−8.0:	2000?	0.004	166	−3 SB	ecl.: 2.92−3.83, 9892 d	Almaaz
ε Lep	5 05.8	−22 22	3.19	1.46	K4 III	14	−2.0	230	0.073	166	1		
η Aur	5 07.0	+41 15	3.18	−0.15	B3 V	15	−1.2	220	0.073	157	+7 V?		Hoedus II
β Eri	5 08.2	−5 05	2.78	0.16	A3 IVn	37	0.4	89	0.128	231	−9		Cursa
μ Lep	5 13.3	−16 12	3.29v	−0.11	B9p IV: (HgMn)	18	−0.4	180	0.043	129	28	var.: 2.97−3.41, 2 d	
β Ori A	5 14.9	−8 12	0.18	−0.03	B8 Ia	4	−6.6	800	0.004	236	+21 SB	B: 7.6, B5 V, 9″; C: 7.6; BC: 0.1″	**Rigel**
α Aur AB	5 17.2	+46 00	0.08	0.80	G6 III + G2 III	77	−0.8	42	0.430	169	+30 SB	composite: A: 0.6; B: 1.1, 0.04″	**Capella**
η Ori AB	5 24.9	−2 23	3.35v	−0.24	B0.5 V + B	4	−3.9	900	0.003	288	+20 SB2	ecl.: 3.31−3.60, 8.0 d; A: 3.6; B: 5.0, 1.6″	
γ Ori	5 25.5	+6 21	1.64	−0.22	B2 III	13	−2.8	240	0.018	221	+18 SB?		Bellatrix
β Tau	5 26.8	+28 37	1.65	−0.13	B7 III	25	−1.3	130	0.178	172	+9 V		El Nath
β Lep A	5 28.6	−20 45	2.81	0.81	G5 II	20	−0.7	160	0.090	185	−14	B: 7.4, 2.6″	Nihal
δ Ori A	5 32.4	−0 18	2.25v	−0.18	O9.5 II	4	−5.4	900	0.002	252	+16 SB	ecl.: 2.14−2.26, 5.7 d	Mintaka
α Lep	5 33.1	−17 49	2.58	0.21	F0 Ib	3	−5.5	1000	0.006	279	24		Arneb
β Dor	5 33.7	−62 29	3.76v	0.64	F7−G2 Ib	3	−4.2	1000	0.007	8	+7 V	Cepheid var.: 3.46−4.08, 9.8 d	
λ Ori A	5 35.6	+9 56	3.39	−0.16	O8 IIIf	3	−4.6	1000	0.006	191	34	B: 5.61, B0 V, 4″	Meissa
ι Ori A	5 35.8	−5 54	2.75	−0.21	O9 III	2	−5.6	1000	0.005	284	+22 SB2	B: 7.3, B7 IIIp (He wk), 11″	Hatsya
ε Ori	5 36.6	−1 12	1.69	−0.18	B0 Ia	2	−6.6	1000	0.004	236	+26 SB		Alnilam
ζ Tau	5 38.1	+21 09	2.97v	−0.15	B2 IIIpe (shell)	8	−2.8	400	0.023	177	+20 SB	ecl., var.: 2.88−3.17, 133 d; B: 5.0, 0.007″	
α Col A	5 39.9	−34 04	2.65	−0.12	B7 IV	12	−1.9	270	0.026	178	+35 V?		Phakt
ζ Ori A	5 41.1	−1 56	1.74	−0.20	O9.5 Ib	4	−5.5	800	0.002	207	+18 SB	B: 4.2, B0 III, 2.4″	Alnitak
ς Lep	5 47.3	−14 49	3.55	0.10	A2 Vann	46	1.7	70	0.023	263	+20 SB?		
κ Ori	5 48.1	−9 40	2.07	−0.17	B0.5 Ia	5	−5.0:	820	0.006	211	+21 V?		Saiph
β Col	5 51.2	−35 46	3.12	1.15	K1.5 III	38	0.2	86	0.405	7	+89 V		Wasn

TABLE OF BRIGHTEST STARS (continued)

Star Name	RA (2007.5) h m	Dec °	V	B–V	MK Type	π mas	M_v	D ly	μ "/yr	PA °	RV km/s	Remarks	
α Ori	5 55.6	+7 24	0.45v	1.50	M2 Iab	8	–5.0:	520	0.028	68	+21 SB	semiregular var.: 0.0–1.3	**Betelgeuse**
β Aur	6 00.1	+44 57	1.90v	0.08	A1 IV	40	–0.2	82	0.055	269	–18 SB	ecl.: 1.89–1.98, 4.0 d (mags. equal)	Menkalinan
θ Aur AB	6 00.2	+37 13	2.65	–0.08	A0p II: (Si)	19	–1.0	170	0.097	149	+30 SB	B: 7.2, G2 V, 4"	
η Gem	6 15.3	+22 30	3.31v	1.60	M3 III	9	–1.8	300	0.068	259	+19 SB	ecl., var: 3.2–3.9, 233 d; B: 8.8, 1.6"	Propus
ζ CMa	6 20.6	–30 04	3.02	–0.16	B2.5 V	10	–2.2	340	0.006	59	+32 SB		Furud
β CMa	6 23.0	–17 58	1.98v	–0.24	B1 II–III	7	–4.0	500	0.014	253	+34 SB	var.: 1.93–2.00, 0.25 d	Mirzam
μ Gem	6 23.4	+22 31	2.87v	1.62	M3 IIIab	14	–1.5	230	0.125	154	55	irregular var.: 2.75–3.02	Tejat Posterior
α Car	6 24.1	–52 42	–0.62	0.16	A9 Ib	10	–5.4	310	0.034	50	21		**Canopus**
ν Pup	6 38.0	–43 12	3.17	–0.10	B8 IIIn	8	–2.4	400	0.010	234	+28 SB		
ε Gem	6 38.1	+16 24	1.93	0.00	A1 IVs	31	–0.6	100	0.061	136	–13 SB		Alhena
γ Gem	6 44.4	+25 07	3.06	1.38	G8 Ib	4	–5.0	900	0.016	195	+10 SB		Mebsuta
α CMa A	6 45.5	–16 44	–1.44	0.01	A0mA1 Va	379	1.5	9	1.324	204	–8 SB	B: 8.5, WDA: 8"; orbit 50.1 y	**Sirius**
ξ Gem	6 45.7	+12 53	3.35	0.44	F5 IV	57	2.2	57	0.224	211	+25 V?		Alzirr
α Pic	6 48.3	–61 57	3.24	0.22	A6 Vn	33	0.7	100	0.275	345	21		
τ Pup	6 50.1	–50 37	2.94	1.21	K1 III	18	–1.9	180	0.079	157	+36 SB		
ε CMa A	6 58.9	–28 59	1.50	–0.21	B2 II	8	–4.1	400	0.002	27	27		**Adhara**
σ CMa	7 02.0	–27 57	3.49v	1.73	K7 Ib	3	–4.7	1000	0.008	284	22	irregular var.: 3.43–3.51	
o² CMa	7 03.3	–23 51	3.02	–0.08	B3 Ia	1	–6.6	3000	0.007	262	+48 SB		
δ CMa	7 08.7	–26 24	1.83	0.67	F8 Ia	2	–7.2	2000	0.008	291	+34 SB		Wezen
L₂ Pup	7 13.8	–44 39	4.42v	1.33	M5 IIIe	16	1.5	200	0.346	18	+53 V?	long-period var.: 2.6–6.2	HR2748
π Pup	7 17.4	–37 07	2.71	1.62	K3 Ib	3	–5.1	1100	0.012	284	16		
δ Gem AB	7 20.6	+21 58	3.50	0.37	F0 IV	55	2.2	59	0.029	241	+4 SB	B: 8.2, K3 V, 0.2"	Wasat
η CMa	7 24.4	–29 19	2.45	–0.08	B5 Ia	1	–7.5	3000	0.008	284	+41 V		Aludra
β CMi	7 27.6	+8 16	2.89	–0.10	B8 V	19	–0.8	170	0.065	233	+22 SB		Gomeisa
σ Pup	7 29.5	–43 19	3.25	1.51	K5 III	18	–1.6	180	0.195	342	+88 SB	B: 8.6, G5: V, 22"	
α Gem A	7 35.1	+31 52	1.93	0.03	A1mA2 Va	63	0.6	52	0.199	239	+6 SB	4"; orbit 445 y; max = 6.5", in 1880;	Castor
α Gem B	7 35.1	+31 52	2.97	0.03	A2mA5 V:	63	1.0	52	0.199	239	–1 SB	min = 1.8", in 1965	
α CMi A	7 39.7	+5 12	0.40	0.43	F5 IV–V	286	2.8	11	1.248	214	–3 SB	B: 10.3, WD ; 2"; orbit 41 y	**Procyon**
β Gem	7 45.8	+28 00	1.16	0.99	K0 IIIb	97	1.1	34	0.629	265	+3 V		**Pollux**
ξ Pup	7 49.6	–24 53	3.34	1.22	G6 Iab–Ib	2	–7.5:	3300	0.033	240	+3 SB		Asmidiske
χ Car	7 57.0	–53 00	3.46	–0.18	B3 IVp (cf. Remarks)	8	–2.0	387	0.042	306	+19 V	Si II strong	
ζ Pup	8 03.8	–40 01	2.21	–0.27	O5 Iafn	2	–6.1	1000	0.033	290	–24 V?		Naos
ρ Pup	8 07.9	–24 20	2.83v	0.46	F2mF5 II: (var)	52	1.4	63	0.100	299	+46 SB	delta Del spec.; var: 2.68–2.87, 0.14 d	
γ² Vel	8 09.8	–47 22	1.75v	–0.14	WC8 + O9 I:	4	–5.8	800	0.007	304	+35 SB2	var.: 1.81–1.87	
β Cnc	8 16.9	+9 10	3.53	1.48	K4 III	11	–1.2	290	0.068	220	22		Tarf
ε Car	8 22.7	–59 32	1.86v	1.20	K3:III + B2:V	5	–4.8	600	0.030	301	2	ecl.?: 1.82–1.94	Avior

TABLE OF BRIGHTEST STARS (continued)

Star Name	RA (2007.5) h m	Dec ° '	V	B–V	MK Type	π mas	Mv	D ly	μ "/yr	PA °	RV km/s	Remarks
o UMa A	8 30.9	+60 42	3.35v?	0.86	G5 III	18	–0.3	180	0.171	230	20	var.?: 3.30?–3.36?
δ Vel AB	8 44.9	–54 44	1.93	0.04	A1 Va	41	0.0	80	0.082	164	+2 V?	B: 5.0, 2"
ε Hya ABC	8 47.2	+6 23	3.38	0.68	G5:III + A:	24	0.0	140	0.198	254	+36 SB	composite A: 3.8; B: 4.7, 0.2"; C: 7.8, 3"
ζ Hya	8 55.8	+5 55	3.11	0.98	G9 II-III	22	–0.2	150	0.101	277	23	
ι UMa A	8 59.7	+48 01	3.12	0.22	A7 IVn	68	2.2	48	0.501	242	+9 SB	Talitha BC: 10.8, M1 V, 4"
λ Vel	9 08.3	–43 28	2.23v	1.66	K4 Ib-IIa	6	–4.8	600	0.026	299	18	var: 2.14–2.30
a Car	9 11.2	–59 00	3.43v	–0.19	B2 IV-V	8	–2.2	420	0.028	283	+23 SB2	HR3659 ecl.?: 3.41–3.44
β Car	9 13.3	–69 45	1.67	0.07	A1 III	29	–1.1	111	0.183	304	–5 V?	Miaplacidus
ι Car	9 17.3	–59 18	2.21v	0.19	A7 Ib	5	–4.4	700	0.019	285	13	Tureis var: 2.23–2.28
α Lyn	9 21.5	+34 22	3.14	1.55	K7 IIIab	15	–1.3	220	0.223	273	38	
κ Vel	9 22.3	–55 03	2.47	–0.14	B2 IV-V	6	–3.9	500	0.012	315	+22 SB	
α Hya	9 28.0	–8 41	1.99	1.44	K3 II-III	18	–2.1	180	0.034	327	–4 V?	Alphard
N Vel	9 31.4	–57 04	3.16	1.54	K5 III	14	–1.3	240	0.034	268	–14	HR3803
θ UMa	9 33.4	+51 39	3.17	0.48	F6 IV	74	2.6	44	1.094	240	+15 SB	
o Leo AB	9 41.6	+9 51	3.52v	0.52	F5 II + A5?	24	0.1	140	0.149	254	+27 SB	Subra A: occ. bin. (mags. equal)
l Car	9 45.5	–62 33	3.69v	1.01	F9-G5 Ib	2	–5.8	2000	0.016	281	+4 V	HR3884 Cepheid var.: 3.28–4.18, 36 d
ε Leo	9 46.3	+23 44	2.97	0.81	G1 II	13	–1.6	250	0.048	252	+4 V?	Ras Elased Australis
υ Car AB	9 47.3	–65 06	2.92	0.29	A6 II	2	–2.5:	330	0.012	305	14	A: 3.01; B: 5.99, B7 III, 5"
φ Vel	9 57.1	–54 36	3.52	–0.07	B5 Ib	2	–5.5	2000	0.013	293	14	
η Leo	10 07.7	+16 44	3.48	–0.03	A0 Ib	2	–5.5	2000	0.006	189	+3 V	
α Leo A	10 08.8	+11 56	1.36	–0.09	B7 Vn	42	–0.6	78	0.248	271	+6 SB	**Regulus** B: 4.5, 0.1"
ω Leo	10 13.9	–70 05	3.29	–0.07	B8 IIIn	9	–2.1	370	0.032	275	+7 V	
ζ Leo	10 17.1	+23 23	3.43	0.31	F0 IIIa	13	–1.1	260	0.023	124	–16 SB	Adhafera
q Car	10 17.3	–61 22	3.39v	1.54	K3 IIa	4	–4.2	700	0.027	276	8	HR4050 irregular var.: 3.36–3.44
λ UMa	10 17.5	+42 53	3.45	0.03	A1 IV	24	0.4	130	0.170	255	+18 V	Tania Borealis
γ Leo A	10 20.4	+19 48	2.61	1.13	K1 IIIb Fe-0.5	26	–0.7	130	0.342	116	–37 SB	Algieba 4"; orbit 620 y;
γ Leo B	10 20.4	+19 48	3.16	1.42	G7 III Fe-1	26	–1.9	130	0.358	119	–36 V	max = 5", around 2100
μ UMa	10 22.8	+41 28	3.06	1.60	M0 IIIp	13	–1.5	250	0.088	290	–21 SB	Tania Australis
p Car	10 32.3	–61 43	3.30v	–0.09	B4 Vne	7	–2.0:	330	0.021	287	26	HR4140 Ca II emission irregular var.: 3.27–3.37
θ Car	10 43.2	–64 26	2.74	–0.22	B0.5 Vp	7	–3.1	400	0.022	291	+24 SB	nitrogen enhanced
μ Vel AB	10 47.1	–49 28	2.69	1.07	G5 III + F8:V	28	–0.9	116	0.085	125	+6 SB	A: 2.72; B: 5.92, 2"
ν Hya	10 50.0	–16 14	3.11	1.23	K2 III	24	–0.3	140	0.215	24	–1	
β UMa	11 02.3	+56 21	2.34	0.03	A0mA1 IV-V	41	0.4	79	0.087	70	–12 SB	Merak
α UMa AB	11 04.2	+61 43	1.81	1.06	K0 IIIa	26	–1.3	124	0.138	239	–9 SB	Dubhe A: 1.86; B: 4.8, A8 V, <1"
ψ UMa	11 10.1	+44 27	3.00	1.14	K1 III	22	–0.5	147	0.075	245	–4	
δ Leo	11 14.5	+20 29	2.56	0.13	A4 IV	57	1.3	58	0.197	133	–20 V	Zosma

TABLE OF BRIGHTEST STARS (continued)

Star Name	RA (2007.5) h m	Dec ° ′	V	B−V	MK Type	π mas	Mv	D ly	μ ″/yr	PA °	RV km/s	Remarks	
θ Leo	11 14.6	+15 23	3.33	0.00	A2 IV (K-line var.)	18	−0.2	180	0.104	216	+8 V		Chort
ν UMa	11 18.9	+33 03	3.49	1.40	K3 III Ba0.3	8	−3.2	400	0.036	309	−9 SB	B: 9.5, 7″	Alula Borealis
ξ Hya	11 33.4	−31 54	3.54	0.95	G7 III	25	0.0	130	0.211	259	−5 V		
λ Cen	11 36.1	−63 04	3.11	−0.04	B9.5 IIn	8	−2.5	410	0.039	258	−1 V		
β Leo	11 49.4	+14 32	2.14	0.09	A3 Va	90	1.9	36	0.511	257	0 V		Denebola
γ UMa	11 54.2	+53 39	2.41	0.04	A0 Van	39	0.2	84	0.094	86	−13 SB		Phad
δ Cen	12 08.8	−50 46	2.58v	−0.13	B2 IVne	8	−3.1	400	0.034	249	+11 V	irregular var.: 2.51–2.65	
ε Crv	12 10.5	−22 40	3.02	1.33	K2 III	11	−2.3	300	0.073	278	5		Minkar
δ Cru	12 15.5	−58 47	2.79v	−0.19	B2 IV	9	−2.6	360	0.039	255	+22 V?	var.: 2.78–2.84, 0.15 d	
δ UMa	12 15.8	+56 59	3.32	0.08	A2 Van	40	1.4	81	0.102	88	−13 V		Megrez
γ Crv	12 16.2	−17 35	2.58	−0.11	B8 III	20	−0.9	160	0.163	276	−4 SB		Gienah Ghurab
α Cru A	12 27.0	−63 08	1.25	−0.20	B0.5 IV	10	−4.0	320	0.030	236	−11 SB	sp. var.?	Acrux
α Cru B	12 27.0	−63 08	1.64	−0.18	B1 Vn	10	−3.6	320	0.031	248	−1	4″; unknown slow orbit: 6″ in 1826	Acrux
δ Crv A	12 30.3	−16 33	2.94	−0.01	B9.5 IVn	37	−2.0	88	0.255	236	+9 V	B: 8.26, K2 V, 24″	Algorab
γ Cru	12 31.6	−57 09	1.59v	1.60	M3.5 III	37	−0.7	88	0.269	174	21	var.: 1.60–1.67	Gacrux
β Crv	12 34.8	−23 26	2.65	0.89	G5 II	23	−0.5	140	0.059	179	−8		Kraz
α Mus	12 37.6	−69 11	2.69v	−0.18	B2 IV–V	11	−2.3	310	0.043	248	+13 V	var.: 2.68–2.73, 0.090 d	
γ Cen A	12 41.9	−49 00	2.95	−0.02	A1 IV	25	−0.1	130	0.190	268	−6 SB	0.6″; orbit 84 y; min = 0.2″, in 1931; max = 1.7″	
γ Cen B	12 41.9	−49 00	2.85	−0.02	A0 IV	25	−0.1	130	0.190	268	−6 SB		
γ Vir AB	12 42.0	−01 29	2.74	0.37	F1 V + F0mF2 V	85	2.2	39	0.567	271	−20 SB	A: 3.48; B: 3.50; 0.7″ (near periastron)	Porrima
β Mus AB	12 46.7	−68 09	3.04	−0.18	B2 V + B2.5 V	10	−2.2:	420	0.041	233	+42 V	A: 3.51; B: 4.00, 1″	
β Cru	12 48.2	−59 44	1.25v	−0.24	B0.5 III	9	−4.0	350	0.042	246	+16 SB	var.: 1.23–1.31, 0.24 d	Becrux
ε UMa	12 54.4	+55 55	1.76v	−0.02	A0p IV: (CrEu)	40	−0.2	81	0.109	95	−9 SB?	var.: 1.76–1.78, 5.1 d	Alioth
δ Vir	12 56.0	+3 21	3.39	1.57	M3 III	16	−0.5	200	0.474	263	−18 V?		Auva
α² CVn A	12 56.4	+38 17	2.85	−0.06	A0p (SiEu)	30	0.4	110	0.242	282	−3 V	B: 5.6, F0 V, 20″	Cor Caroli
ε Vir	13 02.6	+10 55	2.85	0.93	G9 IIIab	32	0.4	100	0.274	274	−14		Vindemiatrix
γ Hya	13 19.3	−23 13	2.99	0.92	G8 IIIa	25	−0.6	130	0.081	127	−5 V?		
ι Cen	13 21.0	−36 45	2.75	0.07	A2 Va	56	1.4	59	0.351	255	0		
ζ UMa A	13 24.2	+54 53	2.23	0.06	A1 Va	42	0.3	78	0.122	102	−6 SB2	B: 3.94, A1mA7 IV–V, 14″	Mizar
α Vir	13 25.6	−11 12	0.98v	−0.24	B1 V	12	−3.6	260	0.054	232	+1 SB2	var.: 0.95–1.05, 4.0 d; mult. 3.1, 4.5, 7.5	Spica
ζ Vir	13 35.1	−0 38	3.38	0.11	A2 IV	45	1.6	73	0.287	277	−13		Heze
ε Cen	13 40.4	−53 30	2.29	−0.17	B1 III	9	−3.3	400	0.028	232	3		
η UMa	13 47.8	+49 17	1.85	−0.10	B3 V	32	−1.8	101	0.127	264	−11 SB?		Alkaid
μ Cen	13 50.0	−41 43	3.41	−0.22	B2 V	7	−2.4	500	0.035	227	+9 SB		
ν Cen	13 50.1	−42 31	3.47v	−0.17	B2 IV–V pne	6	−2.8	500	0.034	220	+9 SB	variable shell: 2.92–3.47	
η Boo	13 55.0	+18 22	2.68	0.58	G0 IV	88	2.4	37	0.370	190	0 SB		Mufrid

TABLE OF BRIGHTEST STARS (continued)

Star Name	RA (2007.5) h m	Dec ° '	V	B–V	MK Type	π mas	Mv	D ly	μ "/yr	PA °	RV km/s	Remarks
ζ Cen	13 56.0	–47 20	2.55	–0.18	B2.5 IV	8	–2.9	400	0.072	232	+7 SB2	var.: 0.61–0.66, 0.16 d; B: 3.9, 1"
β Cen AB	14 04.4	–60 25	0.58v	–0.23	B1 III	6	–5.5	500	0.030	221	+6 SB	**Hadar**
π Hya	14 06.8	–26 43	3.25	1.09	K2 IIIb	32	0.2	101	0.049	163	27	
θ Cen	14 07.1	–36 24	2.06	1.01	K0 IIIb	54	0.1	61	0.738	225	1	Menkent
α Boo	14 16.0	+19 09	–0.05	1.24	K1.5 III Fe–0.5	89	–0.6	37	2.281	209	–5 V?	high space velocity **Arcturus**
ι Lup	14 19.9	–46 06	3.55	–0.18	B2.5 IVn	9	–1.7	400	0.014	266	22	
γ Boo	14 32.4	+38 17	3.04	0.19	A7 IV+	38	1.0	85	0.189	322	–37 V	Seginus
η Cen	14 36.0	–42 11	2.33v	–0.16	B1.5 IV pne	11	–2.8	310	0.049	226	0 SB	variable shell: 2.30–2.41
α Cen B	14 40.1	–60 52	1.35	0.90	K1 V	742	6.2	4	3.678	281	–21 V?	[AB 9"; orbit 80 y; min = 2", in 1955; max 22"
α Cen A	14 40.1	–60 52	–0.01	0.71	G2 V	742	4.2	4	3.678	281	–25 SB	C: Proxima, 12.4, M5e, 2° **Rigil Kentaurus**
α Lup	14 42.4	–47 25	2.30v	–0.15	B1.5 III	6	–4.1	500	0.026	220	+5 SB	var.: 2.29–2.34, 0.26 d
α Cir	14 43.1	–65 00	3.18	0.26	A7p (Sr)	61	1.9	54	0.302	218	+7 SB?	B: 8.6, K5 V, 16"
ε Boo AB	14 45.3	+27 03	2.35	1.34	K0 II–III+A0 V	16	–2.6	210	0.054	289	–17 V	A: 2.50; B: 4.66, 3" Izar
β UMi	14 50.7	+74 07	2.07	1.46	K4 III	26	–1.1	126	0.036	286	+17 V	Kochab
α² Lib	14 51.3	–16 04	2.75	0.15	A3 III–IV	42	0.7	77	0.130	237	–23 SB	Zubenelgenubi
β Lup	14 59.0	–43 10	2.68	–0.18	B2 IV	6	–3.5	500	0.057	221	0 SB	
κ Cen	14 59.7	–42 08	3.13	–0.21	B2 V	6	–2.8	500	0.033	215	+8 SB	
β Boo	15 02.2	+40 22	3.49	0.96	G8 IIIa (cf. Remarks)	15	–0.7	220	0.056	235	–20	Ba 0.4, Fe –0.5 Nekkar
σ Lib	15 04.5	–25 19	3.25v	1.67	M2.5 III	11	–1.9	290	0.087	237	–4	semiregular var.: 3.20–3.46 Brachium
ζ Lup	15 12.8	–52 08	3.41	0.92	G8 III	28	0.1	120	0.128	237	–10	
δ Boo	15 15.8	+33 17	3.46	0.96	G8 III Fe–1	28	0.6	117	0.143	144	–12 SB	
β Lib	15 17.4	–9 25	2.61	–0.07	B8 IIIn	20	–1.0	160	0.101	275	–35 SB	Zubeneschemali
γ TrA	15 19.6	–68 42	2.87	0.01	A1 IIIn	18	–0.8	180	0.067	243	–3 V	
γ UMi	15 20.7	+71 48	3.00	0.06	A3 III	7	–0.1:	150	0.031	308	–4 V	Pherkad
δ Lup	15 21.9	–40 40	3.22	–0.23	B1.5 IVn	6	–2.8	500	0.036	207	0 V?	
ε Lup AB	15 23.2	–44 43	3.37	–0.19	B2 IV–V	6	–2.5	500	0.024	232	+8 SB2	A: 3.56; B: 5.04, <1"
ι Dra	15 25.1	+58 56	3.29	1.17	K2 III	32	0.8	102	0.020	311	–11	Ed Asich
α CrB	15 35.0	+26 41	2.22v	0.03	A0 IV (composite)	44	0.3	75	0.151	127	+2 SB	ecl.: 2.21–2.32, 17 d Alphecca
γ Lup AB	15 35.6	–41 11	2.80	–0.22	B2 IVn	6	–2.8	600	0.035	207	+2 V	A: 3.5; B: 3.6, <1"; similar spectra
α Ser	15 44.6	+6 24	2.63v?	1.17	K2 IIIb CN1	45	0.9	73	0.143	72	+3 V?	var.? Unuk al Hai
μ Ser	15 50.0	–3 27	3.54	–0.04	A0 III	21	0.3	160	0.094	253	–9 SB	
β TrA	15 55.8	–63 27	2.83	0.32	F0 IV	81	2.3	40	0.438	205	0	
π Sco A	15 59.3	–26 08	2.89	–0.18	B1 V + B2 V	7	–3.0	500	0.028	198	–3 SB2	A: occ. bin.: 3.4 + 4.5, 0.0003" sep.
T CrB	15 59.8	+25 54	10.08v	1.34	gM3: + Bep	0	–9.3	–	0.013	327	–29 SB	recurrent nova 1866 (mag. 3), 1946 (mag. 2)
η Lup A	16 00.6	–38 25	3.42	–0.21	B2.5 IVn	7	–2.5	500	0.040	213	+8 V	A: 3.47; B: 7.70, 15"
δ Sco AB	16 00.8	–22 39	2.29	–0.12	B0.3 IV	8	–4.4:	520	0.027	202	–7 SB	AB: sep. < 1"; C: 4.9, B2 IV–V, 8" Dschubba

TABLE OF BRIGHTEST STARS (continued)

Star Name	RA (2007.5) h m	Dec ° '	V	B–V	MK Type	π mas	Mv	D ly	μ "/yr	PA °	RV km/s	Remarks	
β Sco AB	16 05.9	−19 50	2.56	−0.06	B0.5 V	6	−4.2	500	0.022	196	−1 SB	A: 2.78; B: 5.04, 1"; C: 4.93, 14"	Graffias
δ Oph	16 14.7	−3 43	2.73	1.58	M1 III	19	−0.8	170	0.153	198	−20 V		Yed Prior
ε Oph	16 18.7	−4 43	3.23	0.97	G9.5 IIIb	30	0.8	110	0.089	64	−10 V		Yed Posterior
σ Sco A	16 21.6	−25 37	2.91v	0.13	B1 III	4	−4.8:	520	0.025	201	+3 SB	var.: 2.86–2.94, 0.25 d; B: 8.3, B9 V, 20"	
η Dra A	16 24.1	+61 30	2.73	0.91	G8 IIIab	37	0.7	88	0.064	338	−14 SB?	B: 8.7, 6"	
α Sco A	16 29.9	−26 27	1.06v	1.86	M1.5 Iab	5	−5.8	600	0.024	197	−3 SB	irregular var.: 0.88–1.16; B: 5.37, 3"	Antares
β Her	16 30.5	+21 28	2.78	0.95	G7 IIIa	22	−0.5	150	0.100	260	−26 SB		Kornephoros
τ Sco	16 36.4	−28 14	2.82	−0.21	B0 V	8	−3.1	400	0.026	198	+2 V		
ζ Oph	16 37.6	−10 35	2.54	0.04	O9.5 Vn	7	−4.3	500	0.026	28	−15 V		
ζ Her AB	16 41.6	+31 35	2.81	0.65	G1 V	93	2.5	35	0.614	310	−70 SB	A: 2.90; B: 5.53, G7 V, 1.1"	
η Her	16 43.2	+38 54	3.48	0.92	G7.5 IIIb Fe-1	29	0.1	112	0.089	158	+8 V?		
α TrA	16 49.5	−69 02	1.91	1.45	K2 IIb-IIIa	8	−5.0	400	0.044	141	−3		Atria
ε Sco	16 50.6	−34 18	2.29	1.14	K2 III	50	0.1	65	0.661	247	−3		
μ¹ Sco	16 52.4	−38 04	3.00v	−0.20	B1.5 IVn	4	−4.1	800	0.031	202	−25 SB2	ecl.: 2.94–3.22, 1.4 d	
κ Oph	16 58.0	+9 22	3.19	1.16	K2 III	38	1.1	86	0.293	268	−56		
ζ Ara	16 59.2	−56 00	3.12	1.55	K4 III	6	−4.5	600	0.037	200	−6		
ζ Dra	17 08.8	+65 42	3.17	−0.12	B6 III	10	−2.0	340	0.033	310	−17 V		Aldhibah
η Oph AB	17 10.8	−15 44	2.43	0.06	A2.5 Va	39	0.8	84	0.102	22	−1 SB	A: 3.0; B: 3.5, A3 V, 1"	Sabik
η Sco	17 12.7	−43 15	3.32	0.44	F2 V:p (Cr)	46	1.4	72	0.286	175	−27		
α Her AB	17 15.0	+14 23	2.78v	1.16	M5 Ib-II	9	−3.5:	1400	0.035	348	−33 V	semiregular var.: 2.7–4.0; B: 5.4, 5"	Rasalgethi
π Her	17 15.3	+36 48	3.16	1.44	K3 IIab	9	−2.2	370	0.029	276	−26		
δ Her	17 15.3	+24 50	3.12	0.08	A1 Vann	42	1.2	79	0.159	188	−40 SB	B: 8.8, 9"	
θ Oph	17 22.5	−25 00	3.27v	−0.19	B2 IV	6	−3.1	600	0.021	188	−2 SB	occ. bin.: 3.4, 5.4; var.: 3.25–3.31, 0.14 d	
β Ara	17 25.9	−55 32	2.84	1.48	K3 Ib-IIa	5	−4.1	600	0.024	182	0		
γ Ara A	17 26.0	−56 23	3.31	−0.15	B1 Ib	3	−5.7:	650	0.011	170	−3 V	broad lines for Ib; B: 10.0, 18"	
β Dra A	17 30.6	+52 18	2.79	0.95	G2 Ib-IIa	9	−2.9	360	0.026	301	−20 V	B: 11.5, 4"	Rastaban
υ Sco	17 31.3	−37 18	2.70	−0.18	B2 IV	6	−3.5	500	0.032	182	8 SB		
α Ara	17 32.4	−49 53	2.84	−0.14	B2 Vne	13	−1.8	240	0.075	199	0 SB		
λ Sco	17 34.1	−37 07	1.62v	−0.23	B1.5 IV	5	−3.6:	360	0.029	178	−3 SB2	ecl.?, var.: 1.62–1.68, 0.21 d	Shaula
α Oph	17 35.3	+12 33	2.08	0.16	A5 Vm	70	1.3	47	0.255	157	+13 SB?		Rasalhague
θ Sco	17 37.9	−43 00	1.86	0.41	F1 III	12	−3.0	270	0.016	90	1		Sargas
ξ Ser	17 38.0	−15 24	3.54	0.26	F0 IIIb	31	0.9	110	0.076	216	−43 SB		
κ Sco	17 43.0	−39 02	2.39v	−0.17	B1.5 III	7	−3.6	500	0.030	194	−14 SB	var.: 2.41–2.42, 0.20 d	
β Oph	17 43.8	+4 34	2.76	1.17	K2 III	40	0.7	82	0.164	345	−12 V		Cebalrai
μ Her A	17 46.8	+27 43	3.42	0.75	G5 IV	119	3.6	27	0.808	202	−16 V	BC: 9.78, 33"	
υ¹ Sco	17 48.1	−40 08	2.99	0.51	F2 Ia	2	−8.0:	4000?	0.006	171	−28 SB		

TABLE OF BRIGHTEST STARS (continued)

Star Name	RA (2007.5) h m	Dec ° '	V	B−V	MK Type	π mas	Mv	D ly	μ "/yr	PA °	RV km/s	Remarks
G Sco	17 50.4	−37 03	3.19	1.19	K2 III	26	−0.6	130	0.064	58	25	HR6630
γ Dra	17 56.8	+51 29	2.24	1.52	K5 III	22	−1.1	150	0.025	213	−28	Eltanin
ν Oph	17 59.4	−9 46	3.32	0.99	G9.5 IIIa	21	0.0	150	0.118	184	13	
γ² Sgr	18 06.3	−30 25	2.98	0.98	K0 III	34	0.1	96	0.192	196	+22 SB	Nash
η Sgr A	18 18.1	−36 46	3.10v	1.50	M3.5 IIIab	22	−0.1	150	0.210	218	+1 V?	irreg. var.: 3.05–3.12; B: 8.33, G8: IV:, 4"
δ Sgr	18 21.5	−29 49	2.72	1.38	K2.5 IIIa	11	−3.3	300	0.050	127	−20	Kaus Meridionalis
ε Ser	18 21.7	−2 54	3.23	0.94	K0 III–IV	53	1.4	62	0.890	218	+9 V?	
ε Sgr	18 24.7	−34 23	1.79	−0.03	A0 II:n (shell?)	23	−1.4	140	0.129	194	−15	Kaus Australis
α Tel	18 27.5	−45 58	3.49	−0.18	B3 IV	13	−1.0	250	0.048	198	0 V?	
λ Sgr	18 28.4	−25 25	2.82	1.02	K1 IIIb	42	0.4	77	0.190	193	−43	Kaus Borealis
α Lyr	18 37.2	+38 47	0.03	0.00	A0 Va	129	0.6	25	0.348	35	−14 V	Vega
φ Sgr	18 46.1	−26 59	3.17	−0.11	B8 III	14	−1.0	230	0.052	89	+22 SB	
β Lyr	18 50.4	+33 22	3.52v	0.00	B7 Vpe (shell)	4	−4.1	900	0.002	180	−19 SB	Sheliak; similar companion, 0.1"; ecl.: 3.25–4.36, 13 d
σ Sgr	18 55.7	−26 17	2.05	−0.13	B3 IV	15	−2.4	220	0.056	166	−11 V	Nunki
ξ² Sgr	18 58.2	−21 06	3.52	1.15	K1 III	9	0.1	400	0.035	111	−20	
γ Lyr	18 59.2	+32 42	3.25	−0.05	B9 II	5	−3.3	600	0.007	288	−21 V	Sulaphat
ζ Sgr AB	19 03.1	−29 52	2.60	0.06	A2 IV–V + A4:V:	37	1.1	90	0.014	266	+22 SB	Ascella; A: 3.2; B: 3.5, <1"
ξ Aql A	19 05.8	+13 52	2.99	0.01	A0 Vann	39	0.9	83	0.095	184	−25 SB	
λ Aql	19 06.6	−4 52	3.43	−0.10	B9 Vnp (kB7HeA0)	26	0.6	130	0.090	193	−12 V	
τ Sgr	19 07.4	−27 40	3.32	1.17	K1.5 IIIb	27	−0.4	120	0.255	192	+45 SB	
π Sgr ABC	19 10.2	−21 01	2.88	0.38	F2 II–III	7	−3.1	400	0.035	180	−10	Albaldah; A: 3.7; B: 3.8; C: 6.0, <1"
δ Dra	19 12.6	+67 40	3.07	0.99	G9 III	33	0.6	100	0.130	44	25	Nodus Secundus
δ Aql	19 25.9	+3 08	3.36	0.32	F2 IV	65	2.6	50	0.267	72	−30 SB	Deneb Okab
β Cyg A	19 31.0	+27 59	3.36	1.09	K3 II + B9.5 V	8	−2.3	390	0.002	153	−24 V	Albireo; B: 5.11, 35"; C: Δm = 1.5, 0.4"
δ Cyg AB	19 45.2	+45 09	2.86	0.00	B9.5 III	19	−0.7	170	0.069	45	−20 SB	B: 6.4, F1 V; 3"
γ Aql	19 46.6	+10 38	2.72	1.51	K3 II	7	−2.6:	330	0.016	83	−2 V	Tarazed
α Aql	19 51.1	+8 53	0.76	0.22	A7 Vnn	194	2.1	17	0.662	54	−26	Altair
η Aql	19 52.9	+1 02	3.87v	0.63	F6–G1 Ib	3	−4.3	1000	0.009	131	−15 SB	Cepheid var.: 3.48–4.39, 7.2 d
γ Sge	19 59.1	+19 31	3.51	1.57	M0 III	12	−0.9	270	0.070	69	−33	
θ Aql	20 11.7	−0 48	3.24	−0.07	B9.5 III	11	−1.4	290	0.037	79	−27 SB2	
β Cap A	20 21.4	−14 45	3.05	0.79	K0: II: + A5: V:n	9	−1.4	300	0.039	86	−19 SB	Dabih; A: mult.: 4.0 + 4.3 + 4.8 + 6.7, <1"
γ Cyg	20 22.5	+40 17	2.23	0.67	F8 Ib	2	−4.1:	520	0.001	27	−8	Sadr
α Pav	20 26.2	−56 43	1.94	−0.12	B2.5 V	18	−2.1	180	0.087	169	+2 SB	Peacock
α Ind	20 38.1	−47 16	3.11	1.00	K0 III CN−1	32	0.1	101	0.090	39	−1	
α Cyg	20 41.7	+45 18	1.25	0.09	A2 Ia	1	−7.5:	1500	0.005	11	−5 V	Deneb
η Cep	20 45.4	+61 52	3.41	0.91	K0 IV	70	2.7	47	0.827	6	−87	

TABLE OF BRIGHTEST STARS (continued)

Star Name	RA (2007.5) h m	Dec ° ′	V	B−V	MK Type	π mas	Mv	D ly	μ ″/yr	PA °	RV km/s	Remarks
β Pav	20 45.6	−66 11	3.42	0.16	A6 IV	24	0.6	140	0.041	295	10	
ε Cyg	20 46.5	+34 00	2.48	1.02	K0 III	45	0.7	72	0.484	47	−11 SB	Gienah
ζ Cyg	21 13.3	+30 15	3.21	0.99	G8 IIIa Ba 0.5	22	0.2	150	0.052	181	+17 SB	
α Cep	21 18.8	+62 37	2.45	0.26	A7 Van	67	1.4	49	0.159	71	−10 V	Alderamin
β Cep	21 28.8	+70 36	3.23v	−0.20	B1 III	5	−4.0:	820	0.016	38	−8 SB	Alfirk; var: 3.16−3.27, 0.19 d; B: 7.8;13″
β Aqr	21 32.0	−5 32	2.90	0.83	G0 Ib	5	−3.5	612	0.020	105	7	Sadalsuud
ε Peg	21 44.6	+9 55	2.38v	1.52	K2 Ib	5	−5.2	700	0.030	81	+5 V	Enif; irregular var: 0.7−3.5 (flare in 1972)
δ Cap	21 47.5	−16 06	2.85v	0.18	A3mF2 IV:	85	2.2	39	0.394	138	−6 SB	occ. bin.: 2.81−3.05, 1.0 d, 3.2 + 5.2
γ Gru	21 54.4	−37 20	3.00	−0.08	B8 IV−Vs	16	−1.1	200	0.104	99	−2 V?	
α Aqr	22 06.2	−0 17	2.95	0.97	G2 Ib	4	−4.3	800	0.016	104	+8 V?	Sadalmelik
α Gru	22 08.7	−46 55	1.73	−0.07	B7 Vn	32	−0.9	101	0.198	139	12	Alnair
θ Peg	22 10.6	+6 14	3.52	0.09	A2mA1 IV−V	34	1.0	97	0.277	83	−6 SB2	Baham
ζ Cep	22 11.1	+58 14	3.39	1.56	K1.5 Ib	4	−4.2	700	0.015	58	−18 SB	
α Tuc	22 19.0	−60 13	2.87	1.39	K3 III	16	−2.2	200	0.071	237	+42 SB	
δ Cep A	22 29.5	+58 27	4.07v	0.78	F5−G2 Ib	3	−4.4	1000	0.012	67	−16 SB	prototype Cepheid var: 3.48−4.37, 5.4 d
ζ Peg	22 41.8	+10 52	3.41	−0.09	B8.5 III	16	−0.7	210	0.080	96	+7 V?	Homam
β Gru	22 43.1	−46 51	2.07v	1.61	M5 III	19	−1.4	170	0.138	92	2	irregular var: 2.0−2.3
η Peg	22 43.4	+30 16	2.93	0.85	G8 II + F0 V	15	−1.2	210	0.025	148	+4 SB	Matar
ε Gru	22 49.0	−51 17	3.49	0.08	A2 Va	25	0.4	130	0.126	120	0 V	
ι Cep	22 49.9	+66 14	3.50	1.05	K0 III	28	0.6	115	0.137	209	−12	
μ Peg	22 50.4	+24 38	3.51	0.93	G8 III	28	0.8	120	0.152	104	14	Sadalbari
δ Aqr	22 55.0	−15 47	3.27	0.07	A3 IV−V (wk λ4481)	20	−0.1	160	0.047	242	+18 V	Skat
α PsA	22 58.1	−29 35	1.17	0.14	A3 Va	130	1.6	25	0.373	116	7	Fomalhaut
β Peg	23 04.1	+28 07	2.44v	1.66	M2 II−III	16	−1.7	200	0.236	53	+9 V	Scheat; irregular var: 2.31−2.74
α Peg	23 05.1	+15 15	2.49	0.00	A0 III−IV	23	−0.9	140	0.073	121	−4 SB	Markab
γ Cep	23 39.7	+77 40	3.21	1.03	K1 III−IV	72	2.1	45	0.168	337	−42	Alrai

THE NEAREST STARS
By Alan H. Batten

The most important changes to the table for this year comprise one addition, one removal, and one adjustment of a star's position in the table consequent on a more reliable parallax determination. The newcomer is GJ 3323, found just below GJ 1116 A and B, which are the first entries under the horizontal line drawn in the table. On the other hand, BD –13° 637B has been removed; its spectrum has been shown to be that of a giant star and the parallax (which was uncertain) must be unreliable. The star is considerably farther away than was previously thought. Finally, Teegarden's star (2MASS 0253+16 in the table), which has been included for the past few years on the basis of a preliminary parallax determination, has been shown, as was suspected, to be somewhat farther away; it has been dropped from seventh place in the table to thirty-sixth and now appears just above DENIS 1845–63. The absolute magnitude has been adjusted to the new distance and an error in the proper motion has been corrected. Errors of sign in the space velocities of Wolf 424A and BD +15° 2620 have been corrected, and a few minor adjustments made to magnitudes and spectral types of other stars (remember that both these are variable for many of the stars listed). Some stars for which no radial velocities are listed in SIMBAD, nevertheless have radial velocities listed in the Gliese-Jahreiss catalogue, and I have added velocities for them to the table. In general, velocities can be assumed to be the same for the two members of a binary, although there may be small differences caused by the combination of observational errors and orbital motion. The usual caveats about uncertainties still apply; in particular LP 944–20 and GJ 745 may actually be beyond the limit of this table.

The *annual parallax* of a star is the difference between its direction as seen from Earth and the Sun. Astronomers began to look for stellar parallax as soon as they began to take seriously the idea that the Sun, and not Earth, is the centre of the planetary system. The great distances of the other stars ensured, however, that determination of parallax would be beyond the powers of early telescopes. James Bradley (1693–1762) came close to succeeding and correctly deduced that even the largest parallaxes must be less than 2″, but about another century was to elapse before success was achieved. Then, between 1838 and 1840, Bessel, Struve, and Henderson all published trustworthy parallaxes for three different stars. Two of those star systems, α Cen (Henderson) and 61 Cyg (Bessel), are indeed so close to us that they appear in this table. Struve measured the parallax of Vega, which, although a relatively close neighbour of the Sun, lies some distance beyond the limit adopted here. Progress in measuring other parallaxes remained rather slow until it became possible, toward the end of the 19th century, to apply photography to the problem.

A table like the one presented here (pp. 265–266) looks rather static, but if we think on a long enough time scale, the stars within the sphere of approximately 19-ly radius, centred on the Sun, are changing all the time — moving in and out of the sphere. Proxima Centauri has not always been our nearest neighbour nor will it always be, even though it is at present coming closer to us. Calculations by R.A.J. Matthews some time ago indicated that 32 000 years ago L 726-8 was closer to us and that in another 33 000 years Ross 248 will be closer. More recent calculations by García-Sanchez and others, based on *HIPPARCOS* measurements, extend the picture over some tens of millions of years. Seven million years ago, Algol would have been featured in this table; it also would have been appreciably brighter in the sky than Sirius now is. In 1.4 million years, Gliese 710 (now over 60 ly away from us) will be only 1.3 ly away and a moderately bright naked-eye star. All such calculations are approximate, of course, because there are still uncertainties in our knowledge of the distances and motions of the stars.

Massive hot stars are relatively rare. Ignoring white dwarfs, which are not massive, only Sirius, Procyon, and Altair, in this table, are hotter and more massive than the Sun, and only α Cen equals the Sun in these respects. Most of the objects listed are very faint, cool stars; five (ε Ind B and C, at 11.8 ly; LP 944-20 at 16.2 ly; and the faint companion to DENIS 1845–63B at 12.5 ly and BD –21°1377, or GJ 229 B, at 18.8 ly) are brown dwarfs—not massive enough for thermonuclear reactions to be ignited in their centres, and producing energy only by their gravitational contraction. They are very cool, faint, and difficult to detect, "shining" mostly in the infrared. There may be other such objects within the volume of space represented in this table, but thorough searches have not yet revealed them. There is some evidence for a substellar companion to van Maanen's star, for which an approximate period of 1.6 years is proposed, but not enough is known yet to justify including it in the table. Three objects, G 208-44 B, DENIS 1048-39, and 2MASS 1835+32, are very close to the borderline between true stars and brown dwarfs.

In 2004, I extended the table from its traditional limit of about 17 ly (5 parsecs) to just over 19 ly (very nearly 6 parsecs). Almost all the objects listed here may be found in either the *HIPPARCOS* catalogue or the *Yale Catalogue of Trigonometric Parallaxes;* a few have either been discovered or recognized as nearby objects since the publication of those two catalogues. I have preferred *HIPPARCOS* parallaxes when they are available, even though a few stellar parallaxes have been measured even more accurately with the Hubble Space Telescope. I have quoted *HIPPARCOS* parallaxes to the nearest tenth of a milliarcsecond, and ground-based determinations of parallax are only to the nearest milliarcsecond. Exceptions to this rule are the parallaxes of 2MASS 1835+32 and DENIS 1048–39, both ground-based measurements. The convention is not entirely fair to ground-based measurements—the best modern ones are comparable in accuracy with *HIPPARCOS* measures—but it helps the reader appreciate the contributions made by *HIPPARCOS* to our knowledge of stellar distances. The full value of any parallax given to the nearest tenth of a milliarcsecond was used in computing the distance, even if the last digit does not appear in the table. That is why, occasionally, a star may appear to be out of order in the table: the parallax has been rounded up, but the distance was computed from the unrounded value. With this year's additions, the table contains 51 single stars, 16 pairs (including common-proper-motion pairs but not the possible companion to van Maanen's star), and 5 triples (α Cen A and B with Proxima; L 789-6, a pair whose brighter component is a spectroscopic binary; ε Ind A, B, and C; G 208-45 with G 208-44 A and B; and o² Eri A, B, and C). This total does not include planetary companions, discussed below. Some new data have been added for stars already in the old table. A few other objects are known for which there is good reason to suppose that they lie within the volume of space represented in the table, but I shall not add them until trigonometric parallaxes are determined for them.

Spectral types and magnitudes of brown dwarfs require some comment. Although some brown dwarfs have very late M spectral types, two new spectral classes, L and T, have been created. L-type brown dwarfs have effective temperatures between about 2200 K and 1500 K; T-type objects are cooler still. Often only infrared magnitudes are given for these stars. Listing such magnitudes would make these objects appear misleadingly bright. In recent years I tried to estimate a visual magnitude for LP 944-20; however, I have come to the conclusion that *any* entry in the magnitude column could be misleading, so I have not given any magnitude for the five brown dwarfs in the table. The visual magnitude given for DENIS 1048-39 is based on an observed *B* magnitude and an estimated colour index for its given spectral type; it is also uncertain.

Some nearby stars are known to have planetary companions, particularly ε Eri, BD +36° 2147 (Lalande 21185) and BD -15° 6290. 61 Cyg and, as mentioned above, van Maanen's star, may also have such companions. The evidence is not as strong for many other stars that were once believed to have planets, especially Barnard's star. A thorough search of the system of α Cen A and B with Proxima, our nearest neighbours, failed to provide any certain evidence of planets and has set severe limits on what sort of planets the system could contain.

Subject to these comments, the table is arranged as previously. Successive columns give the name or designation of the star, the right ascension (**RA**) and declination (**Dec**) for equinox J2000.0, the parallax (π) in milliarcseconds, and the distance (*D*) in light-years. (If you prefer the scientific unit of parsecs, just take the reciprocal of the parallax; one parsec is approximately 3.26 ly.) Subsequent columns give the spectral type (**Sp.**, in the MK system whenever possible (see p. 252)), the total proper motion (μ) in milliarcseconds per year, the position angle of the proper motion (θ) measured in degrees from north through east, the total space motion, relative to the Sun, (*W*) in kilometres per second for those stars with known radial velocities, and the apparent and absolute visual magnitudes (*V* and *M*$_V$, respectively). Distances of *HIPPARCOS* stars are given to 0.01 ly and of the others to 0.1 ly. Again, I stress that we rarely know distances that precisely. Except for stars new to the list, I have usually retained the spectral types previously used. The K and M stars were classified by R.F. Wing some years ago. Recent reclassification resulted in few significant changes. Many M-type stars are flare stars, variable in both magnitude and spectral type. The space motion is given the same sign as the radial velocity (+ for recession). This is a little misleading for the two components of BD +59°1915, whose radial velocities are small and which are travelling together, despite the difference in sign of their space motions. Several of the radial velocities are based on only one or two observations and are the least reliable data in the table. The velocities of the centres of mass of the binaries α Cen, Sirius, Procyon, and 70 Oph are, however, reasonably well known. I have taken magnitudes from *HIPPARCOS* whenever possible, except for 70 Oph, for which the *HIPPARCOS* value appears to refer to the total light of the system. Magnitudes quoted to only one decimal are not photoelectrically determined.

HIPPARCOS has determined parallaxes and proper motions separately for each component of some binary systems. The components of α Cen have the same parallax, but those of 61 Cyg are different; the components of Procyon are between them in distance, and BD +59°1915 B turns out to be closer than its brighter companion. The two components of the common-proper-motion pair CD −25°10553, included in earlier versions of this table, have been removed because further analysis makes it doubtful they are as close as previously thought. I have suppressed parallax and proper-motion entries for those components of binaries for which separate determinations were *not* made, sometimes condensing the entry to a single line. Only the fainter component of BD −15° 6346 appears in the table since it forms an optical pair with its brighter companion.

There is no uniform nomenclature for these predominantly faint stars; some have many different names. I have used the names I thought most familiar, preferring proper names, Bayer letters or Flamsteed numbers, BD and other Durchmusterung designations. In the newer section of the table, I have often used GJ numbers. These refer to the *Catalogue of Nearby Stars,* originally compiled by Wilhelm Gliese and now maintained by Hartmut Jahreiss. I could extend the use of GJ numbers, but readers might be put off by finding, for example, Sirius called "GJ 244," and it takes some time for new discoveries (DENIS 1048-39) to be assigned a GJ number. (All stars that were in Gliese's original catalogues are given the same number in GJ lists, so, for example, Gliese 229 B and GJ 229 B are the same star.) Designations beginning with L refer to catalogues of proper-motion surveys compiled by W.J. Luyten, as do those beginning with LP (from Palomar observations). Designations beginning with G (not GJ) are from catalogues compiled by H. Giclas and colleagues at the Lowell Observatory. DENIS and 2MASS are acronyms for modern surveys in the infrared. Respectively, they are Deep-Sky Near Infrared Survey and Two-Micron All-Sky Survey.

As usual, either the compiler or the editor will be glad to be notified of errors or omissions. The extension of the table (below the line) is perhaps particularly likely to contain errors or to be incomplete. The revisions of the table were made easier by the access to the SIMBAD and *HIPPARCOS* catalogues provided by the Canadian Astronomy Data Centre. I also made use of the online version of the GJ catalogue and of a recent (2001) paper by Oppenheimer et al. in the *Astronomical Journal,* which lists stars within 8 parsecs north of declination −35°.

Editor's Note: For more information, see A.H. Batten, "Our Changing Views of the Solar Neighbourhood," *JRASC, 92* (1998), pp. 231–237.

TABLE OF NEAREST STARS

Name	RA (2000) h m	Dec ° '	π mas	D ly	Sp.	μ mas/y	θ °	W km/s	V	M_V
Sun					G2V				−26.72	4.85
Proxima	14 30	−62 41	772.3	4.22	M5.5Ve	3 853	281	−29	11.01	15.45
α Cen A	14 40	−60 50	742.1	4.40	G2V	3 709	277	−32	−0.01	4.34
B					K1V	3 724	285	−32	1.35	5.70
Barnard's	17 58	+4 42	549.0	5.94	M5V	10 358	356	−139	9.54	13.24
Wolf 359	10 56	+7 01	419	7.79	M6.5Ve	4 702	235	+55	13.46	16.57
BD +36°2147	11 03	+35 58	392.4	8.31	M2+V	4 802	187	−104	7.49	10.46
Sirius A	6 45	−16 43	379.2	8.60	A1Vm	1 339	204	−18	−1.44	1.45
B					DA2				8.44	11.33
L 726-8 A	1 39	−17 57	373	8.7	M5.5Ve	3 360	80	+52	12.56	15.42
B					M5.5Ve			+53	12.96	15.82
Ross 154	18 50	−23 50	336.5	9.69	M3.6Ve	666	107	−10	10.70	13.33
Ross 248	23 42	+44 09	316	10.3	M5.5Ve	1 588	176	−84	12.27	14.77
ε Eri	3 33	−9 27	310.8	10.50	K2V	977	271	+22	3.72	6.18
CD −36°15693	23 06	−35 51	303.9	10.73	M2V	6 896	79	+108	7.35	9.76
Ross 128	11 48	+0 48	299.6	10.89	M4+V	1 361	154	−26	11.12	13.50
L 789-6 ABC	22 39	−15 18	290	11.2	M5+Ve	3 256	47	−80	12.32	14.63
61 Cyg A	21 07	+38 45	287.1	11.36	K5V	5 281	52	−108	5.20	7.49
Procyon A	7 39	+5 13	285.9	11.41	F5IV–V	1 259	215	−21	0.40	2.68
B					DF				10.7	13.0
61 Cyg B	21 07	+38 45	285.4	11.43	K7V	5 172	53	−107	6.05	8.33
BD +59°1915 B	18 43	+59 38	284.5	11.47	M4V	2 312	323	+39	9.70	11.97
A			280.3	11.64	M3.5V	2 238	324	−38	8.94	11.18
BD +43°44 A	0 18	+44 01	280.3	11.64	M2V	2 918	82	+51	8.09	10.33
B					M4V			+54	11.10	13.34
G 51-15	8 30	+26 47	276	11.8	M6.5Ve	1 270	238	+24	14.81	17.01
2MASS 1259–43	12 59	−43 36	276	11.8	M8–9	1133	306			
ε Ind A	22 03	−56 47	275.8	11.83	K4Ve	4 705	123	−90	4.69	6.89
Ba					T1	4 697	122			
Bb					T6					
τ Cet	1 44	−15 56	274.2	11.90	G8V	1 922	296	−37	3.49	5.68
L 372-58	3 36	−44 31	273	11.9	M5.5V	828	115	−25	13.03	15.21
L 725-32	1 12	−17 00	269.1	12.12	M5.5Ve	1 372	62	+37	11.60	13.75
BD +5°1668	7 27	+5 14	263.3	12.39	M4V	3 738	171	+70	9.84	11.94
2MASS 0253+16	2 53	+16 53	261	12.49	M6.5V	5107	138		15.40	17.48
DENIS 1845–63 A	18 45	−63 57	260	12.5	M8.5V	2558	74.8		17.4	19.5
B					T5.5					
Kapteyn's	5 12	−45 01	255.3	12.78	M1VIp	8 671	131	+294	8.86	10.89
CD −39°14192	21 17	−38 52	253.4	12.87	M0Ve	3 455	251	+69	6.69	8.71
Krüger 60 A	22 28	+57 42	249.5	13.07	M3.5V	990	242	−30	9.59	11.58
B					M4Ve	851	243	−32	10.3	12.3
DENIS 1048–39	10 48	−39 56	247.7	13.16	M8V	1 541	231	−31	(17.0)	(19.0)

TABLE OF NEAREST STARS (continued)

Name	RA (2000) h m	Dec ° '	π mas	D ly	Sp.	μ mas/y	θ °	W km/s	V	M_V
Ross 614 A	6 29	−2 49	242.9	13.43	M4.0Ve	930	132	+25	11.1	13.0
B					M5.5V				14.3	16.2
BD −12°4523	16 30	−12 40	234.5	13.91	M4V	1 189	185	−27	10.10	11.95
CD −37°15492	0 05	−37 21	229.3	14.23	M2V	6 100	113	+128	8.56	10.36
Wolf 424 A	12 33	+9 01	228	14.3	M5+Ve	1 811	277	+38	13.10	14.89
B					M7	1 764	279		13.4	15.2
van Maanen's	0 49	+5 23	227.0	14.37	DG	2 978	156	+82	12.37	14.15
L 1159-16	2 00	+13 03	224	14.6	M4.5Ve	2 096	148	−54	12.26	14.01
L 143-23	10 45	−61 12	222	14.7	M4	1 657	348		13.87	15.60
BD +68°946	17 36	+68 20	220.9	14.77	M3.5V	1 310	194	−36	9.15	10.87
LP 731-58	10 48	−11 20	221	14.8	M6.5V	1 645	158	−36	15.60	17.32
CD −46°11540	17 29	−46 54	220.4	14.80	M3V	1 050	147	−25	9.38	11.10
G 208-45	19 54	+44 25	220	14.8	M6Ve	660	139		14.01	15.72
44 A					M6Ve	681	142		13.47	15.18
44 B					M5.5				16.76	18.47
BD −15°6346B	23 07	−14 52	216.5	15.07		140	53		12.24	13.92
L 145-141	11 46	−64 50	216.4	15.07	DC:	2 688	97		11.50	13.18
G 158-27	0 07	−7 32	213	15.3	M5–5.5V	2 028	204	−62	13.74	15.38
BD −15°6290	22 53	−14 16	212.7	15.34	M5V	1 174	125	+28	10.16	11.80
BD +44°2051 A	11 05	+43 32	206.9	15.77	M1V	4 511	282	+122	8.73	10.31
B					M5de				14.40	15.93
BD +50°1725	10 11	+49 27	205.2	15.90	K7V	1 452	250	−42	6.60	8.16
BD +20°2465	10 20	+19 52	205	15.9	M3.5Ve	491	264	+16	9.43	10.99
CD −49°13515	21 34	−49 00	202.5	16.11	M2V	819	183	+22	8.66	10.19
LP 944-20	3 40	−35 26	201	16.22	≥M9V	439	176	+14		
CD −44°11909	17 37	−44 19	198.3	16.43	M4V	1 176	217	−66	10.94	12.43
o² Eri A	4 15	−7 39	198.2	16.46	K1V	4 088	213	−106	4.43	5.92
B					DA	4 070	212	−100	9.52	11.01
C					M4.5Ve	4 079	213	−107	11.17	12.66
BD +43°4305 A	22 47	+44 20	198.1	16.47	M4−Ve	841	237	−20	10.05	11.53
70 Oph A	18 05	+2 30	196.6	16.59	K0V	971	173	−24	4.20	5.67
B					K4V				5.99	7.46
Altair	19 51	+8 52	194.4	16.78	A7V	661	54	−31	0.76	2.20
GJ 1116 A	8 58	+19 46	191	17.1	M8Ve	820	262	−40	14.06	15.45
B					M5.5	820	263		14.92	16.31
GJ 3323	5 02	−6 57	188	17.34	M4V	769	227	+46	12.16	13.53
GJ 3379	6 00	+2 42	186	17.5	M4	300	86	+56	11.33	12.68
GJ 445	11 48	+78 41	185.5	17.57	M3.5	885	57	−121	10.78	12.12
BD +15°2620	13 45	+14 53	184.1	17.71	M1.5	2 298	129	+61	8.46	9.79
LP 816-60	20 53	−16 58	182.2	17.89	MV	308	174		11.41	12.71
GJ 169.1 A	4 31	+58 59	181.4	17.97	M4	2 439	147	+63	11.08	12.37
B					DC			+64	12.44	13.73
GJ 251	6 55	+33 16	181.3	17.98	M3	831	241	+42	9.89	11.18
GJ 402	10 51	+6 48	177.5	18.37	M4	1 141	224	+31	11.66	12.91
2MASS 1835+32	18 36	+33 00	176.5	18.47	M8.5	759	186		18.27	19.50
BD −3°1123	5 31	−3 41	175.7	18.55	M1.5V	2 228	160	+61	7.92	9.14
GJ 754	19 21	−45 33	175.2	18.61	M4.5	3 111	165		12.23	13.44
BD −8°4352	16 55	−8 20	174.2	18.71	M3Ve	1 208	223	+38	9.04	10.24
σ Dra	19 32	+69 40	173.4	18.80	K0V	1 839	161	+57	4.70	5.89
BD −21°1377A	6 11	−21 52	173.2	18.82	M1V	727	191	+20	8.14	9.33
B					T6.5V					

DOUBLE AND MULTIPLE STARS
By Brian D. Mason

Approximately 85% of stars are found in double or multiple systems. While the first detection of double systems dates back to the early 17th century, it was not until systematic work with large-aperture telescopes was done (notably by Sir William Herschel) that the physical rather than the optical nature of these systems was ascertained. The larger the aperture of the telescope, the closer the stars that can be separated under good conditions. The resolving power in arcseconds can be estimated as $120/D$, where D is the diameter of the telescope objective in millimetres. Astronomers using long-baseline optical interferometry have measured double-star separations less than a milliarcsecond ($0.001''$).

The double stars in the following table, were selected to cover a wide variety of interests. While wide or slowly moving pairs are good for evaluating optical performance or estimating seeing, with the preponderance of inexpensive, large-aperture telescopes and the availability of interferometry for the amateur (in *Sky & Telescope* see the articles by A. Maurer, p. 91, March 1997, and H.A. McAlister, p. 34, November 1996), closer systems have been added to the list. Of the 40 listed systems, 4 have separations less than one arcsecond and 7 more between one and two arcseconds. A pair of binaries with white dwarf secondaries (α CMa and α CMi) is included to demonstrate the detection difficulty imposed by a large magnitude difference. Eight of the systems are found south of the equator. Since many of the stars selected exhibit significant motion, the predicted position angles and separations are given for both 2008.0 and 2009.0. PA (Position Angle) is the angular direction of the fainter star (B) from the brighter (A), measured counterclockwise from north (*clockwise* in an optical system having an *odd* number of reflections). Note that data for 2008.0 have been changed for some systems due to improvements in orbit calculations or more recent measurements. For systems with no orbit determination the most recently measured position is tabulated. Also included are notes on selected systems. If no 2009.0 data are provided, there is no calculation (orbit or linear) of the motion (if any) of this double. The 2008.0 data are the most recently published.

Other double stars appear in THE NEAREST STARS (pp. 262–266) and THE BRIGHTEST STARS (pp. 252–261) sections in this Handbook. Recently an electronic journal for double-star observing was started at the University of South Alabama (see www.jdso.org). The *Journal of Double Star Observations* is a good source for free information on double and multiple stars.

Notes on some double and multiple stars in the table:

α **UMi:** Polaris is a Cepheid variable and thus one of the most important stars for determining the cosmic distance scale. The parameters for AB are given in the table. The wider AC ($40''$) and AD ($80''$) pairs were discovered by Burnham in 1884 and lost until 2005, when they were recovered by amateur astronomer Jim Daley. At magnitudes 13 and 14 they are quite a challenge! The long-known astrometric companion to this bright Cepheid was finally resolved by Nancy Evans and colleagues with the Hubble Space Telescope.

33 Ori: This is a relatively fixed pair, having shown no significant motion since it was discovered by F.G.W. Struve in 1831. As a result, it is a good test object for optical performance and seeing characterization.

α **CMa:** The companion to Sirius is a difficult target, usually observable only during periods of exceptional seeing, when you can use the highest magnification and move the primary off the field of view. The white dwarf secondary, predicted by Bessel and first observed by Alvan Clark, remains a challenging target for visual observers. For more information on Sirius B, see Alan MacRobert's article in the March 2001 *Sky & Telescope,* p. 24.

α CMi: Like Sirius, Procyon has a white dwarf companion. It was first detected in 1840 by the variation in the proper motion of the star but not resolved until 1896 by Shaeberle with the 36-in. refractor of Lick Observatory. For more information on doubles near Procyon, see Sissy Haas's article in the April 2001 *Sky & Telescope,* p. 102.

σ² UMa: Previous observers claimed a marked colour difference and that the secondary was variable, both of which are uncertain. The system is quite slow moving and the orbital period is very uncertain.

ξ UMa: Many "firsts" are associated with this system. It was one of the first discovered systems (Herschel), one of the first systems whose motion led to the discovery of the physical (rather than optical) nature of double stars (Struve), and the first to have an orbit calculated for it (Savary). Always relatively wide and with an obvious position angle change of 6° per year, this is a system that will never fail to please, observing season to observing season. For more information on this system, see Roger Griffin's article in the October 1998 *Observatory.* (In the MAY ALL-SKY MAP on p. 312, ξ UMa is nearest to the letter "S" in the word "BERENICES.")

α Cru: This brilliant double star is located at the bottom of the Southern Cross. According to Allen it was "discovered to be double by some Jesuit Missionaries sent by King Louis XIV to Siam in 1685." Aitken credits it to Father Fontenay at the Cape of Good Hope (en route to Siam?). In any event, it was not until the 19th century that the first measure of all components in the triple were made by James Dunlop at Parramatta Observatory in New South Wales. Several other large Δ*m* companions were detected by Andrei Tokovinin with adaptive optics. Physicality of these new pairs is not certain.

α Cen: Our closest neighbour is a quick-moving double star. The brighter component is a near twin of the Sun, while the B component is cooler. The C component, Proxima, which is slightly closer to the Sun, is an extremely faint red dwarf, 2.2° away. For more information on Proxima Cen, see Alan MacRobert's article in the March 2003 *Sky & Telescope,* p. 22.

ε Boo: In addition to the pair described here, there is an unresolved spectroscopic binary and a faint (V ~ 12) and wide (ρ ~ 177″) companion. An astute Handbook reader noted a magnitude discrepancy for this pair, which is corrected here.

κ Her: The 2008-9 predictions for this pair are based on a linear solution of the relative motion of these stars. A new catalogue of these pairs, which can be found at ad.usno.navy.mil/wds/lin1.html has recently been prepared. These linear systems should provide very precise calibration of rotation and plate scale parameters.

α Sco: Antares is a double system consisting of a cool supergiant and a hot dwarf star. A significant colour difference may be seen if you can overcome the large magnitude difference (4.4).

ε Lyr AB and **CD:** The double-double never fails to impress. The pairs are roughly orthogonal to each other and all quite bright with small magnitude differences. The CD pair is almost due south separated by ~3.5′. The C pair has a close companion, discovered by speckle interferometry, at a separation of about 0.1″. While there are not enough measures of this close pair to calculate an orbit, non-linear motion is indicated.

β Cyg: Also known as Albireo. If a neophyte doubts the colour of stars, this jewel of the summer sky should change that view. Appearing as brilliant yellow and a deep blue, this wide double has shown no apparent motion. The A component has two close companions, discovered by speckle interferometry, one at a separation of about 0.4″ and the other at 0.1″. (In the JULY ALL-SKY MAP on p. 313, β Cyg lies at the south end of the stick pattern for CYGNUS.)

ζ Aqr: This central star in the "water jar" asterism saw closest approach in the mid-1970s and is now slowly opening up. Recent data indicates it may have a shorter period and a more eccentric orbit than the current best solution indicates, so continued observation is warranted. The A component also has a closer astrometric companion with a period of 26 years, as described by Wulff Heintz, the recently deceased "Swarthmore Orbit Machine," who produced more orbits than any other binary-star astronomer and observed more pairs than all but one.

TABLE OF DOUBLE AND MULTIPLE STARS

	RA (2000) Dec			Magnitudes			2008.0		2009.0		
							PA	Sep.	PA	Sep.	Period
Star	h	m	° ′	comb.	A	B	°	″	°	″	a
ζ Psc	1	13.7	+07 35	4.8	5.2	6.2	62	22.70			
γ Ari	1	53.5	+19 18	3.8	3.9	3.9	0	7.40			
α Psc	2	02.0	+02 46	3.9	4.3	5.2	266	1.78	265	1.78	933
γ And AB	2	03.9	+42 20	2.0	2.1	4.8	63	9.57			
γ And BC	2	03.9	+42 20	4.5	4.8	6.0	101	0.30	101	0.28	64
α UMi*	2	31.8	+89 16	2.1	2.1	9.1	233	18.56			
33 Ori*	5	31.2	+03 18	5.5	5.8	6.9	28	1.83			
λ Ori	5	35.1	+09 56	3.3	3.5	5.5	44	4.44			
α CMa*	6	45.1	−16 43	−1.5	−1.5	8.5	98	8.04	95	8.44	50
α Gem	7	34.6	+31 53	1.6	2.0	2.9	58	4.50	58	4.58	445
α CMi*	7	39.3	+5 14	0.4	0.4	10.8	169	2.23	196	2.18	41
ζ Cnc AB	8	12.2	+17 39	5.0	5.6	6.0	46	1.03	42	1.04	60
ι Cnc	8	46.7	+28 46	3.9	4.0	6.6	308	30.67			
σ² UMa*	9	10.4	+67 08	4.8	4.9	7.9	351	4.08	350	4.11	1 141
ψ Vel	9	30.7	−40 28	3.6	4.0	4.8	87	0.61	95	0.74	34
γ Leo	10	20.0	+19 50	2.3	2.6	3.8	126	4.61	126	4.61	619
ξ UMa*	11	18.2	+31 32	3.8	4.3	4.8	226	1.64	219	1.62	60
α Cru*	12	26.6	−63 06	0.2	0.8	1.2	114	4.00			
24 Com	12	35.1	+18 23	4.8	5.1	6.3	270	20.24			
ζ UMa	13	23.9	+54 56	2.0	2.2	3.9	153	14.31			
α Cen*	14	39.6	−60 50	−0.3	0.0	1.3	237	8.29	241	7.53	80
ε Boo*	14	45.0	+27 04	2.5	2.6	4.8	343	2.93			
η CrB*	15	23.2	+30 17	5.1	5.6	6.1	147	0.53	158	0.56	42
κ Her*	16	08.1	+17 03	4.8	5.1	6.2	13	27.01	13	26.99	
α Sco*	16	29.4	−26 26	1.0	1.0	5.4	277	2.65	277	2.65	1 218
λ Oph	16	30.9	+01 59	3.6	4.0	5.0	35	1.45	36	1.45	129
α Her	17	14.6	+14 23	3.3	3.5	5.4	104	4.65	104	4.65	3 600
τ Oph	18	03.1	−8 11	4.8	5.3	5.8	284	1.65	284	1.64	257
70 Oph	18	05.5	+02 30	3.8	4.0	6.0	134	5.42	133	5.58	88
ε Lyr AB*	18	44.3	+39 40	4.7	5.0	6.1	348	2.38	348	2.37	1 804
ε Lyr CD*	18	44.3	+39 40	4.6	5.2	5.5	79	2.36	79	2.37	724
β Cyg*	19	30.7	+27 58	2.9	3.1	5.1	54	34.72			
16 Cyg	19	41.8	+50 32	5.3	6.0	6.2	133	39.67	133	39.68	18 212
δ Cyg	19	45.0	+45 08	2.9	2.9	7.9	221	2.66	220	2.67	780
ε Dra	19	48.2	+70 16	3.9	4.0	6.9	19	3.16			
β Cap	20	21.0	−14 47	2.9	3.0	6.1	267	206.00			
τ Cyg	21	14.8	+38 03	3.7	3.8	6.3	248	0.74	241	0.76	50
μ Cyg	21	44.1	+28 45	4.4	4.7	6.1	315	1.70	316	1.68	789
ζ Aqr*	22	28.8	−0 01	3.7	4.4	4.6	177	2.14	175	2.20	587
δ Cep	22	29.4	+58 25	4.0	4.1	6.3	191	40.61			

*See the preceding note.

VARIABLE STARS

By Arne A. Henden and Elizabeth O. Waagen

Variable stars reveal many stellar properties. Depending upon their type, variables can tell us their mass, radius, temperature, luminosity, internal and external structure, composition, and evolutionary history. In addition, the systematic observation of variable stars is an area in which amateur astronomers can make a valuable contribution to astronomy.

For beginning observers, charts of the fields of four different types of bright variable stars are shown below. On each chart the magnitudes (with decimal point omitted) of several suitable comparison stars are shown. A brightness estimate of the variable is made using two comparison stars, one brighter, one fainter than the variable. The magnitude, date, and time of each observation are recorded. When a number of observations have been made, a graph of magnitude versus date can be plotted. The shape of this "light curve" depends upon the type of variable. Further information about variable star observing is available from the American Association of Variable Star Observers (AAVSO), 25 Birch St, Cambridge MA 02138-1205, USA (email: aavso@aavso.org; Web site: www.aavso.org).

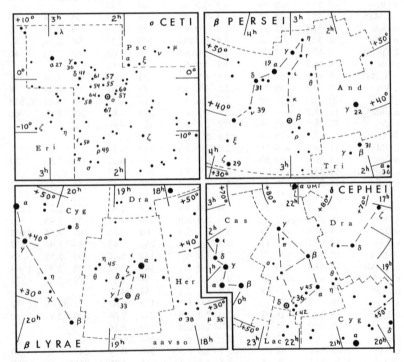

Table 1 (p. 272) is a list of long-period variables, brighter than magnitude 8.0 at maximum and north of −20°. The first column (the Harvard designation of the star) gives the position for the year 1900: the first four characters give the hours and minutes of right ascension, the next three the declination in degrees. The **Max.** column gives the mean maximum magnitude. The **Min.** column gives the mean minimum magnitude. The period **(Per.)** is in days. **Epoch** gives the predicted date of the earliest maximum occurring this year; by adding multiples of the period to this epoch, the dates of subsequent maxima can be found. These variables may reach maximum two or three weeks before or after the epoch and may remain at maximum for several weeks. This table has been prepared with AAVSO observations.

Table 2 overleaf lists stars that are representative of some other types of variables. The data for the preparation of the predicted epoch of maximum for Cepheids are taken from the online edition of the *General Catalogue of Variable Stars,* at www.sai.msu.su/groups/cluster/gcvs/gcvs, the data for eclipsing binaries are from the online edition of *Rocznik Astronomiczny Obserwatorium Krakowskiego 2005,* at ftp://ftp.oa.uj.edu.pl/pub/rocznik/2005, and the data for RR Lyr are based on private communication with N.N. Samus (2005).

DESCRIPTION OF VARIABLE-STAR TYPES

Variable stars can be divided into two main classes: intrinsic variables, in which the variation is due to changes of a single star, and extrinsic variables, in which the variation is due to interaction of multiple stars or objects within a stellar system. There are many cases of overlapping variability types, such as a Mira pulsating variable as part of an eclipsing binary system. Intrinsic variables fall into three main classes: (1) pulsating stars, in which periodic expansion and contraction of the stellar surface occur; (2) eruptive variables, in which solarlike flares occur; and (3) rotating stars, in which shape distortion or star spots cause variation. Extrinsic variables consist of two main classes: (4) binary systems, in which variability is caused by orbital motion or mass transfer, and (5) cataclysmic variables, in which accretion onto a compact object can cause it to go into outburst. With modern detectors, about one percent of all stars are found to be variable. Brief and general descriptions of the major types in each class are given below.

(1) Pulsating Variables

δ *Scuti stars* are variables that have both radial and nonradial pulsation modes with periods from 0.01 to 0.2 days and amplitudes from barely measurable to nearly a full magnitude. They are of A-F spectral types. Typical representative: CY Aquarii.

Cepheids are variables that pulsate with periods of 1 to 70 days. They have high luminosity, and the amplitude of light variation ranges from 0.1 to 2 magnitudes. The prototypes of the group are located in open clusters and obey the well-known period–luminosity relation. They are of late F spectral class at maximum and G to K at minimum. The later (cooler) the spectral class of a Cepheid at minimum, the longer is its period. Typical representative: δ Cephei.

RR Lyrae stars are pulsating, giant variables with periods ranging from 0.2 to 1.2 days and amplitude of light variation between 0.5 and 2 magnitudes. They are usually of A spectral class. Typical representative: RR Lyrae.

RV Tauri stars are supergiant variables with a characteristic light curve of alternating deep and shallow minima. The periods, defined as the interval between two deep minima, range from 30 to 150 days. The amplitude of light variation may be as much as 3 magnitudes. Many show long-term cyclic variation of 500 to 9000 days. Generally, the spectral classes range from F-G at maximum to K-M at minimum light. Typical representative: R Scuti.

Long-period—Mira Ceti variables are giant variables that vary with visual amplitudes from 2.5 to 5 magnitudes or more. They have well-defined periodicity, ranging from 80 to 1000 days. They show characteristic emission spectra of late spectral classes M, C, and S. Typical representative: o Ceti (Mira).

TABLE 1—LONG-PERIOD VARIABLE STARS NORTH OF −20°

Variable		Max. m_v	Min. m_v	Per. d	Epoch 2008	Variable		Max. m_v	Min. m_v	Per. d	Epoch 2008
0017+55	T Cas	7.9	11.9	445	Oct. 27	1425+39	V Boo	7.0	11.3	258	Jun. 4
0018+38	R And	6.9	14.3	409	Jul. 11	1432+27	R Boo	7.2	12.3	223	May 3
0211+43A	W And	7.4	13.7	397	May 31	1517+31	S CrB	7.3	12.9	361	Sep. 26
0214−03	o Cet	3.4	9.3	332	Jan. 23	1546+39	V CrB	7.5	11.0	358	Feb. 26
0228−13	U Cet	7.5	12.6	235	Apr. 13	1546+15	R Ser	6.9	13.4	357	Oct. 20
0231+33	R Tri	6.2	11.7	266	Mar. 31	1606+25	RU Her	8.0	13.7	484	Aug. 23
0430+65	T Cam	8.0	13.8	374	Jun. 26	1621+19	U Her	7.5	12.5	406	Oct. 4
0455−14	R Lep	6.8	9.6	432	Oct. 18	1621−12	V Oph	7.5	10.2	298	May 6
0509+53	R Aur	7.7	13.3	459	Jan. 30	1632+66	R Dra	7.6	12.4	245	Jun. 10
0549+20A	U Ori	6.3	12.0	372	Feb. 11	1647+15	S Her	7.6	12.6	307	Apr. 15
0617−02	V Mon	7.0	13.1	335	Jul. 3	1702−15	R Oph	7.6	13.3	302	Jun. 20
0653+55	R Lyn	7.9	13.8	379	Jun. 11	1717+23	RS Her	7.9	12.5	219	Apr. 28
0701+22A	R Gem	7.1	13.5	370	Dec. 22	1805+31	T Her	8.0	12.8	165	Feb. 21
0703+10	R CMi	8.0	11.0	338	Jan. 8	1811+36	W Lyr	7.9	12.2	196	Apr. 2
0727+08	S CMi	7.5	12.6	332	Feb. 11	1833+08	X Oph	6.8	8.8	334	Jan. 18
0811+12	R Cnc	6.8	11.2	362	Sep. 17	1901+08	R Aql	6.1	11.5	270	Mar. 2
0816+17	V Cnc	7.9	12.8	272	Jul. 6	1910−17	T Sgr	8.0	12.6	392	Jun. 13
0848+03	S Hya	7.8	12.7	257	Mar. 15	1910−19	R Sgr	7.3	12.5	269	Nov. 8
0850−08	T Hya	7.8	12.6	288	Jul. 8	1934+49	R Cyg	7.5	13.9	426	Nov. 21
0939+34	R LMi	7.1	12.6	372	Dec. 29	1940+48	RT Cyg	7.3	11.8	190	Jan. 12
0942+11	R Leo	5.8	10.0	313	Jan. 5	1946+32	χ Cyg	5.2	13.4	407	Nov. 3
1037+69	R UMa	7.5	13.0	302	May 27	2016+47	U Cyg	7.2	10.7	465	Nov. 10
1214−18	R Crv	7.5	13.8	317	Mar. 18	2044−05	T Aqr	7.7	13.1	202	Jul. 9
1220+01	SS Vir	6.8	8.9	355	Jul. 16	2108+68	T Cep	6.0	10.3	390	Dec. 31
1231+60	T UMa	7.7	12.9	257	May 9	2137+53	RU Cyg	8.0	9.4	234	Apr. 17
1233+07	R Vir	6.9	11.5	146	Jan. 7	2301+10	R Peg	7.8	13.2	378	Jan. 10
1239+61	S UMa	7.8	11.7	226	Apr. 16	2307+59	V Cas	7.9	12.2	228	Jul. 12
1315+46	V CVn	6.8	8.8	192	Sep. 27	2315+08	S Peg	8.0	13.0	319	Mar. 3
1327−06	S Vir	7.0	12.7	378	Jan. 30	2338−15	R Aqr	6.5	10.3	387	Dec. 18
1344+40	R CVn	7.7	11.9	328	Oct. 21	2353+50	R Cas	7.0	12.6	431	Dec. 21
1425+84	R Cam	8.3	13.2	270	Feb. 14	2357−15	W Cet	7.6	14.4	351	Jul. 17

TABLE 2—OTHER TYPES OF VARIABLE STARS

Variable		Max. m_v	Min. m_v	Type	Sp. Cl.	Period d	Epoch 2008 UT
0053+81	U Cep	6.7	9.8	Ecl.	B8 + gG2	2.493 0937	Jan. 2.08*
0258+38	ρ Per	3.3	4.0	Semi R	M4	33–55, 1100	
0301+40	β Per	2.1	3.3	Ecl.	B8 + G	2.867 321	†
0355+12	λ Tau	3.5	4.0	Ecl.	B3	3.952 952	Jan. 2.10*
0608+22	η Gem	3.1	3.9	Semi R	M3	233.4	
0619+07	T Mon	5.6	6.6	Cep	F7–K1	27.024 649	Jan. 21.88
0658+20	ζ Gem	3.6	4.2	Cep	F7–G3	10.150 73	Jan. 9.84
1544+28	R CrB	5.8	14.8	R CrB	cFpep		
1710+14	α Her	3.0	4.0	Semi R	M5	50–130, 6 y	
1842–05	R Sct	5.0	7.0	RV Tau	G0e–K0p	144	
1846+33	β Lyr	3.4	4.3	Ecl.	B8	12.940 922	Jan. 12.63*
1922+42	RR Lyr	6.9	8.0	RR Lyr	A2–F1	0.566 885‡	Jan. 1.46
1947+00	η Aql	3.5	4.3	Cep	F6–G4	7.176 641	Jan. 6.71
2225+57	δ Cep	3.5	4.4	Cep	F5–G2	5.366 341	Jan. 1.40
1416+19	T Tau	9.6	10.8	INT	F8Ve–K1IV–Ve(T)		
0530–05	T Ori	9.5	12.3	INA	B8–A3EpV		
0539+09	FU Ori	8.7	9.8	FU	F2peI–II		
0749+22	U Gem	8.6	15.5	UGSS	Pec(UG) + M4.5V		
1946+35	CI Cyg	8.9	12.2	ZAND	Pec Bep + M5III		
2138+43	SS Cyg	8.0	12.5	UGSS	K5V + (Pec)UG		

*Minimum

†Algol; predictions for all minima in 2008 are given in THE SKY MONTH BY MONTH section (pp. 97–119).

‡Changing period (period revised for 2008)

Semiregular variables are giants or supergiants showing appreciable periodicity accompanied by intervals of irregularities of light variation. The periods range from 30 to 1000 days with visual amplitudes not more than 1 to 2 magnitudes in general. Typical representative: R Ursae Minoris.

(2) Eruptive Variables

Eruptive variables are those with flares occurring in their chromospheres, along with shell mass ejections and other stellar wind phenomena. The ejected matter can cause brightness drops as well.

FU Orionis variables are young stars with accompanying cometary nebulae. Usually they have large-amplitude fluctuations that may take years to complete. Typical representative: FU Orionis.

T Tauri variables are young stars that have not yet reached the Zero Age Main Sequence. They are characterized by irregular variations of several magnitudes, often accompanied by emission lines and Algol-like fadings, probably due to dust. Typical representative: T Tauri.

UV Ceti stars are late-type dwarfs that display flare activity. The flares can range from several tenths of a magnitude to many magnitudes in size, lasting a few minutes. Typical representative: UV Ceti.

R Coronae Borealis stars are highly luminous variables that have nonperiodic drops in brightness from 1 to 9 magnitudes due to the formation of "carbon soot" in the star's atmosphere. The duration of minima varies from a few months to years. Members of this group have F to K and R spectral class. Typical representative: R Coronae Borealis.

Irregular variables are stars that at times show only a trace of periodicity or none at all. Often, poorly studied stars are placed in this category. Typical representative: RX Leporis.

(3) Rotating Variables

Rotating variables are stars with nonuniform surface brightness, caused by star spots, mass outflow, or even shape distortion.

Gamma Cassiopeiae variables are rapidly rotating B stars with mass outflow, forming equatorial rings or disks that can cause temporary fading episodes. Typical representative: γ Cassiopeiae.

RS Canum Venaticorum variables are rapidly rotating stars, usually close binary systems that undergo small amplitude changes in light that may be due to dark or bright spots on their surface. Eclipses may also be present in such systems. Typical representative: RS Canum Venaticorum.

(4) Binary Systems

Binary systems are composed of two or more stars or planets around a star, in which the orbital plane is oriented such that one object crosses the disk of another object. These are usually divided into four main classes: detached, semi-detached, contact, and transiting. The first three relate to whether two stars overfill their Roche lobes or are completely isolated from one another.

Detached systems are those in which the two stars are completely isolated from one another. Light curves usually show constant light between eclipses; eclipse depth can be quite large, depending on the relative brightness of the stellar pair. Typical representative: β Persei (Algol).

Semi-detached systems have one member (the donor) overflowing its Roche lobe, with mass accreting onto the second star. Typical representative: U Cephei.

Contact binaries have both members within a common envelope. These stars often exhibit ellipsoidal variations, with the light curves continuously varying throughout the orbit. Typical representative: β Lyrae.

Transiting systems are a new class of binary, in which a planet crosses the disk of the parent star. These variations are quite small (a few hundredths of a magnitude at best), but give a great deal of information about the host star and about the transiting planet. Typical representative: HD 209458.

(5) Cataclysmic Variables

This category contains both explosive and novalike variables. These typically show outbursts caused by thermonuclear runaway on either the star surface or on an accretion disk. They are a product of accretion from one star of a binary system onto the other star, usually a compact object such as a white dwarf or neutron star.

Novae are close binary systems that consist of a normal star and a white dwarf and increase 7 to 16 magnitudes in brightness in one to several hundred days. After the outburst the star fades slowly, returning to initial brightness in several years or decades. Near maximum brightness the spectrum is generally similar to A or F giants. Typical representative: CP Puppis (Nova 1942).

Supernovae increase in brightness by 20 or more magnitudes due to a gigantic stellar explosion. The general appearance of the light curve is similar to novae. Typical representative: CM Tauri (supernova of 1054 AD and the central star of the Crab Nebula).

U Geminorum types are dwarf novae that have long intervals of quiescence at minimum with sudden rises to maximum. Depending upon the star, the amplitude of eruptions ranges from 2 to 6 magnitudes, and the duration between outbursts tens to thousands of days. Most of these stars are spectroscopic binaries with periods of a few hours. Typical representative: SS Cygni.

Z Camelopardalis types are variables similar to U Gem stars in their physical and spectroscopic properties. They show cyclic variations interrupted by intervals of constant brightness ("stillstands") lasting for several cycles, approximately one-third of the way from maximum to minimum. Typical representative: Z Camelopardalis.

SU Ursae Majoris types are dwarf novae similar to U Gem and Z Cam stars in their physical and spectroscopic properties. They have frequent, faint, and narrow eruptions that last from one to a few days, along with infrequent, bright, and long eruptions—"superoutbursts" that last 10 to 20 days. During superoutbursts, there are small-amplitude, periodic variations—"superhumps," 2% to 3% longer than the orbital period of the system. Typical representative: SU Ursae Majoris.

VARIABLE STAR OF THE YEAR—EPSILON AURIGAE
By Arne A. Henden and John R. Percy

Epsilon Aurigae [HR1605, HD31964, A8Ia-F2epIa + (?), V = 2.92–3.83, RA 5h 02 min, Dec +43° 49′ J2000] is a remarkable Algol-type eclipsing binary system. As it contains a supergiant component, it is also classified as a "VV Cephei system." Epsilon Aurigae's variability was discovered by Fritsch, a German pastor, in 1821, with a period and light curve obtained by Schmidt and Argelander during the next eclipse in 1848. It remains an enigma in many ways—especially with regard to the nature of the second component.

The orbital period is 27.1 years, so each eclipse is observed by a new generation of astronomers and instrumentation. The eclipse lasts for two years; it is a leisurely affair. The most recent eclipse, in 1982–84, was the first that could be observed with space telescopes such as *International Ultraviolet Explorer*. It also coincided with the time when photoelectric photometry could be done routinely by amateur astronomers. At third magnitude, it was too bright for the first generation of CCD cameras at professional observatories.

The supergiant component is of interest because it pulsates irregularly on a time scale of tens of days, as many yellow supergiants do. The CHARM optical interferometer gives 2.1 mas as the diameter of the primary component, and astrometry from the *HIPPARCOS* satellite yields a trigonometric distance to the system of 625 pc.

The greatest mystery is the nature of the invisible (to date) secondary component. It is generally agreed that the secondary star (or stars) is not optically visible, partly because it is surrounded by a huge doughnut-shaped disk of dust, seen nearly edge-on. At mid-eclipse, the disk obscures about half the photosphere of the supergiant, dimming it by 0.8 magnitude, but there is a brightening of the system at mid-eclipse, which is what suggests a central hole in the doughnut. The masses of the two components appear to be similar, about 15–20 solar masses, though the masses are still somewhat controversial. No secondary eclipse has ever been detected. The binary separation is about 25 AU.

The supergiant, normally expected to be massive, may have lost much of its mass to the disk and to the secondary star(s). The secondary component could be massive, but not very luminous, if it was actually two stars. [Two stars of a given mass are much less luminous than one star with twice the mass.] Two orbiting stars might also cause a puffing out or "fattening" of the disk, sufficient to eclipse half the photosphere of the primary, and hide the central stars from view.

It is almost time for the next eclipse! First contact is early summer 2009; second contact is in autumn 2009. Mid-eclipse is in August 2010. It is not too early to start observing this star, especially because of the pulsational variability of the supergiant component, never in itself studied thoroughly. The period is about 67 days, with a V-band amplitude of about 0.1 magnitude. A. Arellano Ferro (MNRAS 1985, 216, 571) gives the best study of the pulsational characteristics, highlighting the lack of good photometry, especially outside of eclipse. We need to follow the pulsational behaviour over the upcoming years to see what it is like prior to, during, and after the eclipse.

FIGURE 1 *Light curve of Epsilon Aurigae during the 1982-1984 eclipse. Note that the eclipse lasted for almost two years, and the slight brightening at mid-eclipse. The other variations, during eclipse, are due to the pulsation of the supergiant star. From MacRobert (1985 Sky & Telescope).*

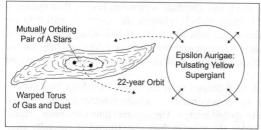

FIGURE 2 *Model of Epsilon Aurigae, based on the light curve above. The "hole" in the torus explains the brightening at mid-eclipse. Jeff Dixon Graphics, after MacRobert (1985).*

Of course, professional astronomers will have an array of new technology to study the 2009–11 eclipse, notably optical interferometers and adaptive-optics systems on large telescopes, which may be able to "image" the system. Because of the intriguing mysteries of this bright system, many professional teams will be formed to monitor the eclipse. But, as always, skilled amateur observers can help, and, in fact, will be essential because bright stars are notoriously difficult to observe with big telescopes.

The AAVSO is running a multi-year campaign starting in the fall of 2007 and will have finding charts, suggested comparison stars, and observing hints available on their Web site. This will be an ideal target for a wide-angle CCD system, or for the new near-infrared photometers that are becoming available. Visual observations are always welcome during the eclipse; see if you can beat that magical 0.1 magnitude error barrier for this bright system!

STAR CLUSTERS
By Anthony Moffat and Peter Jedicke

The study of star clusters is crucial to the understanding of stellar structure and evolution. For most purposes, it can be assumed that the stars in a given cluster formed nearly simultaneously from the same parent cloud of gas and dust. Thus the basic factor that distinguishes one star in a cluster from another is the quantity of matter each contains. When comparing one cluster with another, it is essentially only the age and the chemical composition of their stars that differ. But what makes one cluster *appear* different from another in the sky is mainly the degree of concentration and regularity, the spread in magnitude and colour of the member stars, all of which vary mainly with age, and the total number of stars. Extremely young clusters are often irregular in shape, with clumps of newly formed stars pervaded by lanes of obscuring dust and bright nebulosity (e.g. the Orion Nebula around the Trapezium Cluster). The oldest clusters, which have not yet dissipated and have not been torn apart by external forces, tend to be symmetric in shape, with only the slower-burning, low-mass stars remaining visible; the massive stars will have spent their nuclear fuel and passed to the degenerate graveyard of white dwarfs, neutron stars, or black holes, depending upon their original mass.

The star clusters in the following tables were selected as the most conspicuous. Two types can be recognized: *open* and *globular*. Open clusters often appear as irregular aggregates of tens to thousands of stars, sometimes barely distinguishable from random fluctuations of the general field. Ranging in age from very young to very old, open clusters are concentrated toward the disk of the Milky Way and generally contain stars of chemical abundance like the Sun.

Sometimes we observe loose, extended groups of very young stars. Using precise methods of photometry, spectroscopy, and kinematics, we see that these stars often have a common, but not necessarily strictly coeval, origin. Such loose concentrations of stars are called *associations*. Dynamically, they are generally unbound over time scales of the order of ten million years, being subject to the strong tidal forces of passing clouds and the background Milky Way Galaxy. Often, they contain subconcentrations of young open clusters (e.g. the double cluster h and χ Persei of slightly different ages despite their proximity, in the association Per OB1, which stretches over some 6° of the sky), with a strong gradient in age as the star formation process rips through them from one edge to another. In view of their sparse nature, we do not consider it appropriate here to list any of the 100-plus catalogued Milky Way associations.

Globular clusters, on the other hand, are highly symmetric, extremely old and rich agglomerations of up to several million stars, distributed throughout the galactic halo but concentrated toward the centre of the Milky Way Galaxy. Compared to the Sun and other disk stars, they tend to be much less abundant in elements heavier than hydrogen and helium. For the larger and brighter globular clusters, the observer's goal is to see them well enough to distinguish a generous sprinkling of individual stars against a diffuse glowing background. Large telescope apertures and good skies will help resolve globular clusters. Higher powers are helpful for identification of smaller, more distant globular clusters.

The following table lists all well-defined open clusters in the Milky Way Galaxy with diameters greater than 40' and/or integrated magnitudes brighter than 5.0, as well as the richest clusters and some of special interest. The apparent integrated photographic magnitude (m_{pg}) is from Collinder, the angular diameter (**Diam.**) is generally from Trumpler, and the photographic magnitude of the fifth-brightest star (m_5) is from Shapley, except where in italics, which are new data. The distance (**Dist.**) is mainly from Becker and Fenkart (*Astr. Astrophys. Suppl. 4* (1971), p. 241). The earliest spectral type of cluster stars **(Sp)** is a measure of the age as follows: expressed in millions of years, O5 = 2, B0 = 8, B5 = 70, A0 = 400, A5 = 1000, F0 = 3000, and F5 = 10 000. Complete source lists of open clusters can be found at **obswww.unige.ch/webda**.

OPEN CLUSTERS

NGC/ other†	RA (2000) h m	Dec ° ′	Mag. m_{pg}	Diam. ′	Dist. m_5	10^3 ly	Sp	Remarks
188	0 44.0	+85 21	9.3	14	14.6	5.0	F2	Oldest known
752	1 57.8	+37 41	6.6	45	9.6	1.2	A5	
869	2 19.0	+57 10	4.3	30	9.5	7.0	B1	h Per
884	2 22.4	+57 07	4.4	30	9.5	8.1	B0	χ Per, M supergiants
Perseus	3 22	+48 36	2.3	240	5	0.6	B1	Moving cl.; α Per
Pleiades	3 47.1	+24 08	1.6	120	4.2	0.41	B6	M45, best known
Hyades	4 20	+15 38	0.8	400	3.9	0.15	A2	Moving cl. **, in Taurus
1912	5 28.6	+35 50	7.0	18	9.7	4.6	B5	M38
1976/80	5 35.4	−5 23	2.5	50	5.5	1.3	O5	Trapezium, very young
2099	5 52.4	+32 32	6.2	24	9.7	4.2	B8	M37
2168	6 08.8	+24 21	5.6	29	9.0	2.8	B5	M35
2232	6 26.5	−4 45	4.1	20	7	1.6	B1	
2244	6 32.4	+4 52	5.2	27	8.0	5.3	O5	Rosette, very young
2264	6 41.0	+9 53	4.1	30	8.0	2.4	O8	S Mon
2287	6 47.1	−20 44	5.0	32	8.8	2.2	B4	M41
2362	7 18.8	−24 56	3.8	7	9.4	5.4	O9	τ CMa
2422	7 35.6	−14 30	4.3	30	9.8	1.6	B3	
2437	7 41.8	−14 49	6.6	27	10.8	5.4	B8	M46
2451	7 45.4	−37 58	3.7	37	6	1.0	B5	
2516	7 58.3	−60 54	3.3	50	10.1	1.2	B8	
2546	8 12.5	−37 39	5.0	45	7	2.7	B0	
2632	8 40.1	+20 00	3.9	90	7.5	0.59	A0	Praesepe, M44
IC 2391	8 40.3	−53 03	2.6	45	3.5	0.5	B4	
IC 2395	8 41.0	−48 11	4.6	20	10.1	2.9	B2	
2682	8 50.4	+11 50	7.4	18	10.8	2.7	F2	M67, very old
3114	10 02.6	−60 07	4.5	37	7	2.8	B5	
IC 2602	10 43.3	−64 23	1.6	65	6	0.5	B1	θ Car
Tr 16	10 45.2	−59 42	6.7	10	10	9.6	O3	η Car and Nebula
3532	11 06.4	−58 39	3.4	55	8.1	1.4	B8	
3766	11 36.1	−61 37	4.4	12	8.1	5.8	B1	
Coma	12 25.1	+26 06	2.9	300	5.5	0.3	A1	Very sparse
4755	12 53.6	−60 20	5.2	12	7	6.8	B3	κ Cru, "Jewel Box"
6067	16 13.3	−54 13	6.5	16	10.9	4.7	B3	G, K supergiants
6231	16 54.0	−41 48	3.5	16	7.5	5.8	O9	O supergiants, WR stars
Tr 24	16 57.0	−40 40	3.5	60	7.3	5.2	O5	
6405	17 40.1	−32 13	4.6	26	8.3	1.5	B4	M6
IC 4665	17 46.7	+5 44	5.4	50	7	1.1	B8	
6475	17 53.9	−34 48	3.3	50	7.4	0.8	B5	M7
6494	17 56.9	−19 01	5.9	27	10.2	1.4	B8	M23
6523	18 03.1	−24 23	5.2	45	7	5.1	O5	M8, Lagoon Nebula
6611	18 18.9	−13 47	6.6	8	10.6	5.5	O7	M16, nebula
IC 4725	18 31.7	−19 15	6.2	35	9.3	2.0	B3	M25, Cepheid U Sgr
IC 4756	18 39.3	+5 27	5.4	50	8.5	1.4	A3	
6705	18 51.1	−6 17	6.8	12.5	12	5.6	B8	M11, very rich
Mel 227	20 11.2	−79 19	5.2	60	9	0.8	B9	
IC 1396	21 38.9	+57 30	5.1	60	8.5	2.3	O6	Tr 37
7790	23 58.4	+61 13	7.1	4.5	11.7	10.3	B1	Cepheids CEa, CEb, and CF Cas

† IC = Index Catalogue, Tr = Trumpler, Mel = Melotte ** Basic for distance determination

The table below lists all the globular clusters in the Messier list and most of the globular clusters with a total apparent visual magnitude brighter than about 8.0. A table of Milky Way Galaxy globular cluster data is available on W.E. Harris's Web site: physwww.mcmaster.ca/~harris/WEHarris.html. The apparent diameter (**Diam.**) is from Cragin, Lucyk, and Rappaport (*Deep Sky Field Guide To Uranometria 2000.0*, Willmann-Bell, 1993). The concentration class (**Conc.**) is from I to XII, where I is the most compact and XII the least. The integrated spectral type (**Int. Sp. T.**) varies mainly with the abundances. An observer who can see stars down to the magnitude given in the **V(HB)** ("horizontal-branch" magnitude) column has a good chance of being able to resolve the globular cluster; this information is from Djorgovski and Meylan (*Structure and Dynamics of Globular Clusters*, Astronomical Society of the Pacific, 1993, p. 341).

GLOBULAR CLUSTERS

NGC	M/ other	RA (2000) h m	Dec ° '	Mag. m_v	Diam. '	Conc.	Int. Sp.T.	Dist. 10^3 ly	V(HB)
104	47 Tuc	0 24.0	−72 04	3.95	30.9	III	G4	15	14.06
362		1 03.2	−70 50	6.40	12.9	III	F9	28	15.40
1851		5 14.0	−40 02	7.14	11.0	II	F7	46	16.10
1904	79	5 24.1	−24 31	7.73	8.7	V	F5	42	16.20
2808		9 11.9	−64 51	6.20	13.8	I	F7	30	16.19
3201		10 17.6	−46 24	6.75	18.2	X	F6	17	14.75
4590	68	12 39.5	−26 44	7.84	12.0	X	F2	33	15.60
4833		12 59.5	−70 52	6.91	13.5	VIII	F3	20	15.45
5024	53	13 12.9	+18 10	7.61	12.6	V	F6	60	16.94
5139	ω Cen	13 26.8	−47 28	3.68	36.3	VIII	F5	17	14.52
5272	3	13 42.2	+28 22	6.19	16.2	VI	F6	35	15.65
5904	5	15 18.5	+2 04	5.65	17.4	V	F7	26	15.11
6093	80	16 17.0	−22 58	7.33	8.9	II	F6	33	15.86
6121	4	16 23.6	−26 31	5.63	26.3	IX	F8	14	13.35
6171	107	16 32.5	−13 03	7.93	10.0	X	G0	21	15.70
6205	13	16 41.7	+36 27	5.78	16.6	V	F6	21	14.95
6218	12	16 47.1	−1 56	6.70	14.5	IX	F8	24	14.90
6254	10	16 57.1	−4 05	6.60	15.1	VII	F3	20	14.65
6266	62	17 01.2	−30 06	6.45	14.1	IV	F9	22	15.90
6273	19	17 02.6	−26 16	6.77	13.5	VIII	F7	28	16.95
6333	9	17 19.2	−18 30	7.72	9.3	VIII	F5	27	16.10
6341	92	17 17.1	+43 08	6.44	11.2	IV	F2	26	15.05
6388		17 36.3	−44 44	6.72	8.7	III	G2	37	16.90
6397		17 40.7	−53 40	5.73	25.7	IX	F4	9	12.90
6402	14	17 37.6	−3 14	7.59	11.7	VIII	F4	29	17.50
6541		18 08.0	−43 42	6.30	13.1	III	F6	13	15.10
6626	28	18 24.5	−24 52	6.79	11.2	IV	F8	19	15.68
6637	69	18 31.4	−32 20	7.64	7.1	V	G2	28	16.20
6656	22	18 36.3	−23 54	5.10	24.0	VII	F5	10	14.15
6681	70	18 43.2	−32 17	7.87	7.8	V	F5	29	15.60
6715	54	18 55.0	−30 28	7.60	9.1	III	F7	89	17.71
6752		19 10.9	−59 58	5.40	20.4	VI	F4	17	13.85
6779	56	19 16.6	+30 11	8.27	7.1	X	F5	33	16.20
6809	55	19 40.1	−30 57	6.32	19.0	XI	F4	20	14.35
6838	71	19 53.8	+18 46	8.19	7.2	†	G1	13	14.44
6864	75	20 06.0	−21 55	8.52	6.0	I	F9	61	17.45
6981	72	20 53.5	−12 32	9.27	5.9	IX	F7	55	16.99
7078	15	21 30.1	+12 10	6.20	12.3	IV	F3	34	15.86
7089	2	21 33.5	−0 50	6.47	12.9	II	F4	40	16.05
7099	30	21 40.4	−23 10	7.19	11.0	V	F3	26	15.10

† Originally thought to be an open cluster; never assigned a concentration class

AN EXAMPLE: NGC 3603
A SOUTHERN GALACTIC OPEN CLUSTER THAT CONTAINS THE MOST MASSIVE STAR EVER WEIGHED IN A BINARY

Although far to the south, introducing such an exciting cluster as NGC 3603 may draw attention from northerners on their travels below the equator or on their Web-surfing rides. Southerners may be aware of it already, given the extreme richness of the Southern Milky Way. NGC 3603 is a very dense, young (about one million years old) open cluster, slightly surpassing even the famous central fuzzball cluster R136 at the heart of the Tarantula Nebula, which houses 30 Dor in the Large Magellanic Cloud. NGC 3603 and R136 are essentially clones of each other. But at "only" 20 000 light-years distance in Carina, NGC 3603 is seven times closer than R136 and thus essentially 49 times (i.e. 7 squared) easier to resolve on the sky. This explains why in pre-*Hubble* times, R136 was mistakenly labelled as the most luminous and massive single star known—a superstar with 3000 solar masses!

At RA 11h 15.1 min, Dec −61.3 (2000), NGC 3603 is a little further down the Carina Arm from the famous Carina Nebula, which contains the exotic Eta Carinae, a highly unstable luminous blue variable that some believe may be on the verge of a supernova. NGC 3603 contains some 50 O-type stars, all in a region a couple of light-years across, some of which are among the hottest and most luminous O-stars known, ranging up to type O2. In addition, NGC 3603 also contains three Wolf-Rayet stars (A1, B, and C in the figure) that are on average almost a full magnitude brighter than the brightest O stars in NGC 3603. These are not ordinary "classical" WR stars in the helium-burning phase of a massive star. Rather, they contain hydrogen at near-solar abundance, so they are actually believed to be H-burning main-sequence stars, with WR-like emission lines in their spectra as a result of the winds made by their extremely high and UV-intense luminosities. This being the case, their extreme brightness then suggests that they must be very massive. Indeed, recent studies by one of the authors (AM) and his collaborators, has shown that star A1 is a 3.77-day eclipsing binary, whose orbit reveals stars of 114 and 84 solar masses, the former being the most massive star so far weighed in a binary.

Multicolour HST image of NGC 3603 (W. Brandner, A.K. Grebel, Y.-H. Chu, and NASA) with insert showing a zoom of the central core with the three known WR stars marked.

AMATEUR SUPERNOVA HUNTING
By Rev. Robert Evans

The first discovery of a supernova by an amateur astronomer was by G. Romano of Italy (SN 1957B in NGC 4564); this discovery was photographic. The first visual discovery was by J. Bennett of South Africa (SN 1968L in M83). In Australia in 1980, the author began systematic visual searching using a simple 250-mm backyard telescope and made two discoveries the following year. K. Okazaki of Japan, who discovered two supernovae, one each in 1983 and 1984, was one of several Japanese amateurs to mount systematic photographic searches at that time.

By the late 1980s, most of the supernovae brighter than 15th magnitude were being found visually by amateurs. In the early 1990s, professional astronomers started using supernova studies to address major problems in cosmology; at that time, they depended largely upon amateur searches to provide them with the best and brightest supernovae in nearby galaxies. These nearby supernovae provided much of the benchmark information needed for studying supernovae at remote distances, which led to independent estimates for the expansion, age, and fate of the universe.

CCD Supernova Hunting

In the last few years, the cost of charge-coupled devices (CCDs) has fallen to the point where many amateurs can afford to use them on computer-controlled telescopes. Some of these amateurs are hunting supernovae with resounding success. There are a number of advantages to using telescopes with CCDs and computer control:

(1) You can observe in locations with some light pollution or in the presence of fairly strong moonlight.

(2) With a computer to direct the telescope to individual galaxies, it is no longer necessary to know the sky well.

(3) With appropriate computer control of the telescope, you can sit in a warm room facing the computer screen.

(4) If your equipment is good enough, it will find supernovae without your presence.

(5) Stars as faint as 18th or 19th magnitude become accessible, which includes most supernovae in nearby galaxies plus the brighter supernovae in many distant galaxies, out to about 300 million light-years.

Using a CCD brings so many thousands of galaxies within range that you will never have enough time to observe them all! However, you will need reference materials for all the galaxies on your observing list—even if you make the reference images yourself—so that you can tell when a new object appears near a galaxy.

Visual Supernova Hunting

Visual supernova hunting has a number of advantages over using a CCD:

(1) The equipment is less expensive than that needed for CCD work.

(2) An experienced visual observer usually knows the location and the normal appearance of many target galaxies and can thus work through observations of galaxies at 10 times the speed of anyone using a CCD on an amateur telescope. Professional-standard CCDs are quicker but are still much more expensive than those used by amateurs.

(3) You become very familiar with the night sky. (Personally, I think this is a great benefit of visual searching.)

(4) Amateurs who rely on computers to find galaxies are deceived by technology into being ignorant of the sky. Thus, when the technology fails (as it does from time

to time), the search halts, since the observer does not know where to locate target galaxies. A visual observer who knows the sky is immune to this problem.

There are, however, special requirements:

(1) A reasonably dark observing site is needed.

(2) Your telescope needs to be easily manageable so that you can locate objects quickly, and the aperture needs to be big enough so that you can see down to about 15th magnitude. You can then observe all the nearby galaxies (out to, say, 100 million light-years). You will then be able to see most supernovae in galaxies out to about 25 million light-years and the brighter supernovae out to 100 million light-years or more. But, naturally, your chances of success decrease with the distance of the galaxy. Fainter supernovae in any given galaxy may be more numerous than the brighter ones, although the latter are the most interesting, scientifically.

(3) As in CCD searches, charts or suitable photographs of all your target galaxies are needed, so that you can tell when a new object appears.

Verification and Reporting

Verification of any suspected new discovery is vitally important. The first step is to check any suspect against all available photographs, CCD images, or charts of that galaxy. Measure carefully the offset of the new star from the nucleus of the galaxy. Watch the object for any possible movement against nearby stars. Note the time of your discovery (UT). It is necessary to have a team of other observers who can make independent observations of the new object, and who will do so immediately, if asked. These other observers must also have enough galaxy resources so that they can eliminate anything that is not a supernova, and they should be spread out over a number of locations in case bad weather puts any one observer out of action.

The Central Bureau for Astronomical Telegrams has issued instructions describing how much verification is needed about any possible new supernova, and these should be consulted (see **www.cfa.harvard.edu/iau/cbat.html**). CCD observers need at least five observations covering 24 hours. A visual observer should have independent observations by people who know what they are doing. And even after the Central Bureau has been notified, spectra will probably need to be obtained through one of the main observatories before the Bureau will finally announce a discovery.

When notifying the Central Bureau, provide full details of all observations of the new object: the name and location of the person making the report, the discoverer's name and location, details of the reference materials consulted, details concerning the equipment used, universal time of all observations, name and position of the galaxy, offset and brightness of the supernova, and similar details about each verifying observation. Observers who are not already known at the Bureau should be especially thorough in detailing and supporting their report. All discoveries can be emailed to the Central Bureau at **cbat@cfa.harvard.edu**.

Much helpful advice is available in the *AAVSO Supernova Search Manual,* which is available from the AAVSO, 49 Bay State Road, Cambridge MA 02138, USA, for the cost of postage only. It can also be viewed at **www.aavso.org/observing/programs/sn/supernovasm.shtml**.

Editor's Note: Robert Evans, who made his first supernova discovery in 1981, holds the record for visual discoveries of supernovae: 40. Ten of these were found using a 250-mm telescope, 8 using a 310-mm telescope, 19 with a 410-mm instrument (all "backyard" variety Newtonians), and 3 using the 1.02-m telescope at Siding Spring Observatory (Australian National University). In addition, he has discovered 4 supernovae (plus a comet) on U.K. Schmidt films taken as part of a special supernova search, all in 1996, and one on a European Southern Observatory Red Survey Schmidt film.

EXPIRED STARS
BY ROY BISHOP

Stars are where the action is, and the action is fuelled by gravitation and thermonuclear fusion. Gravitation, the midwife and undertaker, forms a star, heats it to the temperatures necessary to ignite successive stages of fusion reactions, and when nuclear fuel runs out, crushes the ashes of the star into one of three final states: white dwarf, neutron star, or black hole. Thermonuclear fusion, powered by the strong binding energy of protons and neutrons, merely delays the onset of further collapse and higher temperatures. In the case of our Sun, the first and by far the longest delay, the "hang-up" provided by hydrogen-to-helium fusion, is already half over.

White Dwarfs

Stars comparable to our Sun have insufficient gravity to reach the temperatures necessary to form nuclei heavier than carbon or oxygen. When the thermal support pressure generated by fusion wanes, gravity gradually crushes the central portion of the star. If the mass of this core is less than 1.4 solar masses (a limit discovered by a leading astrophysicist of the 20th century, Subramanyan Chandrasekhar), the collapse halts at a very hot, Earth-sized remnant known as a white dwarf. At this point, the squeeze of gravity is offset by *electron degeneracy pressure,* an intrinsic aspect of the wave–particle nature of matter and the same pressure responsible for the stability and size of an atom. However, in the case of a white dwarf, the pressure is such that the electrons are not tied to individual atomic nuclei but occupy the whole star. In this sense, the star has become a giant atom. In physics jargon: electrons are fermions (i.e. they obey Fermi–Dirac quantum statistics) and hence abide by the Pauli Exclusion Principle, which dictates that no two electrons can occupy the same quantum state. This results in an immense pressure, sufficient to prevent further collapse, provided the mass is less than the Chandrasekhar limit. White dwarf diameters are about 1% that of our Sun, which has a nearly water-like average density (1 g/cm^3). Thus a cubic centimetre of white dwarf material has a mass near 100^3 g or one tonne (like a Toyota Echo crushed into a sugar cube).

Because of their immense thermal energy and small surface area, white dwarfs cool extremely slowly. The universe is not yet old enough for any white dwarf to have cooled sufficiently to become a "black dwarf." Also, white dwarfs are intrinsically very faint; thus only those close to the solar system can be seen.

Only one white dwarf is easily observable with a small telescope: **Omicron 2 Eridani B** (also designated 40 Eridani B), located 16.5 light-years from Earth. Omicron 2 Eridani A, the bright (mag. 4.4) companion to the dim (mag. 9.5) white dwarf, is shown on the JANUARY ALL-SKY CHART on p. 310: o^2 Eri A is the eastern (left-hand) member of the close pair of stars located due west of the word "Rigel." Omicron 2 Eridani B, the white dwarf, is located only 83″ east-southeast of o^2 Eri A (position angle ≈110°). Remarkably, stars A and B are accompanied by a third star, a faint (mag. 11.2) red dwarf star, o^2 Eri C, which resides only 9″ north of B. (There is a brighter and closer white dwarf, the companion of Sirius, α CMa B, but it is usually lost in the glare of Sirius. See THE NEAREST STARS (pp. 262–266) and DOUBLE AND MULTIPLE STARS (pp. 267–269) for more information on both of these stellar systems.)

For the observer with a small telescope, o^2 Eri B is the only Earth-sized object visible in the depths of interstellar space, the only visible object with a mass density far exceeding that of ordinary matter, the only accessible star no longer powered by nuclear reactions, and the only star that has expired and can still be seen.

Neutron Stars

For a large star of about eight or more solar masses, energy-releasing reactions end in its centre with the fusion of silicon nuclei into iron. Iron has the most tightly bound nucleus (per nuclear particle) and hence is no good as a fuel for further fusion. Electron degeneracy pressure supports the inert iron core until silicon fusion in a surrounding shell supplies enough additional iron to push the inert core over the Chandrasekhar limit. Gravity then overwhelms electron degeneracy pressure, and the core collapses in less than a second, so quickly that, momentarily, the outer layers of the star stay where they were. Gravitation-induced temperatures in the core rise past 10^{10} K, sufficient to disassemble heavy nuclei synthesized over the life of the star. This absorbs energy, accelerating the collapse. Also, electrons attain sufficient energy to combine with protons to form neutrons and neutrinos, another energy-absorbing reaction that also removes electrons, further hastening the collapse.

Provided the infalling mass is less than about three solar masses, like a hammer striking an anvil, when the core reaches a diameter of about 20 km the infall is violently arrested by a combination of *neutron* degeneracy pressure and the short-range repulsive nature of the strong nuclear force, the same agents that govern the size and structure of the nuclei of atoms of ordinary matter. With a diameter 500 times smaller than that of a white dwarf, the density at this stage is 500^3 larger, 100 million tonnes per cubic centimetre (like an aircraft carrier crushed to the size of the ball of a ballpoint pen). That is the density of ordinary atomic nuclei. The star's core has effectively become a gigantic nucleus, composed primarily of neutrons.

The abrupt rebound of the nearly rigid central core reverses the infall of the adjacent layers, turning the implosion into a spectacular explosion, a Type II supernova. The explosion mechanism is complex and not yet well understood, but appears to involve interactions with the immense numbers of neutrinos generated in the neutron production, and possibly acoustic waves generated by vibrations of the core as it is pummeled by infalling material within a second of its formation. The gravitational energy released in the sudden collapse of the couple of solar masses now locked in the central neutron star is about 10^{46} J. This is far more energy than our Sun will produce in its entire 10-billion-year lifetime.

Over the next several thousand years, the remnants of the outer layers of the star form an expanding, glowing cloud of gas and dust, seeding interstellar space with the heavy chemical elements (oxygen, silicon, iron, uranium, etc.) synthesized in its outer layers both before and during the supernova explosion. The potassium ions moving in the neurons of your brain as you read these words emerged from such a conflagration some 5 billion years ago.

No neutron stars are visible in a small telescope, although one is *indirectly* visible in the **Crab Nebula**, M1. The Crab supernova was a bright, naked-eye star in the skies of Earth in the year 1054 AD, although it had taken 6000 years for the light of the explosion to reach our planet. The nebula we see today is the expanding debris cloud as it was nearly 1000 years after the initial explosion.

The Crab Nebula glows across the electromagnetic spectrum, from radio waves to gamma rays, powered by the rapid but decreasing spin of the neutron star at its centre. The glow of the debris cloud is like the glow of a red-hot disk brake slowing the spin of a wheel. The visible light from the cloud is *synchrotron radiation* emitted by electrons as they spiral in the tangled magnetic field of the neutron star. Nowhere else in the heavens is such an exotic light visible in a small telescope, polarized light with the brilliance of a thousand suns, emitted not by atoms but by free electrons being flung about by a spinning neutron star. The neutron star itself is known as a *pulsar* because it flashes 30 times per second, in step with its spin. However, even if the Crab pulsar were bright enough to be visible in a small telescope, the flashing would not be apparent because, as in a motion picture or cathode-ray tube monitor, the flicker is too rapid for the eye to follow.

Colour photographs of the Crab Nebula reveal a celestial gift: a package of bluish synchrotron radiation wrapped in the loops of a tattered red ribbon—fragments of the shattered star, fluorescing in hydrogen-alpha light. Unfortunately, the luminance of the fluorescence is below the threshold for vision in the red part of the spectrum. Thus all we can see is the ghostly cloud of synchrotron radiation.

The Crab Nebula is located 1° northwest of the star ζ Tau, at the tip of the east horn of Taurus. In the JANUARY ALL-SKY CHART on p. 310, the nebula is the tiny circle of dots 5 mm to the right of the cross marking the summer solstice (SS). In a telescope the nebula appears merely as a small glowing cloud, but to the knowledgeable observer, this synchrotron radiation brake of a spinning neutron star is an object for profound contemplation.

Black Holes

Stars whose masses are greater than about 20 solar masses likely retain more than 3 solar masses in their imploding cores. This is sufficient that gravitation will overwhelm not only the degeneracy pressure of electrons, but also the highly incompressible nature of nuclear matter. Within seconds spacetime itself closes around the imploding stellar core, removing all but the core's gravitational field from the observable universe. The star has become a black hole.

The earliest and best candidate for a stellar black hole is **Cygnus X-1,** one of the strongest galactic X-ray sources in the sky. Cygnus X-1 is the invisible companion of a star that can be seen in a small telescope: HDE 226868, an O9.7Iab star, a very luminous, very hot supergiant located several thousand light-years from the Sun. It orbits its nearby, unseen companion with a 5.6-day period. The mass of the companion is between 10 and 16 solar masses, far too large for it to be a white dwarf or neutron star. X-rays are generated as material from the supergiant falls toward the invisible companion. The X-rays extend to energies of 100 keV and vary on time scales as short as milliseconds, indicative of a very compact companion.

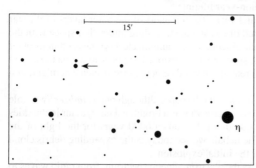

At 9th magnitude, the supergiant HDE 226868 is visible in any small telescope. It is less than half a degree from the 4th-magnitude star η Cygni, which is the star in the neck of the swan, next to the "C" in CYGNUS on the SEPTEMBER ALL-SKY CHART on p. 314. Any low magnification will more than encompass the field shown in the **finder chart** at the left.

North is upward, η Cygni is at the lower right, and HDE 226868 is indicated by the small arrow. The chart magnitude limit is about 13. Although HDE 226868 is a blue supergiant, in telescopes of sufficient aperture this star appears orange because of interstellar dust between us and the star.

All that is to be seen is the hot supergiant, but the view will be worth the search if you know that at this same location in the field of your telescope lurks one of the most likely candidates for a black hole, a knot in the fabric of spacetime where a giant star has vanished. No painting, computer simulation, or Hollywood movie can match this observation.

NEBULAE AND GALAXIES

GALACTIC NEBULAE
BY WILLIAM HERBST

The following objects were selected from the brightest and largest of the various classes to illustrate the different types of interactions between stars and interstellar matter in our galaxy. *Emission regions* (HII) are excited by the strong ultraviolet flux of young, hot stars and are characterized by the lines of hydrogen in their spectra. *Reflection nebulae* (Ref) result from the diffusion of starlight by clouds of interstellar dust. At certain stages of their evolution stars become unstable and explode, shedding their outer layers into what becomes a *planetary nebula* (Pl) or a *supernova remnant* (SN). *Protostellar nebulae* (PrS) are objects still poorly understood; they are somewhat similar to the reflection nebulae, but their associated stars, often variable, are very luminous infrared stars that may be in the earliest stages of stellar evolution. Also included in the selection are three *extended complexes* (Comp) of special interest for their rich population of dark and bright nebulosities of various types. In the table S is the optical surface brightness in magnitude per square second of arc of representative regions of the nebula, and m^* is the magnitude of the associated star.

NGC	M	Con	RA (2000) h m	Dec ° '	Type	Size '	S mag/sq″	m^*	Dist. 10^3 ly	Remarks
1435		Tau	3 47.5	+24 05	Ref	15	20	4	0.4	Merope nebula
1535		Eri	4 14.2	−12 45	Pl	0.5	17	12		
1952	1	Tau	5 34.5	+22 01	SN	5	19	16v	4	"Crab" + pulsar
1976	42	Ori	5 35.3	−5 24	HII	30	18	4	1.5	Orion Nebula
2070		Dor	5 38.6	−69 05	HII	20	—	13	200	Tarantula Nebula
ζ Ori		Ori	5 40.8	−1 56	Comp	2°			1.5	Incl. "Horsehead"
2068	78	Ori	5 46.8	+0 02	Ref	5	20		1.5	
IC 443		Gem	6 17.6	+22 36	SN	40			2	
2244		Mon	6 32.4	+4 52	HII	50	21	7	3	Rosette Nebula
2261		Mon	6 39.1	+8 43	PrS	2		12v	4	Hubble's Variable Neb.
2392		Gem	7 29.2	+20 54	Pl	0.3	18	10	10	Clown Face Nebula
2626		Vel	8 35.6	−40 38	Ref	2	—	10	3	
3132		Vel	10 07.0	−40 25	Pl	1	17	10	—	Eight-Burst
3324		Car	10 37.5	−58 38	HII	15	—	8	9	
3372		Car	10 45.1	−59 41	HII	80	—	6v	9	Carina Nebula
3503		Car	11 01.3	−60 43	Ref	3	—	11	9	
3587	97	UMa	11 14.8	+55 01	Pl	3	21	13	12	Owl Nebula
—		Cru	12 51	−63	Dark	6°	—	—	0.5	Coal Sack
5189		Mus	13 33.5	−65 58	Pl	2.6	—	10	—	
ρ Oph		Oph	16 25.6	−23 27	Comp	4°			0.5	Bright + dark nebula
6514	20	Sgr	18 02.4	−23 02	HII	15	19		3.5	Trifid Nebula
6523	8	Sgr	18 03.6	−24 23	HII	40	18		4.5	Lagoon Nebula
6543		Dra	17 58.6	+66 37	Pl	0.4	15	11	3.5	
6618	17	Sgr	18 20.9	−16 11	HII	20	19		3	Horseshoe Nebula
6720	57	Lyr	18 53.6	+33 03	Pl	1.2	18	15	5	Ring Nebula
6726		CrA	19 01.7	−36 54	PrS	5	—	7	0.5	
6853	27	Vul	19 59.5	+22 43	Pl	7	19	13	3.5	Dumbbell Nebula
6888		Cyg	20 12.3	+38 25	HII	15				
γ Cyg		Cyg	20 22.2	+40 16	Comp	6°				HII + dark nebula
6960/95		Cyg	20 45.6	+30 42	SN	150			2.5	Cygnus loop
7000		Cyg	20 58.9	+44 19	HII	100	22		3.5	North America Nebula
7009		Aqr	21 04.1	−11 23	Pl	0.5	16	12	3	Saturn Nebula
7027		Cyg	21 07.1	+42 14	Pl	0.2	15	13		
7129		Cep	21 43.0	+65 06	Ref	3	21	10	2.5	Small cluster
7293		Aqr	22 29.6	−20 48	Pl	13	22	13		Helix Nebula

THE MESSIER CATALOGUE
By Alan Dyer

Charles Messier's Catalogue provides a selection of the best and brightest deep-sky wonders for Northern Hemisphere viewers. Messier compiled his list in the late 1700s to aid prospective comet hunters. Some of these objects he discovered himself, some were first seen by other astronomers of the day, while a few (the Pleiades and the Beehive) were known since antiquity. The Messier numbers do not follow an ordered sequence across the sky. Rather, they are numbered in the order he discovered and catalogued them. Although he intended to, Messier never did publish a list with entries renumbered in order of right ascension.

In our version of the Messier Catalogue, we've listed the objects by season *for the evening observer,* grouping the objects within their respective constellations. The constellations are then listed roughly in order of increasing right ascension, that is constellations farther to the east and which rise later in the night are farther down the list. This is to help plan the sequence of an evening's Messier hunt.

The identity of some Messier objects is controversial. There is evidence that M91 and M102 are mistaken observations of M58 and M101, respectively. M104 and M109 were found by a colleague, Pierre Mechain, and reported to Messier for inclusion in his Catalogue. NGC 205, one of the companion galaxies to M31, the Andromeda Galaxy, was apparently found by Messier but never included in his Catalogue. Modern-day observers have dubbed this object M110. In our list, we have included 110 entries, including two objects that some have suggested as alternative candidates for M91 and M102.

Modern-day Messier hunters often wonder what telescopes Messier used. The largest were 190-mm and 200-mm reflectors. However, their speculum metal mirrors would have had the equivalent light-gathering power of a modern 80-mm to 100-mm reflector. He also used a number of 90-mm refractors. Today, a dark site and a good 80-mm refractor or 100-mm reflector should be sufficient for completing the entire list. Objects M6 and M7 are the most southerly, while M74 and M76 are often considered the faintest and most difficult. M83's low altitude and diffuse appearance make it a challenge for Canadian observers north of 50° latitude.

The columns contain the Messier number, the object's NGC (New General Catalogue) number, the constellation, the type of object, its equinox J2000.0 coordinates, visual magnitude m_v, and angular size in minutes of arc (planetary nebula sizes are given in seconds of arc ($''$)). Entries marked "**!!**" are showpiece objects. OC = open cluster; GC = globular cluster; PN = planetary nebula; EN = emission nebula; RN = reflection nebula; E/RN = combination of emission and reflection nebula; SNR = supernova remnant; G = galaxy (E = elliptical, I = irregular, SA = normal spiral, SB = barred spiral, S0 = lenticular). Data are taken from *The Deep Sky Field Guide to Uranometria 2000.0* (published by Willmann-Bell, Inc., 1993), compiled by Murray Cragin, James Lucyk, and Barry Rappaport from a variety of contemporary catalogues. Some sizes have been rounded to two significant figures. Also recommended as an excellent guide is *The Messier Objects,* by Stephen James O'Meara (Cambridge University Press, 1998).

> *The RASC offers observing certificates for members who observe the 110 objects in the Messier list or the 110 objects in the Finest NGC list (see pp. 290–292). For beginners or observers using binoculars the Society also offers the "Explore the Universe" Certificate. Contact your local Centre or the RASC National Office (see p. 10) for details.*

NUMERICAL LISTING OF MESSIER OBJECTS

M#	Sky	Con	M#	Sky	Con	M#	Sky	Con	M#	Sky	Con	M#	Sky	Con
1	Win	Tau	23	Sum	Sgr	45	Win	Tau	67	Spr	Cnc	89	Spr	Vir
2	Aut	Aqr	24	Sum	Sgr	46	Win	Pup	68	Spr	Hya	90	Spr	Vir
3	Spr	CVn	25	Sum	Sgr	47	Win	Pup	69	Sum	Sgr	91	Spr	Com
4	Sum	Sco	26	Sum	Sct	48	Win	Hya	70	Sum	Sgr	92	Sum	Her
5	Spr	Ser	27	Sum	Vul	49	Spr	Vir	71	Sum	Sge	93	Win	Pup
6	Sum	Sco	28	Sum	Sgr	50	Win	Mon	72	Aut	Aqr	94	Spr	CVn
7	Sum	Sco	29	Sum	Cyg	51	Spr	CVn	73	Aut	Aqr	95	Spr	Leo
8	Sum	Sgr	30	Aut	Cap	52	Aut	Cas	74	Aut	Psc	96	Spr	Leo
9	Sum	Oph	31	Aut	And	53	Spr	Com	75	Sum	Sgr	97	Spr	UMa
10	Sum	Oph	32	Aut	And	54	Sum	Sgr	76	Aut	Per	98	Spr	Com
11	Sum	Sct	33	Aut	Tri	55	Sum	Sgr	77	Aut	Cet	99	Spr	Com
12	Sum	Oph	34	Aut	Per	56	Sum	Lyr	78	Win	Ori	100	Spr	Com
13	Sum	Her	35	Win	Gem	57	Sum	Lyr	79	Win	Lep	101	Spr	UMa
14	Sum	Oph	36	Win	Aur	58	Spr	Vir	80	Sum	Sco	102	Spr	Dra?
15	Aut	Peg	37	Win	Aur	59	Spr	Vir	81	Spr	UMa	103	Aut	Cas
16	Sum	Ser	38	Win	Aur	60	Spr	Vir	82	Spr	UMa	104	Spr	Vir
17	Sum	Sgr	39	Sum	Cyg	61	Spr	Vir	83	Spr	Hya	105	Spr	Leo
18	Sum	Sgr	40	Spr	UMa	62	Sum	Oph	84	Spr	Vir	106	Spr	CVn
19	Sum	Oph	41	Win	CMa	63	Spr	CVn	85	Spr	Com	107	Sum	Oph
20	Sum	Sgr	42	Win	Ori	64	Spr	Com	86	Spr	Vir	108	Spr	UMa
21	Sum	Sgr	43	Win	Ori	65	Spr	Leo	87	Spr	Vir	109	Spr	UMa
22	Sum	Sgr	44	Spr	Cnc	66	Spr	Leo	88	Spr	Com	110	Aut	And

SEASONAL LISTING OF MESSIER OBJECTS

M#	NGC	Con	Type	RA (2000) Dec h m ° ′	m_v	Size ′	Remarks
The Winter Sky							
1	1952	Tau	SNR	5 34.5 +22 01	8.4	6 × 4	!! famous Crab Neb. supernova remnant
45	—	Tau	OC	3 47.0 +24 07	1.2	110	!! Pleiades; look for subtle nebulosity
36	1960	Aur	OC	5 36.1 +34 08	6.0	12	bright but scattered group; use low pow.
37	2099	Aur	OC	5 52.4 +32 33	5.6	20	!! finest of 3 Auriga clusters; very rich
38	1912	Aur	OC	5 28.7 +35 50	6.4	21	look for small cluster NGC 1907 0.5° S
42	1976	Ori	E/RN	5 35.4 −5 27	—	65 × 60	!! Orion Nebula; finest in northern sky
43	1982	Ori	E/RN	5 35.6 −5 16	—	20 × 15	detached part of Orion Nebula
78	2068	Ori	RN	5 46.7 +0 03	—	8 × 6	bright featureless reflection nebula
79	1904	Lep	GC	5 24.5 −24 33	7.8	8.7	200-mm telescope needed to resolve
35	2168	Gem	OC	6 08.9 +24 20	5.1	28	!! look for sm. cluster NGC 2158 0.25° S
41	2287	CMa	OC	6 47.0 −20 44	4.5	38	4° south of Sirius; bright but coarse
50	2323	Mon	OC	7 03.2 −8 20	5.9	16	between Sirius & Procyon; use low mag.
46	2437	Pup	OC	7 41.8 −14 49	6.1	27	!! contains planetary nebula NGC 2438
47	2422	Pup	OC	7 36.6 −14 30	4.4	29	coarse cluster 1.5° west of M46
93	2447	Pup	OC	7 44.6 −23 52	≈6.2	22	compact, bright cluster; fairly rich
48	2548	Hya	OC	8 13.8 −5 48	5.8	54	former "lost" Messier; large, sparse cl.

SEASONAL LISTING OF MESSIER OBJECTS (continued)

M#	NGC	Con	Type	RA (2000) h m	Dec ° '	m_v	Size '	Remarks
The Spring Sky								
44	2632	Cnc	OC	8 40.1	+19 59	3.1	95	!! Beehive or Praesepe; use low power
67	2682	Cnc	OC	8 50.4	+11 49	6.9	29	one of the oldest star clusters known
40	—	UMa	2 stars	12 22.4	+58 05	8.0	—	double star Winnecke 4; separation 50″
81	3031	UMa	G-SAab	9 55.6	+69 04	6.9	24 × 13	!! bright spiral visible in binoculars
82	3034	UMa	G-I0	9 55.8	+69 41	8.4	12 × 6	!! the "exploding" galaxy; M81 0.5° S
97	3587	UMa	PN	11 14.8	+55 01	9.9	194″	!! Owl Nebula; distinct grey oval
101	5457	UMa	G-SABcd	14 03.2	+54 21	7.9	26 × 26	!! Pinwheel Gal.; diffuse face-on spiral
108	3556	UMa	G-SBcd	11 11.5	+55 40	10.0	8.1 × 2.1	nearly edge-on; paired with M97 0.75° SE
109	3992	UMa	G-SBbc	11 57.6	+53 23	9.8	7.6 × 4.3	barred spiral near γ UMa
65	3623	Leo	G-SABa	11 18.9	+13 05	9.3	8.7 × 2.2	!! bright elongated spiral
66	3627	Leo	G-SABb	11 20.2	+12 59	8.9	8.2 × 3.9	!! M65 and NGC 3628 in same field
95	3351	Leo	G-SBb	10 44.0	+11 42	9.7	7.8 × 4.6	bright barred spiral
96	3368	Leo	G-SABab	10 46.8	+11 49	9.2	6.9 × 4.6	M95 in same field
105	3379	Leo	G-E1	10 47.8	+12 35	9.3	3.9 × 3.9	bright elliptical near M95 and M96
53	5024	Com	GC	13 12.9	+18 10	7.5	12.6	150-mm telescope needed to resolve
64	4826	Com	G-SAab	12 56.7	+21 41	8.5	9.2 × 4.6	!! Black Eye Gal.; eye needs big scope
85	4382	Com	G-SA0⁺	12 25.4	+18 11	9.1	7.5 × 5.7	bright elliptical shape
88	4501	Com	G-SAb	12 32.0	+14 25	9.6	6.1 × 2.8	bright multiple-arm spiral
91	4548	Com	G-SBb	12 35.4	+14 30	10.2	5.0 × 4.1	some lists say M91 = M58, not NGC 4548
98	4192	Com	G-SABab	12 13.8	+14 54	10.1	9.1 × 2.1	nearly edge-on spiral near star 6 Com. B.
99	4254	Com	G-SAc	12 18.8	+14 25	9.9	4.6 × 4.3	nearly face-on spiral near M98
100	4321	Com	G-SABbc	12 22.9	+15 49	9.3	6.2 × 5.3	face-on spiral with starlike nucleus
49	4472	Vir	G-E2	12 29.8	+8 00	8.4	8.1 × 7.1	very bright elliptical
58	4579	Vir	G-SABb	12 37.7	+11 49	9.7	5.5 × 4.6	bright barred spiral; M59 and M60 1° E
59	4621	Vir	G-E5	12 42.0	+11 39	9.6	4.6 × 3.6	bright elliptical paired with M60
60	4649	Vir	G-E2	12 43.7	+11 33	8.8	7.1 × 6.1	bright elliptical with M59 and NGC 4647
61	4303	Vir	G-SABbc	12 21.9	+4 28	9.7	6.0 × 5.9	face-on two-armed spiral
84	4374	Vir	G-E1	12 25.1	+12 53	9.1	5.1 × 4.1	!! w/ M86 in Markarian's Chain
86	4406	Vir	G-E3	12 26.2	+12 57	8.9	12 × 9	!! w/ many NGC galaxies in Chain
87	4486	Vir	G-E0-1	12 30.8	+12 24	8.6	7.1 × 7.1	the one with famous jet and black hole
89	4552	Vir	G-E	12 35.7	+12 33	9.8	3.4 × 3.4	elliptical; resembles M87 but smaller
90	4569	Vir	G-SABab	12 36.8	+13 10	9.5	10 × 4	bright barred spiral near M89
104	4594	Vir	G-SA	12 40.0	−11 37	8.0	7.1 × 4.4	!! Sombrero Galaxy; look for dust lane
3	5272	CVn	GC	13 42.2	+28 23	5.9	16.2	!! contains many variable stars
51	5194/5	CVn	G-SABc	13 29.9	+47 12	8.4	8 × 7	!! Whirlpool Galaxy; superb in big scope
63	5055	CVn	G-SABc	13 15.8	+42 02	8.6	14 × 8	!! Sunflower Galaxy; bright, elongated
94	4736	CVn	G-SAab	12 50.9	+41 07	8.2	13 × 11	very bright and comet-like
106	4258	CVn	G-SABbc	12 19.0	+47 18	8.4	20 × 8	!! superb large, bright spiral
68	4590	Hya	GC	12 39.5	−26 45	7.7	12	150-mm telescope needed to resolve
83	5236	Hya	G-SABc	13 37.0	−29 52	7.6	16 × 13	large and diffuse; superb from far south
102	5866?	Dra	G-SA0⁺	15 06.5	+55 46	9.9	6.6 × 3.2	or is M102 = M101? (look for 5907)
5	5904	Ser	GC	15 18.6	+2 05	5.7	17.4	!! one of the sky's finest globulars
The Summer Sky								
13	6205	Her	GC	16 41.7	+36 28	5.7	16.6	!! Hercules Cluster; NGC 6207 0.5° NE
92	6341	Her	GC	17 17.1	+43 08	6.4	11.2	9° NE of M13; fine but often overlooked
9	6333	Oph	GC	17 19.2	−18 31	7.6	9.3	smallest of Ophiuchus globulars
10	6254	Oph	GC	16 57.1	−4 06	6.6	15.1	rich globular cluster; M12 is 3° NW
12	6218	Oph	GC	16 47.2	−1 57	6.8	14.5	loose globular cluster near M10
14	6402	Oph	GC	17 37.6	−3 15	7.6	11.7	200-mm telescope needed to resolve
19	6273	Oph	GC	17 02.6	−26 16	6.7	13.5	oblate globular; M62 4° south
62	6266	Oph	GC	17 01.2	−30 07	6.7	14.1	asymmetrical; in rich field

SEASONAL LISTING OF MESSIER OBJECTS (continued)

M#	NGC	Con	Type	RA (2000) Dec		m_v	Size	Remarks
Summer Sky (cont)				h m	° ′		′	
107	6171	Oph	GC	16 32.5	–13 03	8.1	10.0	small, faint globular
4	6121	Sco	GC	16 23.6	–26 32	5.8	26.3	bright globular near Antares
6	6405	Sco	OC	17 40.1	–32 13	4.2	33	!! Butterfly Cluster; best at low power
7	6475	Sco	OC	17 53.9	–34 49	3.3	80	!! excellent in binocs or rich-field scope
80	6093	Sco	GC	16 17.0	–22 59	7.3	8.9	very compressed globular
16	6611	Ser	EN + OC	18 18.6	–13 58	—	35 × 28	Eagle Neb. w/ open cl.; use neb. filter
8	6523	Sgr	EN	18 03.8	–24 23	—	45 × 30	!! Lagoon Nebula w/ open cl. NGC 6530
17	6618	Sgr	EN	18 20.8	–16 11	—	20 × 15	!! Swan or Omega Nebula; use neb. filter
18	6613	Sgr	OC	18 19.9	–17 08	6.9	10	sparse cluster; 1° south of M17
20	6514	Sgr	E/RN	18 02.3	–23 02	—	20 × 20	!! Trifid Nebula; look for dark lanes
21	6531	Sgr	OC	18 04.6	–22 30	5.9	13	0.7° NE of M20; sparse cluster
22	6656	Sgr	GC	18 36.4	–23 54	5.1	24	spectacular from southern latitude
23	6494	Sgr	OC	17 56.8	–19 01	5.5	27	bright, loose open cluster
24	—	Sgr	starcloud	18 16.5	–18 50	4.6	95 × 35	rich star cloud; best in big binoculars
25	IC 4725	Sgr	OC	18 31.6	–19 15	4.6	32	bright but sparse open cluster
28	6626	Sgr	GC	18 24.5	–24 52	6.8	11.2	compact globular near M22
54	6715	Sgr	GC	18 55.1	–30 29	7.6	9.1	not easily resolved
55	6809	Sgr	GC	19 40.0	–30 58	6.4	19.0	bright, loose globular cluster
69	6637	Sgr	GC	18 31.4	–32 21	7.6	7.1	small, poor globular cluster
70	6681	Sgr	GC	18 43.2	–32 18	8.0	7.8	small globular 2° east of M69
75	6864	Sgr	GC	20 06.1	–21 55	8.5	6	small and distant; 59 000 ly away
11	6705	Sct	OC	18 51.1	–6 16	5.8	13	!! Wild Duck Cl.; the best open cluster?
26	6694	Sct	OC	18 45.2	–9 24	8.0	14	bright, coarse cluster
56	6779	Lyr	GC	19 16.6	+30 11	8.3	7.1	within a rich starfield
57	6720	Lyr	PN	18 53.6	+33 02	8.8	>71″	!! Ring Nebula; an amazing smoke ring
71	6838	Sge	GC	19 53.8	+18 47	8.0	7.2	loose globular; looks like an open cluster
27	6853	Vul	PN	19 59.6	+22 43	7.3	>348″	!! Dumbbell Nebula; a superb object
29	6913	Cyg	OC	20 23.9	+38 32	6.6	6	small, poor open cluster 2° S of γ Cygni
39	7092	Cyg	OC	21 32.2	+48 26	4.6	31	very sparse cluster; use low power
The Autumn Sky								
2	7089	Aqr	GC	21 33.5	–0 49	6.4	12.9	200-mm telescope needed to resolve
72	6981	Aqr	GC	20 53.5	–12 32	9.3	5.9	near the Saturn Nebula, NGC 7009
73	6994	Aqr	OC	20 59.0	–12 38	8.9p	2.8	group of 4 stars only; an "asterism"
15	7078	Peg	GC	21 30.0	+12 10	6.0	12.3	rich, compact globular
30	7099	Cap	GC	21 40.4	–23 11	7.3	11	toughest in 1-night Messier marathon
52	7654	Cas	OC	23 24.2	+61 35	6.9	12	young, rich cl.; faint Bubble Neb. nearby
103	581	Cas	OC	1 33.2	+60 42	7.4	6	three NGC open clusters nearby
31	224	And	G-SAb	0 42.7	+41 16	3.4	185 × 75	!! Andromeda Gal.; look for dust lanes
32	221	And	G-E2	0 42.7	+40 52	8.1	11 × 7	closest companion to M31
110	205	And	G-S0/E5 pec	0 40.4	+41 41	8.1	20 × 12	more distant companion to M31
33	598	Tri	G-SAcd	1 33.9	+30 39	5.7	67 × 42	large, diffuse spiral; requires dark sky
74	628	Psc	G-SAc	1 36.7	+15 47	9.4	11 × 11	faint, elusive spiral; tough in small scope
77	1068	Cet	G-SABab	2 42.7	–0 01	8.9	8.2 × 7.3	a Seyfert galaxy; with starlike nucleus
34	1039	Per	OC	2 42.0	+42 47	5.2	35	best at low power
76	650/51	Per	PN	1 42.4	+51 34	10.1	>65″	Little Dumbbell; faint but distinct

THE FINEST NGC OBJECTS

By Alan Dyer

Those looking for an observing project beyond the Messier Catalogue turn to the New General Catalogue (NGC). The NGC contains 7840 entries and forms the core database of today's computerized backyard telescopes. To match the Messier Catalogue, this list contains 110 of the finest NGC objects visible from midnorthern latitudes. The seasonal order is similar to that used in the Messier list, and there is no overlap. While the brightness of the best NGCs rivals many Messier targets, at least a 200-mm telescope is required to see all 110 objects on this list. Most are easy; a few are challenging.

The NGC was originally published by J.L.E. Dreyer in 1888, a work that expanded upon Sir John Herschel's 1864 "General Catalogue." Supplementary "Index Catalogues" were published by Dreyer in 1895 and 1908. The first IC extends the NGC with another 1529 objects discovered visually between 1888 and 1894. Most are faint, elusive targets. (To provide a flavour of this extension to the NGC, one entry from the first IC is included on this list, IC 289.) The Second Index Catalogue contains 3857 entries, most discovered photographically between 1895 and 1907.

The *Sky Atlas 2000.0*, the sets of index card charts called *AstroCards*, *The Night Sky Observer's Guide Vol. 1 and 2* by Kepple and Sanner, and the *Uranometria 2000.0* star atlas (the latter two published by Willmann-Bell, Inc.) are recommended finder aids. Most planetarium and deep-sky charting computer programs, as well as computerized telescopes, include all the objects on this list and many more.

Notation below is as in the Messier list. Magnitudes (m_v) are visual, with the exception of those marked "p," which are photographic, or blue, magnitudes. Most galaxies appear smaller than the sizes listed. For open clusters, the number of stars (*) is also given. Data are taken from *The Deep Sky Field Guide to Uranometria 2000.0* (see the introduction to the Messier list), with some sizes rounded to two significant figures.

SEASONAL LISTING OF FINEST NGC OBJECTS

#	NGC	Con	Type	RA (2000) Dec h m ° '	m_v	Size '	Remarks
The Autumn Sky							
1	7009	Aqr	PN	21 04.2 −11 22	8.3p	>25″	!! Saturn Nebula; small bright oval
2	7293	Aqr	PN	22 29.6 −20 48	7.3	>769″	!! Helix Nebula; large, diffuse; use filter
3	7331	Peg	G-SAb	22 37.1 +34 25	9.5	10 × 4	!! large, bright spiral galaxy
4	7635	Cas	EN	23 20.7 +61 12	—	15 × 8	Bubble Neb.; very faint; 0.5° SW of M52
5	7789	Cas	OC	23 57.0 +56 44	6.7	15	!! 300*; faint but very rich cluster
6	185	Cas	G-E3	0 39.0 +48 20	9.2	14 × 12	companion to M31; small and faint
7	281	Cas	EN	0 52.8 +56 37	—	35 × 30	!! large faint nebulosity near η Cas
8	457	Cas	OC	1 19.1 +58 20	6.4	13	80*; rich; one of the best Cas. clusters
9	663	Cas	OC	1 46.0 +61 15	7.1	16	80*; look for NGCs 654 and 659 nearby
10	IC 289	Cas	PN	3 10.3 +61 19	13.3	>34″	dim oval smudge; use nebula filter!
11	7662	And	PN	23 25.9 +42 33	8.3	>12″	!! Blue Snowball; annular at high power
12	891	And	G-SAb	2 22.6 +42 21	9.9	13 × 3	!! faint, classic edge-on with dust lane
13	253	Scl	G-SABc	0 47.6 −25 17	7.6	30 × 7	!! very large and bright but at low altitude
14	772	Ari	G-SAb	1 59.3 +19 01	10.3	7.3 × 4.6	diffuse spiral galaxy
15	246	Cet	PN	0 47.0 −11 53	10.9	225″	large and faint with mottled structure
16	936	Cet	G-SB	2 27.6 −1 09	10.2	5.7 × 4.6	near M77; NGC 941 in the same field

SEASONAL LISTING OF FINEST NGC OBJECTS (continued)

#	NGC	Con	Type	RA (2000) Dec		m_v	Size	Remarks
				h m	° '		'	
Autumn Sky (cont)								
17	869/884	Per	OC	2 21.0	+57 08	≈5	30/30	!! Double Cluster; 315*; use low power
18	1023	Per	G-SB0⁻	2 40.4	+39 04	9.3	8.6 × 4.2	bright lens-shaped galaxy near M34
19	1491	Per	EN	4 03.4	+51 19	—	25 × 25	visually small and faint emission nebula
20	1501	Cam	PN	4 07.0	+60 55	11.5	52"	faint; dark centre; look for NGC 1502
21	1232	Eri	G-SABc	3 09.8	–20 35	10.0	6.8 × 5.6	face-on spiral; look for NGC 1300 nearby
22	1535	Eri	PN	4 14.2	–12 44	9.6p	>18"	bright planetary with blue-grey disk
The Winter Sky								
23	1514	Tau	PN	4 09.2	+30 47	10.9	>114"	faint glow around 9.4ᵐ central star
24	1931	Aur	E/RN	5 31.4	+34 15	—	4 × 4	haze surrounding four close stars
25	1788	Ori	RN	5 06.9	–3 21	—	5 × 3	fairly bright but diffuse reflection nebula
26	1973+	Ori	E/RN	5 35.1	–4 44	—	≈20 × 10	NGC 1973-5-7 just N. of M42 and M43
27	2022	Ori	PN	5 42.1	+9 05	11.9	>18"	small, faint & distinct with annular form
28	2024	Ori	EN	5 41.9	–1 51	—	30 × 30	bright but masked by glow from ζ Ori
29	2194	Ori	OC	6 13.8	+12 48	8.5	8	80*, fairly rich; look for 2169 nearby
30	2371/2	Gem	PN	7 25.6	+29 29	11.3	>55"	faint double-lobed planetary; use filter
31	2392	Gem	PN	7 29.2	+20 55	9.2	>15"	!! Clown Face or Eskimo Nebula
32	2237+	Mon	EN	6 32.3	+5 03	—	80 × 60	!! Rosette Neb.; very large; use filter
33	2261	Mon	E/RN	6 39.2	+8 44	var	3.5 × 1.5	Hubble's Variable Neb.; comet-shaped
34	2359	CMa	EN	7 18.6	–13 12	—	9 × 6	bright; look for 2360 & 2362 nearby
35	2440	Pup	PN	7 41.9	–18 13	9.4	>14"	almost starlike; irregular at high power
36	2539	Pup	OC	8 10.7	–12 50	6.5	21	50*; rich cluster; near M46 and M47
37	2403	Cam	G-SABc	7 36.9	+65 36	8.5	26 × 13	!! very large & bright; visible in binocs.
38	2655	Cam	G-SAB0	8 55.6	+78 13	10.1	6.0 × 5.3	bright ellipse with starlike nucleus
The Spring Sky								
39	2683	Lyn	G-SAb	8 52.7	+33 25	9.8	8.4 × 2.4	nearly edge-on spiral; very bright
40	2841	UMa	G-SAb	9 22.0	+50 58	9.2	6.8 × 3.3	!! classic elongated spiral; very bright
41	3079	UMa	G-SBc	10 02.2	+55 41	10.9	8.0 × 1.5	edge-on spiral; NGC 2950 nearby
42	3184	UMa	G-SABc	10 18.3	+41 25	9.8	7.8 × 7.2	large, diffuse face-on spiral
43	3877	UMa	G-SAc	11 46.1	+47 30	11.0	5.1 × 1.1	edge-on; same field as χ UMa
44	3941	UMa	G-SB0°	11 52.9	+36 59	10.3	3.7 × 2.6	small, bright and elliptical
45	4026	UMa	G-S0	11 59.4	+50 58	10.8	4.6 × 1.2	lens-shaped edge-on near γ UMa
46	4088	UMa	G-SABbc	12 05.6	+50 33	10.6	5.4 × 2.1	nearly edge-on; NGC 4085 in same field
47	4157	UMa	G-SABb	12 11.1	+50 29	11.3	7.1 × 1.2	a thin sliver; NGC 4026 and 4088 nearby
48	4605	UMa	G-SBcp	12 40.0	+61 37	10.3	6.4 × 2.3	bright, distinct edge-on spiral
49	3115	Sex	G-S0⁻	10 05.2	–7 43	8.9	8.1 × 2.8	Spindle Galaxy; bright and elongated
50	3242	Hya	PN	10 24.8	–18 38	7.8	>16"	!! Ghost of Jupiter; small but bright
51	3003	LMi	G-Sbc?	9 48.6	+33 25	11.9	5.2 × 1.6	faint elongated streak
52	3344	LMi	G-SABbc	10 43.5	+24 55	9.9	6.9 × 6.4	diffuse face-on barred spiral
53	3432	LMi	G-SBm	10 52.5	+36 37	11.2	6.9 × 1.9	nearly edge-on; faint flat streak
54	2903	Leo	G-SABbc	9 32.2	+21 30	9.0	12 × 6	!! very large, bright elongated spiral
55	3384	Leo	G-SB0⁻	10 48.3	+12 38	9.9	5.5 × 2.9	same field as M105 and NGC 3389
56	3521	Leo	G-SAb	11 05.8	–0 02	9.0	12 × 6	very large, bright spiral
57	3607	Leo	G-SA0°	11 16.9	+18 03	9.9	4.6 × 4.1	NGC 3605 & 3608 in same field
58	3628	Leo	G-Sb pec	11 20.3	+13 36	9.5	14 × 4	large edge-on; same field as M65 & M66
59	4111	CVn	G-SA0⁺	12 07.1	+43 04	10.7	4.4 × 0.9	bright lens-shaped edge-on galaxy
60	4214	CVn	G-I AB	12 15.6	+36 20	9.8	10 × 8	large irregular galaxy
61	4244	CVn	G-SAcd	12 17.5	+37 49	10.4	17 × 2	!! large distinct edge-on spiral

SEASONAL LISTING OF FINEST NGC OBJECTS (continued)

#	NGC	Con	Type	RA (2000) h m	Dec ° '	m_v	Size '	Remarks
Spring Sky (cont)								
62	4449	CVn	G-I Bm	12 28.2	+44 06	9.6	5.5 × 4.1	bright with odd rectangular shape
63	4490	CVn	G-SBd p	12 30.6	+41 38	9.8	6.4 × 3.3	Cocoon Gal.; bright spiral; 4485 in field
64	4631	CVn	G-SBd	12 42.1	+32 32	9.2	16 × 3	!! large edge-on; with companion 4627
65	4656/7	CVn	G-SBm p	12 44.0	+32 10	10.5	20 × 3	!! in field with 4631; NE end curves up
66	5005	CVn	G-SABbc	13 10.9	+37 03	9.8	5.8 × 2.8	bright elongated spiral near α CVn
67	5033	CVn	G-SAc	13 13.4	+36 36	10.2	10 × 5	large bright spiral near NGC 5005
68	4274	Com	G-SBab	2 19.8	+29 37	10.4	6.7 × 2.5	NGCs 4278/83/86 in same field
69	4414	Com	G-SAc	12 26.4	+31 13	10.1	4.4 × 3.0	bright spiral with starlike nucleus
70	4494	Com	G-E1-2	12 31.4	+25 47	9.8	4.6 × 4.4	small bright elliptical
71	4559	Com	G-SABc	12 36.0	+27 58	10.0	12 × 5	large spiral with coarse structure
72	4565	Com	G-SAb	12 36.3	+25 59	9.6	14 × 2	!! superb edge-on spiral with dust lane
73	4725	Com	G-SABab	12 50.4	+25 30	9.4	10 × 8	very bright, large spiral
74	4038/9	Crv	G-SB/IB	12 01.9	−18 52	≈10.4	≈5 × 3 ea.	"Antennae" interacting galaxies
75	4361	Crv	PN	12 24.5	−18 48	10.9	>45"	small and bright; with 13ᵐ central star
76	4216	Vir	G-SABb	12 15.9	+13 09	10.0	7.8 × 1.6	nearly edge-on; with NGC 4206 and 4222
77	4388	Vir	G-SAb	12 25.8	+12 40	11.0	5.7 × 1.6	with M84 and M86 in Markarian's Chain
78	4438	Vir	G-SA0/a	12 27.8	+13 01	10.2	8.9 × 3.6	paired w/ NGC 4435 to form the "Eyes"
79	4517	Vir	G-Scd	12 32.8	+00 07	10.4	9.9 × 1.4	faint edge-on spiral
80	4526	Vir	G-SAB0°	12 34.0	+7 42	9.7	7.1 × 2.9	between two 7th mag. stars
81	4535	Vir	G-SABc	12 34.3	+8 12	10.0	7.1 × 6.4	near M49 and 0.75° N of NGC 4526
82	4567/8	Vir	G-SAbc	12 36.5	+11 15	≈11	≈3 × 2 ea.	"Siamese Twins" interacting galaxies
83	4699	Vir	G-Sab	12 49.0	−8 40	9.5	4.4 × 3.2	small & bright; look for NGC 4697 3° N
84	4762	Vir	G-SB0°?	12 52.9	+11 14	10.3	9.1 × 2.2	flattest galaxy known; 4754 in same field
85	5746	Vir	G-SA?b	14 44.9	+1 57	10.3	6.8 × 1.0	fine edge-on near 109 Virginis
86	5466	Boo	GC	14 05.5	+28 32	9.0	11	loose class XII; like rich open cl.; faint
87	5907	Dra	G-SAc	15 15.9	+56 20	10.3	12 × 2	!! fine edge-on with dust lane; near 5866
88	6503	Dra	G-SAcd	17 49.4	+70 09	10.2	7.3 × 2.4	bright elongated spiral
89	6543	Dra	PN	17 58.6	+66 38	8.1	>18"	Cat's Eye Nebula; with 10.9ᵐ central star
The Summer Sky								
90	6210	Her	PN	16 44.5	+23 49	8.8	>14"	blue starlike planetary
91	6369	Oph	PN	17 29.3	−23 46	11.4	>30"	"Little Ghost"; look for 6309 nearby
92	6572	Oph	PN	18 12.1	+6 51	8.1	8"	tiny bright blue oval
93	6633	Oph	OC	18 27.7	+6 34	4.6	27	sparse wide field cluster; IC 4756 nearby
94	6712	Sct	GC	18 53.1	−8 42	8.2	7.2	small globular; look for IC 1295 in field
95	6781	Aql	PN	19 18.4	+6 33	11.4	>109"	pale version of the Owl Nebula, M97
96	6819	Cyg	OC	19 41.3	+40 11	7.3	9.5	150*; faint but rich cluster in Milky Way
97	6826	Cyg	PN	19 44.8	+50 31	8.8	>25"	!! Blinking Planetary; 10.6ᵐ central star
98	6888	Cyg	EN	20 12.0	+38 21	—	18 × 13	Crescent Nebula; faint; use nebula filter
99a	6960	Cyg	SNR	20 45.7	+30 43	—	70 × 6	!! Veil Nebula west half; use filter!
99b	6992/5	Cyg	SNR	20 56.4	+31 43	—	72 × 8	!! Veil Nebula east half; use filter!
100	7000	Cyg	EN	20 58.8	+44 20	—	120 × 100	!! North America; use filter & low power
101	7027	Cyg	PN	21 07.1	+42 14	8.5	15"	unusual protoplanetary nebula
102	6445	Sgr	PN	17 49.2	−20 01	11.2	>34"	small, bright and annular; near M23
103	6520	Sgr	OC	18 03.4	−27 54	7.6p	6	60*; small; dark nebula B86 in same field
104	6818	Sgr	PN	19 44.0	−14 09	9.3	>17"	"Little Gem"; annular; NGC 6822 0.75° S
105	6802	Vul	OC	19 30.6	+20 16	8.8	3.2	50*, at east end of Brocchi's Cluster
106	6940	Vul	OC	20 34.6	+28 18	6.3	31	60*; fairly rich cluster in Milky Way
107	6939	Cep	OC	20 31.4	+60 38	7.8	7	80*; very rich; NGC 6946 in same field
108	6946	Cep	G-SABcd	20 34.8	+60 09	8.8	13 × 13	faint, diffuse face-on spiral near 6939
109	7129	Cep	RN	21 42.8	+66 06	—	7 × 7	faint reflection neb. around sparse cluster
110	40	Cep	PN	0 13.0	+72 32	12.4	>37"	unusual red planetary; 11.6ᵐ central star

DAVID LEVY'S DEEP-SKY GEMS
BY DAVID H. LEVY AND LEO ENRIGHT

Observers who have completed the Messier Catalogue and the Finest NGC Objects List are fortunate that David Levy is now willing to share a list of his favourite deep-sky objects—those that particularly attracted his attention during his 40 years of comet hunting. The objects on this list are numbered as they are in his book, *Deep Sky Objects: The Best and Brightest From Four Decades of Comet Chasing*, (Prometheus Books, New York, 2005, 362 p.) where his 384 objects are numbered chronologically, in the order of their being located in the night sky by the author. Renumbering the objects would have added needless confusion, and would have abandoned the ready reference to the wealth of information in the book. U is the chart in *Uranometria 2000.0*.

This list has been shortened to 156 objects, in order to harmonize with conventions of previously published RASC observing lists. Specifically, the following objects have been deleted: 76 objects south of Dec –30 degrees, 58 objects that appear in the Messier Catalogue, 59 objects found on the Finest NGC Objects list (L1 being the single exception), and 10 objects found on the Deep-Sky Challenge Objects list. In addition, 16 double or variable stars, 4 asterisms, 2 photographic objects, and the Gegenschein were deleted, though observing them is strongly encouraged. Refer to the book for information about these additional objects. This list is truly "RASC-friendly" with all the objects readily visible from Canada.

Levy 384 deserves special note. Just as the terms "Plaskett's Star" and "Kemble's Cascade" recognize astronomers of the past, so also the term "Levy 384" is now the recognized name for a previously unnamed asterism.

SEASONAL LISTING OF DAVID LEVY'S DEEP-SKY GEMS

L#	Sky	L#	Sky	L#	Sky	L#	Sky	L#	Sky	L#	Sky	L#	Sky
1	WIN	59	AUT	135	SPR	182	SPR	210	SPR	255	SPR	300	SPR
5	SPR	62	AUT	136	SPR	183	SPR	211	SPR	256	WIN	314	AUT
6	SUM	64	AUT	137	SPR	184	SPR	212	SPR	257	SPR	315	SPR
8	WIN	81	AUT	138	SPR	185	SPR	213	SPR	259	SPR	317	SPR
19	SUM	82	SPR	145	SPR	186	SPR	214	SPR	260	SPR	325	AUT
27	SPR	83	SPR	147	SUM	187	SPR	215	SPR	261	SPR	326	SPR
28	SPR	95	WIN	149	SUM	188	SPR	217	SPR	262	SUM	331	SPR
29	SPR	96	WIN	156	SUM	189	SPR	219	SPR	263	AUT	334	SUM
31	AUT	98	SUM	158	WIN	190	SPR	220	SUM	266	SPR	337	SPR
34	AUT	99	AUT	159	WIN	191	SPR	223	AUT	267	SPR	338	AUT
35	WIN	110	SUM	160	WIN	192	SPR	224	AUT	268	SPR	340	AUT
36	SUM	112	AUT	161	WIN	193	SPR	225	WIN	270	SUM	341	AUT
37	SPR	114	WIN	162	WIN	195	WIN	226	WIN	271	SUM	342	AUT
38	AUT	116	WIN	163	SPR	196	SPR	231	SPR	273	WIN	367	AUT
41	SPR	121	SPR	164	SPR	201	SPR	232	SPR	276	AUT	369	WIN
42	SPR	123	WIN	165	SPR	202	SPR	236	SUM	277	AUT	381	SPR
44	WIN	124	WIN	167	SPR	203	SPR	238	AUT	278	AUT	382	SPR
50	WIN	125	WIN	169	SPR	204	SPR	239	AUT	280	AUT	384	WIN
51	SPR	129	SPR	170	SPR	205	SUM	240	AUT	281	AUT		
53	AUT	130	SPR	171	SPR	206	SUM	243	SUM	282	AUT		
55	AUT	131	SPR	172	SPR	207	SUM	245	SUM	284	AUT		
56	AUT	133	SPR	178	SPR	208	SUM	247	AUT	286	WIN		
57	AUT	134	SPR	181	SPR	209	SPR	249	AUT	296	WIN		

DAVID LEVY'S DEEP-SKY GEMS

L#	NGC	RA (2000) Dec h m ° ′		m_v	Size (′)	U	Remarks
The Autumn Sky							
31	514	01 24.1	+12 55	11.7	3.9 × 2.9	173	Easily seen galaxy in Pisces
34	488	01 21.8	+05 15	10.3	5.5 × 4.0	217	Elongated galaxy in Pisces
38	7753	23 47.1	+29 20	12.0	3.2 × 1.7	92	Slightly elongated galaxy in Pegasus
53	752	01 57.8	+37 41	5.7	50	169	Very large open cluster in Andromeda
55	7664	23 26.6	+25 04	12.7	3.0 × 1.7	333	Galaxy in Pegasus
56	270	00 50.6	−08 39	12.1	2.0 × 1.7	262	Galaxy in Cetus
57	7723	23 38.8	−12 58	11.2	2.8 × 1.9	304	Galaxy in Aquarius
59	524	01 24.8	+09 32	10.2	3.5 × 3.5	173	Round galaxy in Pisces
62	898	02 23.3	+41 57	12.9	1.8 × 0.5	91	Elongated galaxy in Andromeda
64	404	01 09.4	+35 43	10.3	6.1 × 6.1	91	Round galaxy near Beta Andromedae
81	147	00 33.2	+48 30	9.5	15.0 × 9.4	60	Comet-like galaxy; satellite of M31
99	949	02 30.8	+37 08	11.8	3.3 × 2.1	93	Very cometary galaxy in Triangulum
112	7023	21 00.5	+68 10	7.0	10 × 8	32	Unusual-looking nebula in Cepheus
223	150	00 34.3	−27 48	11.3	3.4 × 1.6	306	Elongated galaxy in Sculptor
224	IC 1830	02 39.1	−27 27	11.9	1.9 × 1.5	310	Galaxy in Fornax
238	578	01 30.5	−22 40	11.0	3.9 × 2.2	308	Elongated galaxy in Cetus
239	247	00 47.1	−20 46	9.2	19.0 × 5.5	306	Very elongated galaxy in Cetus
240	157	00 34.8	−08 24	10.4	4.0 × 2.4	261	Elongated "Amoeba Galaxy" in Cetus
247	7217	22 07.9	+31 22	10.1	3.5 × 3.0	122	Round galaxy in Pegasus
249	7457	23 01.0	+30 09	11.2	4.1 × 2.5	124	Elongated galaxy in Pegasus
263	7006	21 01.5	+16 11	10.5	2.8	209	Globular cluster in Delphinus
276	7814	00 03.3	+16 09	10.6	6.0 × 2.5	170	Elongated galaxy in Pegasus
277	7184	22 02.7	−20 49	11.2	6.5 × 1.4	346	Very elongated galaxy in Aquarius
278	474	01 20.1	+03 25	11.5	10.0 × 9.2	217	Galaxy near galaxy NGC 470 in Pisces
280	7721	23 38.8	−06 31	11.6	3.3 × 1.3	304	Elongated galaxy in Aquarius
281	7727	23 39.9	−12 18	10.6	5.6 × 4.0	304	Round galaxy in Aquarius
282	7314	22 35.8	−26 03	10.9	4.2 × 1.7	347	Elongated galaxy in Piscis Austrinus
284	718	01 53.2	+04 12	11.7	2.4 × 2.0	218	Round galaxy in Pisces
314	7457	23 01.0	+30 09	11.2	4.1 × 2.5	124	Elongated galaxy in Pegasus
325	IC 1795	02 26.5	+62 04	−	40 × 15	17	Bright nebula in Cassiopeia
338	1042	02 40.4	−08 26	11.0	4.2 × 3.3	215	Galaxy in Cetus
340	1134	02 53.6	+13 00	12.1	2.3 × 0.8	175	Round galaxy in Aries
341	755	01 56.4	−09 04	12.6	2.8 × 1.1	264	Elongated galaxy in Cetus
342	91	00 21.8	+22 25	13.7	2.2 × 0.8	126	Galaxy in Andromeda, in galaxy cluster
367	613	01 34.3	−29 25	10.0	5.2 × 2.6	352	Special galaxy in Sculptor
The Winter Sky							
1	1931	05 31.4	+34 15	13.0	4 × 4	97	A "Finest"condensed nebula in Auriga
8	1624	04 40.4	+50 27	13.0	5 × 5	40	Cluster with nebulosity in Perseus
35	2420	07 38.5	+21 34	8.3	10	139	Open cluster in Gemini
44	1333	03 29.2	+31 25	−	6 × 3	94	A weird reflection nebula in Perseus
50	1579	04 30.2	+35 16	−	12 × 8	96	Reflection nebula in Perseus
95	1999	05 36.5	−06 42	10.0	2 × 2	271	Diffuse nebula in Orion
96	2681	08 53.5	+51 19	10.3	5.3 × 3.5	44	Galaxy in Ursa Major
114	1637	04 41.5	−02 51	10.8	3.4 × 2.6	224	Comet-like round galaxy in Eridanus
116	2158	06 07.5	+24 06	8.6	5	136	Compact cluster near M35 in Gemini
123	1600	04 31.7	−05 05	10.9	2.3 × 1.5	223	Round, diffuse galaxy in Eridanus
124	2174	06 09.7	+20 30	−	40 × 30	137	Large field of dust in Orion
125	2023	05 41.6	−02 14	−	10 × 10	226	Nebula near Zeta Orionis
158	IC2194/6/7	07 33.7	+31 19	(12.5)	−	(100)	Three of the Castor Cluster of galaxies
159	2264	06 41.1	+09 53	3.9	20	183	Christmas Tree Cluster in Monoceros
160	2254	06 36.6	+07 40	9.1	4	182	Open cluster and star chain in Monoceros
161	2245	06 32.7	+10 10	−	5 × 4	182	Comet–like bright nebula in Monoceros
162	2252	06 35.0	+05 23	7.7	20	227	Open cluster; like rope of stars, in Monoceros
195	2419	07 38.1	+38 53	10.3	4.1	100	"Intergalactic Wanderer" in Lynx
225	1187	03 02.6	−22 52	10.7	5.2 × 3.0	311	Round galaxy in Eridanus
226	2613	08 33.4	−22 58	10.5	7.6 × 1.9	321	Edge-on galaxy in Pyxis

DAVID LEVY'S DEEP-SKY GEMS (CONTINUED)

L#	NGC	RA (2000) Dec h m ° '	m_v	Size (')	U	Remarks
The Winter Sky (cont)						
256	IC 2367	08 24.2 −18 46	12.5	2.3 × 0.5	321	Galaxy in Puppis
273	1746	05 03.6 +23 49	6.1	42	134	Beautiful open cluster in Taurus
286	1360	03 33.3 −25 51	9.4	6.5	312	Beautiful planetary nebula in Fornax
296	2362	07 18.8 −24 57	4.1	8	319	Open cluster in Canis Major
369	IC 2177	07 05.1 −10 42	—	120 × 40	273	Reflection nebula, northeast of Sirius
384	Levy 384	08 15.6 −13 58	—	2	(275)	Compact asterism in Puppis (Special!)
The Spring Sky						
5	5676	14 32.8 +49 28	11.2	3.7 × 1.6	77	Small elliptical galaxy in Bootes
27	5377	13 56.3 +47 14	11.3	4.1 × 2.3	76	Galaxy near Big Dipper's handle
28	5473	14 04.7 +54 54	11.4	2.2 × 1.7	49	Comet–like galaxy near M101 in UMa
29	5474	14 05.0 +53 40	10.8	6.0 × 4.9	49	Galaxy near M101 in Ursa Major
37	3055	09 55.3 +04 16	12.1	2.0 × 1.1	234	Comet–like galaxy in Sextans
41	3810	11 41.0 +11 28	10.8	3.8 × 2.6	192	Round galaxy in Leo
42	4340	12 23.0 +16 43	11.2	3.7 × 3.1	193	Galaxy near NGC 4350 in Coma Berenices
51	Arp 321	09 38.9 −04 52	(12.5)	—	(233)	"Larry, Moe, & Curly" galaxies in Hydra
82	5634	14 29.6 −05 59	9.4	4.9	287	Globular cluster in Virgo
83	5638	14 29.7 +03 14	11.2	2.3 × 2.1	242	Comet–like galaxy in Virgo
121	5846	15 06.4 +01 36	10.0	3.0 × 3.0	243	Galaxy in Virgo
129	U 5373	10 00.0 +05 20	11.3	5.5 × 3.7	234	Sextans B galaxy; local group member
130	3198	10 19.9 +45 33	10.3	9.2 × 3.5	72	Very elongated galaxy in Ursa Major
131	2964	09 42.9 +31 51	11.3	3.2 × 1.8	103	Galaxy contains Mrk 404 in Leo
133	3070	09 58.0 +10 22	12.3	1.6 × 1.6	189	Round galaxy, near NGC 3069, in Leo
134	4319	12 21.7 +75 19	11.9	2.8 × 2.1	9	Galaxy near 4291 & 4386 in Draco
135	4256	12 18.7 +65 54	11.9	4.1 × 0.8	25	Edge-on galaxy in Draco
136	3738	11 35.8 +54 31	11.7	3.2 × 2.8	47	Galaxy near M97 in Ursa Major
137	3718	11 32.6 +53 04	10.8	10.0x 4.7	47	Elongated galaxy in Ursa Major
138	3953	11 53.8 +52 20	10.1	6.0 × 3.2	47	Very elongated galaxy in Ursa Major
145	4473	12 29.8 +13 26	10.2	3.7 × 2.4	193	Very elongated galaxy in Coma Berenices
163	2775	09 10.3 +07 02	10.1	4.6 × 3.7	187	Round galaxy in Cancer
164	3486	11 00.4 +28 58	10.5	6.6 × 4.7	106	Round galaxy in Leo Minor
165	3245	10 27.3 +28 30	10.8	2.9 × 2.0	105	Elongated galaxy in Leo Minor
167	3310	10 38.7 +53 30	10.8	3.5 × 3.2	46	Round galaxy in Ursa Major
169	2986	09 44.3 −21 17	10.6	4.1 × 3.4	323	Round galaxy in Hydra
170	4651	12 43.7 +16 24	10.8	3.5 × 2.3	194	Round galaxy in Coma Berenices
171	4450	12 28.5 +17 05	10.1	5.0 × 3.4	148	Elongated galaxy in Coma Berenices
172	4689	12 47.8 +13 46	10.9	3.7 × 3.2	194	Elongated galaxy in Coma Berenices
178	4596	12 39.9 +10 11	10.4	4.6 × 4.1	194	Elongated galaxy in Virgo
181	3887	11 47.1 −16 51	10.6	3.5 × 2.4	292	Round galaxy in Crater
182	4636	12 42.8 +02 41	9.5	7.1 × 5.2	239	Galaxy with bright core in Virgo
183	4818	12 56.8 −08 31	11.1	3.4 × 1.4	284	Very elongated galaxy in Virgo
184	5147	13 26.3 +02 06	11.8	1.6 × 1.5	240	Round galaxy in Virgo
185	5248	13 37.5 +08 53	10.3	6.2 × 4.6	196	Round galaxy in Bootes
186	5371	13 55.7 +40 28	10.6	4.1 × 3.2	76	Round galaxy in Canes Venatici
187	5020	13 12.6 +12 36	11.7	3.0 × 2.6	195	Elongated galaxy in Virgo
188	4591	12 39.3 +06 01	13.0	1.6 × 0.8	194	Elongated galaxy in Virgo
189	5127	13 23.8 +31 34	11.9	2.3 × 1.7	109	Round galaxy in Canes Venatici
190	4956	13 05.1 +35 11	12.4	1.5 × 1.5	109	Round galaxy in Canes Venatici
191	4772	12 53.5 +02 10	11.0	2.7 × 1.3	239	Galaxy in Virgo
192	4536	12 34.5 +02 11	10.6	6.4 × 2.6	239	Very elongated galaxy in Virgo
193	4129	12 08.9 −09 02	12.5	2.3 × 0.7	283	Elongated galaxy in Virgo
196	5694	14 39.6 −26 32	9.2	3.6	332	Tombaugh's Cluster in Hydra
201	3865	11 44.9 −09 14	12.0	2.0 × 1.6	282	Diffuse galaxy in Crater
202	5427	14 03.4 −06 02	11.4	2.6 × 1.8	286	Galaxy, interacting with 5426, in Virgo
203	5668	14 33.4 +04 27	11.5	3.2 × 2.8	242	Comet–like galaxy in Virgo

DAVID LEVY'S DEEP-SKY GEMS (CONTINUED)

L#	NGC	RA (2000) Dec		m_v	Size	U	Remarks
		h m	° '		(')		
The Spring Sky (cont)							
204	5850	15 07.1	+01 33	10.8	4.6 × 4.1	243	Comet-like galaxy in Virgo
209	3049	09 54.8	+09 16	12.1	2.3 × 1.5	188	Comet-like galaxy in Leo
210	4685	12 47.1	+19 28	12.6	1.5 × 0.9	149	"Winking galaxy" in Coma Berenices
211	4779	12 53.8	+09 44	12.4	1.9 × 1.7	194	Round galaxy in Virgo
212	4795	12 55.0	+08 04	12.1	1.9 × 1.7	194	Round galaxy in Virgo
213	4623	12 42.2	+07 41	12.2	2.0 × 0.7	194	Very elongated galaxy in Virgo
214	4713	12 50.0	+05 19	11.7	2.9 × 1.8	194	Elongated galaxy in Virgo
215	4688	12 47.8	+04 20	11.9	4.0 × 4.0	239	Very large galaxy in Virgo
217	3923	11 51.0	–28 48	9.6	6.9 × 4.8	368	Elongated galaxy in Hydra
219	3309	10 36.6	–27 31	11.0	4.4 × 3.1	325	Hydra I galaxy cluster (five members)
	3311	10 36.7	–27 32	10.9	4.0 × 3.6		
	3312	10 37.0	–27 34	11.8	3.4 × 1.1		
	3314	10 37.4	–27 41	12.8	1.5 × 0.8		(actually two spirals!!)
	3316	10 37.6	–27 36	12.6	1.4 × 1.2		
231	5364	13 56.2	+05 01	10.5	6.6 × 5.1	196	Elongated galaxy in Virgo
232	5068	13 18.9	–21 02	9.6	7.1 × 6.6	330	Very large galaxy in Virgo
255	5016	13 12.1	+24 06	12.8	1.7 × 1.3	150	Round galaxy in Coma Berenices
257	4866	12 59.5	+14 10	11.2	5.5 × 1.2	194	Elongated galaxy in Virgo
259	4722	12 51.5	–13 19	12.9	1.5 × 0.7	284	Round galaxy in Corvus
260	4519	12 33.5	+08 39	11.8	3.5 × 2.3	194	Galaxy in Virgo
261	5350	13 53.4	+40 22	11.3	3.1 × 2.5	76	Galaxy in Canes Venatici
266	5962	15 36.5	+16 37	11.3	2.6 × 1.8	199	Round galaxy in Serpens
267	5247	13 38.1	–17 53	10.1	5.2 × 3.2	331	Beautiful, diffuse spiral in Virgo
268	5690	14 37.7	+02 17	11.8	3.3 × 1.0	242	Very elongated galaxy in Virgo
300	3226	10 23.4	+19 54	11.4	2.5 × 2.2	144	Galaxy in Leo
315	5146	13 26.5	–12 19	12.3	1.8 × 1.2	285	Round galaxy in Virgo
317	5838	15 05.4	+02 06	10.9	3.5 × 1.6	242	Elongated galaxy in Virgo
326	4570	12 36.9	+07 15	10.9	4.3 × 1.3	194	Comet–like elongated galaxy in Virgo
331	3319	10 39.2	+41 41	11.1	6.9 × 4.0	72	Graceful spiral galaxy in Ursa Major
337	0957–	10 01.3	+55 54	15.5	—	45	Famous double quasar in Ursa Major
	+561A/B						(gravitational lens; distinct in 16″ reflector)
381	U5470	10 08.5	+12 18	10.2	12.0 × 9.3	189	Dwarf elliptical galaxy in Leo
382	U6253	11 13.5	+22 10	12.0	15.0 x12.5	146	Galaxy in Leo

The Summer Sky

L#	NGC	RA (2000) Dec		m_v	Size	U	Remarks
6	6229	16 47.0	+47 32	9.4	4.5	80	Compact globular cluster in Hercules
19	6207	16 43.1	+36 50	11.5	3.0 × 1.1	114	Spiral galaxy near M13 in Hercules
36	6364	17 24.5	+29 24	12.9	1.5 × 1.2	115	Comet-like galaxy in Hercules
98	6709	18 51.5	+10 21	6.7	13	205	Open cluster in Aquila
110	6760	19 11.2	+01 02	9.1	6.6	251	Globular cluster in Aquila
147	6638	18 30.9	–25 30	9.1	5	340	Globular cluster in Sagittarius
149	6553	18 09.3	–25 54	8.1	8.1	339	Faint globular cluster in Sagittarius
156	6934	20 34.2	+07 24	8.7	5.9	208	Globular cluster in Delphinus
205	6106	16 18.8	+07 25	12.2	2.3 × 1.2	201	Galaxy in Hercules
206	6118	16 21.8	–02 17	11.7	4.6 × 1.9	246	Galaxy in Serpens
207	6384	17 32.4	+07 04	10.4	6.4 × 4.3	203	Galaxy in Ophiuchus
208	6426	17 44.9	+03 00	11.1	3.2	248	Globular cluster in Ophiuchus
220	6910	20 23.1	+40 47	7.4	7	84	Open cluster in Cygnus
236	6181	16 32.3	+19 50	11.9	2.3 × 0.9	156	Galaxy in Hercules
243	6440	17 48.9	–20 22	9.1	5.4	338	Globular cluster in Sagittarius
245	6781	19 18.4	+06 33	11.4	>1.8	206	Planetary nebula in Aquila
262	6814	19 42.7	–10 19	11.2	3.0 × 3.0	297	Round galaxy in Aquila
270	6535	18 03.8	–00 18	10.5	3.6	249	Globular cluster in Serpens
271	6287	17 05.2	–22 42	9.3	5.0	337	Globular cluster in Ophiuchus
334	6342	17 21.2	–19 35	9.8	3	338	Globular cluster near M9 in Ophiuchus

DEEP-SKY CHALLENGE OBJECTS

By Alan Dyer and Alister Ling

The beauty of the deep sky extends well past the best and brightest objects. The attraction of observing is not the sight of an object itself but our intellectual contact with what it *is*. A faint, stellar point in Virgo evokes wonder when you try to fathom the depths of this quasar billions of light-years away. The eclectic collection of objects below is designed to introduce some "fringe" catalogues while providing challenging targets for a wide range of apertures. Often more important than sheer aperture are factors such as the quality of sky, quality of the optics, use of an appropriate filter, and the observer's experience. Don't be afraid to tackle some of these with a smaller telescope.

Objects are listed in order of right ascension. Abbreviations are the same as in the Messier and NGC lists, with DN = dark nebula. Three columns have been added: **UI** and **UII** respectively list the charts where you'll find that object in the original edition and the 2001 second edition of *Uranometria 2000.0;* the last column suggests the minimum aperture, in millimetres, needed to see that object. Most data are taken from *Sky Catalogue 2000.0, Vol. 2*. Some visual magnitudes are from other sources.

#	Object	Con	Type	RA (2000) Dec h m ° '	m_v	Size '	UI	UII	Min. Aper. mm
1	NGC 7822	Cep	E/RN	0 03.6 +68 37	—	60 × 30	15	8	300

large, faint emission nebula; rated "eeF"; also look for E/R nebula Ced 214 (associated w/ star cluster Berkeley 59) 1° S

#	Object	Con	Type	RA/Dec	m_v	Size	UI	UII	mm
2	IC 59	Cas	E/RN	0 56.7 +61 04	—	10 × 5	36	18	200–250

faint emission/reflection nebula paired with IC 63 very close to γ Cas.; requires clean optics; rated as "pF"

| 3 | NGC 609 | Cas | OC | 1 37.2 +64 33 | 11.0 | 3.0 | 16 | 17 | 250–300 |

faint patch at low power; high power needed to resolve this rich cluster (also look for Trumpler 1 cluster 3° S)

| 4 | IC 1795 | Cas | EN | 2 24.7 +61 54 | — | 27 × 13 | 17 | 29 | 200 |

brightest part of a complex of nebulosity that includes IC 1805 and IC 1848; use a nebula filter

| 5 | Maffei I | Cas | G-E3 | 2 36.3 +59 39 | ≈14 | 5 × 3 | 38 | 29 | 300 |

heavily reddened galaxy; very faint; requires large aperture and black skies; nearby Maffei II for extremists

| 6 | NGC 1049 | For | GC | 2 39.7 −34 29 | 11.0 | 0.6 | 354 | 175 | 250–300 |

Class V globular in dwarf "Fornax System" Local Group galaxy 630 000 ly away; galaxy itself invisible?

| 7 | Abell 426 | Per | Gs | 3 19.8 +41 31 | 12–16 | ≈30 | 63 | 43, A4 | 200–300 |

Perseus galaxy cluster 300 million ly away; mag. 11.6 NGC 1275 Perseus A at centre; see close-up chart A4

| 8 | NGC 1432/35 | Tau | RN | 3 46.1 +23 47 | — | 30 × 30 | 132 | 78, A12 | 100–150 |

Pleiades nebulosity (also includes IC 349); brightest around Merope; requires transparent skies and clean optics

| 9 | IC 342 | Cam | G-SBc | 3 46.8 +68 06 | ≈12 | 17 × 17 | 18 | 16 | 200–300 |

large and diffuse face-on spiral; member of UMa–Cam cloud (Kemble's Cascade of stars also on this chart)

| 10 | NGC 1499 | Per | EN | 4 00.7 +36 37 | — | 145 × 40 | 95 | 60 | 80–125 RFT |

California Nebula; very large and faint; use a wide-field telescope or big binoculars plus H-beta filter

| 11 | IC 405 | Aur | E/RN | 5 16.2 +34 16 | — | 30 × 19 | 97 | 59 | 200 |

Flaming Star Nebula associated with runaway star AE Aurigae; see Burnham's Handbook p. 285 (also look for IC 410)

| 12 | HH 1 | Ori | E | 5 36.3 −06 45 | ≈14.5 | 8″ | 271 | 136 | 250 |

Herbig-Haro 1; best with no filter at 250× or more; bipolar jets from forming star; not plotted; 2.5′ SW NGC 1999

| 13 | IC 434 / B 33 | Ori | E/DN | 5 40.9 −2 28 | — | 60 × 10 | 226 | 116 | 100–150 in dark sky! |

B 33 is the Horsehead Nebula, a dark nebula superimposed on a very faint emission nebula IC 434; use H-beta filter

| 14 | Sh 2-276 | Ori | EN | 5 48 +1 − | — | 600 × 30! | 226 | 116 | 100–150 RFT |

Barnard's Loop; SNR or interstellar bubble? difficult to detect due to size; use filter and sweep with wide field

| 15 | Abell 12 | Ori | PN | 6 02.4 +9 39 | ≈13 | 37″ | 181 | 96 | 250–300 |

plotted on UII as PK 198.6–6.3; on NW edge of μ Orionis; OIII filter required

| 16 | IC 443 | Gem | SNR | 6 16.9 +22 47 | — | 50 × 40 | 137 | 76 | 250–300 |

faint supernova remnant very close to η Gem.; use filter (also look for NGC 2174 and Sh 2–247 on this chart)

| 17 | J 900 | Gem | PN | 6 25.9 +17 47 | 12.2 | 8″ | 137 | 76 | 200 |

Jonckheere 900; bright starlike planetary; plotted as PK 194.2+2.5 in UII; use OIII filter & high power

| 18 | IC 2177 | Mon | E/RN | 7 05.1 −10 42 | — | 120 × 40 | 273 | 135 | 200–300 |

Seagull Nebula; large, faint; contains bright patches Gum 1 (−10°28′), NGC 2327 (−11°18′) & Ced 90 (−12°20′)

DEEP-SKY CHALLENGE OBJECTS (continued)

#	Object	Con	Type	RA (2000) h m	Dec ° '	m_v	Size '	UI	UII	Min. Aper. mm
19	PK 205 +14.2	Gem	PN	7 29.0	+13 15	≈13	~700″	184	95	200–250
	Medusa Nebula or Abell 21; larger than plotted in UI; impressive in large aperture w/ OIII filter									
20	PK 164 +31.1	Lyn	PN	7 57.8	+53 25	≈14	400″	43	26	250
	extremely faint with two small components; use OIII filter; sometimes confused with nearby NGC 2474–75									
21	Leo I	Leo	G-E3	10 08.4	+12 18	9.8	10.7 × 8.3	189	93	300
	dwarf elliptical; satellite of Milky Way; very low surface brightness; 0.3° N of Regulus! requires clean optics									
22	Abell 1367	Leo	Gs	11 44.0	+19 57	13–16	≈60	147	72, A11	300–400
	cluster of some 30 or more galaxies within a 1° field near 93 Leonis; Copeland's Septet nearby									
23	NGC 3172	UMi	G-?	11 50.2	+89 07	13.6	0.7 × 0.7	2	1	250
	"Polarissima Borealis"—closest galaxy to the north celestial pole; small, faint, and otherwise unremarkable									
24	NGC 4236	Dra	G-SBb	12 16.7	+69 28	9.6	18.6 × 6.9	25	13	200–250
	very large, dim barred spiral; a diffuse glow (NGC 4395 on UII chart #54 a similar large diffuse face-on)									
25	Mrk 205	Dra	Quasar	12 21.6	+75 18	14.5	stellar	9	5	300
	Markarian 205; a faint star on SW edge of NGC 4319; centre of redshift controversy									
26	3C 273	Vir	Quasar	12 29.1	+2 03	12≈13	stellar	238	111	250–300
	at 2–3 billon ly away, one of the most distant objects visible in amateur telescopes; magnitude variable									
27	NGC 4676	Com	Gs	12 46.2	+30 44	14.lp	2 × 1	108	53	250
	"The Mice" or VV 224—two classic interacting galaxies; very faint double nature detectable at high power									
28	Abell 1656	Com	Gs	13 00.1	+27 58	12–16	≈60	149	71, A8	250–300
	Coma Berenices galaxy cluster; very rich; 400 million ly away; brightest member NGC 4889; see close-up chart A8									
29	NGC 5053	Com	GC	13 16.4	+17 42	9.8	10.5	150	71	100–200
	faint and very loose globular 1° SE of M53; requires large aperture to resolve; difficult in hazy skies; class XI									
30	NGC 5897	Lib	GC	15 17.4	–21 01	8.6	12.6	334	148	150–200
	large and loose; easily hidden in hazy skies at higher latitude; brightest stars mag 13.3, main branch mag 16.3									
31	Abell 2065	CrB	Gs	15 22.7	+27 43	≈16	≈30	154	69	500 in superb sky!
	Corona Borealis galaxy cluster; perhaps the most difficult object for amateur telescopes; 1.5 billion ly away									
32	NGC 6027	Ser	Gs	15 59.2	+20 45	≈15	2 × 1	155	69	400
	Seyfert's Sextet (6027 A–F); compact group of 6 small and very faint galaxies; see Burnham's Handbook p. 1793									
33	B 72	Oph	DN	17 23.5	–23 38	—	30	338	146	80–125 RFT
	Barnard's dark S-Nebula or "The Snake"; opacity of 6/6; 1.5° NNE of θ Ophiuchi; area rich in dark nebulae									
34	NGC 6791	Lyr	OC	19 20.7	+37 51	9.5	16	118	48	200–250
	large, faint but very rich open cluster with 300 stars; a faint smear in smaller instruments; Type II 3 r									
35	PK 64 +5.l	Cyg	PN	19 34.8	+30 31	9.6	8″	118	48	200
	Campbell's Hydrogen Star; very bright but very starlike; also catalogued as star BD +30°3639									
36	M 1-92	Cyg	RN	19 36.3	+29 33	11.0	12″ × 6″	118	48	250–300
	Minkowski 1-92 or Footprint Nebula; bright, starlike reflection nebula; double at high mag.; associated star invisible									
37	NGC 6822	Sgr	G-Irr	19 44.9	–14 48	≈11	10.2 × 9.5	297	125	100–150
	Barnard's Galaxy; member of the Local Group; large but very low surface brightness; requires transparent skies									
38	Palomar 11	Aql	GC	19 45.2	–8 00	9.8	3.2	297	125	200–300
	brightest of 15 heavily reddened GCs found on Sky Survey; magnitude is misleading; 11 Terzan GCs more challenging									
39	IC 4997	Sge	PN	20 20.2	+16 45	10.9	2″	163	84	200
	bright but starlike planetary; the challenge is to see the disk! blink the field with and without a nebula filter									
40	IC 1318	Cyg	EN	20 26.2	+40 30	—	large	84	32, A2	80–150 RFT
	complex of nebulosity around γ Cygni; multitude of patches in rich starfield; use a very wide field plus filter									
41	PK 80 –6.1	Cyg	PN?	21 02.3	+36 42	13.5	16″	121	47	250
	the "Egg Nebula"; a very small proto-planetary nebula; can owners of large telescopes detect polarization?									
42	IC 1396	Cep	EN	21 39.1	+57 30	—	170 × 140	57	19	100–125 RFT
	extremely large and diffuse area of emission nebulosity; use nebula filter and very wide field optics in dark sky									
43	IC 5146	Cyg	E/RN	21 53.5	+47 16	—	12 × 12	86	31	200–250
	Cocoon Nebula; faint and diffuse; use H-beta filter; at the end of the long filamentary dark nebula Barnard 168									
44	NGC 7317–20	Peg	Gs	22 36.1	+33 57	13–14	≈1 ea.	123	46	250–300
	Stephan's Quintet; 0.5° SSW of NGC 7331; easy to pick out 3 or 4 (also look for "companions" to 7331)									
45	Jones 1	Peg	PN	23 35.9	+30 28	12.1	332″	124	45	250–300
	plotted as PK 104.2 –29.6 in UII; large dim glow; OIII filter required									

SOUTHERN-HEMISPHERE SPLENDOURS

BY ALAN WHITMAN

Any serious deep-sky observer yearns to experience the far-southern sky, the home of the finest emission nebula (the Eta Carinae Nebula), the most obvious dark nebula (the Coalsack), arguably the best open cluster (NGC 3532), the most impressive globular cluster (47 Tucanae), the biggest and brightest globular cluster (Omega Centauri, although it is likely the core of a small galaxy absorbed by the Milky Way), the galaxy that offers amateur telescopes hundreds of targets within it (the Large Magellanic Cloud), and the closest naked-eye star (Alpha Centauri), just to name a few. Here is a checklist of "must-see" splendours, rated with one to three exclamation marks, plus 17 other significant objects. The author has observed all of these objects under fine, dark skies. Fans of a particular class of deep-sky object will probably want to add some members of that class that are too faint or featureless to include here.

Declination –35 was chosen as the cutoff for this list. However, three slightly more northerly objects that greatly benefit from being viewed higher in the sky were included, notably M83, because it is one of the finest face-on spiral galaxies in the southern sky, but its three spiral arms are not well seen from Canada. Countries like Australia, Chile, and Namibia offer the best views of these magnificent objects. However, most objects on the list can be viewed from the southern Caribbean; many are visible from Hawaii or from the Florida Keys; and some, including Omega Centauri, Centaurus A, and the many glorious clusters in the tail of Scorpius, can be appreciated from the American Southwest. February through April are the preferred months for a southern observing run, since there are no far-southern splendours (those with exclamation marks) located between 20h and 0h of right ascension.

Data for open and globular clusters are from Archinal and Hynes's 2003 reference book *Star Clusters,* with the two noted exceptions. Data for other objects are mostly from Malin and Frew's highly recommended 1995 guidebook *Hartung's Astronomical Objects for Southern Telescopes,* 2nd ed. The dimensions of galaxies and nebulae and a few other numbers are mostly from various lists in the *Observer's Handbook* or from Sinnott's 1988 work, *NGC 2000.0.* Various sources, including private communications, have provided some difficult-to-obtain data.

Notation used below is mostly as defined on p. 286; in addition, * = star or stars, CC = concentration class of a globular cluster (see p. 247), Ast = asterism, and DN = dark nebula. Numbers without a prefix in the **NGC** column are NGC numbers.

#	NGC	Con	Type	RA (2000) h m	Dec ° '	Size m_v	'	Remarks
1	55	Scl	G-Sc	0 14.9	–39 11	7.9	32 × 6	! in 100-mm scope: diffuse splinter
2	104	Tuc	GC	0 24.1	–72 05	4.0	50	!!! 47 Tuc; yellow core in 370-mm scope
3	β	Tuc	Dbl*	0 31.5	–62 58	4.4, 4.5	27″	! both blue-white
4	SMC	Tuc	G-Im	0 52.6	–72 48	2.3	3.6°	!!! many NGCs included
5	300	Scl	G-Sc	0 54.9	–37 41	8.1	22 × 16	face-on spiral; low surface brightness
6	362	Tuc	GC	1 03.2	–70 51	6.8	14	! Milky Way GC beside SMC; CC III
7	p	Eri	Dbl*	1 39.8	–56 12	5.8, 5.8	12″	! both yellow-orange dwarfs
8	1097	For	G-SBb	2 46.3	–30 17	9.3	13 × 8	! in 300-mm scope: bar and tough arms
9	θ	Eri	Dbl*	2 58.3	–40 18	3.2, 4.4	8.3″	! both white
10	1313	Ret	G-SBc	3 18.3	–66 30	8.9	9 × 7	in 370-mm scope: bar, one spiral arm
11		For	Gal Cl.	3 22.7	–37 12	—	—	position is for bright 1316, Fornax A
12	1365	For	G-SBc	3 33.6	–36 08	9.5	14 × 10	!! in 300-mm scope: bar with 2 spiral arms
13	f	Eri	Dbl*	3 48.6	–37 37	4.9, 5.4	8.1″	! yellowish stars
14	1566	Dor	G-Sc	4 20.0	–54 56	9.4	13 × 9	! in 250-mm scope: 2 classic spiral arms
15	ι	Pic	Dbl*	4 50.9	–53 28	5.6, 6.5	12.5″	! very nice yellow pair
16	1851	Col	GC	5 14.1	–40 03	7.1	12	! brightest centre of any GC; CC II
17	LMC	Dor	G-SBm	5 23.6	–69 45	0.1	7.2°	!!! many nights' work for large apertures
18	2070	Dor	EN/OC	5 38.7	–69 06	5.4	20	!!! Tarantula Nebula; "spider legs" easy

SOUTHERN-HEMISPHERE SPLENDOURS (continued)

#	NGC	Con	Type	RA (2000) Dec h m	° ′	Size m_v	′	Remarks
19	γ	Vol	Dbl*	7 08.7	−70 30	3.9, 5.4	14.1″	! gold and light green pair
20	2451	Pup	Ast	7 45.4	−37 57	2.8	50	! not a true OC; nice contrast with 2477
21	2477	Pup	OC	7 52.2	−38 32	5.8	20	! 300*; arcs of 12th-mag.–13th-mag. stars
22	2516	Car	OC	7 58.0	−60 45	3.8	22	!! 100*; resembles the Beehive but richer
23	γ	Vel	Dbl*	8 09.5	−47 20	1.8, 4.3	41″	! 4*; 1.8-mag. star is brightest Wolf-Rayet
24	2547	Vel	OC	8 10.2	−49 14	4.7	25	! The Heart Cluster (description by Dyer)
25	IC 2391	Vel	OC	8 40.3	−52 55	2.6	60	! o Vel Cluster; bright stars; fine in binocs
26	2808	Car	GC	9 12.0	−64 52	6.2	14	! brightest CC I; like a pile of sand
27	3114	Car	OC	10 02.7	−60 06	4.2	35	! 120*; four arcs of stars in binocs
28	3132	Vel	PN	10 07.7	−40 26	9.2	0.8	Eight-Burst Nebula; colourless
29	3199	Car	EN	10 17.1	−57 55	9.0	22	! crescent formed by Wolf-Rayet star
30	3201	Vel	GC	10 17.6	−46 25	6.9	20	star chains right through core; CC X
31	3293	Car	OC	10 35.8	−58 14	4.7	5	!! Gem Cluster; EN/RN/DN involved
32	3324	Car	EN	10 37.3	−58 38	6.7	15	two-lobed nebula
33	IC 2602	Car	OC	10 43.0	−64 24	1.6	100	! θ Car Cl, a.k.a. the Southern Pleiades
34	3372	Car	EN	10 45.1	−59 52	2.5	80	!!! Eta Carinae Nebula[A]
35	3532	Car	OC	11 05.5	−58 44	3.0	50	!!! oblate; finest OC?; needs a wide field
36	3699	Cen	PN	11 28.0	−59 57	11.3	1.1	dark rift visible in 200-mm scope
37	3766	Cen	OC	11 36.3	−61 37	5.3	15	! triangular; 60*; λ Cen Nebula nearby
38	3918	Cen	PN	11 50.3	−57 11	8.1	0.2	! the Blue Planetary; round
39	—	Mus	DN	12 25	−72	—	3° × 12′	! the Dark Doodad; near 4372 and γ Mus
40	4372	Mus	GC	12 25.8	−72 39	7.2	19	! CC XII (size is from NGC 2000.0)
41	α	Cru	Dbl*	12 26.6	−63 06	0.8, 1.2	3.9″	! blue-white pair; 3rd star 4.9 mag. at 90″
42	DY	Cru	Red*	12 47.4	−59 42	9v	—	! Ruby Crucis; 3′ W of β Cru; B−V is 5.8
43	—	Cru	DN	12 51	−63	—	6°	!!! Coalsack; forms head of the Emu DN
44	4755	Cru	OC	12 53.6	−60 21	4.2	10	! Jewel Box; sparse in small apertures
45	4833	Mus	GC	12 59.6	−70 52	6.9	14	! CC VIII (magnitude is from W.E. Harris)
46	4945	Cen	G-Sc	13 05.1	−49 28	8.4	20 × 4	! in 500-mm scope: dark lane on SW edge
47	5128	Cen	G-S0	13 25.5	−43 01	6.8	26 × 20	!! Cen A; merging spiral and elliptical[B]
48	5139	Cen	GC	13 26.8	−47 29	3.9	55	!!! Omega Cen; huge rich oval; CC VIII
49	5189	Mus	PN	13 33.5	−65 59	9.5	2.6	! the Spiral Planetary; use OIII filter
50	M83	Hya	G-SBc	13 37.0	−29 52	7.6	16 × 13	!! in 200-mm: bar, 1 arm; 370-mm: 3 arms
51	5286	Cen	GC	13 46.4	−51 22	7.4	11	! CC V; bluish PN 5307 nearby
52	5460	Cen	OC	14 07.6	−48 18	5.6	35	25 straggling*; trapezoidal asterism in S
53	α	Cen	Dbl*	14 39.6	−60 50	0.0, 1.3	8.1″	!! rapidly closing yellow pair: 22″–1.7″
54	5927	Lup	GC	15 28.0	−50 40	8.0	6	CC VIII; pair with Nor GC 5946
55	B228	Lup	DN	15 45	−34	—	4° × 20′	! an unknown wonder; opacity 6
56	5986	Lup	GC	15 46.1	−37 47	7.6	10	200-mm resolves large core; CC VII
57	6025	TrA	OC	16 03.6	−60 25	5.1	15	! triangular, in three clumps
58	6067	Nor	OC	16 13.2	−54 13	5.6	15	! 100*; many pairs
59	6087	Nor	OC	16 18.9	−57 54	5.4	15	! 40*; embedded in Norma Star Cloud
60	6124	Sco	OC	16 25.3	−40 40	5.8	40	100*; many trios around circumference
61	6231	Sco	OC	16 54.2	−41 50	2.6	14	!! ζ, 6231, and Tr 24 form the False Comet
62	6242	Sco	OC	16 55.5	−39 28	6.4	9	23*; good for small scopes
63	6259	Sco	OC	17 00.7	−44 39	8.0	15	like a fainter M11; 120*
64	6281	Sco	OC	17 04.8	−37 53	5.4	8	25*; shines in modest scopes
65	6302	Sco	PN	17 13.7	−37 06	9.6	1.5 × 0.5	Bug Nebula; bright core; knots at tips
66	IC 4651	Ara	OC	17 24.7	−49 55	6.9	10	! loops and chains of 70 equal-mag. stars
67	6388	Sco	GC	17 36.3	−44 44	6.8	10	450-mm scope resolves faint stars; CC III
68	6397	Ara	GC	17 40.7	−53 40	5.3	31	!! easily resolved 10th-mag. stars; CC IX
69	6541	CrA	GC	18 08.0	−43 42	6.3	15	! huge outer halo; CC III
70	6723	Sgr	GC	18 59.6	−36 38	6.8	13	! CC VII; part of fine complex below
71	6726–7	CrA	RN	19 01.7	−36 54	—	9 × 7	! 7th-mag. stars involved[C]
72	6752	Pav	GC	19 10.9	−59 59	5.3	29	!! easily resolves 11th-mag. stars; CC VI[D]
73	7582	Gru	G-SBb	23 18.4	−42 22	10.2	4 × 1	brightest member of Grus Quartet

[A] Chevron-shaped dark lane, many other DN involved, including Keyhole Nebula; tiny orange mag. 5 (variable) Homunculus Nebula at centre; four OC involved

[B] Prominent broad dark lane; 370-mm scope reveals thin bright streak within the dark lane

[C] Part of !! complex with GC 6723, DN Bernes 157 (55′ long, opacity 6), variable RN 6729 (involved with R CrA), headlight Dbl* Brs 14 (mags. 6.6, 6.8 at 13″), and Dbl* γ CrA (both yellow-white, mags. 4.9, 5.0 at 1.3″ and widening)

[D] Curving star chains converge to a tiny central peak; very tight group of four 12th-mag. galaxies 1° SE

DARK NEBULAE
BY PAUL GRAY

Dark nebulae, often appearing as "holes in space," are fascinating to observe. The following is a representative selection of visually observable dark nebulae. The **minimum aperture** in millimetres is what observers have found to be necessary to see each nebula; however, many may be observable with smaller apertures under excellent skies. Quality of optics, the observer's experience, and full dark adaptation are often more important than the size of the aperture. Some objects will also benefit from the use of a filter because they are superimposed upon a bright nebula.

Objects are listed in order of right ascension. The column **UI/II** lists the charts in the *Uranometria 2000.0*, editions 1 and 2, respectively, that contain the object; *italics* indicate that the object is not actually marked in the given chart. The **opacity** is based on a scale of 1 to 6, with 6 being the easiest to observe; no objects of opacity 1 or 2 are listed, since these objects are very difficult to observe visually. Two objects (L 889 and L 896) are from the *Lynds Catalogue*, one (LG 3) is from the *Le Gentil Catalogue*, and one is uncatalogued; all others are from the *Barnard Catalogue*. Showpiece objects are marked "!!". For further information, including finder charts and images, and to view or submit an observation report, visit **www.rasc.ca/handbook/resources.shtml**.

#	B	Con	RA (2000) h m	Dec ° '	UI/II	Size '	Min. Opacity	Aper. mm	Remarks
1	5	Per	3 48.0	+32 54	95/60	22 × 9	5	200	1° NE of o Per
2	211/3	Tau	4 17.2	+27 48	133/78	12 × 110	3	200–250	narrow NW–SE lanes, faint bkgd starfield
3	33	Ori	5 40.9	–2 28	226/116	6 × 4	4	100–150	Horsehead Nebula; use H-beta filter
4	34	Aur	5 43.5	+32 39	98/59	20	4	200	2° W of M37; spider-like appearance
5	35	Ori	5 45.5	+9 03	181/96	20 × 10	5	150–200	near FU Ori and bright nebula Ced 59
6	37	Mon	6 33	+11	182/96	3°	5	150 RFT	near NGC 2245, 2247; try binoculars
7	40	Sco	16 14.7	–18 59	335/147	15	3	250	in bright nebula IC 4592; 50' NE of ν Sco
8	44	Oph	16 40.0	–24 04	336/146	35 × 300	6	10 × 70	large dark rift; naked eye in superb sky
9	59	Oph	17 11.4	–27 29	337/146	60	6	10 × 70	3° SW of θ Oph; part of stem of Pipe Nebula
10	64	Oph	17 17.2	–18 32	337/146	20	6	150–200	30' W of M9; causes darkening of M9
11	68	Oph	17 22.6	–23 44	338/146	3	6	200	small; near B72; region rich in dark nebulae
12	70	Oph	17 23.6	–23 58	338/146	4	4	200	small; near B72; region rich in dark nebulae
13	72	Oph	17 23.6	–23 38	338/146	30	6	80–125	!! the Snake; "S" shape; 1.5° N of θ Oph
14	78	Oph	17 33	–26	338/146	3°	6	eye	!! Pipe bowl, "Prancing Horse" hindquarters
15	84A	Sgr	17 57.5	–17 40	339/146	16	5	150–200	1.5° N of M23; try for extensions to S
16	85	Sgr	18 02.6	–23 02	339/145	5	4	100	!! dark lanes inside Trifid Nebula (M20)
17	86	Sgr	18 02.7	–27 50	339/145	4	5	200	!! Ink Spot; nice pair with NGC 6520 5' E
18	87	Sgr	18 04.3	–32 30	377/163	12	4	200	Parrot's Head; 2° S of γ Sgr
19	88	Sgr	18 04.4	–24 07	339/145	2	4	200	on edge of M8; *not* Burnham's "Dark Comet"
20		Sgr	18 04.5	–24 14	339/145	2 × 1	4	200	Burnham's "Dark Comet"; use filter
21	303	Sgr	18 09.2	–24 07	339/145	1	5	200–250	inside IC 4685; use filter; challenging
22	92/3	Sgr	18 15.5	–18 11	339/145	12 × 6	6	7 × 50	!! on NW edge of Small Sgr Star Cloud, M24
23	103	Sct	18 39.2	–6 37	295/126	40 × 40	6	10 × 70	on NW side of Scutum star cloud
24	104	Sct	18 47.3	–4 32	250/105	16 × 1	5	150–200	20' N of β Sct; a checkmark shape
25	108	Sct	18 49.6	–6 19	295/125	3	3	200	30' W of M11; rich region
26	112	Sct	18 51.2	–6 40	295/125	20	4	200	30' S of M11; also look for B114, B118
27	133	Aql	19 06.1	–6 50	296/125	10 × 3	6	100	on Scutum star cloud; very dark spot!
28	142/3	Aql	19 40.7	+10 57	207/85	80 × 50	6	10 × 50	!! Barnard's famous "E" cloud
29	145	Cyg	20 02.8	+37 40	119/48	6 × 35	4	200	triangular shape
30	L 889	Cyg	20 24.8	+40 10	85/48	100 × 20	–	7 × 50	within γ Cygni Nebula, IC 1318
31	L 896	Cyg	20 37	+42	85/48	6°	–	eye	"Northern Coalsack"
32	150	Cep	20 50.6	+60 18	56/20	60 × 3	5	250	curved filament 1.6° S of η Cep
33	353	Cyg	20 57.1	+45 32	85/32	20 × 10	5	100	in N of North America Nebula; B352 in field
34	LG 3	Cyg	21 00	+53	85/32	12°	–	eye	!! "Funnel Cloud Nebula"; best after Coalsack
35	361	Cyg	21 12.9	+47 22	86/32	20	4	100	cluster IC 1369 to N; try for 1°-tendril to W
36	365	Cep	21 34.9	+56 43	57/19	22 × 3	4	200	in IC 1396; indistinct "S" shape; use filter
37	163	Cep	21 42.2	+56 42	57/19	4	4	200	in IC 1396; use filter
38	168	Cyg	21 49.0	+47 29	86/31	100 × 20	5	7 × 50	large E–W lane; Cocoon Nebula at E end

GALAXIES: BRIGHTEST AND NEAREST
By Barry F. Madore

External galaxies are generally of such low surface brightness that they often prove disappointing objects for the amateur observer. However, it must be remembered that many of these galaxies were discovered with very small telescopes and that the enjoyment of their discovery can be recaptured. In addition, the central concentration of light varies from galaxy to galaxy, making a visual classification of the types possible at the telescope. Indeed, the type of galaxy as listed in Table 1 (p. 268) is in part based on the fraction of light coming from the central bulge of the galaxy as compared to the contribution from a disk component. Disk galaxies with dominant bulges are classified as Sa; as the nuclear contribution declines, types of Sb, Sc, and Sd are assigned until the nucleus is absent at type Sm. Often the disks of these galaxies show spiral symmetry, the coherence and strength of which is denoted by Roman numerals I through V, smaller numbers indicating well-formed global spiral patterns. Those spirals with central bars are designated SB, while those with only a hint of a disk embedded in the bulge are called S0. A separate class of galaxies that possess no disk component are called ellipticals and can only be further classified numerically by their apparent flattening, with E0 being apparently round and E7 being the most flattened.

Environment appears to play an important role in determining the types of galaxies we see at the present epoch. Rich clusters of galaxies, such as the system in Coma, are dominated by ellipticals and gas-free S0 galaxies. The less dense clusters and groups tend to be dominated by the spiral, disk galaxies. Remarkably, pairs of galaxies are much more frequently of the same Hubble type than random selection would predict. Encounters between disk galaxies may in some cases result in the instabilities necessary to form the spiral structure we often see. M51 (the Whirlpool) and its companion, NGC 5195, are an often-cited example of this type of interaction. In the past, when the universe was much more densely packed, interactions and collisions may have been sufficiently frequent that entire galaxies merged to form a single large new system; it has been suggested that some elliptical galaxies formed in this way.

Table 1 lists the 40 brightest galaxies taken from the *Revised Shapley-Ames Catalog*. As well as their designations, positions, and types, the table lists the total blue magnitudes, major and minor axis lengths (to the nearest minute of arc), one modern estimate of their distances in 10^6 ly, and their radial velocities corrected for the motion of our Sun about the galactic centre. Although the universe as a whole is in expansion, there are parts that are still bound together (or at the very least, held back in their expansion) by gravity. These groups and clusters are, in essence, representative of the largest material structures in the universe. Recently, large-scale flows of material have been reported, far in excess of the velocities expected due to the perturbing presence of other galaxies and clusters of galaxies. Either there are exceedingly large concentrations of matter yet to be discovered just beyond our limited view of the world, or the universe has had a much more interesting history than our present theories indicate. The brightest and nearest galaxies in Table 1 may be moving not only as a result of the universal expansion, but also through very complex interactions with distant parts as yet only postulated but not seen.

TABLE 1—THE 40 OPTICALLY BRIGHTEST SHAPLEY-AMES GALAXIES

NGC/IC	Other	RA (2000) Dec h m s	° ′	Type	Magnitude B_T	Size ′	Distance 10^6 ly	Rad. Vel. km/s
55		0 15 08	−39 13.2	Sc	8.22	32 × 6	10.	+115
205	M110	0 40 23	+41 41.3	S0/E5pec	8.83	22 × 11	2.4	+49
221	M32	0 42 41	+40 51.9	E2	9.01	9 × 7	2.4	+86
224	M31	0 42 45	+41 16.5	Sb I–II	4.38	190 × 60	2.4	−10
247		0 47 10	−20 45.6	Sc III–IV	9.51	21 × 7	10.	+604
253		0 47 36	−25 17.4	Sc	8.13	28 × 7	14.	+504
SMC		0 52 38	−72 48.0	Im IV–V	2.79	320 × 185	0.2	+359
300		0 54 53	−37 41.2	Sc III	8.70	22 × 16	7.8	+625
598	M33	1 33 53	+30 39.2	Sc II–III	6.26	71 × 42	2.2	+506
628	M74	1 36 42	+15 47.2	Sc I	9.77	10 × 10	55.	+507
1068	M77	2 42 41	0 00.9	Sb II	9.55	7 × 6	82.	+510
1291		3 17 19	−41 06.5	SBa	9.42	10 × 8	49.	+512
1313		3 18 16	−66 29.9	SBc III–IV	9.37	9 × 7	17.	+261
1316	Fornax A	3 22 42	−37 12.5	Sa (pec)	9.60	12 × 9	98.	+1713
LMC		5 23 36	−69 45.4	SBm III	0.63	645 × 550	0.2	+34
2403		7 36 54	+65 35.9	Sc III	8.89	22 × 12	12.	+299
2903		9 32 10	+21 29.9	Sc I–III	9.50	13 × 6	31.	+472
3031	M81	9 55 34	+69 04.1	SbI–II	7.86	27 × 14	12.	+124
3034	M82	9 55 54	+69 40.7	Amorphous	9.28	11 × 4	12.	+409
3521		11 05 49	−0 02.0	Sb II–III	9.64	11 × 5	42.	+627
3627	M66	11 20 15	+12 59.1	Sb II	9.74	9 × 4	39.	+593
4258	M106	12 18 57	+47 18.4	Sb II	8.95	19 × 7	33.	+520
4449		12 28 12	+44 05.8	Sm IV	9.85	6 × 4	16.	+250
4472	M49	12 29 47	+7 59.8	E1/S0	9.32	10 × 8	72.	+822
4486	M87	12 30 50	+12 23.6	E0	9.62	8 × 7	72.	+1136
4594	M104	12 40 00	−11 37.4	Sa/b	9.28	9 × 4	55.	+873
4631		12 42 05	+32 32.4	Sc	9.84	16 × 3	39.	+606
4649	M60	12 43 40	+11 33.1	S0	9.83	7 × 6	72.	+1142
4736	M94	12 50 54	+41 07.1	Sab	8.92	11 × 9	23.	+345
4826	M64	12 56 45	+21 41.0	Sab II	9.37	10 × 5	23.	+350
4945		13 05 26	−49 28.0	Sc	9.60	20 × 4	23.	+275
5055	M63	13 15 50	+42 01.7	Sbc II–III	9.33	13 × 7	36.	+550
5128	Cen A	13 25 29	−43 01.0	S0 (pec)	7.89	26 × 20	23.	+251
5194	M51	13 29 53	+47 11.9	Sbc I–II	8.57	11 × 7	36.	+541
5236	M83	13 37 00	−29 52.0	SBc II	8.51	13 × 12	23.	+275
5457	M101	14 03 13	+54 21.0	Sc I	8.18	29 × 27	25.	+372
6744		19 09 46	−63 51.3	Sbc II	9.24	20 × 13	42.	+663
6822		19 44 57	−14 47.7	Im IV–V	9.35	16 × 14	2.2	+15
6946		20 34 51	+60 09.4	Sc II	9.68	12 × 10	22.	+336
7793		23 57 49	−32 35.4	Sd IV	9.65	9 × 6	14.	+241

The nearest galaxies, listed in Table 2, form what is known as the Local Group of Galaxies. Many of the distances are still quite uncertain. However, in the present *Hubble Space Telescope* era these galaxies are prime targets for a generation of astronomers intent on accurately determining each of their distances to the best possible precision.

TABLE 2 — THE NEAREST GALAXIES — OUR LOCAL GROUP

Name	RA (2000.0) Dec h m ° '		Magnitude B_T	Type	Distance 10^6 ly
Milky Way Galaxy	—	—	—	Sb/c	—
IC 10	0 20.4	+59 17	11.8	IBm	2.6
NGC 147	0 33.2	+48 30	10.36	dE5	2.0
And III	0 35.3	+36 31	13.5	dE	2.4
NGC 185	0 38.9	+48 20	10.13	dE3 pec	2.4
M110 = NGC 205	0 40.4	+41 41	8.83	S0/E5 pec	2.4
M31 = NGC 224	0 42.7	+41 16	4.38	Sb I–II	2.4
M32 = NGC 221	0 42.7	+40 52	9.01	E2	2.4
And I	0 45.7	+38 01	13.5	dE	2.6
SMC	0 52.7	–72 49	2.79	Im IV–V	0.2
Sculptor	1 00.2	–33 42	10.5	dE	0.3
LGS 3	1 03.8	+21 53	18.0	Irr	2.4
IC 1613	1 04.8	+2 07	10.00	Im V	2.4
And II	1 16.5	+33 26	13.5	dE	2.4
M33 = NGC 598	1 33.9	+30 39	6.26	Sc II–III	2.2
Fornax	2 39.9	–34 32	9.1	dE	0.4
LMC	5 23.7	–69 45	0.63	SBm III	0.2
Carina	6 41.6	–50 58	—	dE	0.6
Antlia	10 04.0	–27 20	16.2	dE	4.0
Leo I	10 08.5	+12 19	11.27	dE	0.8
Sextans	10 13.0	–1 36	12.0	dE	0.3
Leo II	11 13.5	+22 09	12.85	dE	0.8
Ursa Minor	15 08.8	+67 12	11.9	dE	0.2
Draco	17 20.1	+57 55	10.9	dE	0.3
Sagittarius	19 00.0	–30 30	15.5	IBm:	0.1
NGC 6822	19 45.0	–14 48	9.35	Im IV–V	1.7

Editor's Notes:

(1) Aside from those famous companions of the Milky Way Galaxy, the Large Magellanic Cloud (LMC), and the Small Magellanic Cloud (SMC), there is only one galaxy beyond our own that is easily visible to unaided human eyes: M31, the Andromeda Galaxy (730 kpc or 2.4 Mly distant). M33, the Triangulum Galaxy, can also be seen, but this is a difficult observation. To locate M31, see the NOVEMBER ALL-SKY MAP on p. 315, where the tiny cluster of six dots above the first "A" of "ANDROMEDA" indicates its location. With modest optical aid (e.g. binoculars) a dozen or more of the galaxies listed in Table 1 can be seen by experienced observers under dark skies. With a 250-mm telescope, the quasar 3C 273, at one thousand times the distance of M31, can elicit a noticeable signal in the visual cortex (see p. 263).

(2) An interesting article by G. Lake entitled "Cosmology of the Local Group" appears in *Sky & Telescope,* December 1992, p. 613.

(3) The National Aeronautics and Space Administration/Infrared Processing and Analysis Center (NASA/IPAC) Extragalactic Database (NED) is a comprehensive compilation of extragalactic data for over 7.6 million distinct extragalactic objects. The database includes most major catalogues and offers references to and abstracts of articles of extragalactic interest that have appeared in most major journals. Also online are over 21 million photometric measurements and over 2 million images. It is possible to search the main NED database for objects selected by catalogue prefix, position, type, or redshift. The database is available at:

nedwww.ipac.caltech.edu

A knowledgebase of review articles and basic information is available at:

nedwww.ipac.caltech.edu/level5

GALAXIES WITH PROPER NAMES
BY BARRY F. MADORE

Below are the catalogue designations and positions of galaxies known to have proper names which usually honour the discoverer (e.g. McLeish's Object), identify the constellation in which the galaxy is found (e.g. Andromeda Galaxy), or describe the galaxy in some easily remembered way (e.g. Whirlpool Galaxy).

Galaxy Name	Other Names / Remarks	RA (2000) h m	Dec ° '
Ambartsumian's Knot	NGC 3561, UGC 06224, ARP 105	11 11.2	+28 42
Andromeda Galaxy	M31, NGC 224, UGC 00454	0 42.7	+41 16
Andromeda I		0 45.7	+38 01
Andromeda II		1 16.5	+33 26
Andromeda III		0 35.3	+36 31
Antennae Galaxy	Ring Tail, NGC 4038/39, ARP 244	12 01.9	–18 52
Antlia Dwarf	AM 1001-270	10 04.0	–27 20
Aquarius Dwarf	DDO 210	20 46.9	–12 51
Arp's Galaxy		11 19.6	+51 30
Atoms For Peace	NGC 7252, ARP 226	22 20.8	–24 41
Baade's Galaxies A & B	MCG+07-02-018/19	0 49.9	+42 35
Barbon's Galaxy	Markarian 328, ZWG 497.042	23 37.7	+30 08
Barnard's Galaxy	NGC 6822, IC 4895, DDO 209	19 44.9	–14 48
Bear's Paw (Claw)	NGC 2537, UGC 04274, ARP 6	8 13.2	+46 00
BL Lacertae		22 02.7	+42 17
Black Eye Galaxy	M64, NGC 4826, UGC 08062	12 56.7	+21 41
Bode's Galaxies	M81/82, NGC 3031/4, UGC 05318/22	9 55.7	+69 23
Burbidge Chain	MCG-04-03-010 to 13	0 47.5	–20 26
BW Tauri	UGC 03087, MCG+01-12-009	4 33.2	+5 21
Carafe Galaxy	Cannon's Carafe, near NGC 1595/98	4 28.0	–47 54
Carina Dwarf		6 41.6	–50 58
Cartwheel Galaxy	Zwicky's Cartwheel, MCG-06-02-022a	0 37.4	–33 44
Centaurus A	NGC 5128, ARP 153	13 25.5	–43 01
Circinus Galaxy		14 13.2	–65 20
Coddington's Nebula	IC 2574, UGC 05666, DDO 81	10 28.4	+68 25
Copeland Septet	MCG+04-28-004/05/07 to 11, UGC 06597, UGC 06602, ARP 320, NGC 3745/46/48/50/51/53/54†	11 37.8	+21 59
Cygnus A	MCG+07-41-003	19 59.4	+40 43
Draco Dwarf	UGC 10822, DDO 208	17 20.2	+57 55
Exclamation Mark Galaxy		0 39.3	–43 06
The Eyes	NGC 4435/8, UGC 07574/5, ARP 120a,b	12 27.7	+13 03
Fath 703	NGC 5892	15 13.7	–15 29
Fornax A	NGC 1316, ARP 154	3 22.7	–37 12
Fornax Dwarf	MCG-06-07-001	2 39.9	–34 32
Fourcade-Figueroa	MCG-07-28-004	13 34.8	–45 33
The Garland	S of NGC 3077 = UGC 05398	10 04.2	+68 40
Grus Quartet	NGC 7552/82/90/99	23 17.8	–42 26
GR 8 (Gibson Reaves)	UGC 08091, DDO 155	12 58.7	+14 13
Hardcastle's Galaxy	MCG-05-31-039	13 13.0	–32 41
Helix Galaxy	NGC 2685, UGC 04666, ARP 336	8 55.6	+58 44
Hercules A	MCG+01-43-006	16 51.2	+4 59
Hoag's Object		15 17.2	+21 35

† Position errors caused these to be historically marked as nonexistent in the NGC and RNGC.

GALAXIES WITH PROPER NAMES (continued)

Galaxy Name	Other Names / Remarks	RA (2000) h m	Dec ° '
Holmberg I	UGC 05139, DDO 63	9 40.5	+71 11
Holmberg II	UGC 04305, DDO 50, ARP 268	8 19.3	+70 43
Holmberg III	UGC 04841	9 14.6	+74 14
Holmberg IV	UGC 08837, DDO 185	13 54.7	+53 54
Holmberg V	UGC 08658	13 40.6	+54 20
Holmberg VI	NGC 1325a	3 24.9	−21 20
Holmberg VII	UGC 07739, DDO 137	12 34.7	+06 17
Holmberg VIII	UGC 08303, DDO 166	13 13.3	+36 12
Holmberg IX	UGC 05336, DDO 66	9 57.6	+69 03
Horologium Dwarf	Schuster's Spiral	3 59.2	−45 52
Hydra A	MCG-02-24-007	9 18.1	−12 06
Integral Sign Galaxy	UGC 03697, MCG+12-07-028	7 11.4	+71 50
Keenan's System	NGC 5216/16a/18, UGC 08528/9, ARP 104	13 32.2	+62 43
Kowal's Object		19 29.9	−17 41
Large Magellanic Cloud	Nubecula Major	5 23.6	−69 45
Leo I	Regulus Dwarf, UGC 05470, DDO 74, Harrington-Wilson #1	10 08.5	+12 18
Leo II	Leo B, UGC 06253, DDO 93, Harrington-Wilson #2	11 13.4	+22 10
Leo III	Leo A, UGC 05364, DDO 69	9 59.3	+30 45
Lindsay-Shapley Ring	Graham A	6 42.8	−74 15
Lost Galaxy	NGC 4535, UGC 07727	12 34.3	+8 11
McLeish's Object		20 09.7	−66 13
Maffei I	UGCA 34	2 36.3	+59 39
Maffei II	UGCA 39	2 42.0	+59 37
Malin 1		12 37.0	+14 20
Mayall's Object	MCG+07-23-019, ARP 148	11 03.9	+40 50
Mice	NGC 4676a/b, UGC 07938/9, IC 819/20, ARP 242	12 46.1	+30 44
Miniature Spiral	NGC 3928, UGC 06834	11 51.8	+48 41
Minkowski's Object	ARP 133 (NE of NGC 541)	1 25.8	−01 21
Pancake	NGC 2685, UGC 04666, ARP 336	8 55.6	+58 44
Papillon	IC 708, UGC 06549	11 33.9	+49 03
Pegasus Dwarf	UGC 12613, DDO 216	23 28.5	+14 44
Perseus A	NGC 1275/6, UGC 02669	3 19.8	+41 31
Phoenix Dwarf Irr.		1 51.1	−44 26
Pinwheel Galaxy	see also Triangulum Galaxy	1 33.9	+30 39
Pinwheel Galaxy	M99, NGC 4254, UGC 07345	12 18.8	+14 25
Pinwheel Galaxy	M101, NGC 5457, UGC 08981, ARP 26	14 03.3	+54 22
Pisces Cloud	NGC 379/80/82-85, UGC 00682/3/6-9, ARP 331	1 07.5	+32 25
Pisces Dwarf	LGS 3	0 03.8	+21 54
Polarissima Australis	NGC 2573	1 42.0‡	−89 20
Polarissima Borealis	NGC 3172, ZWG 370.002	11 50.3‡	+89 07
Reinmuth 80	NGC 4517a, UGC 07685	12 32.5	+0 23
Reticulum Dwarf	Sersic 040.03	4 36.2	−58 50
Sagittarius Dwarf		19 30.0	−17 41
Sculptor Dwarf	MCG-06-03-015	1 00.2	−33 42
Sculptor Dwarf Irr.		0 08.1	−34 34

‡The high declination of these objects makes the RA particularly uncertain.

GALAXIES WITH PROPER NAMES (continued)

Galaxy Name	Other Names / Remarks	RA (2000) h m	Dec ° '
Seashell Galaxy	Companion to NGC 5291	13 47.4	−30 23
Sextans A	UGCA 205, MCG-01-26-030, DDO 75	10 11.0	−4 41
Sextans B	UGC 05373, DDO 70	10 00.0	+5 19
Sextans C	UGC 05439	10 05.6	+00 04
Sextans Dwarf		10 13.1	−1 37
Seyfert's Sextet	Serpens Sextet, NGC 6027/6027a-e, UGC 10116	15 59.2	+20 46
Shapley-Ames 1		1 05.1	−6 13
Shapley-Ames 2	NGC 4507	12 35.1	−39 55
Shapley-Ames 3	MCG-02-33-015	12 49.4	−10 07
Shapley-Ames 4	UGC 08041	12 55.2	+0 07
Shapley-Ames 5	MCG-07-42-001	20 24.0	−44 00
Shapley-Ames 6		21 23.2	+45 46
Siamese Twins	NGC 4567/4568	12 36.5	+11 15
Silver Coin	Sculptor Galaxy, NGC 253, UGCA 13	0 47.6	−25 18
Small Magellanic Cloud	Nubecula Minor	0 52.7	−72 50
Sombrero Galaxy	M104, NGC 4594	12 39.9	−11 37
Spider	UGC 05829, DDO 84	10 42.6	+34 27
Spindle Galaxy	NGC 3115	10 05.2	−7 42
Stephan's Quintet	NGC 7317-20, UGC 12099-102, ARP 319	22 36.0	+33 58
Sunflower Galaxy	M63, NGC 5055, UGC 08334	13 15.8	+42 02
Triangulum Galaxy	Pinwheel, M33, NGC 598, UGC 01117	1 33.9	+30 39
Ursa Minor Dwarf	UGC 09749, DDO 199	15 08.8	+67 12
Virgo A	M87, NGC 4486, UGC 07654, ARP 152	12 30.8	+12 23
Whirlpool Galaxy	Rosse's Galaxy, Question Mark Galaxy, M51, NGC 5194/5, UGC 08493/4, ARP 85	13 29.9	+47 12
Wild's Triplet	MCG-01-30-032 to 34, ARP 248	11 46.8	−3 49
Wolf-Lundmark-Melotte	MCG-03-01-015, DDO 221	0 02.0	−15 28
Zwicky #2	UGC 06955, DDO 105	11 58.4	+38 03
Zwicky's Triplet	UGC 10586, ARP 103	16 49.5	+45 30

Catalogues:

AM *Catalogue of Southern Peculiar Galaxies and Associations,* by H.C. Arp and B.F. Madore, Cambridge University Press (1987).

ARP *Atlas of Peculiar Galaxies,* H. Arp, *Ap. J. Suppl. 14,* 1 (1966).

DDO *David Dunlap Observatory Publ.,* S. van den Bergh, II, No. 5, 147 (1959).

IC *Index Catalogue,* J.L.E. Dreyer, *Mem. R.A.S.* (1895–1910).

MCG *Morphological Catalogue of Galaxies,* B.A. Vorontsov-Velyaminovet al., Moscow State University, Moscow (1961–1974).

NGC *New General Catalogue of Nebulae and Clusters of Stars,* J.L.E. Dreyer, *Mem. R.A.S.* (1888).

RNGC *The Revised New General Catalogue of Nonstellar Astronomical Objects,* J.W. Sulentic and W.G. Tifft, University of Arizona Press (1973).

UGC *Uppsala General Catalogue of Galaxies,* P. Nilson, *Nova Acta Regiae Societatis Scientiarum Upsaliensis,* Ser. V: A, Vol. 1, Uppsala, Sweden (1973).

UGCA *Catalogue of Selected Non-UGC Galaxies,* P. Nilson, Uppsala Astronomical Observatory (1974).

ZWG *Catalogue of Galaxies and Clusters of Galaxies,* F. Zwicky et al., Vol. 1–6, California Institute of Technology (1961–1968).

RADIO SOURCES
By Ken Tapping

There are many types of cosmic radio sources, driven by a wide variety of processes. Some are thermal, that is, producing radio emissions because they have a temperature above absolute zero. Others involve the interaction of high-energy electrons with magnetic fields or complicated interactions of waves with plasmas. There are radio spectral lines from some atoms (such as the 21-cm emission from cosmic hydrogen) and an ever-increasing number of discovered molecular lines originating in cold, dense parts of the interstellar medium.

In this article we list cosmic radio sources that can be observed using small radio telescopes. Flux densities are listed for frequencies of 0.1, 0.5, 1, and 4 GHz (wavelength 3 m, 60 cm, 30 cm, and 7.5 cm respectively). The latter frequency corresponds to highly sensitive and easily available 3.7–4.2 GHz satellite TV receivers for radio astronomy. The unit of flux density used is the Jansky (Jy), where 1 Jy = 10^{-26} W·m^{-2}Hz^{-1}. In the table, m denotes visual magnitude, and z redshift.

The main solar system radio sources are the Sun, the Moon, and Jupiter. The Sun produces strong thermal emission, with enhanced emission from active regions. Flares produce intense radio bursts of seconds to minutes in duration. The flux densities for the undisturbed (quiet) Sun are 20 000, 25 0000, 450 000, and 800 000 Jy. The lunar emission is thermal and equivalent to a mean blackbody temperature of about 225 K. Flux densities are 5, 120, 480, and 8000 Jy. Wavelengths shorter than about 3 cm originate close to the lunar surface and show the temperature variations over the lunar day. Longer wavelengths come from farther down, where the temperature remains more constant. Jupiter is a bright radio source at metre wavelengths, producing strong bursts of emission.

For more information see: *Radio Astronomy*, by J.D. Kraus (Cygnus-Quasar Books, Powell, Ohio, 1986); *Astronomy*, 5 (12), 50 (1977); *JRASC*, 72, L5, L22, L38,... (1978); and *Sky & Telescope*, 55, 385 and 475, and 56, 28 and 114 (1978). Some maps of the radio sky can be found in *Sky & Telescope*, 63, 230 (1982). Some projects to try are described in *Radio Astronomy Projects*, by William Lonc (Radio-Sky Publishing, 1997). Relevant information can be found on the following Web sites: UK Amateur Radio Astronomy Network (**www.ukaranet.org.uk**) and the Society of Amateur Radio Astronomers (**www.qsl.net/SARA**).

Source	RA (2000) Dec h m ° ′		Flux Densities Jy	Remarks
3C10	0 25.3	+64 08	180/85/56/10	remnant of Tycho's Supernova (1572)
W3	2 25.4	+62 06	—/80/150/134	IC 1795; complex, bright HII region; OH emission
3C84	3 25.4	+41 32	40/25/17/47	NGC 1725, Seyfert galaxy; $m = 12.7$, $z = 0.018$
Fornax A	3 20.4	−37 22	900/160/110/40	NGC 1316, galaxy; $m = 10.1$, $z = 0.006$
Pictor A	5 19.9	−45 47	440/140/100/50	galaxy; $m = 15.8$, $z = 0.034$
Taurus A	5 34.5	+22 01	1450/1250/1000/360	Crab Nebula; remnant of 1054 supernova
Orion A	5 35.3	−5 25	90/200/360/330	Orion Neb.; HII star-forming region; OH, IR source
3C157	6 17.6	+22 42	360/195/180/20	IC 443; supernova remnant
Puppis A	8 20.3	−42 48	650/300/100	supernova remnant
Hydra A	9 18.1	−12 05	390/110/65/25	galaxy; $m = 14.8$, $z = 0.052$
3C273	12 29.1	+2 03	150/57/49/30	brightest quasar; $m = 13.0$, $z = 0.158$
Virgo A	12 30.8	+12 23	1950/450/300/170	M87, elliptical galaxy with jet
Centaurus A	13 25.4	−43 02	8500/2500/1400	NGC 5128; galaxy; $m = 7.5$, $z = 0.002$
3C295	14 11.4	+52 12	95/60/28/10	galaxy; $m = 20.5$, $z = 0.461$
Hercules A	16 51.2	+5 01	800/120/65/11	galaxy; $m = 18.5$, $z = 0.154$
Gal. Centre	17 42.0	−28 50	4400/2900/1800	strong, diffuse emission from galactic centre
Sagittarius A	17 42.5	−28 55	100/250/200/336	compact source at gal. cen.; assoc. with black hole?
Cygnus A	19 59.5	+40 44	15500/4000/2100/370	strong radio galaxy
Cygnus X	20 22.6	+40 23	400/150/30/70	complex region
Cassiopeia A	23 23.4	+58 49	25000/4500/2800/806	supernova remnant

MAPS OF THE NIGHT SKY
BY ROY BISHOP

The maps on the following seven pages cover the entire sky. Stars are shown down to a magnitude of 4.5 or 5, that is, those that are readily apparent to the unaided eye on a reasonably dark night.

The first six maps are drawn for latitude 45°N but are useful for latitudes several degrees north or south of this. They show the hemisphere of sky visible at various times of year. Because the aspect of the night sky changes continuously with both longitude and time, while time zones change discontinuously with both longitude and time of year, it is not possible to state simply when a particular observer will find that his or her sky fits exactly one of the six maps. The month indicated above each map is the time of year when the map will match the "late evening" sky. On any particular night, successive maps will represent the sky as it appears every four hours later. For example, at 2:00 or 3:00 on a March night, the May map should be used. Just after dinner on a January night, the November map will be appropriate. The centre of each map is the *zenith*, the point directly overhead; the circumference is the horizon. To identify the stars, hold the map in front of you so that the part of the horizon you are facing (west, for instance) is downward. (The four letters around the periphery of each map indicate compass directions.)

The southern sky map is centred on the south celestial pole and extends to 20°S declination at its periphery. Thus there is considerable overlap with the southern areas of the other maps. Note that the orientation of the various names is generally inverted compared to that on the first six maps. This is in recognition that most users of this Handbook will be residents of the Northern Hemisphere and will make use of the southern sky map when they make trips to the tropics. Thus in "normal" use this map will be read in an area above its centre, unlike the first six maps, which are normally read below their centres. The months indicated around the edge of the map may be used to orient it to each of the preceding six maps and have the same "late evening" significance as explained above. Tick marks around the edge of the map indicate hours of right ascension, with hours 0, 3, 6, etc., labelled. Starting at the centre of the map, the series of small crosses along 0h right ascension indicates southern declinations 90°, 80°, 70°,..., 20°. With the aid of a drawing compass, an observer in the Northern Hemisphere can quickly locate a circle, centred on the south celestial pole, which represents the southern limit of his or her sky.

On all seven maps, stars forming the usual constellation patterns are linked by straight lines, constellation names being given in uppercase letters. Three constellations (Horologium, Mensa, and Microscopium) consist of faint stars; hence no patterns are indicated and the names are placed in parentheses. Small clusters of dots indicate the positions of bright star clusters, nebulae, or galaxies. The pair of wavy dotted lines indicates roughly the borders of the Milky Way. Small asterisks locate the directions of the galactic centre (GC), the north galactic pole (NGP), and the south galactic pole (SGP). LMC, SMC, and CS signify, respectively, the Large Magellanic Cloud, the Small Magellanic Cloud, and the Coal Sack. Two dashed lines appear on each of the first six maps. The one with more dashes is the celestial equator. Tick marks along this indicate hours of right ascension, the odd hours being labelled. The line with fewer dashes is the ecliptic, the apparent annual path of the Sun across the heavens. Letters along this line indicate the approximate position of the Sun at the beginning of each month. Also located along the ecliptic are the Northern Hemisphere vernal equinox (VE), summer solstice (SS), autumnal equinox (AE), and winter solstice (WS).

JANUARY ALL-SKY MAP

Notes:

MARCH ALL-SKY MAP

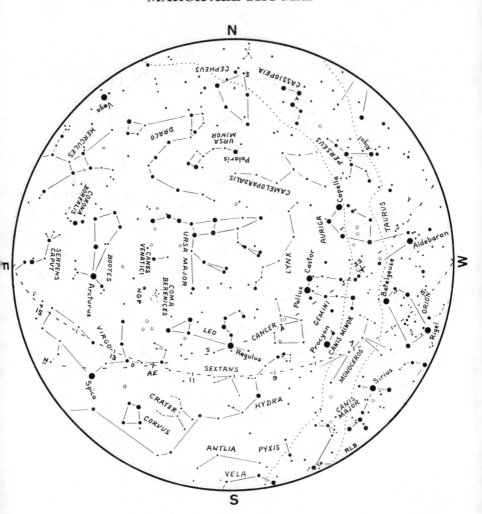

Notes:

MAY ALL-SKY MAP

Notes:

JULY ALL-SKY MAP

Notes:

SEPTEMBER ALL-SKY MAP

Notes:

NOVEMBER ALL-SKY MAP

Notes:

THE SOUTHERN SKY

Notes:

This page intentionally left blank.

OBSERVER'S HANDBOOK 2009
ORDER FORM

(The *Observer's Handbook* for the year 2009 will be
available in September 2008.)

MAIL-ORDER PRICE PER COPY FOR ORDERS OF 1–4 COPIES:

Destination	Unit Price	Shipping & Handling		GST†		Total
Canada	$25.95 Cdn.	+ $4.00 Cdn.	+	$1.80 Cdn.	=	$31.75 Cdn.
United States	$25.95 U.S.	+ $6.00 U.S.			=	$31.95 U.S.
Elsewhere	$25.95 U.S.	+ $13.50‡ U.S.			=	$39.45 U.S.

† GST registration number 119126282
‡ shipped via airmail
Bulk-order pricing is available upon request. Prices are subject to change without notice.

Please send............... copies of the 2009 *Observer's Handbook*.

Name ....

Address ....

....

....

Payment Enclosed $ .... [ ] Cheque [ ] Money Order

[ ] Visa [ ] MasterCard [ ] Amex

Number ....

Expiry .... Signature ....

Name ....

Telephone (..........) ....

Email ....

Order on the Internet using your credit card at www.store.rasc.ca

or send this order form to:

Royal Astronomical Society of Canada
136 Dupont St
Toronto ON M5R 1V2
Canada

Phone: (416) 924-7973; in Canada only: (888) 924-7272
Fax: (416) 924-2911
Email: mempub@rasc.ca

To order any of the other publications of the RASC, please contact the Society or visit
www.store.rasc.ca.

This page intentionally left blank.

INDEX

"MM" denotes the monthly pages of THE SKY MONTH BY MONTH on pp. 96–119.

INDEX (continued)

"MM" denotes the monthly pages of THE SKY MONTH BY MONTH on pp. 96–119.

INDEX (continued)

INDEX (continued)

"MM" denotes the monthly pages of THE SKY MONTH BY MONTH on pp. 96–119.

HHF-4474 12-10-07

UNION COUNTY COLLEGE

3 9354 00185246 2

For Reference

Not to be taken from this room

CRANFORD

2008 HOLIDAYS AND SPECIAL DATES

New Year's Day	Tue.	Jan. 1		
Islamic New Year	Thu.	Jan. 10		
Martin Luther King Jr. Day (U.S.)	Mon.	Jan. 21		
Winter Star Party, Florida Keys	Mon.	Feb. 12	– Sat.	Feb. 17
Chinese New Year	Thu.	Feb. 7		
Presidents' Day (U.S.)	Mon.	Feb. 18		
Good Friday	Fri.	Mar. 21		
Easter Sunday	Sun.	Mar. 23		
First Day of Passover	Sun.	Apr. 20		
International Astronomy Week	Mon.	May 5	– Sun.	May 11
International Astronomy Day	Sat.	May 10		
Victoria Day (Canada)	Mon.	May 19		
Riverside Telescope Makers Conference, Calif.	Fri.	May 23	– Mon.	May 26
Memorial Day (U.S.)	Mon.	May 26		
Texas Star Party, Fort Davis, Texas	Sun.	Jun. 1	– Sun.	Jun. 8
RASC General Assembly, Toronto*	Thu.	Jun. 27	– Sun.	Jul. 1
Canada Day	Tue.	Jul. 1		
Independence Day (U.S.)	Fri.	Jul. 4		
Stellafane Convention, Springfield, Vermont	Thu.	Jul. 31	– Sun.	Aug. 3
Mount Kobau Star Party, Osoyoos, B.C.	Sat.	Aug. 2	– Sun.	Aug. 10
Civic Holiday (most of Canada)	Mon.	Aug. 4		
Starfest, Mount Forest, Ontario	Thu.	Aug. 7	– Sat.	Aug. 9
Butterpot Star Party, St. John's, Newfoundland	Fri.	Aug. 8	– Sun.	Aug. 10
Saskatchewan Star Party, Cypress Hills, Sask.	Thu.	Aug. 28	– Sun.	Aug. 31
Nova East, Smileys Provincial Park, N.S.	Fri.	Aug. 29	– Sun.	Aug. 31
Labour Day	Mon.	Sep. 1		
First day of Ramadân	Tue.	Sep. 2		
Alberta Star Party, Caroline, Alberta	Thu.	Sep. 25	– Sun.	Sep. 28
Fall 'N' Stars, Belleville, Ontario	Fri.	Sep. 26	– Sun.	Sep. 28
Rosh Hashanah	Tue.	Sep. 30		
Yom Kippur	Thu.	Oct. 9		
Thanksgiving Day (Canada)	Mon.	Oct. 13		
Columbus Day (U.S.)	Mon.	Oct. 13		
Halloween	Fri.	Oct. 31		
Remembrance Day (Canada)	Tue.	Nov. 11		
Veterans Day (U.S.)	Tue.	Nov. 11		
Thanksgiving Day (U.S.)	Thu.	Nov. 27		
Christmas Day	Thu.	Dec. 25		
Boxing Day (Canada)	Fri.	Dec. 26		
Islamic New Year	Tue.	Dec. 30		

*The 2008 General Assembly is being hosted by the Hamilton, Mississauga, and Toronto Centres
See pp. 12–14 for Web sites and geographical coordinates of the listed star parties.